DUTCH CULTURE OVERSEAS
Colonial Practice in the Netherlands Indies, 1900-1942

FRANCES GOUDA

DUTCH CULTURE OVERSEAS

Colonial Practice in the Netherlands Indies, 1900-1942

EQUINOX PUBLISHING (ASIA) PTE LTD
No 3. Shenton Way
#10-05 Shenton House
Singapore 068805

www.EquinoxPublishing.com

**Dutch Culture Overseas:
Colonial Practice in the Netherlands Indies, 1900-1942**
by Frances Gouda

ISBN 978-979-3780-62-7

First Equinox Edition 2008

Copyright © 1995 by Amsterdam University Press.
This is a reprint edition authorized by
the original publisher, Amsterdam University Press.

Printed in the United States

1 3 5 7 9 10 8 6 4 2

All rights reserved. No part of this publication may be reproduced, stored in a retrieval system, or transmitted in any form or by any means, electronic, mechanical, photocopying, recording or otherwise without the prior permission of Equinox Publishing.

Contents

Introduction		1
Chapter One	Trying to Reconstruct the Dutch East Indies, 1900-1942: *The History of Colonial Culture and the Vagaries of Human Memory*	11
Chapter Two	A Cunning David amidst the Goliaths of Empire: *Dutch Colonial Practice in the Indonesian Archipelago*	39
Chapter Three	Educating Indonesian Girls in Java and Bali: *The Infatuation with Aristocratic Culture and the Invisibility of Women in the Desa*	75
Chapter Four	The Native 'Other' as the Medieval, Childlike, and Animal 'Self' (or as Fundamentally Different): *Evolutionary Ideas in Dutch Colonial Rhetoric in Indonesia*	118
Chapter Five	Gender, Race, and Sexuality: *Citizenship and Colonial Culture in the Dutch East Indies*	157
Chapter Six	Indies Pavilion in Flames: *The Representation of Dutch Colonialism at the International Colonial Exposition in Paris, 1931*	194
Epilogue	"Paradise Lost": *Nostalgia and the Re-Imagined Community of the Dutch East Indies*	237
Notes		243
Index		296
Postscript		305

For thousands upon thousands of years, we —humankind — have told ourselves tales and stories, and these were always analogies and metaphors, parables and allegories; they were elusive and equivocal; they hinted and alluded, they shadowed forth in a glass darkly.

Doris Lessing, *Under My Skin. My Autobiography to 1949* (1994)

Acknowledgements

Research for this book was generously supported by a Grant-In-Aid from the American Council of Learned Societies (1990), a Fellowship-In-Residence from the Woodrow Wilson International Center for Scholars in Washington D.C. (1990-1991), and a Fellowship from The Harry Frank Guggenheim Foundation (1992-1993). I am extremely grateful to these institutions for their faith in this project. The exhilarating intellectual adventure of plotting and planning the book began in 1988, when I attended the Southeast Asian Studies Summer Institute at the University of Hawaii in Honolulu, where Mbak Erlin taught me first-year *bahasa Indonesia* in an expert — and cheerful — manner. During the same memorable summer, James Collins gave insightful lectures about language and civility in Indonesian society: *budi bahasa*. He became an encouraging friend and colleague in the process, as did Jennifer Krier.

Being interested in Indonesia, whether its colonial past or its contemporary culture, invariably brings most of us in contact with Cornell University. Norman Cantor, in his *Inventing the Middle Ages. The Lives, Works, and Ideas of the Great Medievalists of the Twentieth Century*, described the world of Ithaca, New York, as a gloomy "Valhalla of the North," perched on a "bleak, high precipice over Laka Cayuga, surrounded by ice and snow." I can easily envision upstate New York in the depth of winter as a glum and frosty place. However, despite its location in a frigid winter landscape for many months of the year, to me Cornell University represents a perennially warm source of critical guidance. Benedict Anderson and Saya and Takashi Shiraishi have commented on drafts of papers and answered myriad questions; all have given me a sense of going to graduate school yet again, but this time in southeast Asian Studies and via a series of correspondence courses. Audrey Kahin and Dolina Millar, too, have been considerate and kind. The example of meticulous scholarship embodied in Cornell's tradition of Indonesian Studies has become a model I have tried to emulate as much as possible.

In Washington D.C., where most aficionados of Indonesian society function within the orbit of either the U.S. State Department in Foggy Bottom or the political establishment on Capitol Hill, I found few people who are truly interested in Indonesia's colonial history *per se*; their focus tends to revolve around the political economy of contemporary Indonesia or its place in international relations. One notable exception is Joel Kuipers, who has been an astute critical reader of several chapters, for which I am very thankful. David Turcotte rendered yeoman research assistance during my year as a Fellow at the Woodrow Wilson International Center for Scholars; he unearthed treasure troves of obscure articles and books in the Library of Congress and transported them to the Smithsonian Castle. Mary Brown Bullock, the former Director of the Woodrow Wilson Center's Asia Program, as well as Kirsti Hastings and Craig Garby, assisted in making the 1990-1991 academic year a memorable experience.

John Bowen, Mott Greene, Nancy Smith Hefner, Robert Hefner, Rita Smith Kipp, Herman Lebovics, Pamela Pattynama, David Pollen, Danilyn Fox Rutherford, Toby Volkman, and Charles Zerner provided editorial counsel, critical commentary, and knowledgeable insights. Ann Stoler's remarkable work set a formidable theoretical standard. Kitty Preyer, whose interest in Indonesian history is avocational but heartfelt, nurtured and cheered on the progress of this research project from Cambridge, Massachusetts. Gary Price, as always, listened to a flurry of half-baked ideas while the manuscript was in progress. In his incisive analytical mode he engaged all my intellectual quandaries and commented on an endless series of drafts; Gary, in other words, is again very much part of this book.

In the Netherlands, P.J. Drooglever's thoughtful review of an earlier version of the manuscript prodded me to think through an array of interpretations. The encouragement of Saskia de Vries and Peter van Roosmalen the director and production editor of Amsterdam University Press, rendered the final stages of work on this book enjoyable. Steven Vink, the head of the photography section of the Royal Tropical Institute (KIT) in Amsterdam, made the search for photographs both efficient and pleasant; the same holds true for Petra van Bergen-Godthelp in the photography division of the Royal Institute of Linguistics and Anthropology (KITLV) in Leiden. Paul Koedijk generously shared his prodigious knowledge of archival sources and secondary scholarship. Ernst Heins, the curator of the Jaap Kunst archives in the Musicology Department at the University of Amsterdam, served as an informative guide to the complex personal relationships — which were bathed in petty rivalries and displayed a "bitchy side," as Benedict Anderson noted in the 25th anniversary issue of *Indonesia* — that characterized the Dutch community of Java and Bali *liefhebbers* (enthusiasts and amateur scholars) in the 1920s and 1930s.

My mother and older sisters may read the first chapter and disagree with some of my personal recollections and observations. If so, I can only counter with a historian's typical, and probably unsatisfactory, response: history and memory are utterly subjective things! All of them have shared in my excitement about this intellectual enterprise, though, and showered me with family warmth during my regular research trips to the Netherlands. I am especially indebted to Ria Gouda, who functioned as a veritable newspaper-clipping service during the past few years and dispatched across the Atlantic Ocean an endless stream of articles and books.

In terms of spelling Indonesian words in either the antiquated, Dutch-Malay fashion or in the modern format of Bahasa Indonesia, I have followed the practice of Dutch historians who maintain the version contained in historical sources or contemporary literature. When remembering Dutch colonial usage of Malay words, I have also reproduced the old-fashioned rendition. When I refer to the names of cities or regions or do not cite a specific source, however, I have used contemporary Indonesian spelling. As an alternative to natives, *inlanders*, or indigenous peoples I occasionally describe them as Indonesians. I employ the terms *Indië*, the Dutch East Indies, the Netherlands Indies, or colonial Indonesia interchangeably to designate the territory more or less under Dutch control since the beginning of the twentieth century, until independence.

Finally, Elsbeth Locher-Scholten has acted as a colleague in the true sense of the word. Her own impressive scholarly work on such wide-ranging topics as the Ethical Policy, the historiography of Dutch imperialism, women and mediation, Dutch attitudes towards Indonesian domestic servants, concubines, and women workers, or the incipient expansionism of Japan in the 1930s, has informed this book from beginning to end. Elsbeth has been unstinting in her substantive comments, suggestions, and kindness. In gratitude and friendship, this book is dedicated to her.

INTRODUCTION

One of the inspirations for this book was a description of a free-floating conversation between Christopher Hitchens and Simon Schama, published in the magazine *Interview* in May of 1989. In the middle of what was clearly a pleasant afternoon of adventurous food and intellectual sparring in Harvard Square in Cambridge, Massachusetts, Hitchens posed a question to Schama he supposedly had "always wanted to ask." Dutch culture, he said, is forever represented "as a model of highly evolved religious tolerance and political pluralism. How is it that the Dutch diaspora —Indonesia, Surinam, South Africa — is so disfigured by violence and bigotry?"

Schama's response was interesting, although not entirely surprising. Because the small, water-logged Dutch Republic did not possess any natural resources, he said, the nation during the early modern era depended almost entirely on commerce and shipping. Alienating Catholics, Jews, or Mennonites through the establishment of a Calvinist theocracy within the national borders of the wheeling and dealing United Provinces would not produce the kind of unimpeded social interaction that was conducive to profitable trade. When Dutch Calvinists departed for exotic places elsewhere in the world, however, "they went by the book." Of course the intransigent *Boers* in South Africa followed their own convoluted path: "you could say it was an aspect of a general Dutch tendency, which is one of self-invention."[1]

Schama predictably pointed to the "Golden Age" of the Dutch Republic as the source of Hitchens' observation that Holland has often functioned as a paragon of political virtue and lack of religious prejudice in European history. Relative to other nations in the early modern period, the seventeenth-century Republic, indeed, represented a haven of "tolerant secularism." But it comprised a safe harbor in which ships and oceans, barges and rivers, merchants and sea captains, ledgers and trade — and what Oliver Rink has called "greed and guilders" — played the starring roles.[2] The Dutch Republic's religious and political pluralism, in other words, issued forth from practical exigencies and mundane realities rather than being the result of high-minded commitments. "Ordinary people," even if they lived in an "extraordinary age," faced an array of mostly pedestrian problems in daily life, which they tried to resolve to their best advantage. If these "common" citizens collectively produced "uncommon" cultural results, however, this does not automatically constitute evidence of a heroic spirit of magnanimity.[3]

Nonetheless, Schama's idea that Dutch men and women have a tendency to reinvent themselves in different habitats in other parts of the world is very intriguing. He had argued in the *Embarrassment of Riches. An Interpretation of Dutch Culture in the Golden Age*, after all, that the luminous civilization of the seventeenth-century Dutch

Republic emanated from a Protean feat of self-creation, arising as it did from an amorphous assemblage of towns and villages to become the sumptuous, sparkling "star of the baroque world."[4] If the birth of the opulent culture of the seventeenth-century Dutch Republic resembled an act of parthenogenesis, then this unique Dutch habit of self-invention may also have operated in different geographic locations.

Since the early modern era, Dutch notions of civil society, or the Dutch community's flexible and relatively charitable, attitudes towards non-Calvinists, were "scattered," as in the Greek word *diaspeirein*, to remote corners of the earth. In some cases this physical journey of a chaotic assortment of Dutch cultural values to distant places — to New York State in colonial North America, for instance, or to Michigan in the nineteenth century — endowed "Dutchness" with subtle new meanings.[5] In other cases, Dutch political customs and traditions were warped in the course of migrating to exotic locales. In their Great Trek to Transvaal, the South African *Boers* embarked on a solitary cultural trajectory; they recreated themselves as "God's people" and seemed to turn into ghoulish caricatures of "Dutchness" in the process.[6] As Anthony Trollope observed dryly in 1878: "The Dutch *Boer* is not what he is because he is Dutch or because he is a *Boer*, but because circumstances have isolated him."[7] The word "scattering" accurately captures this complex pattern of Dutch cultural translation and, in some instances, complete metamorphosis.

In her recent, widely discussed book, *Nationalism: Five Roads to Modernity*, Liah Greenfield has emphasized that any nation's "social reality is intrinsically cultural" and filled with *ressentiment*, referring to the diffuse mixture of contradictory feelings such as affinity and rancor, or attachment and envy, that forge the affective bonds of citizens not only with each other but also with the nation-state and the outside world.[8] This characterization aptly captures the chameleon-like or "Janus-face" quality of almost all forms of nationalism — being both friendly and bellicose, or communal and authoritarian at the same time.[9] It also underscores that the advent of nationalism entails a creative leap of faith: citizens' "fuzzy" sense of community is transformed into solidarity with a clearly defined nation, as if the nation is imagined into existence through a collective act of "conjuring."[10]

But Greenfield's sophisticated meditation on the evolution of nationalism entirely glosses over the crucial fact that the possession of a colonial empire in two of her case studies, England and France, also became a constitutive element in the formation of nationalism. Governing an empire in these two countries, as well as in others such as the Netherlands, represented a "protracted, almost metaphysical obligation," as Edward Said has noted in his *Culture and Imperialism*.[11] Or, in Antoinette Burton's recent formulation, "national and imperial identities were co-dependent," since a distinctive "national version of imperialism" constituted a moral yardstick with which to measure differences in national style.[12] African critics, moreover, have emphasized the need to consider the nation as a "key middle term," to cite Kwame Anthony Appiah's phrase, in deciphering the relationship between concepts of racial purity and ideas about literature that both convey and authenticate a particular national identity.[13]

All these analyses of nationalism, of course, are a far cry from the "woolier" visions of German Romantics in the early nineteenth century, who insisted on either a visceral or a mystical basis of nationalism and glorified "an ineluctable root of nationhood" which partitioned one *Volk* from another.[14] However, rather than being grounded in some primordial force, national culture acquires its real significance in the humdrum routines of daily life that sanction and sustain a particular use — or abuse — of political power. Besides, acknowledging the imbrication of empire in definitions of national identity should automatically inspire us to think about the ways in which nationalism, if twisted and turned into a new shape in a totally different landscape, immediately reconfigured the meanings and manifestations of this cauldron of patriotic sentiments, too.[15] In other words, the transplantation of a "structured moral community," as Richard Johnson has typified a nation, into a different soil type in a new climate indelibly altered the kinds of moral imaginings or cultural values that managed both to germinate and flourish.[16]

In addition, using the concept *ressentiment* in a Dutch setting may be a misnomer, because cultural tensions within Dutch society, especially those articulated in religious affiliation, were formally acknowledged and neutralized through a Byzantine process of institutionalization. However volatile these domestic cultural strains may have been, the Dutch state, resembling a gifted conductor of a symphony orchestra, has maintained social harmony by re-fashioning various contentious factions into political entities that possess a co-equal voice in the body politic. This Dutch accommodation differed from that of many other countries, where diversity often tended to surface in antagonism to an official mainstream culture.[17] Such patterns of legitimating cultural differences within the boundaries of Dutch society, however, were deformed beyond recognition in the colonial enterprise. Hence, the "claims, performances, and recognitions in the name of [Dutch] nationhood" in the alien arena of southeast Asia can yield revealing insights into what Herman Lebovics might call the "true" nature of Dutch national identity and its cultural permutations as a result of *diaspeirein*.[18]

An editorial in *The Spectator* of London on September 8, 1894, bluntly addressed the issue of "Dutch Culture Overseas":

> The Dutch, who are at home an efficient people, make a horrid mess of their foreign possessions ... Something in the Dutch irritates the dark races profoundly, and one wonders what it is. It is said to be their cruelty; but they are no more cruel than the native leaders themselves, and it is certainly no want of efficiency. We suspect it is the feeling which induces them to treat dark men exactly as if they were animals, sometimes kindly and sometimes cruelly, but always with a grave immovable contempt; but then what does that feeling arise from? It is wholly apart from the insolence of the French, and the passionless aloofness of the English, and the rigidity of the Germans, and suggests the dominance of some idea.[19]

When we think about the word *diaspeirein*, it immediately conjures up "the scattering" of Jews to areas outside Palestine since the sixth century B.C. But this was hardly a voluntary migration. Instead, the compulsory dispersion of Jews was the bitter consequence of persecution and anti-Semitism. Similarly, the "African diaspora," as the term is used in contemporary African-American discourses in the United States, was enforced, too, by the horrific practices of the slave trade, in which Dutch sea captains played a significant role. Webster's Collegiate Dictionary (1975), though, provides an additional, and more generic, definition of the concept diaspora. It states that the word refers to "decentralization, as of religious or national groups living outside their homeland but maintaining [or renegotiating] their cultural identity."

This definition serves as the guiding inspiration for this book. It is also the explication that prompts anthropologists who focus their scholarly attention on Indian and Pakistani communities in Britain or the United States to talk about the "south-Asian diaspora."[20] The diaspora of south Asians has often been grounded in people's unforced decision to emigrate to other parts of the world that are not as rigidly stratified and caste-based and might make upward mobility possible, even if desperate poverty restricts human agency and coerces hungry people to make drastic decisions. Occasionally, historians or political scientists who study the ubiquitous Chinese communities of merchants and traders in many southeast Asian cities also use the term "Chinese diaspora." In other words, both south Asian and Chinese emigrants entered a diaspora in search of a better life, whether they were in pursuit of economic opportunities or yearned to be liberated from caste or status constraints.

Such a dream also motivated a large number of Dutch folk who ventured towards the Dutch East Indies. Aside from earnest civil servants dispatched to the opposite side of the globe to administer the great Dutch empire in southeast Asia, many others were either *gelukzoekers* or *fortuinzoekers*: people in search of happiness and freedom, or adventure and financial fortune. They surrendered to "wanderlust" and gave in to a desire to be far away from the soggy, cramped homeland. Many Dutch migrants to the Indonesian archipelago yearned to see tropical nature at sunrise and sunset and to live amidst the palm trees or in wide open spaces that embodied "radical differentness (*het gans andere*)," enabling them either to find or to rediscover the "true ground" of their personal identities.[21]

Few religious seekers ended up in *Indië*, although this did not necessarily imply that the "phlegmatic Dutch" displayed less religious fervor in the missionary arena than their "ardent" Iberian rivals.[22] But since its early days in Asia, the Dutch East India Company's (VOC) directors hired missionaries themselves and made them accountable to its administrative directives; as Charles Boxer has intimated, in the expansion of the Dutch empire overseas, the VOC secured the preeminence of Mammon over God.[23] However, in terms of the private spirituality of Dutch residents in colonial Indonesia, the dictates of traditional Christianity tended to become more relaxed, and many Dutch men and women were inclined to absorb a diffuse mixture of indigenous cosmology into their daily lives. In the course of their expatriate journey, the inclusive "original language" of Dutch culture they brought along withered away due to "the exhaustion of distance" and became, instead, the garbled speech of Dutch colonial mastery and racial *apartheid*.[24] In sum, Dutch "dreams of adventure" in the luxuriant

Introduction

Java's north coast at sunset. From W.H. Van Helsingen, ed., Daar wordt wat groots verricht... Nederlandsch-Indië in de XXste eeuw (Amsterdam: Elsevier, 1941)

tropical universe of southeast Asia were translated into what we might today consider the bewildering "deeds of empire."²⁵

Even though concrete answers remain elusive, in the chapters that follow I engage a range of broad questions, such as: how did Dutch East Indies' "ethical" residents envision their idealistic efforts to nurture, tutor, and instruct Indonesians in order to guide them towards maturity and, perhaps, eventual autonomy? Why and how were citizens of a small and politically insignificant European nation capable of representing as natural and normal their paternalistic dominance over ancient civilizations in places such as Java and Bali? To what extent did Dutch colonial residents embrace vulgar notions of evolutionary biology, and how did they talk about and explain the cultural differences between themselves and the so-called "primitive" indigenous people of the Indonesian archipelago?

I also examine the ways in which the Netherlands articulated and portrayed its unique colonial style to the outside world in general or, more specifically, represented the Dutch East Indies at the grand spectacle of the International Colonial Exposition in the Bois de Vincennes in Paris in 1931. How did the conviction that Java, and later, the entire Indonesian archipelago, embodied both "the sheet anchor and the mainstay

Balinese peasants at work. Photo: Paul Spies (Coll. Rudolf Bonnet, Koninklijk Instituut voor de Tropen [KIT], Amsterdam)

of the Dutch ship of state," as Taco Roorda called it in 1841, inflect the rhetoric of government officials in the Netherlands as well as the Dutch East Indies?[26] In which ways did the pivotal importance of the Indies in the collective mentality of the Dutch nation modulate the justifications of colonial rule? And how is the complex history of Dutch colonial culture in Indonesia both "imagined" and "reimagined" — which often means either romanticized or vilified — in the contemporary Netherlands?

I explore, too, a series of issues related to Dutch as well as Indonesian women and their interactions with European men in an effort to understand the "gendering" practices of colonial governance in the Dutch East Indies. In virtually every colonial settler society, the social and sexual behavior of women constituted a cornerstone of European domination. Colonial administrators engaged in a constantly changing process of formulating norms for suitable feminine behavior and defining forms of proper family life for both European and indigenous women. Women's compliance with — and only very occasional resistance to — these moral dictates and sexual prescriptions comprised a fundamental aspect of most European communities in Asia or Africa.

The cultural grammar of colonial rule assigned to white wives and daughters the role of defending the social pecking order and articulating the moral superiority of European civilization in their daily lives. As such, white women bolstered the inviolability of "the colonial tradition," which was grounded in the dogma of racial superiority as well as the preeminence of Western culture. Indigenous women, too, were seen as embodying "tradition." They functioned as the "guarantors" of cultural practices that were deemed original and authentic; native women's daily lives made up the "discursive playing field" on which colonial rulers acted out and championed their national version of imperialism.[27] Similarly, changes in the gendered distribution of power due to economic or political factors beyond the control of indigenous people also expressed themselves in subtly shifting women's roles in ethnic ceremonies or religious rituals.[28] In the process, indigenous women tended to shoulder the triple burden of native patriarchal practices, European colonial mastery, and the dubious treatment by Indies *njonjas* or British *memsahibs* (colonial matrons).

These explorations are not meant as a response to the prominent Dutch journalist Rudy Kousbroek's cheeky attempt, in the past few years, to ignite an intellectual firestorm by accusing women's historians of a deliberate effort to obfuscate the cruelty and vengefulness, or the vanity and carnality, of white-skinned and mixed-blood colonial matrons in the Dutch East Indies.[29] He claims that practitioners of women's studies are reluctant to acknowledge the more objectionable aspects of female behavior. They are presumably mired in a feminist discourse that emphasizes either a generic, female victimology or celebrates women's ways of knowing and bonding as intrinsically more compassionate than men's. Feminist scholars, Kousbroek asserts, convey a Victorian image of white women as "pathetically helpless creatures on a pedestal, born to suffer and barely competent in securing their daily survival, uncontaminated by all the evils of the world and, of course, devoid of libido."[30]

Even though Kousbroek's ability to influence the collective Dutch memory of the nation's colonial past may be "worth more than that of a hundred historians," this particular challenge resembles a tempest in a teapot rather than a firestorm.[31] A wide range of women's historians in the past decade have argued straightforwardly that European women in either British India or the Dutch East Indies were part and parcel of an intrusive system of colonial domination: they used and abused their positions of power over indigenous people just as men did.[32] Kousbroek's quandary — whether women were more than, or just as, ruthless and racist as men in their conduct towards Indonesian underlings — comes across as a misguided one, at least to me. Both *deugd* and *ondeugd* (virtue and vice) flourished indiscriminately among men and women in the Dutch East Indies. As much as circumstances allowed, all colonial residents in the Indies tried to craft their own sense of individual morality, even if the meanings ascribed to feminine virtue yielded a resonance or entailed behavioral injunctions that differed from definitions of masculine rectitude.

Invoking Rudyard Kipling's dictum that "the female of the species is more deadly than the male" or quoting Willem Walraven's vivid letters about white women's supercilious treatment of Itih, his beloved Sundanese wife, does not tell us much about the differential roles assigned to, and embraced by, European women in the imperial drama of white-skinned protagonists and brown-skinned subalterns.[33] After all, few if any Dutch women literally or figuratively whipped Javanese or Chinese contract laborers into shape on tobacco and rubber plantations, simply because they did not work as planters on the east coast of Sumatra in the early twentieth century. But within the European family circle, where wives and mothers wielded the scepter, a large

Djamal temple in Bali (Coll. Bonnet, KIT)

number of white women mistreated or humiliated their domestic servants, which was just as egregious. The Indo-European writer Loes Nobel, for example, in several of her terse but beautiful short stories collected in *Gebroken rijst* (Cracked Rice), contrived a disturbing character in the person of the imperious *tante Betty* (Aunt Betty) — a hard-hearted Indies *njonja* who slapped, shamed, or shrieked at her domestic servants if given the slightest provocation.[34]

However, does it make sense to contemplate whether in the cosmic equation of justice — or injustice — the psychological damage done to household servants by women was worse than, or equal to, the physical harm to coolies perpetrated by men? We can also speculate, of course, whether women might have flogged and flailed helpless coolies in the same way that some men did, if and when they would have been forced to suffer the same exhaustion or frustrations which Deli planters endured in the course of their sweaty toil among the rubber trees and tobacco plants. Such counterfactual propositions might be both titillating and intellectually satisfying. They are not very useful, however, in telling us more about the particular agency of white women within a carefully designed "colonial project" which only male politicians and civil servants, or technocrats in government employ and businessmen in the private sector, had erected and managed.[35]

Instead, my questions will focus in a low-key fashion on whether, even if female behavior was as problematic as male conduct, Dutch women conceived of their colonial roles differently from their husbands, fathers, or sons. As was the case with Indonesians, European women, too, were defined as "the other," although they embodied the "inferior sex within the superior race."[36] How did this gendered positioning of women in Western culture shape their visions of colonial society and mold their sense of place within it? Which notions of proper "womanhood" inspired the well-intentioned Dutch women who advocated the creation of or taught in schools for Javanese or Balinese girls and were wholeheartedly committed to the "uplifting" of the *inlandse vrouw* (indigenous woman)? How did European men's time-honored practice of living with a *njai*, an Indonesian housekeeper *cum* concubine — the women who functioned as the primary progenitors of the archipelago's large Eurasian population — affect Dutch women's equanimity?[37] What were the prevailing notions about interracial reproduction and cultural citizenship in the twentieth century, and did they bias European women's attitudes in ways that diverged from male perspectives?

In probing these questions, I hope to portray Dutch colonial culture as a multi-faceted and pluralistic phenomenon. In doing so we have to keep in mind, of course, Sancho Panza's pithy statement to Don Quixote in the musical *The Man of La Mancha* that it makes little difference whether the stone hits the pitcher or whether the pitcher hits the stone, because the end result is always bad for the pitcher! But instead of representing colonialism only as a faceless behemoth of political and economic subjugation imposed upon innocent native victims, I want to emphasize the ways in which European colonialism was always intertwined with indigenous traditions and tried to "reshape" native customs and traditions in its own image.[38] Europeans' cultural grammar — or "the rhetoric of empire" — commanded the power to "enframe" the reality of colonized peoples and lands in such a way that the West could stake its claim over them and secure them as a "standing reserve."[39] As Nicholas Thomas argued in 1994 in *Colonialism's Culture. Anthropology, Travel and Government,* virtually every form of colonialism hinged on cultural processes, and its intrusions and fictions were almost always conceived of and "energized through signs, metaphors, and narratives."[40]

Dutch colonialism in *Indië*, in other words, resulted from an eclectic fusion — albeit a volatile one, filled with subliminal tensions — of a wide range of European mentalities and unique local conditions. It yielded a culture that encompassed much more than a monolithic ideology intent on disguising or vindicating European modes of domination; instead, Dutch colonial culture in the Indonesian archipelago was also "expressive" and "constitutive" of colonial relationships themselves.[41] As a result, the "scattering" of Dutch cultural values and their translation into the abrasive language of power in southeast Asia in the twentieth century resurfaced as a Babylonian confusion of tongues, which transformed the meanings of "Dutchness" in a European context by transcribing them into the contested realities of colonial society in the Indonesian archipelago.

CHAPTER ONE

TRYING TO RECONSTRUCT THE DUTCH EAST INDIES, 1900-1942:

The History of Colonial Culture and the Vagaries of Human Memory

All of us ... all human beings, are in the shackles of our imaginations, tied up by our imaginations ... [but] if we really try very hard to liberate ourselves from the shackles, if we use every possible means, we are sure to be released from the shackles.[1]

Armijn Pane, *Belunggu* (In Shackles), 1940

When I was a child, growing up near Haarlem in the Netherlands, certain Indonesian (*Maleis*) words and phrases surfaced in our family quite regularly. Bananas were routinely called *pisang* and when they had gotten too ripe to eat, my mother described them as *boesoek*, while cucumbers were often referred to as *ketimoen*. When I was overly confident about something I might be told I was too full of *branie*, and if I asked for yet another cookie or a piece of chocolate, my mother would forever claim they were *habis* (finished). When my parents and sisters and I would come home from an outing or a trip, my father might turn to my mother in a gesture of mock despair and say *tidak ada koentji* — I do not have a key. My parents asked us whether we were *senang* (content, happy) and when we had a sisterly argument, it could be smoothed over as a temporary *tidak tjotjok* (not meshing, or not getting along).

My three older sisters and I all tried to eat *sambal*, too, and being able to mix bigger globs of the chili pepper sauce into our rice became a mark of distinction or a sign of bravery. The most confusing memory I have is being called a *binatang*, who caused everyone nothing but *soesah*. When I was little, I had convinced myself that these were terms of endearment: I imagined grown-ups thought I was a sweet child who gave other people only pleasure. It was not until 1988, when I attended an intensive Indonesian language program at the University of Hawaii, that I learned the real meaning of this phrase: adults had called me an animal who generated nothing but trouble!

More poignant memories of the Dutch colonial history in Indonesia also entered the emotional universe of my childhood. My very best friend in grade school was born in Berastagi in Sumatra, and had lived during her early years on a tobacco plantation in an area we call the land of the Karo Bataks today. Her guitar-playing and much-beloved father had worked as a prisoner of war on the Burma railroad. His infrequent stories about having made music on a makeshift string instrument for groups of emaciated, hollow-eyed forced laborers in Burma with the famous *cabaretier* Wim Kan — a towering icon of the Dutch popular theater in the post-World War II era — impressed me greatly. I also remember vividly how vehement my friend's father was in his refusal to see the movie "The Bridge over the River Kwai," a life-devouring structure which he had helped to build. The movie would undoubtedly trivialize or romanticize the desperate suffering of the men who had actually lived the story, he said.[2] Her mother described *Indië* as a horrible place — a *pokkenland* (a pox-ridden country), she called it — not unlike other Dutch women who remember their Indonesian experience as a "haunting nightmare" in an environment full of mystery and unfathomable dangers.[3]

Many friends of my parents, too, had endured but survived the dehumanizing conditions of the Japanese internment camps in the Indies during the war, whereas my oldest sister's father-in-law had been forced to labor in a grisly coal mine in Japan itself. Her mother-in-law, however, had refused to obey the Japanese command that all European women enter an internment camp. Instead, she dyed her hair black and covered her young son's blond hair with sundry disguises such as a tea cosy and set off on her bicycle to embark on a courageous journey with her little boy in tow. They survived the war by hiding in the houses of an array of Indonesian friends in various *kampongs* (urban neighborhoods). In my adolescent imagination, she was a heroic woman. But the suffering endured in the Indies during World War II by many of the adults I encountered while I was growing up, only obliquely hinted at on very rare occasions, hung over social gatherings as a cloud of mystery, or so it seems to me in retrospect. Amidst the banter and laughter of large get-togethers I thought I could detect in some of these "aunts" or "uncles" a sudden moment of sadness or catch a glimpse of a despondent, faraway look. It made me view all these jovial, familiar people with a mixture of awe and curiosity.

Although my parents did not spend too many years in the Dutch East Indies prior to World War II, where my oldest sister was born in 1941, their memories of those halcyon days in the tropics lingered palpably, since they were not overshadowed by horrific camp experiences. However, ours was not at all a genuine "Indies" family of diehard former colonials, who, having returned to the chilly climate and watery Dutch landscape on the North Sea in the post World War II era, collectively drowned in nostalgia. The bittersweet yearning that *krontjong* music celebrates — the longing for a cherished land or a sweetheart beyond reach and songs exulting in the paradoxical message that "although I am at home, I savor my feelings of homesickness" — did not arouse melancholy sentiments in my sober parents.[4] Nor was ours a family that felt estranged from the small-scale coziness of Dutch social life and buried itself in wistful reminiscences about *tempo doeloe*, the good old days in the Dutch East Indies, as a diversionary tactic. I did not grow up in a household decorated with the tangible artifacts of a colonial past, with shadow puppets on the wall or batik tablecloths and ikat curtains everywhere.

Nonetheless, my parents' short stint in the Dutch East Indies left an indelible mark on their lives and, indirectly, on their four daughters. In old family photo albums we could see black-and-white pictures, yellowed by time, of my sun-tanned father, dressed in shorts and knee socks, lounging in a rattan lazy chair on the veranda of a white-washed, typically Indies bungalow. We gazed at other photographs of our attractive young mother sitting on a mountainside near Berastagi, surrounded by healthy-looking Dutch friends who luxuriated in the natural splendor and breathtaking vistas of Sumatra. We perused posed pictures of our parents in front of a waringin tree as well as more informal snapshots of groups of young married couples around a dinner table, raising their glasses in a toast for the camera. There was also a lonely picture of a beautiful Javanese woman in *sarong* and *kebaja* — named *baboe* Siti, my mother told us — who was my oldest sister's nanny and carried her as an angelic golden-haired baby in her arms.

Our parents, especially my father, would sometimes tell us about their years in the pre-war Dutch East Indies, and his tales evoked for me an exhilarating world of conscientious, hard work in a land of plenty. His stories portrayed a society that had encouraged my parents to forge strong bonds of friendship with other youthful men and women who had also recently arrived from Holland, and he remembered it as an era of existential independence, productivity, and energy. After all, they had left for the Indies at the tail end of the Great Depression — a period when even the most well-endowed and gifted young people had difficulty finding employment in the Netherlands. But in colonial Indonesia my parents found both professional opportunities and a personal sense of purpose. It had liberated them from the moral scrutiny of my grandparents and small-town social pressures, and it enabled them to create a brand-new life together, entirely on their own terms.

As a child, I remember listening to a "long, melodious string" of exotic names of places and institutions: Batavia, the capital city in which my parents had become officially engaged, Medan, the town on the east coast of Sumatra where they were married; the Tjikini hospital in which my mother had worked as a nurse and Berastagi, the invigorating mountain resort where she had recuperated from exhaustion.[5] The melody of strange-sounding names concluded with Surabaya, the city where my oldest sister was born, and Tretes, a Dutch hill station in the cool mountains above Malang to which my mother and sister had moved when Japanese planes began to bomb Surabaya. I recall studying the brownish pictures in the photo albums, with their funny, serrated edges and frayed corners, whose subjects, dates, and places my father had identified underneath in his neat handwriting. When I was young I did not wonder about the millions of Indonesian people who never appeared in any of the photographs, with the exception of the solitary picture of *baboe* Siti with my oldest sister cradled in her arms. I guess I must have guilelessly absorbed my parents' recollection that Indonesians tended to be invisible, serving mostly as a silent backdrop to the hustle and bustle of the Dutch colonial community in which they lived and worked.

Now that I am an adult and a historian who has tried to think seriously about the distinctive nature of twentieth-century Dutch colonial culture in the Indonesian archipelago, I am both puzzled and slightly embarrassed, once in a while, by my failure to notice the almost total absence of Indonesian faces in the family photographs I poured over during childhood. How could I be so blind? Why didn't I ask specific questions about *baboe* Siti, or about the other servants — the *kukkie*, *kebon* and *djongos*

Trying to Reconstruct the Dutch East Indies, 1900-1942

The author's parents on their weddingday in Medan, 1940

The author's oldest sister in the arms of the baboe, 1941

(the cook, gardener, and male servant) — within my parents' household? This kind of discomfort in hindsight, of course, is a silly, and basically false, emotion, because it presumes that the sensibilities we have acquired as adults should have been naturally present in childhood. It is an example of what Doris Lessing in her recent autobiography has called the difficulty of reconciling "child time" with "adult time."[6] Instead, most children notice what they are taught to see and value. A need for approval molds a child's powers of observation, while parents' or older siblings' shared sense of propriety influences the kinds of questions a child will innocently probe.

In a more immediate personal context, Paula Gomes, in her moving book *Sudah, laat maar* (Enough, let it be) has recorded with touching precision the dilemma of a young Dutch girl's acceptance of the unequal relationship with her beloved Indonesian nanny who slept, as was custom, on a mat besides her bed. On one occasion she remembers sitting in bed looking at a book with pretty pictures, when she invited the *baboe* to come sit next to her so they might look at the book together. But the *baboe* stayed on her mat on the floor, shaking her head and beginning to giggle: "the *baboe* belonged below, on the floor, and even though it flashed through my mind: why, really? I accepted the situation."[7]

Paula Gomes's deceptively simple challenge, resembling a fleeting, if suppressed, glimmer of insight — why, really? — is the basic question that sustains this book. Unlike Paula Gomes, I have no personal memories of Dutch colonial society in Indonesia. I was born after my parents had survived the trying separation of World War II and had safely returned to Holland. The war had dispatched them to opposite corners of the earth for more than three years. My father had spent the war years as an officer in the Dutch navy, based mostly in Trincomalee in Ceylon (Sri Lanka). My mother had managed to leave the Dutch East Indies on one of the very last transport ships to end up, by way of Perth (Australia), San Francisco, New York, and Caracas (Venezuela), on the Caribbean island of Curaçao in the Dutch West Indies — with two tiny babies by then. I appeared later, while they were busily reconstructing their traditional lives in a very familiar Dutch setting. My questions issue from a different source. They combine the diffuse memories of childhood tales about the Indies as a world of lush tropical abundance, populated by the most gentle and pliable people on earth, with the more disciplined intellectual queries of a historian interested in the particular nature of Dutch history or Dutch culture in diaspora.

My version of Gomes's question: why, really?, entails, above all, a wish to understand the wide range of mentalities, myths, and rhetorical practices that buttressed Dutch colonial rule in the Indonesian archipelago and endowed it with an aura of naturalness and normalcy. As a curious historian I have pestered various people who lived in the Indies before World War II, now quite elderly, with questions in the course of the past six years. With an array of soothing preambles, such as: I am not at all interested in exposing "colonial exploitation" in the past —*koloniale uitbuiterij*, a phrase that has acquired haunting overtones in contemporary Dutch discussions — I tried to give assurances that I simply wanted to know more about the nature of Dutch colonial practice in the Indies. Invariably they looked at me with suspicion and shrugged their

The author's parents (father on the left) reunited after World War II in New York, December, 1945

shoulders, only to give me a frustrating and perhaps typically Dutch answer: that is simply the way it was! (*zo was het nu eenmaal*). Sometimes, I am afraid, they silently conjured up yet another quintessentially Dutch thought when I bothered them with these vexing questions: if you just act normal, you are already crazy enough! (*doe maar gewoon, dan ben je al gek genoeg*).

I wonder whether these Dutch phrases function as an equivalent to what a nineteenth-century Russian intellectual might have called "the tragedy of fate." As Rudy Kousbroek has recently reminded us, human beings with little sense of autonomous control over the course of their life tend to invent the magic potion of an inescapable "fate" or an inexorable human "destiny." But they drink this comforting elixir merely to explain their own "lack of determination and character" or to render themselves immune to current or retroactive criticism. Appealing to fate, Kousbroek suggested, absolves us from personal responsibility and enables us to exonerate our own questionable behavior by blaming neutral outside forces such as circumstances, dumb luck, or destiny; it allows us, in other words, to ascribe culpability to anyone or anything but ourselves.[8] Indeed, if a silly throw-away line such as *zo was het nu eenmaal* — which often seems accompanied not only by a shrug of the shoulders but also a slow, sheepish grin — is a droll Dutch rendition of valiant Russian struggles with a "tragic fate," then many among us might benefit, as Kousbroek wryly recommended, from a rereading of Ivan Turgenev.

But each and every one of these elderly people are perfectly decent Dutch folks, who embody all the cultural and political virtues one commonly associates with "Dutchness." Perhaps some among them might grumble in silence about the Dutch welfare state's overly generous provisions to foreign immigrants into overcrowded Holland, whether they hail from the former Dutch colony Surinam or from Sri Lanka, Ghana, or Bosnia; but on the whole they are broad-minded and kind-hearted people. However, even the most innocent questions about their past identities and attitudes as Dutch colonial residents of the Indonesian archipelago seemed to raise all sorts of hackles.

In some cases this reluctance issued from the fact that these former Dutch East Indies' residents had never envisioned themselves as "rulers" but simply as refugees from the Great Depression in the European metropole, who finally found a sense of self-confidence and professional success in southeast Asia. In other cases their unwillingness to reminisce may stem from a psychological incapacity to think about life in the Dutch East Indies because the recollections of the humiliation endured in a Japanese internment camp during World War II has obscured all other memories. Yet other people's reticence may have derived from the troubling questions raised in the late 1960s and again, in recent years, about the culpability of the Dutch nation *vis-à-vis* Indonesia.

As most human beings acknowledge, confronting and articulating memory in a truthful fashion can be both a liberating and a harrowing process — what Meena Alexander has recently called "the exhilarating dangers of memory."[9] A natural tendency resides in many of us to suppress recollections of the personal ordeals of childhood that linger on as aching thorns in the psychic flesh of adult life; instead, we are inclined to embellish the uncomplicated, happy ones. The same desire to gloss over traumatic historical experiences affects collective memory, too.[10] A country with neither a record of foreign aggression nor a strident military tradition — and a nation that has always prided itself on a long history of tolerance and civic-mindedness — constitutes no exception in this regard. The burdens of history and the "anxieties (*Unbehagen*) of culture," in the sense that Sigmund Freud attached to it, weigh as heavily on the shoulders of small nations as on those of large, powerful ones.[11] But memory is hardly ever cast in stone: its meanings are malleable and constantly reconfigured over time. Mundane realities at later historical moments either nurture or restrain the willingness of younger generations to unearth and scrutinize some of the more problematic actions of their forebears.

On the one hand, as Ian Buruma wrote in 1994 in his *Wages of Guilt. Memories of War in Germany and Japan*, growing up in the Netherlands in the post-World War II era among elders who had suffered either Nazi atrocities in the European metropole or endured Japanese abominations in the Indies was "to know that one was on the side of the angels."[12] On the other hand, Dutch historical memory in recent years has become mired in a murky emotional morass of "shock, outrage, and shame" about revelations of Dutch cruelty during the post-war independence struggle in Indonesia — a set of visceral reactions just as incapable of yielding a calm and reasoned understanding.[13]

To a Dutch person living on the other side of the Atlantic Ocean, this kind of polarization of historical memory comes across as a quaint, and perhaps typical, national habit. The attempt at a collective reckoning with the colonial past is full of "moralizing, criticizing, discussion, and debate." The motto "complain, protest, object, and appeal" converts serious, if critical, historical scholarship into something resembling a national emergency that demands a vigilant moral opinion from everyone, regardless of whether such views are grounded in a thorough knowledge of the facts.[14] As the military historian Petra Groen recently noted with a hint of caustic humor, people in Holland have "a certain propensity to engage in moral discussions."[15] Besides, particular segments of public opinion in the Netherlands also endow novels and other forms of fiction, if situated in the baroque setting and evocative emotional world of the colonial community in the Indies, with the power to ridicule or insult the honor of any citizen of the contemporary Netherlands.

The whimsical wordplay in the title of a recent, and quite irreverent, guidebook to contemporary Dutch culture written by a sardonic Anglo-American team — *The Un-Dutchables. An Observation of the Netherlands, its Culture and its Inhabitants* — alludes to the self-righteous FBI crusaders within American culture, "The Untouchables," who engaged in an uncompromising battle with Chicago's wicked Mafia during Prohibition in the 1920s. A similar aura of a herculean struggle between the forces of good and evil is summoned up in the current, impassioned efforts to assess the realities of the Dutch colonial past or the ill-fated "police actions," as they had been labeled euphemistically, during the post-World War II era.

As the Dutch nation during the Nazi occupation of World War II split apart between either brave resistance fighters or active collaborators, so is contemporary public opinion about the record of Dutch colonialism in Indonesia stuck in a quagmire of sadly polarized views. During World War II, when numerous "Righteous Christians" in the Netherlands defied the Nazis and helped Jews — a fact commemorated in the impressively long list of Dutch names on the wall of the Yad Vashem Memorial in Jerusalem or in the Holocaust Museum in Washington D.C. — the Dutch nation also produced a sizable group of volunteers for Hitler's Waffen SS. Today, the public controversy over the culpability of Dutch colonial rule in Indonesia is also caught in a web of antagonistic moral judgments. This combative discourse — obsessed as it is with exposing either guilt or innocence, as if historical "Truth" is contained in a black box that only needs to be uncovered and put on display — again weighs down the process of coming to terms with historical realities, at both an individual and a collective level. Hence, personal interviews have not yielded much insight into the ways in which the unique mixture of European moral sensibilities and Indonesian circumstances transformed the identity of Dutch people in colonial southeast Asia. As a result, my pursuit of the thorny question, why, really? has relied on the traditional written sources of historians — such as archival records, memoirs, novels, journal articles and newspapers — rather than the interviewing techniques more commonly employed by either anthropologists or sociologists.

Dutch East Indies society was hardly an equitable, civic-minded community that incorporated Indonesians as partners in civil society; as a result, it deviated from the perceived quintessence of "Dutchness" in the European metropole. The characteristics we tend to associate with Dutch political culture and social practices in the European metropole — religious tolerance, broad-mindedness, early forms of freedom of thought, "communitarian" or "consociational" democracy, pragmatism, or free trade — did not form the foundation of Dutch behavior in colonial Indonesia.

In a European context, the cultural representation and meaning of being Dutch were rooted in an unwavering faith in civic freedom and neutrality, or in the liberal acceptance of political and religious difference. "Dutchness," in other words, resided in a political universe ordered by time-honored habits of accommodation, compromise, and the honest bargaining over contested space. Once uprooted and divorced from the cultural lineage of the Dutch nation in the European metropole, however, such cultural representations became empty gestures, as if "true" Dutch values were lost in translation. In a colonial arena, it appeared, the moral visions and behavioral norms of Dutch men and women were transformed and came to be grounded, instead, in a belief in their white-skinned, cultural superiority.

Rather than resolving conflicting visions of hierarchy or contested cultural claims through even-handed negotiation, which was customarily viewed as a normal Dutch "style," colonial residents in Indonesia tended to rearrange prevailing notions of command and subordination in a quixotic and arbitrary fashion.[16] As Anath Abeyesekere has recently observed with regard to a different context but a similar quandary, Captain James Cook, when he was at home in eighteenth-century England, appeared to be a grave, steady man — "a gentle navigator with a decent, plump Englishwoman as a wife" — but aboard ship he was a "despot" and in his treatment of Polynesian people he behaved like a lunatic and a "brute."[17] In the same way, a number of compassionate, civic-minded Dutchmen who had lived quiet lives with sweet, chubby housewives in Holland transformed themselves into hard-hearted human beings upon their migration to the Indies.

Dutch colonial "lords" thus relegated Indonesians to a position of illiterate "bondsmen," as subalterns who were incapable, either for the time being or permanently, of mastering the social idiom and cultural vocabulary of the West.[18] It was true that in the twentieth century a small number of Western-educated Indonesians were endowed with a civil status equal to Europeans (*gelijkgesteld*, or *staatsblad Europeanen*). Dutch colonial society bestowed Eurasians, too, with European citizenship if their white-skinned fathers formally acknowledged them. Nonetheless, *gelijkgestelde* Indonesians were not really embraced as peers in Indies' society who could enjoy the same cultural prerogatives as full-blooded Europeans. The Dutch colonial civil service carefully studied, co-opted, and reshaped the ancient customs and legal traditions of Indonesians (*adat*), so they might reflect more comfortably the interests of the colonial community and provide labor power for the profitable export economy.[19] Hence, in the 1920s and 1930s, Dutch government officials imprisoned well-educated and refined Indonesian nationalists, without due process of law, in internment camps for voicing an independent political opinion and disrupting Dutch notions of order and political harmony. In another context, some Dutch planters approached Javanese and Chinese contract laborers on the rubber and tobacco plantations on the east coast of Sumatra as "beasts who somewhat resemble human beings" whom they could therefore abuse without moral qualms.[20]

As the thoughtful Indonesian nationalist Sutan Sjahrir wrote in 1936, in the Indies "the official idea of a 'concentration camp' has not yet been institutionalized; it thus lags behind Nazi-Germany. But Germany could have learned a lot about the creation of such institutions by studying the practices of Boven Digoel."[21] This was the controversial camp where Indonesian political leaders who were reputedly the most dangerous to the state (*staatsgevaarlijk*) had been confined in the late 1920s and 1930s. An editorial in *The New Republic* in October, 1945, in fact, described the Tanah Merah camp of Boven Digoel with more than a bit of hyperbole: *The New Republic* labeled Boven Digoel as "one of the world's most terror-ridden concentration camps in a swampy, malaria-infested jungle" of Dutch New Guinea.[22] Published after Allied troops had not only liberated the Nazi concentration camps in Poland and Czechoslovakia during the late Spring of 1945 but had also broadcast their horror at what they had uncovered, this American assessment was certainly a tendentious and loaded one.

While a comparison of Captain James Cook's behavior among Polynesian peoples in the Pacific with the conduct of Dutch planters on the east coast of Sumatra is unlikely to arouse the ire of many citizens of the contemporary Netherlands, the analogy between the Dutch East Indies and Nazi-Germany constitutes a "forbidden metaphor."[23] It is true that the proverbial permeability of Dutch culture has implied a constant need "to define and redefine what Dutchness really means."[24] This shifting historical necessity to forge and refashion national identity has often entailed a process of designating the essence of Dutch political culture relative to that of others. In 1991, in fact, a nationwide, multi-disciplinary research program, generously funded by the Netherlands' equivalent of the American National Endowment for the Humanities, began to contemplate Dutch culture and identity in the face of a blurring of national boundaries that might come in the wake of the growing unity of the European Community.[25]

Even within an explicitly comparative approach, though, certain analogies seem unproblematic, while others appear to do nothing but rankle and cause distress. Hence, an exploration of the "Englishness" of Captain Cook's eccentric behavior in a Polynesian environment comprises a legitimate parallel; it is an analogy that might shed light on the "Dutchness" of white-skinned Europeans' dubious treatment of coolies on tobacco and rubber plantations in Deli. But in the post-World War II era, any homology between Dutch colonial mastery in Indonesia and the Third Reich has been taboo: it conjures up a simile that is beyond the pale of accepted rhetorical practices.

For example, Henk van Randwijk, a founder and editor of the anti-German, underground newspaper *Vrij Nederland* during World War II, wrote on July 26, 1947, that "two years after Hitler's defeat we have not yet forgotten that armed violence can be used to defend injustice and ungodliness ... because I am a Dutchman I say no! to the brutality that we currently perpetrate in Indonesia."[26] Van Randwijk invoked the "higher standard" of human decency and moral integrity he had used during the war to condemn the Nazi regime and he simply proceeded to apply the same ethical principles to the Dutch government's actions in Indonesia. But despite his stature as a pivotal figure in the anti-Nazi Dutch resistance, Van Randwijk's judicious comparison with Hitler produced commotion and calumny, causing a split in *Vrij Nederland*'s editorial board and eventually effecting a reduction, albeit minor, in the number of subscribers.[27]

Van Randwijk, however, was not alone in summoning the Hitler analogy. In December, 1948, an Australian delegate to the meeting of the Security Council of the United Nations in Paris in December, 1848, employed the same "forbidden metaphor." He accused the Dutch government of committing acts of cruelty in Indonesia that "were worse than what Hitler had done to the Netherlands."[28] This linguistic proscription continues to be alive and well in the contemporary Netherlands. When Graa Boomsma said recently that the members of the Dutch military during the Indonesian independence struggle "were not SS officers, no, but because of the things they did they could be compared [with SS officers]," or when he wrote in 1992 that "Boven-Digoel existed long before Hitler had established the concentration camps Buchenwald or [Bergen] Belsen," he overstepped, yet again, a rhetorical boundary.[29] Because he had allegedly offended former colonial residents' sense of propriety by misrepresenting the meaning of the Dutch political record in colonial Indonesia, Boomsma and the journalist who interviewed him were accused of libel and subsequently tried in a court of law.

But regardless of the homologies we invoke, it is hard to ignore or deny that Dutch definitions of cultural citizenship as they functioned in northern Europe were recast in a colonial context. Hence, we must try to decipher the transcription of Dutch ideas about belonging to the community, or about inclusion and exclusion, into the ideology of colonial mastery in the Indonesian archipelago. In the setting of the Dutch East Indies the mostly communitarian definitions of citizenship in the Netherlands itself were transformed into a rigid classification of Europeans and natives (*inlanders*), which relegated the millions of Indonesians to an opaque territory on the opposite end of an enormous colonial divide, where they could be inscribed with various forms of otherness.

In colonial Indonesia, the concern with the collective economic well-being of the small Dutch nation in Europe, surrounded by powerful neighbors, was translated into a vision of Indonesians not as members of the same community, but as beasts of burden who bolstered the invincibility of the Dutch colonial "citadel" without being allowed to share in the material or cultural spoils of victory.[30] It was the agricultural labor power of Indonesians that directly sustained the wealth of an exclusive, Dutch bastion in the tropics and nurtured the prosperity of the mother country in the European metropole.

The Dutch, of course, were not alone in their colonial vocation in Asia. It makes sense, therefore, to think comparatively, on occasion, about the different colonial histories of other Western nations in Asia. Indeed, in almost every imperial setting, European dominion in Asia intervened in indigenous institutions and cultural practices by introducing new forms of civil society and proclaiming "politics" to be the solitary preserve of white civil servants and their native retainers. Colonial regimes also selectively maintained many elements of the pre-colonial world, depending on their utility.

Through a process of "freezing the wolf in sheep's clothing," to use the picturesque phrase Nicholas Dirks coined, colonialism disguised its own intervention by either ossifying or rearranging the meaning of certain indigenous customs or by reorienting the function of native institutions. Accordingly, colonial rule established a form of cultural "dominance without hegemony." Even though it was an uneven and incomplete process at best, colonial culture tried to offer a ratification of the social structure it had created by neglecting certain practices or reinforcing other cultural meanings and successfully passing them off as "The Tradition."[31]

Inevitably, the Western reconfiguration of indigenous customs was different in each national context, and such variations depended on an imperial power's definition of its civilizing mission — or *mission civilisatrice* — as well as on the distinctive nature of the pre-colonial *ancien régime*. After all, British, French, or Dutch colonial administrators imposed a wide range of dissimilar European expectations upon colonized territories, since diverse political and cultural factors, located exclusively in the European arena, influenced the attitudes and actions of European emissaries to the colonies. For instance, the need for government revenue in the European metropole, or the relative significance of the search for international prestige through imperialist expansion defined the specific style of a colonial community. The composition and ethnographic training of civil servants, or industrialized Europe's hunger for capitalist markets, also molded colonialists' visions and influenced their practices.[32]

Equally relevant was the extent to which Europeans absorbed the rhetoric of biological evolution, which enabled them to approach indigenous people as helpless children or to envision them as a species stuck at an earlier stage of the evolutionary process. Invariably, the relative importance of Europeans' missionary zeal to convert the indigenous population to Christianity played a role, too. While the *conquistadores* embarked on their colonial mission in Latin America armed with both the sword and the Bible, Paul van 't Veer has aptly written, the French wielded not only the sword but also their firm belief in the superiority of French civilization. The Dutch and the British, on the other hand, arrived in the colonies waving their muskets while scribbling furiously in their financial ledgers.[33]

Similarly, structural conditions unique to each colonized country affected the specific nature of colonial practice. For example, a region's ethnic diversity or religious heritage occupied a conspicuous place of importance; what mattered, too, was whether it possessed raw materials and other economic resources or was integrated into the world economy. The alliances or malleability of a country's indigenous elites constituted issues of equal significance, whereas the length of time a certain region had been colonized also influenced the ways in which European civil servants, planters, businessmen or women functioned in the colonies. It was the specific interaction between European expectations and local conditions that created a unique colonial culture; its particularity hinged on a distinct hybrid of European values and Asian circumstances — what Ann Stoler has called "homespun creations" in which European moral values and patterns of behavior acquired novel political meanings.[34]

But Dutch colonial residents internalized these diffuse forces at a concrete level in their humdrum, daily routines. Even though we might like to remember our personal histories in more dramatic terms, the average human life unfolds more often as a chaotic —and alas, quite pedestrian — "sprawl of incidents" rather than as a grand epic.[35] Instead of acting as the fearless protagonists of a coherent story, human beings resemble "wounded creatures [with] cracked lenses, capable of only fractured perceptions."[36] For the average Dutch person in colonial Indonesia, this was perhaps even more true, because a career in the Indies implied a sense of intellectual isolation, Willem Walraven wrote: it meant living on a gently flowing "tributary" or a sleepy "side street," far removed from the main "source" of honest self-criticism.[37]

The prosaic realities of the expatriate experience defined Dutch men's and women's behavior; it shaped their mode of thinking and turned many among them into different people.[38] Normal human beings of "flesh and blood, with individual histories and a unique set of qualities" forged their own utterly "banal" responses to the exigencies of their new tropical milieu.[39] Ideas about the intrinsic superiority of the West constituted an organic part of Europeans' newly crafted, "homespun" identities in the Indies. Given the "strange interdependence between thoughtlessness and evil," as Hannah Arendt has described it, many Dutch folk in the Indies translated the technological sophistication of the West into a vision of the world that "naturally" entailed white-skinned dominance over brown-skinned people, too.[40]

Through their command over the cultural grammar of daily life in colonial societies, Europeans concocted a subtly changing set of clichés about the native "other," whether in Java or elsewhere. From "inscrutable" they mutated into "primal but predictable Orientals": superstitious, devious, spineless, or effeminate. But these fickle stereotypes could be altered yet again whenever it served a different imperial agenda, and thus Javanese superstitions might become an expression of their inborn spirituality; on occasion, their lack of education was transformed into an innate Oriental wisdom, or "cowardice" became "timidity" and could be rendered as evidence of the inherently pacific nature of the Javanese.[41]

In 1917, the architect Thomas Karsten addressed these trenchant issues in a thoughtful short article on "Racial Delusions and Racial Consciousness":

> Dutch people in Europe harbor no intense racial prejudice. Why would they? ... Holland's greatest virtue resides in the arena of culture: it has an honorable history of being a haven for refugees from other nations ... But here, race is poised against race. Here, climate and nature are not nurturers of his natural tendencies or needs, but rather, their enemies. The Indies force him to relinquish all sorts of mores and values he has always viewed as natural. Only when he arrives here does he understand that these familiar habits constitute an intrinsic part of his identity, both as an individual and as a racial type. Unknowingly the milieu in which he was born and raised had also endowed his life with an organic sense of meaning or of self-worth. When this milieu is suddenly lacking, his standards fail him. There is more: everything he does entails an inner-conflict, both substan-

tively and morally — because colonizing, even if it appears logical and inevitable, subjectively remains unnatural as well as illegitimate. As a result, he feels deeply threatened, whether consciously or unconsciously, in his most personal values. Hence, racial delusions provide a wonderful solution — the exaggerated estimation of the value of his own kind, of his own work, and of the labors of his own people![42]

But the process of forging newly configured, colonial identities and moral personalities, whether male or female ones, kindled a combustible kettle of differences. Different Dutch women and men championed or excused their superior position of power in the colonies in myriad, and internally contested, ways. Indeed, an understanding of the intransigence of Dutch colonial society in Indonesia in an era of growing nationalist agitation forces us, I would argue, to examine the contradictions in the imaginings of "the nation" and the musings about the multiple meanings of cultural citizenship, which competed with each other in a continual effort to validate colonial mastery.

This bedlam of distinctive visions coaxed some Indies men and women into repudiating the Dutch colonial manipulation of millions of indigenous peoples, to invoke Karsten's words, as "subjectively unnatural and illegitimate." But other Europeans engaged in a series of convoluted justifications that managed to endow European dominance with an aura of both normalcy and permanence, perhaps in an effort to sublimate their misgivings through "hypocrisy" or "bluff."[43] They invented an ostentatious "world of pretense" which either blurred or solidified the boundaries between ruler and ruled in an unpredictable fashion. By establishing a "theater" of imaginary linkages, most Dutch residents in the Indies converted a social world that was grounded in polar extremes of rich and poor, of white and brown, of us and them, into a spellbinding "working harmony" that presumably managed to "enchant" all participants.[44]

The colonial domain in southeast Asia loomed larger than life in the collective *mentalité* of the Dutch nation: as an American political scientist observed in the late 1930s, it "saturated" the whole being of the mother country.[45] The Indies served as a tangible reminder of an era when the seventeenth-century Dutch Republic had performed a starring role in the world-wide coliseum of politics and commerce. But towards the end of the nineteenth century Holland became acutely aware of its "schizophrenic" international position: in Asia the nation could flaunt its prestige as a "colonial heavyweight," while in the European metropole its stature represented that of a puny "lightweight."[46] Only the continued possession of the colonies could assuage the oversensitivity of "a small nation with a great past" and verify its claim to be a mouse that could still roar.[47] The importance of the Indies, in other words, bolstered Holland's assertion to be a valuable second-string player in international affairs, and the Dutch nation hoped to substantiate this claim by trying to administer its empire with more wisdom and discretion than other colonizing powers. The so-called *Ethische Politiek* (Ethical Policy), however, which was enunciated in 1900 and officially inspired Dutch policies in the Indonesian archipelago in the twentieth century, produced a sad irony. Its idealism was soon overshadowed by a deep-seated fear of Indonesian nationalism, which tended to deflect the Ethical Policy's honorable intentions of creating more schools for Indonesians, delivering better health care, and bringing about political decentralization.⁴⁸ The Ethical Policy was meant to be an optimistic fresh start, initiated in response to a barrage of criticism voiced in the late nineteenth century, when journalists, scholars, and politicians from both sides of the ideological spectrum had begun to reproach the systematic and highly successful Dutch exploitation of its Indonesian possessions.

After all, relative to other colonial powers in Asia the *cultuurstelsel* (system of forced cultivation of cash crops), implemented by Governor-General Johannes van den Bosch around 1830, had been enormously effective in generating income for the Dutch nation. In 1851-1860, for instance, it reached the astronomical figure of 31 percent of aggregate government revenue.⁴⁹ Thanks to the cultivation system *Indië* came to resemble, in the words of the nineteenth-century novelist Multatuli, "a beautiful horse with a thief mounted on top."⁵⁰ When the mother country rejoiced in its last "bloodsoaked" *batig slot* (surplus income) from the Indies in 1877, according to the Social-Democrat Josef Emanuel Stokvis the Dutch nation had earned a grand total of 823 million guilders since Van den Bosch's first transmission of profits in 1831; other critics guessed it was an even higher amount.⁵⁰

In a response full of soul-searching and contrition, the Ethical Policy proposed that the Dutch role in the Indies, instead, ought to be one of moral *voogdijschap* (custody or guardianship): colonial policy should focus on educating and "uplifting" the Indonesian population.⁵² In fact, in the annual Royal Oration before the Dutch Estates-General in 1901, the young Queen Wilhelmina had spoken of a new "moral mission" for the Dutch colonial administration in the Indies. Rather than viewing the colonies merely as patrimony and a profitable cash cow, the Ethical Policy implied a novel dedication on the part of the Dutch colonial administration to the development of schools and medical services, transportation, and other infrastructural improvements for the native population.⁵³ The Minister of Colonial Affairs wrote to the Queen in 1904 that a lasting, undisturbed possession of the colonies could best be secured through "a peaceful, righteous, and enlightened administration."⁵⁴ And the new *Encyclopaedie van Nederlandsch-Indië*, published in various installments since 1917, proclaimed that the Ethical Policy had inaugurated a "modern" stage in the colonial relationship between the Netherlands and the Indies: no longer based on materialistic exploitation, "Dutch colonial policy would be conducted honestly and unselfishly in the interest of the colonized peoples and their country."⁵⁵

Scores of civil servants trained at the University of Leiden after 1901, under the intellectual aegis of famous Islamic scholars and knowledgeable *adat* specialists such as Christiaan Snouck Hurgronje and Cornelis van Vollenhoven, absorbed this perspective on Dutch colonial obligations as a high-minded, moral imperative.⁵⁶ Authoritative voices within the civil service began to call for an integration of native district chiefs and regents in the day-to-day governance of the colonies, who should be incorporated into one comprehensive hierarchical structure rather than being relegated to a contiguous one.⁵⁷ Unflappable "ethical" colonial officials worked with all their might at enriching educational opportunities for indigenous people or at curtailing epidemic disease among them; they rolled up their sleeves to help in the colonial state's engineering efforts at expanding irrigation systems, building roads and bridges, or improving sanitation.

Many a Dutch civil servant in the Indies did much better than merely espouse a soft-hearted, "teary-eyed ethical stance" (*huilerige ethiek*). Indeed, some of them harbored in their souls a veritable "sacred fire (*feu sacré*) which burns because of their empathy and love for the simple peasants in the countryside (*kromo*)," the dedicated Resident of Rembang, G.L. Gonggrijp, wrote in January, 1913.⁵⁸ In other words, a large number of ethical progressives in the Indies became "humanitarian dreamers" or "bourgeois aesthetes": idealists who truly wanted to serve and support, to edify and educate, or to help and heal, but they were "perched on the edge of a volcano" and foresaw nothing of what the future might bring.⁵⁹ To some extent reminiscent of the rhetoric of Radical Tories in England, the ethical stance was avuncular in intent and practice.

However, despite their romantic goals and regardless of a profound knowledge of the wide range of ethnic traditions and cultural practices within the Indonesian archipelago, many of these didactic civil servants also continued to perceive Indonesians as childlike and ignorant about the complexities of the world (*weltfremd*) and thus in need of Western tutelage for at least another generation or two. These lingering attitudes found expression in the painfully slow assimilation of Indonesians into the upper echelons of the Dutch civil service. In 1940, for instance, of the 3,039 high-level positions in the colonial bureaucracy, only 221 were held by Indonesians.⁶⁰ Being the exact opposite of a humanitarian dreamer, the penultimate Governor General of the Dutch East Indies, Bonifacius Cornelis de Jonge, grotesquely exaggerated such jaundiced perspectives on the naiveté of Indonesians in the 1930s. Censured by left-of-center critics as a "reactionary who was completely blind to internal relationships within *Indië*," De Jonge envisioned himself as the father of a family with an enormous number of little children; he exemplified the motto that there was only one system of good governance: "I am the boss — and I will feed you [*inlanders*] your pablum."⁶¹ Not surprisingly, the next-to-last Governor General opined in July, 1933, that Indonesians would not be ready for independence, and the Dutch would therefore need to stay on as overlords, for "another three hundred years."⁶² Moreover, in their daily administrative routine, well-intentioned civil servants encountered cantankerous opposition from planters and conservative businessmen who accused them of losing sight of Dutch national interests and the imperative logic of Western capitalism.

A denunciation of the Ethical Policy from Dutchmen in the opposite ideological corner of Socialism delivered another salvo of criticism. In 1917, the fervent socialists Henk Sneevliet and Asser Baars, for example, sneered that in its mature stage, capitalism forced its defenders in colonial societies in Asia or Africa to talk about "rights" in addition to "duties." The running dogs of Western capitalism, they contended, invented the hollow slogan of "self government" and concocted the delusion of "popular representation" as diversionary tactics. The twentieth-century ethical posture of white-skinned colonial masters was nothing but an epiphenomenon of the youthful liberalism of a burgeoning European bourgeoisie. The so-called Ethical Policy of the Dutch colonial regime, Sneevliet and Baars noted in a startling metaphor, resembled "the false pearls and fake diamonds with which a decrepit, worn-out old man curries the favors of a vain child." Socialists, instead, offered a luxuriant panorama of the political future, which could be compared to a handsome and idealistic "young dreamer's stormy declaration of love."[63]

Similar "counter voice[s]," to use Elsbeth Locher-Scholten's fitting phrase, within the chorus of pro-and-contra arguments continued to sound their antiphonal song, both loudly and softly, until the bitter end in 1942.[64] Several oppositional journals, which raised deeply moral questions about the nature of the colonial relationship, waxed and waned. In 1931, a social-democratic critic scorned the Dutch proclivity to indulge in the intellectual "luxury of sociological, psychological — even illogical — philosophizing" about the nature of colonial societies. The sophisticated, erudite treatises about cultural synthesis and the much vaunted association between the fragile Eastern soul and the Western spirit of ingenuity were in reality nothing but hagiography (*heldenzang*), "singing the praises of the Dutch civil service, its caution, its painstaking solemnity, and its even-keeled courtesy."[65]

An inspector of secondary education in the Indies who had formerly served as the principal of the HBS (European High School) in Semarang, Z. Stokvis, ridiculed such over-intellectualized tomes. He dismissed these books as truly absurd because they glossed over the fact that "we" invented and continued to monopolize the mechanisms of power. "We" monitored, spied on, arrested, and incarcerated; "we" silenced any Indonesian who had the temerity to disagree with "our" presumably beneficent vision of colonial rule.[66] Another reviewer also repudiated books such as the massive volume written by Arnold Dirk Adriaan de Kat Angelino in 1930 as a "psychologically inept, naively inhumane" (*onmenschkundig, naief-onmenschelijk*) disquisition. Because the West had perpetrated "injustice and violence" upon the East, the Occident was "bothered by a most irksome thing, a [guilty] conscience," which exposed the West to a level of criticism that was both appropriate and "deserved." Nonetheless, De Kat Angelino's book resembled the fancy footwork of "a rhetorician who muddles the truth" rather than the labor of an artist who "amplifies reality."[67]

In due course, not only a collective fear of the nationalist movement but also a repressive policy of *rust en orde* (tranquility and order) obscured the idealistic endorsement of the Ethical Policy, especially in the wake of the Communist insurgency in Java and western Sumatra in late 1926 and early 1927. This uprising came as a surprise to the Dutch colonial regime, notwithstanding the presence of an invasive police apparatus that carefully monitored what were called "extremist" groups.[68] Since the earlier years of the twentieth century, a wide array of nationalist organizations had emerged in Indonesia. The earliest association was *Boedi Oetomo* (Beautiful Endeavour), an alliance of Javanese aristocrats founded in 1908, which sponsored a mild form of nationalism. Since many among its members had been drafted into the middle-ranks of the colonial bureaucracy which kept alive their hope for future promotions, traditional feudal rulers (*priyayi*) in Java were reluctant to bite the hand that fed them. As a result, the island's elite walked a political tightrope that was suspended in a liminal space between the hierarchical values of the Dutch colonial civil service and Javanese popular culture, which would spawn a variety of political factions enthralled with more radical forms of nationalism.

Sarekat Dagang Islam (Islamic Union) was created three years later and claimed as many as two million members by 1918.[69] *Sarekat Islam's unprecedented ability to mobilize the orang kecil* (literally "little people," i.e. the common folk), especially in Java, turned the organization's leaders into a forceful voice of criticism of the "colonial administrative order and all its trappings: Dutch superiority, *priyayi* arrogance, and the social barriers imposed upon native society."[70] Members of the Islamic Union openly expressed their antagonism towards "the *priyayi* cultural matrix" of Javanese society; in the vernacular press, they criticized both the feudal aristocracy and their Dutch colonial patrons. Hence, *Sarekat Islam* emerged as a potent populist organization that both startled and preoccupied Dutch colonial authorities.[71]

Mixed-blood European settlers were also mobilized politically and rallied around the *Indische Partij* and *Insulinde* and later, around the Indo-European League (*Indo-Europees Verbond*). Myriad ethnic groups created their own political and cultural organizations, too. At the same time, some activists within the Indonesian nationalist movement considered themselves unapologetic Communists imbued with lofty dreams of social justice and economic equality, even if the *Partai Komunis Indonesia* (the Indonesian Communist Party or PKI) would not mushroom into the largest Communist party in south-east Asia until the decades following World War II.[72]

These new nationalist organizations, with varying degrees of patience, urgency, or "extremism," embraced the goal of eventual independence for Indonesia. Acting out of dread and a sense of foreboding — a sentiment that emerged as the telling slogan "The Indies Torn, Calamity Born," or in Theodore Friend's translation, "The Indies Lost, Disastrous Costs" (*Indië Verloren, Rampspoed Geboren*) in the post-war era — the Dutch government in The Hague, instead of responding in a constructive fashion to the demands of the nationalist movement, nervously reasserted its imperial authority.[73] The colonial regime in the Indies, meanwhile, became more peremptory in its treatment of renowned Indonesian leaders by summarily imprisoning them on the basis of the Governor General's extraordinary powers, without due process of law or a judicial hearing; at the same time, the colonial state imposed an even stricter system of surveillance on nationalist groups.

Ultimately, the government in The Hague rejected the reasonable Soetardjo petition of 1936, which had already been accepted by the Indies *Volksraad* (People's Council), the *Duma*-like parliament in which elected Dutch and Indonesian delegates could play an advisory political role. The fate of the Soetardjo petition composed a "depressing story" with an unhappy ending.[74] This mild-mannered proposal envisioned Indonesian independence in ten years but affirmed in articles 1 and 2 "that the centuries-long history of joint material and ideological (*ideëel*) interests ... requires an intimate and heart-felt cooperation between the two parts of the commonwealth...."[75] The government in The Hague, however, could not bring itself to seize this felicitous opportunity and fostered, instead, "the growing sense of [racial] superiority" of the European community in the Indies, as an Indonesian member of the *Volksraad* called it, "which paralyzes the masses."[76] Before 1942, in other words, "the colonial apparatus of power and control functioned as the slopes of a mountain that contained the churning mountain stream" of nationalist sentiments "within its riverbeds." After 1942, "the mountains suddenly disappeared and the buoyant river swelled to the extent that it flooded the entire valley."[77]

Indonesians, of course, were hardly alone in their desire for autonomy in Asia. In the 1920s and 1930s, nationalist movements blossomed in many neighboring countries — in the nearby Philippines, for example, as well as in India and French Indo-China — which proceeded to struggle for national independence after the defeat of the Japanese at the end of World War II by resisting the return of their former colonial rulers. Before the outbreak of the second World War, the Japanese had shrewdly cultivated the growth of nationalist sentiments through the prophesy of a "new dawn for Asia" and by nurturing the desire for an "Asia for Asians only," even if an occasional prophetic counter-voice within Indonesia itself warned that this credo in the mouth of the Japanese empire really meant "Asia for Japan." The Javanese poet and essayist, Noto Soeroto, for instance, had already written in early 1920 that the Japanese "rape" of Korea in 1910 and "the tragedy of the Korean people" should serve as a cautionary tale for other peoples in Asia.[78]

Towards the late 1920s, Dutch political rhetoric and action were modulated less and less by humanitarian scruples, especially among an increasingly vocal group of Dutch colonial residents who belonged to the reactionary *Vaderlandsche Club* (Patriotic Club).[79] Another segment of the colonial community clung to its optimistic agenda and continued to approach its role in the Indies primarily as one of teaching, guiding, and nurturing. Many others, such as my parents, floated somewhere in an oblivious middle, mostly concerned with hard work and achieving psychological autonomy or economic security. Gradually, however, an undercurrent of anxiety infected the Dutch colonial community. This European population was estimated at approximately a quarter of a million people. It constituted only 0.35 percent or so of Indonesia's total population, but it was a European enclave that was quite extensive in comparison to the number of British or French settlers who lived and worked in other Asian colonies.[80]

The Ethical Policy had brought scores of teachers, engineers, and doctors to the Indies after 1900, whereas the tail-end of the bleak professional job market in the Netherlands during the Great Depression induced a new generation of young Dutch men and women to try their luck in the Indies instead. Escaping from the economic "slump" of the 1930s, hopeful new arrivals from Holland may have been appalled at the defensive atmosphere and racial prejudice they found. Returning to their precarious existence in Europe was out of the question, however, and many among them felt they had no other option but to adjust to the mores of the emphatic "white civilization" in the Indies; some ensconced themselves so firmly in this white-skinned stronghold that they made old-time residents look like sentimental "native lovers" in the process.[81] In sum, the steady influx of European residents since the turn of the century, who viewed their colonial sojourn as merely a temporary one (*trekkers*) and withdrew into an increasingly racist white community, began to displace the "*blijver*" community of permanent settlers which regarded the Dutch East Indies as its beloved home and had created a distinctive mestizo culture.[82]

Again, what is ultimately at stake in any analysis of culture, whether in the classic Western tradition or in a colonial context, is the conundrum of historical memory and human agency, and the visions of self and the "other" that are part and parcel of membership in a particular national community. It was true, of course, that colonial residents' cultural knowledge did not shape individual behavior separate and apart from either Dutch political culture or social structure. Processes of incorporation and segregation, both in Europe and in the colonies — or the right to determine who truly belonged and could achieve full-fledged citizenship in the nation — exerted an indelible impact; definitions of private rights and public obligations also influenced the behavior of Dutch men and women in the Indies. Invariably, the social attitudes they inherited in Holland or the cultural knowledge they employed were transformed in the course of their activities in the lush, tropical milieu of Dutch East Indies' society.[83] But the significance of these cultural processes resonated differently at a personal level and affected the commonplace, day-to-day realities of people's lives in diverse ways, all the more so because they lived in a world rife with political friction and teeming with contending opinions.

These internal political divisions became increasingly palpable during the twilight years of Dutch authority in the Indonesian archipelago, especially during the 1920s and 1930s. These acrimonious disagreements continued to tear apart the Dutch nation in the post-war era, when Indonesians waged a bloody battle for independence. During the past ten years they have resurfaced again, when questions about Dutch guilt, or the ruthlessness of Holland's colonial practices in the past, have again preoccupied the public imagination in the contemporary Netherlands.

My unsuccessful efforts to engage my parents' elderly friends in a genuine conversation occurred during the past five years. Aside from the occasional tendency of the human mind in old age to become fuzzy and fragmented, the reticence to discuss their personal recollections of life in the Dutch East Indies may also have been tangled up with this painful public discussion about the brutality of Dutch colonial rule. A tentative outbreak of soul-searching had erupted in the late 1960s, as the controversial Vietnam War raged and younger generations throughout the world engaged in passionate protests against the brazen "neo-colonial" actions of their elders. But when a philospher at the University of Groningen in the Netherlands added to the slogan "Johnson Murderer" the refinement "according to the standards of the Nuremberg trials," he was judged liable to a charge of having insulted the head-of-state of a nation that was a political ally.[84]

In Holland itself the ferment surrounding the Vietnam War yielded an initial crack in the wall of silence. For the first time Dutch public opinion warily broached the topic of that "nasty little war," as Professor Nicolaas Beets called the Dutch military battle with the Indonesian Republic in the post-war era in a tongue-in-cheek fashion.[85] A television news program in 1967 interviewed a former participant in the "police actions" of 1947 and 1948, who reported having witnessed acts of torture, summary executions, and the callous destruction of innocent women and children in villages.[86] The Vietnam-War turmoil also coincided with an official, parliamentary discussion in 1969 of Dutch military conduct in Indonesia after World War II during the so-called "police actions": the *excessennota*, or an inquiry into excessive military violence. The parliamentary debate circled gingerly around the tip of the iceberg. The soothing adage *à la guerre comme à la guerre* — which presumably absolved people who had engaged in nasty, war-time behavior from moral blame — prevented many centrist or conservative members of parliament, despite the pleas of representatives on the left, from pushing the official investigation any further.[87]

But since the early 1980s a tempestuous public discussion has surfaced periodically. At once poignant and vitriolic, waves of controversy have crashed onto the shores of Dutch public opinion in the wake of the publication of several new scholarly books that analyzed the history of Dutch colonialism in Indonesia. The historical memory of the former Dutch East Indies, it appeared, still tugs at the heart strings of a large number of people in the contemporary Netherlands. Despite the passage of time, dispassionate judgment continues to be elusive, and an avalanche of highly emotional responses to the new scholarship has tumbled onto the pages of both the popular press and scholarly journals.

Among the books that reignited the flames of controversy was Lou de Jong's history of the Dutch East Indies in the twentieth century, which comprised the latest installment of his monumental *History of the Kingdom of the Netherlands during the Second World War*.[88] De Jong proved to be a harsh critic of Dutch colonial policy. He also argued that some sectors of the Dutch military had been extremely vicious during the "police actions" in 1947 and 1948, which had attempted to neutralize the independent Indonesian Republic in order to perpetuate Dutch colonial dominion in southeast Asia. De Jong's allegation of unnecessary cruelty was a bitter pill to swallow for the very young military officers and soldiers who had fought the fight against Indonesian independence, many of whom are still alive today.

Dispatched to the Indies from a Dutch nation ravaged by the Nazi occupation, most of these young men had engaged in a nightmarish battle with the nationalist forces, an experience that in many cases still haunts their memories. It was true that thoughtful Christian missionaries had advocated a peaceful evolution of Indonesian independence, to which the Dutch nation should voluntarily and energetically contribute. The Dutch Communist Party, too, without the Labor Party's support, was a lonely force in mounting protests. A wildcat strike of trolley workers in Amsterdam, for example, partially crippled public transportation in the city to try to prevent the troops from leaving.[89] It was also true that an extraordinarily large number of military inductees became conscientious objectors or deserters.[90] But all together more than 100,000 young men, including volunteers, sailed off to Indonesia. They went not only to defend their red-white-and-blue flag but also to assert the Dutch nation's "natural" right to preserve its empire from internal chaos, which meant during the painful, postwar *bersiap* period the protection of vulnerable women and children against the murderous rage of gangs of Indonesian nationalists. Once there, these callow Dutch lads landed in a world of "tropical surrealism": they hovered on "the edge of an abyss" because they were forced to confront an evasive enemy who moved about in a slippery "black hole they could not even see."[91]

The memories of these events are still raw; hence, the popular response to De Jong's accusations in newspapers and television programs was agitated and shrill. A second book that unleashed a tempest of outrage, disbelief, or sorrow was Jan Breman's cool analysis in 1987 of labor management practices on the European plantations on the east coast of Sumatra: *Taming the Coolie Beast: Plantation Society and the Colonial Order in Southeast Asia*.[92] Breman's work presented testimony of colonial planters' savage treatment of their Asian subordinates on the immense rubber and tobacco plantations that had literally and figuratively been carved out of the Sumatran jungle. The book chronicled the dehumanizing conditions imposed on imported Javanese and Chinese coolies, who were forced to engage in backbreaking labor from sunrise to sunset and were routinely beaten into submission, starved, and held in a never-ending cycle of contractual bondage.[93]

Breman's findings echo the despair of the Dutch socialist Henk Sneevliet, who had argued in a court of law in Semarang in 1917 that many among his white-skinned, "racial compatriots had degenerated into a bombastic type of *parvenu*, for whom brown-skinned human beings hardly belong to the same biological species."[94] On the opposite end of the political spectrum even A.W.F. Idenburg himself, during his tenure as Governor General a few years earlier, had expressed a similar view that European planters in Sumatra were a woefully "unsympathetic kind of people. Cynical in the extreme, they harbor the opinion that coolies are substandard creatures."[95] Christian missionaries, too, registered their alarm about the "life-threatening danger" they faced if they defended the interests of the natives against "the injustice and the outrageous, dissolute behavior" of European colonialists, because a true missionary could never join the ruling race as a loyal "party member" (*partijganger*).[96]

The most shocking revelation of Breman's book, however, was his publication of the Rhemrev report, the results of an official inquiry by a Department of Justice official, J.T.L. Rhemrev, into labor practices on Sumatra's east coast which the reigning Governor General of the Dutch East Indies (Rooseboom) had commissioned in May of 1903. Rooseboom had been galvanized into action by a short, if inflammatory, book entitled *De millioenen uit Deli*, written by a feisty lawyer in Medan, J. van de Brand, whose *J'Accuse* disclosed the scandalous conditions on Sumatra's plantations.[97] After Rhemrev had submitted his exposé to the Governor General in 1904 — which elicited a comment in the margin from then-Minister of Colonial Affairs Idenburg that it was "a distressing story of suffering and injustice" — the government skillfully suppressed it, and the report remained out of sight and out of mind until Breman unearthed it and published it in 1987.

However, the ubiquitous Idenburg — who was a devout member of the Dutch Reformed Church and a prominent political figure in the conservative Anti-Revolutionary Party — had steadfastly defended the coolie regulation in Sumatra's plantation belt for many years.[98] He proposed in 1911 that as long as coolie labor contracts with penal sanction existed, the threat of punishment should not be rendered "illusory." Idenburg even instructed the Dutch civil servant in charge of Sumatra's east coast to reduce the nutrition of coolies convicted of an infraction of their labor agreements, to avoid a situation in which they might view their judicial conviction as "a liberation from the merciless yoke" that had tethered them on tobacco or rubber plantations.[99] After he had read a few English-language pamphlets about "Dutch cruelty" in Deli, Idenburg sent them to Abraham Kuyper — the founding father and ideological commander-in-chief of the Anti-Revolutionary Party — in the Netherlands. In response, Kuyper wrote that he did not pay any credence to those "little English books about Dutch brutality," if only because "our own Dutchmen cause unbelievable damage with their own vitriol."[100] These two hyper-Christian political soulmates discussed the allegations of Dutch planters' barbaric behavior in cryptic, veiled language, carefully avoiding a formal acknowledgement of the widespread abuses in Deli. It also appeared that government officials, responsible for the subsequent conspiracy of silence regarding the record of inhumanity chronicled in Rhemrev's inquiry, justified their decision by arguing that the few bad things that occurred in colonial Indonesia in the past should be locked up in history's Pandora's box and "covered with the cloak of charity."[101]

With the publication of Lou de Jong's analysis and three years later, Breman's study, the proverbial cat had escaped from the bag: Dutch soldiers had committed questionable acts of violence in 1947 and 1948, while the Rhemrev report provided incontrovertible evidence of the Dutch government's complicity in a colonial reign of terror on the east coast of Sumatra. These revelations, it seemed, substantiated the accusations that stalwart critics on the left had leveled against Dutch governance throughout the entire archipelago. In the post-Independence era, social democrats in the Netherlands could barely concede that the Dutch in the Indies had wrought anything that was even remotely beneficial: Dutch imperial control in Indonesia had yielded nothing but the most flagrant example of racism and exploitation. Others recognize that the historical record may have been a bit more contradictory and complex, while yet another segment of contemporary public opinion was reassured that the Dutch administration of the Indies displayed a series of positive features, too. Nonetheless, these kinds of strident categorical indictments have not fostered a public discussion that might be able to address Paula Gomes's low-key, but compelling, question.

Instead, the historical discussion has been converted into a stand-off between two firmly entrenched camps, whose emotions have boiled over and whose ideological armor prevents them from seeking a *rapprochement* that might yield a thoughtful exploration of the complicated and contested Dutch legacy in the Indies. It produced the sorry spectacle of the "Committee for the Historical Restitution of Honor to the Dutch East Indies" (*Comité Geschiedkundig Eerherstel Nederlands-Indië*), representing as many as 60,000 members, who filed a class-action lawsuit against the Dutch government in the mid-1980s because taxpayers' money had subsidized De Jong's research.[102] After all, not every former colonial was "a rotten bastard" (*rotschoft*), a tongue-in-cheek headline in the social-democratic *Volkskrant* announced.[103] This misguided polemic has reached another fever pitch since June of 1994, when a court of law adjudicated the libel case against the novelist Graa Boomsma and the journalist who interviewed him for employing the "forbidden" analogy between Dutch participants in the "police actions" of 1947 and 1948 and Hitler's SS officers.[104] Fortunately the court displayed the wisdom to acquit the two defendants.

Obviously, such rigid black-or-white judgments are not very productive and do not convey the inherently chaotic and contradictory nature of the historical record. Many former colonial residents, either knowingly or against their better judgment, engaged in forms of behavior that would never have passed political muster or survived moral scrutiny in the European metropole. Others departed for the Indies to build bridges and irrigation systems, to teach in boarding schools for aristocratic Javanese girls, or to serve as medical personnel in clinics and hospitals. Many of these idealistically inclined people clung to an exuberant conviction that "they were accomplishing something great over there."[105] Yet others worked in business offices in the private sector that were not dramatically different from the milieu they would have encountered if they had stayed behind in either Amsterdam or Rotterdam. There were also a considerable number of Dutch civil servants, intellectuals, and missionaries who harbored a life-long scholarly infatuation with various Indonesian cultures. These Java or Bali *liefhebbers* (serious amateur scholars), Toraja specialists, or Batak experts contributed an enormous amount of valuable academic knowledge that still forms the intellectual foundation, today, of contemporary scholarship on modern Indonesia.

Besides, many Dutch women who arrived in southeast Asia after the turn of the century skated blithely on top of the opaque surface of indigenous life and were ensconced in an isolated European community. My mother was a good example. Because she worked long hours as an obstetric nurse, she did not have much time left over to learn much about indigenous cultures; neither did she become a deft speaker of Malay, since she lived in a mostly Dutch-language environment during the years she spent in the Indies. She was far from unique in this regard. Most Dutch *singkies*, as she called newcomers like herself, mastered not much more than *brabbel maleis*: an elementary lingo akin to what Southern Rhodesians called "kitchen kaffir," which tended to formulate mostly imperative sentences: Do this, Bring that, Go there, Stay here![106] Many Dutch women would recite a little ditty, which often they had learned on the boat to the Indies, to clarify their lack of linguistic skills: *satoe* is one, *batoe* is stone, *mati* is dead, *roti* is bread, *jalan* is to walk, *beli* is to buy, and what you don't know remains the same." My father, whose Malay was much more fluent, taught me two additional lines to this silly rhyme that were a bit *risqué*, which scandalized my mother.

There was no such thing as a standard Indies experience, nor can we speak of a generic Dutch cultural style or undifferentiated colonial guilt. Human agency is always contingent, forever molded by an unruly combination of individual sensibilities and social pressures, further complicated by a variety of other factors such as education, individual background, or political ideology. Our duty as historians, I would argue, is to disentangle, as best as we can, this mixture of pushes and pulls. It was a turbulent medley of both rational opinions and ill-defined prejudices or fears that guided Dutch people's behavior in the Indies and sustained Dutch colonial culture; this should be the focus of the historian's inquiry — not moral condemnation or "the historical restitution of honor to the Dutch East Indies," but simply the effort to shed light on Paula Gomes's disarming question: why, really?

Be that as it may, the public imagination of the Dutch nation in recent years has become embroiled in its own version of a *Historikerstreit* about the memory and representation of its colonial past in Indonesia. While the Dutch may have been clever colonialists, as Eric Hobsbawm recently implied in *The Age of Extremes. A History of the World, 1914-1991*, they did not heed the political lessons of the English withdrawal from India or the decolonization of other parts of the British Empire. England shrewdly recognized that by graciously and ceremoniously relinquishing formal power, it could maintain a palpable, if informal, influence in its former colonies and avoid a traumatic schism in the process.[107]

Hobsbawm added, though, that "the Dutch were rather better than the British in decolonizing their 'Indian' Empire without partitioning it."[108] This, however, was not a matter of choice; prominent Dutch civil servants and politicians in the Indies in the post-World War II period became "fascinated" with the new project of designing a federal state of Indonesia.[109] But their frantic, last-minute attempts at social and political engineering produced little more than an intricate castle in the sand that could hardly withstand the oceanic tide of the nationalist movement. A conservative former civil servant mocked the overwrought post-war efforts to build the United States of Indonesia as a "synthetic creation that was richer in fantasy than in insight ... a chimera, a deliberate dismemberment of the symbiosis that had grown organically under the protection of the Dutch flag!"[110]

Since then, Dutch public opinion has followed with keen attention the ebb and flow of modern Indonesian politics following independence. Even though the Dutch struggled desperately between 1945 and 1949 to turn the relentless undercurrent of decolonization before they formally acknowledged the autonomy of the Indonesian nation state, a host of nostalgic social connections have lingered on. On various occasions during the early 1950s, the Dutch press indulged in a frenzy of *ad hominem* attacks on Sukarno and other leaders of the independent Republic. Using a metaphor that could only be applied to non-Dutch "others," one news magazine even compared Sukarno's manipulation of public opinion with the Nazi propaganda of Joseph Göbbels.[111] Yet, the convoluted attachments of many Dutch men and women to Indonesia endured. And despite President Sukarno's intrepid actions and defiant proclamations of the late 1950s and the early 1960s, designed to sever once and for all the umbilical cord between the Netherlands and its legendary, magical *Indië* of bygone days, the emotional and cultural bonds are far from ruptured.

In February, 1990, for instance, the Dutch government threatened to withhold 13 millions dollars of foreign aid to Indonesia if the Suharto government proceeded with the execution of four palace guards, implicated in the bloody transition of political power (*kudeta*) in 1965, who had been incarcerated during the previous twenty-five years. In response, the Vice Speaker of the Indonesian House of Representatives, R. Soekardi, initially stated that he could not believe that the Dutch government had really decided to withdraw its commitment of financial aid to Indonesia "because the two countries need each other."[112] But when the Dutch foreign policy establishment actually suspended foreign aid in the wake of the Dili massacre on East Timor in 1992, the New Order regime resolutely abolished the IGGI — the Inter-Governmental Group on Indonesia, which the Netherlands had dominated — in an effort to muzzle the moralistic Dutch voice in internal Indonesian affairs.

At the same time, the publicity surrounding the "Festival of Indonesia" in the United States, officially sponsored by the Suharto government in 1991, which dazzled American audiences in Washington D.C., New York, Houston, and San Francisco with gorgeous art exhibits and spectacular dance performances, made no reference to the colonial past. The Festival entirely glossed over the long history of Dutch control.[113] Instead, it displayed Indonesian ethnic cultures as pristine and completely untarnished by more than 300 years of Dutch presence, as if the Dutch colonial past is a "concluded chapter that has been erased from Indonesians' collective conscience."[114] The Festival's total silence about the Dutch colonial legacy lent some credibility to Rudy Kousbroek's brusque statement that in Indonesia people do not "do" history for its own sake, not out of "resentment or shame, not because people do not want to be reminded of the past, no, simply because the past has disappeared: it does not exist."[115] The value of history, in other words, does not really depend on its facility to reveal the past. Instead, history's meaning hinges more on its prophetic powers and its ability "to inscribe the future."[116]

In another context, the memory of Dutch colonial rule is invoked as a justification of some of contemporary Indonesia's political flaws. In February of 1990 Umar Kayam, a prominent Indonesian intellectual and professor at Gadjah Mada University in Yogyakarta, boldly urged the New Order government to permit greater freedom of political expression, although he conceded that Indonesians were not yet accustomed to uncensured political debate "due to their long history of Dutch colonialism."[117] He challenged Indonesia's opaque authority structure — "a system of politics among princes," a commentator called it recently —which excludes all but a handful of the nation's 190 million inhabitants.[118]

While speaking the truth, Umar Kayam's invocation of the colonial past was undoubtedly designed to mitigate the personal risks involved in questioning the New Order state — a palpable hazard that was reconfirmed, in June of 1994, when the Suharto administration closed down three magazines (*Tempo*, *Detik*, and *Editor*) because of their criticism of government policies and corruption.[119] During the Spring of 1994, the

Suharto regime initiated "Operation Cleansing" — a badly chosen name with haunting overtones reminiscent of Serbians' "ethnic cleansing" practices in Bosnia — supposedly to wipe out street crime. But the target of "Operation Cleansing" quickly expanded from pickpockets and petty thieves to "economically and politically motivated criminals" such as academics, journalists, and labor organizers.[120] The government has arrested and imprisoned human rights activists, too, without much consideration for due process of law.

Despite Indonesia's reluctant membership in the United Nations' Human Rights Commission since early 1991, and its promise to set up a national Human Rights Commission in early 1993, the New Order administration persists in trying to convince the outside world that in Indonesia, human rights are "respected in accordance with the special traits of [our] national culture." In response, Pramoedya Ananta Toer did not mince words. He dismissed this culturally relativist conception of human rights as "out-of-date rubbish." It is the equivalent to pronouncing "us dead under civil law," he scoffed, "or marginalizing us as pariahs."[121] The obsession with forging and maintaining a distinct national identity in which Islam is allowed to play a growing role inflects Indonesia's response to the Western world's demand for greater human rights. Taufik Abdullah, meanwhile, has wondered whether this concern resembles a national neurosis that strangles the evolution of a viable and democratic body politic in the process.[122]

In the government's imagination these courageous people, struggling for free political discussion, human rights, and an independent labor movement, personify a subversive tribe of "goblins of sectarianism" who must be rooted out.[123] Vice-President Try Sutrisno has even branded them as "a new generation of Communists" or "new traitors" requiring the eagle-eyed surveillance of the army.[124] The "feudal" New Order state is presently so leery of any form of criticism that when a human-rights activist made a joke in a seminar at the Islamic University in Jakarta in August, 1994, quipping that "in Indonesia, we don't have general elections, but we have an election of generals," he was immediately arrested.[125] The Suharto government in recent times, the poet W.S. Rendra has suggested, behaves like a fiendish but fainthearted spider that frantically tries to constrict the voice of public opinion by spinning a "tyrannical" web of unpredictability.[126] Hence, few people would question Umar Kayam's intellectual integrity, or that of anyone else, in appealing to the Dutch colonial past as a partial explanation for the less than open political discourse of contemporary Indonesia.

An occasional historian in the Anglo-American scholarly world, in fact, has argued that among all the former colonial powers in Asia, the Dutch, despite their "great virtues and economic achievements," have generated the most virulent "hostility" among their previous colonial subjects.[127] But Indonesians seem to make an analytical distinction between their memories of the exploitative relationships inherent in a colonial system, on the one hand, and their recollections of the Dutch nation and its people, on the other. Quietly ordained by the Suharto government, the idea prevails that the history of both colonial subjection and the bloodthirsty *kudeta* of 1965 are behind them: there is no need to belabor the memory of either sequence of troubling historical events — or "to dredge up old cows from the creek" (*oude koeien uit de sloot halen*), to use an eccentric Dutch expression.[128]

In Indonesians' historical memory, the truth about the Dutch colonial legacy may be ominous and black, but it does not merely function as a fertile breeding ground of bitter animosity. The contemporary meaning of the colonial past probably resides somewhere in a dull, gray area in the middle. The long period of Dutch colonial governance has exerted a lingering impact, however erratic and uneven, on the political culture of contemporary Indonesia, which modern-day Indonesians acknowledge with a mixture of emotions ranging from rancor to indifference, depending on the purpose it might serve. While in official nationalist historiography Dutch colonialism is often depicted as "the devil incarnate," in the imagination of run-of-the-mill Indonesian citizens the Netherlands probably resembles little more than a loud-mouthed, if "toothless," lion.[129] In contemporary Indonesia's negotiations with a powerful Western world, the United States and the United Nations Human Rights Commission — or the World Bank and the International Monetary Fund — are much more significant than opinionated little Holland. After all, the task of building a newly independent nation is a monumental one. Rehashing the negative repercussions of Dutch colonial rule in the context of modern Indonesian politics converts historical memory, in many instances, into little more than an instrumental device.

Similarly, any approximation of the truth about the history of Dutch colonial culture also occupies a cloudy space in-between collective guilt and dreamy nostalgia, or in-between the universal "rotten bastardry" of all Dutch colonial residents in the Indies and sanguine memories of the good life of hard-working, decent Dutch burghers in the tropics. Binary opposites of this sort neither enable a fruitful discussion nor foster a deeper understanding. As most people realize, history can function as the one-dimensional mirror of Snow White's evil stepmother: it divulges only what we want to see and confirms all the myths we harbor about ourselves. But history also constitutes a multi-dimensional crucible — it refracts, distorts, obscures, or enlightens, depending on one's location and perspective. The historian's task, it seems to me, is trying to retrieve "the style of the imagined community" of the past, to use Benedict Anderson's pertinent phrase, in all its messy diversity and contested realities.

Of course many of us who are serious about being historians find ourselves chasing shadows or tilting at windmills. Even though we can plumb the depths of revealing source materials, most historians realize that any reconstruction of a historical reality is an inherently subjective exercise. We can only concoct a deeply personal vision and obtain a frustratingly partial view of the past. Every nation's past, after all, is inundated with a flood of endless contradictions. The historical record of each and every national community reveals both human decency and distressing examples of human depravity. History is almost always filled with big victories and resounding defeats or with nasty little fights and lukewarm reconciliations. History is also replete with moments of ideological certitude that alternate with instances of existential doubt and despair.

But for historians, however fragmentary our memories inherently are, trying to remember is an imperative, as the Hebrew Bible repeats over and over again, because forgetting, Joseph Yerushalmi has warned us, will inspire the irrevocable wrath of God.[130] Historians with a more secular mindset might see themselves as "physicians of memory." Just as a doctor has a mandate to intervene because a sick patient requires urgent attention, regardless of the medical theories or technical equipment at his or her disposal, so the historian should try to act under a moral obligation to resuscitate, purge, heal, and keep alive a "nation's memory, or that of mankind."[131] What would have been the use of an officially sanctioned, public discussion about the nation's sensibilities that spurred on the frenzied "police actions" in 1947 and 1948, the Dutch journalist Anil Ramdas asked in January, 1995? His answer was very simple: to make Dutch people acknowledge that they have no legitimate reason to feel "holier" than anyone else.[132]

Chapter Two

A Cunning David Amidst the Goliaths of Empire:

Dutch Colonial Practice in the Indonesian Archipelago

When history calls upon small nations to engage with energy and intelligence in the demanding work of empire, a little country such as Holland provides better guarantees than larger nations to implement the appropriate policies. Bigger European countries have a proclivity to use brute force in colonial administration — a blunt violence that is grounded in their self-assurance as a society that can wield superior political and military might. Large countries tend to ignore the gradual adjustment process and evolutionary development that indigenous people must go through in order to achieve a higher level of civilization.[1]

J.C. van Eerde, "Omgang met inlanders," 1914

"The greater the weakness" in the international political arena of European nations trying to foster the evolution of native peoples, wrote Professor Johan Christiaan van Eerde, the Director of the Anthropology section of the Colonial Institute in Amsterdam in 1914, the more earnest would be their efforts "to acknowledge and accommodate the cultural predilections of members of indigenous societies." Van Eerde asserted that those European colonial powers that could rely on their "reckless sense of strength (*domme kracht* or *plomp geweld*) to impose their own will and determination" on vulnerable, primitive people would be less likely to recognize the unique, if fragile, nature of indigenous cultures. As a result, he concluded, such nations would fail to nurture the organic development of indigenous people in order to enable them to flourish.[2]

Besides its relative political frailty in the European metropole, Dutch observers also invoked the physical vulnerability of Holland's water-logged provinces, half of them submerged below sea level, to explain the Netherlands' unique role in the imperial enterprise. Centuries of courageous struggle to protect their "own square foot of ground," not only against the ferocious North Sea but also against the *realpolitik* pursued by domineering neighbors, gave willful Dutchmen the ability to maintain themselves, too, amidst an ocean of indigenous peoples in southeast Asia. The Dutch nation had acquired a special blend of characteristics that rendered its colonial civil service an exemplary one, and all of this combined to make Holland eminently suitable for a leadership role in forging a positive synthesis between West and East, a function "world history has entrusted to Holland."[3]

This was the legend of the peerless colonial civil service which the semi-official spokesman of Dutch colonialism, Arnold Dirk Adriaan de Kat Angelino, theorized in 1930. His massive scholarly tome, sponsored by the Ministry of Colonial Affairs and translated into both French and English within the next two years, constituted a "gigantic official memorandum (*nota*)" on the virtuosity of the Dutch colonial civil service that became the "Holy Bible of the official mind."[4] Civil servants in the Indies embodied the "apotheosis of the superior and honest Dutch bureaucratic style." His book celebrated the Dutch civil service as a sturdy "silent force" which had molded indigenous societies into a model of economic efficiency and social stability.[5] De Kat Angelino exalted European administrators' gentle cooperation with their "younger Indonesian brothers," which would bring about cultural fellowship in the "foreseeable future." Yet, the completion of this cultural synthesis would take a very long time, while he was hardly convinced that this journey would automatically lead to independence. Instead, reaching the end of the path of cultural association would merely bestow upon Indonesia at some vague point in the future the "honor of becoming an autonomous member of the Kingdom of the Netherlands."[6]

Van Eerde's and De Kat Angelino's pronouncements echoed the call to arms which the prominent legal scholar and *adat* law expert at the University of Leiden, Cornelis van Vollenhoven, had issued in 1910. With Weberian overtones, Van Vollenhoven announced that Holland's "vocation" should be to nurture world peace and to promote international cooperation.[7] It was a function the Dutch Republic had performed with great political agility and moral prestige until 1700 or so, only to be reduced to relative oblivion thereafter. The "calling" of the Dutch nation in the twentieth century, Van Vollenhoven intoned, was to reclaim and reinvigorate this vital historical destiny. Because of its small size and pacific traditions, Holland was not guilty of participating in the insidious game of international power politics that mighty nations played with arrogance and aplomb. If the Netherlands did not seize the auspicious opportunity to perform once again the leading role of facilitator and mediator in international relations, Holland's fate would be to remain a country that was both trivial and dull (*duf*) or desultory and sluggish (*gebluscht*).[8]

Van Vollenhoven's rousing peroration was designed to awaken the Dutch nation from its nineteenth-century hibernation and its obsessive focus on internecine, domestic struggles; it should do so by reasserting its Solomonic vocation in international affairs. His high-minded exhortation both reflected and legitimated the earnest arguments of many other Dutch and foreign writers concerning Holland's empire in southeast Asia. Even though Holland was a mouse in its European habitat, it was a lion in an imperial setting. But the Dutch lion in colonial Indonesia was not depicted as one to roar, rant, and rave. Instead, in the popular imperial imagination the Dutch lion represented a clever beast which was the symbol of Dutch national identity and ruled its den with cunning and insight, with wisdom and imagination.

Accordingly, Dutch colonial civil servants exulted in their ethnographic knowledge of native peoples. The distinct configuration of *adat* among each ethnic group — referring to the particular patterns of social and spiritual bonds grounded in custom and convention, in form and feeling, and in unique definitions of prestige and deference — they insisted, should both be cultivated and protected.[9] By learning as much as possible about the cultural practices, cosmology, and local languages of the many different ethnic groups of the archipelago, most Dutch civil servants hoped to carry out their philanthropic agenda and act out their "ethical" convictions. In doing so, many among them approached their task of colonial governance as conscientious parents who were intimately familiar with the quaint habits and peculiar psychology of their native offspring, thus assuring that Indonesia would stay under Dutch tutelage for centuries to come.

Hence, the basic point of this chapter is simple and straightforward: the Netherlands, as a diminutive democracy in northern Europe, which played only a cameo role in the grand theater of powerful European nations, was, in fact, a colonial giant. This paradox provided Dutch burghers in the colonial diaspora of the twentieth century with an urgent sense of mission. Owing to Holland's small population and its undistinguished military presence in Europe, Dutch colonial administrators could not rely on crude power or brute force. Instead, many among them saw their primary role as one of governing their districts with more anthropological learning, greater cultural sensitivity, and better political skills than any other imperial power in Asia.

The Dutch, in other words, had to employ the ingenuity of David in order to maintain themselves among the Goliaths of Empire. By displaying an appropriate mixture of ingenious political judgment and cultural wisdom in the governance of its southeast Asian colonies, the Indies provided Holland with the most important reason "why and how a small nation can be great."[10] Dutch colonial rule in the Indies became both a serious intellectual "project" and a carefully designed "poignant monument," as Jacques van Doorn has recently called it, in which the glorification of local *adat* or the *desa* (village) community and the respectful study of indigenous cultures did not merely serve Machiavellian purposes.[11]

The prominent Dutch economist George François Elbert Gonggrijp, for example, insisted that for Holland the meaning of the Indies epitomized an immense ethical challenge, because the Indies invited the Netherlands "to deploy all the integrity and intellectual talents it could muster."[12] A former lieutenant-colonel in the Royal Dutch East Indies Army concurred in 1938 that Dutch authority in the Indies, with its population of nearly 70 million and a minuscule military presence of only 30,000 soldiers, was rooted in "moral force" rather than "military prowess." It was common knowledge, after all, that a small country such as Holland could not have the slightest belligerent intentions, either in Europe or in the East, but if Dutch colonial rule were to collapse, it would inevitably lead to nothing but "chaos in the Indies."[13]

The propaganda of the Netherlands Chamber of Commerce in New York carried this theme of Holland's political insignificance in Europe versus its prominent position in colonial affairs to even greater rhetorical heights: "the paradox of the political weakness of the mother country" in light of the enormous size of its overseas empire formed the Netherlands' unique "strength as a colonial power." In a lengthy and self-congratulatory report issued in 1924, the Netherlands Chamber of Commerce stated that the Dutch East Indies underscored "the truth of the philosophical dictum about the harmony of contrasts: a small mother country and a wealthy colonial empire ... the inhabitants of the mercantile 'Low Countries' as masters of agriculture on the mountainside." Their business spirit and their "calm, well-balanced temperament," the report claimed, rendered Dutch colonizers "superior" to other imperialist nations.[14]

In an effort to encourage the investment of foreign capital in Indonesia, the report proudly announced that Holland wished to provide economic access to her overseas territories to "those nations which have no colonies of their own, and in this way [Holland] demonstrates to a narrow-minded, egotistic world the practical solution to conflicts in the colonial sphere." The report confessed — with a somewhat disingenuous *mea culpa, mea maxima culpa* — that the economic history of the Dutch East Indies during the previous 300 years had journeyed along a path "through the narrow valleys of self-interest and the depth of grinding exploitation." But the language of atonement for past transgressions gave way to a jubilant plea: the time was ripe for Holland to reach "the summit of *freiwirtschaftliche* (free-trade) policy" and to enact its pioneering role in the "internationalization of economic life."[15]

This remarkable report alluded to the fundamental ambivalence of historical memories about the Dutch imperial project. As far as the *mise en valeur* (economic productivity) of its overseas possessions was concerned, the Netherlands had been, in the words of a modern-day historian, "the most imperialistic nation," but it was also the "least imperialistic" one, since the Dutch state voluntarily surrendered its settlements in Africa shortly before the final partition of the continent in 1872 and abstained from an official policy of expansion since then.[16] Accordingly, Dutch imperialism, several contemporary political scientists and historians have concluded, was of an accidental — or an "abstemious" or "reluctant" — variety and displayed a more "informal character" than the combative imperial adventures into pristine territory of other European nations in the late nineteenth century.[17] The somewhat oxymoronic phrase "ethical" imperialism, or imperialism "with a moral calling," for instance, has also been employed to chronicle the bloody Dutch subjection of the southern half of Bali in 1906.[18]

Contemporary historians' use of euphemistic language, though, derives most likely from the honorable tradition of Dutch neutrality, tolerance, and lack of belligerence in the European arena, thus yielding the impression that the designation Dutch imperialism was a contradiction in terms. After all, the territorial boundaries of the Dutch colonial possessions in southeast Asia were informally agreed upon — and unchallenged — during the era of international rivalry and the frantic European search for colonial possessions after 1870. The gradual "rounding off" (*afronding*) of Dutch colonial rule into the archipelago's outer regions was portrayed as neither arousing the same kind of jingoistic nationalism nor dictating a policy of military aggression commonly associated with the imperialist agendas of larger European nations. This kind of historical representation has even raised the rhetorical question whether such a phenomenon as "Dutch imperialism ever really existed?"[19]

However, the process of "colonial sub-imperialism," to use Fieldhouse's characterization, involved not only a variety of non-violent political negotiations with independent native rulers, but also entailed a series of ad hoc military campaigns, which caused the loss of many lives among both Dutchmen and Indonesians, ranging from Aceh in Northern Sumatra to Lombok and Bali.[20] Despite such palpable violence, the expansionism of the Dutch colonial state in the late nineteenth century was often depicted as a series of delicate political maneuvers and subtle cultural transactions between wily, sensitive, and above all, knowledgeable, colonial administrators, on the one hand, and indigenous sultans, regional chiefs, and local potentates, on the other.

Since the late nineteenth century, Dutch colonial governance revealed a remarkable symmetry between the desire for knowledge (*le désir de savoir*) and the desire for power (*le désir de pouvoir*). The burgeoning respect for *adat* law and the painstaking ethnographic study of the cultural traditions of Indonesian ethnic groups constituted what Sheldon Pollock has recently described as an "extreme and often transparent instance" of knowledge that both generated and sustained "power," while bolstering the forms of colonial domination that shaped the very concept of "power."[21] In other words, *adat* scholarship in colonial Indonesia, which had become deeply entrenched by the 1920s, was unequivocally beholden to the logic of colonial rule. In comparison, the development of anthropology as an academic discipline in Britain seemed to emerge more autonomously from nineteenth-century intellectual developments in biology, natural history, or moral philosophy. Relatively speaking, the British colonial administration of countries such as India was less self-consciously implicated in the anthropological project of understanding the cultural or evolutionary differences between Europeans and so-called primitive peoples elsewhere in the world. English civil servants in India — although less so in Africa — occasionally dismissed academic anthropologists as "suspicious characters."[22] In general, British anthropology responded more directly to the theorizing, hypothesizing, or model-building of biologists or natural philosophers than to the exigencies of empire.[23]

Similarly, French colonial scholarship, from its inception more acutely aware of the political friction between the theoretical claims of ethnology and the descriptive, classificatory orientation of ethnography, issued from a palpable intellectual quest to test the relevance of universal laws of social progress in particular empirical contexts or "*champs d'expérience*" (fields of experience).[24] Towards the end of the nineteenth century, the French colonies in North Africa, Indo-China, or Madagascar emerged as ideal experimental laboratories in which French colonial administrators could gauge the functioning of grand social theories and measure or index their differential refraction within particular socio-cultural milieux.[25] But the French colonial empire also served, its peripetetic architect Louis-Hubert-Gonzalve Lyautey announced, as a breeding ground for a reinvigorated French national energy, a nursery of a uniquely French cultural "flair" (*élan*).[26] Through a rigorous process of comparison, ethnological scholarship would yield crucial insights into the "true" nature of French cultural achievements and reveal both its essence and its inherent superiority.[27]

Dutch ethnography, instead, was more deliberately dedicated to furnishing accurate and practical information to colonial civil servants responsible for the administration of the Dutch empire in southeast Asia.[28] "Oriental" learning and ethnographic scholarship, in terms of the prevailing definition of the substantive "fields of anthropological study" as well as the choice of theoretical perspectives, followed neatly in the footsteps of the socio-cultural and political preoccupations of the Dutch East Indies' bureaucracy.[29] Despite palpable internal differences, colonial civil servants' shifting perceptions of effective governance, or the particular visions of modernity they embraced, had an indelible impact on scholarly definitions of Indonesian ethnic traditions. Bureaucratic and administrative concerns inflected ethnographic efforts to understand and describe indigenous cultures, while ethnographers supplied basic knowledge to civil servants.[30]

In the process, both ethnographers and administrators "localized, fractured, and restated" Indonesian cultural forms, which were thus "drained," to cite Oliver Wolters, of some of their original meanings.[31] Dutch "Oriental" knowledge, in other words, conformed to Edward Said's dictum and "particularized" all things Indonesian by splicing them into "manageable parts."[32] While it is probably correct to note that in many colonial settings the data and insights of anthropologists were either "dispensible" and often "too esoteric for government use," this was perhaps less true in the Dutch East Indies.[33]

The distinctive nature of Dutch anthropology — which was characterized by its "accuracy, concreteness, pertinacity, modesty, caution, breadth of interest, and a simply amazing control of the historical, literary, and linguistic tools of Indonesian scholarship" — issued unambiguously, it seemed, from the political requirements of colonial administration.[34] In the Dutch imperial imagination, fastidious "Oriental" scholarship was portrayed not only as an intellectual mechanism considered essential to the endurance of colonial mastery; it was also viewed as the most advantageous alternative to the blunter instruments of military prowess and political arrogance deployed by more influential European nations. Knowledge was the handmaiden of power, whereas a display of authority without knowledge would quickly degenerate into the mindless saber-rattling of imperial Goliaths.

Accordingly, espionage activities, intelligence gathering efforts, or the "counter-insurgency research" of Orientalist scholars accompanied the late nineteenth-century expansion of Dutch dominance beyond Java. The work of Christiaan Snouck Hurgronje — who has been described as either an opportunistic adventurer, a bigamist, and a devious spy or as an erudite professor of Islamic religion and culture at the University of Leiden — constituted a controversial example. His scholarly advice eased the incorporation of various outer regions into the Dutch East Indies empire, especially during the colonial state's protracted struggle with the volatile Acehnese in Northern Sumatra.[35] Edward Said, for his part, identified Snouck Hurgronje as a "simple and clear" example of an Islamicist whose Orientalist scholarship crystallized, above all, his "national identity."[36]

Dutch officials were inclined to interpret ethnographic exploration and military reconnaissance as two sides of the same coin. Beginning in 1879, the Indies colonial state began to commission an array of linguistic officers and started to employ serious scholars who advised the government on Islamic law or native, Chinese, and Arabic affairs; in the next decades, the government became the sponsor of an elaborate archeological research agency and an ethnomusicological archival center, too. Professor Van Eerde summed up the situation in a comprehensive review of Dutch ethnographic literature, written in English for an international audience, in 1927: "no group of less civilized peoples has been so well described, so much studied and made so accessible to ethnological science as the peoples of the Dutch East Indian archipelago."[37]

Many foreign commentators confirmed this uniquely Dutch imperial imagination. The American anthropologist, Raymond Kennedy, for instance, argued in 1942 that the distinguished record of even-handed patience and broad-minded cultural understanding of the Dutch in the crucial question of race relations in the colonies had bestowed upon them a highly respected voice in post-World War II plans for the Orient. In the near future, when East and West may finally meet on equal terms, Kennedy maintained that the Netherlands will serve as a shining example in "showing the way to the new era of tolerance and the brotherhood of man."[38] And in 1943, a high-ranking U.S. State Department official asserted that it was a generally accepted opinion that "the Dutch have made the best [colonial] administrators" in the world.[39] Observers abroad, it appeared, whether in England, France, or the United States, tended to corroborate the Dutch pride in their judicious colonial governance. What intrigued foreign specialists on Dutch colonial affairs most, though, was the spectacular success of the Dutch in the Indonesian archipelago to extract an abundance of agricultural products, profits, and revenues from its overseas domain, as if the Dutch East Indies constituted a prolific "Frisian milk cow which the Dutch government milked with great care."[40]

The triumphant *mise en valeur* of the Dutch East Indies, as the French called the profitable use of indigenous labor, was a perennial source of either barely suppressed envy or begrudging admiration. Between 1891 and 1904, for instance, no less than twenty-five French study missions, or *missions d'enquête*, visited colonial Indonesia. Participants in these various fact-finding excursions focused their attention on topics ranging from Dutch political administration and patterns of land tenure to the technical details of specific irrigation projects. They also investigated Dutch colonial museums of archeology, the available tourist facilities in the Indies, or the railroad network on Java.[41] Moreover, the bi-weekly *Quinzaine Coloniale*, which served as the magazine of *Union Coloniale Française* (French Colonial Union), published a regular feature entitled "The Netherlands Indies." In these columns the editors offered a steady stream of flattering news about the intricacies of the cultivation of rubber, tobacco, or cacao on European plantations and the management of the indigenous labor force. They also lauded the splendor of the government-sponsored botanical gardens in Buitenzorg (Bogor) or complimented the sophisticated legal and linguistic training of Dutch civil servants.[42]

On the whole, most French observers were compelled to acknowledge, perhaps with a certain amount of rancor, that little Holland, despite its insignificance in European politics, could present to the rest of the world, "without fear and with legitimate pride, the magnificent fruits of its patient and tenacious efforts" in the administration of its overseas possessions.[43] The French expert on Colonial Affairs, Joseph Chailly-Bert, asserted in 1927 that he routinely told students enrolled in his courses on comparative colonialism at the *Ecole des Sciences Politiques* in Paris that if they wanted to acquire both "unparalleled learning and a prominent reputation" at the same time, they should learn to read and speak Dutch and examine the writings on Dutch colonial administration in order to translate or "rewrite them for the use of our compatriots."[44] In doing so, he intoned, they would render an immense service to their country and engage in a splendid intellectual task.

The English-speaking world painted a comparable rose-colored picture. That the Dutch were a clever colonial power whose possessions in Asia had generated profits and revenue beyond anyone's wildest dreams became a well-known fact after the middle of the nineteenth century, especially following the publication of a widely read book by the Englishman J.W.B. Money, called *Java, or How to Manage a Colony*, in 1861. Money's book captivated the fancy of King Leopold II of Belgium, for example, who literally and figuratively went shopping for a colonial empire in 1862 after reading it.[45] Since then Clive Day's and John Sydenham Furnivall's thoughtful analyses of Dutch colonial practice also entered the Anglo-American scholarly universe, which reiterated, with some caveats, the generally positive assessment of the Dutch administration of the Indies.[46] English-speaking visitors to Java, meanwhile, waxed rhapsodically about the endless beauty and natural order of the Indonesian countryside. "Java, as little Holland itself, is cultivated from edge to edge like a tulip garden," wrote Eliza Scidmore in *Java, the Garden of the East*; "all the valleys, plains, and hillsides are planted in formal rows, hedged, terraced, banked, drained, and carefully weeded as a flower bed."[47]

Above all, English-language accounts extolled the "thoroughness" of Dutch colonial governance and congratulated Dutch civil servants on their intimate familiarity with the social particularities and cultural traditions of the each ethnic group.[48] Despite its small size and its trivial role in the politics of the European metropole, both England and France were forced to embrace little Holland as a peer and partner in colonial affairs. And when an occasional foreigner criticized the Indies government for being stingy in providing education and health care or faulted the colonial state for exacting antidiluvian forms of feudal labor service from the native population, Dutchmen shrugged their shoulders and dismissed it as mere "jealousy of little Holland's large and lucrative empire."[49]

Obviously, the enormous discrepancy in the geographic and demographic size of the Netherlands and its colonial empire in southeast Asia was striking. Tiny Holland consisted of a narrow tract of land in Europe that occupied less than 16,000 (15,963) square miles. Indonesia, in contrast, embraced approximately 13,000 islands which covered an aggregate territory of approximately 735,000 square miles and were dotted for a stretch of about 3,000 miles along either side of the equator. The entire population of the Netherlands in 1909, when the political and military expansion into the outer regions of the Indonesian archipelago had more or less come to an end, reached no more than a paltry 5.8 million people.[50] The total indigenous population of the Dutch East Indies during the same year has been estimated at somewhere between 37 and 40 million, of which about 30 million people lived on Java and Madura alone.

By the time the Dutch East Indies' census of 1930 was completed, providing somewhat reliable population figures for the first time, the overall population of both Java and the outer regions had risen to a grand total of at least 59.1 million, while the population of the Netherlands had grown to 7.9 million.[51] These grotesquely incongruous numbers underscore the unequal —or unnatural — relationship between a mother country that was both a physical and allegorical dwarf and its colonial progeny that had reached gigantic proportions.[52]

In terms of its real economic worth to the mother country as well as the ways in which its meaning was inscribed in the Dutch public imagination, Java had become a glorious ship which Holland's capable captains had commanded to a grand victory — or in Furnivall's more truthful and precise formulation, the "life belt that kept especially the Dutch treasury afloat."[53] Relative to other colonial powers in Asia, the Dutch *cultuurstelsel* — the system of compulsory cultivation of cash crops such as coffee, cane sugar, and indigo, and, to a lesser extent, tobacco, tea, or spices, which were transported and sold on the European market through state monopolies — had been most effective in generating government revenue. For example, during the period 1830-50, 19 percent of Dutch government revenue derived from the Indies, a figure that grew to 31 percent in 1851-60, only to decrease to 24 percent in 1861-70 and to 13 percent during the following decade of 1871-1880.[54]

Some nineteenth-century liberal economists as well as many modern-day historians have excoriated the cultivation system for wreaking havoc among the Javanese peasantry and for reducing the "beautiful island of Java to unparalleled wretchedness and misery," especially in the 1840s when devastating crop failures caused widespread famine, epidemics, and death.[55] Others, instead, have praised the Dutch improvements to irrigation and transportation networks necessary for the large-scale production of cash crops; they also applauded the stimulus to internal trade and the increased circulation of money, which enabled peasants to absorb a rudimentary understanding of the logic of the capitalist market and nurtured a blossoming sense of indigenous entrepreneurship.[56] In the official historical record of modern Indonesia, however, the cultivation system functions as the most notorious evidence of Dutch greed and systematic exploitation.

For the Netherlands, meanwhile, Java emerged as the "jewel in the Dutch crown," since the valuable commodities such as coffee and tea, produced through labor services imposed upon the native population, yielded handsome prices on the international market and eventually generated the necessary capital to catapult the Dutch economy in the European metropole into the ranks of the modern industrialized world. Thanks to a variety of infrastructural innovations in industry and education, or railroads and waterways, which were financed to a great extent with the profits derived from the Indies, Dutch society in 1900 was no longer a stagnant economic backwater. Not long before the turn of the century, Holland had been submerged in a "deep slumber"; in the mind's eye of many Dutch citizens, the nation had stagnated since the "golden" glory of the seventeenth-century Republic of Rembrandt and Vermeer had faded.[57] But thanks to the phenomenal wealth that the rich volcanic soil of the Indies spewed forth — what Cees Fasseur has bluntly called *andermans geld* (other people's money) — the Netherlands had managed to recoup its former economic vitality around the turn of the century which, indirectly, may also have helped the Dutch nation to recover some of its previous international prestige.[58]

The data on the tangible financial benefits the Netherlands continued to derive from its enormous colonial domain in southeast Asia confirmed these impressions. Although government monopolies had been replaced by private enterprise and capitalist agriculture near the turn of the century, the Indonesian colony endured as a profitable source of income. According to Theodore Friend, during the interbellum period the Dutch nation relied for as much as one-seventh of its overall income on the earnings, dividends, salaries, pension payments, and currency transfers from the Indies (see Table 2-1). Audrey and George Kahin have recently argued that this proportion was about one-fifth, or that the Indies economy yielded 20 percent of Dutch national income.[59] According to W.H. van Helsdingen in 1945, who had served as President of the *Volksraad* prior to World War II, on average an annual sum of 700 million guilders had flowed from Indonesia to the Netherlands during the interbellum period.[60] Even if we judge these estimated numbers as inflated, they nonetheless may have constituted the highest earnings ratio of any imperial nation in the world. With the exception of British India, neither the English nor the French earned profits in their colonies that achieved the same magnitude; in many colonial contexts they mostly suffered financial loss.[61]

In the collective Dutch imagination, though, the proportion of Indies-derived income was even greater than the already substantial figure of 14 or 20 percent: a large number of policymakers or professionals as well as more humble citizens were convinced that the national dependence on earnings generated by the Indies was as high as 40 or 50 percent.[62] As a former mayor of the city of Rotterdam melodramatically overstated the case in March of 1928: "Imagine our colonial empire gone, and our small country can no longer feed its children. Imagine if we were to lose it all, our entire position in the world will fall to pieces."[63] The somber Dutch refrain, *Indië verloren, rampspoed geboren* (the Indies torn, disaster born) was more than mere rhetorical posturing on the part of those who advocated an aggressive stance against Indonesian nationalists.[64] The fear of losing the Indies became engraved in the collective subconscience of Dutch society, an anxiety that grew steadily as the budding strength of the Indonesian nationalist movement in the 1920s and 1930s raised the specter of either Indonesian dominion status or complete independence from the mother country.

Hence, the significance of the Indies was blown out of proportion: if Indonesia would gain independence, some people lamented, Holland would be reduced to the same frivolous position in world politics as Denmark! This underlying concern fostered the conviction that the Dutch midget could maintain its authority in southeast Asia most effectively by slowly educating and uplifting its giant offspring. But this long, drawn-out process of guidance should rely on a thorough understanding of the "structural core" of Indonesian cultures.[65] As a result, a distinct sense of pride in civil servants' profound knowledge of Indonesian conditions, customs, and languages came to define the Dutch style of colonial governance. Or, to use the quaint mixture of classical and maritime metaphors of a Dutch *adat* scholar in the late 1920s: between the "Scylla" of European dominance and the "Charybdis" of indigenous patterns of authority, clever Dutchman, with their long-standing experience as a small but spirited seafaring people, had identified a "perfectly navigable passage" and would sail the tricky waters of colonial dominion in the Indonesian archipelago for a very long time to come.[66]

When the *adat* expert Bernard ter Haar made this statement in 1928, he did not take into account the further expansionism of Japanese political power and military might throughout Asia. However, a mere fourteen years later, the Japanese abruptly cut off the access routes of even the most competent Western navigators on the vast oceans of European colonial rule in Asia. Once Indonesia's independence became an irrefutable fact in December, 1949, Indonesians began to traverse the treacherous waters of political governance by themselves — no longer as subordinate shipmates of the Dutch, but as captains in command of their very own ship of state. But perhaps the lasting impact of Indonesians' long-standing apprenticeship under Dutch skippers, with their unique seafaring style, was more palpable than post-independence politicians may have wished to acknowledge.

Clifford Geertz, for instance, recently argued that Suharto's New Order government in contemporary Indonesia has attempted to "culturalize" ethnic, economic, and religious differences as much as possible in order to conflate contending ideological or religious world views into a single vision.[67] The modern Indonesian state under Suharto, in other words, tries with all its formidable might to pacify political conflicts and placate economic antagonism by glorifying the cultural unity of the Indonesian Republic and accentuating its homogenous national identity. This implies, too, that the Jakarta government attempts to shroud its raw political power in a seductive and disarming "cultural guise."[68]

During the last three decades the Suharto regime has relegated *politik* to the seditious extremities of the body politic; it tends to redefine "politics" as synonymous with individual selfishness and deliberate attempts to subvert the socio-cultural harmony of the nation. The New Order's incantatory slogan of progress and economic development on a capitalist model — *pembangunan* — hardly aspires to bring about cultural change or social transformation. Instead, *pembangunan* constitutes a streamlined carnival of state-sponsored building projects that tries to render the status quo both palatable and "real"; development programs are designed as high-tech "floats in a parade" intent on celebrating the cultural cohesion of the nation by presenting examples for "popular emulation" throughout the archipelago.[69]

Category of Income	1925-34	1938
1. Dividends and interest[a]	179	155
2. Salaries, wages, pensions (private enterprise)	36	29
3. Salaries, pensions, etc. (civil service)	26	26
4. Currency transfers to families	9	5
5. Shipping	67	63
6. Exports, 75% of total value[b]	81	75
7. Trade in colonial products; misc.[c]	60	35
8. Undisbursed profits[d]	30	40
Total primary income	488	428
Total secondary income (70% of 1-7, excluding 8)	321	272
Total Indies-derived income	810	700
Total Netherlands national income	5,500	5,100
Indies-derived income as a percentage of national income	14,7%	13,7%

SOURCE: Adapted from Derksen and Tinbergen, 'Berekeningen over de economische betekenis.'
[a] Consisting of: dividends from Dutch companies working in the Netherlands East Indies (G117 million); interest on government bonds received from NEI (G29 million); interest, private companies (G4 million); and interest on loans made by the Dutch government and the Nederlandse Bank to the NEI government (G5 million).
[b] To allow for improved raw materials, 25% has been deducted.
[c] Revenues from international trade, conducted in the Netherlands, in products such as tobacco, teak, chinchona, and sugar; consequences of noncontrol of large oil companies; and some minor sources of revenue.
[d] Very rough estimate.

Aggregate Netherlands' Income Derived from the Dutch East Indies, in Millions of Guilders
From: Theodore Friend, *The Blue-Eyed Enemy. Japan Against the West in Java and Luzon, 1942-1945* (Princeton: Princeton University Press, 1988), p. 18.

However, the Suharto government's resourceful cultural policies in present-day Indonesia have an unambiguous historical precedent. After all, the Dutch colonial regime, from the late nineteenth century until the Japanese occupation of the archipelago in 1942, employed a comparable conception of efficient governance by designating ethnic identities and sanctioning particular "traditions." The political project of incorporating new regions and ethnic groups beyond the island of Java into the political unit of the Dutch East Indies in the twentieth century was similarly "culturalized." Hence, the Dutch state inscribed its political record of empire-building in the twentieth century with neutral meanings that were grounded in the idea of negotiation and respect for local *adat*.

In the eyes of a substantial sector of the Dutch colonial community, the clarion call since the turn of the century for the material and spiritual "uplifting" of the native population required a careful assessment of local needs. The creation of a national infrastructure based on "cultural synthesis" hinged on the implementation of a policy of "differentiation according to [local] circumstances"; hence "cultural synthesis" defined colonial practice in the twentieth-century Dutch East Indies.[70] Not symbiosis but synthesis was the desired course of action. Symbiosis automatically implied that Europeans' "inborn sense of superiority" would impose a *tjap Belanda* (stamp of Dutchness) on indigenous peoples and might suffocate the uniqueness of their vibrant local cultures in the process.[71] Synthesis, instead, entailed a policy of strategically adapting Dutch colonial policies to the cultural particularities of each ethnic group in the archipelago. The idea of cultural synthesis also included an administrative pattern of bestowing self-government upon traditionally autonomous regions, of promoting decentralization, and establishing administrative divisions based on traditional Indonesian units of authority or juridical domains.

After centuries of self-interested exploitation of the Indies, especially Java, the Dutch nation wished to pay its "debt of honor," as Queen Wilhelmina called it in her annual oration before the Dutch Parliament in 1901, to Indonesians. Although Holland was not unique in this regard, no other colonial power "confessed its guilt as eloquently or donned the cloak of contrition as publicly" as did the Netherlands.[72] But the debt of honor would be paid through magnanimous social policies that would elevate the material well-being of Indonesians by forging a genuine cultural harmony between West and East.

In this conception, cultural harmony, association, or synthesis entailed a happy marriage between the systematic, and above all, sensitive insights of European civil servants and pristine Indonesian customs and institutions that had organically grown over time and would continue to do so under Dutch tutelage. There were only two ways, De Kat Angelino argued in 1930, in which a European nation could impose respect upon less sophisticated people: they could do so by either brandishing a "mailed fist" or by exhibiting "actual merit." The latter, he intoned, consisted of a commitment of all the mental, moral, intellectual, and material capacities of the West in an honest effort to adjust them to "Oriental" conditions.[73]

Accordingly, Dutch colonial civil servants should withhold neither political support nor the appropriate decorum from time-honored Indonesian institutions, since doing so would unjustly give them the appearance of being ineffective. The essential task of colonial management was to designate the "proper field of activity of indigenous organisms, and suitably ordering" their position and influence in society.[74] Only by respecting the organic diversity of Indonesians' lives — and by orchestrating the proper role of all the individual organisms that compose the whole — could Dutch colonial administrators nurture, arrange, and oversee the "right functions, the right organs, the right ligaments."[75]

Indirectly, echoes of the *ordeningsgedachte* in the Netherlands itself — the emerging notion of social regulation — reverberated in the Indies. Since the turn of the century, the idea burgeoned that the problems of Holland's modern industrial democracy in the European metropole could best be handled through sensitive technocratic planning or low-key corporatist regulation.[76] The "character formation" of citizens should be carefully nurtured and their "political morality" ought to be cultivated through a conscious process of proper instruction and social guidance.[77] Endowing the chaotic assemblage of human relations among the various religious and political factions or status groups within the Dutch nation with their appropriate "forms" (*vormgeving*) entailed a greater reliance on a cadre of expert planners. It also meant trying to relieve the executive burden of parliamentary decision-making, which not only constituted a cumbersome process but also rested on the shoulders of well-meaning politicians whose managerial skills were dubious.[78] Hence, in the mother country and perhaps even more so in its southeast Asian colonies, governance came to be approached as the task of public officials who coordinated and mediated — or "agglomerated, disaggregated, recombined, intermixed, and reordered" — the complexities of day-to-day social life.[79]

In the colonial arena this vision of social and cultural management produced technocratic tendencies and yielded a "Saint-Simonian" ambience, to cite Van Doorn's characterization of the Indies bureaucratic climate.[80] As the natural world revealed a kaleidoscope of different animal and plant species, so the political universe of the Dutch East Indies encompassed a cornucopia of distinctive cultural organisms and deeply entrenched social phenotypes. Governing a colonial domain characterized by such a mind-boggling variety of ethnic groups required careful analysis and the judicious construction of taxonomies or, to use the phrase Oswald Spengler had coined, "cultural morphologies."[81] Since hiding behind the bluster of Western military power was not an option available to the Dutch colonial state, civil servants had no choice but to use the meticulous scholarly methods of a botanist. Their primary chore, it seemed, was to identify, label, and categorize the forms, structures, tissues, and functions of cultural practices throughout the Dutch East Indies with the precision of a biologist engaged in the classification of the plant kingdom.

Since "culture" was embedded in different natural environments, too, it was equally necessary to delineate and chart, resembling the scrupulous labors of a cartographer, the boundaries between the divergent geographic habitats in which particular forms of *adat* flourished. The central notion of nineteen or twenty distinctive *adat* law circles (*kringen*) in the Indonesian archipelago, based mostly on linguistic criteria as well as other measures such as irrigation methods in rice cultivation, served as an organizing principle which enabled ethnographers to allocate to each system of *adat* its "proper place."[82]

Moreover, the cultural habits of peoples and tribes in diverse regions also exhibited, in both an evolutionary and a taxonomical sense, incremental layers of cultural complexity and different levels of civilization.[83] Hence, the interaction between specific physical milieux and the particular stage of cultural development displayed by various ethnic groups furnished an additional rank-ordering mechanism. This kind of ecological determinism supplied a further intellectual tool that could yield insights into the relationship between the structural environment in which particular ethnic groups lived, their distinctive habits or the relative degree of sophistication they had achieved, and the passage of time.

In 1914 Professor Van Eerde, in this context, raised a question about the definition of ethnic "character traits" and their transmission over time: the deep-seated passivity and pliability of the average Javanese peasant, he argued, had been reinforced by a climate "forged through centuries of oppression by higher castes, ranks, and rulers, which had made their meekness an inherited characteristic." The Dutch colonial state, he advised with a Lamarckian evolutionary aura, should now surround the humble *tani* (peasants) in the countryside with a new cultural environment that might alter the essence of the personality of Java's "little people" (*orang kecil*), who would then pass their newly acquired psychological attributes on to subsequent generations.[84]

Of course the Dutch colonial community's disquisitions "on the subject of Java's" hallowed elite also enveloped the sultanates of Surakarta (Solo) in central Java — or of Yogyakarta, for that matter — with a particular cultural milieu that inflected the character and decorum of Java's aristocracy. The majestic rulers of *tanah Jawa*, or "Javaland," were imagined as living in a timeless "fantasy" world. Dutch civil servants in central Java projected onto Surakarta's two *kraton* (Sultans' courts) a range of phantasmagoric illusions. They conceived of the central Javanese courts as mythical "model realms ruled by kingly monarchs and animated by their own customs, ceremoniousness, and appearance of order" which would be delivered from one illustrious sultan to the next.[85] Courtly retainers who chronicled *kraton* traditions, meanwhile, "domesticated" the lumbering emissaries of Dutch colonial authority by converting them into fictitious members of the family, or what John Pemberton has called "ritual-in-laws," capable of displaying linguistic subtleties and genteel sensibilities that were akin to the Sultan's innate refinement.[86]

The imposition of Dutch supremacy upon a widening sphere of ethnic groups throughout the archipelago fostered this process of cross-fertilization between Dutch colonial visions of *adat* and their indifferent "appropriation" by local people themselves.[87] In a variety of regional settings, Dutch interpretations of the meaning of *adat* were somewhat idiosyncratic and frequently harked back to a diffuse and hazy past, a tendency that often issued from the need for a more rational administrative hierarchy. Bureaucratic aspirations prompted Dutch civil servants to reinvigorate obsolete ethnic institutions or revive archaic positions of power. Colonial administrators justified these *adat* inventions — or re-inventions — by appealing to the "impartial" authority of ethnographic research, although it did not really matter whether pragmatic civil servants, Dutch *liefhebbers* (amateur scholars), or erudite *adat* experts had produced the necessary historical knowledge of local culture.[88]

Hence, the reconfiguration of local *adat* for bureaucratic purposes was translated into the nonpartisan, scholarly idiom of cultural history and archaeology or into the neutral, scientific language of botany and cartography. The expansion of colonial mastery since the late nineteenth century was de-politicized and represented dispassionately as a series of discreet cultural transactions and intricate "natural" adjustments. Culture, in a Dutch colonial lexicon, resulted from a conscious process of human negotiations, as if it signified a man-made and deliberately contrived bundle of economic and political relations. The only entries listed under "culture" in the second edition of the presumably definitive *Encyclopaedie van Nederlandsch-Indië* (Encyclopedia of the Dutch East Indies), published and expanded between 1917 and 1935, consisted of *cultures, cultuurdiensten* (cultural services), *cultuurmaatschappijen* (culture companies), *cultuurpapier* (culture paper), and *cultuurstelsel* (cultivation system), which was more or less true, too, for the Encyclopedia's scholarly Supplements issued in 1927, 1932, and 1935. No entry could be found for *beschaving* (civilization) either.[89]

"Culture" in the setting of colonial Indonesia was typically associated with the creative agency of Europeans: it referred to agricultural enterprise on a technological, profit-maximizing Western model, while the plural word *cultures* alluded to the cultivation of rubber, tobacco, coffee, tea or sugar on European plantations; the term culture as in "culture paper" or "*cultuurstelsel*" denoted particular forms of financial credit or signified the compulsory production of cash crops exported via government monopolies. But the word culture also functioned as a metaphor for Europeans' skillful orchestration of native traditions. The civil servant J.J. Wesseling, for example, used such an explicitly musical trope to describe Dutch creative usages of indigenous *adat*. "The traditional authority of the nobility and semi-nobility" in southern Sulawesi, he wrote, constituted an "important instrument" for the Dutch colonial regime. "Playing this musical instrument with expertise and patience" could, in certain instances, either create discordant sounds or produce a "surprisingly harmonious song."[90]

The concept of culture as either an anthropologist or a historian might approach it was explicated, instead, through such entries as *adat, adatrecht, adatrechtspraak*, and *adatregelingen*, which converted the idea of "culture" into an inventory of neatly wrapped packages. *Adat*, the Encyclopedia asserted, entailed an assortment of "customs and practices that guide every aspect of indigenous life: social relations, agriculture, treatment of the sick, judicial arrangements, ancestor worship, burial of the dead, games and popular entertainment, etc."[91] However, the Encyclopedia's listing for *adat* was immediately disaggregated and deconstructed. While the word *adat* proper designated "pure indigenous (Indonesian) customs," among Muslim natives these traditions were juxtaposed with the injunctions of Islamic law (*hoekoem*, or *sarat, sjarat, oekoem*), which they tended "to see as opposites." Moreover, *adat* varied dramatically between the disparate ethnic groups throughout the archipelago, the *Encyclopaedie* proclaimed, and exhibited different behavioral norms and social implications. *Adat* was also called by "distinctive names, such as *bowo* in Nias, *bitjara* among the Karo Bataks, *oegari* in southern Batakland, *oekoe* on Sumba, or *kebiasaan* in the Minahassa region."[92] Hence *adat*, as the embodiment of the socio-cultural norms and spiritual practices of the indigenous population, was an inherently fragmented and regionally differentiated phenomenon. *Adat* represented the tangible, day-to-day reality of native customs and conventions in the archipelago, which displayed an endless array of variations, peculiarities, and differential levels of complexity.

A Cunning David Amidst the Goliaths of Empire

Central Javanese Regenten. From: Daar wordt wat groots verricht..

The idea of cultural fragmentation became one of the clichés, almost an apodictic statement, about the native inhabitants of the Dutch East Indies; thus, the successful management of cultural differences in order to construct a harmonious whole emerged as one of the central obligations of the Dutch East Indies civil service.[93] In this context, the *Encyclopaedie van Nederlandsch-Indië* catalogued many other fascinating Dutch idiosyncracies. The entry for *landaard* (regional or ethnic identity), for instance, was deflected to a listing in a different volume entitled *verdeeling* (classification or division), which elaborated in great detail on the rationale behind the complicated definitions of Dutch East Indies citizenship.[94] The minimalist entry for animism, recording only a few desultory remarks about the anthropological ideas of Edward Burnett Tylor and Arnold van Gennep, was deflected to the listing *heidendom* (paganism), which provided a painstaking inventory of regionally precise and ethnically specific beliefs in natural spirits, origin myths, fertility rites, patterns of cannibalism, and forms of ancestor worship; this lengthy overview covered the entire spectrum of the archipelago ranging from Sumatra, Borneo, Celebes, and Eastern Indonesia to the heartland of Dutch colonial society, Java.[95]

Dutch officials, in fact, had newly identified and ennobled *adat* and *adat* law as a venerable subject of intellectual analysis around the turn of the century: *De ontdekking van het adatrecht* (The Discovery of *Adat* Law), as Professor Cornelis van Vollenhoven called it straightforwardly in 1908.[96] As the most renowned authority on *adat* law, Van Vollenhoven, who taught at the University of Leiden from 1901 to 1933, had trained many of the ethically inspired and ethnographically sophisticated colonial civil servants in the twentieth century. He observed that during the previous centuries, officials had failed to acknowledge that "the indigenous populations had their art, their achievements, or their emotions. All we heard about Java," he complained, "was that it was mercilessly hot, that one suffers from fever and can possibly encounter tigers and wild boars, but no one reported on the meaning of the village community (*desa*) in indigenous life or how native families lived."[97]

Before the turn of the century, Dutch colonial administrators had approached *adat* in an amateurish fashion as if it were a "hodge podge" or a "grab bag of loosely connected rules" that did not constitute a coherent whole. Many civil servants, in trying to record the actual situation of a particular ethnic culture, had displayed the worst kind of "dilettantism," since they also proceeded to invent an elaborate evolutionary history through "conjecture, fantasy, and hypothesis" without any real knowledge of the facts.[98] *Adat*, in every ethnic context, did not follow a progressive or linear model of development, nor did it automatically attain higher levels of complexity and civilization over time. Instead, Van Vollenhoven wrote, *adat* everywhere was composed of three elements: some customs and traditions were like "previously cultivated fields (*stoppelveld*) that have reverted back to wilderness; other *adat* injunctions are fertile fields still under cultivation," whereas yet others resembled ancient, gnarly "tree trunks that are beginning to send out new shoots."[99] Thus, the codification of *adat* law, too, should change constantly, Van Vollenhoven suggested; serious scholars might have to reexamine and revise their descriptions of local *adat* law every fifteen years or so![100]

Although Van Vollenhoven conceded that *adat* was not "a holy cow," he argued that the colonial administration should engage in "expert examination" and incorporate indigenous social prescriptions and customary law in its administrative procedures whenever appropriate and wherever it could.[101] Since many of the immaculate systems of *adat* in regions beyond Java were not yet corrupted by the nefarious influences of "tyrannical rule" or the dislocations of the "cultivation system" — and because they were still uncontaminated by either "government encroachment or private industry such as sugar production, which crushes and distorts everything" — the outer islands revealed the true nature of customary law in all its pristine glory.[102]

In his inaugural address upon assuming the chair of "Muslim Law and Other Popular Institutions and Customs of the Netherlands Indies" at the University of Leiden in 1901, Van Vollenhoven stressed the urgent need to gather methodically all the factual data in order to assemble a precise classification of regional customary law in the archipelago. The primary task at hand, he suggested, was to conduct a systematic headcount of cultural differences, to draw a detailed map, or to build a *musée des imaginaires* which could accommodate and exhibit the dizzying diversity of *adat* artifacts.[103] Otherwise, he warned, comparative jurisprudence would degenerate into nothing but a series of scholarly fictions, or "scientific castles in the air," that were fabricated from either "the whole cloth of Darwinian slogans" or contrived on the basis of half-baked academic disciplines still in their infancy, such as sociology, comparative ethnography, or socio-ethnology.[104] The systematic collection of factual details on *adat*, instead, would yield a deeper and more profound level of understanding about indigenous cultures in order to probe such worthy questions as: "what is the meaning of Oriental institutions and mores for native people themselves? Which human feelings or expectations are embodied in *adat*, and how is *adat* related to people's past history or to their emotional temperament and their thought processes?"[105] However, Van Vollenhoven cautioned that:

> Our goal is not to engage in *adat* scholarship for its own sake, nor is it our aim to impede the economic development of the Indies in order to protect or coddle as curiosities certain quaint forms of *adat* (*vertroetelde adatcuriosa*). Our noble purpose is to establish both good legal institutions and a well-organized administration, neither of which can be created without knowledge of popular mentalities and popular legal institutions.[106]

In short, the task of Dutch *adat* law experts was to enumerate and index the data on each separate realm of customary law. This would lead to the construction of an overall taxonomy that might enable European civil servants and their native retainers to employ the kind of judicial reasoning that fostered, as much as possible, due process of law across the enormous expanse of the archipelago.[107] *Adat* law should function as the foundation of colonial jurisprudence in the Indies. As Cees Fasseur recently joked: Dutch legal officers were expected to personify an earlier incarnation of Herbert von Karajan conducting a *gamelan* orchestra with musicological insight and tonal sensitivity![108]

Questions of comparative jurisprudence and the fragmentation of local customary law, Van Vollenhoven wrote, replicated the intellectual quandaries of Dutch East Indies' linguistic officers. When a language scholar recognized that his knowledge of Latin grammar did not enhance his understanding of the speech of the Timorese, he did not ask the people of Timor to conceive of an appropriate grammatical system, nor did he employ the morphological principles of Latin to analyze and clarify the Timorese language. Instead, a Dutch expert in linguistics attempted to construct a Timorese orthography and grammar by reviewing the available information on differences and analogies with neighboring languages.

In a similar fashion, European civil servants could not resolve questions of equity and justice only through a further interrogation of village elders or native wise men about local *adat*; neither should they use the principles of Roman law to impose a set of legal rules upon particular ethnic groups. Rather, Van Vollenhoven maintained, *adat* scholars should try to uncover the common denominators shared by the widest range of indigenous systems of customary law in order to identify a basic skeleton of *droit commun coutûmier* (customary law) applicable throughout the Indonesian archipelago.[109] But this bare-bones framework could only emerge inductively from thorough "Oriental" wisdom and the cautious interpretation of empirical data. By devising a "catalogue of cultural traits" and collecting vital ethnographic data, Dutch *adat* scholars should try to produce detailed historical documents that recorded the realities of native cultures for posterity.[110] Eventually, it would be up to a bona fide "Javanese or Buginese William Blackstone" with a passionate interest in legal questions to inculcate in his compatriots a genuine love and understanding for their own customary law.[111]

Van Vollenhoven was a human being with "remarkable intuitive gifts," who managed to master foreign languages in an effortless, "playful" manner. He understood native cultures "from the inside out" because he was a devoutly religious person who could easily fathom native peoples' spiritual imaginings and instinctively grasp their social sensitivities and moral judgments of right and wrong.[112] He professed his commitment to study "systematically, historically, and comparatively the legal structures of the world" (*rechtsgeheel der aarde*) and to endow future generations with "the architectonic insights of [empirical] science."[113] However, *adat* scholars should not impose Western analytical categories or social scientific reasoning deductively, because such a theoretical approach would convert the rambling epistemological edifice of *adat* law systems into a majestic architectural monument that was in reality nothing but a house of cards. In sum, Van Vollenhoven's vision embraced the diffusionist style of early twentieth-century anthropology and constituted a striking example of what David Ludden has recently labeled "Orientalist empiricism."[114]

Christiaan Snouck Hurgronje addressed a similar issue in his official advice to the Indies government in 1904. Dutch legal officials' inefficient — or worse, capricious — adjudication of indigenous defendants in the past, he argued, could only be attributed to their lack of social interaction and psychological contact with regional cultures. European judicial officers rarely understood the defendants' language; it was even less common for Europeans to muster any comprehension of "the normal thought processes of indigenous people." Until the turn of the century, Dutch civil servants' encounters with native society had been much too perfunctory to equip them with the kinds of insights that were essential to a proper judgment of legal disputes. They had no inkling of "the motives, actions, and expressions" of native peoples, whose spiritual life remained a hermetically sealed book to them.[115] In contrast, sophisticated native judges of aristocratic provenance who had benefitted from an enlightening European education, the controversial scholar of Islam pointed out, could instinctively evaluate defendants' testimony, a capacity well-trained European legal officers sometimes managed to replicate but could hardly ever exceed.[116]

An administrative post in the Indies, Snouck Hurgronje proclaimed, required both the versatility and talent to serve simultaneously as diplomat, judge, police chief, tax inspector, economist, agricultural engineer, medical doctor, ethnographer, and linguist. Dutch civil servants and judicial officers should demonstrate the highest intellectual caliber and deploy the greatest cultural agility: merely average human beings (*doorsneemensen*) would simply not suffice. They should become polished, university-trained "indologists," who had absorbed a rich and varied academic curriculum which incorporated subjects such as Indonesian geography, history, and religions, Islamic and *adat* law, the principles of linguistics, and the study of Malay and/or Javanese as well as other indigenous languages.

When push came to shove, though, few civil servants were able to apply their sophisticated indological training in the field. The civil servant J.V. de Bruyn, for example, after completing a scholarly doctoral dissertation on Hindu-Javanese archeology at the University of Leiden in the early 1930s, ended up supervising the construction of bicycle paths on western Ceram in one of his early civil-service assignments. Even if he became famous as the "Jungle Pimpernel" in New Guinea during World War II, De Bruyn's early administrative posts hardly plumbed the depths of his impressive indological credentials. "I was not really trained" in the civil engineering of roads or bicycle lanes, he allowed with a hint of dry humor, but "governing means accomplishing all the things that need to be done."[117]

Snouck Hurgronje's vision remained both a Eurocentric and a paternalistic one, even though he insisted that the ultimate agenda of well-educated indologists was to render themselves more invisible and dispensable over time. While he asserted that it had to be done sooner rather than later, Snouck Hurgronje nonetheless cautioned that avuncular civil servants should relinquish their administrative power to Indonesians gradually, with all the sensitivity and deliberation they could muster.[118] In contrast, the social-democrat Jozef Emanuel Stokvis was much more emphatic; every European in the Indies, he wrote in 1923, had to do his utmost "to make himself completely superfluous as rapidly as possible!"[119] Snouck Hurgronje argued that Dutch civil servants should initiate native judges, administrators, doctors, and engineers in the efficient ways and technological know-how of the West through a harmonious process of intellectual and cultural fusion. In due course this synthesis would spawn a cohort of native Indonesians who could wield authority on their own. Especially in the labyrinthine court system of the archipelago the number of Europeans should be reduced, because they should make way for more indigenous legal officials. The time was ripe, as Snouck Hurgronje summarized the situation in 1904, to recognize that "it is unacceptable to continue to treat native pupils who have evolved into full [intellectual] maturity (*vollen wasdom*) as children, merely because their brothers are still illiterate."[120]

Van Vollenhoven's and Snouck Hurgronje's emphasis on greater "Oriental" erudition — whether it was ethnographic and linguistic learning or meticulous datagathering to inspire a more enlightened understanding of indigenous cultural practices — differed from the late nineteenth-century French faith in social science. Arnold van Gennep had called for serious, social-scientific research on "semi-civilized societies" as an essential precondition for anyone wishing to render "the work of colonization durable." His contemporary, Lucien Lévy-Bruhl, was equally adamant about the utility of sociology and the scientific method.[121] But "true" social science, they asserted, should be emancipated and divorced from the mundane practicalities of colonial administration in particular cultural domains, be it Indo-China, North Africa, or Madagascar.

Social-scientific expertise, Van Gennep and Lévy-Bruhl implied, issued from a profound understanding of the classical Western tradition ranging from Plato and Aristotle to Descartes, Rousseau, and Durkheim. Every graduate of the *Ecole coloniale* (training school for colonial civil servants) in Paris was steeped in Western philosophy, French literature and history and, above all, knowledge of Roman law, which were viewed as indispensable to the task of colonial governance. Roman jurisprudence, French theorists of colonialism were convinced, had a universal relevance, even in primitive societies, since it produced a transcendent judgment of right and wrong, regardless of its shifting social contexts.[122] In the process, they posited an abstract, universalist "colonial type."[123]

If detailed "Oriental" learning and a familiarity with native languages and cultures were relevant at all, they served as means to mollify the resistance of the colonized or to ease their pacification. There were French administrators, of course, who tried to be an exception to the rule, such as Léopold Sabatier's valiant efforts to preserve the sanctity of local culture in the rugged Central Highlands of Vietnam in the 1920s. But in the colonial imagination of an average French civil servant, the purpose of collecting basic information about the native "other" tended to serve a specific purpose, which was to stifle the vibrancy of wasteful or extravagant local traditions and to hasten the process of making colonial territories economically profitable.[124] Accordingly, the resolution of practical problems in the French colonial theater hinged on Western reason, disciplined thinking, and the application of European scientific principles, not on local knowledge. The expectation was that the French colonies would develop, both economically and culturally, once a sufficient number of natives had learned French and embraced the inherent superiority of French civilization — in other words, had become "evolved" natives (*evolués*). The French, after all, posted signs in public places, whether in Saigon or Guadeloupe, that the speaking of indigenous languages was forbidden! (*il est défendu de parler la langue indigène ici*).[125]

Notwithstanding the twenty-five official "missions of inquiry" that had been dispatched to the East Indies to study Dutch administrative style and economic management in the late nineteenth century, and despite of the flurry of complimentary information about the Netherlands Indies disseminated in French colonial magazines such as the *Quinzaine Coloniale*, most French observers failed to see a fundamental aspect of Dutch colonial governance. By leaving native customs and traditions intact, they functioned as essential building blocks that formed the foundation of the profitable economic structure of the Dutch East Indies. By seducing the indigenous aristocracy or inducting local rulers into the Dutch colonial bureaucracy and adjusting Western rationality to Eastern circumstances, the *mise en valeur* of the Indies had emerged as the first among equals. French colonial policymakers, however, chose to ignore both the implications of the Dutch example as well as the critiques of powerful French intellectuals within the European metropole. Emile Durkheim, for example, had warned against judging the value of human institutions on the basis of some arbitrarily defined Western ideal; instead, the merits of indigenous customs and conventions should be evaluated on the solitary criterion of their successful adaptation to the milieu from which they arose.[126] Lyautey's was a lonely voice among the actual designers of the French imperial project: the French should respect and utilize ingrained ethnic traditions and local practices, he argued, otherwise colonial administrators would be confronted with nothing but a graveyard of indigenous institutions and "social dust."[127] On the whole, though, Durkheim's and Lyautey's vision of colonial administration as an intricate social art was overshadowed by colleagues who approached it as a magnificent engineering feat that would reveal the genius of French civilization to native peoples everywhere.

In the late 1930s, Georges Henri Bousquet, who was a Professor at the University of Algiers, forcefully articulated this Western engineering model, which allegedly exemplified the superiority of the French colonial mission in comparison with Dutch colonial practice. He faulted the Dutch state in Indonesia for not demonstrating the same kind of "high and majestic idealism" or "claims to glory" as the French. Whereas Frenchmen wished to spread the grandeur of French civilization and to communicate the literary beauty of the French language to *indigènes* as much as possible, even if "a negro from Gabon or a Laotian cannot become a gentleman in Chateauroux," Bousquet had reputedly never met a Dutch resident of the Indies who had a "noble conception of colonization."[128]

To his amazement, the Dutch did not at all try to impose upon colonial subjects their language or religion, their conceptions of law or civilization. The Dutch, instead, wanted to deprive their indigenous pupils of contact with the outside world and prevent an intellectual grasp of the splendors of European culture among the natives. This, he wrote, was "undoubtedly due to a lack of imagination" on the part of the Dutch and their shortage of faith in the preeminence of Western thought. It was their own fault, Bousquet opined, that Indonesian nationalists had chosen the Malay language as a "terrible psychological weapon" to combat Dutch influence in the archipelago.[129] Because Dutch colonial administrators neither harbored a desire to broadcast the benefits of European culture nor wished to engage in a "civilizing mission in its highest sense," their social role in the Indies — "such as it is," he added snidely — would soon disintegrate.[130]

Although the French appeal to Western social-scientific theory and deductive reasoning in the colonial enterprise had a distinctly alien resonance to scholars in Leiden, it did not fall entirely on deaf ears among the members of the newly created department of indology at the University of Utrecht — whom Leiden professors mocked as the "petroleum faculty." Nurtured and financed in 1925 by the guardians of capitalist interests in the Indies such as the *Bataafse Petroleum Maatschappij* (later Royal Dutch Shell) and sundry rubber and tobacco producers, the training program in Utrecht was intended to supply a conservative counterweight to the "library extremists" in Leiden — a variation on the theme of parlor socialists — who were dangerous because they fed their indology students too much "hyper-ethical pablum." Student-pranksters in Leiden during the early 1930s responded by ridiculing their "oil-soaked" or "rubberized" counterparts in Utrecht with a parody on Marlène Dietrich's wildly popular lyric *Ich bin von Kopf bis Fuss auf Liebe eingestelt*: "From Head to Toe I am Disposed toward Rubber!"[131]

Leiden's academic establishment presumably indoctrinated aspiring civil servants with a precious fondness for native culture and an exaggerated deference to indigenous peoples. Professors in Leiden sowed "seeds of doubt" about the legitimacy and permanence of Dutch rule in the sprawling archipelago, even if the Indies body politic was nothing but a "Dutch creation" that had only achieved a semblance of national coherence thanks to the blessings of Dutch colonial administration.[132] Hence, French liberal sociologists' call for a social-scientific approach to colonial societies, based on Western rationality and analytical categories, had a familiar ring to the "petroleum faculty" in Utrecht; it echoed their efforts to imbue Indies civil-servants-in-training with respect for neo-classical economics and to endow them with a desire to defend the logic of the capitalist marketplace.

While Leiden's orientation continued to inflect colonial practice in Indonesia until the bitter end, it also revealed problematic overtones, despite its honorable intentions. The emphasis on the internal differences and fragmentation of ethnic cultures indirectly yielded a "divide and rule" colonial policy. In trying to reinforce the political sovereignty and local pride of the various regions of the archipelago, the Indies state hoped to quell the burgeoning sense of supra-ethnic national identity among all Indonesians, whether they were Javanese or Acehnese, Minangkabau or Menadonese. As Prime Minister Hendrik Colijn, who continued to sound an authoritative, if screeching, voice in colonial affairs, proclaimed in 1937, no coherent, national unity could be found in the Indies. Resembling an "ayatollah from the polder," he was convinced that he maintained a personal pipeline with God and was capable of articulating His will on earth.[133] He proclaimed in the Second Chamber in The Hague during the parliamentary discussions on the Soetardjo petition that the primary task of colonial governance was to train the separate ethnic populations of the Indies for "local and regional citizenship, expressed in participation in, and care for, their own daily interests."[134]

From a purely human point of view, Colijn judged the goal of Indonesian independence "unlogical"; from a religious perspective he viewed it as "unwarranted." Why should independence be the "highest reward for centuries of labor on the part of the best human resources of our nation?" After all, God in His wise counsel had brought Holland and the Indies together. The revelation of God's word spoke to the Dutch nation through the inexorable flow of history, Colijn claimed, and "we must preserve that which history has consecrated."[135] God in His infinite wisdom had revealed through the evolution of history that Indonesians were not yet ready to manage an independent state, he concluded. For the sake of Indonesian people themselves, Dutch colonial authority should persist in its heroic efforts to show them the way and guide the native population on their journey towards intellectual adulthood. Not surprisingly, Colijn's strident voice did not go unchallenged. When "the fox preaches the Gospel," one of his fellow orthodox Protestants commented sarcastically a few years later, "farmers should watch out for their chickens."[136]

The Royal Decree of November 16, 1938, which was mostly the brainchild of Prime Minister Colijn and his Minister of Colonial Affairs (Welter), explained the government's rejection of the Soetardjo petition. At this stage, the decree pronounced, granting a higher level of autonomy to the Indies would be the wrong response to an "artificially created political longing." However understandable, even commendable, this political yearning might be, actual independence could only result from a slow, natural process of "ripening" that was grounded in the "economic strength (*draagkracht*) and intellectual development of the broad strata of the population."[137] And this gradual process of maturation would take many decades, if not centuries.

As a result, the colonial administration in the 1920s and 1930s covertly nurtured the internal rivalry between the predominant Javanese and other ethnic groups. Dutch officialdom gently nourished a sense of Javanese "conceit" that was articulated, for example, in an editorial in the magazine of the young-Javanese movement, *Wederopbouw*, in 1920: "the longing for [Indonesian] unity has always emanated from Java, because Java is the cradle of all existential expressions in this archipelago."[138] Some sectors of the Indies political establishment quietly applauded Javanese nationalists' tendency to treat their Minangkabau brethren as "almost Western" philistines, as secret *agents provocateurs* on behalf of European culture, simply because they did not idolize the consecrated icons of Javanese culture, such as "Borobodur, Arjunawiwaha, or the Panji tales," in the same rapturous way.[139] Besides, Minangkabau men entered the colonial bureaucracy not for "the glory of service," as Javanese *priyayi* might anoint their mid-level administrative roles, but as artful entrepreneurs, who quickly figured out the "name of the game and played it to their greatest personal advantage."[140] By delicately reinforcing the Javanese aristocracy's self-image as philosophical "thinkers" and romantic "dreamers," the colonial administration made it easier for *priyayi* with nationalist aspirations to look down on Sumatrans as overly "sober" and too deeply ensconced in the messy business of "practical politics and economics."[141]

The Dutch policy of nurturing the Western education of upper-class Javanese men vicariously preserved, too, the enormous social gap between nationalists and *kromo*—

the millions of humble, poverty-stricken peasants in the countryside. As a Sundanese journalist, Darna Koesoema, noted in March of 1917 in a caustic commentary on his Malay translation of Henk Sneevliet's controversial *Zegepraal* (Victory) article, which glorified the Russian proletariat's success in the first phase of the Russian Revolution: "More than a few sophisticated Javanese men routinely utter the words *tjinta bangsa* (I love the people). So far, however, I don't see many among them who are willing to sacrifice themselves for the general cause. The attitude of *brani kerna bener* — I have courage because I have justice on my side — does not yet flourish with abandon."[142]

In his polemical "Victory" article Sneevliet had written:

> Do the [Russian] victory bells peal loudly enough to reach the cities and *desas* of this country? Here live people in a land which nature has blessed like no other. Here live people in want and ignorance ... people who produce riches which for centuries have flowed into the savings accounts of overlords in Western Europe, primarily into the banks of the small nation that governs this country. Here live people who suffer and endure ... People of Java, the Russian Revolution contains lessons for you, too! The Russian people were poor and illiterate like you; they also bore centuries of oppression. They won a victory only because of their unrelenting struggle against a government that was grounded in violence and duplicity ... Serving freedom is a strenuous task: it is a service that does not tolerate weakness, ambivalence, doubt, or insecurity. It commands the entire personality and requires determination and, above all, courage! Do the bells of joy now reverberate in our hearts? Shall those who sow the seeds of propaganda for the radical political and economic mass movement in the Indies [now] double their efforts? ... Shall they persist in their work, despite the attempts to suppress the movement for freedom? If so, then the people of Java can only achieve what the Russian people have accomplished: Victory![143]

Obviously this was an explosive call to arms, issued a mere twenty-four hours after the first telegrams from Saint Petersburg had reached faraway Semarang. To express his excitement about the monumental events in Russia, Sneevliet had rushed his article to the editors of *De Indiër*, which was the unofficial but widely circulated newspaper of the eclectic nationalist organization "Insulinde." He decided not to wait for the next installment of *Het Vrije Woord*, the more radical magazine of the Indies Social Democratic Association, which he had molded to conform to his theoretical stance and political vision. On the pages of *Het Vrije Woord* he had opened a floodgate of criticism of government policies and "so-called" ethical politicians; he had also openly praised popular acts of rebellion against colonial domination and capitalist exploitation. The audience of *Het Vrije Woord*, however, was narrow and limited. The magazine addressed primarily a small "debating club of Dutch socialists." Instead, Sneevliet chose the *De Indiër* as his forum because he wanted his rousing appeal to be heard far and wide.[144]

About two months later, in June of 1917, jittery colonial officials charged Sneevliet with "inciting or encouraging sentiments of hatred, animosity, and contempt towards the government of the Dutch East Indies," which constituted an indictment on the basis of the infamous *haatzaai artikelen* — the statutes regulating the propagation of hatred. A second accusation alleged he had "aided and abetted a crime through the dissemination of printed material." The prosecutor in Semarang justified his demand that Sneevliet be placed in preventive custody by appealing to the precedents of Minami and Mas Marco Kartodikromo, who had been incarcerated upon being charged with similar violations of the restrictive press laws, or *persdelicten*. The actual court case took place in November, 1917: it constituted the first explicitly political trial of a *totok* (European-born) Dutchman in the Indies.[145]

But Henk Sneevliet's gritty commitment to a socialist labor movement or his devotion to raise the economic position of desperately poor Javanese peasants also represented a discomfiting example to many Javanese intellectuals. As the chairman of the *priyayi* nationalist organization *Boedi Oetomo*, Dr. Radjiman, noted in 1914: "Mr. Sneevliet paints a picture of such vivid color that it hurts [our] eyes even to look at it."[146] Hence, throughout the 1920s and 1930s the colonial establishment was keenly aware of the deep ambivalence of Javanese notables' response to the idea of a populist movement. And by pursuing a pattern of surreptitiously reinforcing such entrenched social divisions or by bolstering mindless cultural stereotypes about other ethnic groups, the Dutch colonial regime could sow internecine discord and dampen the fraternal spirit of the nationalist movement.

Prior to 1942, the self-serving logic of these public and clandestine Dutch efforts at "divide and rule" was not lost on American diplomats stationed in Batavia.[147] As one of them noted: the Dutch emphasis on regional autonomy would "separate the sheep from the goats" and splinter the desire for Indonesian independence on a national scale in order "to ensure Holland's sovereignty of the islands as a whole."[148] In response, during his theatrical defense oration at his political trial in 1930, Sukarno conjured up a mythical antidote to the Dutch policy of *divide et impera* (divide and rule): the goddess *Merdeka* (freedom, independence) who would instruct her Indonesian worshippers in the sacred knowledge "united we stand, divided we fall."[149]

Sukarno's idea of "unity in diversity" found a potent expression in the fiery postwar independence struggle. Nonetheless, in 1947, in a curiously disconcerting anthology entitled *Indië roept* (The Indies beckon) published at the height of anti-colonial agitation in Indonesia, the editors in the Netherlands noted sheepishly that "we have to confess that the Dutch never cultivated a sense of solidarity among the different parts of the empire, neither did they promote tolerance in the area of religion nor nourish the mutual appreciation of the [different] races." The same editors, however, still called upon young Dutch men and women to travel to the other side of the globe to fulfill their "humanitarian duty" in *Indië*, despite the fact that an independent Indonesian Republic had been unilaterally proclaimed as much as two years earlier.[150] Even a year later, in 1948, in the midst of the political acrimony and bloodshed unleashed by the Dutch police actions, five lengthy articles on tropical medicine appeared in the *Nederlandsch tijdschrift voor geneeskunde*, the principal Dutch medical journal, which were motivated, too, by a desire to mobilize the idealism and expand the intellectual horizons of bright young physicians in Holland "to whom the fate of a new *Indië* would be entrusted!"[151]

Also in the missionary arena the idea of inter-ethnic "solidarity" or a sense of "mutual appreciation" between the different "races" of the archipelago had rarely been promoted. Instead, the different evangelical "fields" where either Protestants or Catholics could try to accomplish their good deeds and pursue their missionary goals were prudently designated and partitioned. It was true that during its nearly 200 year presence in Java, evangelical activity had not really constituted a "priority" of the Dutch East India Company.[152] But once the transformation of the Dutch presence in Java from a makeshift bazaar into a decorous empire had taken place, Dr. Johannes Theodorus van der Kemp — "a sinful libertine who, after experiencing an epiphany," had embraced God's command — took the initiative to found a Dutch Missionary Society in Rotterdam in 1797 (*Nederlands Zendeling Genootschap*).[153] There may have been about 70,000 indigenous Christians in the Dutch southeast Asian empire in 1797; however, the same estimate suggested that only five preachers remained in Java to cater to their spiritual needs or to nurture the sick and elderly.[154] As a result, the official administrative organization of missionary efforts in the Indies did not begin to take actual shape until the mid- to late-nineteenth century.

The formal regulation of the missionary enterprise coincided with the flurry of sub-imperialist, military ventures into the outer regions and conformed to the emerging ideology of "preserving quaint cultures and establishing an imperial sense of space."[155] Out of fear that Christian missions might provoke resentment or incite active resistance among Muslims — a possibility already acknowledged by the Directors of the Dutch East India Company — the policy of non-interference in Islamic regions initially lingered on.[156] Article 177 of the Indies constitution of 1925, which reiterated the policies stipulated in the organic laws (*staatsregeling*) of 1854, required that the office of the Governor General furnish each missionary with a special permit to enter the archipelago. Article 177 also specified that the Indies government should designate a clearly circumscribed terrain where all the different missions could engage in their efforts at teaching, healing, and baptizing the natives in the name of the Father, the Son, and the Holy Ghost.[157]

In the twentieth century, the Indies government abandoned its "suspicion and indifference" towards missionary activity, if only because a recognition dawned that the missions rendered services of "public use, such as caring for the sick, providing general and vocational education, and studying local languages and traditions;" in short, missionaries accomplished important "cultural labor" (*cultuurarbeid*).[158] As a result, the worries about the risks of missionizing in Muslim areas faded a bit. In September, 1906, a "Missionary Consul" joined the ranks of other foreign diplomats assigned to Batavia, whose duty entailed the representation of the political interests of the myriad missionary societies in the Indies and to negotiate on their behalf with secular authorities.[159]

To respond in the most proficient manner to the Great Commission of Matthew 28: "Go ye therefore and teach all nations" in the name of a benevolent Christian God, the

Indies became an intricately stitched patchwork of separate fields. What Benedict Anderson has described as clearly delineated "proselytizing zones" determined where each independent missionary society could try to sow the seeds of God's grace in pagan pastures and "carry the Gospel into heathen darkness."[160] As a result, the Christian missions' impact throughout the colonial era was inherently "splintered," while its moral voice in the formulation of Dutch colonial policy was muted.[161]

These distinct domains were meticulously divided between the "sovereign circles" of various Protestant and Catholic missionary orders from Holland as well as Lutheran, Pietist, Methodist, or Baptist missionary societies with headquarters in either Germany and Switzerland or in England and America.[162] The mostly Muslim island of Java, for example, resembled a busy beehive of missionary zeal in the 1920s; it sheltered six different Catholic mission districts of more or less equal size, divided between Jesuits in both Batavia and Semarang, Crutched Friars in Bandung, missionaries of the Holy Heart in Purworejo, Lazarists in Surabaya, and Carmelites in Malang. At the same time, Dutch Protestant missionary districts, painstakingly apportioned between Mennonites, Orthodox Calvinists, Dutch-Reformed missions and an occasional semi-independent local organization — such as the one in Salatiga — sustained by the Netherlands Mission Society, oversaw a grand total of 39,577 missionary communities and managed 210 schools and 38 hospitals.[163]

Despite their deep involvement in the social and spiritual well-being of a wide variety of Indonesian ethnic groups, the Christian missions' attitudes towards the nationalist movement vacillated until the unequivocal end of colonial rule seemed in sight.[164] As Willem Walraven wrote in 1939, the church had always been "the mistress and servant of the ruling powers" and had forever preached too much heaven and too little earth. Instead of trying to improve conditions for the common folk, he growled, God's disciples on earth moralized about patience and resignation and only sermonized about the need "to await one's heavenly rewards."[165] In 1945, however, when Indonesians' desire for independence was indelibly written on the wall, Christian missionaries in Indonesia were suddenly urged to make sure that the "righteousness of the Kingdom of God would not atrophy": church authorities called upon them to shed "all traces of spiritual imperialism." Bathed in "blood and tears, in grief and humiliation," Indonesians wished to liberate themselves from the "clutches of a rigid and sterile past," efforts which colonial rule had diabolically hindered and restrained. God's mandate, as issued to his shepherds on earth, was to rejoice in a "strong and healthy" flock rather than a "weak and subservient" one. Thus missionaries, based on purely theological grounds, should never feel at home in the "demonic reality" of the colonial relationship; accordingly, with vigor and compassion they should contribute to the "radical suspension" of such an impious system of greed and injustice.[166]

Until Indonesian nationalists "radically" destroyed it, however, the Dutch East Indies mushroomed into a "hypertrophied colonial dependency" anxiously watched over by dutiful Dutch doctors: the colony could serve as an archetypal example of Alphonse Daudet's *Port Tarascon*.[167] The canny British scholar of colonialism, John Sydenham Furnivall, might have interpreted this assiduously crafted Dutch colonial project as the "Fashioning of Leviathan." It was an enterprise bent on fabricating an "artificial" society filled with passive subjects manipulated into submission by the "art" of government, which converted the calculation of self-interest into a series of uncompromising dictates by shrouding them in a natural sheen of inevitability.[168]

Even in the microcosm of colonial prisons, Dutch authorities imposed social hierarchies and fostered the preferential treatment of prisoners who hailed from an elite background. Eventually they created a honeycomb of internment camps which separated intellectual, "academically trained" Indonesian nationalists from their less-educated comrades. This Foucaultian "carceral" structure subverted the potential of refurbishing prisons into a "Mecca" or a communist "boiling pot," as was the case in French Indo-China.[169] Dutch penal policy, instead, consciously tried to avoid converting prison camps into "a training ground of the Indonesian progressive movement, where parochial and undeveloped regionalisms might become a modern Indonesian nationalism."[170]

The Hobbesian force capable of binding together this eclectic mélange of regional cultures and conflicting ethnicities within the stretched-out archipelago was to wave the Netherlands' red-white-and-blue banner and to extol Dutch administrative acumen from Sabang to Merauke. "Over the magnificent tropical beauty of the Indies environment, populated by demanding and diverse indigenous peoples, flies the flag of our beloved great little country," an ecstatic Dutchman wrote in the early twentieth century. And when Dutch citizens behold their nation's red-white-and-blue flag, their pride surges and "their souls soar with lofty emotions and they feel themselves becoming bigger, stronger, and better when they contemplate their monumental task in the Indonesian archipelago."[171] The great duty of the representatives of this little country was to manage its gigantic empire with discretion, wisdom, and above all, judicious negotiating skills, since the use of blunt military force was not a viable political option. Even though Dutchmen might be "strangers" to the inhabitants of the Indonesian archipelago because they came from "over there" (*disana*), as the arch-conservative chairman of the *Vaderlandsche Club* pontificated in the *Volksraad* in 1932, the economic skills and benevolent actions of these very same Dutch outsiders had made it possible for people "here" (*disini*), whether they lived in Java or Sumatra, the Minahassa or the Moluccas, "not to be strangers to one another."[172]

The idea of association or the procedures of cultural synthesis — shaped, in part, by the political and military weakness of Dutch society in the European arena — were exalted as a distinctive feature of Dutch national identity and a healthy imperial imagination. The last conciliatory and semi-idealistic Governor General, A.C.D. de Graeff, for example, due to his alleged "tempestuous, demonstrative preference" for the native (*inlander*) above the European, was diagnosed in 1930 with "dissociative tendencies," as if he suffered from a neurological disease or displayed a psychiatric abnormality. De Graeff had turned the label "hyper-ethical" into a pejorative epithet because, as his detractors proposed, he languished in a "dry, theoretical inactivity in the face of nationalist [or] racist intrigues."[173]

Cultural synthesis constituted the core of imperial ideology in the twilight years of Dutch colonial rule. In fact, according to the theorist of Dutch colonialism, De Kat Angelino, the realization of cultural association in the Indies constituted the evidence of the "collective genius" of the Dutch nation. This did not sound any different from Lord Lugard's paean to the British "Dual Mandate" in Nigeria, which presumably issued forth from "the genius of our race to colonize, to trade, and to govern."[174] But De Kat Angelino repeated this claim as recently as 1961. As he wrote in a remarkable volume of essays, *Balans van beleid. Terugblik op de laatste halve eeuw Nederlands-Indië* (Evaluation of Governance. Retrospective on the Last Half-Century of the Dutch East Indies), which Henk Maier recently called an "eerie and authoritative" retroactive justification of Dutch colonial rule:[175]

> Only a people such as the Dutch ... who had never been united by power from above but whose society had organically evolved from hundreds of boroughs, hamlets, villages, Hanseatic cities, city states, polder boards, or provinces into a full-fledged nation state, could have erected a system for which a blueprint in the theoretical literature was nowhere to be found. Only a people who had embraced in their daily lives a variety of autonomous institutions, languages, dialects, religions, sects, mores, habits and customs, dress and architecture, were capable of such an accomplishment. For centuries the Dutch have acknowledged the culture and history of others, while they displayed a heart-felt compassion for outsiders. This created a situation in which the differences of nations, races, classes, religions or status did not produce an unbridgeable gap. Free of cultural or other feelings of superiority, only people like the Dutch, with an instinctive certainty and spontaneous sensitivity that was reinforced by their daily administrative labors, could conceptualize and implement such an ingenious system. In sum, the method of cultural synthesis flowed naturally in the lifeblood of the Dutch nation!"[176]

Van Vollenhoven and Snouck Hurgronje as well as their intellectual disciples were convinced that a pattern of direct observation, precise measurement, and the cataloguing of individual cultural systems was a more reliable guide to thinking about Indonesian society than deductive, social-scientific reasoning. The policies of the Indies state, too, should be grounded in scrupulous empirical evidence of "Oriental" conditions. The only way in which Dutch colonial governance would be effective and lucrative depended on the state's ability to monitor the lives — and mobilize the labor power — of the many different ethnic groups of the archipelago.

Paradoxically, despite their identification with the progressive idealism of the "Ethical Policy," the empiricist approach and the suspicion of half-baked academic disciplines still in their "infancy" (*kinderschoenen*) endowed the life's work of Leiden *adat* experts with a conservative aura; their approach, in fact, resembled the monographic techniques of nineteenth-century social investigators in France such as Frédéric Le Play and Gustave le Bon, or Léopold de Saussure and Louis Marin.[177] The profusion of *adat* law studies, conducted at Van Vollenhoven's behest, were inspired by a quest to preserve, in their untainted authentic glory, the primordial cultural identity or the social norms and forms of hundreds of different ethnic groups. Genuine anthropological inquiries —questions about material culture and the diffusion of certain entrenched practices, or the reasons for either the similarity or diversity of social customs and spiritual beliefs within the vast Indonesian archipelago and their change over time — were often left to foreigners and relegated to "a science of left-overs."[178]

Clifford Geertz has referred to *adat* as residing in a space "halfway between social consensus and moral style," but the Dutch colonial scrutiny of local systems of *adat* throughout the archipelago emphasized their formal rules rather than their functioning as a shifting array of ceremonial canons or cultural conventions that were forever in flux.[179] In accentuating the legal components of *adat*, Dutch colonial scholars replicated the tendency of British civil servants in Malaysia and elsewhere to render ethnic customs and traditions primarily as a series of fixed legalistic rules or a compilation of stable historical practices. In Malaysia, the transmutation of *adat* into a set of documented legal precedents eased the imposition of British civil administration, which was grounded in a uniquely British pattern of common law. British jurisprudence, after all, was circumscribed by precedents and resolved legal conflict by appealing to the accumulated historical record of judicial opinions and resolutions.[180]

In contrast, Dutch society was based on Roman jurisprudence and did not depend on legal precedents. One of the fundamental principles of the Dutch civil code was, and continues to be, the fact that "custom does not bind" unless the law specifically promulgates it.[181] In Roman law, prescriptions of legality and illegality hinged on an exhaustive inventory of normative principles that stipulated in minute detail the idealized rules for proper human conduct, which were contained in civil and criminal codes. But a community's consensus as to what comprised acceptable versus unacceptable behavior — or legal versus illegal actions — inevitably changed in the course of history, and practicioners of Roman law engaged in a never-ending process of revising and adapting statutory law to conform to new definitions of appropriate social demeanor. Hence, in a colonial setting, the attempts to comprehend and transcribe the fluid meanings of *adat* — its social rituals and mythological significance, or its shifting "moral style" over time — should have played a larger role in Dutch ethnographic scholarship.

Of course a sizable group of Dutch civil servants amassed an encyclopedic knowledge about native cultures and languages, which yielded a colonial administration that admirably adjusted European rule to the particularity of local conditions. However, under Van Vollenhoven's intellectual stimulus, academic *adat* experts or civil servants with intellectual inclinations yearned to uncover in each specific region what Geertz has called "the *Ur* society concept" by searching for a cultural quintessence through a "cake of custom" approach.[182] It was as if the average Dutch analyst was convinced that underneath the visible top layer of social habits and spiritual beliefs lay buried an essentialist cultural matrix: some kind of elusive, if vital, wellspring that had both directly and indirectly nourished and guided all later cultural developments. We might say that Dutch *adat* scholars viewed Indonesian cultures as thick, complicated "texts" from which the first layer of writing had been erased to make room for fresher ones but which nevertheless left that first tier of inscription faintly visible.

The Javanologist Willem Huibert Rassers, for example, saw the *wayang purwa* as an archetypal "document" that disclosed the submerged, oblique *oervorm* (*Ur* form) of Javanese society: an ancient totemistic, sacred rite that contained the gist of its culture.[183] He maintained that the *wayang* comprised a home-grown Javanese "cultural asset" (*cultuurbezit*); although Hinduized through the grand epics of the *Mahabharata* and the *Ramayana*, it nonetheless disclosed the underlying principles of Javanese culture.[184] Similarly, in his ebullient correspondence with either the German ethnomusicologists Erich von Hornbostel and Curt Sachs or Indonesia specialists in many fields, Jaap Kunst unfailingly pondered what the *Ur* scales and tonal prototypes of certain forms of ethnic music in the Indonesian archipelago might be.

Hence, throughout his frenetic musicological career in the Indies Kunst listened to, and painstakingly recorded, a wide variety of local musical traditions. In analyzing his findings, he considered such questions as: did the ancient Chinese wind-quintet comprise the foundation of Javanese music?[185] Was *slendro* of Hindu, south-Asian provenance? Or did the word *slendro* derive from *Cailendra* and might therefore be viewed as a homespun, *Ur* musical form? Did *pelog* emerge from Polynesian sources or did it constitute an authentic Balinese or eastern Javanese musical expression?[186] The well-known Dutch archeologist Willem Frederik Stutterheim, with whom Kunst exchanged a long string of affectionate letters in which they explored personal matters while trying to solve intellectual puzzles, shared his quest to locate the mainspring of the cultures of the archipelago. Stutterheim enthused in a letter to Kunst on July 13, 1925, "both of us are dedicated to the same task: we are both searching for the primordial culture (*stamcultuur*) of Indonesians and I think we are on the right track!"[187]

Ethnic musical traditions and cultural origins, in Kunst's vision, were intimately linked: they unlocked a window of understanding to an "alien soul." He raised a variety of thoughtful issues about the relationship between music and ethnology; he hinted, for instance, at the question as to whether those ethnic musical forms that embraced fixed rhythms and fixed pitches were more likely to engage in harmonious social activity or "team work" than ethnic cultures that performed atonal or arhythmic music.[188] To be able to explore such questions, Kunst insisted, indigenous musical practices should be shielded from deformation by the West. During one of his early field trips on which the Dutch painter Rudolf Bonnet accompanied him, Kunst had cringed when he was forced to listen to a German missionary on the island of Nias conducting a choir of indigenous Christians which sang a four-part Bach chorale. When it was finally over he remarked ruefully that he did not know whom to pity more: poor Johann Sebastian Bach or the poor people of Nias![189]

In 1934, however, Kunst returned to the Netherlands, never to see his cherished ethnomusicological archive in Batavia — nor his beloved Indies — again. In his *Proeve van een autobiografie* (Autobiographical Explorations) written later in life and dedicated to his wife and children, he described the emotional anguish he felt due to a sense of foreboding that he might have to leave his life's work behind. On the boat back to

Jaap Kunst and a variety of Indonesian musical instruments. From: Jaap Kunst. Tradional Music and its Interaction with the West (Amsterdam: Royal Tropical Institute and University of Amsterdam/Ethnomusicological Centre "Jaap Kunst," 1994)

Holland he confessed to being "in a grievous mental state," suffering from what "German psychiatrists call free-floating fears" (*frei flottierende Angste*). Once settled in Holland again, he poignantly admitted it took him close to three years to reconcile himself to a much less thrilling existence, cut off from the profusion of the different sounds of music throughout the Indonesian islands he adored and wanted to protect from Western corruption.[190]

But Kunst continued to write with love and sensitivity about myriad musical traditions in Indonesia. He received numerous invitations to give lectures on ethnomusicology throughout Europe; on several occasions he would repeat Curt Sachs' insight that in the ancient world "time and space, substance and power" were beyond mankind's control. However, human beings had always created sound by themselves. Through music, whether communicated via melodious incantations, measured ca-

Rudolf Bonnet in Bali, 1953 (Coll. Bonnet, KIT)

dences, or pounding rhythms, they could claim a responsibility for "either strengthening or imperiling the equilibrium of the world." Thus the correctness of pitches and scales constituted a core element in the origins of every social community in the world: music comprised "an essence of all cultural expressions."[191]

In ways that were similar to their musicological colleague, ethnographically inclined civil servants registered in minute detail all the social injunctions and moral dictates of each cultural microcosm. But they were less likely to consider the disputed meanings of *adat* and its contested practical ramifications in daily life. On the whole, the *adat* law monographs which Dutch civil servants and other scholars produced tended to record previously uncodified rules through an endless series of consultations with village elders. In the process, Dutch analysts of native traditions displayed an inclination to ossify or freeze what they judged to be a social consensus. As a result, they converted the diverse systems of local *adat* throughout the archipelago into an essentialist, static, and more or less predictable status quo.

By assuming an unambiguous correspondence between the formal structures of social life and the existential or cosmological implications they engendered, the diversity of ethnic cultures could be "wrapped" in neat intellectual packages and stacked and rearranged, or assembled and unpacked, at will.[192] Cultural synthesis, in a Dutch administrative idiom, used the "thick" description of each unique system of *adat* as the indispensable pillars and posts of its colonial edifice. Resembling an adroit political architect, in the 1920s and 1930s the Dutch East Indies state tried to remodel its skill-

"Young Siulu of Saua, Nias," drawing made by Rudolf Bonnet during his field trip to Nias with Jaap Kunst, 1930 (Coll. Bonnet, KIT)

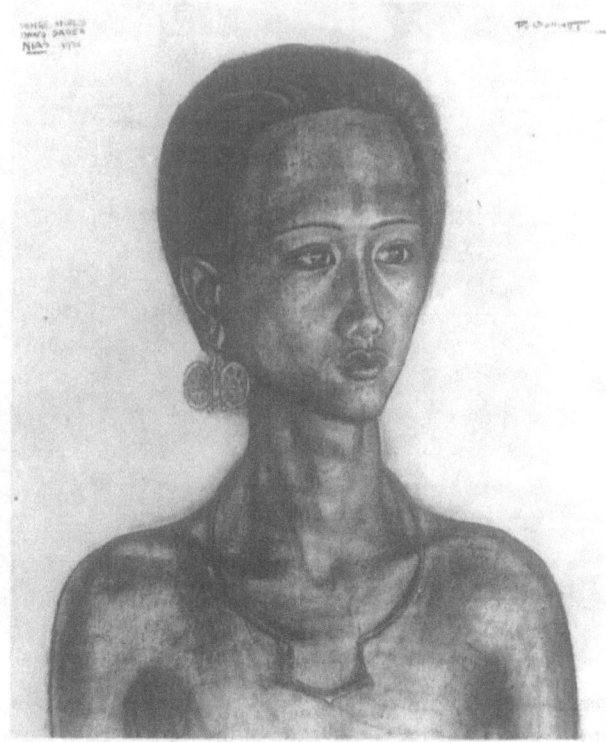

fully crafted tropical household, not only to harness the growing number of educated Indonesian nationalists who requested entry but also to muzzle their demand for a political voice in its internal management. Eventually, Indonesians' polite plea for a co-equal voice in the body politic escalated into a "passionate embrace of *merdeka* (freedom, independence)." As Piet Korthuys wrote in 1947, *merdeka* began to function in Java as an "incomprehensible, magical word without content," a term that unhinged "all the primitive, bloodthirsty instincts of hatred and produced a delirious, dangerous drunkenness."[193] In this bruising post-war pursuit of *merdeka*, however, the Dutch colonial residence proved to be nothing but a flimsy "glass house," as Pramoedya Ananta Toer has labeled it, that only held together because of Dutch police surveillance. The Japanese easily trampled this frail, transparent structure in 1942, while the Indonesian independence movement irreversibly shattered its remains during the post-World War II era.[194]

CHAPTER THREE

EDUCATING INDONESIAN GIRLS IN JAVA AND BALI:

The Infatuation with Aristocratic Culture and the Invisibility of Women in the Desa

The young Javanese girl, today, engages in a pioneering effort and she commands our admiration ... She has embraced a giant struggle: not only a battle with ingrained, archaic *adat*, but also with the egotism of men. With melancholy eyes the average Javanese man observes the emancipation of his sister or daughter. He will cease being the lord and master, because she will no longer serve as a slave who pliantly submits to his will. She will not allow herself to be traded like a commodity any more. In the future she won't tolerate a second wife at her husband's side. The evolution of the Javanese woman opens up glorious perspectives for Javanese society. With the blessing of education, her soul will unfold like a blossom in the sunlight: she will resemble a melati flower and exude in ever-widening circles her exquisite fragrance ... With poignant confidence Javanese parents entrust their daughters to the support and direction of the white woman, since a Javanese girl's steps upon this unfamiliar path must be guided to prevent her from going astray and losing her way. She requires instruction and new knowledge: a magnificent field of labor awaits European women, who can sow the seeds of wisdom in the guileless, receptive mind of a Javanese girl, yielding a rich harvest that will dignify Javanese society in the future![1]

"Het Javaanse meisje," *De Taak*, 1918.

Education for girls, the editorial in *De Taak* proposed in 1918, would enable young girls in Java to unfold like resplendent "melati flowers" who would blossom and radiate their delicate perfume throughout Javanese society in order to transport it to new heights. But melati flowers, however lusciously fragrant they might be, had few practical meanings in the strenuous day-to-day existence of the millions of simple peasant women in the rice fields. In their discussion of the education of "the Javanese girl," in other words, *De Taak*'s progressive editors were primarily thinking about upper-crust daughters rather than humble girls in the *desa* or *kampong*, who labored from dawn to dusk and had little time either to rejoice in the beauty of education or to linger over the delicious scent of jasmine flowers.

The same focus on aristocratic girls influenced the attitudes of "ethical" Dutch men and women who dedicated their labors of love to the education of *de inlandse vrouw* (the native woman). Accordingly, in this chapter I examine the ways in which European interpretations of the aristocratic sensibilities, characteristic to certain parts of the Indonesian archipelago, permeated Dutch ideas about the appropriate education for Indonesian girls in the twentieth century. During the decades after the year 1900 or so, the idealistic clarion call for the general "uplifting" (*opheffing*) of Indonesian people through the improvement of "the position of native women" inspired the creation of an elaborate series of private educational institutions. These schools were specifically designed to instruct Javanese girls and to prepare them for their housewifely duties and maternal destiny. However, most altruistic Dutch women who engaged in sincere educational efforts on behalf of indigenous girls and had entered this "magnificent field of labor," as *De Taak* called it, embraced a feudal, hierarchical model, which shaped their vision of educated womanhood.

Many Dutch women who were teachers or social workers in Indonesia, especially in Java and Bali, fell hopelessly in love with the dignity and refinement of Javanese *priyayi* (aristocratic) society or the artistry of "authentic" caste-based culture in Bali.[2] In a sizable group of Dutch women and men this "Orientalist" infatuation had arisen after reading the aristocratic Raden Adjeng Kartini's expressive and poignant letters, written in ornate Dutch prose, that had been published in 1911. The beloved memory of Kartini hovered directly over many Dutch residents' enthusiastic efforts to "uplift" the lives of indigenous women in Java and, indirectly, in Bali. Hence, the private educational institutions they established — or the definitions of appropriate schooling and knowledge they embraced — resided in the distinctly hierarchical universe of the Javanese feudal aristocracy.

Harking back to the history of medieval Europe, in a Dutch historical imagination feudalism seemed to imply a set of mutual obligations, in which labor services were exchanged for protection: *noblesse oblige*. Assuming the existence of a similar set of reciprocal relationships in feudal Java, Dutch progressives expected that the education of the daughters of the Javanese nobility or upper-caste Balinese would naturally "trickle down" to poor women in the *desa* and the *kampong*. However, by romanticizing medieval lords' supposed commitment to nurture and shelter their social inferiors as a *quid pro quo* for labor services rendered, Dutch educators twisted the social realities and distorted the meaning of Western feudalism. A tendency to look upon the European feudal past through a "golden haze" as a reciprocal world of chivalry and deference, of paternalism and obedience, colored their perspectives.[3]

Noblesse oblige, however, whether in the context of the European Middle Ages or in its reinvented and feminized Victorian version of the late-nineteenth century was hardly the lofty expression of a "humanitarian sensibility" or a pristine "charitable impulse"; it had never registered European lords' or ladies' magnanimous inclination to reward humble people for their Herculean labors.[4] *Noblesse oblige*, instead, tended to confirm the existence of a rigid hierarchy. The very idea of "noble duty" sustained a deeply divided social order in which the blessed few of aristocratic birth or exalted economic, political, and cultural standing bestowed some of their symbolic gifts — but rarely real resources — upon the many poor peasants whose backbreaking work made the asymmetrical system possible.

Educating Indonesian Girls in Java and Bali

Raden Adjeng Kartini. From: Jubileum-verslag uitgegeven ter gelegenheid van het 25 jarig bestaan der Vereeniging Kartinifonds te 's Gravenhage, 1913-27 Juni-1938 (The Hague: Raad van beheer, 1938)

A Kartini school. From: Jubileum-verslag... Vereeniging Kartinifonds

A similar misconstruction colored Dutch educators' vision of the feudal customs and traditions in Java; they imposed the same illusory notions of mutuality upon the unyielding hierarchy of Javanese society, where peasants, in the words of Clifford Geertz, "clung" to local *priyayi* primarily because the latter radiated a "magical-mystical aura." In the eyes of common Javanese folk toiling in the ricefields, *priyayi* possessed sublime virtues that adorned them with a "blinding halo." Their spiritual enlightenment was expressed in decorous display and entrenched in intricate patterns of "politesse," which managed both to mesmerize and enthrall local peasants. *Tani* (peasants) in the countryside felt beholden to *priyayi* as hallowed superiors, to whom they gladly paid tribute in a ritual and material sense. Javanese feudal civilization, in other words, was built upon the "diligence" of peasants and the "peagantry" of aristocrats.[5]

The Dutch "Orientalist" romance with Java or Bali required that schooling for indigenous girls respected, if not revered, the distinctive features of these forms of patrimonial *adat* and indigenous religions. The exquisite task of educating young Javanese girls, wrote a Dutch female teacher in 1913, required that a European instructor did not behave like a "mistress" or "ruleress." Instead, she should observe with care and sensitivity "the development of her female pupils, their habits, their experience in the family circle, their thought processes and the influences which until now have shaped them — because it is necessary to adjust Western culture to Eastern civilization."[6] Thirty years later, the feverish attempts among Bali lovers to create a Hindu-Bali school was justified on the grounds that girls, "who are our future mothers, should enjoy an education that fosters reverence for old Balinese institutions and conceptions. This respect should not be based on fear of magical dangers but on an appreciation that is grounded, instead, in an elementary understanding of the principles which constitute the foundation of Balinese views of life, nature, and the cosmos."[7]

However, all these well-intentioned educational ventures designed to show regard for the integrity of indigenous cultures relegated desperately poor women in the *desa* or *kampong* to a position of silence and invisibility. Neither the idea nor the reality of *noblesse oblige* prevailed in the asymmetrical world of Java or Bali. The social distance between *priyayi* and ordinary folks — whether they were called *wong cilik* (Javanese for humble people in the countryside), *kromo* or *orang kecil* (Malay for illiterate people without rank, status or wealth), or *volksvrouwen* (Dutch for women of the people) — was inviolable and wide. In subtle ways, the Dutch East Indies government tried to preserve this social detachment.

After 1893, the colonial state had erected a labyrinthine educational structure that almost forty years later, in the official propaganda accompanying the Dutch pavilion at the 1931 *Exposition coloniale internationale* in Paris, was still described, with an odd sense of misplaced pride, as a "chaotic" cornucopia of different types of schools.[8] The government created, among many other institutions, first-class native schools for the sons and daughters of aristocrats and the well-to-do — converted into "Dutch native schools" (*Hollands-Indische Scholen*) in 1914, when instruction in the Dutch language was introduced — and second-class native schools, which taught students in Malay and vernacular languages, for ordinary people's children. All schools were based on a co-educational model, but girls attended with less frequency since Javanese parents objected to their daughters's presence in a classroom with boys.[9] On the basis of gender, the students in public and private Dutch Native Schools were divided as follows:

Indonesian Students in Public *Hollands-Indische Scholen*[10]

Year	Boys	Girls
1915	18,970	3,490
1925	28,722	10,195
1929-30	29,984	11,917
1934-35	31,231	15,492
1939-40	34,307	19,605

Indonesian Students in Private *Hollands-Indische Scholen*[11]

Year	Boys	Girls
1915	1,195	1,049
1925	14,529	6,258
1929-30	14,055	6,941
1934-35	14,077	8,355
1939-40	15,915	10,838

Even in the regionally diverse and more elementary village schools, founded locally to prepare native students for government educational institutions, a mere 8 percent of the students in Java and Madura were female. Only 5,114 girls, as compared to 66,125 boys, attended in 1910, a ratio that was still more or less the same in 1915, when 18,619 girls and 242,436 boys were students in *desa* schools.[12] Among the tiny number of natives pupils who attended public European primary schools in the Indies — all of whom hailed from an elite background — boys consistently outnumbered girls, although not to the same degree as in the Dutch native schools. In private European Schools, the division between native boys and girls who were enrolled achieved parity towards the end of the colonial era.

Indonesian Students in Public *Europese Lagere Scholen*[13]

Year	Boys	Girls
1900	1,327	218
1905	3,244	508
1910	2,915	548
1915	3,339	858
1920	4,029	1,358
1925	2,932	1,424
1929-30	2,036	1,362
1934-35	2,063	1,698
1939-40	2,080	1,954

Indonesian Students in Private *Europese Lagere Scholen*[14]

Year	Boys	Girls
1900	50	20
1905	143	40
1910	189	58
1915	248	97
1920	565	201
1925	586	235
1929-30	375	340
1934-35	537	529
1939-40	542	574

Some *priyayi* sons were thus drawn into the modern world, especially the few among them who had attended Dutch Native Schools or, even more exceptional, the *Europese Lagere School* (European Primary School) or the *Hogere Burger School* (European High School). To many of them the meaning of traditional culture lost some of its "natural" coherence — or its metaphysical wholeness — since it was now juxtaposed with Western values and European technology, which opened up new intellectual prospects and provided fresh political options. Young men boldly called themselves *kaum muda* (community of the young), a defiance that issued from their sophistication and modernity relative to their parents, who had not enjoyed the benefits of Western education.[15] Having mastered a Western cultural lexicon and being young and "modern" entailed a liberation from the blind, unquestioned obedience sons owed their fathers, perhaps resembling a psychological patricide. The "anti-feudalism" of the members of "Young Indonesia" and other student organizations hinged on a generational rebellion against the deferential, *kaum ningrat* perspectives of their elders, whose august aristocratic names in Java often ended with *ningrat*. Exalting modernity was "almost exclusively an issue of fathers," who were still hopelessly entangled in a hierarchical web spun by the Indies civil administration. Young nationalists suspected their elders of having embraced the values of "them," *kaum sana*, the colonialists "over there."[16] As a result, they were uncertain whether fathers — or in a comparable manner, overly Westernized Indonesian intellectuals — could be counted on as members of "us, our community, here" (*kaum sini*).[17] As Mohammad Hatta declared in a speech in 1927, perhaps a little tactlessly, elders' bureaucratic worldview lulled them into complacency because they continued to be "hypnotized" by Dutch colonial values.[18]

For women the situation was fundamentally different. An unspoken consensus among even the most progressive members of the Dutch colonial community prevailed that women, above all, emblematized "tradition," because they "naturally" lived it in their daily rituals of family, work, and religion. Women tended to be the ones who interceded between "innovation and tradition" and who mediated between the pushes of the future-oriented, modern world and the pulls of backward-looking traditions.[19] This vision confirmed the opinions of genteel members of Java's upper crust. Kartini's sister Kardinah, for instance, asserted in 1914 that the strength of a culture resided in "the preservation of women's purity." She was convinced that women would always function as the "guardian angels" of the spiritual values and cultural dictates of Javanese tradition.[20]

Indonesian women, moreover, served as a metaphor for what Sara Suleri has called "alterity": they functioned as "discursive icons" in the cultural grammar of Dutch colonialism.[21] A Western and essentially middle-class vision of women's maternal destiny and housewifely duties merged with respect for *adat*. "Tradition" emcompassed a jumble of personal habits or cultural customs that were imperceptibly in flux. Women's rituals and routines in daily life, in turn, constituted a yardstick with which to measure the meaning and "authenticity" of tradition. Hence, intricate changes in women's lives, over time, revealed a complex pattern of complicity between indigenous patriarchal dictates and Western ideas about "bona fide" native cultures.

But the Oriental traditions the Dutch admired and wished to nurture were the gracious manners of high-born Javanese, as if *priyayi* daughters were "pieces of eccentric furniture" or "exotic plants" the Dutch gleefully displayed in their salons.[22] Colonial debates over the ways in which *adat* defined the position of indigenous women routinely served as the basis for a Western rearticulation of what they deemed "genuine" cultural norms and forms. By dressing up ethnic traditions according to European tastes and sensibilities in Western cultural attire, Dutch colonial residents neatly collected and intellectually appropriated Javanese or Balinese cultures in order to arrange them in a taxonomy that rendered them more manageable to the Dutch colonial regime.[23] By inventing and extolling a pattern of reciprocity that presumably characterized feudalism, whether in a Western or in an Eastern setting, Europeans could focus their educational efforts on aristocratic girls and simply conjecture that they would "naturally" disseminate their newly acquired learning among the millions of Javanese and Balinese women of lower social status.

Relieving the "tradition" of village women's exhausting labor in rice fields, though, or alleviating the colonial "tradition" of women's exploitation on tea plantations or in coffee factories, entered the Dutch colonial imagination in only the most peripheral fashion. Poor women, it seemed, were either "forgotten" or "unnoticed."[24] "Ethical" members of the colonial community deplored the ignorance and economic illiteracy of modest women in the villages. If and when the suffering of desperately poor women in the *desa* came into focus, it was described with the bland euphemism "lesser" or "diminished welfare" (*mindere welvaart*).[25] But the story about the *mindere welvaart* of Javanese peasants and their families did not assign an instrumental role, for example, to the land hunger of the sugar industry. Sugar factories in densely populated north-central and eastern Java eagerly swallowed up rice fields and reduced peasants to increasingly smaller lands or transformed them into underpaid and overworked employees on sugar estates. Instead, in the Dutch colonial imagination, the hardship of destitute women was transcribed into a neutral, depersonalized narrative that depicted *mindere welvaart* as the inevitable result of their economic irrationality or inferior housekeeping skills.

At the same time, Dutch social workers, who engaged in noble efforts to save Eurasian (*Indo*) pauper girls from moral corruption and sexual promiscuity, repudiated their native mothers as inherently immoral, which echoed the derogatory opinions of the Javanese upper class. In general, even the most progressive Javanese aristocrats slighted *kromo*, on occasion, as "stupid" or as a "simple soul."[26] In the words of Kartini, they endowed aristocratic superiors with "powers no mere humans could ever possess."[27] In his remarkable novel about the mysterious tensions of Indies life, *De Stille Kracht* (The Hidden Force) published in 1900, Louis Couperus portrayed the same slavish devotion that peasants lavished upon a local Javanese regent, who was "a silent, spiteful, secretive fanatical *wayang* (shadow) puppet, with his reputation as saint and sorcerer, stupidly idolized by the people in whose welfare he took no interest and who adored him for the glamour of his ancient name."[28] But this aristocratic disdain hinged on a vision of humble village folk as *masih bodoh* — "still stupid," meaning still untutored or not yet educated, rather than *kromo* being congenitally dumb or simply crude and uncivilized (*kurang ajar*). *Masih bodoh* did not constitute a "fixed" personality trait; rather, it was a fluid social condition that could be improved.[29]

Nonetheless, the Dutch rhetoric about Indonesian *volksvrouwen*, which alternately emphasized their inexperience or their depravity, paralleled the condescending attitudes of the indigenous ruling classes. In the restless and constantly shifting "gaze of empire" the meaning of cultural difference and otherness was equally malleable and contingent. Europeans, in this particular instance, ascribed the label "primitive" as a symbolic opposite to what it meant to be sophisticated and "Western" exclusively to women of the people. Dutch colonials incorporated *priyayi* daughters, meanwhile, into a familiar pecking order that mirrored Western sensibilities about status, the representation of culture, and gracious manners.[30]

The powerful legacy of Kartini, the refined and well-informed daughter of a prominent aristocratic family in Java, exerted an indelible impact on colonial definitions of educated womanhood in a self-consciously "modern" guise. "I have been so anxious to make the acquaintance of a modern girl" — or to meet a girl belonging to "the new age" — Kartini wrote excitedly in her first missive to the Dutch feminist Stella Zeehandelaar.[31] Through her lively correspondence with an assortment of "ethical" Dutch women friends, Kartini came to embody all the goals of modernity that Dutch educators aspired to fulfill.

In a long and gushy letter on July 5, 1903, to a Dutch female teacher named Mien Bosch, for instance, Kartini had written that "I want you to get to know the soul of our naive, childish people (*naif kind-volk*) and learn to love it." She emphasized that the young students who attended the little school she had established in Jepara for the daughters of *boepati* (district heads), *jaksa* (judicial officers) and *wedono* (village heads) in the vicinity, near Java's northern coast, provided vivid evidence of the fact that *inlanders* "are receptive to educational development." She regaled her Dutch friend and fellow-educator with exuberant stories about her "wonderful task, which is to lead those clean, young hearts and to form those youthful characters: the students are quick, receptive, clever and, at the same time, so obedient."[32]

Referring to the general native efforts to educate themselves, she cited the example of a young Sumatran boy, proud to be the *primus inter pares* — or the valedictorian — of his European High School class, who is "filled with faith and ideals, full of illusions, to work for his people." While describing this young man's hopes and dreams, though, Kartini made a curious statement about "his" people and "his" racial brothers and sisters (*rasgenoten*), leaving ambiguous whether his otherness derived from his Sumatran ethnicity or whether his differentness issued from the fact that he was an ordinary *inlander* not belonging to her *priyayi* world. In saying that he wished to "incite his racial kin to dedicate themselves to a collective ideal, the elevation of the indigenous race (*inlandse ras*)," Kartini, perhaps inadvertently, revealed her ambivalence by hinting at the social distance she sensed between her own elevated status and Indonesians of common descent.[33]

Since her death in 1904 during the delivery of her first child, at the tender age of twenty-five, Kartini has been lionized as the guiding light of the emancipation of Indonesian women and a founder of the Indonesian nationalist movement.[34] Shortly after Independence, for instance, the Indonesian wife of a prominent Dutch journalist gave a lecture on "The Position of the Indonesian Woman." As a patriotic Indonesian she glorified "Unity in Diversity" but relished, too, her ethnic identity as a Minangkabau woman from west Sumatra. Invoking Biblical language and comparing Kartini's role to Moses who led the Isrealites out of the land of Egypt, as described in Deuteronomy 6:23, she told her Dutch audience that "it was Kartini, this immortal woman, who guided us from darkness to light, who steered us through the eye of the storm into calm waters, who escorted us through struggle to achieve honor, who nurtured us in our suffering to bring us joy."[35] In fact, in contemporary Indonesia, Kartini's birthday is a national holiday and she is still commemorated, every year, as a legendary heroine, a righteous pioneer, and an early visionary of the Indonesian independence struggle. Kartini's letters constitute a "documented ideal" for Indonesian women — a constant reminder of the need to strive for women's emancipation.[36]

As Danilyn Rutherford has recently shown with keen insight, the Old Order government of Sukarno bestowed upon the aristocratic Kartini a sense of genuine, populist commitment to "the people" or "the masses" (*rakyat*) as fellow Javanese and co-equal victims of Dutch colonial oppression.[37] As evidence of her yearning to transcend the bifurcated feudal rigidity of Java, Pramoedya Ananta Toer's reading of Kartini celebrated her egalitarian sentiments and her pledge to work for the collective well-being of *all* Javanese, whether rich or poor, whether *priyayi* or peasants, as if she were "an honorary member of the proletariat."[38] Kartini, Pramoedya argued, was eager to break down the social cleavages of Javanese society in order to envision an undivided nation that could rise above differences in birth and status. Kartini's symbolic meaning to Suharto's New Order, however, has an entirely different resonance: by endowing her with patronizing *priyayi* feelings of responsibility and affection for her people — or *bangsa*, in other words, her father's retainers — historians or biographers of Kartini since the bloody 1965 coup have mobilized Kartini's legacy to legitimate Suharto's patrimonial New Order.[39]

In the early twentieth century, her premature death had also deeply affected "ethically" inspired European colonial residents of the Indies — all the idealistic Dutch men and women who were dedicated to "uplift" and improve the collective welfare of indigenous peoples by protecting them from "injustice and arbitrary treatment" — with whom she had become friends.[40] Kartini had captured the fancy and sparked the imagination of her "ethical" Dutch soulmates. One of them described her as "a miraculous phenomenon .... Anyone who comes into contact with the indigenous cultures of the archipelago is constantly reminded of her gentle seriousness, her kindness, her innate artistic talents, her quickness of mind, and her elegance."[41] Kartini's touching letters, primarily to Rosa Manuela Abendanon-Mandri, the wife of the former Director of Education, Religion, and Industry of the Dutch East Indies, Mr. Jacques Henry Abendanon, were edited selectively and published in 1911 in the Netherlands with the evocative, and quintessentially Javanese, title *Door duisternis tot licht* (from

Rosa Manuela Abendanon-Mandri later in life (Coll. Koninklijk Instituut voor Taal-, Land-, en Volkenkunde [KITLV], Leiden)

Darkness to Light). Almost immediately, the collection of letters achieved an enormous success among the Dutch reading public.

The book's royalties, along with generous private donations and government subsidies, financed the creation of the Kartini Foundation in 1913, which by 1916 had opened seven private schools — in Semarang (1913), Batavia (1914), Madiun (1914), Buitenzorg (1914), Malang (1915), Cirebon (1916), and Pekalongan (1916) — devoted exclusively to the basic education of daughters of indigenous notables.[42] The official motto of the Kartini Foundation confirmed its loyalty to Kartini's heritage and fame: the Foundation was committed to "the elevation (*verheffing*) of the Javanese woman as advocated by Raden Adjeng Kartini." As a logical sequence the Van Deventer Foundation, founded in 1917, followed in its wake and organized boarding schools in Semarang, Malang, Bandung, and Solo for "the advanced (*voortgezet*) education of Indonesian girls" in order to train Javanese women as schoolteachers.[43]

*Jacques Henri Abendanon.
From: Jubileum-verslag...
Vereeniging Kartinifonds*

A Van Deventer school. From: Jubileum-verslag... Vereeniging Kartinifonds

In the 1920s it became clear that parents who could not afford to send their daughters to Kartini and Van Deventer schools or to European schools or Dutch native schools had few alternatives. Accordingly, the Kartini Foundation opened three *istri* schools, or second-class native schools for girls, in Buitenzorg (1924), Batavia (1927), and Meester Cornelis (1928). Conforming to the curriculum of the government-sponsored second-class native schools, albeit supplemented with courses in home economics designed to "prepare indigenous girls for their future task as housewives," the *istri* schools quickly attracted a considerable number of female students.[44] Nonetheless, as a percentage of the total female population of Java, the number of girls who actually attended either official government schools or Kartini and Van Deventer schools was miniscule; the same was true for the more simple *istri* schools or *desa* schools. On the whole, Javanese women, even more so than men, remained overwhelmingly illiterate throughout the era of Dutch colonial rule.[45]

Although limited in their reach, the Kartini and Van Deventer Foundations joined the philanthropic ranks of an intricate network of charitable trusts that had been created to provide educational opportunities to gifted Indonesians in an effort to carry out the "ethical" policy's dictates. Since 1911 the Max Havelaar Foundation, for example, granted subsidies to promising upper-class Indonesian men to study at institutions of higher learning in the Netherlands, pending the establishment of a university in Indonesia itself. The Tjandi Foundation, also instituted in 1913, pursued a more broadly conceived mandate of encouraging bright Indonesians to "elevate themselves intellectually and spiritually" through interest-free loans.[46] Indeed, within a little more than ten years of her untimely death, Kartini's reputation had spawned, either directly or indirectly, a concerted effort on the part of Dutch progressives to ennoble the intellectual stature of Indonesians, as long as they belonged to the gracious *priyayi* world.

In her intelligent, revealing, and intermittently passionate letters, written in florid Victorian Dutch, Kartini deplored the evils perpetrated upon women in traditional Javanese society.[47] She lamented the illiteracy that prevailed among women, owing to the absence of any educational opportunity for girls; she denounced, too, the practice of polygamy and the compulsory marriages often foisted upon Javanese women who were sometimes still in their very early teens.[48] "We, Javanese girls, are not allowed to have ideals," she wrote bitterly, because we can only indulge in one dream, and that "is to be forced into marriage either today or tomorrow with a man our parents consider appropriate."[49] Dutch commentators, meanwhile, concurred that it was "curious" that women in higher social circles had a "worse fate" than humble women in rural villages, who acted as the boss of their families and often reduced their husbands to weak-kneed, simpering boys. To the amazement of some Dutch observers, the day-to-day existence of simple Javanese peasants showed that the moral strength, ingenuity, and general cleverness of wives in the *desa* was even more palpable than "among Western peoples!"[50] "Traditional" marriage rituals in small-town, rural Java, meanwhile, incorporated ceremonial practices hinting at a boisterous contestation of power between men and women (*rebutan*), which conceded that the domestic harmony of the bridal couple would hinge on a life-long accommodation between two equally feisty partners.[51]

But eventually, in 1903, Kartini had to agree, with misgivings she disclosed in touching letters to her Dutch friends, to a marriage her father had negotiated for her. She confided that she wanted a husband who would be "an equal, a friend, a comrade," and she was certain her husband-to-be would play all those roles. She professed, however, that she did not really "yearn to be a bride" and had never longed for this particular future.[52] In trying to reconcile herself to her arranged marriage, perhaps, or as an attempt to heal the lingering rift with her father, Kartini became more involved with mysticism and Islam. Although in a memorandum about education written in early 1903 she still warned of the ominous danger that Islamic propaganda in native schools "might incite the opposition of the fanatical elements" of the population — a fear the Dutch colonial community anxiously and wholeheartedly shared — before her death in September of 1904 she had adopted a more devoutly Islamic stance.[53]

But she was and remained, above all, an upper-class Javanese woman; her perspectives on the world around her and the aspects of Javanese *adat* she fulminated against were those that restricted the freedom of *priyayi* daughters but privileged their brothers, who were destined to enter the bureaucratic hierarchy as indigenous retainers of the Dutch colonial regime. Tradition in Java implied "everything for the man, and *nothing* for the woman," she lamented, "that is our law and custom."[54] But Kartini rarely established a linkage between her own predicament and the somber reality of Javanese women's lives in the *desa*, who toiled from sunrise to sunset in rice fields or on the European-owned tea, coffee, or sugar plantations that dotted the Javanese landscape. Neither did she reveal much compassion for the 4 percent of the total female labor force, which worked as servants of European families or in aristocratic households in order to eke out only the most meager existence.⁵⁵ She commanded and scolded underlings without moral qualms, as if it was entirely natural and legitimate for her to do so.⁵⁶

While exulting in the flawless artistry and innate elegance of Javanese culture, Kartini also harbored great admiration for Western civilization. In her letters she did not specifically criticize the Dutch colonial state, although she was occasionally negative about certain aspects of colonialism in general. Every now and then Kartini mocked the pretentiousness of Dutch women when they behaved as "proud madams," who gave a "cold shoulder" to the Javanese and looked upon them with "cool disdain;" some ostentatious Dutch women, she admitted, treated their colonial subjects like a "kind of vermin" (*ongedierte*) simply because they were white and prominent (*kandjeng njonjas*) only by accident, thanks to their marriage to important men who could claim the appellation "your excellency."⁵⁷

But in most of her letters Kartini was effusively grateful to Dutch "ethical" comrades-in-arms for being allies in her struggle against "the rusty and deeply entrenched views (*ingeroest en oeroud*) and archaic customs and traditions" of Java.⁵⁸ She rejoiced in her letter to Mien Bosch, for instance, that "for the Dutch in Indonesia much that is beautiful and glorious remains to be done: that the Netherlands may fulfill this task, voluntarily assumed, with love and dedication!"⁵⁹ She wished for a harmonious and productive "synthesis" of the best features of the cultural grammar of West and East, in order to formulate a new social vocabulary that would grant aristocratic women more latitude within the feudal and hierarchical universe of Javanese *priyayi* culture.

In fact, Kartini employed a subtle evolutionary rhetoric by invoking the Mendelian notion of the blending and mutation of species. The Javanese, she pleaded, should absorb the finer things of European civilization, not to suppress or replace their own exquisite culture, but to fortify or "ennoble" it: "through the cross-fertilization of either plants or animals of different types, one can obtain an improved plant or animal species." She then posed a predictable question: would not the same be true for human morality? If the positive features of Western civilization were to be blended with the good qualities of Javanese culture, would not a more "elevated morality" be the logical result?⁶⁰

Raden Adjeng Kartini's aristocratic biases echoed the emerging orientation of Dutch political strategies in twentieth-century Indonesia. More emphatically than before, after the turn of the century Dutch policies tended to intensify the feudal patterns of command and subordination, both in Javanese society and elsewhere. Of course, Dutch colonial authorities were not unique, in this regard. Following the Sepoy Mutiny of 1857, the British colonial state in India also sought to preserve the subcontinent as a patrimonial order by codifying and rank ordering India's traditional hierarchical patterns of authority and subservience. British government policy in India in the 1860s began to incorporate the formerly independent rulers and princes of autonomous territories throughout the subcontinent as Queen Victoria's "Loyal Indian Feudatories," who, through the Queen's Viceroy in India, owed her deference and allegiance.[61]

Towards the end of the nineteenth century the Dutch colonial state in Indonesia embraced a comparable vision of effective governance in order to fulfill its desire for *rust and orde* (tranquility and order). The Indies government introduced Western-style hereditary rights to rank and office, for instance, in an attempt to undermine typically Javanese conceptions of power. In the cosmology of Java, power hovered as a finite quality in the universe, as if it were a brilliant glow radiating from a clearly discernable source of illumination.[62] In Javanese eyes, power concentrated in a specific person who visibly possessed such attributes as serenity, refinement, and masculine prowess. Questions about the legitimacy of power or the orderly transition of authority were mostly irrelevant, since power could be contested at any historical juncture. Individual men embodied power — and assimilated the potency of their predecessors — if they perceptibly absorbed it and conveyed authority to peers and subordinates in the outside world. Hence, "sacred bonds" and "hallowed privileges" united *priyayi* with diffident, even reverent, local peasants, who accepted aristocrats' superior status as natural.[63] Aristocratic wives indirectly affirmed this alliance by symbolizing their spouses' virility and charisma through prodigious fertility and gracious demeanor.[64]

However, this conception of power proved to be a stumbling block to the Dutch colonial regime with its penchant for legalistic rules and statutory prescriptions. Hence, the implementation of a system of hereditary rights to positions of power in the colonial bureaucracy tended to produce a neat and tidy succession of authority; these rights would subvert the elite's traditional sources of prestige, while reifying the patrimonial hierarchy of Java at the same time. This process of re-feudalization would yield the kind of order and predictability the Dutch East Indies government both sought and valued. Selectively providing educational opportunities, too, fostered the dislocation of the traditional elite by nurturing a vicarious, European-defined sense of status among Java's notables. As an elderly woman in Java today remembers angrily about the colonial era: the Dutch allowed only high-born children to attend school, and "they did this to keep the loyalty of Java's leadership class, by giving them extra privileges and turning them against the peasants."[65]

After the incorporation of the entire island of Bali into the Dutch colonial empire in the early twentieth century, the Indies government also reinvigorated "exotic" Bali's traditional Hindu caste system by reviving its ancient nomenclature and restoring the power positions of the island's ancestral rulers. The colonial civil service could thus hide behind the slender if refined shoulders of high-caste Balinese, who used the resurrection of their traditional prerogatives with abandon. They expanded their landholdings at the expense of 94 percent of the island's inhabitants who were both without caste (*kasteloos*) and controlled only the smallest plots of land to cultivate rice. Balinese rulers also began to demand new and exquisite forms of deference, while imposing more feudal labor services upon an already desperately poor peasantry.[66]

Claiming to protect the island from Christian missionaries in order to preserve "authentic" Balinese culture for posterity in all its artistic glory, the Dutch colonial

Colonial Practice in the Netherlands Indies, 1900-1942

Walter Spies in Bali, 1935 (Coll. Bonnet, KIT)

"Balinese men with their fighting cocks," drawing by Walter Spies, 1930 (Coll. Bonnet, KIT)

Kris dance in Pagutan, Bali, 1930.
Photo: Walter Spies
(Coll. Bonnet, KIT)

state attempted to convert Bali into a "living museum."⁶⁷ The island would be an open-air exhibit featuring expensively restored temples and special "Hindu-Bali schools," which would teach children Balinese dance, gamelan music, drawing, and Hindu religion and philosophy.⁶⁸ The attempt to safeguard "authentic" Balinese culture and society by conserving it in a pristine bell jar —the "Balinization (*Balisering*) of Bali" — surrendered the island to the anthropological imagination and erotic fantasies of a large contingent of north Americans and Europeans, with Margaret Mead, Gregory Bateson, Jane Belo, Colin McPhee, Rudolf Bonnet, and Walter Spies as only the most visible among them. Both men and women from the West hovered around — or fell in love with — the handsome and charismatic Walter Spies, a painter and architect of German-Russian origins, who functioned as the nucleus of the bohemian circle of intellectuals and artists from the West in Ubud in south-central Bali.⁶⁹

Westerners could thus enshrine Bali as a romantic paradise and concoct fantastic stories about the essence of "The Balinese Character," about ancient village democracies, and the happy and harmonious integration of art and religion in daily life. In Bali, as one rhapsodic European wrote,

> There exist neither schools nor schoolteachers, but everyone can read and write. Bali knows neither art academies nor museums, but almost everyone is an artist.

"Balinese woman," drawing by Miguel Covarrubias, 1935. From: Sujeta Neka, The Development of Painting in Bali (Ubud: Yayasan Dharma Seni Museum Neka, 1989)

I have never heard a priest give a sermon, but all the Balinese people are more truth-loving, honest, and honorable than Europeans. There are no police, but no one steals. Bali possesses neither professors nor universities; nevertheless, there are many philosophers. Infants never cry and children are never naughty, even if mothers and fathers appear totally unconcerned with raising their children.[70]

These fairy tales, however, often degenerated into horror stories with pornographic overtones. Depicting a "natural" Bali that resembled the erstwhile Tahiti of Paul Gauguin, such seductive narratives portrayed a world uncontaminated by stultifying Victorian mores. It was an arcadian landscape in which Western voyeurs — or what the American anthropologist Raymond Kennedy called "prostitute-hunting tourists in the last Paradise" on earth — could feast on nubile bodies and bare breasts, rejoice in the gorgeous physicality of Balinese men and disclose their residual homoerotic desires, and presumably take part in an uninhibited sexuality.[71] The new *Encyclopaedie van Nederlands-Indië* confirmed this impression in 1917: "The Balinese are candid, lively, and sincere .. They enjoy life, laugh easily, are loyal, hospitable, and eager to learn ... [but generally] Balinese erotic tendencies can prompt them to engage in extremely vile acts, although it should be noted that these vices are more prevalent in higher social circles than among the common people."[72] The Dutch colonial regime,

Educating Indonesian Girls in Java and Bali

Balinese landscape at dawn. Photo: Paul Spies (Coll. Bonnet, KIT)

Young Balinese dancer (Coll. Bonnet, KIT)

meanwhile, could congratulate itself for having created "tranquility and order" in one of the most densely populated places in the entire world, where social tensions and desperate poverty were palpable and diseases such as tuberculosis and syphilis were endemic.

In Java, too, twentieth-century colonial policies had a notable impact on daily life. The increasingly ornate differentiation of the Javanese language, for instance, and the veneration of *krama* and *krama inggil* — high-polite and very-high-polite speech levels, which underscored the social distance between the Javanese aristocracy and commoners who spoke a robust, graphic *ngoko* (low Javanese) — were evidence of sly colonial attempts to re-feudalize the Javanese aristocracy. While *krama* resembled a refined linguistic instrument that was "artistically but artificially" adjusted to articulate the elevated spiritual life of Java's upper class, *ngoko* embodied the "artless, unaffected" gift of the people, which expressed the "earthy vitality, the spontaneity and tumultuous charm of popular life."[73]

This critique, ironically, has an oddly "modern" ring to it. In recent years, several cultural commentators in contemporary Indonesia — if they dare to speak at all — have deplored the tendency of the New Order government to silence the clatter and din of real life. As Gunawan Mohamad lamented in 1992, the arid, stilted style of official speech in Suharto's Indonesia has stripped *bahasa Indonesia* of its "shape and smell, color and form, grit and graffiti, and its rumpus and commotion."[74] Earlier in the twentieth century, a comparable development occurred. Subtly encouraged by what Benedict Anderson has called the "schoolmarmish pedantry" of the Dutch colonial administration, *priyayi* not only exacted baroque forms of courtesy (*hormat*) from subordinates but also converted *krama* into a "morbid, deformed phenomenon" or "a pathological" language full of affectations.[75]

The Dutch insistence on the legitimacy of *hormat* and *krama inggil* divorced Java's genteel upper crust more and more from the "authentic" values of Javanese society and the linguistic practices of the millions of compliant peasants in the countryside. The Javanese elite's demand for a more bombastic display of deference on the part of underlings served as a compensation for their loss of "real" authority due to *priyayi*'s cooptation into the colonial bureaucracy.[76] The Dutch colonial administration expressed its reverence for the high style of central Java's notables, too, by adorning its most exalted rulers with an "immense ceremonial arsenal" of honorific titles, ribbons, medals, grand-crosses, insignia, and other emblems of "knighthood."[77] Kartini, because she may have divined this trend early on, mentioned mischievously in one of her letters that "it is especially in the company of Europeans who understand our language and our *adat* that we deliberately and more often address her [a cousin] as 'Your Highness'."[78]

Thus, Kartini's aristocratic perspective, or her tendency to gloss over the gloomy existence of Javanese peasant women in the *desa* — whom she described as belonging to a "naive childish people" living in a universe very different from hers —revealed a curious symmetry with both the administrative orientation of the Dutch colonial state as well as the more liberal outlook of some of the "ethical" members of the Dutch colonial community. Having been kept under lock and key inside her father's compound since the age of twelve, she was imprisoned in a gilded cage until her father selected a suitable husband for her.[79] She had endured this "horrible" period in "dumb despair." Wherever she turned, she remembered later, she confronted "closed doors" and all her valiant efforts yielded nothing but a collision with a "cold, stone wall."[80] She could only learn about the outside reality of Java by reading Dutch magazines and books although, as the daughter of her father's secondary wife (*garwa selir*, which is sometimes also given the meaning of concubine, perhaps mistakenly), she had a deeply personal connection with her biological mother's common origins in village life.

In the hushed formality of *priyayi* culture, *selir* wives should be silent and unseen: they were permitted only to whisper and to cast furtive glances. Often she served as little more than a glorified domestic servant; besides, a husband could send away a *selir* wife at a moment's notice and force her to leave her children behind.[81] As Pramoedya wrote in his novel *Gadis Pantai* (The Girl from the Coast), "she had to keep still — no one wanted to hear her voice ... she had to keep her eyes to the ground because she did not know what she was allowed to look at and what she wasn't."[82] Through an identification with her mother's subordinate status Kartini may have acquired some populist leanings, which might have made it difficult to keep straight who was "us" and who was "them," as if her "mixed-up audiences" elicited "mixed-up metaphors."[83] If her emotional solidarity with her mother produced such egalitarian sensibilities, Kartini would have taken care not to divulge them to the European women friends with whom she corresponded.

But it was above all the Dutch language that became the prism through which she observed the "other" world beyond her father's restrictive home. The only source of consolation she could find in the "prison" of her aristocratic household (*kabupaten*) were the Dutch books and magazines in the monthly box of reading materials (*leestrommel*), to which she was not denied access.[84] This incongruous position placed Kartini in liminal territory; she appeared to drift in a never-never land, as far removed from the "crazy" Hollanders as she felt alienated, according to one of her letters, from the "stupid" Javanese.[85]

Although she indicated that she "liked to observe" the Javanese people and tried "to come into contact with them as much as possible" by visiting them in their village shacks, Kartini confessed that the people in the *desa* stared at her "somewhat strangely (*wat vreemd*)."[86] Accordingly, when she passionately advocated the creation of educational opportunities for Indonesian girls, she was talking about women like herself, not the illiterate young girls toiling in rice fields who looked at her "strangely" — probably owing to a mixture of subservience and fear — from across an insurmountable social divide.

The irony, though, was that among peasants in the countryside, the independent agency of women was explicitly acknowledged. Dynastic considerations and a scrupulous concern with the convoluted distinctions of rank and status circumscribed the lives of *priyayi* women with a Byzantine code of conduct. Even though *adat*, in theory, endowed them with prerogatives similar to the privileges common women in the *desa* enjoyed, they had to preserve the dignity and "charisma" of their aristocratic standing. Thus upper-class women in Java, restricted as they were to their paternal household and later, to their husband's residence, had less leeway to act upon the rights both *adat* and *hukum* (Islamic law) granted them.[87]

The delicate task of personifying and maintaining family prestige in the eyes of peers affected peasant women in different ways, and they relished a certain freedom in their day-to-day existence which their aristocratic counterparts did not possess. With some regional variations, Javanese *adat* generally embraced bilateral inheritance arrangements for daughters and sons in village communities. In the case of divorce, the belongings of husband and wife tended to be equally divided, and *adat* recognized women's right to control their own property and sanctioned women's activities in the economic realm beyond the household.[88] Women in the *desa* traded, bartered, and controlled family finances. Hunger and poverty, of course, engendered their independent economic agency, and most women in Java — which was true, too, for casteless women in Bali — worked from daybreak to nightfall to supplement their family's income.[89] But due to their superior knowledge of the world outside the village and their role as mediators, or "cultural brokers," with a cash economy, if it existed, most Javanese peasant women had a license far greater than their aristocratic or European superiors in trying to shift the barriers, or renegotiate the behavioral restrictions, their family or community might impose upon them.[90]

While *priyayi* daughters were literally and figuratively immured within the ideological walls of Javanese patriarchy which modulated their access to the outside world, such boundaries between private and public behavior, whether imagined or real, did not encumber the lives of Javanese peasant women to the same extent. In the late nineteenth century, however, some colonial voices began to reorient definitions of women's proper place on a Western model by incorporating *all* women, whether white or indigenous, whether high-born or of humble descent, into the domestic realm. As usual, this did not occur without contentious debate, because another faction of the colonial community argued that women's work in Java, whether during the day or throughout the night, was an utterly "natural" institution sanctioned by Javanese *adat*. In order to guarantee a steady supply of cheap labor on the lucrative coffee, tea, and sugar plantations that punctuated the Javanese landscape, this contingent of the Dutch voices invoked the so-called "essentialist" differences between Eastern and Western women.[91] Not surprisingly, these euphemistic debates about the "natural" habit of women's work in Java concealed a wide range of ulterior motives.

Nonetheless, it was the palpable memory of the sophisticated if fragile Kartini that served as the primary source of enlightenment and inspiration to many female members of the "ethical" Dutch colonial community, not the reality of poor but plucky peasant women in the countryside. In the eyes of her Dutch fellow travelers, Kartini epitomized the *summum bonum* of "enlightened" Dutch colonial rule in a "modern" guise without losing her stylish Javanese identity: she embodied the tangible results of a culturally sensitive but solid education. It was her narrative on Javanese traditions — which, in her view, resulted from a culture that imposed loathsome constraints on women — which defined Dutch women's perceptions of their educational task. As a result, the Dutch women who directed Kartini Schools or taught in Van Deventer boarding schools envisioned their educational efforts in a vertical, hierarchical design. They concocted a "trickle down" model of educational development, expecting that the daughters of *priyayi* and other native officials in the colonial bureaucracy, whom they cultivated intellectually, would harbor a sense of obligation and desire to pass on their own cherished learning to women in the *desa*. In the 1920s and 1930s, when parents of more "modest social origins" (*uit lagere standen*) began to request admission to the Kartini and Van Deventer schools for their daughters, the Dutch colonial state, instead, created new schools for less well-born native girls, thus upholding the ironclad social hierarchy of Javanese society.[92]

The statement of principles, issued at the birth of the Kartini Foundation in 1913, envisioned the creation of Dutch-Javanese day schools for girls between the ages of six and twelve, which would provide "simple, character-building education designed especially for female pupils." The schools would acknowledge and respect their Eastern "religious feelings" and their parents would have to pay a "relatively high tuition" to assure that the schools would attract students from families that have already reached a certain "level of development" and to make it known that a good education required financial sacrifice. The statement also expressed the hope that eventually students would register a "serious longing for more advanced education."[93] The Van Deventer boarding schools, founded a few years later, presumably responded to this "serious longing" — an intellectual desire that was perceptible. For example, 550 female students eager to earn teaching degrees applied to the public Normal School in Purwakarta in June, 1917, but due to a lack of space only 21 young women could be admitted. The creation of Van Deventer schools, a Javanese observer noted, meant that private foundations were fulfilling a task that should really be carried out by the government.[94]

Both the Kartini and Van Deventer schools, however, walked an intellectual tightrope between two models of educational development in colonial societies. On the one hand, the blueprint of a distinctly Western education bestowed upon the Javanese elite was designed to nurture a class of "evolved" natives, who would gradually learn to lead their nation, under benevolent Dutch patronage, along the appropriate path. On the other hand, the "Orientalist" model championed a vision of education that "associated" or blended Western knowledge and technology with Javanese formality, spirituality, and hierarchy by adjusting the former to the latter.[95]

At the turn of the century, the initial impetus of the "Ethical Policy" in Java emphasized Western education for the elite. Towards the 1920s, however, a distinct "Orientalizing" tendency emerged. Many Dutch men and women began to plead for an educational system that sought more connections with the "native milieu" so that natives "would not be alienated from their cultural roots."[96] "Orientalism" in colonial Indonesia produced strange ideological bedfellows.[97] A large number of conservative colonial residents espoused such "Orientalist" notions, because they sought a guarantee that the intellectual and political "awakening" of the Javanese would occur only at a snail's pace. Socialists and other critics of Dutch colonial policies, meanwhile, also advocated practical Eastern education that might enable simple folk in rural villages to expand the rice harvest, to improve irrigation, or to cultivate new crops.

Occupying a hazy middle ground between the political right and left, the ethically inspired but paternalistic — or maternalistic — progressive segment of the Dutch colonial community supported Western education for native men; however, they were captivated by the "Orientalist" prototype as far as the education of girls was concerned. Among the enthusiastic supporters of Kartini and Van Deventer schools, the rallying cry was to show genuine respect for native culture. Thus, Javanese *priyayi* sons were recruited into the colonial bureaucracy and instructed into the ways of Western administrative procedures. Javanese girls, meanwhile, ought to remain "natural" and uncontaminated by European values, except that *priyayi* daughters should no longer be treated as pawns in a marital chessgame designed purely to further their fathers' interest in enhancing their families' status and prestige.[98]

Recognizing that it would be difficult, a Dutch teacher should nevertheless "uplift her native student by allowing her to remain a native." Dutch educators should honor and cultivate all aspects of Javanese culture and ought to be "obliged to study Javanese customs and habits and encourage students to wear native dress." Again, this official ideology was akin to upper-class Javanese attitudes. The progressive husband of one of Kartini's sisters, Achmad Sosrohadikoesoemo, wrote in 1916 that schools should not foster the metamorphosis of girls into flamboyant "pseudo-European women" but should produce, instead, "real modern Javanese women" who would be equally at home in either European or Javanese circles. Any girl who took on the brash style or liberated airs of a European woman, however, would be "lost to the cause," and all girls attending schools should be forbidden from wearing European clothing.[99]

Despite this official credo, which true believers of the ethical movement embraced wholeheartedly, the Director of the Van Deventer school in Semarang, Mrs. F.A. Volkers-Schippers, added some caveats. The only practices that deserved to be suppressed, she noted, were those that Westerners could unequivocally condemn, and she produced a litany of complaints: "child marriages, teeth filing, giving big parties, wearing jewelery often bought with borrowed money, eating with one's hands all sorts of food prepared and sold on the street, not to speak of other evils such as opium, alcohol, and gambling." But the fears of "too much Westernization" in the schools, she bluntly informed the Board of Directors of the Kartini Foundation in The Hague in 1924, proved nothing more than that certain Dutch teachers "are not intellectually equipped for their task;" it did not mean that the system of providing genuine Javanese education to girls in the Dutch language was flawed.[100]

One of the moving forces behind the valiant Dutch efforts on behalf of the education of Indonesian girls was Elisabeth (Betsy) van Deventer-Maas. Until 1897 she and her husband had lived in Java, where fate had "smiled upon them" and they had found both happiness and wealth, while the Indies, in return, had earned their undying "love and gratitude." To them, this profound sense of appreciation became a "debt of honor," and both Van Deventers were convinced that the cultural links between the native population and Dutch civilization should be strengthened. But Coenraad van Deventer's goal was not to set the masses in motion himself. He clung to his conviction that "Java's children" (*landskinderen*) should guide such movements themselves: they, alone, could bless their country, not European outsiders.[101]

Betsy van Deventer-Maas and her husband were among the founders of the Kartini Foundation in 1913, and after her husband's death in 1915, she was instrumental in the creation of the Van Deventer Foundation's boarding schools. While living in The Hague in the Netherlands, she converted the schools into objects of her constant solicitude and faithful attention until her death at the advanced age of eightyfive in 1942. She was a woman much beloved and admired for "her caring heart," who had embraced her beautiful life's work, according to a friend, without any trace of "militant feminism." To the contrary, Betsy had secured the admiration and respect of Dutch society, both in Europe and in southeast Asia, "only through her splendid feminine modesty."[102]

Betsy van Deventer-Maas had also established close connections with important Javanese aristocrats. In the sumptuous commemorative volume proffered to Mangkoe Nagoro VII in 1939, to celebrate his elevation to the Sultanate of the Mangkunegaran realm in Solo twenty-four years earlier, she rejoiced in her long-standing friendship with the Sultan. The *Triwindoe-Gedenkboek* was a beautifully illustrated album in which a wide range of Europeans expressed their misty-eyed admiration for the high style of "Javaland" by paying homage to one of its most debonair rulers; they did so with sentimental poetry, worshipful essays, or even in special musical compositions, such as a sonata for piano and violin composed in honor of the Sultan.[103] Betsy's message was a sober entry in comparison to the other effusive or pretentious contributions. She remembered that she and her husband Coenraad had gotten to know Mangkoe Nagoro VII in 1912 in Solo. "Their rapport had become more intimate" during the Sultan's sojourn in the Netherlands in 1913-1915, when he agonized over "the difficult choice whether to stay in Holland for further study or return to his fatherland." Since then, the creation of the Van Deventer school in Solo had reinforced their ties, because "the Sultan and the *Ratoe Timoer* (his wife) bestowed upon the school their strong support."[104]

Betsy van Deventer-Maas carried on a lively correspondence with Dutch school directors and teachers in Java as well as with the indigenous students during the late 1920s and the 1930s. She received a steady stream of information about the schools and the trials and tribulations of both the European teachers and their Javanese pupils. She also received a cornucopia of stilted, official photographs of the various graduating classes from the different schools, or gifts, such as the present of a basket of special Javanese fruit dispatched via airplane from Batavia to the Netherlands in 1937 on the occasion of her eightieth birthday.[105] The black-and-white photographs portrayed groups of girls with earnest, dignified faces, whether they were dressed in traditional *sarung* and *kebaya* or in fashionable European clothes. But especially the letters from students are exceptional documents, often written in a charming Dutch prose with only an occasional grammatical or idiomatic lapse, in which they conveyed their pride in having mastered the cultural idiom of the colonial elite but also registered, on occasion, a certain sense of insecurity about the meaning and implications of the education they had received.

One student, Sri Wahijah, wrote to Betsy van Deventer-Maas in 1931 that she was now the proud owner of three diplomas, "the weapons I need to defend myself as I follow upon my life's path. Now I can stand on my own two feet, earn my own bread, and support my parents. How wonderful to think of having my own class, my own students! Now I am worth something to this society, to this overwhelming life; I have fervently looked forward to this moment, although I am also a bit afraid."[106] Another girl named Srijoewati mentioned in a letter in 1930 that she had forever "yearned to leave school quickly in order to earn my daily bread myself, but now that we are adults and have to leave school in order to stand on our own two feet we realize what a delightful experience our boarding school years have been." Sri Martini, a few years later, informed Mrs. Van Deventer-Maas that she could only "hope and pray that I can properly serve you, your deceased husband, and our school by employing all the good things I have learned in order to transmit them to other women and girls."[107]

Certain quaint phrases resurfaced in almost all students' letters, such as the expression "to earn one's own daily bread" — a bizarre figure of speech in a society in which people ate nothing but rice — or "to stand on one's own two feet." But some of the letters also conveyed, in between the lines, a silent subtext of anxiety about their ambiguous position as young women trained in Dutch schools but who were now forced to find a niche for themselves in the "courtly and decorous world" of a *priyayi* society obsessed with status and gentle refinement.[108]

A young girl named Adi, for instance, sent a remarkable six-page letter in 1932 from Yogyakarta to the ex-Director of the Van Deventer school in Solo, who was on medical leave in Holland. She entertained her former teacher with stories about teaching first grade in her father's nationalist school, an independent institution the Dutch colonial state scornfully referred to as a "wild" school because it had refused to adopt the government-sanctioned lesson plans. Instead, these autonomous Javanese institutions had developed a curriculum that constituted a mixture of ultra-modern Western educational ideas with instruction in traditional Javanese arts and history, thus combining "new and old, radical and conservative."[109]

The intellectual father of the *taman siswa* movement (garden of pupils), Ki Hadjar Dewantoro (Soewardi Soerjaningrat), had chastised the indigenous "bourgeoisie's" tendency to worship Western expertise and fluency in Dutch cultural grammar. He rebuked a particular kind of Javanese *parvenu* "who is always bent on conspicuous display and material gain and who fails to appreciate any form of education that does not incorporate Dutch-language instruction." Thus he advocated that the obsessive Western orientation of certain social circles in Java should be cured through the establishment of schools that promoted knowledge of, and fostered pride in, their own culture.[110]

Javanese teachers established and controlled such "wild" schools themselves, with neither subsidies nor interference from the Dutch colonial administration. The first of

Coenraad Theodoor van Deventer. From: Jubileum-verslag... Vereeniging Kartinifonds

these *taman siswa* schools had been founded in Yogyakarta in 1922, but they spread like wildfire beyond central Java. Ten years later, despite the government's introduction of the Wild School Ordinance in September, 1932, representing a futile attempt to restrict these intractable educational institutions, the *taman siswa* movement already incorporated 166 schools with approximately 11,000 Javanese students.[111] The government's annual report on education in 1936 listed as many as 1,663 "wild schools" which enrolled 114,000 students. For 1937 the report cited a grand total of 1,961 schools which taught 129,565 pupils, while in 1941, the number of native students receiving Dutch-language instruction in "wild" schools, located within and beyond Java, may have been as high as 230,000.[112]

Java was not alone in witnessing a stealthy expansion of independent schools that self-consciously tried to stay outside the orbit of Dutch governmental control. In the Minangkabau region of western Sumatra, a comparable flourishing of autonomous educational institutions took place during the same period. Even though they were more explicitly beholden to Islamic *ulama* (teachers) than in Java and devoted more time to Koranic instruction, *kaum muda* schools in Minangkabau country also eagerly fostered in their students "the idea of individual rationality (*idjtihad*) and the spirit of

Mangkoe Nagoro VII during his stay in the Netherlands as a young man. From: Triwindoe Gedenkboek Mangkoe Nagoro VII (Soerakarta: Comité Triwindoe Gedenkboek, 1939)

reform."[113] Very quickly, the implementation of the "Wild School Ordinance" sparked spontaneous opposition in both Java and western Sumatra.[114]

The Indies government's public claim in trying to hinder the proliferation of all these "wild" schools was its wish to protect the natives from "the quacks and snake-oil salesmen in the educational arena." Its more deep-seated concern, however, issued from *taman siswa*'s potential production of a "proletariat of discontented semi-intellectuals" who might disseminate anti-Dutch propaganda.[115] But in the face of an oppositional alliance of progressive teachers, nationalist politicians, and even more conservative Islamic teachers, the government beat a hasty retreat by suspending its enforcement of the Wild School Ordinance a mere six months later, in February 1933.[116] Both *taman siswa* and *kaum muda* schools became thriving institutions; they induced in students a burgeoning sense of pride in their native cultures. While Dutch educational efforts, according to a modern-day Indonesian critic, were designed merely to satisfy the need for native civil servants who had absorbed the intellectual ways of the West, these indigenous independent schools were committed to raising "the cultural standards of [all] the people of Indonesia!"[117]

With regard to her work in her father's nationalist school in Yogyakarta, Adi joyfully announced in her letter to her former head mistress that she had formed a "Girls Study Club" for female students who were at least fourteen years old. Deploying the distinctive rhetoric of the Kartini and Van Deventer schools, she mentioned that "we want to help each other with domestic training in sewing, cooking, and hygiene, in short, we want to learn everything we need to know in order to fulfill our duty as housewives." Then, in a striking narrative shift, she told her former teacher about the Muslim fasting month (*puasa*) which had just ended: "we fasted the entire time, which required a lot of exertion." But at the end, during *lebaran*, "we honored our grandparents and parents by giving them a *kniekus*" —an Islamic rite of obeisance called *sunkeman*, which often entailed a kiss on the knee (*ngaras*).[118] In return, Adi received the blessing (*pangèstu*) of her elders in exchange for her act of supplication: "we passionately begged them for forgiveness for all the mistakes we had made during the past year. I wish you could have been there to observe this spectacle (*schouwspel*): presumably we now begin the next year with a pure heart."[119]

What is so interesting about Adi's letter was the uncanny way in which she juxtaposed a Western vocabulary to describe the need to teach sewing and hygiene in order to equip her pupils for their housewifely destiny, on the one hand, with her description of the solemn family ritual marking the end of the arduous month of spiritual atonement and purification, on the other. Adi resided in a social space full of contradictions. She hovered in a liminal terrain in between the Dutch colonial world that had trained her and the atmosphere of Islamic religious rituals and the proud spirit of Javanese cultural identity and national revival of her father's *taman siswa* school. She could only resolve her ambiguous position, it seemed, by indulging in escapist fantasies. Adi admitted that was she was building "castles in the air" (*luchtkastelen*) that her ex-teacher might wish to open a new school, "with her former students as teachers, preferably in a cool place such as Magelang." She also confessed that she dreamt about going to the city of Bandung in west Java to earn additional teaching degrees in English and Dutch, but then she lamented that her father "cannot pull it off [financially] because I have so many younger brothers and sisters."[120]

Binti, Adi's friend, former classmate, and fellow teacher at the "wild" school in Yogyakarta, touchingly revealed a similar ambivalence. She deplored not yet having received a teaching assignment in a government school, even though she desperately needed the salary to help support her mother and younger siblings because her father had recently died. She said she was biding her time teaching at the nationalist school where they paid her "only a little pocket money for her efforts." But then Binti suddenly seemed to switch her sense of allegiance, and *they*, the underpaid but idealistic Javanese teachers and their native students of the *taman siswa* school, became *us*: "it all depends on us, Javanese . . teaching at this school pleases me, because it makes me feel so free just to be among ourselves (*zo onder onsjes*)!"[121]

Many other *priyayi* graduates of the Van Deventer school, though, expressed fewer qualms about the value of their European schooling, as if their initiation into the exalted world of advanced, Dutch-language education provided straightforward evidence of their elite status. Their elevated training and knowledge of Dutch validated the inbred sense of superiority of *priyayi* daughters, whose social distance from women in the *desa* or *kampong* replicated the great divide between Europeans and peasants. Some of them conveyed, perhaps unwittingly but with exceptional clarity, their cultural detachment or social aloofness from the harsh realities of daily life among simple Javanese folk, especially during the era of the Great Depression in the early 1930s.

Soeparni, for example, mentioned in a letter from Tegal in 1932 that due to the Depression, she saw a lot of suffering around her. Owing to the dwindling employment opportunities of native labor in sugar factories or on coffee and tea plantations, which comprised the embattled export sector of Java's economy, an enormous number of Javanese workers were rendered jobless and hungry. Even though "we have a poorhouse in town," Soeparni wrote, "poverty-stricken people still bother us (*hebben last van*) by coming to the house every day to ask for alms. Especially before and during *lebaran* the number of beggars overwhelmed us and everywhere schools and offices are closed and teachers and employees are fired . . as a result, many people leave town to look for work elsewhere. Numerous houses are empty and no longer rented: what a disaster for the owners!"[122] Soeparni's loyalties were transparent, and the dislocation and human misery spawned by the Great Depression affected only "others," not herself.

In the same year her friend Sarlyne, also living in Tegal in 1932, wrote blithely to her former teacher that she and her friends had started a tennis club with mostly European members. "I am one of the youngest, and we play once a week on the court of the *Mangkoe* (local ruler). I have learned to swim but aside from sports, I only help my mother a bit with her household duties and with sewing. Right now I am learning to make *batik*, which I find boring."[123] Sarlyne obviously interacted and played sports with European girls on a regular basis, a fact Petrus Johannes Gerke would have applauded. This civil servant, who enjoyed an illustrious Indies career between 1910 and 1935 in the General Secretariat, the Office of Native and Arabic Affairs, and the Department of Finance had argued, after all, that the best way to initiate the cream of the crop —or, as he called it, the *crème de la crème* — of young Javanese womanhood in the spirit of the West was "to encourage them to have close contacts with civilized, European women outside the context of school as well." Gerke claimed that the European education of indigenous girls was becoming increasingly important because young

Javanese women should be transformed into good partners for "the growing number of young men who have enjoyed the benefits of a Western education."[124]

It was true that *priyayi* sons, if they had been taught in exclusive European schools or in Dutch native schools, also stood in the midst of a cultural maelstrom, where the ebb of Western influences and the flow of Javanese tradition buffeted them about. Young men, however, had more flexibility in resolving these contradictions by making public, political choices. In contrast, their European-trained sisters, caught in the feudal web of Javanese restrictions imposed on girls in their teens —an age when their parents customarily tried to arrange advantageous marriages for them — harbored two competing inner voices. They were forced to negotiate between the loud and imperious Dutch voice they had heard in school, which had encouraged them "to earn their own daily bread" and transmit their valuable learning to women of the people but had also urged them, paradoxically, to fulfill their maternal destiny. The soft-spoken mellifluous speech of their ancestral Javanese world, in contrast, praised them for their modesty and compliance with indigenous patriarchal traditions.

They may have been standing on their "own two feet," but it seemed as if they had one foot firmly planted in the hybridized world of the twentieth-century Dutch East Indies, while their other foot was tied to, or bound by, archaic Javanese *adat*. "Western-educated youth occupies a small peninsula" in between two separate oceans of competing ideological values that "both beckon and sow anxiety at the same time," the Dutch fiction writer M.A.M. Renes-Boldingh scribbled in a maudlin novel, entitled *Adat*, about the very different universe of Christian Karo Bataks in northern Sumatra. One of the novel's main characters, in fact, used the exact same trope. "We straddle a boundary, with one foot in the old world and the other foot in the new one: it produces a yearning for freedom as well as a fear of letting go of the old [traditions]."[125] Both Christian Karo Bataks in Medan or graduates of the Kartini and Van Deventer schools, in other words, inhabited what Homi Bhabha as well as Michael Taussig have recently called an "in-between space" located in the interstices of colonial societies. These young, Western-educated Indonesians resided in a chaotic domain halfway between East and West — a territory full of mimicry and contestation which spawned cultural "overlap and displacement."[126]

In Java, however, *priyayi* customs did not encourage unmarried girls to venture into the world beyond their paternal household. Neither did Javanese hierarchical traditions stimulate married women, whose contacts with "women of the people" probably entailed little more than overseeing servants, to muster a great deal of compassion with peasant women who lived on the other side of an immense feudal divide. After all, *adat* dictated that *priyayi* women "should never work, especially not for the common folk."[127] Besides, Javanese tradition prescribed that upon marriage, aristocratic women should break all personal ties with their previous lives, because the emotional attachments of childhood might encumber their romantic devotion to their new husbands. Being forced to sever all formal connections with the past also implied they should try to forget a personal history that had included a sophisticated and expensive Western education.[128]

It would not be until the 1930s that the plight of overburdened, overworked, and silently suffering women in Java's villages and rural areas came into sharper focus among members of the "ethical" Dutch community. In 1932, the ex-director of the Van Deventer boarding school in Semarang, Mrs. F.A. Volkers-Schippers, started a monthly magazine, entitled *Widoeri*, for former students of the Kartini and Van Deventer schools who were called upon to share their precious learning with the *volksvrouw* (woman of humble origins) and thus give her a better lease on life. As *Widoeri*'s founder wrote in 1937: "Anyone who looks around the Indies must understand that now that the *priyayi* woman has enjoyed ample opportunity to develop herself intellectually, it has become high time for her to try to enhance the fate of the simple Javanese woman and thus improve the fortunes of the entire population."[129]

Even though Mrs. Volkers-Schippers conceded that "the maternal instinct of the average Javanese *volksvrouw* is alive and well," she reputedly discharged her duties as mother and housewife in only the most sloppy and deficient manner. Not only because Javanese mothers of simple origin were often too young and inexperienced, but also because they had no one in their direct environment who could provide them with a good example or "with useful information." Thus, the Dutch teachers who contributed to *Widoeri* summoned the upper-crust graduates of Kartini and Van Deventer schools to emerge from their charmed lives. Even though few *priyayi* daughters were ever forced to cook, sew, or clean themselves, *Widoeri* encouraged them to roll up their dainty sleeves, so to speak, and to descend into the villages and use their ingenuity in trying to teach better housekeeping and culinary skills to uneducated or overburdened subalterns.

The literal meaning of the word *widuri* derives from the Javanese term for a particular kind of shrub, but in this instance, the magazine's title constituted a quaint abbreviation of the Dutch verbs *willen, doen,* and *richten* (to want, to do, and to guide) which formed the fanciful contraction *Wi-doe-ri*. The magazine's subtitle was "*Widoeri*, a journal dedicated to the knowing, capable, and wise woman" (*de wetende, de kundige, de wijze vrouw*). The cute name of the magazine was a reflection of its saccharine content, which combined an endless array of sewing patterns, cooking recipes and nutritional information, or household tips with a patronizing narrative about the cultural illiteracy and misguided economic logic of peasant women. What well-intentioned Dutch authors did, in this remarkable publication, was to invoke all the *priyayi* prejudices and to confirm the innate, feudal sense of superiority of former students towards their Javanese subordinates. By disseminating Western notions, in a language only the daughters of Java's notables could read, about good nutrition, rational economic conduct, and the kind of appropriate motherly behavior that the simple folk in village communities should absorb, they articulated their "trickle down" vision of educated womanhood.

Although intended to arouse empathy and the desire to help, scattered throughout the pages of the magazine were the most condescending observations about peasant women. For example, in 1935, *Widoeri* told its aristocratic audience that:

The mother in the *desa* slogs and slaves away. She carries loads on her back as heavy as lead; in the middle of a pitch-black night she pounds *dedek* (bran) or *djagoeng* (corn) so she can trudge the enormous distance to a *passar* (market) far away where she sells her pathetic products in order to earn a few cents ... if only she would stay at home and learn to care better for her children by meeting her housewifely obligations, then enough time would remain to earn extra income by doing some light agricultural labor or, even more desirable, by spinning, weaving, or making *batik, tritik, djoemplat, plangi* (various ornate forms of decorated cloth) and pottery or baskets.[130]

To enhance the dramatic impact of this narrative, the magazine printed a series of Rient van Santen's evocative drawings of pitiable, bent-over Javanese women, resembling overburdened pack horses, while carrying their crushingly heavy loads. "The woman with her simple basket, in her *slendang* (shawl), straight of limb and body, represents how it should be," was the Dutch author's commentary about the accompanying illustrations, "but this stands in striking contrast with the other human wrecks who struggle forth."[131] An English-speaking woman journalist reported identical imagery in her insipid account of a journey through Java in the 1930s: everywhere she saw "wizened wisps of humanity," with "shrunken little bodies" who carried baskets slung on their backs overflowing with an onerous load of "smooth round stones from the riverbed, each the size of a man's head."[132]

During the next few years the representations of women in the *desa* became neither more compassionate nor truthful. In 1937 *Widoeri* proclaimed "We can only attribute undernourishment in Java to a prevailing lack of knowledge; if only the native woman would value *kedele* (soybeans) more than *ketela* (cassava, yams, and starchy rootcrops) and prefer fruits and green leaves to sweets, then famine would not exact as many victims each time it stalks the island of Java." And in the same year *Widoeri* announced that "the peasant woman's fundamental ignorance prevents her from using her time efficiently; if only she could comprehend her household tasks more clearly, then she and her family might be able to live more economically."[133]

Widoeri's attempts to persuade educated Javanese women to reach out to their poor and illiterate "sisters" in the countryside achieved only minimal success, even though a former inspector of education in the Dutch East Indies claimed in 1940 that the impact of *Widoeri* courses was of a far greater significance than "the direct results might suggest."[134] Albeit different in tone and diction, their former teachers' forceful voices articulated views about the still "stupid" Javanese peasants — as Kartini had labelled them in 1903 and many other Javanese aristocrats continued to do — that resonated their own soft-spoken biases. Because *priyayi* women on their wedding day had to renounce, in a ceremonial "gesture of subjection," their formal ties with their previous life in their parents' household, *Widoeri*'s call to nurture and teach poor peasants violated Javanese conventions.[135] The exhortation to be charitable, in other words, evoked a historical memory of a past experience at the Kartini or Van Deventer schools that *adat* did not encourage them to recall. The admonition to teach common village women, meanwhile, which constituted a form of work, also invited aristocratic women to defy traditions that did not sanction aristocratic women's work.

Despite their self-proclaimed sensitivities to the Eastern context in which they lived, many well-intentioned Dutch women revealed a kind of cultural blind spot to the real meaning of Javanese customs and traditions. In a different setting, a Dutch woman accused the forty-four Javanese girls from good families and "high social status," who were student-nurses in the *Boedi Kemoeliaan* hospital for women and children in Batavia, of being "extremely hardhearted, even cruel," in their treatment of poor sick children. While the average *priyayi* girl "relishes her lessons and is fond of theory," she wrote in 1920, such a native girl should also harbor a heartfelt desire to help her people (*haar volk*), but instead, she is "rude (*grof*) and lacks any sense of duty or responsibility, which forces me to conclude that general human compassion (*algemeene mensenliefde*) is not part of her mentality."[136]

Perhaps it was only someone like the young girl Goenarsih who, after satisfying her culture's expectations by immediately marrying a Javanese doctor upon leaving the Van Deventer school, could reconcile the two disparate and competing inner voices in order to achieve sweet harmony. She followed her doctor-husband to Bali, where she aspired to become the best "doctor's wife" that was humanly possible. Her goal, she wrote, was to help as much as she could "the other women in Bali, who know nothing about health science (*gezondheidsleer*), childbirth, or child care."[137]

The island of Bali, where Goenarsih and her husband moved in 1930, found itself in the eye of an intellectual storm over the nefarious impact of Westernization. A *bandjir* (flood) of Western influences, the Bali "lobby" proposed, was destroying the spontaneity and artistic vitality of the island's culture. A whirlwind of modernity threatened to uproot and cast off its inhabitants, who had become increasingly alienated from their spiritual moorings, which were no longer anchored in old Balinese institutions and cosmology. The plan to create a Hindu-Bali school geared especially towards girls from the upper social strata (*de gegoede stand*), Bali connoisseurs argued, would turn the tide.[138] Moreover, the high-profile artist and long-time Bali resident Walter Spies had offered to donate his services for the design of the Hindu-Bali school in classic Balinese architectural style.[139] The school would thus enhance the physical splendor of the island by adding a new architectural artifact to the "living museum" that was Bali.

Holland's position *vis-à-vis* Bali resembled the relationship of a sophisticated adult who faced "an untrained but artistically gifted child of alien origins," noted the painter Rudolf Bonnet, who also lived permanently in Bali.[140] It would be an "easy trick" (*een klein kunstje*) for high and mighty European rulers to lord their influence over a primitive people and thus obliterate its culture, but Holland would not receive any accolades for trying to do so. Is it not the duty, he asked rhetorically, of a foreign guardian (*voogd*) and educator (*opvoeder*) to provide a group of innocent people with the chance to evolve according to its *own* nature and to renew itself in its *own* direction? The Dutch should recognize, he wrote, that culture and civilization were not the same thing. Religion and art, blended into daily life, constituted culture; proper social relations, knowledge and keen insight, or comfort and hygiene, brought civilization. The

Rient van Santen's drawings of Javanese women. From: *Widoerileergang. Hoe men elementair naai-en huishoudonderricht kan geven aan de volksvrouw op Java* (Batavia: Volkslectuur, 1937)

average Dutch person might be civilized, but on the whole he or she possessed little culture.

Every Balinese man, woman, and child, however, could boast of "a powerful" (*machtige*) culture — each one of them, ranging from high-caste rulers to poverty-stricken peasants without caste, were "natural democrats," all of them "born with remarkable artistic talents" — even if they were relatively uncivilized.[141] The high-minded duty of Dutch colonial rulers was "to support and guide Bali in its evolution towards its *own* cultural destiny," Bonnet concluded, because development in a Western mold would accomplish nothing but to convert the unsullied and innocent Balinese into a pathetic "caricature" of Europeans.[142]

Dutch colonial officials in the 1930s were alarmed by the preference of young upper-caste Balinese men for Javanese wives, allegedly because they could not find sufficiently educated Balinese brides; this pattern, the self-proclaimed protectors of Bali feared, would undermine the resilience of Balinese culture, since women were the ones to transmit cultural knowledge to the next generation.[143] As a renowned Dutch archeologist, an expert on the Hindu origins of Indonesian temple architecture, noted: "from a modern perspective, the intellectual development of Balinese mothers is *nihil*, while their knowledge of their own culture is defective." If we want to preserve Balinese art and culture in all its authentic glory, Willem Frederik Stutterheim argued, we have "to seek its salvation in the education of girls," since many upper-caste Balinese parents acknowledged the "need for boys to be trained in the ways of the West, but prefer a more old-fashioned education for girls."[144]

The indefatigable Ms. C.J.A. Lichtenbelt, who had been the director of a normal school for girls in Blitar in Java, coordinated the frenzied attempt to found a Hindu-Bali school: she behaved like the captain of a ship that might sink at any moment. In her copious correspondence, carried on with academic Bali specialists and colonial officials in both the Indies and the Netherlands, she repeated over and over again that the only way "Indonesian society can flourish is when the development of men goes hand in hand with the elevation of women."[145] This rhetoric, of course, echoed Kartini's exhortations. Even though Ms. Lichtenbelt corresponded with the directors of the Kartini and Van Deventer Foundations in order to raise funds for her Hindu-Bali school, she claimed that Bali was truly exceptional and that the education of Balinese girls could not be a "cliché" of the situation in Java. Bali, she wrote, was a "*unicum*" in the Indonesian archipelago, because it integrated religion in daily life. Java, in this context, revealed a vivid contrast, she maintained, because in Java "religion is not an integral element of culture. In fact, in Java one can hardly speak of a living indigenous culture (*een levende inheemsche cultuur*)."[146]

This ill-conceived pronouncement probably irritated many Dutch devotees of the exquisite elegance of Javanese culture. Nonetheless, they supported the idea that the strength of Balinese customs could best be rejuvenated through the educational advancement of high-caste Balinese women. Most ethical Dutch progressives represented especially upper-class women as the ones embodying tradition in their daily lives, who would impart the "essence" of native cultures to the next generation. This conviction shaped the perspectives of the Java lobby and subsequently, its counterpart in Bali; Dutch-language education, sensitive to its gracious Eastern context, would also allow the daughters of high-caste Balinese to shelter their culture's miraculous artistry for posterity, as it presumably had already accomplished in Java. And eventually, Dutch colonial observers were convinced, they would relieve the ignorance and naiveté of women in the *desa* and *kampong* by teaching them, too, the essential meaning of their culture and cosmology.

A similar kind of complicity between European and indigenous upper-class attitudes affected Dutch efforts to rescue the pauperized daughters of Dutch fathers and Indonesian mothers. In a lecture in 1925 to students and teachers of the Colonial School for Women and Girls in The Hague — a school that prepared Dutch women, about to embark on a new housewifely existence in colonial Indonesia, for their tasks ahead — a female Dutch journalist from Surabaya talked about "the duty of the European woman to the female pauper child in Indonesia." Many young Eurasian girls in the Indies suffered from desperate poverty, Mrs. Van Loo-Rootlieb said; often, they were the daughters of European men and native concubines, whose white fathers had abandoned them. Living in the *kampong*, they soon "degenerated" to the level of native society, since daily existence in the villages or urban neigborhoods of Java was depraved, but above all "sad and miserable."[147] *Indos*, in short, whether male or female, comprised the "sorry wreckage in the ocean of humanity, pushed about by the turbulent waves and fickle undertow of destiny."[148]

All sorts of vices associated with pauperism festered in the *kampong*. A native mother often forced a mixed-blood daughter into prostitution or compelled her to steal, and thus she ran "wild, both morally and sexually" (*zedelijke verwildering*). Indonesian girls matured very early, Mrs. van Loo-Rootlieb asserted, and many of them already bore children at the age of 13 or 14. If we want to save the young pauper girl, she concluded, European women should feel obliged to perform a noble rescue mission and create institutions that could deliver her from a life of dissipation and sin.[149] Thus schools for Eurasian pauper girls would furnish them with useful knowledge so they might become better housewives and mothers who could elevate themselves and their children from the sinful native milieu. Even though "vanity, laziness, and frivolity" played a major role in the lives of not only Indo-European girls but their indigenous mothers, too, dismal economic circumstances were primarily responsible for thrusting them into the arms of various uncouth characters "whose daily bread depends on the seduction of innocent girls."[150]

A fund-raising letter circulated among potential donors in 1919 by an Association in Semarang chartered to establish boarding schools for young *Indo* women confronted the issue directly. The written appeal for financial support — or the *circulaire* — asserted that girls were often helpless victims who had no other option but to surrender "to the evil forces of the slums, where they are physically and spiritually corrupted." The stated goal of the schools hinged on imprinting them with a distinctive "stamp of Dutchness" that might ennoble their spirit and render them as honorable as genuine European girls. In order to liberate teenage *Indo* girls from the sinister influences of their native mothers' environment, which often transformed them into either mercenary harlots or reduced them to "trivial, narrow-minded souls," they should interact with well-bred Dutch teachers.[151]

The Juliana Foundation, which oversaw such an educational institution in Malang and another one in Ambarawa — a school that moved into a specially constructed building in Semarang in 1928 — proved that genteel Dutch women's supervision of "future mothers from socially disadvantaged backgrounds" possessed an "immeasurable value."[152] Many intelligent residents of the Indies harbored doubts about Cesare Lombroso's findings regarding the inherited proclivity of certain human types to engage in crime, a female administrator of the *Pro Juventute* organization in Surabaya conceded in 1936; she noted, however, that the same smart people tend to agree that "women's criminal tendencies often manifest themselves in prostitution." Hence, white women should reach out to this embattled group of young mixed-blood girls, because children's sobs and cries for help, or the emotional turmoil inherent in female puberty, resonated "loudly enough on the sounding board of a [white] woman's soul to make their sadness clearly heard."[153]

The term pauperism had entered the social vocabulary of the European metropole in the nineteenth century with a vengeance. In industrializing Europe, the word pauperism summoned fears of the revolutionary danger embodied in the growing presence of a volatile, wage-earning proletariat in urban areas.[154] In the Dutch East Indies, however, the label pauperism was almost exclusively attached to its large Eurasian population, which one educated estimate placed at 95,000 people in 1905 and 190,000 in 1930.[155] While Dutch colonial residents in public discussions held forth on the poverty, toil, or "lesser well-being" of indigenous women, *Indo* girls were categorized as paupers, who were victims of their "mongrel origins." Young Indo-European women supposedly indulged in too much misguided pride to perform the menial labor of Javanese peasants of common descent, but they manifested "neither the education nor the civilization, neither the knowledge nor the energy" to do the work of Europeans. In a tropical climate, which induced "indifference and indolence," many Eurasian girls languished and quickly "degenerated in a physical and moral sense."[156] Technically classified as Europeans as long as their white fathers legally acknowledged paternity, the native milieu in which *Indo* girls spent their day-to-day existence tended to offset the positive effects of their semi-white ancestry and European blood.[157]

Patterns of inclusion within, or exclusion from, the "European" community in the Dutch East Indies were infinitely complex due to the results of several centuries of interracial reproduction and a well-entrenched tradition of concubinage. Many indigenous women worked as a *njai*, cooking and keeping house for unmarried Dutchmen whom they also served sexually. Concubinage, in fact, had been encouraged and more or less institutionalized ever since a Dutch East India Company policy in 1652 had restricted the immigration of Dutch women and encumbered formal marriages between Dutch men and Javanese women with a series of complicated requirements.[158] As a result, Dutch residents in early twentieth-century Indonesia witnessed, either with equanimity or with chagrin, the outcome of almost three centuries of interracial unions.

The practice of concubinage was still widespread at the turn of the century. It was true it had become less prevalent in Java, but the tradition continued in full force on Sumatra's east coast.[159] A considerable number of women from Japan also served as concubines in Deli; hence, the folktale that *njais* functioned as "walking dictionaries" or attended to *totok* Dutch men as private tutors of Indonesian *adat* was in reality nothing but a figment of the colonial imagination.[160] On the east coast of Sumatra the normal routine, however, was for a European rubber or tobacco planter to pick a pretty Javanese woman from the ranks of newly arrived contract laborers, whether or not she was already married, and oblige her to share his house and bed; after a while some of these arrangements produced one or more children with amber-colored skins. The *njai* might have considered herself relatively privileged, despite the fact that other coolies tended to view her as unclean, polluted by her relationship with a pork-eating and jenever-drinking white "kafir."[161]

Even if mostly male coolies were forced to stand in snake-infested sludge while weeding the long rows of tobacco during the rainy season, women laborers, too, had to work extremely hard when they hunted for caterpillars on tobacco plants in the blazing sun, sorted leaves, or tapped rubber on European plantations. The women selected as a *njai*, instead, spent their equally long working days tending to the household, overseeing other servants, and catering to their masters' whims and wishes. They lived in a daily grind that was full of sexual indignities and other humiliations. Nevertheless, working as a concubine was a far cry from carrying immense piles of leaves on one's head, lugging heavy buckets with rubber, or living in filthy *pondoks* (barracks) overflowing with feuding and gambling Chinese or Javanese coolies.

Sharing quarters with a native housekeeper was still normal practice, too, among military men enlisted in the Royal Dutch East Indies Army (KNIL) throughout the archipelago. Dutch public opinion in the European metropole had concocted a scandalous image of military barracks in the Indies as sleazy dens of iniquity. "In one large room," a former officer in the Indies army wrote tendentiously, "hundreds of soldiers sleep with their girls or housekeepers in beds not even separated from each other by a curtain. Without any sense of propriety they make love, in full view of everyone else, like bulls, stallions, canine studs, tomcats, Congo negroes, Hottentots and such sundry beasts and creatures of nature."[162] Nonetheless, the concubines should not be described as professional prostitutes, the *Encyclopaedie van Nederlandsch-Indië* declared in 1919, even if it was true that "the *njai* residing in military barracks has a supple conception of love."[163] However, as long as the question of prostitution in the Indies was not addressed forcefully, "from a utilitarian point of view, barracks concubinage remains a necessity."[164]

Because the sexuality of Indonesian women was unhampered by Western mores, it was capable of mutating into a "malignant, tropical disease."[165] As a female gynecologist in Yogyakarta opined in 1936: the sexuality of native girls was so fundamentally different from Dutch girls that European ideas of virtue and morality "have no grip on them."[166] As a consequence, the management of prostitution and concubinage seemed to require the skills of an epidemiologist, who should carefully track female sexual behavior in order to contain its patterns of contagion. On the other hand, an earnest participant in a "Pro and Contra" debate in 1918 on concubinage among KNIL personnel in military barracks actually made the argument that sharing a bed with a *njai* enriched and improved the "health and morals" of soldiers. He contended that the presence of housekeepers in soldiers' garrisons prevented an unspeakable "evil" much worse than unmarried cohabitation, such as the abominable, "unnatural acts, whether those committed in private or collective ones, which are far from unknown among the members of the French Foreign Legion."[167]

At any rate, in colonial Indonesia the term pauperism came to be more explicitly linked to the sexual unruliness of Eurasian offspring rather than to the threat of proletarian revolution. Pauperism provoked worries about further interracial reproduction and sexual vice — and the blurring of social categories that might come in its wake — rather than resulting from concerns with anti-capitalist rebellion. It was true, of course, that an entirely different line of reasoning could also be found in the Indies, which articulated positive views of miscegenation. These favorable visions of intermarriage were grounded in the fear that a Western race transplanted into the voluptuous warmth of the tropics was doomed to reach a barren end, unless Europeans reinvigorated their gene pool through procreation with local spouses. This strand of argumentation in both scientific journals and popular literature was linked to neo-Lamarckian evolutionary logic and especially to Gregor Mendel's ideas about hybridity and the progressive mutation of species, which will be explored in greater detail in the next chapter of this book.

However, the biological discussion about racial blending as a means of survival for white-skinned Europeans in a sultry equatorial milieu gave way, in the course of the twentieth century, to an emphasis on the rigid separation of all ethnic groups. Accordingly, the anxieties about *Indo* pauper girls expressed an underlying political significance. To prim and proper Dutch women, newly arrived in the Indies, the ubiquitous Indo-Europeans in the Dutch East Indies represented symbolically the long history of carefree intermarriage and racial eclecticism of Dutch colonial rule in the past. Especially after the turn of the century, when the social sensibilities of the *totok* community became more prominent, *Indos* emerged in the public imagination of Europeans as tangible evidence of the sexual licentiousness and lack of self-discipline of Dutch colonial practice until then.

The southeast Asian tropical heat not only caused material objects to expand or prompt white human bodies either to bloat or to wither away, the sultry climate "also induces notions of morality to become infinitely more tractable than they were in Europe," wrote a stern, judgmental Indies woman in 1914.[168] Invariably this elasticity was ascribed to the embrace of concubinage and mixed marriages as a normal convention, particularly in some of the outer regions.[169] In the twentieth century, though, the growing number of white women born in Holland, who brought with them a keener sense of proper Victorian behavior and family values, altered the tolerant attitudes towards the loose and easy mestizo culture of the Indies; instead, they insisted on a greater racial *apartheid*.[170]

Especially poverty-stricken *Indo* girls epitomized the dangers inherent in the hybridized character of Dutch colonial rule. *Indo* boys, at least before the economic convulsions of the Great Depression of the 1930s, could regularly find employment in the colonial bureaucracy or offices in the private sector as low-level clerks. If white men acknowledged fatherhood of their mixed-blood sons who, as a result, were formally classified as Europeans, colonial mythology incorporated *Indo* boys into the putative whiteness of the Dutch community in the Indies, even though the appeal of this fantasy began to lose its luster during the early 1930s. Mixed-blood girls, in contrast, personified the permanent loose ends of Dutch colonial practice. They symbolized, in their hybrid physicality, the enormous cultural chasm between European virtues of hard work and a newly embraced ethic of sexual self-restraint, on the one hand, and the supposed lethargy and promiscuity of indigenous society, on the other. Moreover, many Dutch colonial residents blamed native mothers for the degeneracy of their olive-skinned daughters. Indigenous women's own "dissolute, adulterous behavior" and "debased character," after all, had induced them to become housekeepers *cum* sexual partners of European men in the first place.[171]

Once these unions had produced offspring, mothers held them in higher esteem because of their ginger-colored complexions and they fostered their semi-European daughters' misguided arrogance and pride and "excited their animal passions." The Javanese upper-classes, meanwhile, had nothing but aristocratic disdain for light-skinned *Indo* children because they belonged to the "low social status" of their mothers.[172] Javanese popular attitudes in the early twentieth century echoed this pejorative, *priyayi* view of Indonesian concubines and their mixed-blood children. They were "low and dirty" women — Jezebels who had defied the dictates of Javanese propriety and were "without culture, moved only by lust." These women possessed no "moral character, selling [their] honor to live easily and in luxury," and they created "families of prostitutes, destined to sink into nothingness" without leaving a trace in the official annals of Javanese history.[173]

A novel sub-text on the perils and risks of miscegenation began to run through twentieth-century colonial discourses, which recorded an alarmist, almost hysterical, narrative. Anyone who has ever "descended into the so-called *kandang ajam* (chicken coop) neighborhoods" — slums that were also referred to as *kandang babi*, or pig pen, communities — inveighed a Dutch female teacher and social worker who had lived for forty years in Java, "will find a world where one child is the stepsister of her second mother, where another child is not the actual progeny of her lawful father, where sometimes Lea and Rachel share the same husband, where a young boy is already a father and where everything revolves around sexual excess and gambling."[174]

Carolien Gunning, the Director of a school for *Indo* paupers in Sukabumi mustered a similarly hackneyed set of images in 1919 in a letter to her father: "children of the same mother but with two different fathers are brought to us, the children of mothers with dubious morals, children whose mothers have abandoned them to follow Dutch soldiers to their next posting ... An officer from a nearby military barrack brought us Juliana, a little girl, and he told us that her native mother abused her terribly."[175] The didactic pronouncements of Dutch social workers about *Indo* girls — or the hortatory language of missionaries — represented native women as unscrupulous and corrupt, thus emblematizing the flip side of the illiteracy or inexperience that was ascribed to most non-aristocratic Indonesian people.

The twentieth-century rhetoric about simple women in the *kampong* or the *desa* — the *volksvrouwen* who composed the silent millions on the islands of Java, Bali, and other regions of the Indonesian archipelago — revealed a remarkable symmetry, whether deployed by *priyayi* daughters educated in Dutch schools, their Dutch women teachers, or social workers struggling to rescue *Indo* pauper girls from doom and damnation. Colonial discourses rendered simple women in the *kampong* and *desa* speechless, a compulsory silence that reputedly derived either from their naiveté or from their congenital immorality. Although capable of graphic and meaningful speech, the cultural grammar of Dutch colonial rule as well as the aristocratic hierarchy of Javanese and Balinese society muzzled women of common descent and depicted them as autistic and faceless subalterns, who lived in a world in which no one had any interest in the clamor of their voices. Their "Orientalist" infatuations gave Dutch colonial residents partial vision and made them East-Indies deaf — *Oost-Indisch doof*, a revealing Dutch expression for those who hear merely what they wish to hear — because the only speech they were eager to listen to consisted of the gentle, melodious tones of *priyayi* daughters, while they shut their ears to the pandemonium of the spontaneous and lively sounds of women in the *desa*.

Because of the victorian emphasis on women's maternal and housewifely destiny, many Dutch observers interpreted the active involvement of Javanese and Balinese women of the people in the economic realm as the direct result of their ignorance. The "gaze of empire" seemed to make them blind to the desperate poverty of simple women in the countryside, who had no choice but to work like packhorses in order to help feed their families.[176] A large number of Dutch observers also failed to recognize the real implications of Javanese *adat* which, if unhampered by pompous and extravagant aristocratic concerns with rank and status, granted women of the people certain rights and freedoms that neither European women nor *priyayi* daughters could enjoy.

In a similar manner, sermonizing about the wicked influence of native housekeepers of Dutch men on their mixed-blood female children tended to gloss over the emotional hardship of the well-entrenched practice of concubinage. Indigenous mothers as well as their *Indo* daughters were often stripped of any form of autonomous agency or subjectivity of their own.[177] Popular wisdom held that the sensual tropical environment and the constant consumption of spicy food excited white men's passions and amplified their libido, which demanded satisfaction from a native mistress in order to avoid sexual corruptions that were infinitely worse, such as random "lechery or sodomy."[178] Colonial rhetoric routinely portrayed both the *njai* and her golden-skinned daughters as empty vessels, devoid of an interior life, who resembled pliable puppets that were pushed and pulled by the capricious sexual desires of European men. A plethora of Indies novels, although advertised as genuine "historical documents" and routinely promoted as "typical" of manners and morals in the Dutch tropics, sustained this imagery of ductile *njai* or perverse *Indo* women in order to sanction a variety of "racial myths and unfounded theories" about blood, sex, and race.[179] Such novels, Toni Morrison has suggested with regard to a comparable literary tradition, stirred up a witch's brew of "darkness, otherness, alarm and [clandestine] desire."[180]

The authors of these "race melodramas" repeatedly conjured up overbearing European men who, without any sense of guilt, viewed their housekeepers as no more than "a necessary evil."[181] White men's physical needs defined the existential reality of an indigenous concubine's life: she reputedly functioned as a torpid receptacle — a listless thing which Dutch men routinely denigrated as an inert "piece of indigenous furniture which they called a *njai*."[182] In the most lurid colonial novels a European master did not treat his housekeeper as a full-fledged human being but he approached her as if she were an obedient and "faithful dog, who waits patiently at her master's feet for a kind look and a pat on the back."[183] A devoted concubine was sometimes represented as having to endure a Dutchman's physical aggression: she bore the brunt of his violent temper tantrums either "because he was merely frustrated with his life or had drunk a glass too much in celebration of a Royal Birthday."[184] Some planters in Sumatra, even after living with a beloved housekeeper in quasi-connubial bliss for long stretches of time, bragged about their ability to dismiss their *njai* whenever they saw fit: "I would throw her out today as easily as I would have eight years ago. Certain personalities attach themselves to such a girl, but the word sentimental does not appear in my emotional dictionary."[185] Although *priyayi* Javanese men could evict their secondary, *selir* wives with the same kind of indemnity, boasting about it would have been an alien idea.

Whether a Dutch master spurned his mistress because he had simply grown tired of her or whether he expelled her because he wished to marry a European woman, he could throw his *njai* out of his house as if she were a tattered, broken chair or he could chase her away like a stray puppy or a mangy dog. The ex-concubine often had no other option but to return to the *kampong* with her lighter skinned children where, by hook or by crook, she tried to survive as best as she could. In sum, the collusion between the Dutch romance with "authentic" Oriental traditions and upper-caste attitudes towards either peasant women or evicted *njai* and their *Indo* daughters proceeded to banish female subalterns and their children to an inscrutable territory. As a result, such poor, voiceless women appeared to live on the other side of an enormous social divide, where they could be inscribed with various forms of otherness. The legal historian Gertrudes Johan Resink has neatly summarized this poignant process of writing official "histories": the Javanese *priyayi* with their *babads*, the European rulers with their *geschiedenissen*, and the modern Indonesian elites with their *sejarahs* compose "a stylized line, in the sense that they are each and all far removed from the letter-blind millions who have so much past but so very little history."[186]

Chapter Four

The Native 'Other' as the Medieval, Childlike, and Animal 'Self' (or as Fundamentally Different):

Evolutionary Ideas in Dutch Colonial Rhetoric in Indonesia

Three centuries ago, the peoples of the Indies were an old population in decline: they had outlived their civilization. This is a very normal biological fact, which transpires everywhere in nature. All living organisms, whether plants, animals, humans, or populations, undergo a cycle of ascent, flourishing, decline, and extinction. No living organism can escape this immutable law. Other peoples in the world today, young and fresh as they are at the apex of their stage of growth, will one day decline and disappear from the face of the earth. This is merely a law of nature, nothing more and nothing less.[1]

P. Fournier, "De Beteekenis van het overheerschingstijdperk,"
Wederopbouw, 1920.

Articulating an evolutionary logic that differed from Fournier's model of rigid biological determinism, a specialist on education in the Dutch East Indies, Dr. G.J. Nieuwenhuis, wrote an iconoclastic article in *Djawa* in 1923, a quarterly magazine issued by the Java Institute in Yogyakarta. The Java Institute was reestablished in 1921 at the behest of a group of Dutchmen and Javanese aristocrats, who chartered it to "stimulate the development of the indigenous cultures of Java, Madura, and Bali in all their possible meanings." The Institute was also commissioned to engage in research on Javanese society in both the past and present, and "to plan the direction for its future development."[2]

In his essay, which was published simultaneously in the *Indische Courant* and in the journal of the conservative *Politiek Economische Bond*, Nieuwenhuis stated that anyone who had ever read Johan Huizinga's *The Waning of the Middle Ages* would inevitably discover many basic parallels between the mystical world view of Europeans in the late medieval period and the mentality of the Javanese in the 1920s.[3] These obvious similarities overshadowed all lingering notions of a fundamental difference between East and West, he continued, whether the latter was rationalized by appealing to variations in either climate and geography or by accentuating racial characteristics and skin color.

Instead, everyone familiar with *The Waning of the Middle Ages*, Nieuwenhuis claimed, was compelled to acknowledge that "the enormous contrasts between the cultural milieu of Holland, on the one hand, and Java, on the other, are primarily determined by a difference in their respective evolutionary stage." Oriental, he concluded, was to a great extent synonymous with the kind of feudal society Europeans had known in the Middle Ages.[4] Of course Indonesian nationalists had a very different perspective on the chronological unfolding of feudalism in East and West. Tjipto Mangoekoesoemo, for instance, stated curtly in 1918 that feudalism and aristocratic prerogatives still existed in Java long after they had faded in Europe simply because "the colonial oppressors had synthetically stimulated and stabilized them!"[5]

At any rate, in his article Nieuwenhuis addressed a perennial theme that absorbed many of the contributors to *Djawa* as well as other Dutch colonial residents throughout the first half of the twentieth century: what was distinctive about the myriad indigenous cultures of Java, Bali, Sumatra and other outlying regions, and what were the fundamental contrasts between East and West? How could Dutch men and women living in the Indonesian archipelago understand and explain the differences between the cultural sophistication of the European world and the alleged backwardness of primitive peoples in southeast Asia — which, after all, legitimated their subjection — even though Java and Bali exposed Westerners to a cultural heritage that was as complex as that of many European societies? And finally, how could citizens of a tiny, insignificant democracy in the European metropole — a clever David among neighboring Goliaths — justify their mastery over millions of people in the vast Indonesian archipelago in southeast Asia?

Dutch colonial residents were hardly alone in their preoccupation with these compelling questions. In a never-ending effort to justify white-skinned dominance over native peoples, British or French colonial rulers in Asia and Africa, too, probed the answer to these questions. The search for a rhetoric of legitimacy that could endow European colonialism with an aura of naturalness tended to be an integral element of imperial domination, regardless of its physical or cultural locale.[6] As a result, the intellectual efforts to explain the otherness of indigenous people revealed a certain degree of similarity, despite palpable disparities in the political values or socio-cultural styles of colonizing nations within the European metropole.

A galaxy of colorful metaphors and images informed Western perspectives on "the" primitive, both in the past and the present. Europeans have depicted native peoples as unruly children, for example, or as mystics who wallowed in a spiritual harmony with nature and reveled in an existential freedom that most citizens of the modern Western world had long since lost. In this construction native people became idealized "strangers in paradise," who lived their daily lives without conflicts and contradictions and were unhampered by private property or divisions of labor.[7] Westerners also portrayed primitive people as representations of the submerged wildness in themselves, embodying an unbridled instinctive behavior, irrationality, or a libidinous license they had learned to curb long ago. White-skinned Europeans viewed primitives, too, as personifications of a primeval cultural identity harking back to an earlier European era. The encounter between the modern Western world and the so-called primitive cultures in a colonial setting yielded a discourse of domination and control, on the one hand, and a "rhetoric of desire," on the other, based on the yearning to implicate "us" with "them."[8]

The effort to understand primitive societies, Tzvetan Todorov and Marianne Torgovnick have recently argued, conjures up both beginnings and endings; such ruminations summon not only nightmares but also pleasant dreams, because contemplating the nature of primitive societies evokes "our origins" while envisioning "our" possible destiny, too: "not one *or* the other, but one *and* the other."[9] Paul Gauguin, for instance, gave one of the most enigmatic paintings he brought back from Tahiti the revealing title *D'où venons-nous? Que sommes-nous? Où allons-nous?* (Where Do We Come From? What Are We? Where Are We Going?). The large canvas unveils a variety of Tahitian women who convey serenity and quiet wisdom: they come across as self-possessed human beings, at ease in their bodies and souls, "who walk about freely in public places" and who may choose either "to accept or to reject men's caresses."[10] The women seem to know who they are, and they gently beckon all viewers to define the contours of their own identities and to contemplate whom they might be.[11]

Gauguin's startling name for his painting elicited the sense of collective possibility implicit in representations of the primitive and alluded to the imbrication of the primitive with the modern, of them with us, or of us with them.[12] At an infinitely more pedestrian level, the Home Video Sales Catalogue of the Public Broadcasting System in the United States during the Summer of 1993 established a similar juxtaposition. Emblazoned on its cover is an announcement for a video series entitled "Millennium: Tribal Wisdom and the Modern World," further advertised by emphasizing that "We have much to learn from primitive cultures foreign to us." Gauguin's question, *d'où venons-nous? que sommes-nous? où allons-nous?* is a refrain that reverberates throughout an otherwise troubling TV documentary narrated by the Anglo-American anthropologist David Maybury-Lewis.

These rhetorics of control and desire were formulated, of course, within the distinct cultural semantics of the West. Judgments about otherness hinged on an intellectual curiosity forged in a uniquely European context, and ideas about cultural difference were articulated by employing a Western scholarly lexicon.[13] Moreover, intellectual inquiries of this kind were often beholden to the logic of colonial mastery. As chronicled in Chapter Two of this book, the overlapping field of interest between anthropology as an academic discipline and as an agency of the budding enterprise of European colonialism in Africa and Asia in the nineteenth century has become a well-charted domain.[14]

Yet the politics of empire did not permeate each scholarly effort or every scientific investigation in a colonial setting. It was true that even "pure" science, such as the refinement of instruments to measure rainfall or intricate experiments in physical chemistry, responded to the utilitarian demands of commercial agriculture. Planters and "merchant princes" in the Indies' private sector went much further than merely subsidizing research into practical problems; instead, they "consistently anticipated government action in the realm of scientific inquiry."[15] The U.S. Governor General of the Philippines in 1931, in fact, was filled with admiration for the Dutch confidence in scientific research and development which was managed and financed by the Indies government in cooperation with the private sector, and he noted that "Java was ahead of the Philippines by 30 or 40 years."[16]

But few "traces of imperialist ideology" guided what the instruments actually measured or how scientists interpreted their results. Some plant biologists affiliated with the Botanical Gardens in Bogor (Buitenzorg), for example, indulged their scientific fascination with tropical botany without necessarily coupling their research to the ceaseless quest for higher crop yields and greater profits on European-owned plantations.[17] Similarly, earth scientists working in the dynamic geological terrain of Indonesia, which straddles several tectonic plates, saw mountains and active volcanoes which none of them had ever encountered in the relatively static landscape of Europe. They analyzed geological layers or rock configurations that differed radically from anything they had seen before, because they could measure the impact of many earthquakes and observe regular volcanic eruptions with alacrity and precision.

This veritable geologists' "paradise" prompted Dutch scientists in southeast Asia to speculate about the formation of the earth, or to venture forth with innovative hypotheses in plate tectonics in ways that revolutionized the basic assumptions of the discipline, regardless of the rationale of colonial rule. Few other episodes in the history of science have shown as clearly "the fortuitous nature of scientific discovery."[18] Hence, Felix Vening Meinesz's and Willem van Bemmelen's geological surveys generated carefully formulated, innovative ideas in geophysics that issued forth from the internal logic of their scientific discipline. Similarly, Joan Voûte's research in double-star astronomy at the privately funded Bosscha Observatory outside Bandung, or the physicist Jacob Clay's discoveries in cosmic rays at the Bandung Institute of Technology, were mostly impervious to the ebb and flow of colonialism's strategic interests.[19]

Imperialist agendas, however, were linked more directly to the revolution in the biological sciences, which, in turn, spurred the development of anthropology. After all, the mid-nineteenth century had given rise to the dissemination of the concept of evolution. Its resulting appropriation by serious social scientists such as Charles Burnett Tylor, or crude Darwinian theorists such as Ernst Haeckel and Herbert Spencer, shaped the anthropological project of defining the essence of primitive societies. A vulgar transcription of evolutionary ideas, meanwhile, equipped the ordinary day-to-day routine of white-skinned Europeans' superiority in a colonial setting with a veneer of normalcy.

Some twentieth-century Dutch colonial residents, for example, were still oddly obsessed with "missing links" and pondered the resemblance between native peoples and clever, anthropomorphic great apes.[20] Others incorporated, in a distorted Spencerian form, the new reasoning of biological evolution and crafted metaphors about the childlike nature or "lesser development" of Indonesians. In addition, Dutch inhabitants of colonial Indonesia considered with care the issue of the tropical environment and its impact on the behavior or evolutionary level of native people. They also contemplated the ways in which the physical and psychological identity of Dutch men and women seemed to transform in the process of adapting to their new tropical milieu, which inundated them with its "exultant, resolutely ecstatic" natural beauty.[21] In short, the search for a rationale that could vindicate European mastery in equatorial southeast Asia induced many Dutch colonialists in twentieth-century Indonesia to concoct a wide range of metaphors, whether knowingly or unwittingly, that comprised a quaint medley of argument derived from old-fashioned natural history as well as more modern evolutionary theories.

Hence, in this chapter I explore the diverse ways in which Dutch residents in Indonesia employed an eclectic mixture of both classical, natural-history arguments that summoned the hierarchical Great Chain of Being as well as novel theories of biological evolution in order to explain the differences between "us" and "them". But as Stephen Jay Gould has recently noted, even well-educated people found it difficult to resist the "allure of physical determinism and 'our' hope for a simple order of things."[22] As a result, through a subtle process of mirroring, the Great Chain of Being was transformed into the "Great Chain of Empire": it was as if the chronological unfolding of European history and colonialism fused with ideas about the evolution of the species.[23]

However, there was no unanimity in Europeans' views; instead, Dutch colonialists broadcast a cacophony of voices that was modulated by factors such as political perspective, social background, or level of education. Whether they worked in the private sector or served as dedicated civil servants colored their perspectives, too. Besides, permanent Indies citizens embraced an outlook that differed from those who saw themselves merely as transient residents or temporary employees. In the course of the 1920s and especially during the 1930s, however, a palpable paranoia about Indonesian nationalism eclipsed the intellectual anarchy of competing opinions. Whether Dutch colonial inhabitants approached the colonized "other" as an unformed child, an underdeveloped species, or an incarnation of a medieval European "self," the white-skinned community began to refashion the Indonesian elite with whom they maintained direct contact more and more as quasi-intellectuals, who manipulated the peasant masses for their own "childlike," selfish purposes.[24] In the hearts and minds of a growing proportion of Dutch East Indies residents, these pseudo-educated upper-class natives began to resemble cocky demagogues —adolescent "roosters who think that by crowing noisily they can accelerate daybreak."[25] Not yet mature enough to realize that a little Western knowledge could hardly transform them into commanding officers of their independent ship of state, native politicians' irrational conviction that they were capable enough to replace their Dutch masters confirmed their infantility and privileged one particular strand of evolutionary thinking.

But before this "hard-wiring" of racial and political attitudes occurred, a pandemonium of diverse opinions percolated throughout the European community in the Indies.[26] In their efforts to lift the veil of otherness and to shed light on the cultural difference between indigenous peoples and themselves, some Dutch colonial inhabitants wondered, for instance, whether some Indonesian ethnic groups constituted a different species, representing a less complex form of life that hovered somewhere between apes and humans in the grand taxonomy of the genus. They were taken aback by the wildness and animality of specific ethnic tribes, which echoed Charles Darwin's reaction to the "absolutely naked [men] bedaubed with paint ... their expression wild, star-

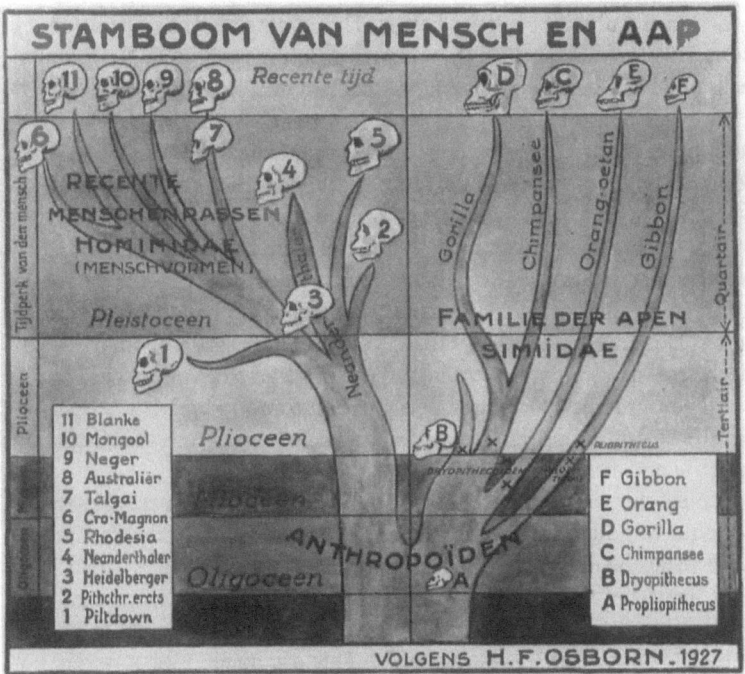

The genealogy of humans and apes according to H.F. Osborn (Album 71/t.o.61,KIT)

tled, and distrustful" whom he encountered on the wind-swept plains and forest-clad mountains of Tierra del Fuego.[27] As he reported in his autobiography, "the sight of a naked savage in his native land" left an indelible impression.[28]

As recently as the 1920s and early 1930s the regular sightings of upright, hairy creatures in the highlands of Sumatra coincided with the lingering fables about the elusive *Orang Kubu* or *Orang Gugu* (Kubu people or Gugu people): human scavengers who reputedly roamed through the same forested highlands. Dutch scouts and explorers in these jungles endowed the furry, ape-like apparitions they saw from a safe distance with human characteristics, too. In fact, local Malay speech labeled them *orang pendek* (short man) or *orang letjo* (dwarf man, or midget man), which prompted Dutch colonial residents to ponder the inherent similarities between evasive indigenous people and orangutans.[29] The great apes' actual name, orangutan or *orang hutan*, literally means "man of the forest" which Webster's Collegiate Dictionary (1975) defines as an "anthropoid ape with a mongoloid look."

After all, when Linnaeus classified the animal kingdom in the mid-eighteenth century based on physical resemblances, he had included both humans and apes in the same category of Anthropomorpha, while fifty years later Lamarck had identified the orangutan as the most likely ancestor of human beings.[30] Thus the cunning, if shy, great apes Dutchmen encountered in the jungles of Sumatra made them wonder whether they had seen animals or human beings. This confusion lent credence to the vision of Indonesians as a different species occupying a lower position on the immutable Great Chain of Being — a rank-ordering mechanism of biological species that Arthur Lovejoy has described as explicitly and vehemently anti-evolutionary.[31]

Lamarckian logic, instead, suggested that the orangutans of Sumatra, perhaps alongside Indonesian natives, occupied the same obscure territory just below Europeans on the evolutionary scale. Although not yet fully human, they were allegedly capable of becoming so by effectively adapting to their natural environment and passing on newly acquired characteristics to future generations — a process biologists have labeled "hereditary morphing" or what behavioral scientists call "phenotypic cloning."[32] It is likely that few Dutch colonial residents had ever thought seriously about the scientific details of the transmission of either phenotypes or genes from one generation to the next. Nonetheless, the homology between great apes and indigenous peoples — and presumably their similar appearances and shared behaviors — was a fertile terrain for the European imagination.[33]

Others contended that the simple and naive populations of either Java, Sumatra, or Bali belonged to the same species as white-skinned Europeans, but embodied an immature and still malleable stage of human development. As a Dutch psychiatrist in Java, Dr. P.H.M. Travaglino, alleged in 1920, adult Javanese men and women exhibited the psychological foibles of children, because "the natives (*inlanders*) are still in an earlier stage of their evolutionary development."[34] This argument probably did not emerge in a vacuum. Whether or not he was aware of it, a quaint new fashion within European psychiatry paralleled his line of reasoning. A small *côterie* of young enthusiasts circling within the intellectual orbit of Sigmund Freud in Vienna was equally fascinated with the psychological implications of the homology between "primitivism and infantility," if only because it might shed indirect light on the early formation of "normal," European personality structures.[35] Travaglino's inquiry thus echoed a similar discussion among *avant garde* psychiatrists in Europe.

Travaglino argued in 1920 that so far, the natural circumstances that enveloped the average Javanese adult had prevented the progressive, natural advancement of higher forms of intelligence and more exalted cultural impulses. Their instincts, he wrote, "are younger in an evolutionary sense," because, over time, the gradual adaptation of the human species to their physical environment bestowed upon mankind a greater capacity for rational thought, more elevated passions and refined, subtle sensibilities. But among the Javanese, instead, all sorts of pre-pubescent "primary instincts" predominated — "the yearning for pleasure and the excessive influence of sexuality" — which Travaglino interpreted as evidence of the puerile nature of the Javanese psyche. The mentality of the Javanese, he asserted, was characterized by "an infinite capacity for unrestrained emotionality, a strong fantasy life, and occasionally an obsessive concentration of their attention" on a particular object. Travaglino also claimed that adult Javanese men and women suffered from "a limited *vigiliteit*" (watchfulness or vigilance), which seemed to be a contradiction of their stubborn tenacity.[36]

Thus the Javanese, in terms of the evolutionary process, represented the developmental level of children (*kinderlijk niveau*), since the structural conditions of their lives had prevented, to a great extent, the natural maturation of more sophisticated impulses, which were of a more recent vintage in an evolutionary sense. The Javanese, he concluded, "have progressed at a slow pace in the evolutionary process (*langzaam voortschrijden in het evolutionaire proces*)."[37] Javanese people, in other words, recapitulated the ontogenetic development of Europeans but had gotten stuck, for the time being, at the level of childhood, which explained the different mentalities of East and West.

Dr. Nieuwenhuis and his soulmates, in turn, placed this evolutionary logic in a temporal — or historical — context. Nieuwenhuis did not neccesarily wish to minimize the cultural distance between Europeans and the colonial "other," but aimed to historicize the differences between the two. He argued that the great cultural divide that separated modern Dutch society in the European metropole in the early 1920s from either the feudal rituals and grandeur of Java's elite, or, on the opposite end of the social spectrum, the backbreaking labor of the Javanese peasantry, was primarily a function of the passage of time. He supported his argument with references to a well-known and much admired book on the history of the late Middle Ages. In *The Waning of the Middle Ages* Huizinga had painted a vivid portrait of an elegiac cultural universe in which religious sentiments "tended to be transmuted into images." He also described medieval human beings' all-consuming faith in symbolic representation, which prompted them to erect "an impeccable order, an architectonic structure [of] hierarchic subordination." Hence, by underscoring the similarities between Javanese culture in the early twentieth century and Huizinga's depiction of medieval religiosity, Nieuwenhuis portrayed Java as a "distant mirror" of the high Middle Ages in Europe.[38]

The pervasive mysticism of Huizinga's late-medieval world was comparable to the cosmology that saturated Java in the twentieth century. Hence, contemporary Javanese society was, above all, an incarnation of a chronologically younger European "self." The honor and deference Javanese peasants bestowed upon Java's ancient rulers echoed the subservience and labor services medieval serfs owed their lord, and the enormous social divide between aristocrats and peasants in Java, in his eyes, was a tangible memory of the rigid feudal hierarchies of the European past. Nieuwenhuis's argument linked the idea of evolution directly to the unfolding of Europe's unique history and he emphasized the fact that primitive people would inevitably recapitulate Europeans' historical, or phylogenetic, development.[39]

Huizinga's emphasis on "Waning" — or the melancholy, autumnal decay implicit in his title — also referred to the inability of late medieval civilization to preserve its monolithic "symbolic identity."[40] In fact, the original Dutch title of the book, *Herfsttij der middeleeuwen*, which can be translated as either the autumnal "Season" or the autumnal "Tide" of the Middle Ages, drew a more explicit analogy with the unfolding of the regular seasons of the year in which the muted, auburn glow of Fall inexorably succeeded the vibrant colors of the fecund heydays of Summer. The title can also be read as a suggestion that historical processes unfolded cyclically, like the relentless ebb and flow of oceanic tides, which was not at all Huizinga's intention.[41]

Again, Huizinga's vision of the Middle Ages' loss of metaphysical coherence reverberated in a twentieth-century Javanese context. Powerful influences from the West undermined the spiritual resonance of the vaunted icons of Javanese culture by converting devotion and worship into an arid, arcane formalism.[42] The majesty of Borobodur, or the hortatory *wayang* stories based on the *Mahabharata*, *Ramayana*, or *Panji* Tales, were allegedly losing their symbolic significance in Java's popular imagination, as if the Javanese spirit had reached the barren "end of its natural path."[43] This, in turn, suggested that Javanese society was simply replicating the loss of cultural cohesion that had caused the decline of the high Middle Ages, as if it were a preordained process of nature.

After reading an early manuscript version in 1918, Cornelis van Vollenhoven, Huizinga's close friend and weekly dinner guest in Leiden on Thursday evenings, effused enthusiastically that his colleague's "magnificent" book had helped him "understand [better] the courts of Surakarta (Solo) and Yogyakarta."[44] But the decomposition of the dead leaves of Autumn fertilized the soil and prepared for the bountiful crops of many summers to come. However, whether Java's alleged cultural "languishing" in the twentieth century would enrich the land in the same way and yield a similar abundant harvest in the future — the crumbling of the high Middle Ages, after all, had nourished the blossoming of the Renaissance — was less obvious.[45] A Dutch civil servant in Amboina, meanwhile, used graphic Huizinga-like imagery in 1930: "death and life, putrefaction and resurrection meet here; relics of native arrangements, of native *weltanschauungen* remain, but it is all more or less decaying. And all of this hidden behind the shadow of European culture."[46]

Nonetheless, Huizinga's celebrated study — "a radiant, if lonely, peacock surrounded by less elegant fowl," an effusive reviewer called it on the occasion of the first anniversary of the author's death in 1946 — seemed to validate the evolutionary model that informed the perspectives of a variety of Dutch people in the Indies.[47] In a prickly polemical exchange in 1918 with Soetatmo Soeriokoesoemo on the pages of *Wederopbouw*, the magazine of the young-Javanese movement dedicated to the "spiritual life" of Java, for instance, the theosophist L.S.A.M. von Römer asserted that "the things one tends to coddle, today, as essential features of the Orient, will eventually disappear."[48] The Indo-European Von Römer, who reveled in his semi-Indonesian identity and his hybrid status in between the Orient and Occident, maintained that the West formerly was at the exact same stage of development the East had finally reached in the early twentieth century.[49] He did not mean to imply that the brown-skinned Javanese, by following the developmental path of the West or by absorbing European modes of thought, would either "acquire a white skin or that it would cause the sun to shine less brightly or that rice would be converted into potatoes."[50]

Alluding to Nieuwenhuis's argument but foreshadowing Fournier's idea that each and every organism in the universe, whether plants, animals, humans, or populations, "is caught in an immutable cycle of ascent, flourishing, decline, and extinction," Von

Römer meant to say that the exaltation of "the so-called essential differences between West and East" paralyzed an understanding of the potential organic evolution of Javanese culture in the future.[51] After all, other peoples — in casu Europeans — had long since left behind the developmental level of the Middle Ages that was identical, "like two drops of water resemble each other," to the quintessential cultural characteristics of the Orient today. In the natural sequence of cultural evolution, however, Javanese society would be reborn just as Europe had acquired new incarnations since the fourteenth century. Eventually, he argued, the culture of Java would regenerate itself, too, but it would do so in its own, unique mode![52]

In 1935 the thoughtful Indonesian nationalist Sutan Sjahrir also invoked the analogy between twentieth-century Indonesia and the European Middle Ages. But he endowed the same corollary with yet another twist, which echoed, to some extent, the nineteenth-century European confidence in the inexorability of "progress." What can the *wayang*, Sjahrir pondered, "filled as it is with elementary symbolism and simple mysticism — which parallels the allegorical wisdom of medieval Europe — still offer us? In truth we cannot accept the so-called essential difference between East and West ... because culturally we are closer [today] to Europe and America than we are to Borobodoer and the *Mahabharata* or to the primitive cosmology of Islam in Java and Sumatra."[53]

Sjahrir, in other words, treated cultural change as a form of unidimensional or teleological growth. From his "ultra-modern" perspective, he seemed to imply that Indonesians in the 1930s could no longer comprehend their existence merely in terms of the *wayang*'s mystical contemplation of the eternal struggle between the Pandawa and Kurawa and the cataclysmic "orgy of bloodshed between close kinsmen" at the end.[54] Just as Europeans had transcended their yearning for the magical "sweet inpouring of Divine Love" or had left behind their Manichean belief in a relentless battle between God and Satan, so had "modern" Indonesians presumably become impervious to the childish magic of the *wayang*.[55]

Be that as it may, Sjahrir's ideas differed yet again from the profusion of views espoused by either Travaglino and Fournier or Nieuwenhuis and Von Römer. The latter's emphasis on the uniqueness of Java's own cultural future, though, surfaced with a vengeance in discussions on Bali. Dutch men and women as well as other Westerners envisioned the idyllic island of Bali as an imagined community that deviated from any society to be found in the West; Bali, therefore, seemed to belong to a "petrified" time or appeared to reside in a realm "beyond" history. The visual beauty of the island, Johannes Fabian has suggested, made it "paradisiacal, hieratic, emblematic — everything but coeval with the Western observer."[56] The artistry, religious vitality, and village democracies presumed to constitute the essence of this island's culture, summoned a historical precedent that was more advanced in a chronological, or an evolutionary, sense. In a modern imagination, Bali did not conjure up the stylized, if inflexible, feudal hierarchy of the Middle Ages, as was the case with Java. Instead, Bali evoked memories of the Italian Renaissance and of the magnificent and dynamic city-state of Florence in the *quattrocento* during Lorenzo di Medici's aesthetic patronage.

Bali epitomized a harmonious world where religion and civil society constituted an integrated, organic unity. Art and architecture served the dual purpose of symbolically representing the glory of the gods as well as enriching the daily lives of Bali's enchanting inhabitants.[57]

Margaret Mead, in fact, portrayed Bali as a "symbol of nostalgia" or as a field of dreams for civilized spectators, which satisfied the desire of disaffected citizens of the modern Western world for a more natural community where art, emotions, and faith spontaneously enveloped daily life.[58] The Canadian musician and composer Colin McPhee compared his love of Bali as a place of inner contentment with American expatriate writers' infatuation with Paris in the 1920s: "everyone carries within him his own private paradise, some beloved territory whose assault is an assault on the heart."[59] However, it was especially the island of Bali, with its artistic splendor, village democracies, and religious equilibrium that prompted Westerners to fathom the possibility of an autonomous developmental trajectory that was an alternative to the evolutionary path Europeans had followed.

This kind of evolutionary perspective on the rank-ordering of cultures and social systems was a relatively new phenomenon that was intimately linked to intellectual developments in both geology and biology in the mid-nineteenth century.[60] With the birth of the concept of "geological time" — or Sir Charles Lyell's recognition that the formation of the multiple layers of the earth issued from a cumulative process that had taken millions of years — it was possible for philosophers or biologists to envision "evolution." Charles Darwin's assertion that the differences between species were not primordial and indelible but rather, "the daughter of time," offered novel intellectual possibilities to Europeans eager to grasp and explain the differences between themselves and indigenous peoples.[61] His contention that in the long sweep of history all species were constantly in flux and forever adjusting to changing structural circumstances, based on natural selection, yielded a new understanding of history.

While Darwin was convinced that evolution was an inherently random process that responded to stimuli in the natural world in a serendipitous and unpredictable manner, Jean Baptiste de Lamarck had emphasized the creative agency of evolution and the transmission of acquired characteristics. Lamarck ascribed to all organisms a subliminal form of agency or a homeostatic yearning for self-improvement, as if he endowed individual living organisms with the same kind of determination that had infused French revolutionaries' efforts to transform society in the late eighteenth century.[62] This was an argument that some social theorists appropriated and embellished around the turn of the century. Ernst Haeckel and Herbert Spencer, as the most prominent among these "scholars," endowed the evolutionary past with a linear sense of progress, as if all history displayed an inherent teleology.

If giraffes, over time, managed to develop elongated necks in order to eat the juicy and nourishing leaves of tall trees, thus allowing the species to thrive and multiply more effectively, then the cultural progress and economic success of white Europeans in the nineteenth century might be conceptualized, too, as resulting from a comparable process of creative evolution.[63] Even though lingering and unanswered questions confounded many evolutionary theorists — such as the reasons for a hungry giraffe's ability, rather than a starving zebra or wildebeest, to generate long necks, or whether the sons of weight lifters would automatically inherit their fathers' muscles — Lamarck's theoretical speculations appealed to social scientists interested in illuminating the fundamental differences between advanced Western societies and backward primitive communities.[64] As Haeckel wrote in 1904, "lower races," such as the Veddahs of India or the Aborigines of Australia, were "psychologically nearer to mammals such as apes and dogs than to civilized Europeans; we must, therefore, assign a totally different value to their lives."[65] From this warped Lamarckian perspective, it became feasible to approach the colonial other as an "ossified European" who embodied the actual genealogy of modern European culture; primitive people thus represented the corporeal or the tangible "documentary" evidence of human evolution.[66]

One might argue, in fact, that the findings of the geologist Lyell and the revolutionary biological theories of Lamarck and Darwin gave birth to and licensed the intellectual discipline of anthropology as we know it today. Only when the notion of geological time, and knowledge of the painstakingly slow evolutionary process of the species, began to inform Europeans' understanding of primitive societies, was it possible for Edward Burnett Tylor, Professor of Anthropology at the University of Oxford, to write in his classic anthropology textbook of 1881: "savage and barbarous tribes often more or less fairly represent stages of culture through which our own ancestors passed long ago, and their customs and laws often explain to us in ways we would otherwise have hardly guessed, the sense and reason of our own."[67] Nineteenth-century anthropology, in Tylor's formulation, infused all human history with an unequivocal purpose: native people elsewhere in the world, Tylor implied, recapitulate the grand spectacle of Europeans' history — *our* history. *We*, the white-skinned residents of the European metropole in the modern era, Tylor maintained in the 1880s, are the only members of the theater's audience who truly understand the unfolding plot of the human drama in primitive societies, because we know how the story ends, since we *are* the end of the story.[68]

Prior to the mid-nineteenth century, Europeans could neither have perceived nor categorized the indigenous peoples they encountered in their natural habitat in either Asia, Africa, or the Americas as earlier historical manifestations of themselves. During the Renaissance Europeans had employed Christianity as an inviolable line of demarcation between the West and heathen others, by relegating the latter to the realm of demonology. Pre-modern biological taxonomies were concocted on the basis of a fixed, vertical order in which only the criteria for the specific hierarchical status or seniority of specific species were a matter of debate. Invariably God was ranked highest and, descending down the "Greater Scale," one could find a sequence of archangels, angels, prophets, saints, and holy men jockeying for position, while mortal human beings always occupied the lowest rung on the ladder. But a late seventeenth-century taxonomist also invented an adjacent "Lesser Scale of Animals," in which he placed human beings at the top, and then wondered whether the elephant, the gorilla, the parrot, or the bee should occupy the second place on the scale.[69] The barbarians Europeans encountered in either Asia or the Americas, meanwhile, would most likely have been classified on the Lesser Scale somewhere halfway between humans and gorillas, elephants, parrots, or bees.

The Enlightenment, in turn, produced new visions of otherness. In the eighteenth century the colonial "other" came to be labeled "ignorant" or "unenlightened," and native peoples' lack of rationality or civilization presumably confirmed the difference between sophisticated citizens of Europe and colonial subjects elsewhere. The primitive mind, eighteenth-century *philosophes* argued, represented the childhood or perhaps the adolescence of the human spirit. Instead of employing reason and logic to resolve problems, primitive people used supplication, sorcery, and mystical associations in their attempt to accomplish goals they could more easily attain through rational calculation.[70] In other words, non-Europeans did not know the "Truth" about the primary significance of human reason; they faltered by appealing to spirits or invoking magic and hence, the anthropology of the Enlightenment was based on a "psychology of error."[71]

In the process of comparing the primitive mind to the infancy of the human spirit, the Enlightenment constructed a vision of indigenous people as peevish children — a typology the Dutch psychiatrist Travaglino still championed in 1920. Childlike natives could not yet comprehend the nature of the enlightened world of adults even if, in due course, they possessed the capacity to absorb the rules of civilized conduct and to embrace the benefits of rational thought. Enlightenment *philosophes* no longer represented indigenous peoples as demons or monsters, whose otherness was immutable; instead, they reconfigured them as objects of Europeans' *mission civilisatrice*. Eighteenth-century analysts thought they could initiate ignorant natives in the enlightened wisdom of the Western world and transform natives into dark-skinned imitations of their exquisitely cultured Western selves.

The subsequent French colonial tendency to categorize indigenous elites as "evolved natives" (*evolués*) — a classification reserved only for those indigenous men who had fully mastered the cultural grammar of Western civilization and had thus become adults and well-educated (*bien élevé*) — did not imply, however, that *evolués* were regarded as full-fledged citizens in an egalitarian body politic. In other words, it did not mean that "evolved" native inhabitants with brown or black skins had achieved rights and obligations that were on a par with white-skinned Europeans. Indigenous intellectuals were merely properly educated natives, whose fluency in the vocabulary of French culture entitled them to the role of intermediary between the colonial rulers and the masses of untutored native subjects. The intellectual discourse of the Enlightenment, however, did not enable Europeans to imagine the possibility that the study of the culture of the colonial other could yield profound knowledge about themselves.

This bifurcated legacy of infantile associative thinking, on the one hand, and adult Western rationalism, on the other, lingered on in twentieth-century colonial Indonesia. The thoughtful Dutch ethnographer F.D.E. van Ossenbruggen, however, qualified this bi-polar assessment. Any person with a "naive mind," he argued in 1925, was easily satisfied with "striking resemblances, which are substitutes for positive, convincing evidence." They treat "visual analogies" between a wide variety of objects, or subjective analogies between two very divergent experiences, as tangible properties or "identities" and adjust their behavior accordingly.[72]

In many places in the archipelago, Van Ossenbruggen cited as one among many other examples, people envision the spread of smallpox as "an ugly man, a negro, or an old woman, who propagates the disease by sprinkling fruit pits or little peas around themselves." This "crude, materialistic, associative thinking" suggested that individuals could save themselves from being infected with smallpox simply by avoiding close physical contact with homely men, people with jet-black skins, elderly women, peas and fruit pits. He wondered, though, whether the "associative thinking" of primitive people differed in too dramatic a fashion from the analogic thought processes of rational, Western men. "A child's blushing cheeks remind us of red apples," he noted impishly, whereas a European peasant, whose village neighbor had emigrated to America and had become fabulously rich, often expected that analogous wealth automatically awaited him purely because he hailed from the same hamlet in the Old World and moved to the same, distant continent![73]

However, the eighteenth-century Enlightenment left yet another, somewhat contradictory, legacy: the imagery of the colonial other as natural and unaffected, as noble savages not yet contaminated by the evils of civilization. Although the emblem of the untarnished and pure "noble savage" is often associated with Jean Jacques Rousseau, he only posited the idea of man in the state of nature as a rhetorical construction. Natural man had never really existed, Rousseau wrote in 1754; nonetheless, it was necessary "to have exact notions" about the state of nature in order "to judge accurately our present state."[74] Thus, natural man lived in abominable conditions: he roamed through the forests without "industry, or speech, or home" and could hardly be distinguished from wretched animals.[75]

Natural man could neither discriminate between virtue and vice nor muster sentiments of justice and morality. Man was not yet fully human in the state of nature: "limited to physical instinct alone, he is nothing, he is stupid." But according to Rousseau, human beings could only become truly human if they were members of a social community: the inescapable paradox was that "society corrupts mankind," but human beings could only be "truly human if they entered into society."[76] Between the original state of nature and modern eighteenth-century society, Rousseau argued, existed an intermediate savage stage. This was a gilded era when human beings no longer constituted indolent animals but had not yet become miserable modern men, and this transitional phase must have been the "happiest and longest-lasting epoch." Savages occupied a charmed domain between primitive bestiality and the "petulant activity of our vanity."[77]

Hence, Rousseau's contradictory perspective endowed Europeans' desire to engage in a *mission civilisatrice* with a melancholy aura and inscribed it with contested meanings, since he represented Western civilization as an intrusive influence that might elevate man from his animal stupor, but would inexorably transform human beings into egotistic and unhappy citizens of the modern world. The Western civilizing mission thus threatened to accelerate but divert the natural evolution of primitive peoples from their own "true" forms of human society, a conviction members of the Bali lobby would avow with great intellectual vigor in the 1920s and 1930s.

In the twentieth-century Dutch East Indies, these multiple conceptions of the colonial other competed with each other. Professor Johan Christiaan van Eerde, the Director of the Ethnology Section of the Colonial Institute in Amsterdam, articulated the dilemma succinctly in the context of the Indonesian archipelago: Europeans' opinions of less developed people, Van Eerde wrote in 1914, tended to oscillate between two extremes. On the one hand, Westerners invented a vision of primitive people as perennially caught in a suffocating tangle of "cruelty, magic, cannibalism, and slavery." On the other hand, they imagined an Elysian Field of virtuous people untainted by civilization and living in "dreamy tranquility and harmony in the mild climate of their natural environment."[78]

The placidity and contentedness of the Javanese could be interpreted as a sign of their unspoiled character. Indeed, some hyper-ethical Dutch colonials saw the Javanese and Balinese or other Indonesians as genuine creatures of nature, who were virtuous, innocent, and capable of living in perfect concord as long as the evils of European civilization had not corrupted them. Some idealistic Dutch residents in both the public and private sector, in fact, feared that they and their fellow Europeans, as purveyors of Western decadence, caused the Javanese to lose their inherent purity and were responsible for making them greedy, petulant, and untrustworthy.

As the progressive civil servant G.L. Gonggrijp — who believed firmly in the Dutch colonial duty to "uplift" and educate Indonesians — insisted that, the genuine, Ur-Javanese were "fundamentally honest."[79] He asserted in December, 1911, that in certain regions of Java where Indonesians' contact with European culture was still superficial, such as in southern Bantam, Priangan, or Banyuwangi, the act of stealing was entirely unknown. In Banyuwangi, Gonggrijp remembered, villagers who had lost something while walking to a rice field or a nearby market, "will simply retrace their steps, only to find the lost object hanging by a string from a tree, which others, who have passed by since, have left untouched." This practice, Gonggrijp concluded, certified the basic decency of the Javanese and their respect for the property of their peers: "people with this kind of custom have a deeply rooted reservoir of elemental honesty."[80]

Twenty years later several Dutch residents reconfirmed this opinion. C.K. Elout mentioned that he had moved at least fifty times while he lived in the Indies; he tended to be scatter-brained, on occasion, and would inadvertently leave behind either a watch, a wallet, a change purse, or things of lesser value. Every time, he wrote, honest *inlanders* would bring them to him, and *totoks*' whining about native people's laziness and stupidity, or Europeans' complaints about the natives "proclivity to steal" only supplied evidence of their own lack of civilization (*beschaving*)![81] A scion of an old-Indies family, Cornelis van Heekeren, made the same observation while stationed as a civil servant in Northern Sumatra in the 1930s. He claimed that "Bataks would not think of stealing even the smallest thing," although he conceded that on "Java this occurred quite regularly."[82]

A long-standing and oft-repeated apodictic pronouncement about the Javanese or other ethnic groups was that their ignorance made them so much more contented and at peace with themselves than civilized people from the West. The simple Javanese may have been destitute and unenlightened, but they possessed an equanimity Westerners could no longer fathom: this was "the *dolce far niente* of the Orient." Primeval Asians were happier and more serene than Europeans could ever be. After all, the Javanese never displayed the boredom, frustration, or nervousness of high-strung Westerners; besides, primitive people also possessed "keener senses and more practiced habits of perception" in comparison to civilized people.[83]

The peripatetic nineteenth-century Javanologist, Taco Roorda, had converted this idea of "natural" emotional composure into an inventive political logic. By disrupting the innate sense of hierarchy among the Javanese, or by infusing the Javanese spirit "with our European conceptions of freedom, Java will be lost to us!"[84] And somewhat later in the nineteenth century a Protestant preacher in Batavia posed a similar rhetorical question: "Why give them education?" He answered his own query: education would only transform the Javanese into a southeast Asian reincarnation of the French Revolution's "Jacobins, who would [immediately] evict us from Java!"[85] This line of reasoning continued well into the twentieth century, and indirectly nurtured the suspicion that too much Western education might sully or destabilize the harmonious nature of indigenous peoples.

The inhabitants of the island of Bali, even more so, emblematized honesty and purity, too. Now that Bali is "in fashion," wrote a Dutch anthropologist in the early 1930s, many Europeans or Americans who felt discontented with their lives in the hustle and bustle of modern Western societies were searching for a utopian alternative, either in the past or in "out-of-the-way" places elsewhere in the world.[86] A certain "cultural lassitude" prompted many men and women in the Western world to yearn for a society that embodied "beauty, transcendence (*verhevenheid*), and cosmic balance." Hence, some of them rejoiced in having found in Bali a modern-day reincarnation of a harmonious community of the past, while others interpreted the serenity of the Balinese "soul" as concrete proof of the possibility of an alternative evolutionary path.[87]

Bali's own grand future would be guaranteed, the Indonesian nationalist Tjipto Mangoenkoesoemo insisted in 1919, if the government fulfilled the primary and necessary condition for "its healthy evolution, and that is *freedom*."[88] Bali, after all, was a society with an "admirably constructed, organic unity."[89] Occasionally scholars characterized Bali as little more than a "continuation of the Majapahit empire of Java without Islam," as the Bali-expert Roelof Goris wrote in 1927; he argued, however, that this vision was myopic, because the island "possesses an undiluted culture in its own right." While the people of Bali acknowledged that they might be distant relatives of the neighboring Javanese, Goris offered, the Balinese were convinced they were Java's "brothers, not their sons."[90]

The true nature of any culture, Dutch protectors of arcadian Bali argued, regardless of its geographic locale, was grounded in a consensus concerning style, which enabled the possibility of unconflicted social interaction and cultural expression. Both an individual and a particular ethnic group (*volk*) could only achieve genuine cultural eloquence in a style that had become "an internalized quality through nature, history, and tradition." This cultural style might change over time, but if it did, "it should issue forth intuitively from innate, creative forces."[91] Thus, Bali should be allowed to plumb the depths of its authentic cultural soul and its distinctive wellspring of spirituality in order to muster new strength for its own unique future. During his visit to Indonesia in September of 1927, a journalist for the nationalist magazine *Timboel* quoted the Indian Hindu philosopher-poet Rabindranath Tagore's attempt to define the religious character of Bali:

> We, Hindus in India, have incorporated the ancient Hindu faith in a philosophical and metaphysical sense, while the Balinese have absorbed it in an aesthetic mode. This is a people of natural artists, with an all-embracing gift for adornment and ornamentation rather than a talent for philosophical contemplation. Their yearning for beauty, their decoration of temples and homes with sculptures and designs — a longing [for beauty] which expresses itself in the embellishment of every little space on the island —courses through the life blood of the Balinese. These genuine artists have scrutinized the human experience in a deeply probing manner and they understand [human destiny] to such a profound degree that in their plastic arts the Balinese achieve a representation of the essence of life with inexorable exactitude (*onverbiddelijke juistheid*).[92]

The Dutch painter Rudolf Bonnet applied comparable reasoning to the more mundane issue of Dutch art education in schools attended by Balinese students. Europeans' rigid teaching practices "stunted and repressed the evolution of the inborn artistic gifts of the Balinese," he wrote from Ubud to the ethnomusicologist Jaap Kunst in Batavia on April 23, 1933. "The didactic guidelines for drawing and art in the curriculum of Dutch native schools," he scoffed, resembled a silly attempt "to prune and mutilate a luxuriant tropical forest in order to convert it into a proper Dutch park with neat little garden paths."[93]

After having served on a jury in charge of awarding prizes to drawings submitted to an art competition for students of the Dutch Indies School in Klungkung, Bonnet noted "that the Balinese students had made pleasant, and in some cases, truly fine drawings." Even though the student-participants in the contest had been given a choice of topics that were both Eurocentric and too confining, everyone agreed, including the two daughters of Governor-General De Jonge who visited the exhibit of the schoolchildren's drawings, that "no Dutch child of the same age could have produced such beautiful works of art."[94]

But in the Balinese artistic imagination of the early 1930s, making an individual drawing on paper with a pen or a brush, either with ink or paint, as a discrete work of art was still a somewhat unfamiliar enterprise. The Balinese, whether young or old, en-

Rabindranath Tagore and Mangkoe Nagoro VII. From: Triwindoe Gedenkboek

visioned artworks as integral elements of an elaborate array of rituals in which "musical and dramatic dance performances [took] precedence."⁹⁵ Being firmly ensconced in the artistic life of central Bali, however, Rudolf Bonnet and his German-Russian friend, Walter Spies, had begun to encourage Balinese craftsmen to take up painting. They founded an artists' league called *Pita Maha*, meaning "great vitality" or "strong determination."⁹⁶ They also helped the association's "new painters" to sell their artworks to the growing number of international tourists who flocked to heavenly Bali in the 1930s. But Spies and Bonnet urged the novice painters to depict traditional Balinese themes, ranging from Hindu festivals and temple dances to tropical landscapes of rice fields and bustling market scenes with smoldering volcanoes in the background. To loosen and cultivate the artistic potential of the "new painters" — and, equally important, to enhance their paintings' appeal to potential buyers from abroad — Spies and Bonnet counseled them to omit the representation of Western themes.⁹⁷

Thus, Bonnet's criticism of the Dutch art-teaching method followed in the school in Klungkung and elsewhere in Bali, entitled *Gauw en Goed* (Quick and Good, or Quick and Competent), was entirely consistent with his nurturing patronage of Balinese painters. He argued that *Gauw en Goed* was not only detrimental to "the development of the personal, inborn artistic style" of Balinese students, but added wryly that in any art form in the Indies, "speed can never accomplish anything." The drawing books used in schools were "full of stupid illustrations and stiffly drawn little lines" demonstrating the dumb Western examples students were forced to copy and reproduce. Thus the art-teaching technique used in the Dutch East Indies should be suspended as far as instructing Balinese children was concerned, Bonnet concluded, so their "Oriental psyche" could soar spontaneously and inspire their artistic development in their own, archetypal Balinese mode.[98]

These lyrical evocations of an innate artistic style or the Balinese "psyche" and "soul" echoed Oswald Spengler's *The Decline of the West*, which had appeared in a second German edition in 1923 and was translated into English in 1926.[99] Spengler, after all, had waxed mystically about the essence of all cultural styles as "seeds," enveloped in hermetically sealed cocoons, that were impervious to the cultural influences or inclinations of the outside world — as if external forces could only engender a "pseudomorphosis."[100] A cultural soul flourished in a definable landscape, to which it remained bound like a biological organism; the soul died when the full sum of its possibilities was actualized in the shape of "peoples, languages, dogmas, arts, states [and] sciences."[101]

Spengler's effort to create the new discipline of cultural morphology was intended to reveal that history was devoid of a fixed point of reference or a teleological purpose; all cultures were self-contained living organisms which experienced their own relentless cycles of growth and decline, as predictable as the annual seasons of Spring, Summer, and Autumn in northern Europe. A critic recently described Spengler as "a good second-rate thinker" with a knack for distilling the research of "first-rate thinkers into readable form."[102] But in a curious contradiction of his own reasoning, Spengler managed to refurbish Huizinga's carefully constructed, and age-specific, image of the "Autumn of the Middle Ages" into a relentless cyclical mechanism with universal applicability.

Hence, the West should not violate Bali's cultural autonomy or rankle its peace of mind; the untarnished Balinese should be allowed to achieve their own cultural destiny. The impact of European civilization on vibrant cultures such as Bali's functioned as a kind of "corrosive acid," Jaap Kunst observed in 1939, or as a "blood transfusion given to a patient with a different blood type," which contaminated, enfeebled, and eventually ruined native culture in its deepest essence.[103] Employing a similar metaphor of physical fitness and toxic infection, the economist Julius Herman Boeke noted that in order "to neutralize the poisonous by-products of Western capitalism" within a dual-economic structure, native communities should be injected with antibodies to allow their immune systems to fight off the contagious diseases of the West.[104] After all, even the most elementary forms of economic production in colonial Indonesia constituted a homeostatic "welfare institution" (*verzorgingsinstituut*) from which the largest possible number of members of the village community or ethnic group should benefit. Economic individualism on a Western model, or the growing rational organization of productive activity in order to pursue greater profits, caused a deadly "collision" with the intrinsic "elasticity" and the economic survival of the *desa*.[105]

Accordingly, European devotees of Balinese culture raised a logical and predictable question. They wondered with a hint of good-natured humor, as did some of their colleagues in Java, whether the cultural endurance of Indonesians would reveal the exact same medical profile as Europeans and simply replicate their life-cycle of health and sickness or life and death. In a historical sense, this produced the quandary whether "the Orient, too, must experience a Renaissance and Humanism? Must it necessarily follow the exact same evolutionary path as the West?"[106] The actual encounter between primitive people and formidable Western values, instead, could yield a re-evaluation and revival of indigenous cultural customs and "both deepen and widen their own traditions and religious imagination."[107] The evolution of indigenous culture would follow its own itinerary amidst the pushes of native traditions and the pulls of "emancipation" on a Western model. Their own heritage, after all, provided the Balinese or the Javanese with "interior and exterior stability," because they held up a "mirror of a nobler past to a colorless present," thus charting the route towards their own "glorious future."[108]

A positive vision of Balinese people as natural and pure inspired Dutch civil servants' empathetic devotion to pristine indigenous peoples, whose innate gentility and sweet disposition deserved the Indies government's protection. The colonial state in Bali, said Victor Emanuel Korn, a civil servant who worked in Bali for many years, should uphold "the three Gs of Religion, Family, and Authority" (*Godsdienst, Gezin, and Gezag*), which added a peculiar Dutch twist to the British imperialist triumvirate of Christianity, Commerce, and Civilization. Every government official had sworn an oath that in the region under his command "the state will not violate the independence of indigenous communities (*inheemsche gemeenten*) in regulating their social and economic interests" nor inhibit or interfere in the archipelago's natural cultural development.[109] Another prominent civil servant, Dr. B.J. Haga, summed up the Dutch view of Bali's condition succinctly:

> If we remember that our full-fledged governance of Bali began only in 1908, we also have to recall that until then Bali was totally free of Western influences. In the past twenty-five years Bali has been forced to adapt to the overwhelming impact of the West in terms of administration, transportation, commerce and industry, a process of adjustment that took European people many centuries. Bali should be given a chance to incorporate these alien forces and convert them into a harmonious whole. This is not an island doomed to die. To the contrary, it will probably generate its own [organic] development in the future.[110]

However, Dutch observers in different regions of the archipelago saw the cruelty, magic, and infantile fantasies of indigenous peoples as testimony of their retarded human development or of their slow progress along the path of evolution. These two competing visions clashed with each other dramatically after the turn of the century. In fact, these contradictory perspectives reverberated in a correspondingly contested discourse in which the "hyper-ethical" language of motherly affection and respect for local *adat* collided with the stentorian masculine voice of other colonials who called for discipline and constant surveillance.

None of these viewpoints, though, suggested that the end of Dutch colonial mastery was imminent. All native people, irrespective of whether they were helpless due to their childlike immaturity, their slow phylogenetic ascension up the evolutionary ladder, or whether they were defenseless owing to the congenital, lesser intelligence of their sub-human species, required either nurturing or control. Whichever biological metaphors they stressed in order to support their position, Dutch colonial residents argued that they should accompany Indonesians on their evolutionary journey, because they were knowledgeable about the path's obstacles and pitfalls. Having traversed the same territory themselves in an earlier stage of their individual and collective development, they could prevent innocent Indonesians from stumbling or getting lost along the way. Moreover, in the case of the Balinese, who had risen above the animal-like state of nature and had managed to construct an artistic and virtuous human community, the Dutch should shield them from the nefarious influences of the West and Christian missionary zeal that might otherwise pollute their pure souls.

A vision of Indonesian peoples as depraved savages — because "*Indië* is a country of monkeys and all the native people are skunks" — required Europeans' constant vigilance, too, in order to protect them from an "involution" that could emanate from their own sordid primal instincts.[111] As one of the characters in P.A. Daum's novel *Nummer Elf* (Number Eleven) pondered: "who dared to call these creatures, in his eyes more ape-like than the tame redskins [in North America], people?"[112] Pramoedya Ananta Toer raised this European perception of the Javanese as monkeys to greater rhetorical heights. In his historical novel *Bumi Manusia* (This Earth of Mankind), the central Javanese character, a thoughtful and charismatic young man named Minke, received his name from a Dutch schoolmaster who bastardized the word monkey into Minke. Besides, another offensive European brute whose gross body was as "big as an elephant" said to Minke that even if he dressed up in fancy European clothes, mixed with Europeans, and spoke a little Dutch, he would always be nothing but a "monkey!"[113] It is possible that these occasional references to the Javanese as monkeys dressed in Western attire may have reminded Indies residents of the tasteless Dutch saying *al draagt een aap een gouden ring, het is en blijft een lelijk ding* (even if a monkey wears a golden ring, it is and remains an ugly thing)!

Repudiating the Javanese or other ethnic groups as monkeys and apes, skunks, lapdogs, or draft animals and other beasts of burden facilitated the vision of all indigenous people as aboriginal creatures, who were physically and intellectually less mature than the Europeans poised at the apex of the evolutionary chain. This homology harked back to pre-nineteenth century biological theory. Until Lamarck and Darwin revolutionized biological notions, the prevailing consensus held that objects of nature formed an immutable chain that ascended without interference from the simplest single-cell organisms to the most complex organisms, i.e. humans. The perception of a similitude between great apes or Malay bears and wild natives who lived in jungles and presumably ate each other — the popular mythology about the wild men of Borneo was a compelling emblem, in this context — conjured up an unchanging hierarchy of the species which relegated the colonial other to a nebulous space somewhere between man and beast.[114]

Again, these intellectual queries relied indirectly on the work of Linnaeus, who had invented an intermediary species called *Homo troglodytes*, which he ranked immediately below *Homo sapiens*, in his *System of Nature*, first published in 1735 and refined many times thereafter. While Linnaeus was quite voluble in his description of *Homo sapiens* in all its diversity, he was terse about *Homo troglodytes*. The latter was only active at night, he wrote, and spoke in hisses and grunts. As Stephen Jay Gould has noted, Linneaus probably concocted *Homo troglodytes* as a compound of exaggerated travelers' reports of "anthropoid apes humanized or native peoples degraded."[115]

Linnaeus's *Homo troglodytes*, it seemed, accentuated the negative pole of Troglodytes' dual nature, which Montesquieu had concocted in his *Lettres Persanes* (Persian Letters) in 1721. Montesquieu had emphasized the difference between his "unenlightened" Troglodytes and the threatening creatures Herodotus had chronicled; Herodotus's Troglodytes were fierce cave dwellers, who lived around the southern coast of the Red Sea and resembled savage beasts rather than human beings. Montesquieu, in contrast, insisted that Troglodytes, before their initiation into the world of "enlightenment," were far from deformed; they were not covered with hair and "shaggy like bears, nor did they hiss, and they had two eyes." But initially they were so "brutal and ferocious," that there was no "principle of equality and justice" among them.[116] Montesquieu's Troglodytes, however, carried within them the capacity for evolutionary change and the ability to become "humane, just, and lovers of virtue" if provided with a proper environment and rational, "enlightened" leadership.[117] Linnaeus, in turn placed his *Homo troglodytes* in a similar murky territory between the unequivocal beastlike nature of Herodotus's feral tribe and their eventual metamorphosis into Montesquieu's gentle Troglodytes.

Almost 200 hundred years later, in Sumatra in the late 1920s, Dutch civil servants still pondered these issues in comparable language, although they were equipped, in the meantime, with a theoretical apparatus expanded by Lamarck, Darwin, and Haeckel. Dutchmen in Sumatra worried about, and were intrigued by, the reported sightings in the regions around Jambi, Kerinci, and Palembang of the legendary *orang pendek*, an upright species which resembled a human being. Similarly, in the Rokan mountains, which was one of the most isolated areas of Sumatra and maintained no contact with either Jambi or Palembang, people also claimed to have caught a glimpse of a comparable scavenger, who walked on his two hind feet through the jungle and was called *orang letjo* (midget man or dwarf man) by local people. This species reputedly "had no hair on his body or at least had only a little hair, like a human being," in the appropriate places. A newspaper article in July, 1932, furnished further details:

> The creature has a rosy brown color and long hair on his head. Based on the description given, the *orang letjo* could be the missing link, thus occupying the po-

sition between human beings and the most highly developed animal species. Because of his great cleverness and rational capacity this creature will not find it hard to hide. It combines an almost human cunning and reason with physical strength, shyness, and agility. Until now mankind has never encountered a creature of this kind!"[118]

The Dutch civil servant Louis Constant Westenenk wrote in a long administrative report about his tenure as Resident of Palembang in 1928 that a tall, hairy, and upright species of approximately one and a half meters tall, which native Sumatrans of the surrounding area called *lolok* or *segoegoe*, had kidnapped a native girl about four years old named Martina Rau. While a search party frantically looked for the child, a day or so later she returned on her own, entirely unharmed; when asked where she had been for such a long time, she answered "I went along with my grandparents" (*toeroet sama nene dan tete*).[119] *Lolok* or *segoegoe*, in other words, resembled friendly members of the human family who gave the little girl the feeling that they were respectful, kindly grandparents.[120]

Westenenk chronicled many other encounters. He mentioned, for instance, that a forester in the jungle near Kerinci in 1927 had seen a "human apparition ... a reasonably short male person (*manspersoon*) with very long hair, an almost black skin color, and stark naked, without any weapons or tools in his hands. Like my native servants, I am positive that it was a human being."[121] Europeans spotted *orang pendek*, too, in the rugged, mountainous area of the Gayo people in northwestern Sumatra. "The *manti*, or so-called *orang pandak* or *pendek*, exists," wrote a captain of police from the Gayo highlands. His footprints "resemble those of a child," and are very different from the footprints of a bear, "with which I am intimately familiar." And a military official with the Dutch topographical service in Jambi in 1929 told of having met in the forest "a creature in the form of a human being, covered entirely with brown hair. His height was approximately 1.30 meter and he had a broad chest of a half a meter wide."[122]

In the semi-darkness of the Sumatran jungle, Europeans thought they confronted a variety of mysterious "human" organisms that constituted an evolutionary puzzle. The eighteenth-century Irishman William Marsden had already described Sumatra's nomadic Kubu people (*orang Kubu*) as "promiscuous" eaters, who devoured everything they encountered in the jungle ranging from deer, rhinoceros, and wild hogs to snakes and monkeys. Marsden also depicted the even more elusive *orang Gugu* as employing a form of speech almost identical to that of orangutans and sporting a torso covered all over with long hair.[123] With their dirty, stringy tresses and bodies lacquered with mud, an adventurer-geologist in Sumatra continued to assert in 1921 that the Kubu people personified man in the original state of nature, who constituted "living fossils" from which Europeans could learn "how the *Urmensch* had existed" and thus infer how modern *Homo sapiens* had evolved over time.

Their lack of intelligible language and their astounding ability to climb trees made the Kubus more akin to the great apes who resided in the forest canopy above them than they were to human beings. The moisture and shadows of the jungle deprived the

Kubus' "life blood of its existential energy"; the dense tropical forest with its abundance of edible vegetation and animals, moreover, prevented Kubu people's capacity to develop a more substantial brain and hampered their facility to engage in rational thought. After all, the "human spirit" of compassion or the spirituality of the "human soul" defined the condition of being truly human, all of which were alien to the Kubus.[124] Due to the profound influence of "space and time," some French and British analysts argued with similar logic that the "gray matter" in the brains of African Negroes was of a more intense shade of gray than the brains of Europeans. The impaired development of Africans' cerebrum presumably derived from a too hasty settling of the bones of the skull at the onset of puberty, which impeded the expansion of their brains and thwarted the maturation of African Negroes' rational faculties in adulthood.[125]

The homology between animals and native people also crept into the language of Dutch men and women who claimed to be sympathetic to Indonesians' plight and wished to expose the degraded conditions of their lives. The writer Madelon Szekely-Lulofs, for instance, in her valiant, if flawed, attempt to write a novel that might provide a poignant portrait of the dehumanizing working conditions of Javanese contract laborers on the rubber and tobacco plantations on the east coast of Sumatra, compared the Javanese to animals throughout. Lulofs equated the fatalism of Javanese coolies —reinforced by their sense of powerlessness in the face of terrifying mistreatment by Europeans — with the passivity of unruffled beasts who did not know any better. The Javanese in Deli "lived like tamed animals" with their "bodies as dark as buffaloes," she wrote in *Coolie*, and their "earnestness was that of an animal which passes its days contented and without desire, trustful of life and therefore happy without being aware of the true meaning of happiness."[126]

Szekely-Lulofs' purpose in writing *Coolie*, she stated with Spenglerian overtones in a foreword to the English edition in 1936, was to explain the soul of "a strange race" that remained an enigma to most Westerners. She also wanted to contemplate "the various shapes adopted by the human soul" in response to different ecological conditions. The brutal environment of Sumatra's plantation belt played a crucial role in her attempt to understand the degree of culture and civilization the Javanese had achieved.[127] Her depiction of Javanese coolies as numb, pacified animals thus flowed directly from a physical milieu that had been created by what she called the "more or less necessary system" of European rubber plantations in Deli.[128] The end result was a depiction of the Javanese plantation workers as organisms of "vegetal passivity." The new material circumstances that immured them had unveiled their true nature and exposed them as beings "without fatherland, without family, without tradition," who replicated the dull, instinctive behavior of buffaloes.[129]

One of Lulofs' contemporaries, though, added a humorous twist to Dutch colonial residents' tendencies to draw analogies between native people and animals or to chortle about the "monkey faces" of *inlanders*. Dutchmen's own bovine facial features and less than intelligent appearance, he joked, reminded him of "the pig sty or the cow stable" in which their own birth cradle must have stood![130] The Indonesian nationalist,

Dr. Soetomo, would have wholeheartedly agreed: he also called Dutch government officials and policemen *karbouwen*: waddling water buffaloes, which were useful but highly uncivilized animals![131]

Meanwhile, the Dutch civil servant stationed in Sumatra, Louis Constant Westenenk, granted the foresters and soldiers who professed to have encountered *orang pendek* in Jambi, Kerinci, the Gayo highlands or the Rokan mountains, the benefit of the doubt. He offered the opinion that all these people had a keen eye and were "trained to observe and analyze facts," and he doubted that they all suffered from fantastical delusions (*aartsfantasten*).[132] Thus, in an earnest and scientific manner, Westenenk proceeded to craft plaster of Paris models of the puzzling creature's footprints in order to dispatch them to the appropriate government officials in Batavia.

On July 1, 1928, Westenenk received an effusive letter from a paleoanthropologist, Professor Eugène Dubois of the Zoological Museum in Amsterdam, who wrote that "on the basis of an analysis of the footprints, I have come to the firm conclusion that we are dealing with the footprints of the Malay bear." He continued to say that:

> We have to rescind, in a physical sense, the homology (*menschähnlichkeit*) between human beings and great apes, but restore the humanity of the *orang pendek* in a psychic sense to the species of the Malay bear. The Malay bear rather than the great ape should be referred to as the *orang pendek*, which will thus provide confirmation of a biological law of the greatest significance: the law of the autonomous phylogenetic perfection of the psycho encephalon.[133]

While serving as a physician with the Royal Netherlands Indies Army who was mesmerized by questions of evolutionary biology, Eugène Dubois, it turned out, had uncovered in 1891 the skull and thighbone of a primitive human form. At first he had labeled his discovery *Anthropopithecus erectus*, or upright man-ape, and then renamed it *Pithecanthropus erectus*, or upright ape-man — better known as "Java Man."[134] Dubois was determined to search in Asia rather than in Europe or Africa for the original mainspring of humanity. He had been inspired by one of Ernst Haeckel's more idiosyncratic assertions, proposing that the first humanoid species had evolved on an Asian equivalent of Atlantis: the lost continent of Lemuria, located near the Indonesian archipelago but which the Indian Ocean had long ago swallowed up again.[135]

His discovery of "Java Man," Dubois contended, confirmed Darwin's speculation that proto-humans had stood upright before they acquired the intellectual faculties of a modern brain. After all, "Java Man" possessed a femur that comprised evidence of a species that had walked erect, on two feet only. Besides, its cranium was considerably larger in size than that of any living anthropoid ape, even if it was analogous in form and structure to the skulls of actual animals still in existence. Although a few zoologists conceded that *Pithecanthropus erectus*'s femur constituted the proof of a species that had stood upright, they were not convinced that it actually belonged to the same organism as "Java Man's" cranium, because Dubois had found the thighbone at a distance of 15 meters from the skull. In fact, some among them raised the possibility that the skull and femur belonged respectively to a great ape and a human being who had died in a lethal struggle with each other.[136] Other biologists dismissed "Java Man's" skullcap as belonging to a human being who was probably "a deformed idiot," while others ascribed the cranium without hesitation to an ape, "probably a large gibbon."[137] Besides, some critics harbored doubts, too, about the venerable geological age of at least one million years Dubois had assigned to his original "Java Man."[138]

At a zoological congress in Leiden in 1895, a large segment of the international community of scientists greeted Dubois' discovery with a healthy skepticism that was fueled, too, by his emerging theory of "saltational cephalization" — or the evolution of the human brain by means of unexpected leaps and bounds.[139] Dubois was persuaded that an upright posture and bipedal locomotion came long before the development of a human-sized brain. Walking on only two rear legs freed a species' front paws, which could then be used for the handling of tools. Employing utensils and implements, in turn, spurred rational thinking about the ways in which the environment could be manipulated to enhance survival, thus enlarging cranial capacity in sudden saltational spurts.[140] Many other evolutionary biologists, however, clung to the "brain first" theory.[141]

In his autobiography, Darwin himself had suggested that the shape of the human skull could be "quite altered" as a result of deep rational thinking and the intensive exercising of the human brain "when the primeval instinct of the barbarian slowly yielded to the acquired tastes of civilized man."[142] But whether an autonomous development of the brain first prompted early humanoids to walk about on only their hind feet in order to liberate their front paws for the deft maneuvering of tools — or whether the causal sequence was the other way around — were issues that continued to baffle evolutionary biologists. As a result, Ernst Haeckel and the French anthropologist Leonce Manouvrier comprised a few lonely voices heralding *Pithecanthropus erectus* as irrefutable evidence of the "missing link" in human evolution.[143] One of Dubois's German detractors, in fact, argued emphatically that *Pithecanthropus erectus* was not the "*Stammvater des Menschen*" (archetypal father of humanity) but rather, an anthropoid ape of the kind that must have been more prevalent in the past and had once upon a time constituted a "parallel form" to human beings.[144]

Thirty-three years later, when scholarly interest in his "Java Man" had long since faded, Dubois seemed to rejoice in having found in the Malay bear in the jungles of Sumatra rather than in neighboring Java the living proof of the linear progression, or the sovereign "phylogenetic perfection," from lower forms of life to modern *Homo sapiens* with its complex brain faculties and unique human conscience.[145] With the quaint scientific term "psycho encephalon" Dubois underscored the difference between the shrewdness and cunning of the highest forms of animals and true intelligence and human consciousness, which he attributed to the most highly evolved *Homo sapiens*, in other words, white-skinned Europeans. Great apes or Malay bears may exhibit an "encephalon," he implied, but they did not manifest the moral or ethical conscience of a "psycho encephalon." The similitude between some indigenous peoples and higher forms of animals, he suggested, hinged on their collective inability to engage in the kind of moral reasoning — or the unique forms of critical "self-awareness" only *Homo*

Colonial Practice in the Netherlands Indies, 1900-1942

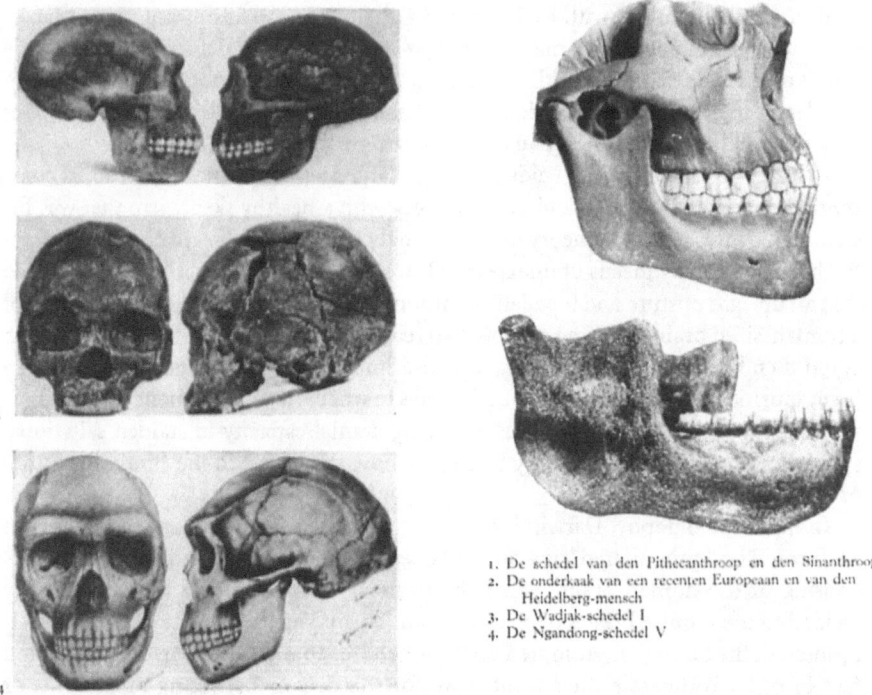

1. De schedel van den Pithecanthroop en den Sinanthroop
2. De onderkaak van een recenten Europeaan en van den Heidelberg-mensch
3. De Wadjak-schedel I
4. De Ngandong-schedel V

The skull of Pithecantropus erectus compared to other paeleontological findings. From: G.L. Tichelman and H.Van Meurs, eds., Indië roept (Amsterdam: Van Holkema & Warendorf, 1947)

sapiens could muster — that was part and parcel of "The Human Condition" in modern Europe.[146]

With this assertion Dubois may have appealed to the arguments of the ebullient Thomas Henry Huxley — a British morphologist who had anointed himself as "Darwin's bulldog" and served as a populist crusader on behalf of Darwinian theory during the second half of nineteenth century.[147] If Dubois had Huxley's combative logic in mind when he discussed the "psycho encephalon" in 1928, he proceeded to distort it. After all, Huxley had written in a tongue-in-cheek fashion that "the power of good and evil — the pitiful tenderness of human affections — raise us out of all real fellowship with the brutes, however closely they may seem to approximate us." But Huxley's rhetorical purpose was to emphasize above all that no "absolute structural line of demarcation" could be drawn between the animals that immediately preceded humans on the evolutionary scale and "ourselves," even if white-skinned Europeans were capable of gentle emotions and forms of reflexivity that were beyond the scope of even the most sophisticated, humanoid apes.[148] In the face of Herbert Spencer's contorted translation of Darwinian evolutionary theory, suggesting that a struggle against one's fellow human beings functioned as a kind of ethical imperative, Huxley became more emphatic. In 1893 he argued resolutely that struggles in nature held no ethical implications whatsoever, except to show human beings how they should *not* behave.

In his emphasis on the "psycho encephalon," Dubois tried to transcend the "exclusive consideration of form" or "the material monism" which characterized the work of Haeckel and his pseudo-scientific fellow travelers in Germany.[149] Dubois also echoed an earlier observation made by the Dutch anatomist Jacob Herman Frederik Kohlbrugge, well-known in Javanese scholarly circles, with whom he had intermittently corresponded. In criticizing evolutionary biologists for basing their arguments about the origins of man almost exclusively on morphological differences or analogies between the species, Kohlbrugge had noted in 1908 that they nonetheless glorified *Homo sapiens* "above all other creatures primarily owing to his psychological characteristics." Instead, the Dutch scientist insisted, it "is our duty to study the psychology of both animals and primitive races."[150]

Charles Darwin himself, as Kohlbrugge probably knew, had also written about the importance of the study of *The Expression of Emotions in Men and Animals* in 1782.[151] But it would be another Dutchman, Niko Tinbergen, who would heed Kohlbrugge's admonition and convert the socio-affective behavior of different species into a lifetime of impassioned scientific inquiry. One of the founders of the academic discipline of ethology — and the first to receive a Nobel Prize in this new field — Tinbergen spent his career studying the instinctual and social behavior of animals and "primitive" peoples. During the early 1930s, for example, Tinbergen participated in a polar expedition to Greenland, where he conducted research on the communal behavior of snow buntings and red-necked phalaropes and analyzed the social interaction of Eskimos and their dogs.[152] Especially since Darwin's writings, both behavioral scientists and biologists have continually tried to ascertain whether animals, ranging from elephants to chimpanzees, are capable of feeling the same emotions of despair and remorse, or empathy and euphoria, that sensitive human beings experience.[153]

Kohlbrugge argued that the physical size of a cranium had nothing to do with either intelligence or the richness of a species' emotional life. A European who learned early in life to use his mind would acquire a more "substantial brain" than a person who did so only minimally, even if their skull sizes were identical. The same held true for primitive people. If they were "instructed since early childhood to exercise their minds," primitives' brow ridges (*Supraorbitalbogen*) might become less prominent, but the circumference of their cranium or the volume of their brain would remain the same. Neither was it true, Kohlbrugge maintained, that a complex pattern of brain furrows (*Gehirnfürchen*) comprised automatic evidence of a higher level of development. If the intensive mental activity of famous European intellectuals generated a more intricate neurological arrangement of brain furrows, Kohlbrugge contemplated, then Javanese Muslims who tried to memorize as many passages from the Koran as humanly possible should reveal the same complex physiological result.[154] Whether or not he was aware of the work of Franz Boas, Kohlbrugge was obviously probing questions that were similar to the German-born American anthropologist. Boas, after all, would make a statement a few years later in an essay on *Kultur und Rasse* (Culture and Race) that "brain size, alone, is not an adequate criterion. Complexity of structure is much more important than mere size!"[155]

But in Kohlbrugge's vision, neither the actual size of the brain nor the intricacy of the brain's neurological configuration could explain people's psychological sense of self. The South-American Carib people in the Dutch colony Surinam, he observed with good-natured cynicism, even though they might become extinct as a species, were convinced they were the most exalted human beings on this earth: they regarded Europeans as elongated, pale-faced creatures who ranked far below them.[156] Accordingly, Kohlbrugge wondered whether "our triumphant, objective" scientific methods had brought the modern Western world no further in several millennia than the standpoint of the Caribs — whom Rousseau had identified as the people most closely resembling man in the state of nature — that "*one* is simply more than the *other*?"[157]

Kohlbrugge was a scholarly personality, who spent a large part of his career in Tosari in Java. He wrote with great intellectual certainty about the psychological attributes of the Javanese and their Dutch overlords (*overheerschers*), even though his expertise was contested by a more illustrious scholar of Indonesian cultures, Christiaan Snouck Hurgronje.[158] He also carried out anthropological "fieldwork" among the Tengger people in Eastern Java, and published a study in French in the journal *L'Anthropologie* in 1897 on this isolated Hindu group living in a remote mountain region of an island that had embraced Islam about five centuries earlier.[159] Kohlbrugge ventured into the field of political economy, too, and produced an analysis in 1909 that tried to answer the question whether "leasing land to sugar factories [was] a blessing or a curse for the Javanese."[160] In addition, he conducted biological research into the musculature and peripheral nervous system of primates; he also studied spermatogenesis and the reproductive behavior of a particular species of bats, and published all his findings in the proceedings of the mathematics and physics division of the prestigious Dutch Academy of Sciences.[161] His large-scale study on the neurological structure of the Javanese brain was illustrated with pull-out charts containing dozens of elaborate brain diagrams.

In addition, Kohlbrugge wrote weighty philosophical treatises about regression and evolution; in 1897 he published a two-volume *magnum opus* on atavism: *Der Atavismus und die Deszendenzlehre* (Atavism and the Theory of Regression) and *Der Atavismus und die Morphologie des Menschen* (Atavism and Human Morphology).[162] In 1908 he composed *Die Morphologische Abstammung des Menschen. Kritische Studie über die neueren Hypothesen* (The Morphological Origins of Man. A Critical Study on the New Hypotheses), in which he displayed a dazzling erudition in the international literature on traditional natural history and the modern theories of evolution and regression. While he published his scientific work either in German or French because it was geared mostly towards an international audience of natural scientists, Kohlbrugge also contributed an occasional article to more popular Dutch-language magazines in the Indies, such as the column "Questions of the Day" (*Vragen van den Dag*) in a weekly colonial newspaper.[163]

On the basis of his voluminous research and his professional experience in the Indies, Kohlbrugge stated repeatedly and unequivocally that environment and upbringing either nurtured the progressive development — or, instead, caused the regression and extinction — of all species, whether humans or animals. At a less lofty evolutionary level, he suggested that the tropical milieu in which individual people lived possessed an ineluctible power either to undermine their emotional equilibrium or to destabilize their racial character. He took part, in other words, in a general discussion in the Indies concerning the influence of environmental factors on human psychology. This debate arose from a "discomfiting awareness" that the ecological surroundings in which human beings functioned could alter their innate identities or modify their "racial essences," thus intimating that racial categories were both "porous and Protean at the same time."[164]

Milieu or tropical climate — what a Dutch psychologist, Paul van Schilfgaarde, called a *deus ex machina* variable in 1925 —acquired major significance in decoding the differences between Europeans and indigenous peoples in the twentieth century. If Dutchmen indulged their cowardly side, Van Schilfgaarde noted, they blamed "the environment for what is in reality the consequence of our misdeeds (*misdragingen*)." In contrast, if they wished to be compassionate, they appealed to the tropical surroundings "to excuse the flaws and shortcomings" of native people. The reality most likely resided somewhere in the middle, he argued, since the human character revealed itself in the manner in which people "experience, acknowledge, accept, serve, contest, or overcome" the physical circumstances of their lives.[165] But it would be simple-minded to argue that the frigid winters of northern climates were responsible for galvanizing Europeans into higher levels of activity or inducing their greater needs and high-minded aspirations. It would be equally unproductive to point to the natural abundance and lush vegetation of the Indonesian archipelago as a solitary explanation of native people's carefree attitudes or their want of ambition.[166]

Nevertheless, Dutch observers routinely established a linkage between the meekness and lack of individualism among the Javanese and the ecological or social climate in which they lived. Any character sketch of the Javanese or any other ethnic group, many European "experts" contended, must be embedded in a detailed description of the village communities in which they spent their day-to-day lives, since a native person, virtually everywhere, was enslaved to the "capricious forces of nature." The average indigenous man or woman was equally subservient to the human tyranny of "gossip and intrigue" in their village communities, which tormented them.[167] Above all, *banjirs* (floods), droughts, earthquakes, volcanic eruptions, or thunder and lightning molded and shaped the mentality of indigenous people. Their simple lives, in other words, were dominated by all sorts of "mysterious" and "dangerous" forces of nature over which they could exert influence only through "ceremonial" exercises and superstitious practices.[168]

A combustible mixture of evolutionary logic and ecological determinism colored the perspectives of scores of twentieth-century Dutch writers, whether they wished to clarify the animist cosmology of native peoples or diagnose the curious illnesses which befell Europeans in the tropics. The former colonial civil servant Samuel van Valkenburg, for instance, who spent most of his prolific academic career as a political geographer in the United States, still propounded in 1939 that the majority of colonized societies, owing to the negative impact of climate and environment on the development of native peoples, would never be able to govern autonomous nations that might become full-fledged members of the world community.[169] But the exotic environment of the Indonesian archipelago emerged as a singularly important factor in illuminating the character and behavior of Europeans in the tropics as well; in fact, it was a hotly debated question among Dutch writers.

Some asserted that Dutch men and women living in a southeast Asian environment, in *Heilig Indië* (the Sacred Indies), achieved a "metamorphosis of the soul" and transformed themselves into big-hearted and open-minded "citizens of the world" (*wereld-burgers*).[170] Amidst the "divine" natural splendor of the Indonesian archipelago, many Dutchmen who were in the prime of their lives labored underneath the tropical sun with "energy and dedication, with strength and steely resolution" for the benefit of the Indies, while younger men strove "with impulsive enthusiasm and warm-blooded passion" to improve the social conditions of Indies society.[171]

An occasional foreign observer concurred with this idealistic assessment. As the Frenchman Joseph Chailly-Bert declared in 1900 in his *Java et ses habitants*: the Dutch in Java became "powerful spirits, devoid of prejudice, with souls cleansed of almost all religious sentiments." Instead, they were captivated with "the idea of *égalité*" and rejected all distinctions of class and caste. Chailly-Bert claimed that the typical Indies person abhorred the memory of the bigotry and intrusive character of social life in small Dutch towns; he wrote that most Dutch people in southeast Asia trembled at the thought of having to move back to "the narrow-minded Protestant milieu" in their country of origin.[172] A German anthropologist told his Nazi audience more or less the same story in 1943; because of the "free and unconstricted air" colonial residents had learned to breathe in the Indonesian archipelago, once they returned to their frosty and petty *Heimat* in Europe they suffered from an irrepressible nostalgia for the wide open spaces of "the land of eternal sunshine, as if for a Paradise Lost."[173]

Others, however, posed the opposite argument that the Indies milieu "oxidized" or "disfigured" Europeans' souls, especially those of younger, "as yet unformed," psyches, whose natures were still "plastic" and could thus be more easily contorted by the sweltering heat of the new habitat that encircled them. If Europeans went to the Indies and adapted to the climate of their tropical surroundings, they would inevitably "regress" and experience a "coarsening of the spirit" and sooner or later pay for it with an "existential unhappiness."[174] The Indies destroyed something in sensitive Dutch people with worthy intentions, because the milieu shattered or warped the "noble elements of their psychic mechanism," and the average Dutch person returned from the Indies with "the strings of his soul either broken or seriously out of tune."[175]

Accordingly, the Medical Journal of the Dutch East Indies (*Geneeskundig Tijdschrift voor Nederlandsch-Indië*) habitually published lengthy, learned articles about the frazzled psychological state or psychiatric afflictions of Europeans in the tropics. After all, human beings' consciousness and soul, wrote the psychiatrist W.F. Theunissen in 1921, had to accomplish much more than what was simply a successful — and hopefully lucrative! —adjustment to the lush, sun-soaked environment in which they found themselves in the Indies. The average Dutch colonial resident was forced to engage in an enterprise that transcended the elementary struggle for existence: "as sunlight does not shine for the sake of the human eye, but the eye owes its existence to the presence of light, so does the human conscience derive its existence from the world in which it is implanted."[176]

But personal character and ego strength (*ikheid*), Theunissen qualified, was a constantly changing entity that either burgeoned or shriveled as a result of its encounter with varying "external influences such as age, climate, or physical health." In the Indies, the psychology of individual Dutch people could suddenly reveal a "rich tapestry" of sensations and feelings; the tropical milieu might unearth a psychological depth or unveil an emotional wisdom that had been submerged in Holland. On the other hand, Europeans' ego strength always ran the risk, too, of shrinking to a "pathetic, underdeveloped *ikheid*" due to the impact of the equatorial heat.[177]

The debate about Europeans' response to the southeast Asian tropical habitat had begun to reach a fever pitch after a previously unknown writer, a man named Bas Veth — who brandished a pen as if it were a weapon "dipped in vitriolic acid," outraged contemporaries exclaimed — published his notorious *Het leven in Nederlandsch-Indië* (Life in the Dutch East Indies) in 1900. A cantankerous personality with literary pretensions, Veth had arrived in the Dutch East Indies in 1879 to work as an apprentice to a trading firm in Makassar, only to write his scathing denunciation of Indies life upon his return to the Netherlands.[178] The opening paragraph of his diatribe set the tone: the Indies were "the incarnation of misery," he wrote. "Good people change into bad ones, all that arrives fresh grows stale, all that blushes becomes pale, all that flourishes withers away, all that sparkles is obscured, all that glows is rendered dull: thoughts, affections, illusions, perceptions." Europeans' bodies and souls inexorably degenerated, Bas Veth fulminated, due to an unconscious and stealthy, if treacherous, process of decay, "like the first stage of a cancer, like beri-beri, diabetes, or pestilence."[179]

The average "Indies man," Veth wrote, was a "recognizable variety of the human race." Whether he actually worked in southeast Asia, lounged in a lazy chair on a steamer in the Suez Canal, or had retired to a grand villa in Bloemendaal, he always exhibited the crude "racial characteristics" of his distinct human type. He was fat and uncouth, his looks were always coarse, and his skin revealed a dirty yellow or dingy gray color. Invariably he was an alcoholic, and his "crass and foul attitudes" (*plat-vuil*) towards women comprised another distinctive attribute of his species, so that the "lovemaking of animals expresses more exalted beauty" than that of a typical boorish Indies man.[180]

Indies women themselves, however, did not fare any better in Veth's harangue, whether they had "$\frac{1}{4}$, $\frac{1}{3}$, or $\frac{1}{2}$ native blood" in their veins, which gave them a *hitam manis* complexion with the lovable appeal of "brown sugar" — or more literally, a "sweet black" tint with a bronzed sheen. This was the glorious golden glow of the *koelit langsep* of Dutch East Indies women that inspired the same kind of poetic licence, he wrote, as the "lily white skin of European beauties." But Veth also denounced seductive and calculating Indies *nonnas*, who ensnared recently arrived Dutch men and bankrupted their upstanding moral character by bending their European psyches out of shape. An interracial marriage, he wrote, was a "fatality," and both mixed-blood Indies women as well as wives of the *inlandse* race, he claimed, always led their guileless European partners to doom and damnation.[181] This foreboding, and often agonizing, leitmotif also resonated in a large number of novels set in the baroque colonial culture of the Indies, such as Louis Couperus' novel *The Hidden Force*, in which the Indies wife Léonie functioned as a shadowy angel of darkness in her Dutch husband's tragic downfall. Her narcissistic sensuality and her apparent invulnerability, "as though she were incapable of suffering ... because no sickness, no anguish, no poverty, no misery existed for her," contributed directly to the psychological collapse and social ruination of the Dutch civil servant Otto van Oudijck. Although he heroically tried to cling to his European faith in reason, logic, and honor, in the end he could not withstand the insidious, contaminating influences of his Indies wife or his mixed-blood children.[182]

The female novelist Augusta de Wit depicted Dutch East Indies' residents in a comparable fashion. In her widely read novel *De godin die wacht* (The Goddess Who Waits), published in 1903, she wrote that the majority of Europeans were only European in the official sense of the word. Even full-blooded Hollanders no longer resembled the energetic and sturdy Dutch folk they once had been. A pale yellowish tint had overtaken their bodies, their limbs had lost strength and their faces had slackened. Indies people's sluggish movements, she determined, constituted the tangible evidence of the "denationalization" of their souls. It was as if the tropical milieu had drained them of their characteristic Western vitality and replaced their bold initiatives with "the kind of fatalistic resignation that was unique to the Indies."[183]

But the worst of it all was that Indies children seemed to inherit these vile racial attributes. European boys and girls growing up in the Indies became the same kind of white-skinned philistines, as if through a natural process of osmosis: they were just as lazy and self-indulgent as their parents. Early in life they already behaved like little tyrants and displayed an undisciplined wildness and precocious sexuality.[184] In their educational develoment, Indies children always lagged behind their peers in Holland who had reached the same age. Children's lack of academic performance in the Indies, however, did not emerge from intrinsically inferior talents; instead, the corrupting influence of the humidity and heat of their tropical habitat was responsible for all their intellectual handicaps.

In addition, the negative impact of the environment was reinforced by their dumb Indies parents, who lacked proper judgment and failed to supervise their children: "Mamma, who does nothing but slouch on a *chaise longue* on the verandah and pappa, who does nothing but drink bitters and jenever, leaving the *baboe* (native nanny) in charge of forming — or rather, mangling — the fragile child's soul."[185] Being too "sultry, too much like a hothouse," the "climatological atmosphere" of the Netherlands Indies could not foster the organic expansion of the human mind. The tropics distorted the relationship between the "physical and mental development of young individuals, which undermines their sense of balance and negatively affects their intellectual achievements."[186] As adults, most children would exhibit all the odious racial properties of the permanently debased Indies man.

The neo-Lamarckian resonance of this discourse was palpable.[187] Indies children naturally acquired the degenerate habits of their parents, as if sons, indeed, inherited the bulging muscles of their weight-lifting fathers. Lamarck, after all, had speculated that the behavioral responses of a particular organism to changes in the environment produced structural modifications that might be passed on "by reproduction to the new individuals which arise." The habits acquired during a lifetime of accommodating the new demands imposed by a different physical habitat endowed an organism with the ability to develop "the organs with which to execute them."[188]

While these theoretical conjectures were often used to explain the favorable adjustment of the human species to the exigencies of their environment, Lamarck had also linked his ideas about evolution to the tricky issue of atavism and regression. Under certain circumstances, Lamarck had intimated, species ran the risk of reverting back to an original type by descending down the evolutionary ladder. Other species might become extinct if they perfected a particularly useful physical trait to the extent that others atrophied — what Stephen Jay Gould has called biology's "little joke."[189] In his critical study on the Morphological Origins of Man, Kohlbrugge similarly speculated that numerous zoological species, which had anatomically evolved and specialized in too one-sided a fashion, had disappeared in the course of history. The same was true for those human races, he argued, that experienced an unbalanced or overly monomorphic physical development: "thus the Weddas (Veddahs) in India, the Aborigines in Australia, and the Papoeas (Papuas) in New Guinea may disappear in the same manner as the giant pre-historic reptiles."[190]

However, the preoccupation with the negative impact of the Indies environment on Europeans spawned a parallel set of arguments that arose in response to the hysterical repudiation of Indies life and its toxic effect on Europeans' souls. It elicited sardonic responses from some people, such as the attorney D.J. van Doorninck. He questioned whether it was true that the southeast Asian milieu brought out all the residual negative features of the Dutch psyche, while Holland's flat and wind-swept landscape in Northern Europe nurtured only its positive qualities. If this reasoning were taken to its logical extreme, Van Doorninck admonished with a certain amount of sarcasm in 1912, a Dutchman who lived in the natural splendor of the Swiss Alps for awhile would return to the Netherlands with a rotten, debauched soul, too![191] On the whole, it was clear that the public condemnation of the Indies climate kindled a scholarly discussion that was cloaked in psychiatric expertise and grounded in medical judgments. Not only did this debate among medical professionals summon Lamarckian notions about regression and atavism, it also echoed arguments about hybridization and biologists' hypotheses concerning the blending or mutation of species, thus incorporating a medley of competing theoretical positions current in early twentieth-century biology.[192]

Hybridity, in Linneaus's original formulation in the eighteenth century, would merge the characteristics of a higher organism with those existing in a lower one; the new combination would merely occupy a new slot in the immutable taxonomy of the species. Hence, the hybrid Indies man was a new intermediate racial type, as Bas Veth and others had proclaimed, who would always exhibit his dissolute character. Whether he sprawled his fat body on the deck chair of a ship in the Indian Ocean or shuffled about the Indies neighborhood of The Hague, this mongrel Indies type invariably disclosed the deficiencies of his species. But it was especially the notion of mutation, initially developed by Gregor Johann Mendel but elaborated, in a Dutch context, by the biologist Hugo de Vries in 1904, that seemed to reverberate.[193]

It was true that Darwin in his chapter on "Hybridism" in the *Origins of the Species* had ventured the tentative opinion that most species would probably become sterile if they interbred.[194] His contemporary, the French physician and anthropologist Paul Broca, conducted prodigious research on hybridity and cross-breeding among animals as well as humans. Broca came to more detailed conclusions. Sex between a Negro and a white woman rarely produced conception, he wrote, but if it did, it "engendered extremely miserable offspring." Sex between a man of a "higher" race with a woman of a "lower" race, however, could occasionally generate a child that was superior to its mother; he implied, though, that such offspring would seldom improve upon the caliber of its racially "superior" father. On the whole, Broca claimed judiciously, most hybrids were destined to retrogress even if some among them turned out well.[195] But Mendel and De Vries revised these judgments. Sooner or later, De Vries maintained, mutation would create a species that rendered it more robust and better equipped to survive in a particular physical habitat than even its parent form; in the long run, it was hybridization that shaped evolution and survival.[196]

In a similar fashion, if white-skinned Europeans wished to maintain their efficiency and productivity in a tropical setting, evolutionary logic implied that Europeans should mutate and adjust creatively to their new physical environment in order to guarantee their natural evolution and endurance as a species. Europeans in equatorial regions should intermarry with indigenous peoples, some Dutch colonial residents argued, thus endowing the mestizo world of Java that had evolved since the mid-seventeenth century with a luster of scientific logic.

"Statistics teach us that a pure Western race in the tropics is doomed to die" unless rejuvenated by vigorous native blood that was accustomed to flow freely in the voluptuous warmth of Indonesia. In the tropics "the old Dutch ancestral tree should develop vigorous new branches" and revitalize its genetic constitution, Mrs. Hissink-Snellebrand insinuated in 1911, but these hybrid offshoots required gentle nursing and careful cultivation to ensure the survival of the tree.[197] Again, milieu and education emerged as the central factors in Europeans' risk of regression. It was not "skin color or blood that produced degeneracy"; rather, Europeans could transcend the negative effects of "climate and upbringing (*opvoeding*)" by modifying the genetic make-up they passed on to their children. In other words, unless they rejuvenated their species through intermarriage, most Europeans in the tropics were eventually destined to sink into oblivion, thus lending an aura of scientific authority to Bas Veth's tirade. The "Oriental deformation" of Europeans' personality and character could only be arrested, Kohlbrugge foretold, if they carefully monitored their responses to the environment in which they had to function.[198]

In 1911 Kohlbrugge offered some highly impressionistic evidence in a further effort to explore the thorny question whether a Western race in the tropics, if it refused to reinvigorate its gene pool with well-adjusted local blood, would lose its procreative vigor. While "the first generation of blond Europeans can be productive [in the tropics]," he wrote, it is doubtful whether their children and grandchildren, if they remain in the Indies, "will be as permanently healthy and fertile (*duurzaam gezond en vruchtbaar*) as the first generation."[199] He stated that it was not interbreeding that produced sterility, as Darwin had speculated; instead, infertility among Europeans was a natural result of living in alien surroundings that were hostile to their reproductive stamina.

Kohlbrugge was not alone in this line of reasoning. In 1900, for example, the French expert on the Dutch *génie colonisateur*, Joseph Chailly-Bert, had also raised the specter that second-generation Europeans in the Indies might be "struck with sterility," and this unexamined truism lived on for at least another thirty years.[200] The children or grandchildren of Europeans in the tropics "usually remain without offspring," wrote the semi-official theorist of Dutch colonialism, Arnold Dirk Adriaan de Kat Angelino, in 1930, hinting at the possibility that they could have avoided their childlessness by refurbishing their genetic resources through interracial procreation.[201] Kohlbrugge, for his part, concluded that nobody could truly answer this question, because "pure-blooded Europeans are rarely found in the Indies" since all second- or third-generation male European residents of the Indies married women who had either Indonesian or Chinese "blood in their veins." Kohlbrugge knew of only one family, consisting of four brothers, who were fourth-generation Indies residents but who could claim to be unadulterated Caucasians; all of them had married completely healthy wives, he intoned with a sense of impending doom, but none of them had been able "to sire any children."[202]

Two years later, in 1913, the fervent Indies nationalist, E.F.E. Douwes Dekker, addressed the issue of miscegenation more bluntly: the colonizers who had crossed the oceans in order to reach southeast Asia, he sneered, did not forget to bring along their "tools of procreation" (*teeltwerktuigen*). In fact, they had used their "tools" with abandon. Our colonial masters, Douwes Dekker scowled in an article written for *De Indiër*, indulged their unbridled "lust" and "nonchalantly bred children" with our country's daughters — bastards, whose being they claimed to ennoble with an "exalted" component of their European blood.[203] However, at more or less the same time, the bi-weekly magazine of the Indies *blijver* association "Insulinde" injected this very same issue with a note of pride. *Insulinde* reminded its audience, most of whom were also mixed-blood permanent residents just like *De Indiër*'s readers, that the Dutch East India Company (VOC) had stopped the emigration of white women to the Indies in the seventeenth century. Instead, Dutchmen were advised to live with or marry indigenous women, because the Company representatives in Java allegedly realized that intermarriage was absolutely necessary for "the *production* of healthy babies and robust children!"²⁰⁴ A late colonial novel continued to invoke the same hackneyed image of the physically well-adapted, hybrid Indies person: "healthy and acclimated, comfortable with the tropical soil and atmosphere, at home in-between the palm trees and the natives but superior to the latter as a queen [or a king] to her subjects."²⁰⁵

In 1930 an earnest medical anthropologist, Dr. P.K. Kroest, still supplied a scholarly basis for such stereotypes in his presentation of preliminary research findings in the Dutch East Indies' Journal of Medicine on "Cross-Breeding in Java." He supplemented his research results with an array of elaborate anthropometric indices pertaining to skin, eye, or hair color as well as measurements of the transmission of either "brachycephalic" or "mesocephalic" skull structures. Kroest concluded that mixed marriages between European men and native women generated offspring who "surpassed the average of their fathers in terms of their *Index cephalicus*" —proving that this hybrid progeny possessed bigger brains than its European ancestors. Indo-Europeans, therefore, were not only physically better equipped to prosper and succeed in the tropical milieu of *Indië*; Kroest intimated, too, that *Indo* descendants might intellectually outstrip their European fathers. Hence, he seemed to contest the assertion of Kohlbrugge and others that actual brain size did not necessarily constitute evidence of a superior intelligence.²⁰⁶

Attitudes such as Kroest's, however, increasingly began to comprise the exceptions to the rule. During the 1930s, when the Dutch East Indies tumbled into a devastating economic depression and the colonial community became more openly fearful of the nationalist movement, the discussion about racial blending and Indo-Europeans changed profoundly. Even as unlikely a source as the famous modernist writer Eduard du Perron, the amber-skinned son of a wealthy, land-owning family in Java who exemplified the hybridity of Indies society, registered the growing European ambivalence about interracial coupling in 1935, despite the fact that Dutch men continued to marry native or *Indo* wives with impunity.²⁰⁷ In his seductive autobiographical novel *Het Land van Herkomst* (Country of Origin) he wrote that "when a European man confronted the smell of coconut oil [from a native woman's hair] on the pillow of his bed, he was forced to recognize how low he had sunk."²⁰⁸

Despite Dutch men's ongoing sexual involvement with native or Indo-European women, a sinister form of evolutionary logic, instead, emerged as the handmaiden of reactionary notions about the racial purity of white-skinned Europeans. After all, Europeans supposedly stood at the apex of the biological hierarchy of the species and should be protected from mixing with, or pollution by, "inferior" races. In some conservative Indies circles, this newly garbled version of evolutionary biology gave rise to the motto, as Danilyn Rutherford has aptly called it, "special spaces for special races" and endowed the policy of "divide and rule" with an aura of scientific legitimacy as well as political urgency.²⁰⁹

A popular version of the scientific language of biology and natural history colored the perspectives of Dutch colonial residents in the Dutch East Indies in the twentieth century. Albeit in an unpredictable or chaotic way, this pseudo-scholarly idiom armed them with a ragtag arsenal of intellectual weapons to legitimate the dominance of white-skinned Europeans over native people in a colonial context. Especially an oversimplified, colloquial transcription of the idea of evolution gave Dutch observers a useful and flexible rank-ordering mechanism, because it invested the political and economic divisions inherent in colonial societies with a quasi-scientific aura of naturalness and inevitability.

Evolutionary rhetoric, it seemed, could explain and illuminate almost all cultural distinctions, even the internal differences between the national character of various European nations. In a discussion of the differential response of the Dutch, British, or Germans to a tropical climate, for example, the Dutchman D.C.M. Bauduin proclaimed in 1927 that the average Englishman in terms of his intellectual capacity "occupies a lower rung on the evolutionary ladder" than a Dutch or a German person. But the British race, wrote Bauduin, had developed into a "standard type of human being of a universally high caliber."[210] German or Dutch people as a collectivity had yet to achieve an evolutionary level that endowed them generically with the same kind of "steady and calm personality" that English men and women displayed across the board. The stereotypical English person, Bauduin concluded, "is what he [or she] is," because in the tropics, despite the dramatic change in environment and the glorified status of white-skinned Europeans, English people maintained "the same phlegmatic identity" as if they were still surrounded by the Yorkshire plains.[211]

However, Western conceptions regarding the presumable reasons for the backwardness of primitive people, or questions about the origins of cultural difference, prompted few Dutch men and women to doubt the legitimacy of colonial dominance in southeast Asia. The representation of Javanese people as ontogenetically stuck at the level of childhood required parental nurture. The portrayal of indigenous cultures as having reached a phylogenetic stage that was comparable to medieval Burgundy or the Italian Renaissance dictated a policy of surveillance in order the help them along their historical path. An emphasis on the sophistication and organic unity of Balinese culture ordained the Dutch government's protection against the contaminating influence of Christian missionaries so that Bali might follow its own evolutionary itinerary. And an argument in favor of the homology between Indonesian natives and great apes or other sophisticated animals — in other words, all those creatures that were not yet capable of the moral reasoning of a "psycho encephalon" or unable to muster the pathos and delicacy that characterized *Homo sapiens* emotional bonds — compared the role of colonial governance to that of a zookeeper.

Regardless of the biological theories they invoked, many Dutch colonial residents presented their continued mastery as more or less immutable. The evolutionary trajectory that primitive Indonesian people in the colonies needed to follow in the future, in their valiant attempts to achieve full-fledged maturity and independence, was exactly the route that Dutch men and women had followed before, both individually and collectively. Accordingly, their continued guidance was not only necessary but, above all, efficient, because Dutchmen's superior knowledge of the road Indonesians still had to travel would keep them out of harm's way and perhaps even expedite their journey.

CHAPTER FIVE

GENDER, RACE, AND SEXUALITY:

Citizenship and Colonial Culture in the Dutch East Indies

In Batavia, Dutch matrons sport immense bellies stuffed to the gills with food; their stomachs are bloated, too, because they take too many siestas and refuse to engage in any kind of physical exercise. In the Dutch East Indies, in fact, activity and work comprise an exclusive attribute of men. Forever in a feverish hurry, men overwork themselves to get rich within a few years in order to retire to a green old age on the borders of the river Maas or along the Frisian polders near the Wadden Sea. With only an occasional exception, their wives, in contrast, allow themselves to be lived with the indolence of chained beasts. They walk around on bare feet and wrap their bodies in only a simple sarong, without a corset; they spend their idle days surrounded by their children as well as a cumbersome, whining crowd of lazy, cheating, or foolish Malay servants."[1]

Robert Chauvelot, Un roman d'amour à Java, 1919

This was the unflattering portrait of Dutch East Indies' matrons (*njonjas*) and their servants painted by the French writer Robert Chauvelot in 1919 in one of his pulp novels. The reality of European women's existence in *Indië*, however, was infinitely more varied and complex than this disconcerting picture of gluttony and idleness. In the course of the twentieth century, a growing number of Dutch and Eurasian women held paying jobs and worked as teachers, nurses, or social workers. In the public transportation sector of the Indies, for example, female employees made up a large and actually favored share of its administrative personnel.[2]

In fact, in a late-colonial anthology about life in the Indies, *Zóó leven wij in Indië* (Such is Our Life in the Indies), a chapter on "The Working Woman" proudly announced that European women, whether they had been born in Holland or in the Indies, were employed as "lawyers, physicians, and dentists, as managers of branches of government, customs officials, clerks, secretaries, bookkeepers, directors of normal schools, [and] inspectors of education ..."[3] Many among these vivacious and independent women pursued productive lives in a colonial culture that still measured their private conduct with a more censorious "moral yardstick" than the sexual behavior of confirmed bachelors or temporarily unmarried men.[4] However, among a total paid labor force of approximately 85,000 Europeans in 1930, only 15 percent consisted of women.[5]

Despite his crude caricature of Dutch *njonjas*, Robert Chauvelot did touch upon an essential theme that affected the lives of many white women in the Indies who were not single, autonomous, or gainfully employed. A kind of gnawing emptiness, or the absense of a clearly defined purpose, enveloped many married women's tropical existence. Above and beyond the supervision of household servants — whom they tended "to command while slouching in their rocking chairs or *krossi malas* (chaise longue)," the solitary, hard-working female member of the Indies *Volksraad* wrote somewhat contemptuously — daily life in the Indies did not pose serious challenges to most Dutch wives, because servants were the ones to buy food, prepare meals, clean, tend to the garden, and watch over fair-skinned Dutch children as eagle-eyed, if indulgent, nannies.[6]

In certain ways the day-to-day existence of Chauvelot's plump Batavia matrons did not differ much from the lives of middle-class women in the European metropole. After all, a gendered, if permeable, separation between a private domain that tended to enclose bourgeois women within family life and a masculine public sphere of industry and politics prevailed in Europe as it did in the colonies. But housewives in the Netherlands itself possessed more leeway in endowing their ordinary routines with a satisfying content. If they wanted to do so, middle-class wives in Holland could engage in charitable activities or take part in church circles or book clubs. Middle-class women could attend an array of concerts and visit museums and the theater or, if they lived in large cities and were bold enough, might participate in suffragist politics. Besides, fewer wives in the Netherlands could rely on nannies to supervise their children. The average bourgeois family in Holland also hired fewer household servants to cook, wash, and scrub, because employing a retinue of domestics constituted a prerogative of only the truly well-to-do. In Europe, in other words, women's lives revolved around some real tasks, which they accomplished either cheerfully or with sullen resentment, but which nevertheless gave them a clearer sense of purpose.

In Batavia, Semarang, Surabaya and elsewhere in the Indies, however a bevy of Indonesian servants took care of most of the mundane requirements of daily life. Hence, Chauvelot's distressing depiction of female passivity and languor contained at least some truths. There were, of course, various Dutch women who used their newly found leisure in extremely fruitful ways; being liberated from the relentless daily grind of household tasks enabled them to explore their residual creativity. Especially if they lived in outlying regions, some among them became skilled botanists and designed luxuriant tropical gardens. Others developed a serious interest in medicine and treated the physical ailments of local people with empathy and expertise, while more artistically gifted or intellectually inclined Dutch women cultivated their talent as painters, gratified their desire to write fiction, or nurtured their ethnographic curiosity about local culture.

But it was infinitely more difficult for white women to pursue such creative avocations if they resided in an obsessively status-conscious colonial city, surrounded not by Chauvelot's fictional chubby matrons but by real-life counterparts, who were probably not as obese as *Un roman d'amour à Java* insinuated.[7] In the major urban communities of the Indies, social frictions tended to arouse European women's passions and a never-ending cycle of rumor and idle chatter provided the diversions typical of the "tropical gothic."⁸ It was a society "filled with distrust, jealousy, and malice," in which even the most trivial event among white residents was "examined with a fine tooth comb, until every silly detail was exposed."⁹

Daily conversations among Europeans were filled with clichés and revolved around an incantatory reconfirmation of universally accepted "verities." In one of her short stories, Margaretha Ferguson parodied a presumably typical Dutch cocktail conversation in the Indies, lubricated by many rounds of jenever and bitters, which repeated the same theme *ad nauseam*: "life is expensive, salaries are too low, the *inlanders* are impudent and arrogant and think they can take care of themselves but they are really too dumb to dance for the devil and will need [us] for at least another hundred years."¹⁰ Besides, some European women "fought each other like polecats" over eligible bachelors, while maintaining status, or showing off wealth as a tangible sign of their husband's economic success, represented a full-time job for many of them.¹¹ Dressing fashionably was extremely important business, too, because only prosperous Batavia matrons had the means to order the latest *haute coutûre* and the fanciest hats from the European metropole, preferably from Paris. But the average member of "the genus *Indische mevrouw*" (Indies madam), according to the judgment of the civil servant Cornelis van Heekeren, was "uneducated, nosy, and obsessed with gossip."¹²

Both in daily life and at official gatherings of the Dutch colonial community an emotional vortex of envy, social snubs, and calumny whirled around most women. In her otherwise unremarkable novel written in 1893, *Bogoriana. Een roman uit Indië* (The Lore of Bogor. A Novel from the Indies), F.J.J.A. Junius, under the pseudonym of Annie Foore, chronicled with painful clarity the petty rivalries of women at a ball in the Governor-General's palace at the turn of the century.¹³ "When they enter, the privileged wives of high-ranking officials stride by their women friends with a smug, triumphant smile, while their husbands can't fail to puff out their chests ... the other women, filled with sweet illusions, whisper to themselves: only one more promotion, only one more death, and then [it is my turn]!"¹⁴ Even the license plates of automobiles, the Indies writer Melis Stoke —who also published under the name Herman Salomonson — bemoaned forty years later, conveyed people's standing in Batavia society: the lower the number, the more elevated one's ranking in the social hierarchy. Number One registered the car of the Governor General, whereas the license plates of the automobiles of the members of the Council of the Indies and of foreign diplomats displayed the next lowest numbers.¹⁵

Hence, whether they inhabited skinny or pudgy bodies, were hyper-active or lazy, or whether they had blushing pink cheeks or skins with a pale auburn tinge, few European women in Batavia ambled around on bare feet or went about in an Indonesian sarong and kebaya.¹⁶ It was likely, though, that the stifling heat and humidity of Java's north coast emboldened many among them to shed their suffocating corsets. Besides, the sultry climate rendered an afternoon siesta a dire necessity, not only for lethargic white women but also for their more ambitious husbands, fathers, or sons, who routinely went to work at the crack of dawn. But the only Dutch women in the twentieth century who continued to wrap a batik sarong nonchalantly around their hips during the morning hours tended to live in rustic outposts, far away from the madding crowd of Europeans in Batavia, Surabaya, Semarang, or Medan. The *totokization* or "Europeanization" of Indies social life outside the central axis of Java and the east coast of Sumatra was often an incomplete process; in some remote, outlying regions, in fact, it may not have occurred at all.[17]

Nonetheless, domestic advice manuals in the twentieth century gently urged newly arrived Dutch women to become more engrossed in the day-to-day running of their households rather than leave it to a "whining crowd" of deceitful Indonesian servants, as Chauvelot intimated. However, as Elsbeth Locher-Scholten has described so vividly, an odd sense of ambivalence pervaded the average guidebook to family life in the Indies. To promote white prestige, the domestic advice literature stressed the importance of learning to speak Malay as quickly as possible and urged white women to immerse themselves in the intricacies of local *adat*. Households that incorporated servants relied on a process of "mutual monitoring," requiring knowledge that went in both directions because servants were steeped in local culture which made white women dependent on them for much more than simple domestic chores.[18] But at the same time, the manuals prodded *njonjas* to function as paragons of virtue to their domestic servants, because "servants are just like big children. Let us try to understand their situation and feel compassion for them: this should inspire us to improve their fate, to uplift them."[19] White women's all-embracing maternal instincts, in other words, should prompt them to nurture and educate their Indonesian servants in the same way they cherished and raised their own children.

In most European households, servants constituted an integral element of both "the white-washed manor house with its open verandahs" as well as the surrounding Indies landscape: they "belong to us" just as much as they belonged to the palm trees swaying in the wind or to "the bamboo forest, the bottomless ravine, the glimmering *sawah* and the sacred *waringin* tree."[20] But the ambiguity of advice manuals resided in the portrayal of servants as passing their daily lives in a fundamentally different world on the other side of a disinfected, neutral middle zone — a "*cordon sanitaire*" — despite their indispensable roles in European households and their intimate involvement in the family circle.[21] "The compound behind the house is their exclusive domain," wrote a Dutch woman who was also active in the suffragist movement in the Indies in 1926. "The two boundary markers at the end of the driveway, with their widely extending low fences, serve as watchtowers and look-out posts" from which the servants observed the happenings of white-skinned family life, which often remained a bewildering spectacle to them.[22]

In the hearts and minds of many *totok* European women, servants' physical proximity provoked eerie feelings of discomfort. As a result, white women's handbooks frequently depicted them, too, as mysterious and untrustworthy, or as unhygienic and dirty, even perverse, in their private habits. Not only domestic advice manuals but also Dutch novels for adolescent girls equated the possession of brown skin with "human fallibility, if not danger." White-skinned people, in contrast, personified competence and safety. If the human failures of Indonesian servants were not too grievous, white

The kokki returns from the market. From: C.W. Wormser, ed., Zóó leven wij in Indië (Deventer: W. Van Hoeve, 1945)

women should "rescue and save" them from making their inevitable mistakes and expect ever-lasting gratitude in exchange.[23] These strains and contradictions were barely hidden beneath the surface; in fact, they absorbed the average Dutch woman's life. Often, however, she was forced to negotiate such tensions in solitude, because many a husband tended to be too tired after a long day's work to listen to the "petty" concerns of his wife and simply wished to drink his jenever and bitters in peace.

Most Dutch men working in private industry and commercial agriculture lived hectic lives. Chauvelot, in his vapid *Un roman d'amour à Java,* was no more charitable toward Dutch colonial men than he was to Indies matrons. He invented a comparable burlesque of dumb, grinning "Batavian giants with bulging muscles," who performed the most physically exhausting work all day but possessed "the mentality of laboring brutes: they rarely talk and think even less."[24] Other men resembled "ambulatory cash registers" and were in a frenzied rush to get rich.[25] But even a considerable number of Indies-born men — those who had no desire whatsoever to return to the Netherlands with a hefty bank account in order to retire in The Hague or a pretty spot "in the polder near the Waddenzee" — worked excruciatingly long hours. Civil servants, too, dedicated seemingly endless days to the strenuous task of colonial governance.

Whether they were blue-eyed newcomers from northern Europe with a reddish, freckled complexion — which made many Indonesians suspect they suffered from ringworm — or mixed-blood, "Indies" characters with olive-colored skins, European men engaged in a concerted effort to forge solidarity across the wide social spectrum of the European community. They incorporated their wives and daughters, too, in a herculean effort to make the white colonial enclave speak with a unanimous voice. However hard they tried, though, Europeans in the baroque social setting of colonial societies could not simply abandon their sensitivity to internal class distinctions. Despite their valiant efforts to pretend that social background did not matter in the Indies, perceptions of class differences, indeed, may have been magnified.[26]

Within the European metropole, members of the upper or middle class rarely met "the other ranks" on a tennis court, across a dinner table, or in social clubs. Women who had to shop for food themselves because their foothold in the middle class was precarious, might view the butchers, greengrocers, or milkmen they faced each day as their social inferiors. If their husbands were rich enough, they engaged "common" folk as servants, who were thus in a clearly circumscribed subservient position. It was true, of course, that in Europe — in the Netherlands or in any other European country — the signs and symbols of class were subtly articulated in sartorial display, style, and speech. But it was particularly the social geography of daily life that delineated class distinctions and imposed a palpable segregation between rich, poor, and people of the middling sort — or rather, between those Europeans who defined themselves as superior to any "other" fellow citizen they might look down upon. In Holland itself, the sensibilities of Dutch men and women were not habitually rankled by encounters with people they perceived as hailing from a dubious class background.

In the Indies, in stark contrast, such social interactions occurred on a daily basis. In big cities on Java or in Medan in northern Sumatra, humble women who had worked as seamstresses in Holland shared a bridge table or the dance floor with pretentious Dutch matrons of upper-class provenance. A middle-class woman with academic training and a lively intellectual imagination could face a dull, barely literate military wife as her only white female counterpart in a remote civil service post. Or in the fiercely competitive world of the plantation belt of Deli on the east coast of Sumatra, a Dutch lady with an impeccable patrician lineage or a wealthy family background might have to defer to a former shop girl she secretly despised as cheap and vulgar, simply because the latter's husband had ascended more rapidly up the administrative ladder of a rubber plantation.[27] As Marie van Zeggelen posed the question, with both anger and despair, about her previous experience as a military wife in a remote and rugged mountain district of Sulawesi in 1910: "why are women in the Indies always restricted only to each other's company and then, for Pete's sake, only on the basis of their rank ... not rank based on their respective ages, no, rank derived from the status of their husbands?"[28]

In their daily lives, "incorporated" European wives were saddled with the role of enforcing subtle hierarchical distinctions, making them protectors of the ontological wholeness of the colonial system, even if they had little to do with its political or economic construction.[29] As such, Dutch women served as foot soldiers — either willingly or with moral qualms — who were in charge of defending an elaborate colonial pecking order that placed indigenous women at the bottom and classified white men at the top. Hence, in their quotidian routines most *njonjas* in colonial Indonesia — as was the case with *memsahibs* in British India — gave concrete expression to a male-defined imperial agenda and knowingly contributed to "the ideological work of gender."[30]

White women's unequivocal exclusion from all official functions in either policy-making or the business world left them with little more than anxieties about servants or petty struggles over social credentials as conferred by men in public life. In the eyes of their spouses or fathers, white women's obsession with social pedigree confirmed, tautologically, the inherent frivolity of women and their unsuitability for any kind of official role. Women themselves, meanwhile, including those whose mother was Javanese but whose father had acknowledged them or those who had acquired European status through marriage, complied with the roles imposed upon them, although it was probably true that some among them acquiesced reluctantly. Willem Walraven, in this context, reported with anguish that one of his lighter-skinned daughters, the oldest one, was ashamed to be seen in public with Itih, her Sundanese mother, because she was certain that full-blooded European women would snicker facetiously and snub them.[31] Upholding the labyrinthine colonial patchwork of rank and status, in fact, bolstered white women's collective sense of superiority over native people, even if they had skin with the luscious warmth of café-au-lait which revealed their Indonesian blood, such as Walraven's daughter. Besides, European women's private conduct thus acquired serious public significance.[32]

In contrast to the British Empire, where English authorities rarely endowed Eurasians with "European" civil status, this was a normal practice in the setting of Dutch colonial society in Indonesia.[33] The universal "whiteness" of Dutch colonial rule should thus be taken with a grain of salt, since "European" identity was hardly reserved for people with white skins only. The offspring of Dutch men and Indonesian women, if fathers legally recognized them, were officially classified as "European," and Japanese residents of the Netherlands Indies had been categorized as "honorary Europeans" since 1899. Accordingly, the hybridized nature of Dutch colonialism in southeast Asia eloquently underscored the imaginary character of the quintessential "whiteness" of colonial mastery.[34] Although presented as a seamless web of "white" European rule, the Dutch community in the Indies incorporated, instead, both *Indo* (Eurasian) assistant clerks and blue-eyed plantation managers, or mixed-blood, rowdy infantrymen in the colonial army as well as university-trained civil servants straight from the Netherlands. In the Indies, these "white" men closed ranks in order to present a unified image to the colonized.[35]

While the racial identity of both Dutch and Indonesian women was inherently fluid because legal classifications could shift as a result of marriage, white men's racial status — as was the case with Eurasian or Japanese men officially categorized as "European" — was indelible and permanent. Thus, the legend of universal "whiteness" was based on a color-blind as well as a class-blind illusion and served as a marker of masculinity.

The fantasy of straightforward social equality among members of the "European" community, an old Indies hand intoned at the turn of the century, supposedly derived from the unique qualities of Indies life. "Here, people need each other more and develop more solidarity . . We only ask: how is the man himself? Is he a decent fellow, a fair human being, or a pleasant conversationalist? Is he a man who knows his mind and keeps his word? . We don't ask whether his father was a shopkeeper or if his grandmother was a charwoman. In the Indies we enlarge our perspectives, we become broad-minded and automatically more humane."[36] In short, colonial culture constructed a myth that it was not *bon ton* to discuss the social background of anyone endowed with an official "European" classification.

Hence, white men with dramatically different class origins in Europe, together with men born and bred in Indonesia whose skins often revealed a darker hue, hid behind a "curtain of impenetrable whiteness."[37] Collectively they erected a bulwark of ideological certainty about their "European" racial and cultural superiority over indigenous subjects. Grounded in masculine patriotism and a cult of the superior rationality of Europeans, this "white" homogeneity supposedly transcended all class differences.[38] Distinctions in social background, so the myth held, could be wished away as merely unpleasant memories of the stratified social world of Europe they had left behind. As Ladislao Szekely, a scion from a formerly well-to-do Jewish family in Hungary who had become a planter in Sumatra, wrote in the early 1930s: in the newly imagined community of the colonies "a new type of man emerged — all Europeans were of one nationality, they were *white*."[39] The blunt Indonesian Communist Tan Malaka, however, added a cynical twist: every ne'er-do-well Dutch wastrel, he scoffed, was a "potential lord of the manor (*grand seigneur*) in Deli."[40]

In the rough and tumble plantation culture of Sumatra's east coast, a motley crew of disparate Europeans reinvented themselves as either tobacco or rubber planters and forged a monolithic facade of white-skinned colonial mastery. This miraculous reincarnation occurred across the board, whether one could quote Caesar in Latin and Homer in Greek and proudly carried a double-barreled last name or an aristocratic title, or whether one spoke in a coarse dialect and hailed from *De Jordaan*, a working-class neighborhood of Amsterdam.[41] Even crude young men of very modest origins in Europe belonged automatically to the Indies "*noblesse de la peau*" (the nobility of the skin).[42]

In the heart of Sumatra's untamed darkness, filled with nothing but mud, crocodiles, and tigers, these supposedly egalitarian white chiefs converted the primordial forest (*oerbos*) into a haven of agricultural progress and a wellspring of "human happiness."[43] "Exuberant and perpetually youthful" Deli was lionized by some of its Dutch inhabitants as a land of legendary proportions where European men with protean strength engaged in "heroic hard work as well as the boisterous pursuit of pleasure."[44] But a fundamentally different judgment about the culture of Deli existed, too: "it was a wanton, frivolous (*wuft*) society in which money, liquor, and a lack of marital morality played the starring roles."[45]

Despite the powerful fiction of unambiguous, white-skinned *égalité* and *fraternité*, Dutch men continued not only to live with native women but also to marry both indigenous and mixed-blood women as a normal practice. As far as concubinage was concerned, the Dutch East Indies were hardly unique. White men had cohabited with native women in most colonial societies in Asia, Africa, or South America; in the words of Ian Buruma, colonial life, virtually everywhere, was "quite literally drenched in sex."[46] But in the Dutch East Indies interracial unions had developed into ingrained features of the cultural landscape: it was part of the "morals and customs of the land that unmarried men, whether highly or lowly placed," lived in concubinage.[47]

The *njai*, above all, was the mother of the large mixed-blood *Indo* population, as Hagar had been "the mother of Ishmael."[48] In addition to concubinage, as late as in 1925, 27.5 percent of all Europeans in Indonesia who married chose either native or mixed-blood spouses, a proportion that remained high until 1940, when it was still 20 percent. Besides, in the 1930s, barely 30 percent of the total population formally classified as "European" had actually been born in Europe.[49] Invariably, many among the remaining 70 percent of Europeans in the Indies had a number of Indonesian ancestors, especially in Java. Amidst a total population in the archipelago of ninety million in 1942, the sociologist Wim Wertheim has estimated that as many as eight to nine million inhabitants had one or more European ancestors, even if only 220,000 were officially endowed with European status.[50]

Many English-speaking visitors felt ill-at-ease in the hybridized social setting of Dutch colonialism in Java. The outward appearance of an easy-going social integration of *Indos* into Europeans' daily life perplexed them and many proper English folk found the visible results of several centuries of intermarriage and interracial reproduction shocking. In 1942 an American anthropologist noted that to "the British, half-castes in Indonesia are beyond the social pale."[51] But the Dutch were simply "realists": they recognized the absurdity of treating Indo-Europeans as a "minority" because hybridity comprised the inevitable result of colonialism, an English-speaking female journalist wrote in her Javanese travelogue in 1942. In comparison, she judged the "peculiar snobbery" of the British, who irrevocably barred Eurasians from all European social spaces in Malaysia or India, as narrowminded as well as misguided.[52] Having been seduced into the veneration of an Oxbridge pedigree or the "mighty mimicry" of its style, upper-class Indian circles shared in this typically British ambivalence about mixed-blood people.[53] As a modern-day Indian political scientist, Zareer Masani, confessed recently: one of the sorry signs of the "colonial hangover" was that "we, affluent Indians, [also] looked down upon the racially hybrid 'Anglos.'"[54]

In Java, in contrast, the life of Europeans had long since been intertwined with the indigenous world and constituted a mestizo civilization; the "Dutch" community in Java had gradually incorporated a medley of Javanese cosmology which intermingled with no-nonsense Dutch practicality, moral self-righteousness, and spiritual anxieties. We cannot deny, of course, that the social sensibilities of blue-eyed women and men, born and raised in Holland and still exuding the pungent smell of the cheese of their country of origin (*totok masih bau kedjoe*) became more prominent in the course of the twentieth century. The old Indies families of Java, "true gentlefolk" renowned for their legendary wealth as well as for their "instinctive courtesy and hospitality," represented a dying breed.[55] As the Indies writer Herman Salomonson (Melis Stoke) noted in 1935:

> The so-called 'Indies families' are becoming increasingly rare. Their imposing landholdings and grand estates lay idle and abandoned; either the Chinese have taken them over or they have been torn down. Their names live on as inscriptions on tombstones in Indies cemeteries. Their names also appear on the roster of foreign residents in elegant seaside resorts in Europe, or they are registered in the tax rolls among the highest taxpayers .. others have ended up in the *kampong*, the place of least resistance, where economic and social degenerates have landed among their descendants (*nakomelingen*).[56d]

Paradoxically, both the idea and the reality of the homespun and syncretic Indies cultural style lingered on until the outbreak of the Second World War, despite the convoluted efforts of right-wing *totoks* in the 1930s to create a clearer separation between all the different racial groups within the archipelago. For instance, a large number of long-term residents with unambiguously Dutch names had a swarthy, un-Dutch appearance, which they often attributed to a legendary, dark-haired Italian or Spanish ancestor in the family; besides, many among them viewed "Holland as if it were a planet in a different galaxy."[57] Some third- or fourth-generation residents of the Indies could not properly pronounce certain Dutch letters or words and spoke *petjoh*, or "crooked" Dutch, eliciting haughty giggles from nervous white women who had recently arrived from the European metropole.

Most seasoned old-Indies hands also tended to be more attentive to supernatural forces than many Holland-born people would care to admit. Indeed, newly arrived Dutch men and women, as well as Western-educated Indonesians, judged them as fatalistic, superstitious, intellectually dull and culturally alien. As late as 1937 the nationalist politician, Sutan Sjahrir, reported somewhat scornfully from his imprisonment on the island of Banda that a full-blooded European woman on the island lived in mortal fear of *tjoeliks* — fabled headhunters who allegedly collected heads on behalf of the government.[58] Sjahrir himself belittled anyone's belief in spirits or phantoms; in the late 1920s he had insisted categorically that no such things as ghosts existed, which clearly represented a "minority view" in Java at that time.[59]

When physical ailments struck, a typical Indies person would ingest native herbal medicines rather than consult a doctor steeped in Western medical knowledge. Besides, expertise about the medicinal properties of natural herbs and roots, whether real or imagined, was a fund of feminine knowledge and perhaps a source of Indies' women's superior ability in coping with their natural environment. Above all, long-term European inhabitants of the Dutch East Indies seemed to possess a different identity. They appeared more serene and naturally at home in both their own bodies and in their tropical habitat, as if they were immune to the sweltering heat and oblivious to the buzzing swarms of mosquitoes or the slithering armies of geckoes on the ceiling. And when the *tokeh* (tree lizard) sounded its "sonorous, deeply probing, human-like" call, many Indies people suddenly held their breath and counted excitedly, in silence, because if the *tokeh* called exactly seven times it would bring a heap of good luck in the future![60]

In an undiplomatic flight of fancy, the American Consul General in Batavia in the late 1920s, Coert du Bois, commented on the exquisite beauty of *Indo* women. In 1928 he wrote to the Secretary of State in Washington, D.C.:

> Half-caste women in the Dutch East Indies are fine physical specimens, varying in skin color from golden brown to nearly white, the constant characteristics being lustrous black eyes and wavy hair. To the average man, the young half-caste woman is physically more attractive than the pure-blooded Dutch woman. This is borne out by the fact that young Dutch bachelors marry half-caste girls with a frequency embarrassing to the conservative Dutch element.[61]

Du Bois seemed unaware of the prurience implicit in his report to the State Department in Washington D.C. Women whose complexion possessed a soft sienna incandescence and whose hair was shiny black comprised a particularly handsome "specimen" of womanhood, he insinuated, which male-defined aesthetic norms ranked higher than pallid, anemic "samples" of femininity. What British colonial residents in India might anxiously call a touch of the tarbrush, the Dutch colonial community in the Indies appraised as a *koelit langsep*: skin with the earthy tint of ripe olives or tangy ginger, with the savory glow of coffee with cream, or with the golden sheen of hammered copper. In pseudo-poetic French the complexion of Indies women was lauded as a *teint basané [avec] une petite couleur de chocolat-au-lait* (a tanned complexion with the color of milk chocolate) or, in the more problematic language of an English-speaking visitor to Java, with the shade of a "good willow calf shoe."[62]

In the eyes of many old-Indies residents such a pale chestnut complexion possessed an irresistible appeal in its own right. In her heart-rending novel, *De maan op het water* (The Moon on the Water), Elvire Spier recently described the sorrow experienced by a little blond-haired girl, born into an old Indies family in the Preanger (Priangan), whose lily-white skin no longer exuded the bronzed radiance of her mother's or grandmother's complexion. Her Sundanese great-grandmother commiserated with her anguish about her rosy-colored cheeks, because a *koelit langsep*, "a golden-colored skin is the greatest gift Allah can bestow upon a woman."[63]

But what the U.S. Consul General failed to mention in his remarkable missive to the Secretary of State was that in the past, some of the mixed-blood daughters of old Indies families were reputed to be the future heirs to considerable colonial fortunes, although this ceased to be the case in the twentieth century. Nonetheless, the secret hope for hidden family wealth may have added fuel to the romantic fire that burned in many a Dutch bachelor's heart, causing his passions to smolder more ardently in the company of amber-skinned Eurasian women with jet black hair than in the vicinity of chalky white, flaxen-haired "specimens" of womanhood.[64]

When Dutch women paired up with Indonesian men, however, the reaction of the European community was less than forgiving, even though it occurred much less frequently. Initially, the 1848 Civil Code for Europeans had stipulated that an Indonesian man who became the legal spouse of a Dutch woman would acquire his wife's European classification through marriage. At a juridical congress in Batavia in 1887, however, legal experts registered their principled objections to this regulation and advocated a policy reversal. Marriages between European women and *inlanders* were undesirable from an "administrative, social, and moral perspective," they claimed. The knowledge that she would be classified on a par with her Indonesian husband's civil status might prevent a pure-blooded European women from taking such an improvident step "if she attaches any value to her social stature as a European lady." Any white girl who willingly "married into the *kampong*" no longer thought or felt like an authentic, dignified European woman, the congress participants asserted, because in the eyes of proper white ladies such an action was both "shocking and degrading."[65]

Hence, a European woman who voluntarily abdicated her honor and humiliated herself by embracing a native groom deserved nothing else but to be surrendered to her own devices. Accordingly, article 158 of the revised statute of 1898, regulating mixed marriages in the Indies, formulated the issue succinctly: any "woman who concludes an interracial marriage acquires the civil status of her husband." In case of divorce and the division of marital property between spouses, the law associated with the civil status of the husband determined the nature of the proceedings.[66] While European men's "invisible bonds" of nationality remained intact regardless of their spouses' racial categorization, a white woman's "conjugal choice" could summarily suspend her membership in the European community.[67] Forty years later Professor Roeland Duco Kollewijn appended to these regulations an absurd coda, underscoring their Kafkaesque character. Indies' law stripped any run-of-the-mill Dutch girl, whether she lived in Leiden, Amsterdam, or Rotterdam, automatically of her European status as soon as she married a Javanese student. Instead, she was classified as an *inlandse* (native woman), Kollewijn wrote in 1939, even if she never set foot in the Dutch East Indies because she and her husband settled permanently in the Netherlands![68]

The relatively sedate debates in Dutch East Indies legal circles towards the turn of the century about the civil status of *inlanders'* Dutch wives echoed some of the shrill rhetoric surrounding the earlier efforts in British India to alter a racially discriminatory clause of the Indian Penal Code. The proposed amendment, known as the Ilbert Bill, would have granted Indian civil servants the right to exercise criminal jurisdiction over British subjects living outside the chief Presidency towns. The Ilbert Bill had unleashed a vitriolic controversy in 1883 and 1884, when opponents maligned the Bill because it would undermine the prestige of "pure and defenseless white womanhood in India," which might be subjected to the impertinent, even vile, attitudes towards women or the crude legal judgments of an ordinary Indian magistrate.[69]

In a similar fashion, the chairman of the legal congress in Batavia in 1887, Mr. M.C. Piepers, raised the possibility of scandal that could erupt if the blue-eyed Dutch wife of

Gender, Race, and Sexuality

Young Indo bride who married a man 30 years her senior (Coll. KITLV)

an Indonesian man had to appear before a native judge in a criminal case. Piepers, in fact, held the opinion that in any interracial marriage, regardless of its gender configuration, the higher civil classification should be conferred upon the lower-status partner.[70] But the other perspective prevailed, and the statute of 1898 codified the "de-Europeanization" of a white woman who, having fallen in love with and married an Indonesian man, had compromised her virtuous womanhood and, as a result, could no longer claim either the approbation or the civil protection of the European community.[71]

In his autobiography, the important early Indonesian nationalist Dr. Soetomo reported in 1917 that his marriage to a Dutch widow — who had come to Java to work as a nurse in an effort to overcome her sadness about the untimely death of her husband —provoked a reaction of derision and outrage among Europeans. His wife, he said, felt compelled to break off contacts with all her compatriots because in general "they did not respect Indonesians" although some amidst them might have treated her husband with kindness and esteem. Their marriage even enraged her beloved older sister, he wrote, who rebuffed him because he was an Indonesian man — a mere *inlander* — who had the gall to fall in love with her honorable younger sibling. They married in an Islamic ceremony, which some Indonesian nationalist comrades celebrated as a "Muslim victory." In his eulogy upon his wife's death seventeen years later, Soetomo commemorated her in poignant language: "As a Dutch woman, my wife loved freedom, justice, and equality, and so she could not endure a situation full of discrimination and she hated to see behavior that could stain the good name of her nation."[72]

The same consternation enveloped Maria Duchâteau-Sjahrir in 1932, when she walked through Medan, dressed in a sarong and kebaya, hand-in-hand with her Indonesian husband, whom she had married, too, in an Islamic wedding rite. Disturbed Europeans would stop her on the street to ask her whether she needed "help." It was true that Duchâteau and Sjahrir had adopted a cheeky, bohemian ethic during their student years in Amsterdam, and they may have wished to provoke or deliberately scandalize the self-satisfied members of a colonial community in Medan — *épater le bourgeois* — that remained hypocritical and racist, despite its pretension to epitomize the dynamic "brave new world" of Indies modernity.[73]

As a result, colonial government officials quickly raised the question of bigamy, since it appeared Maria had not yet properly divorced her ex-husband, Sal Tas, whom she had left behind in Holland. This same issue resurfaced again in the post-war era, when she was married to Sjahrir's brother, Sutan Sjahsam, and lived temporarily in the United States; authorities in The Hague wondered, in fact, whether she had properly surrendered her Dutch passport.[74] In the end Duchâteau and Sjahrir actually lived together as husband and wife for only five weeks, until the authorities put Maria on a ship back to Holland. Sutan Sjahrir's stunning letters to his wife in the Netherlands, though, full of wisdom and erudition written from the grisly prison camp in Boven Digoel and later from his exile on the island of Banda, contain a touching testimony to their short-lived and ill-fated marriage.[75]

The large group of Indo-Europeans that interracial unions had spawned, regardless of the gender configuration that had sired them, started to present a political quandary to the most reactionary Dutch *totok* residents of the Indies, as Consul-General Coert du Bois pointed out in 1928. Although proud of having both a first and a last name and protective of their exalted civil classification as Europeans, *Indos* earned only paltry salaries as low-level clerks in government service or in private industry. Registering his anxiety about the bleak future faced by his oldest mixed-blood son in 1930, Willem Walraven thought he would have few options other than to become an "office yokel or a stupid little railroad employee," because the chance to acquire a genuine profession was reserved for *inlanders* only.[76] When the Great Depression mandated a retrenchment in the size of the bureaucracy, however, or when the faltering profits of private industry ordained a reduction in the labor force, unemployment soared and the poverty among Indo-Europeans acquired heart-wrenching proportions. The growing pauperization of hordes of Indo-Europeans rendered the most "conservative element" of the colony, to use the U.S. Consul General's neutral phrase, more reluctant to embrace *Indos* as junior partners in the Dutch community.[77]

No longer quietly incorporated into the mestizo sociability of the eclectic Indies world, right-wing *totoks* began to view *Indos* as a fuzzy and troubling social category. Conservative Europeans in the colonial community, such as the members of the ultrareactionary *Vaderlandsche Club* (Patriotic Club), started to treat them with greater "racial prejudice" and humiliated them with a wide range of "petty tyrannies" and not so "petty indignities."[78] Because *Indos* increasingly obfuscated the equation of European citizenship with a superior social status that was grounded in relative affluence, they sabotaged the growing need of the *totok* community to taxonomize society into a rigid hierarchy of clearly delineated social and racial groups. "Racial consciousness," in other words, came to be viewed in an increasingly palpable fashion "as the lifeblood of colonial society."[79]

At more or less the same time the *blijver* (settler) community with a large proportion of Eurasians in its midst, began to claim a privileged position for its constituents. Because they were born and bred in the Indies, "they had a moral right to the land of their birth." While the Agrarian Law of 1870 had stipulated that Europeans were not allowed to own land but could only conclude temporary rental agreements and long-term leases, the leader of the Indo-European League (*Indo-Europees Verbond*) insisted in 1931 in the proto-parliament of the Dutch East Indies, the *Volksraad*, that those children "who catch their first glimpse of life on the soil of this country, should be able to retire peacefully in the *desa* with a house and a bit of land."[80] Native nationalists, quite predictably, derided this kind of double talk as a wily attempt to secure, literally and figuratively, the best of both worlds for Indies-born Europeans.

As Danilyn Rutherford has reported, during the 1931-32 session of the *Volksraad*, Muhammad Hoesni Thamrin disparaged the Indo-European League's claim as a devious gimmick "to keep all the privileges of their father's side, i.e. the rights granted him by the constitution, his economic standing, and other [racial] prerogatives," along with the entitlements of their mother's side, such as the right to own land, but none of her "obligations"; this would render the Indo-European "the most privileged of all races" in the archipelago.[81] During the 1935-36 assembly of the *Volksraad*, however, in a much more conciliatory appeal Thamrin urged Indo-Europeans to awaken from their delusions and to face the somber realities of the Dutch policy of divide and rule. A "shared sense of commonly borne injustice" should bind *Indos* to their native brothers and sisters. "In temperament [Indo-Europeans] are more Eastern than Western, [because] the blood of the mother's side flows more vigorously in their veins than that of the father."[82]

In the twilight years of Dutch colonial rule, the multi-colored mestizo society of the Indies acquired new meanings. The blind faith in the universal "whiteness" of the European community, despite the scores of mixed-blood members, lost some of its imaginative power. More palpably than in the past, *Indos* were represented as occupying a shadowy space between white and brown, between master and subaltern: "they roam back and forth between indigenous and European society .. and they comprise an unhappy, discontented, and harmful segment of the population."[83]

It was true that the *Encyclopaedie van Nederlandsch-Indië* had already referred in 1919 to "the dangerous pauper element" or to "crude and rough [*Indo*] paupers, who are the scourge of the *kampong*."[84] But their situation deteriorated markedly during the 1930s, when sophisticated natives with superior European training frustrated Indo-Europeans' livelihoods even further, by threatening to take the limited number of jobs in the bureaucracy or private industry that were traditionally available to them.[85] In a mere ten years, between 1928 and 1938, the proportion of Indonesians among both technical and administrative personnel grew exponentially.[86] And in an era of financial retrenchment, both the Indies public and private sectors were more than happy to remunerate Indo-Europeans on a par with native white-collar employees, since the latter commanded lower salaries. In this context, the social-democrat Marcel Koch made an invidious comparison with the policy of "Indianization" in British India. While in the south-Asian subcontinent this project really entailed the substitution of English employees with Indian workers at more or less the same salary level of the former, in *Indië* it merely meant a policy of paying Indo-Europeans the same pathetic wages customarily dispensed to native workers.[87]

Indos' growing impoverishment during the early 1930s made a segment of the reactionary *totok* community more overtly ambivalent about the large group of "racially desultory" Dutch men and women with creamy cinnamon-colored skins and eyes that resembled shimmering pools of blackness, to paraphrase the lyrical language of U.S. Consul-General Coert du Bois.[88] Despite the enduring habit of intermarriage, Indo-Europeans, especially in the eyes of Dutch residents on the far right of the political spectrum, had transmuted into a potentially disruptive group. Just like young Indonesians, scores of bare-footed *Indo* boys wandered through the streets, "dusty and covered with sores, with their heads shaven due to lice or scabies." When "facing proper (*nette*) people" young *Indos* were just as apprehensive as Javanese youths, because they also saw either "disapproval or pity" in Europeans' eyes.[89] Indo-European boys and men increasingly came to signify a form of seedy if "volatile" masculinity, and the cliché of skulking, shiftless, or swaggering *Indos* "who spoke crooked Dutch and were inept in their rivalry with full-blooded white men" came to be stored in the gloomy attic of right-wing Europeans' imagination. The conservative Dutch colonial community began to immure *Indo* girls and single women, too, within a discursive prison that charged them with either indolence or wanton behavior.[90]

As a result, an increasingly nervous colonial state — haunted as it was by free-floating anxieties about the mushrooming nationalist sentiments that sprouted up in even the most unpredictable nooks and crannies of the Indies political landscape — judged it critical, especially in Java, that the large cluster of Indo-Europeans was firmly ensconced in the European camp. Reactionaries with fascist inclinations, on the other hand, began to conjure up fantasies of relegating Indo-Europeans to an isolated space in a segregated social domain. *Indos* themselves, fearful of being overshadowed and, ultimately, displaced by Western-educated natives, clung to their European status with a fervor that made them passionately faithful to the Queen in Holland, even when their skin was just as brown as that of many full-blooded Indonesians. Hence the symbiotic, inclusive "Indies" nationalism that had inspired the earlier Indo-European organization *Insulinde* gave way to a more one-sided identification with the Dutch ancestry of their fathers. Indo-Europeans' solidarity with their blue-eyed progenitors placed them, willy nilly, in opposition to the burgeoning nationalism associated with their mother's lineage. While in British India Eurasians were becoming the zealous "foot soldiers of Ghandi," a self-congratulatory Dutch observer opined in 1930, "our" *Indos* serve as the staunch and reliable "bodyguards of our authorities."[91]

Ironically, in the course of the 1930s Indo-Europeans found a shaky common ground with reactionary Dutchmen in their advocacy of various colonization schemes.[92] Their collective panacea focused on a plan to relocate groups of destitute "Europeans" from over-populated Java by enabling them to colonize and cultivate empty spaces in the under-populated outer regions of the archipelago. A first exploratory spotlight had targeted the Gayo Highlands in northern Sumatra as a potential migration site. But then the uncharted, virginal land mass of New Guinea, which had long since functioned as the "stepchild" of the Indies administration, was hailed as an ingenious solution: a supposedly vacant universe that emerged as a "fata morgana."[93] One of the two rival Indo-European Colonization Societies — the *Vereeniging voor de Kolonisatie van Nieuw Guinea* (The League for the Colonization of New Guinea) — even composed a ballad, "Our New Guinea Song," with a refrain that celebrated New Guinea as "our new fatherland, dear to our heart. We offer you our blood; to you we pledge our yearning for freedom: we take an oath of loyalty until death [do us part]."[94] According to a scholarly analyst in 1935, the physician Johan Winsemius, the tendency to worship New Guinea as "The Promised Land" on the part of those Indies residents whose existence was full of economic injury and social injustice made eminent sense; the "cult" of New Guinea as an illusory fountain of milk and honey provided a diversionary tactic that offered hope and "consolation," thus making their harsh daily lives more bearable.[95]

European paupers or newly unemployed Indo-Europeans could move to the stone-age world of the *papoeas*, where the 1870 Agrarian Law had not yet been implemented and they could settle on their own lands. They would thus be able to escape from the joblessness and penury that tormented them in the heartland of the colony. In "empty" New Guinea wretched Europeans might recreate themselves as a kind of landed gentry in pristine territory. Rather than descending to the level of ordinary peasants, they would would maintain their "highly civilized, Western" identities and be reborn as self-sufficient yeoman farmers in "God's glorious tropical nature."[96] Ideally, this migration would duplicate the success story of north Queensland in Australia, where "the physical organisms of white Europeans adjusted harmoniously to the different biological stimuli of the tropical environment. Their effective adaptation to the sweltering heat is confirmed by a constant growth in the number of *tropenblanken* (white tropical residents) born to the third or fourth generation."[97]

Obviously, the discourses on the European colonization of New Guinea radically reversed the logic of such people as the anatomist Jacob Herman Frederik Kohlbrugge, who had suggested earlier in the twentieth century that many Europeans might be doomed to lose their procreative power in the tropics. Instead, the triumphant example of sturdy Europeans' adaptation to the environmental rigors of north Queensland portended that white colonists in New Guinea "will simply become a little smaller in stature, while their complexion may acquire a greater pallor and puberty may set in earlier." Nevertheless, the prediction was that Europeans who moved to New Guinea could physically "accommodate the forbidding climate completely by developing a resistence to diseases such as malaria and typhoid." At the same time, based on the Queensland example, "the fertility of white women will be boosted and they will likely recover their ability to give birth to children without any outside help!"[98]

In Java, European paupers or downtrodden *Indos* had been relatively deprived vis-à-vis their wealthier *totok* compatriots, but in comparison to the primitive Papuans they would always be rich, powerful, and superior. Rather than being feared as "potential patricides" in Java, to cite Ann Stoler's clever formulation, russet-skinned *Indos* might become "pastoral patriots" in New Guinea.[99] The reactionary Dutch colonial community, meanwhile, fantasized about the enclosure of an under-class of threadbare Europeans and *Indos* in their very own "sovereign circle," to be replenished with vibrant blood and vital expertise imported straight from Frisian farmers' stock. In the process, they would nurture the agricultural development of a primordial terrain by founding lucrative cattle ranches, dairy farms, and plantations in order to convert backward New Guinea into another Deli.[100] As an inducement, a well-heeled Dutch resident of exemplary "tropical Australia," in fact, offered in 1935 the spectacular price of one hundred Pounds Sterling as a reward for the first fifty kilos of genuine Dutch butter produced in New Guinea.[101]

Eventually, right-wing dreamers imagined, New Guinea might mature into an independent political unit under the direct tutelage of the Dutch crown. Hyper-ethical afflictions and an exaggerated concern with the welfare of the native population had rendered the Indies state weak-kneed in the face of the burgeoning nationalist movement. In New Guinea, the colonial state could reinvent itself and reclaim its masculine vigor, unencumbered by the effeminate empathy for the natives to which many teary-eyed ethical civil servants had surrendered. New Guinea promised to be yet another inhospitable arena in which the stubborn pioneering spirit of "Dutch" men and women in Asia would thrive, because right-wing *totoks*' fantasies about the colonization of New Guinea tended to reconfigure *Indos* as real, unadulterated Europeans. Besides, at some point in the future, the unspoiled jungle might be transformed into a Dutch equivalent of the "white Australia" of north Queensland or eastern New Guinea and evolve into "a second Netherlands in the Far East!"[102]

In the colonial debates about the proper place of Indo-Europeans, feminine figures of speech tended to allude to the lack of power of humble Javanese mothers who had given birth to mixed-blood children while working as a *njai*. Feminine metaphors also seemed to evoke a generic sense of subservience and weakness that was intrinsically related to the subordination of native culture to the omnipotent Western civilization of *Indos' Dutch fathers*.[103] After all, European men had the right to dismiss their housekeepers *cum* mistresses whenever they saw fit. Hence paternal tropes, in contrast, conjured up notions of authority and discipline, of "priggish love of order, hard facts, and hard work."[104] But the usage of such feminine and masculine metaphors both preceded and transcended the particular discourses about Indo-Europeans in the late colonial era. In the Netherlands itself, masculinity had also begun to function as a trope for "energy, boldness, and action" — in other words, for the kind of impetuous flair or irresistible panache (*élan vitale*) that Henri Bergson flaunted in France around the turn of the century.[105] At the same time, on the editorial pages of the nationally distributed daily newspaper *Algemeen Handelsblad*, the flamboyant Dutch journalist Charles Boissevain referred repeatedly to the theme of unbridled masculinity or "imperial machismo." Similar to Bergson in Paris or to the British novelist Henry Rider Haggard, who effused about the urgent need for a revival of "virile energy" or "soldier-like" briskness in the face of the feminine softness and "clap trap sentimentality" of Victorian England, Boissevain also created an imaginary opposite to the effeminate fragility that seemed to be sapping the strength of the Dutch nation:

> The heroic and death-defying courage of our navy and army in *Indië* constitute the salt that preserves the health and vitality of our national spirit. How do nations decline? They degenerate by surrendering in a fey, womanly manner to complaisance. Everything that undermines masculine courage and determination eats at the heart of the nation. In every civilized country, a thousand causes contribute to effeminate frailty and softness, which render many men as nervous as lapdogs and as pacific as [frightened] hares.[106]

Boissevain, in fact, appeared almost consumed with images of masculinity and feminity. Following his long journey through Java and the Padang highlands in 1907 and 1908, he described the exotic Indies fairyland with its gorgeous "golden-bronze" inhabitants in rhapsodic language. The Occident and the Orient, however, belonged together as man and woman. According to Boissevain, the West was strong, energetic, and logical while the East was weak, languorous, and emotional, and the Occidental husband should take his fragile Oriental bride by the hand and escort her through life.[107] But it is clear that these kinds of gendered figures of speech encoded all sorts of unequal social relationships that were not connected to female versus male identity *per se*. Rather, they constituted graphic symbols — universally recognizable — designed to register differences in power, moral style, or cultural sensibilities.[108]

Through the use of metaphor, the idea of gender was dislodged from the tangible realm of physiological distinctions between men and women and emerged, instead, as a narrative tool designed primarily to illuminate social hierarchies. The rhetoric of colonial dominion, in other words, employed a constantly changing array of gendered symbols to underscore differential positions of command and subordination or of intellectual self-discipline and irrational emotionality. In the process, Europeans' agency acquired a flexible range of meanings that was grounded in the fluid emblems and shifting sensibilities associated with either womanhood or manhood. At the same time, colonized peoples, too, were endowed with gendered characteristics; as such, feminine and masculine tropes functioned as integral elements of almost every aspect of social organization or political structure.[109]

The obsessive Boissevain in the European fatherland waxed effusively about the need for a reinvigorated masculinity, and he held up the intractable South-African *Boers* in Transvaal as archetypal examples of Dutch manliness and heroism. Invoking the other side of the gender equation, he endowed the East with a "typically" feminine frailty and thus forever in need of the powerful, masculine guidance of the West. At more or less the same time, however, ethical Dutch administrators in the Indies began to invert or destabilize these stereotypical gendered metaphors. Instead, they summoned gentle, maternal symbols in emphasizing their duty to nurture the welfare of indigenous people and to foster their intellectual and social development.[110] Again, this was hardly a development unique to the Dutch East Indies. Wherever Europeans asserted the validity of colonial rule, whether in British India, French Algeria, the Netherlands Indies or elsewhere, they routinely cited both their fatherly and motherly duties towards their native progeny. "You've done very wrong, but I am still your father and mother," English military officers in India might say to their native subalterns, while British civil servants were actually known as *Ma-Bap*, mother-father, to the residents of their districts.[111]

Discourses fashioned to vindicate colonial regimes suggested a mixture of maternal models of empathetic caring for the welfare of indigenous peoples as well as more explicitly paternalistic equivalents, which emphasized the rigorous training of throngs of native children. This language, it seemed, was invoked to represent colonial societies as a great happy family composed of benevolent, if stern, white-skinned parents who guided their brown-skinned offspring to basic literacy and psychological maturity. In general, Europeans' appeal to family imagery, across the board, intended to bolster the illusion of colonial societies as a natural, organic whole, and parental symbolism constituted a root metaphor that framed and defined the rhetoric of colonial mastery.[112] As Christiaan Snouck Hurgronje wrote critically in 1908, aristocratic Javanese rulers had become taciturn "children of the administrative family" whose brooding silence was imposed upon them.[113]

Hence, a maternalist idiom emerged in the twentieth century alongside a paternalistic vocabulary that was deeply entrenched in the Indies. Bound by a straightforward patrilineal lexicon, refined Javanese aristocrats who served as indigenous retainers of the Dutch East Indies state, for example, were expected to think of local Dutch civil servants as either a "big brother" or "father," whereas they should imagine the Dutch East Indies Governor General as a "grandfather."[114] As late as December 13, 1939, when the Governor of Central Java retired, the oldest Javanese member of the Provincial Council, Soerioadikoesoemo, bade farewell to the departing Dutch civil servant by commemorating that with R.K.A. Bertsch departed "a father, a good father, who had always seriously minded the well-being of his brood (*kroost*)."[115]

Most Indonesians with a formal role in the colonial administration, however, were fully aware that a female Queen on the other side of the globe required the greatest deference of all. The recognition that in the overall hierarchy of authority a female monarch rather than a male Governor General personified the most august symbol of power may have added an aura of ambiguity to Indonesians' understanding of European constructions of power, gender, and parenthood. But this ambivalence captured the ways in which colonial rule, whether knowingly or unconsciously, conflated masculine and feminine emblems of parental authority in order to envelop colonial governance in a comforting aura of family rhetoric.

Europeans' invocation of parental images in a colonial arena tended to appeal implicitly to a series of presumptions about motherhood and fatherhood and to the distinctive manner in which men and women wielded control over their flock of children. On the one hand, parental symbols established a taxonomy of authority, tutelage, and obedience; they served as recognizable signs of the differential positions of power of old and young —or, in a colonial setting, of knowledgeable grown-ups from Europe and ignorant native toddlers. In many cultural contexts, though, "colonial parents" often imposed differential expectations upon their native sons and daughters, and they perceived indigenous women, on the whole, as demanding more protection and requiring less disciplinary rigor than native men.

But the view that indigenous women were always in need of masculine guardianship often merged with a more ambivalent perception of "the natives" in general; as a result, the idiom of colonial mastery was awash in symbolic characterizations of both women, whether white or indigenous, and native people in general as emotional, irrational, irresponsible, lazy, or self-indulgent. Colonial residents depicted indigenous men as capricious children who delighted in foolish games of chance or dazzling religious rituals. At the same time they tended to portray women, both white and women of color, as caring only about ephemeral pleasures or not being educated enough to be interested in any aspect of life beyond the domestic realm. Colonial discourses thus associated femininity with weakness and frivolity; often, all non-white peoples, whether female or male, were identified with infantile helplessness, rendering everyone instinctually dependent on "patriarchal tutelage."[116]

As in other colonial societies in Asia, Dutch civil servants in Indonesia in the early twentieth century relished a sense of seemingly limitless authority in their administrative fiefdoms, although many among them had learned to express the meaning of their power in the "ethical" language of maternal nurturance. They repeatedly rationalized their august positions of command as a desire to educate their indigenous apprentices towards social maturity. Some idealistic civil servants hoped that in the not-so-distant future, the natives' growing intellectual sophistication might render them comparable to educated, Western folk, albeit in their own distinctive "Oriental" way. In many cases, however, civil servants' labors of love did not necessarily incorporate a vision of unequivocal Indonesian autonomy at the end of their arduous journey.

The Dutch colonial administrator J.H. Friedericy, stationed on the Indonesian island Celebes (Sulawesi) in 1924, for instance, wrote at the tender age of twenty-four to his parents in the Netherlands that he could not imagine "a career which imposes greater moral and intellectual demands on a person than the colonial administration." He enthused that "if we want to do our work well, we must immerse ourselves in the mores and customs of every [ethnic] group in every region .. We must be aware of kinship relations, friendships, enmities, and intrigues."[117]

In terms of expanding its administrative territory and solidifying Dutch colonial dominance in the archipelago, Friedericy must have done a fine job in the pristine region of southern Celebes, which had only recently been brought under Dutch control and was not yet tarnished by Western influences. A mere three years later he was the highest government official in a sub-district in southwestern Sulawesi populated by approximately 160,000 people. He lived and worked in a remote district in an adventurous all-male world, riding horses on inspection tours, adjudicating disputes, forging alliances with local chiefs, and gathering ethnographic data for a scholarly dissertation he would defend at the University of Leiden in 1933.[118] Before his marriage to a Dutch woman in 1927, Friedericy either lived alone, was a guest of another civil service family, or shared quarters with other bachelors, surrounded by an exclusively masculine world filled with government retainers and servants.

Most indigenous women, meanwhile, were less restrained by either a real or an imaginary boundary between private and public behavior. They worked on European plantations or in factories, cultivated rice paddies and other crops, helped bring produce to local markets, or they bartered and traded goods, because native women's contributions were crucial to the average family's survival strategies. In the late nineteenth century, however, some colonial voices began to reorient definitions of women's proper place on a Western pattern by incorporating *all* women, whether white or indigenous, into the domestic realm. In other cases, the so-called "essentialist" differences between Eastern and Western women served as a justification for employing Javanese women in coffee, tea, or sugar factories where they worked throughout the night.

The Dutch colonial regime in Indonesia in 1925, for example, discussed in the *Volksraad* the state's regulation of women's industrial work at night, a practice quite common in the ubiquitous and wildly profitable sugar, tea, and coffee industries in Java in the 1920s. Members of the *Volksraad* who supported the abolition of female factory labor at night applied Western conceptions of women's inherent domesticity and their primary duty of caring for their husbands and children; working throughout the night, said one Dutch *Volksraad* member, "affects not only mothers, but also their families adversely, because it compels women to neglect their small children and to become indifferent to the needs of their households."[119]

The opponents of the curtailment of nocturnal labor, however, appealed in classic "Orientalist" fashion to *adat* as a justification for the continued employment of women at night. Women's work, whether in the daytime or at night, they recited, was equal to men's labor and a perfectly natural institution. In comparison, the quintessential "nature" of Dutch women in the European metropole not only made them ill-suited for manual labor, especially during the night, but Western women also lived in a world where men had a deeply ingrained and "serious determination" (*ernstige wil*) to provide for their wives and families.[120] Indonesian men, in contrast, harbored neither the economic means nor the "inner impulse" (*innerlijke aandrift*) to take care of their families. As a consequence, the *Volksraad* members who agitated against a legal restriction of female factory labor at night claimed that all wives and children had to survive on their own, by whatever means.[121] This was an entrenched pattern in native culture, emissaries of European employers' associations announced with great fanfare. Any government interference would imply an unscrupulous violation of customary law: such a measure would undoubtedly encounter "serious opposition from the [native] population."[122]

Despite the Dutch colonial administration's sincere effort to honor the sanctity of indigenous traditions, their meanings could be renegotiated. Hence, as far as Indonesian women were concerned, the cultural grammar of the Dutch East Indies thus revealed a subtle interplay between two parallel discourses. The first one issued directly from Western notions about women's proper place. The second rhetorical theme, meanwhile, derived from constantly shifting European views on the connotations of indigenous norms and forms. Because the political and economic agenda of colonial rule was fluid and changed over time, the European assessment of native practices revealed a similar elasticity.[123] The shifting perspectives on the ways in which *adat* in Indonesia defined the position of indigenous women thus served as the basis for a Western rearticulation of "authentic" cultural norms. As a result, the colonial state's attempts to restructure tradition often entailed a redefinition of the status of women in society.[124]

As elaborated in Chapter Three, the position of non-aristocratic women in Java and various other ethnic cultures of the archipelago presented Dutch administrators with an intricate puzzle. Married women in many *desas* or *kampongs* not only wielded control over their own property, however trifling, they could also engage in legal proceedings on a par with men. In case of divorce, property was split more or less equally, while daughters and sons both had legal status as heirs. As the Frenchman Joseph Chailly-Bert had observed in 1900: "the Orient is full of Bluebeard stories, but in Java, it is the woman who holds the key to the mystery chamber. She is the manager of the household, the trader, and the cashier. She is the one who disposes, dispenses, and reprimands!"[125]

Javanese *adat* obviously granted "women of the people" certain prerogatives that were still elusive to European women. Even though the latter could be elected as members of city councils since the mid-1920s, they possessed less developed rights in marriage and divorce. Besides, relative to women in the Netherlands, who had received the right to vote in 1919, Dutch women in colonial Indonesia lagged behind: they could not participate in elections until exactly one year prior to the Japanese invasion of the Dutch East Indies.[126] The dapper explorer and self-appointed connoisseur of the female condition in many corners of the earth, Richard Francis Burton — who was, in fact, a dreadful misogynist — made a similar observation about Muslim women in the

Middle East; their legal status, he noted, was superior to those of middle-class women in England or British *memsahibs* in colonial societies.[127]

However, the Dutch industrialist's pronouncement in the *Volksraad* in 1925, when the abolition of women's labor at night was at issue, that Javanese culture did not inspire men's desire to provide for their wives and children, may have been a distorted mirror of women's more equal legal status within the household. In this particular context, the gender-based prerogatives of Javanese *volksvrouwen* (women of the people) served colonial objectives, even though Dutchmen would have balked at similar equitable arrangements for their own wives and daughters. The bottom line seemed to be that local tradition, as observed through an adaptable Dutch lens, should ensure the availability of women as a cheap source of labor, both day and night, whenever it was needed in the scores of lucrative sugar factories or tea plantations that dotted the Javanese landscape. At the same time, women's work supplemented the family income of indigenous households, thus legitimizing the low wages European employers paid to indigenous men.

In exactly the same year, however, the People's Council of the Dutch East Indies discussed, too, the question of female eligibility in city council elections. In the context of the parliamentary deliberations, representatives to the *Volksraad* proposed that it "was inconceivable to privilege European women over indigenous women," provided the latter were literate and paid taxes. Accordingly, delegates to the *Volksraad* suggested that native women should receive the same political rights as European women, if only because such entitlements would confer "educational benefits" upon indigenous women and their families.[128] In this instance, formal colonial opinion treated women, whether European or native, generically, and variations in the color of their skin or distinctions in their civil status did not supersede their gender.

Clearly, colonial administrators and *Volksraad* members also either endorsed or repudiated arguments about the "essentialist" differences between Western and Eastern women whenever it suited their purposes. The entanglement of the cultural idiom of the West with constantly changing European interpretations of the meaning of precolonial patriarchal traditions constituted a pliable colonial discourse. Official definitions of the existential realities of women's lives, both white and indigenous, were plastic, too, and could be reconfigured in order to mediate their interaction with either explicit or more diffuse colonial agendas.

As a consequence, the rhetoric of colonial legitimacy tended to conflate images of female malleability, whether of white or indigenous women, with those of indigenous men. The resulting imperial "master" narrative justified not only the power of white skins over brown ones, but asserted the pivotal significance of Western masculine knowledge and order over native ignorance and female unruliness. As Jean-François Lyotard has suggested, "virility claims to establish order," while femininity epitomizes "the compulsion to deride order."[129] Male colonial administrators, whether in Indonesia or in English-speaking colonial societies, often saw themselves as the embodiment of austerity, courage, and self-discipline. Native men, meanwhile, were caricatured as their emotional opposites — as velvety creatures who exuded a "comely, slender sensuality" or displayed a "feline strength and litheness" and who indulged in effeminate emotionality.[130]

The picture of white women as petty and brittle thus replicated the representation of all indigenous people, whether male or female, as weak or lacking self-restraint. As a consequence, colonial civil servants depicted and treated their native wards, across the board, as vulnerable and helpless — politically inept and preoccupied with only "trivial" matters such as home, family, and survival. But, at the same time, European rulers perceived native men as sneaky, subversive, or even potentially explosive; as such they required vigilance, because they could always run *amuk* and threaten the white-skinned colonial community's peace of mind.

White men's anxieties about protecting their wives and daughters from what Edward Said has called the "fecundity," the presumably relentless sexuality and promiscuous desire of indigenous peoples, whether in the Middle East, Asia, or Africa, mingled with growing concerns about race and burgeoning worries about preserving the rigid boundaries between the rulers and the ruled.[131] Even the most cultivated and enlightened European men in the colonies were convinced that indigenous peoples, both male and female, possessed sexual urges which were more "insatiable and uninhibited" than their own; moreover, they could less easily keep their physical urges in check. The gentle and languid sensuality attributed to Javanese men was one of the oft-recurring titillating themes in the colonial literature of the Dutch East Indies.[132] Other controversial *topoi* of colonial officials focused on what they judged to be aberrant sexual practices — such as homosexuality — which supposedly demonstrated the wide moral gulf between degenerate natives and healthy, upstanding Dutchmen.[133]

The *Encyclopaedie van Nederlandsch-Indië* stated matter-of-factly in 1919 that in the Indonesian archipelago "*paederastie* is widespread. The Balinese, under the name *menjelit*, indulge in this perversion in a major fashion ... In Atjeh, the *sedatis*, children between the ages of nine and twelve, who probably hail from the island of Nias, make a business out of participating in this vice publicly [like the *gandroengs* in Bali] ... On Madoera, pederasty occurs in public, without shame, and it is also practiced as a profession on Java."[134] Among the maritime Dayaks, the *Encyclopaedie* mentioned in its entry for priests, "the male shamans (*manang bali*) engage in [homosexual] prostitution and the male priests of the Dayak on the Barito river surrender themselves to unnatural vices ... in Olo-Ngadjoe, the male shamans are called *basirs*, and they sing and dance at festivals and submit their bodies [to the sexual use of men]."[135]

Concerns about these allegedly deviant sexual practices among men reached a fever pitch in late 1938, when they spilled over into an obsessive crackdown — a veritable "witch hunt," Margaret Mead called it — of homosexuals in the white-skinned colonial community.[136] On March 1, 1939, after the Dutch state had gone haywire by flinging accusations of homosexuality at a wide range of distinguished European men — arresting, among many others, such luminaries as Walter Spies, Roelof Goris, and Herman Noosten in Bali — the painter Rudolf Bonnet was in deep despair about the humiliation and anguish heaped upon many of his close friends. He wrote from Ubud, Bali, to the ethnomusicologist Jaap Kunst in Holland that "I finally saw with clarity what people are worth: either they are men in all their base, mean-spirited selfishness or they are men who, in an hour of danger, grow in spiritual resilience and the greatness of their soul."[137]

Bonnet further mentioned to Kunst that the Dutch police had also treated the Balinese in an unduly harsh manner, who "do not understand any of this. They look like frail, frightened birds: after all, a homosexual relationship is nothing special to them!"[138] As the American anthropologist Jane Belo reported in February, 1939, sexuality between men did not constitute a violation of Balinese *adat*: to be *salah mekoerenan* (wrongly married) entailed men's relations with animals, with young girls who had not yet reached maturity, or with higher-caste women. As a result, Belo wrote, the Balinese thought that "the whole white caste" had gone stark raving mad.[139]

Indonesian women, too, were often portrayed as seductive, robust, and completely "natural" in their sensuality — in other words, very different from the ethereal sexuality attributed to victorian Dutch women who arrived from the European metropole. In his attempt to explain the prevalence of interracial coupling between white men and native women, a Dutch psychiatrist gave such liaisons a pathological spin by ascribing white men's physical yearning for brown-skinned women — especially among the many men "who are sadistically inclined" — to the "masochistic tendencies" prevalent among indigenous females. The lack of masochistic sentiments in Dutch women, wrote Dr. Swart Abrahamsz in a newspaper article at the turn of the century, "drives Dutch men into the arms of perennially masochistic native women."[140]

Many Indonesian women also worked for European families as a nursemaid or nanny (*baboe*). In the eyes of European children, the *baboe*'s devotion to them was infinite, and many Dutch men and women who were born and raised in Indonesia remember their *baboe* with tenderness and longing. Dutch children in the Indies lived like little "princelings," Louis Couperus remembered.[141] From the early days, when the *baboe* carried Dutch babies around in a batik *slendang* (shawl), until young adolescents enrolled in an Indies HBS (*Hogere Burger School* or European High School) or sailed off to the other side of the globe to go to school in the Netherlands, she gave them a vicarious sense of intimate belonging to the indigenous world. Thanks to their *baboe* Dutch children made friends with native boys and girls. Fair-haired children learned to play Indonesian games, rode fiery little horses along mountain paths or became experts in *pencak*, a unique Indonesian form of the martial arts.[142] Other rosy-cheeked boys and girls mastered the art of flying fighter kites and "building bird traps, of fishing in brooks along the rice fields and swimming in the local river."[143]

Through their *baboe*, who routinely was "the primary mother figure," Dutch children became aware of "the agility and cruelty, the naturalness and obscenity" of native culture — or, from a distinctly male perspective, its seductively "erotic" nature.[144] The *baboe* instructed Dutch boys and girls as to the ways of the natural world and delighted them with gossip or regaled them with scary stories about phantoms and spirits. She might tell wide-eyed European children about *kuntilanak* or *pontianak*: ghosts in the guise of old women, who descended from trees during the rainy season in order to steal children. Or she may have warned Dutch boys and girls, trembling with a giddy combination of excitement and fear, that after death good people no longer haunt the world but that bad peoples' spirits continue to hover and roam around: the latter could always extend "a withered hand from the grave to reach for a child's soul and cause mischief" in the daily lives of parents or brothers and sisters.[145] In sum, the *baboe* familiarized blue-eyed children with her "being different" (*anderszijn*) and exposed, at the same time, their "otherness" (*andersheid*), while preserving a delicate sense of power that derived from her control of the very "process of initiation."[146]

Not infrequently, Dutch wives, recently settled in southeast Asia, were leery of the many Indonesian women who, as *baboe*, had captured, even monopolized, their children's love and affection, or who had served as concubines of Dutch men. Many big-boned, pink-skinned, and anxious Dutch *njonjas*, physically ill-equipped to cope with the hot and humid tropical climate, were dependent on their small, graceful native servants to teach them how to run a household, to learn to speak Malay, and to understand local *adat*. More often than not, these relationships were characterized by mutual distrust and apprehension.

Predictably, a favorite motif of Dutch colonial fiction at the beginning of the twentieth century was the murderous revenge of the former *njai*, who had been sent back to her family, often with one or more children and either with or without some financial remuneration, after her Dutch master *cum* lover had married a Dutch woman he had met, for instance, during his first home leave in the Netherlands. In some of these narratives, the guileless Dutch wife confronted, with great moral anguish, the physical reality of her husband's illegitimate Eurasian offspring. Once in a while these children tugged at a white woman's heartstrings and aroused maternal feelings to the extent that she insisted they should be raised in the household of their European father.[147] In other novels the Dutch wife could not bring herself to embrace such mixed-blood infants, because the memory of their native mother paralyzed her. But the more gothic plots of colonial fiction conjured up an ex-concubine, banished to a nearby native village, who engaged in a conspiracy with a *njonja*'s new household servants to cast spells, to invoke spirits, or to contaminate an innocent Dutch mistress's food. Natural poison and black magic (*goena goena*) played a prominent role in this theatrical scenario of rejection, envy, retribution, and perhaps contrition in the end.[148]

The most sensational Dutch colonial fiction was equal to the grand melodrama of a Puccini opera. A good example among many others was Thérèse Hoven's sappy novel, written in 1892 under the pseudonym Adinda, *Vrouwen lief en leed in de tropen* (Women's Love and Sorrow in the Tropics), even if it possessed none of Puccini's melodious beauty or dramatic allure.[149] Hoven tells the sorry tale of a naive Dutch girl's confrontation with the perfidity of Dutch East Indies culture; as was presumably true for many Indies marriages, her bridal wreath very quickly turned into a prickly crown of thorns.[150] Her beloved husband, whom she met and married in a whirlwind romance while he was on home leave in The Hague, proved to be an amoral scoundrel. Before his departure for Europe, he had evicted his Madurese *njai* and their young son. But after his return to his administrative post on a coffee plantation in eastern Java with his trusting Dutch partner in tow, he rehired his ex-mistress as the family cook and indulged himself by using her as an occasional lover when his dainty wife was away on a trip.

Not surprisingly, the humiliated former concubine was bent on taking revenge, as a stereotypical woman from Madura was wont to do. She exacted retribution by slowly trying to poison both her master and his delicate blond bride with tiny bamboo fibers added to their daily *rijsttafel*, only to commit suicide in the novel's final unraveling. Because the neophyte Dutch wife could not yet tolerate spicy, Indonesian food and ate a typically Dutch fare of meat and potatoes instead, she was spared her husband's noxious fate and emerged as the novel's tragic heroine. The virtue of the sugary sweet Dutch woman overcame the treachery of Indies life: she adopted the motherless son of her murdered husband, and returned to the Netherlands with a solemn promise to raise the mixed-blood orphan as her own and as an equal to his little, blond half-sister![151]

The *baboe*, too, became an embattled character in some of the written folklore about colonial life, especially during the twilight years of Dutch colonial rule in the Indies. Occasionally the *baboe* was represented as the unwitting nurturer of the dictatorial instincts of five-year old Dutch bullies, who forced her to cater to their whims and wishes.[152] Rudyard Kipling wrote in a similar fashion that the subservient devotion of native nursemaids in British India produced a sense of "omnipotence" in English children.[153] Others began to portray the *baboe* as an outright diabolical figure, and held her responsible for the undisciplined wildness and precocious sexuality of some European boys and girls growing up in the Indies, owing to the "repulsive methods," such as fondling their genitals, she reputedly employed to comfort children when they cried or were in distress. These techniques, outraged Dutch writers intoned, "although quite commonly used among indigenous people themselves, are repugnant according to our Western standards."[154]

In English-speaking colonies, the allegedly superior fecundity and deep-rooted sexual intemperance of the native world — called "the black peril" — was represented as an ever-present menace of white women's contamination by indigenous men's sensuality.[155] In India, some British residents depicted the "unsavory" carnality of native men or the raucous celebration of sexuality in some Hindu festivals as ready, at any time, to invade and assault — or perhaps worse, seduce — virtuous, white womanhood.[156] Due, in part, to the long-standing tradition of eclectic blending of Dutch and native sexuality in colonial Indonesia, however, an equivalent "brown peril" was not a theme that reverberated with the same aura of dread as in India. Dutch masters viewed Javanese and most other native men as inherently gentle and not prone to commit brazen acts of aggression —unless they ran *amuk*, and then, popular wisdom proposed, they tended to murder rather than rape. Besides, fathers may have assumed that the 1898 policy of forcing Dutch women to relinquish their hallowed European status if they embraced Indonesian men would make self-protective white girls think twice before indulging in such impulsive conduct. These kinds of nebulous prejudices soothed the Dutch community's masculine fears of Indonesian men inserting themselves into the fragile sexuality of their fair-skinned wives, daughters, or sisters.

Dust jacket of Madelon Szekely-Lulofs's novel De andere wereld (Amsterdam: Elsevier, 1934)

Nevertheless, Dutch women were sometimes blamed for behaving improperly and thus undermining white prestige; even if it occurred very infrequently, any romantic liaison between Dutch women and Indonesian men provoked uproar and outrage. At a more mundane level, Europeans' homes in the Indies lacked privacy and the "hostile tropical world entered the house through open windows, doorless spaces, and gaping holes," which made many women inside feel exposed and defenseless, while some among them became angry and defiant.[157] In the mind's eye of the male guardians of European imperialism, the heat or loneliness rendered a number of white women, who would otherwise be demure, less so in their dress and demeanor. As such they could inadvertently tempt even the most timid and placid native man who, as a result, might lose control over his sexual impulses. Albeit in a less anxiety-ridden way than in British India, the control of white women's behavior in Indonesia, presented under the guise of protecting them from the specter of its pollution by indigenous men's sexuality, also became a subliminal element of Dutch colonial mastery.

It was true that the increasing number of white women who settled in the colonies at the beginning of the twentieth century provided companionship and brought the emotional comforts of "home," but their arrival augmented anxieties, too.[158] One of the lingering mythologies of British colonialism suggested that European colonialists and natives had coexisted in brotherly harmony until white women appeared in greater numbers and became the shock troops of racism by insisting upon a radical *apartheid*.[159] Some modern historians and contemporary English novelists, in fact, have vilified white colonial wives and daughters as the most "obnoxious" characters in the annals of European imperialism.[160] Similarly, the prolific Dutch journalist Rudy Kousbroek has recently paid much attention to the catty, wanton, and racist behavior of European matrons (or *mems*) in colonial societies.[161] Focusing mostly on European women in the Dutch East Indies, but with an occasional comparative glance cast at British India, he has scorned the idea of women's inherent "loving kindness" or their innate "tolerance of the differentness of others" as nothing but a self-serving invention of modern feminism.[162]

If we tone down his somewhat self-consciously hyperbolic language, Kousbroek is certainly correct when he argues that Dutch women became active defenders of their European social standing and their own preeminence relative to the native population. But whether European *mems* in Indonesia committed crimes of cruelty and racism that were more odious than those of their husbands or fathers represents an assertion that is a bit more problematic. Few, if any, Indies matrons physically beat or caned their domestic servants, even if they slapped them in the face, on occasion, or shamed them psychologically and disgraced their honor. Because of native servants' involvement in the intimacy of Europeans' family life, their subaltern status within colonial society was more overt and perceptible than, for instance, that of poverty-stricken peasants in the countryside. In their daily lives, peasants working in rice fields and living in villages encountered Europeans only sporadically, if at all.

However, not even the most racist and arrogant Dutch woman in the twentieth century had the authority to force landless peasants in eastern Java to work excruciatingly long hours in a sugar factory and pay such a measly wage that they rarely ate more than a bowl of rice with a sad-looking sprinkle of vegetables or dried fish. Nor did any European woman torment Javanese coolies on tobacco plantations in Sumatra if they seemed indolent or unresponsive. But most white women obliged as complicit spectators; their definitions of virtue and morality did not prompt much resistance to the exploitation and human suffering intrinsic to the colonial system. The average woman, in other words, endowed the imperial relations of command and subordination with the same gloss of normalcy or inevitability as men.

It was probably true that many members of "the genus of Indies madams (*Indische mevrouw*)" spent a lot of their time bickering about pedigree, prestige, and propriety. Mostly trivial conversations brightened their daily lives, which unfolded amidst servants who sometimes frightened them and whom, in return, they may have treated with cool disdain. In a different locale but a comparable social setting, the pioneering American anthropologist Hortense Powdermaker mentioned in the 1930s that she

Gender, Race, and Sexuality

Javanese mother and son. From: Justus van Maurik, Indrukken van een totok. Indische typen en schetsen (Amsterdam: Van Holkema & Warendorf, 1898)

would occasionally escape from her isolated research site off the coast of New Guinea to visit with Australian planter families, only to be bored to death by the vapid talk of planters' wives. During dinner, she wrote, the women would spend the entire evening discussing "with great seriousness a new pattern for sewing their husbands' pajamas."[163]

A considerable number of jittery *totok* wives tried to keep the incomprehensible social world of the natives at bay, because it was filled with anxieties about ghosts perched in treetops or spirits hiding behind bushes. Other practices such as polygamy or boys dressed in female clothing vying for the sexual attentions of men were overtly terrifying. Newly arrived white women in the colonies, whether Indonesia, Australian New Guinea, or India, tried to withdraw into the safe harbor of a lily-white domestic scene. They hoped to find solace in a sheltered home life, even if it was characterized by a mixture of fear as well as "a tedious daily routine of mind-numbing boredom," which comprised the ragged edge of colonialism.[164] In some instances, the "burden" of white men in colonial societies was refashioned as a problem of white women's dread, *ennui*, or "infidelity, which, in turn, was a sort of infection [induced] by loneliness and strange places."[165]

Raw and palpable fear, for instance, permeated a telegram that 167 women from various plantations on the east coast of Sumatra dispatched to Queen Wilhelmina in the Netherlands after a Javanese coolie had murdered a white planter's wife by entering her house and slashing her throat with a large butcher's knife on July 6, 1929.[166] The telegram, full of pathos, appealed to the Queen's maternal instincts:

> We, Your Majesty's faithful subjects and residents, outside of all politics, deeply convinced by our womanly instincts of the meaning of these actions, beseech your Majesty, as the mother of our people and as our high hostess, to change the regime, in order to prevent bloody conflicts between our men and fathers and the laboring people who are on the road to insubordination and unruliness, a condition which will bring indescribable grief.[167]

The 167 women signed their telegram to the Queen with the abject greeting: "[from] your Majesty's loyal women subjects .. who are living on the lonely plantations in sorrow and fear."

Despite their claim to be "outside of all politics," the women nonetheless repeated their husbands' negative opinion of Governor-General De Graeff who, in the eyes of hard-boiled European tobacco and rubber planters, was too soft on the natives.[168] They also reiterated a score of mythologies about indigenous men, who allegedly were on the road to mutiny and uncontrollable violence. Their knowledge about Chinese and Javanese coolies, though, was mostly derivative, because white women themselves rarely came into close personal contact with plantation workers. Since the only indigenous men they actually knew were household servants, the women's reference to the unruliness of contract laborers was merely an echo of their husbands' opinion.

When European women entered an alien and intimidating world such as the large tobacco and rubber plantations on Sumatra's east coast or an outlying civil service post, they confronted loneliness, desperation, or fear, compelling them to muster inner resources some did not possess. Absolutely nothing in the previous experience of young women, frequently born and raised in provincial Dutch towns — where only the most conventional and perhaps narrow-minded standards of propriety had guided their existence — prepared them for the emotional and social seclusion of colonial life in rural parts of Java or the outer regions. While surrounded by indigenous people everywhere, both within the home and outside, their feelings of being cast off and abandoned, of course, derived from their yearning for "white" companionship. It was an existence of "unbearable monotony and cruel solitude" in the most "God-forsaken corners of the earth," remembered a former civil service wife who had been stationed in rustic outposts in the Moluccan islands, western New Guinea, and the highlands of Sumatra in the 1920s and 1930s. She said she had to carry loneliness and homesickness with her like a sword of Damocles, wherever she went. In the sweltering tropical heat, she wrote afterwards, she idealized the cold climate of her country of origin and tended to forget about "the frozen faucets and broken pipes of winter." She simply could not reimagine "the frost-bitten feet and tingling fingers of a bone-chilling cold winter's day, or the ferocious North Sea wind that literally took one's breath away." Instead, in the stifling silence and melancholy blackness of a tropical night, she could only recall the refreshing rain of Autumn and yearn for "the well-lit shop windows of a quaint Dutch city street, for traffic, noise, radios and movie theaters."[169]

Other Dutch-born wives of civil servants stationed in similarly remote districts in Borneo (Kalimantan), Celebes (Sulawesi), or the islands in the eastern archipelago, or women who followed their engineering husbands to the oil fields of south-central Sumatra or the tin mines on Singkep or Bangka, were bewildered by their physical environment. Some of them felt intimidated by a scenic landscape that was dotted with smouldering volcanoes, forever threatening to erupt, as Tamboro and Krakatau had done earlier and Kelut, Agung, and many others would do later. Thunder and lightning as well as torrential downpours returned every rainy season to drown life and limb. The vibrancy of the tropical forests resplendent with unfamiliar vegetation and filled with snakes and many strange creatures petrified other women, especially since nearby jungles broadcast a perpetual concert of piercing sounds emitted by exotic birds or ferocious beasts one could not even see.

European wives, meanwhile, lived in permeable tropical houses and stayed behind with servants as domestic companions, because their husbands went either on inspection tours or put in longer stints in faraway tin mines. Whether they had any medical training or not, Dutch women often functioned as the local "doctor" in districts with no physicians; they ran impromptu medical clinics which brought them face to face with the physical afflictions and habits of the native population, which they viewed, on occasion, as either incomprehensible or shocking.[170]

Fear and isolation — and their antidotes, courage and companionship — were the crucibles of white women's emotional and social lives. Some Dutch women relished their autonomy and were thrilled to be liberated from the suffocating social rituals — or, as they said, the hypocrisy — of the European community in cities on Java. Many colonial wives shed their victorian corsets and stockings with a sense of relief and reveled in the physical freedom of wearing only a loose batik sarong. Others rejoiced in the novelty of their isolated residence and nourished a genuine interest in native culture. Some *totok* wives, however, could not overcome a palpable nostalgia for the flat Dutch landscape of their childhood with its weeping willows, windmills, gabled rooftops, and chilly climate; a sizable number among them continued to fantasize about the coziness of basking in the glow of burning embers in a fireplace located in their ancestral home on a cobble-stoned street in a picturesque Dutch town.[171] Others plain and simply lost their minds. A wife of a low-level civil servant in Central Borneo, for example, reported in the early 1930s that her predecessor had "gone absolutely insane from the loneliness."[172]

Flink, dapper, kordaat, kranig (sturdy, plucky, fearless, gutsy) — endless variations on the theme of personal courage — were the words men used to describe wives who were sturdy enough to withstand the solitude and who could flourish regardless of the psychological hardships of life in remote areas.[173] Even though men have traditionally appropriated courage as an exclusively masculine attribute (one Dutch verb for being courageous, in fact, is *zich vermannen*, which means literally "to be[come] like a man"), women who thrived in the isolation of colonial outposts received a red badge of courage — or rather, as Virginia Woolf called it, "the red feather" of bravery.[174]

Although Dutch female missionaries were rare in colonial Indonesia — the Dutch Missionary Society did not formally appoint women evangelists until the second decade of the twentieth century or so — British colonies gave some bold and strong-willed European women a chance to dedicate their lives to teaching, nursing, and missionizing among indigenous peoples.[175] Despite their good intentions, such European women nonetheless contributed to a male-defined imperial agenda by representing their female students as downtrodden and blameless victims of native men's destructive social practices or sexual perversions.[176] In India, for instance, a variety of tough-minded *memsahibs* devoted their idealistic efforts to winning over the souls of their young female pupils and, in the process, they ran hospitals and managed schools. In Africa, too, some English women became serious ethnographers and wrote about female ritual knowledge, marital practices, or the social position of women in particular ethnic groups. Other English women emerged as crusaders for reform, lobbying legislators on behalf of the abolition of what they perceived to be horrific practices such as cliterodectomy or polygamy. But in the process, they displayed an often unquestioned faith in the superiority of Western standards of sexual propriety, thus inadvertently widening the colonial divide between white and native women.[177]

In the rare case that an Indo-European Women's Association in colonial Indonesia allowed for the inclusion of full-blooded native women as well, the latter were permitted to join provided they could "energetically contribute to the goals and progress of the organization," which was to protect the status of "European" women and girls in the Indies. This criterion excluded the tens of millions of Indonesian *volksvrouwen* in the archipelago; it probably implied that only a few wives of low-level native civil servants requested membership, perhaps because they thought they might be able to enhance their husband's career in the colonial bureaucracy through personal contacts and female friendships.[178] It was not likely, though, that refined, *priyayi* wives would have seized the opportunity to mingle with "European" women whom they tended to perceive as the female descendants of Dutch men and their common-born native housekeepers. Hence, such an organization preserved the great divide between white and native women.

Clearly, the position of European women in Indonesia and other colonies was rife with contradictions. They were not merely silent fellow-travelers of their fathers or spouses, who were the ones to codify the rules of colonial domination. White women, in fact, performed crucial roles as supporting actresses in the ceremonial display and ostentatious rituals of Western superiority; a large number of European women were enthusiastic purveyors of imperial culture in their own right, even if some among them did so with a troubled conscience. Colonial wives were indispensable to Europeans' assertion of greater cultural refinement and moral integrity, despite the fact that women were mostly marginal to the never-ending process of fashioning or reshaping the political agenda or statutory content of colonial traditions.

Colonial men mobilized their wives and daughters to shoulder the task of upholding the internal hierarchy and moral dignity of the white community, but were quick to blame women for any reputed loss of white status. Since women were held responsible for preserving the unpolluted whiteness of the European community, their private conduct in the domestic realm was converted into a symbolic public phenomenon that affected the very foundation of colonial mastery. While Dutch men could live with native housekeepers and sire mixed-blood children without too much moral censure, the colonial community tended to vilify or ostracize a Dutch woman who became sexually involved with an Indonesian man.

It was a situation that yielded a curious paradox. Dutch women's daily lives transpired in a domestic universe that was carefully segregated from the political and economic world of men. But the male-defined meanings attached to their ultimate private actions, instead, conjured up a permeable boundary between the private and public sphere, because female sexuality had serious public consequences. As far as their paramount intimate choices were concerned, the realms of private and public were reframed as fungible categories, because European women's proper sexual behavior, less so than men's, was charged with upholding the untainted whiteness and moral dignity of the colonial community.

This irony suggests that white women's private spaces were never truly private, since husbands or children could almost always enter them whenever they pleased, while the masculine "gaze of empire" defined the significance of white women's sexual decisions and marked the perimeters of their personal universe.[179] Dutch men, meanwhile, continued to sleep with or marry Indonesian and mixed-blood women with impunity, until the bitter end of Dutch colonial rule in the Indonesian archipelago. Thus, the intimate demeanor of white as well as indigenous women in the Indies was embedded in, or intertwined with, an official imperial project.

As colonial culture became obsessively concerned with making visible the palpable difference between ruler and ruled, and did so increasingly through spectacular pomp and circumstance, women's acceptance of more rigid sexual boundaries between the "European" community and native society was essential.[180] Since both Dutch and Indonesian women's racial identities were far from immutable and could change in the wake of marriage, interracial unions became a growing cause for concern among colonial policymakers in the twentieth century.[181] The control of the private "space" of female sexuality and child-bearing was therefore crucial to the unchallenged Dutch mastery of the political and material resources of the colony.[182] In sum, the increasing surveillance of not simply the sexuality, but above all the reproductive capacity, of both white and native women became part and parcel of an overall concern with reserving for the European community the material spoils of victory of colonial rule.

It is hard to deny that some aspects of the particular story of Dutch women in colonial Indonesia were distinctive. The long history of cohabitation, relatively free of moral reproach until the year 1900 or so, between Dutch men and Indonesian women —and the eclectic, multi-colored Indies civilization it had spawned— found no parallel in English-speaking colonial societies. It was a culture that valued sociability and treasured the display of knowledge about the colonial "other," especially in Java. Many Europeans in the colonial heartland knew something, however shallow their insights may have been, about *adat* and native manners and morals, about shadow puppets, gamelan music, herbal cures, or about the popular belief that magical powers hovered over the wondrous natural world in which they collectively lived. In few other colonial societies, moreover, was it considered normal for white women outside big cities to wear native dress in their daily routine. British colonial matrons in India, even those stationed in the remotest corners of the empire, would have been stunned and perhaps horrified if one in their midst would have come calling at tea time wearing an Indian sari.

At the same time, however, the experience of Dutch women in Indonesia is comparable to that of European women in most other colonial societies, whether elsewhere in Asia or in Africa. Except for a few rebellious free spirits among them, most white women were ensnared in a net of behavioral prescriptions which their fathers, husbands, and sons had woven and put in place: a set of standards that dictated women's private conduct and endowed it with major public significance. While they may have spoken different languages or harbored very different social styles and cultural sensibilities, almost all white women in a colonial setting were voluntarily on center stage in supporting, ceremonial roles that bestowed legitimacy upon the unfolding imperial drama.

The postmodern emphasis on difference and fragmentation — or on the uniqueness of each locality — has made us wary of the totalizing tendencies of some feminist disquisitions about *the* female condition, in particular, and the globalizing proclivity of Western humanistic scholarship, in general. Obviously this new sensibility should be applauded even if it sometimes creates the impression that historians should return to an earlier empiricist mode that celebrated the singularity of each historical event by glorifying history's inherent diversity, anarchy, and cacophony of voices. But the new faith in knowledge derived from "the local" is not simply old wine in new bottles. Neither is it a call to return to the cultural relativism of earlier generations of anthropologists, or to a historiographical style that merely wishes to provide a taste of the texture of a particular historical moment in a narrowly bounded place. Instead, the project of gender and colonial history aims to establish taxonomies of power and genealogies of knowledge that illuminate the contestation, as well as the collusion, implicit in each particular colonial encounter.

However, the piecemeal truths and the patchwork of endless differences between specific microcosms — what Alan Liu has aptly called "the romanticism of detail" — have meanings that transcend their narrow confines.[183] When Europeans, whether from Holland, England, or elsewhere, observed native traditions through an imperialist looking glass, they tended to see only what they wished to see. Often, when they did not understand or were frightened by indigenous customs, they reconfigured both the reality and significance of such cultural practices as an imaginary projection of their own interests. The cultural grammar of colonial rule, in other words, assigned meanings that rose above the particularity of a specific locale. Virtually everywhere, colonial cultures imposed upon white wives and daughters — whether their bodies were tall and gangly or short and stocky — the duty to defend the social pecking order and to express the moral superiority of European civilization in every aspect of their daily lives. Indigenous women, too, embodied "Tradition." They suffered under three different sets of behavioral norms that constrained their arduous lives. As a result, most of them endured a tough existence that was circumscribed by native patriarchal practices, white-skinned colonial mastery, and the supercilious treatment of European *mems*.

CHAPTER SIX

INDIES PAVILION IN FLAMES:

The Representation of Dutch Colonialism at the International Colonial Exposition in Paris, 1931

... Thirty-four million visitors! Rabbit catchers who dreamt about hunting elephants. Heroes in bed slippers envisioning themselves as intrepid explorers of distant, exotic continents. Cuckolded men fantasizing about submissive women. Shivering housewives who imagined living in sultry climates. Bankrupted folks plotting revenge. Short, fat, white men who looked down on tall, lanky black men . . Young boys pretending to be compassionate missionaries and little girls daydreaming about romantic interludes . . the most extraordinary spectacle in all of French history....[1]

Erik Orsenna, De koloniale tentoonstelling, 1989

The highly acclaimed Dutch presence at the International Colonial Exposition in 1931 embodied a national effort. In a circumspect manner the Dutch delegation represented its distinctive colonial style to the European public, which descended upon the elaborate Festival of Empire in the Bois de Vincennes by the millions. The Dutch exhibits in Paris involved a delicate process of internal soul-searching as to what made Dutch management of its overseas colonies unique and different from the colonial practices of other European nations. The tangible result consisted of an ingeniously designed Dutch pavilion, which was located on the borders of the Lac Daumesnil at the heart of the Exposition terrain and resembled an eclectic, fairy-tale castle.

French newspapers as well as journalists from other countries admired the Dutch palace as the most artistic building of the entire Exposition. Being an imaginative architectural structure fashioned to convey the "multi-cultural" nature of the Netherlands' empire in southeast Asia, the pavilion served as a metaphor for the Dutch pride in being able to forge political unity among the diversity of sophisticated ethnic cultures and religions that flourished in the Indonesian archipelago. Perhaps the building was intended to be an architectural demonstration of the kinds of ideas which Professor A.S. Oppenheim had articulated in his radio address on New Year's Eve a few years earlier: "Holland shows its most attractive features in *Indië*. Which other nation of only six to seven million inhabitants has mastered to the same extent the art of recreating a region of islands with tens of millions of inhabitants ... into a miraculously livable empire, furnished with all sorts of modern amenities and tokens of European civilization?" This exemplary Dutch colonial domain, he continued, had been nurtured into existence "by a corps of civil servants whose dedication, integrity, and genuine desire

Indies Pavilion in Flames

Sketch of Netherlands pavilion at the World's Fair in Chicago, 1933 (Archives P.A.J. Moojen, KITLV)

Sketch of Netherlands paviljon at the World's Fair in Chicago, 1933 (Archives P.A.J. Moojen, KITLV)

to serve the *res publica* cannot be surpassed by any other group of civil servants anywhere in the world!"[2]

While most other colonizing powers partipating in the grand, colonial festival in the Bois de Vincennes in 1931 merely reproduced and embellished the architecture that was typical to their imperial territories, whether it entailed a replica of a picturesque grass hut from Oceania or the recreation of a magnificent Cambodian temple, the Dutch display in Paris comprised a truly creative synthesis. Intended to symbolize the concept of cultural association between East and West, the ornate and inventive Dutch pavilion stood in striking contrast to the other exhibits at the Exposition, with Angkor Wat as its towering centerpiece. Ironically, two years later at the general World's Fair in Chicago, the central Dutch pavilion again comprised a flamboyant, Indies-inspired structure, although the Chicago Fair was not at all a specific celebration of colonialism. Rather than replicating a typical Amsterdam canal house with gabled rooftops or another example of authentic Dutch architecture, the Netherlands building in Chicago in 1933 would again be adorned with a Minangkabau roof which combined with a central facade that evoked the ancient Hindu temples of the Dieng plateau in central Java, while gentle water buffaloes and fierce Balinese dragons guarded the entrance. The possession of the Indies, in other words, also influenced the Dutch self-representation at the 1933 World's Fair in the United States, even if the glories of colonialism did not constitute an official theme of Chicago's exhibition of technological progress in the modern world.[3]

At the International Colonial Exposition in the Bois de Vincennes, however, the life-size recreation of the classic Cambodian temple of Angkor Wat was meant to function as the fairground's visual hub in order to communicate the centrality of France among all the colonizing nations. On the rare sunny mornings and many chilly afternoons during the Spring and Summer of 1931 — which proved to be an exceptionally rainy year —throngs of well-dressed Parisians and foreign tourists or timid, frumpy visitors from the provinces beheld this amazing sight.[4] A recreation of Angkor Wat had also constituted the proud central pavilion of the French Colonial Exposition in the city of Marseille in 1922. At that time the temple had imbued European spectators with awe; some among them had celebrated it as the fulfillment of a primordial dream "to see the silvery glow of the moon scatter her rays over the mysterious ruins of Angkor."[5] Therefore, Exposition organizers in 1931 simply repeated an earlier recipe for success. The temple was again resurrected in all its intricate glory, but this time on the borders of a scenic lake on the outskirts of the city of Paris.

Once more its faithful reproduction was a startling apparition amidst the fragrant, blossoming lilacs of a sprawling urban park that had been transformed into a "fairyland, a magical city absolutely unique in this world, where Parisians become intoxicated with marvels and exotic visions."[6] A lyrical Dutch newspaper correspondent stationed in Paris called the Bois de Vincennes in the Spring of 1931 a world bathed in a kaleidoscope of luminous colors. Next to the chalky whiteness of the North-African buildings, he was dazzled by the contrasts of "the reddish brown Madagascar palace, the earthy red of West Africa's structures, the bright red, green, yellow, and gold of the Indo-Chinese pavilions, and the deep gray of Angkor Wat."[7]

The life-size reconstruction of Angkor Wat, the Exposition's Official Guidebook in 1931 informed the visiting public, was based on a Cambodian monument that had originally been erected in the twelfth century A.D. as a temple to Vishnu. However, King Jahyavarman VII — a ruler who was portrayed as the southeast Asian "Sun King," a Khmer equivalent to the powerful Louis XIV —had soon thereafter converted it into a Buddhist inner sanctum, while Angkor Wat also came to exalt the hallowed memory of another great Cambodian monarch, Suryavarman II.[8]

Few representations lionizing a radiant king and his worshipful retainers adorned the walls of Angkor Wat. Despite their sophisticated artistic and technical talents, Khmer sculptors had not used their art primarily to celebrate the accomplishments of venerated secular rulers nor had they tried to glorify the enlightenment that Hindu deities may have spread among their followers. Instead, they had covered the monument with symbols of undiluted power and unbridled control, chiseled in stone for posterity.[9] The temple's *bas reliefs* revealed humans, monkeys, and elephants engaged in mortal combat; they featured prisoners of war led off in chains to slavery. Angkor Wat, in short, portrayed seemingly helpless people being bludgeoned to death for reasons that remained an enigma of cruelty to most French spectators.

In the mind's eye of the French men and women who meandered through the festival grounds in the Bois de Vincennes, Angkor Wat's monumental stature may have echoed the imposing dimensions of the very familiar Notre Dame cathedral in the heart of Paris.[10] Perhaps some of them even envisaged a likeness between Angkor Wat's stone carvings of strange animals and Notre Dame's rows of bizarre gargoyles. The heads of oxen crowning the tall tower of the Madagascar pavilion may have suggested such an analogy with Nortre Dame's gargoyles, too. Perched on the edge of Notre Dame's roof, these weird little demons sported grotesque mouths which spewed forth rainwater, insects, or dead birds on unsuspecting pedestrians on the walkways below. An occasional Parisian might have wondered why medieval stone-carvers had inserted these ominous creatures into the holiness of a grand Christian basilica dedicated to the glory of God.

But Notre Dame was also filled with crucifixes depicting a sadly suffering Christ and images of gentle saints who populated the cathedral's brilliant stained-glass windows. When imagining Notre Dame, French men and women may have automatically conjured up the somber sounds of devotional Gregorian chants or the celestial music of Palestrina's or Pergolesi's *Stabat mater*. They might also have envisioned the cathedral's kindly, black-robed priests who celebrated mass and prayed for God's forgiveness and the salvation of Parisians' souls. Notre Dame, in other words, exhibited a comforting Christian iconography, while Angkor Wat embodied an awesome, if stark, vision of an exotic world: a giant temple *cum* funerary monument with golden towers that were shrouded in incomprehensible beastly and human violence.

The posters advertising the Colonial Exposition promised its guests a "tour of the world in one day." The daily newspaper *L'Echo de Paris* printed an advertisement on

Colonial Practice in the Netherlands Indies, 1900-1942

The recreation of Angkor Wat at the Colonial Exposition in the Bois de Vincennes in Paris, 1931 (Coll. Roger Viollet, Paris)

The Duke and Duchess of York visit the Colonial Exposition, 1931 (Coll. Roger Viollet)

April 6, 1931, that covered the entire front page, announcing that when the Colonial Exposition would open its gates in one month, visitors would embark on "the most beautiful journey across the world!" They would encounter:

> A splendid, lively spectacle that will include marvelous architecture, exotic life in its picturesque and colorful setting, arts, handicrafts, and the fauna and flora from all over the world ... All sorts of enchantments: brightly lit night-time *fêtes* and nautical, military, and equestrian festivals ... Filled with attractions [such as] theaters, concerts, films, a scenic railway, restaurants, cafés and cabarets, tearooms, dancing, etc. etc., and finally, a modern zoological garden. [The Exposition will be] an incomparable intellectual, economic, and social manifestation: it shall present an awe-inspiring atlas [of the world] and, at the same time, a panorama of our entire colonial history.[11]

Strolling along paths lined with newly planted palm trees, spectators could wander from an Algerian or Tunisian *souk* to a village of Bamoum huts in Cameroon; half-way in between they came face-to-face with the flamboyant, reddish-brown palace from Madagascar adorned with gigantic ox heads. Multi-colored fish and other strange-looking animals from the sea swam, slithered, and squirmed in an aquarium in the *Palais Permanente des Colonies*, while a zoo in naturalistic style exposed visitors to the miracles of nature in the world beyond Europe.[12] Sightseers could behold graceful, supple dancers from Cambodia who moved to the ethereal sounds of xylophones and flutes, only to be whipped into a frenzy by the pounding rhythms of Senegalese drums around the corner. One could taste the savory foods, mint or green teas, and unique sweets from the different parts of the Empire or overindulge in potent drinks that flowed in a Moroccan café.[13] Predictably, the Dutch pavilion offered a tasty *table de riz* (*rijsttafel* or "rice table") consisting of dozens of spicy dishes.[14] The restaurant *Warong Djawa* in The Hague supervised the preparation of this authentic Indonesian fare, while a *djongos* (steward or waiter) on loan from the shipping company the Rotterdamsche Lloyd served the aromatic platters with traditional Javanese decorum.[15]

In the evenings, a sparkling sound and light show transformed the exhibition terrain into a *chiaroscuro* universe that was vaguely reminiscent of a Rembrandt painting. Rembrandt, after all, had used the juxtaposition of light and darkness as a "magic device" to render the intangible more visible.[16] In a much less artful manner and with an opposite purpose in mind, the "Sound and Light" show in the Bois de Vincennes scattered magical patterns of shadow and light across the nocturnal blackness of the Exposition's pagodas and minarets in order to cloak the pavilions in mystery and surprise. Hence, spectators who ambled through the Bois de Vincennes in the evening marveled at a "symphony" of sound and light that enveloped the Exposition's unconventional architecture.[17]

Perhaps it prompted tourists to pretend they were surrounded by the flickering shadows and starry skies of a haunting tropical night, albeit without the nuisance of a buzzing swarm of mosquitos, which "fostered quiet contemplation, but rarely imparted serenity."[18] Despite the make-believe of embarking on a romantic, night-time

Colonial Practice in the Netherlands Indies, 1900-1942

Madagascar pavilion at the Colonial Exposition in Paris, 1931 (Coll. Roger Viollet)

promenade through the inexhaustible beauty of the tropics, the average visitor to the Exposition probably had an inkling of the frightening animals — whether ferocious tigers or charging rhinoceroses, poisonous snakes or giant spiders — one could encounter in the lush forests or barren deserts near the equator. But this awareness may have added a slightly piquant edge to their sightseeing excursion across the Exposition grounds after nightfall.

The towering presence of Angkor Wat constituted the visual core. The temple evoked the alien universe of southeast Asia. Perhaps the average sightseer at the Exposition had a clue that Annam, Cochin-China, Cambodia, and Laos — or, in a colonial locution, "Indo-China" — constituted an outpost of European imperialism, presumably functioning as a beachhead of French civilization in between the chaos of humanity in India and the ominous human hordes on the vast plains of China. Indo-China was part of "Greater France," of course, but most French visitors to the Colonial Exposition in 1931 had only a cursory knowledge about this most distant of all French territories overseas.

Algeria, at least, had been under French political influence for exactly one hundred years. North Africa had acquired an inchoate sense of familiarity in the course of time even to small-town or rural citizens in provincial France, if only because a neighbor's cousin, for example, had been dispatched across the Mediterranean as a military con-

Indies Pavilion in Flames

Indo-Chinese pavilions at the Colonal Exposition in Paris, 1931 (Coll. Roger Viollet)

script. Moreover, the visible presence of courageous black-skinned soldiers in the French trenches during the Great War from 1914 to 1918 had settled colonized indigenous peoples from Africa even more in the public imagination of metropolitan France. Since the mid-nineteenth century, the French colonial state in Algeria had implanted itself in the "affairs of local communities" in ways that were far more intrusive than its Turkish predecessors had ever deemed possible or desirable.[19] As a result, Algeria and the adjoining Arabic cultures on Africa's northern coast, a mere stone's throw away from France on the other side of the Mediteranean, had entered the French popular imagination with a particular set of stereotypes. The image of Algeria and later, Tunisia, and Morocco, summoned a world filled with imposing, if treacherous, saber-rattling men on horseback surrounded by furtive, veiled women, who shielded their sensuous beauty from the impudent gaze of Western men.

At first, French pioneers in Algeria tended to celebrate North Africa and the Middle East as the world of Egyptian pharaohs or Moses crossing the Red Sea — in other words, as the "cradle of Western civilization."[20] But soon they converted it into the colorful domain of Shéhérazade and *A Thousand and One Nights*. Audacious photographers switched the focus of their camera's lens from recording the monumental colonnades of Baalbek or the sleek beauty of the pyramids to the enigmatic charm of

Postcard sent to Paris from Algeria, 1910

Algerian women.[21] Since the development of photography in the second half of the nineteenth century, an ever-expanding stream of black-and-white postcards mailed from across the Mediterranean had brought Algeria, and later Tunisia and Morocco, closer to home. Yet most photographs of the Magreb and the Near East, whether they conveyed the Spartan splendor of the landscape or highlighted the shrouded charisma of Arabic women, were "symbolic representations" designed to neutralize the "real" social conflicts implicit in colonial domination. Hence, the postcards depicting Arabic peoples or the scenery of the Islamic world that saturated the public domain of metropolitan France broadcast a set of alluring and "usable" images; in the process, these black-and-white pictures managed to render the French colonial project palatable to the average citizen.[22]

As a result, North Africa in the French popular imagination comprised more than a foreign "dreamland, where unfathomable mysteries dwell and cruel and barbaric scenes are staged."[23] Instead, North Africa came to symbolize a manageable "feminine Orient: the universe of Salomé, Salammbô, Queen Saba and Queen Dido, and above all of Shéhérazade."[24] Regardless of whether citizens in France viewed the colonized Arabic universe with either intimacy or reserve, as soon as the disparate communities of the Magreb fell into the fold of the French empire, in the public's perception they quickly lost their "sovereign" political and cultural identities, too.[25] An official within the Morocco section of the French Ministry of Foreign Affairs articulated this jaundiced view succinctly: "the curve of evolution is inclining more and more towards Paris." It was in the illustrious direction of Paris rather than towards "the East that the great mass of North Africans are turning their expectant eyes."[26]

In contrast, Annam, Cochin-China, Cambodia, or Laos seemed to reside in a different galaxy altogether. The cultural atlas of Southeast Asia was infinitely more complex than the rectangular boundaries, drawn arbitrarily through the Sahara desert, that punctuated the map of Algeria and its neighbors in North Africa. Besides, Indo-China was a more recent addition to the French imperial family, but it remained an elusive, distant relation; its distinctive cultures and ethnic diversity still constituted an intricate puzzle to observers in the European metropole. The typical traveler through the unfamiliar landscape of the Colonial Exposition in 1931 might have gleaned from the popular press only a few facile clichés which characterized remote Indo-China as a world filled with "peaceful if carefree Cambodians, poetic but lazy Laotians, docile if deceitful Annamites, or erudite but decadent Mandarins."[27] Besides, the fact that head-

Advertisements for the Colonial Exposition, to be officialy opened on May 6, 1931, in L'Echo de Paris, April 6 and April 11, 1931

Colonial Practice in the Netherlands Indies, 1900-1942

"If you lift my skirt you can see the arts of colonies." Postcard for sale at the Colonial Exposition in Paris, 1931 (Coll. Moojen, KIT)

lines in French newspapers rarely referred to cultural issues but instead featured regular articles on the "ruthless Communist propaganda" that incited these hapless people to "rebel against us" did not pique the curiosity of the average reader to learn more about the existential realities of Indo-Chinese peoples.[28]

The Exposition opened officially on May 6, 1931, to a public whose appetite for the "exotic" had been wetted by the many catchy advertisements printed in daily newspapers or an avalanche of seductive photographs published in illustrated magazines during the previous months. Although the voyeuristic exhibition of dark-skinned people from either Africa or Asia to citizens of the European metropole had a time-honored history, the media in 1931 seemed intent on reinventing the wondrous appeal of the *indigènes* on display in the Bois de Vincennes. The Exposition embodied a major invest-

Indigenous people from New Guinea playing billiards at the Colonial Exposition in Paris (Coll. Roger Viollet)

ment, both financially and psychologically, in the glory of the French empire. It was crucial, therefore, to stimulate the curiosity of the public, whether in France or abroad, in order to prompt as many people as possible to buy a ticket to enter the fairgrounds and thus make the Festival a financial as well as an ideological success. Accordingly, the organizers of the Exposition blanketed the city of Paris with posters, depicting a close-up of the faces of colonized people in a solemn, if stylish, manner. Daily newspapers, meanwhile, conjured up an exuberant language filled with promise and excitement about the journey through alien cultures that awaited all potential sightseers at the Exposition. By training the gaze of anonymous multitudes of Europeans upon the glamorously exotic people brought together in the Bois de Vincennes, the French state — and *ergo*, other colonizing powers as well — could manifest its "ability to command, order, and control objects and bodies" from all over the globe.[29]

The essential purpose of the Colonial Exposition was the disclosure and celebration of European political and cultural power, which had presumably touched even the darkest and most backward corners of the earth. It functioned more explicitly as "a vehicle for government propaganda" than previous World Fairs or International Exhibitions. Beginning with the glorious industrial bazaar in the Crystal Palace in London in

1851, such Expositions indulged, too, in a "periodic, lavish display" of national accomplishments.[30] But they appealed to visitors as independent agents and potential consumers whose acquisitive tastes could only be enticed, not dictated, through a demonstration of alluring industrial products or handicrafts.

Since the Crystal Palace Show, participants in subsequent World Fairs carefully described the value of all the exhibited items and attached price tags registering their cost. In fact, during the Universal Exposition in Paris in 1900, some critical Frenchmen lampooned the assembly of exotic people and animals which mixed chaotically with tacky commercial advertisements and information about the price of consumer goods. In the Trocadéro one could find "the Acropolis as a next-door neighbor to the Golden Horn and the Suez Canal almost bathing the Hindu forest." The animal circus entertained the public with "camels that bowed, kneeled, and danced" for crowds of spectators who were busily buying lemonade or beer from hawkers while they inspected the hundreds of rugs, suspended from the walls of a large hall, that were for sale and had "their prices prominently marked!"[31]

The 1931 Colonial Exposition's mission, instead, did not focus on the arousal of the acquisitiveness and consumerism of the public. Aside from the postcards, books, and other memorabilia tourists could buy in kiosks or the delectable food and drink they could purchase in the restaurants and cafés in the Bois de Vincennes, no price labels had been attached to any of the artifacts on display in the pavilions, simply because they were not for sale. Instead, the colonial Festival's aim was to imbue the public with an indelible awareness of the raw power of colonizing nations to dominate native peoples as they saw fit, which ironically duplicated, *writ large*, the unchecked forms of power chiseled in stone in Angkor Wat's sculptures. Rather than approaching spectators as discriminating consumers with economic or political judgments of their own, the informational exhibits at the Colonial Exposition welcomed sightseers as passive observers who were unable to form independent opinions about the strange people and objects they confronted, as if their minds were blank slates that could be inscribed with any kind of meaning.

However, neither the sensational verbal and visual imagery in the popular media nor the organizers' earnest efforts at public education in the Exposition's Official Guidebook could convert the European public's vacuous impressions into a more profound knowledge. The same was probably true for the gigantic Information Center (*Cité des informations*), which was filled with ethnographic and history texts, brochures, posters, postcards, and a movie theater for documentary films. The reading materials disseminated through a novel contraption, the highly publicized *bibliobus* — which was an ambulatory library mounted on top of a truck — could not transcend the public's prurient perspectives either.[32] The Exposition's sincere attempts to educate its audience were probably not very effective in displacing the fantasies or overcoming the visceral impact of the exoticism that inundated sightseers at the Exposition. In a certain way the Festival in the Bois de Vincennes seemed to augur "Disneyland," with the poignant difference that undisguised Asians and Africans of

Balinese dancer at the Colonial Exposition. Photo: A. Harlingue (Coll. Moojen, KIT)

flesh and blood, with real thoughts and feelings, were forced to masquerade in the same roles as Mickey Mouse and Donald Duck.

Tzvetan Todorov recently noted that "real" knowledge tends to be "incompatible with exoticism."[33] The great divide between "us" and "the others" (*nous et les autres*), whether in the past or in the present, can only be transcended through deep, detailed understanding. But the mind-boggling diversity of cultures, jampacked together into an aesthetically pleasing, seamless web in the Bois de Vincennes — an example on a massive scale of what James Clifford has called a "modernist collage" —was hardly conducive to such "true" knowledge.[34] The quaint rituals and exotic beauty of colonized men and women from Asia or Africa, however stunning their physical appearance might be, automatically raised the issues of difference and hierarchy, of superiority and inferiority.[35] Echoes of some of Guy de Maupassant's more lurid short stories may have resonated, such as "Marroca," in which he portrayed an Arabic woman "as a splendid girl of an animal but superb type ... [which] made her a sort of inferior yet magnificent being."³⁶

In Western eyes, the daily existence of indigenous peoples from colonized countries, albeit fascinating as well as entertaining, was radically divorced from their own straight-laced lives. The irrevocable otherness of the people on display at the Colonial Exposition left European observers with few options other than turning them into ideal-types of exoticism that stood entirely outside their own lived experience. Hence, the Exposition's dramatic representation of Indo-Chinese cultures merely confirmed the great divide between their own cosmopolitan Western identities and the differentness of *petite Anna, p'tite Annamite* and *ma Tonkiki, ma Tonkinoise*, as the popular French ditty called them lovingly, even if Angkor Wat's regal architecture exposed the French public to an august southeast Asian history that was as ancient and distinguished as their own.³⁷

Angkor Wat and the nimble-fingered female dancers from Cambodia or Laos, though, were not alone in representing the unfamiliar universe of southeast Asia in the Bois de Vincennes. The Dutch pavilions and refined dancers and musicians from Bali, too, symbolized yet another distant bulwark of Western civilization. The Dutch empire in southeast Asia, covering an elongated chain of islands not far from French Indo-China, constituted a similar Western "balcony on the Pacific wedged between the two great reservoirs of humanity in India and China."³⁷ Little Holland, after all, was the third largest colonial power in the world, and its dominion in Indonesia was a time-honored as well as an extremely lucrative one. To many French colonial theorists the profitable Dutch economic productivity (*mise en valeur*) of Indonesia was a paragon of efficiency that other colonizing nations should try to emulate.³⁹ In fact, to some spokesmen for the French empire the lucrative agricultural economy established in Java and Sumatra served as a source of barely hidden envy; they conceded that "the Dutch are not liars when they promote the legend that their colonies represent the most splendid and best maintained ones" in the world.⁴⁰ Again, the French were hardly alone in this assessment. It was a salutary perspective on Dutch colonialism that also lingered on among a section of the American foreign-policy establishment, which claimed as late as 1942 that "Dutch [colonial] administration was the model in many ways."⁴¹ However, *La Tribune Indochinoise*, the official newspaper of a Vietnamese nationalist party that advocated anti-colonialism through constitutional reform, gave an ominous twist to this Dutch reputation for brilliance. The French may go "to school in the country of Queen Wilhelmina because the Dutch have standing and fame as masters in the matter of colonization," a journalist named Nam Dan, who called himself the "friend of the Indo-Chinese people," wrote caustically on May 16, 1931. But he added that "everyone knows that there will soon be a time when the Dutch East Indies shall also be intensely exercised by Communism, a time when peace can only be restored through extremely flexible and liberal policies."⁴²

The Indonesian writer Matu Mona, whose 1938 Malay novel *Spionnagedienst. Patjar Merah Indonesia* (Espionage Service. The Indonesian Scarlet Pimpernel) partly transpired in Paris during the Exposition, emphasized that in the judgment of most visitors, the Indo-Chinese and Indonesian delegations stood out as exceptional.[43] He wrote that:

> The Exposition was extraordinary. People from the East were being introduced to the bourgeoisie of the Western world in order to disclose their civilization. But they were displayed in such a manner that in the eyes of Western people they nonetheless looked like savages without manners, except in one or two cases. The Indo-Chinese received a lot of attention because of their dancing and music, as did the musicians and .. dancers from ... Bali, from whose sounds Western musicians profited greatly.[44]

The Exposition's organizers, in their deliberate efforts to make the carnival of empire a truly international one, had gone to great lengths to welcome the Dutch delegation, especially after the supreme colonial power in the world, Great Britain, had declined to participate, citing as an excuse its grave financial troubles generated by the Great Depression.[45] While French Exposition managers had responded with a mixture of anger and annoyance to the British refusal, the progressive editors of the anti-colonial journal *Timboel* in Java gave England's decision not to participate a different twist. "We do not think it is at all coincidental that the British have declined to take part in the Colonial Exposition's parade of power; being the most competent of all Western colonizers, Britain tends to understand best the warning signals and changing needs of our times."[46]

Amidst the clutter of both temperate and more inflammatory pro-independence publications in Indonesia in the 1920s, *Timboel* was a nationalist magazine published by the Indonesian Study Club in Solo. The editors received a regular subsidy from the Sultan's court (*kraton*) to produce the bi-monthly journal in which they waged a constant battle of words against an array of Dutch political policies in the Indies. But *Timboel* was especially exercised about Dutch actions towards the majestic Sultans' courts in central Java, and throughout its six-year life span *Timboel* never ceased to call upon the colonial administration to grant greater autonomy to the decorous palaces in their city of Solo.[47] As a result, aside from lambasting the Exposition's Organizational Committee in the Indies for its boorish treatment of the central-Javanese courts, *Timboel* sneered sarcastically in June of 1931 that in general, little Holland performed the role of Cinderella in the Bois de Vincennes and functioned as a "bridesmaid to the most naive and most shamelessly conservative of all the colonial powers in the world."[48]

Being forced to serve as the chief acolyte to the majesty of French colonialism, however, also produced some rancor in proud Dutchmen in the European metropole. The general secretary of the Dutch Exposition committee, Dr. L.J. van der Waals, complained in 1932 that the French, in the last few years, had tried to situate themselves "at the apex of all the colonial powers. Neither the Netherlands nor England should allow themselves to be dragged along, because the French devote all their efforts, as was the case with the actual Exposition itself, only to the exaltation of the glory of France itself! (*la gloire de la France*)"[49]

But "the magnificent Dutch effort, a veritable *tour de force*" acted as the only "rival" to Angkor Wat at the Exposition, because the Dutch had produced a pavilion that gave eloquent testimony to the "riches of Insulinde."[50] The Dutch representation occupied a grand total of three hectares of the fair grounds and had required the enormous sum of fifteen million francs, which was the equivalent of a million-and-half guilders.[51] The official opening of the Dutch exhibits took place on May 8, and was one of the "most intelligently organized."[52] The main palace covered six-hundred square meters and revealed a facade of more than one hundred meters in width which possessed "such finesse and elegance" that it was "one of the most remarkable" structures — as well as the biggest — at the Exposition.[53]

The exterior of the central building incorporated a hodge-podge of disparate architectual styles from the archipelago. Wooden carved doors from a Hindu temple in southern Bali combined with a roof with upward-pointing corners typical of a Minangkabau house from western Sumatra; the canopy of the building also alluded to the overhanging, layered roofs of a typical Javanese mosque. The entire structure, in turn, was blanketed with 750,000 ironwood *sirappen* (shingles) from Borneo; the fifty-meter high spires were modeled on a Balinese *meru* — the turrets of a Hindu temple — but also seemed to refer to the low, integral towers of the classic Javanese mosques in Demak or Cirebon. Being stretched skyward for fifty meters, however, made the Balinese pagodas look like skinny, inverted staircases reaching for the heavens, which clashed with the apparent solidity of the massive building.[54]

L'Echo de Paris described the Netherlands' fairy-tale chateau in gushy language in a front-page article on April 11, 1931:

> If you take the direction opposite to Angkor Wat, an extraordinary building rises up before you, and you are lifted off your feet, as if transported by a miracle. The same magnificence, the same nobility; the dragons guarding this pink and violet palace are the cousins of those who watch over the steps of the monumental stairway leading up to the lacquered portals of Angkor Wat ... Nonetheless, when you have recovered from your surprise and look a bit closer at this enchanted palace entwined with flowers and dragons, you see the difference at once. Here we are in Insulinde; over there we are in Indo-China. Insulinde is one of the most mysterious parts of the world: architecture, plastic arts, music — all this is virginal and pure to our Occidental eyes.[55]

The *Nieuwe Rotterdamsche Courant* appraised the building as a model of "balance, serenity ... and seriousness," which symbolized the essential nature of "our" colonial identity. The monumental structure "is composed of different architectural styles linked to each other by Dutch building motifs; hence we see the work of ordering and association which the Netherlands accomplishes among the people of the Indonesian archipelago [epitomized in the pavilion]."[56] The Dutch palace, both literally and figuratively, constituted a deliberate example of James Clifford's "modernist collage." The pavilion's connective tissue that fused the archipelago's bricolage of architectural styles together resembled the modernist building techniques of the Amsterdam school

The Netherlands pavilion at the Colonial Exposition. Photo: Braun & Cie (Coll. Moojen, KIT)

and "De Stijl" movement. Reminiscent of the Bauhaus architecture of Walter Gropius or the severe hyper-modern designs of Mies von der Rohe, the simple structural lines and square angles that constituted the pavilion's unifying theme may have served as a metaphor for the Dutch colonial administration's rational forms of authority, which had presumably amalgamated the many disparate Indonesian ethnic cultures into a coherent political entity.

Mounting an exhibition, the *Nieuwe Rotterdamsche Courant* noted on May 7, is above all "the art of conjuring up an illusion," and the Indies architect, W.J.G. Zweedijk had succeeded magnificently in crafting a "patrician palace."[57] Initially Zweedijk had wished to construct a "real" replica of Borobodur, which could have served as an "authentic" southeast Asian companion to Angkor Wat. Apparently he abandoned this idea because of its "impracticality," which was a fortuitous decision because he received many accolades for the architectural marvel he designed as an alternative to the reproduction of Borobodur.[58] The *Algemeen Handelsblad* complimented the Dutch pavilion as the "*clou*" to the Exposition, and quoted the opinion of an anonymous French journalist that Angkor Wat constituted a mere "imitation" of the original, while the Dutch building represented a genuine "creation." The newspaper applauded the building for exuding a sense of "calmness and mystery inspired by the contemplative Buddha of *tjandi Mendoet* (Mendut temple), who looks down on us, hurried visitors."[59]

Side view of the Netherlands pavilion. Photo: Chevojon frères (Coll. Moojen, KIT)

The ever-critical journalists at *Timboel*, in contrast, harbored a very different opinion of this giant palazzo with its "rose-colored, varnished walls, its lilac and eggplant-colored roof, and its pillars encircled by tropical flowers that seem to have cast off their terrestrial appearance only to transform themselves into living things."[60] They called the building a "pseudo-clever but nevertheless sorry mongrel — a mishmash that proves that its designers have no sense whatsoever of the function and appeal of any of their architectural examples."[61] The pavilion conveyed none of the aesthetic sensitivities of the famous Indies architect Thomas Karsten, who had pointed to the ways in which public buildings should express "the unique style and harmony" that enveloped everything in Javanese thought and deed, drama and milieu.[62] Nor did it incorporate the Dutch East Indies architect Henri Maclaine Pont's insight that "the mastery of Javanese architecture resides in its self-restraint in which bold, simple lines predominate, while detail and rich ornamentation are reserved for spaces where they can be admired from up close."[63] Thus the *Timboel* writers judged the building "worse than their bleakest expectations." But they added: "Who cares? Bourgeois Paris is flabbergasted because it does not know any better!"[64]

Surrounding the principal pavilion were examples of the daily lives of other ethnic groups such as typical Toraja and Batak dwellings and a Minangkabau rice shed as well as a coop with chickens, geese, and other tropical fowl; a Balinese theater had also been erected to set the stage for the performances of the delicate *legong* dancers and *gamelan* musicians. The private sector had organized a series of exhibits, too, celebrating the capitalist triumphs of plantation agriculture. After all, initially spices, and later coffee, tea, rubber, tobacco, sugar, and quinine had funneled the extraordinary wealth generated by the archipelago's fertile volcanic soil directly into Dutch bank accounts.

But the irresistible centerpiece of the Dutch representation was the enormous pavilion at the center, which unfurled two spectacular dioramas of Java and Bali. It unveiled, too, a diorama of Curaçao and a reproduction of the cathedral of Paramaribo in Surinam, even though the Dutch West Indies seemed to function mostly as an afterthought in the Dutch parade of its colonial empire. The pavilion was also filled with extraordinary artifacts. The viewer confronted "a promiscuity of objects" ranging from gold swords and sacred daggers to silver necklaces or tiaras encrusted with rubies, diamonds, and other precious stones.[65] The interior was further adorned with priceless wooden carvings and unique ceremonial statues. The dark blues and browns of antique batik sarongs from Java saturated the inside of the building with earth tones, while the deep reds of embroidered cloth from Palembang, *ulos* from Batak land, and a collection of stunning *ikat* from eastern Indonesia added a burgundy glow. The exhibition inside the pavilion also introduced a variety of original paintings and striking, black-and-white murals created especially for the occasion. In addition, it proudly showed a plethora of unique geographic maps and rare navigational charts drawn up by famous seventeenth-century Dutch cartographers. Fragile, first-edition travel journals recording dauntless Dutchmen's voyages of discovery in Asia and the Americas during the early modern era were on display, too.[66]

As the *Nieuwe Rotterdamsche Courant* opined, it was "an exquisitely tasteful" collection, which had been borrowed from institutions such the Arts Society in Batavia and the Ethnographic Museum in Leiden. The private collection of Mr. P.A.J. Moojen, the official Dutch delegate in Paris and an artistic adviser on the construction of the Dutch pavilion, had supplied a large number of textiles and artifacts, too.[67] In fact, the incendiary group of Surrealists who agitated against the Exposition, drawn in by the intellectual charisma of such literary luminaries as Louis Aragon, André Breton, Paul Eluard, or Yves Tanguy, singled out the Dutch exhibition of beautiful objects as the ultimate, and thus most perverse, "*acte manqué* on the part of capitalism." If all of this were to be destroyed, the Surrealists insisted that "the most precious documentation of the intellectual life of Malaysia (sic) and Melanesia (sic)" would be annihilated.[68]

The year 1931, in this context, seemed to be a peculiar moment to stage an ostentatious international celebration of European colonialism. Since the beginning of the decade, the world economy had tumbled into a Great Depression, and most European colonial powers faced grave social and structural problems, both at home and overseas. French economic relations with its empire overseas, however, revealed a unique profile in this regard. While exports to Britain from their colonial possessions in such

The "Sumatra house" at the Colonial Exposition. Photo: Chevojon frères (Coll. Moojen, KIT)

places as Uganda and Nigeria had dropped by a disastrous 50 percent — a percentage that more or less held true for Dutch East Indies' exports to the Netherlands and the rest of the world, too —French imports of agricultural products and other primary materials from its empire, in contrast, grew dramatically from 37.5 percent in 1929 to 71.2 percent in 1938.[69]

Hence, the Spring of 1931 was as appropriate a season as any to infuse the French public with a more palpable emotional connection with the golden era of colonial France. The Sumatran writer Matu Mona, for his part, asserted in his novel that "the Exposition was filled to overflowing with wealthy visitors (*kaoem hartawan*) from all over Europe, because the economic depression (*malaise*) had not yet reached its peak and was not yet felt by the kings of money (*kaoem radja-radja oeang*)."[70] Because of the influx of tourists, the city of Paris "beautified" itself to welcome and impress the millions of foreign guests who descended upon its urban landscape: "above the newly repaved boulevards, illuminated globes are suspended at regular intervals, while the water fountains on the Boulevard Saint-Michel and the Place de la Concorde have received a color treatment that adds an even greater artistic element to the Parisian

Interior of the Netherlands pavilion. Photo: Braun & Cie (Coll. Moojen, KIT)

décor."[71] *Le Figaro* waxed effusively that "Paris, the queen of capitals and resplendent in her grace and loveliness, is going to sheathe herself in the mantle of royalty again; for the sake of both the heart and the spirit, [Paris] will ply all her powers of seduction."[72]

Buses, trams, and even a special boat service on the Seine connected the heart of the City to the colonial fairgrounds located on its eastern outskirts. The newly constructed No. 8 line of the metropolitan subway system connected the central underground station at Drouot with the Porte-Dorée near the Bois de Vincennes. This new subway line could "transport an average of 40,000 travelers per hour, who do not even have to switch trains in the course of their journey."[73] Encouraged by this easy access, chic bourgeois couples, often accompanied by one or two well-behaved children, converged upon the festival of empire in huge numbers. According to Matu Mona, rich foreigners came all the way "from America and from Eastern continents, principally from India, especially to see the Exposition."[74] *L'Echo de Paris* announced in late June that Parisians or wealthy visitors from abroad could buy tickets from the wife of Paul Reynaud, the Minister of Colonial Affairs, for the astronomical cost of one-hundred francs apiece, to "the most brilliant and greatest celebration of the colonial season" that would take place in the Bois de Vincennes on July 6th, featuring "Cambodian and Laotian dancers, Annamite and Cochin-Chinese theater, the most celebrated tamtams from black Africa, dancing from Oceania, etc. etc."[75]

A few of the middle-class spectators who were intrigued with modern technology may have been outfitted with small box-like cameras, which the French called "Kodaks," to try to imitate the beautiful photo reportages they had seen in *L'Illustration* or

Spectators at the Colonial Exposition observing a performance by African dancers (Coll. Roger Viollet)

Le Petit Parisien.[76] The magazine pictures they admired prior to their "tour of the world in one day" might have muted Parisians' ambivalence about the strangeness of colonized people. Photographs, after all, express a surreptitious form of power: they possess the ability "to appropriate time and space" and "to decontextualize" all the people who live their daily existence within a particular place at a specific moment.[77] Photographs, in the words of Walter Benjamin, estrange observers from reality in their very attempt to capture it.[78] By converting the culture, architecture, and physicality of *indigènes* into a socially neutral "pastiche" of aesthetic "curiosities," these photographs enabled the French public to visualize the native "other" as a stylized object of beauty or a "blissfully simple creature."[79]

The photographic representations of colonized people from Asia or Africa isolated them from their opaque natural surroundings and depicted them, instead, as living in a transparent, "brightly different" world that was bathed in an "imagined sensuality and luxurious beauty."[80] By visually divorcing "exotic" people from the intricate realities of their day-to-day existence, European photographers and their audience could project an array of aesthetic or erotic fantasies upon the lives of *indigènes*; in the process, European spectators could translate the meaning of Asians' or Africans' lives into the familiar cultural grammar of the West. Hence, the amateur photographers among the middle-class sightseers who toured the Exposition could personally attempt to replicate this process of cultural transcription. Taking snapshots of their flustered wives and giggling children while they sat on the steps of Angkor Wat or stood in front of a village from Gambia, flanked by drum-playing or spear-bearing Africans dressed in costumes that revealed a lot of bare skin, allowed bourgeois photographers to insert their own refined, Western selves into the eccentric world of the natives.

At any rate, whether they actually carried cameras or were merely equipped with picnic baskets and baby carriages, middle-class French families and prosperous tourists from abroad were inundated with educational materials in the massive Information Center during their circumnavigation of the Exposition's wide world of non-Western civilizations. While these informative brochures were not very effective in fostering a deeper cultural knowledge of colonized people, they were quite successful in glorifying the civilizing mission of colonizing nations. In the French case, the pamphlets self-consciously induced national pride and made the average visitor aware of the importance of the overseas empire in the continued preeminence of the French nation in Europe. At the same time, middle-class families spent a healthy day in the fresh air of a Parisian park while rejoicing in a personal sense of sophistication relative to the hundreds of picturesque indigenous peoples in their colorful attire who danced, made music, or served as stately honor guards.[81]

More humble families, possibly with a larger number of noisier children in tow, could also muster the fare for either the bus or the subway and afford the three-franc ticket — the equivalent of one liter of ordinary wine (*vin ordinaire*) — to enter the Exposition.[82] Solid working-class denizens of the nearby, proletarian neighborhoods on the city's east side as well as reasonably well-off provincial families from the environs of Paris were among the six million French sightseers who admired the exotic sights in the Bois de Vincennes, although few, if any, carried cameras or could pay for an expensive ticket to the night-time feasts. Perhaps they felt slightly intimidated by the educational materials they received. Besides, the ornate temples or ox-headed spires they saw and the many black or golden-skinned people they encountered may have overwhelmed them.

Nonetheless, it was likely that working-class or peasant families also returned home with a vicarious feeling of contentment. Their own lives of hard work and meager rewards were probably harsh and far from perfect, if only because many bourgeois households lived in much greater material comfort than they did on the basis of less strenuous work; yet their existence compared favorably with the strange lives and bizarre habits of the *indigènes* they had seen on display at the Colonial Exposition.[83] As the Exposition's chief organizer, Louis-Hubert-Gonzalve Lyautey envisioned, the Exposition could reduce class envy and enhance the "social peace" of the city.[84] Jean de Castellane, the president of the Municipal Council of Paris, offered a similar pronouncement. In a "spirit of brotherhood and patriotic solidarity people will come to this radiant décor in a verdant Parisian park to examine, appreciate, and admire the embodiment of a truly integrated France."[85]

At a more practical level he gloated about the extension of the subway system to the working-class *quartiers* in the eastern part of the City, which would "survive as a durable enrichment of our patrimony." Similarly, he rejoiced in the fact that the *Musée permanent des colonies* would forever adorn this poorer section of Paris.[86] But De Castellane seemed eager to transcend such mundane considerations in order to rise to greater rhetorical heights. He said that the Exposition would imbue rich as well as poor Parisians with a burgeoning sense of pride in the "Homeric Odyssey of the white race to every corner of the earth, a journey that has transformed barbarian continents into civilized places." Citizens on both sides of the economic divide, he predicted, would embrace each other and unite in a collective appreciation of French accomplishments overseas.[87]

Of course the Dutch delegation also came to Paris armed with a hefty information booklet about the Indies. Obviously written in French, it was filled with complimentary stories and flattering data. The Colonial Institute in Amsterdam had produced this substantial brochure specifically for dissemination at the Paris' Colonial Exposition. It stressed the fact that the people of Java or Bali were far from "illiterate and uncivilized." In fact, the Javanese and Balinese, the Dutch propaganda material for the Paris Exposition emphasized, had forged "a culture that is more ancient than that of western Europeans." Java and Bali, aside from elegant palaces presided over by refined Muslim sultans as well as magnificent Hindu temples, also possessed both a proper alphabet and an impressive literary tradition — "unprinted, to be sure, but nonetheless of great value."[88]

However, the Exposition booklet also stated that until recently, native intellectuals in Indonesia had demonstrated a "complete lack of interest" in trying to understand the meaning of their own ancient cultures.[89] Thankfully, during the past few decades "the assiduous labors of two generations of European scholars" had exposed native intellectuals to the value and beauty of their own secular Hindu-Javanese origins. "The development of an active scientific and scholarly life" in the Dutch East Indies since the turn of the century functioned not only as a source of "well-being for the average native person," but more importantly, it "revealed to all of them the forces that still slumber in their own souls." The eventual creation of a university in Batavia with a curriculum in languages and literature would presumably become "the germ that will propagate a renaissance of Hindu-Javanese culture" in the future![90] Founding a real university in the Indies was an urgent necessity, the *Nieuwe Rotterdamsche Courant* had suggested a few years earlier, because reality had shown that bringing young Indonesians to study at Dutch universities posed "a political problem." Such eager, if gullible, young men went socially and ideologically astray, and they began "to espouse extreme forms of nationalism because Moscow searches for Revolution against the West through its mobilization of Asians."[91]

Hence, the plans for offering a language and literature curriculum in the Indies, already amply discussed in earlier colonial educational congresses in The Hague in 1919 and 1924, framed the need for a university with a faculty in the humanities in Batavia as one that would focus primarily on "indigenous cultures and their evolutionary history." The astringent editors at *Timboel* insisted they did not want a university intent on inscribing Indonesian students with a "stamp of Dutchness" (*tjap Belanda*). When criticizing the Ministry of Education's Memorandum of 1930 on "The Creation and Organization of a Faculty of Letters," they joked that the carefully planned humanities curriculum actually looked like an "à la carte menu" for a sumptuous European dinner with an endless series of courses.[92] Obviously, what role Dutch language, literature, and history would play in a university with a humanities and social science curriculum — whether it would be central or merely auxiliary — comprised a hotly debated issue.

A large number of experts were convinced that Dutch civilization should function as the intellectual foundation of the humanities taught in a university in Batavia. Others warned against too much "Hollando-centrism" and spoke dismissively of Dutch cultural imperialism, fearful it would stifle or misdirect Indonesians' independent efforts to analyze and describe their own society and history. Hence, Dutch language and literature should merely be a medium that galvanized Indonesians into "forging their own independent cultural existence."[93] As an editorial in the neo-ethical journal *Kritiek en Opbouw* (Critique and Construction) implored in 1940, those who "prayed from the bottom of their hearts" that Dutch culture would remain the "Western yeast that activates the growth of Indonesian cultures" should be aware that this ferment could only thrive as a catalytic agent if it was embedded in a policy of emancipation (*ontvoogding*). The leavening of Indonesian cultures in a Dutch mold would not occur unless accompanied by a strategy of uplifting the economic condition of the popular masses. Dutch social-welfare policies on behalf of the Indonesian population, in other words, should serve as supplementary enzymes that would trigger the creation of a society with a "normal social structure."[94]

This interminable, impassioned debate was finally concluded when it could accomplish little more than confirm its own obsolescence. The Faculty of Letters in Batavia, when established at long last in 1940-1941, was hovering on the edge of an abyss only to be overtaken by the Japanese juggernaut in 1942. The officially embraced goal of the short-lived institution of higher learning in the humanities, though, was to provide Indonesians with an impulse to study the development of their own cultures rather than a curriculum that "would urge Indonesians to absorb Western civilization."[95]

If the French organizers of the *Exposition coloniale* in 1931 were aware of this arcane, drawn-out debate, or if they had been fully familiar with the Dutch ambivalence about imposing their own European civilization upon their colonial subjects, it probably mystified them. Ernest Lavisse's old history textbook, reissued again in 1936 and used in thousands of public primary schools throughout France, for example, impressed upon French grade-school students that "France wants little Arab children to be taught in the same way and just as well as little French children. This proves that France is good and generous to the peoples it submits" in its colonial territories.[96] Pondering the propriety of imposing French cultural values upon primitive peoples in north Africa or southeast Asia did not enter the French imperial imagination as often.[97] Besides, the colonial policymakers within the Ministry in Paris studiously ignored both the "singularly acerbic" and more charitable critiques leveled against French assimilationist policies, which came from a variety of ideological corners.[98]

Even highly placed colonial administrators criticized French governance of its overseas territories for destroying native social traditions and replacing "the rigorous hierarchy of yesterday with a well-intentioned but emasculated [French] one today." The Governor General of French West Africa in Dakar, Joost van Vollenhoven — a naturalized French citizen born to Dutch parents in Algiers, who had made a meteoric rise through the ranks of the colonial civil service — noted ruefully in late 1917 that once upon a time Africans had welcomed the "liberation" that French colonial protection promised to bring about. He deplored, however, that "these days" they neither "like us nor trust us."[99]

But to many French officials overseas, the superior beauty of the French language and the preeminence of French civilization was only too self-evident. To be sure, earnest research into the intricacies of native traditions was relevant, but mostly because such knowledge functioned as a mechanism to accelerate the acculturation of indigenous populations into Greater France and, in the process, expedite their economic productivity (*mise en valeur*).[100] As far as the mission to civilize was concerned, a journalist for the newspaper *L'Homme Libre* proclaimed, "France has done more than any country in the world. No one can deny us our good faith, our profound desire .. and our great, idealistic flair (*élan*) . . to bring to our brothers of all colors the essential principles of our civilization."[101]

Clearly, the officially sanctioned posture of Dutch colonial rule at the Exposition differed in subtle ways. Instead, the educational bulletin handed out by the Dutch delegation represented Holland's colonial method and style as scrupulously respectful of indigenous cultures. Amidst the zoo-like quality of the Exposition and its eroticized "wrapping" or materialistic "packaging" of primitive cultures from Africa or Asia, the Dutch pamphlet, in contrast, stressed the Netherlands' reverence for ancient Indonesian traditions.[102] In fact, the perceptive editors of *Timboel* had already addressed the bifurcated character of these kinds of International Exhibitions in 1927. On the one hand, any such event constituted "an international commodities market engaged in peddling the industrial and handicraft wares" produced in each country; on the other hand, an Exposition also functioned as a "cultural fair, publicizing the artistic talents of different peoples." Unless those two missions were kept separate, *Timboel* warned, any Exposition quickly degenerated into a "parade of eccentricities (*rariteteitenuitstalling*) that reduces 'culture' to nothing but a fringe that functions as the trimming on the edge of the industrial center."[103]

Hence, the way in which the Dutch could distinguish themselves from the enterprises of other colonizing nations represented in the Bois de Vincennes was to emphasize their careful study and profound understanding of the complexity of native cultures. As the Dutch Minister of Colonial Affairs Koningsberger had stressed in his initial announcement of the Dutch participation in the Paris Exposition: Holland rejoiced in entering "the peaceful competition of nations and peoples." But he added that "our" country preferred to reveal its important role in the world economy by means of "carefully considered, business-like, and refined exhibitions rather than ostentatious displays."[104] Both Koningsberger and the chairman of the Dutch organizing committee, former Governor-General Dirk Fock, invoked the idea of *noblesse oblige*: Holland had to show the world that its affectionate, paternalistic commitment to its southeast Asian colonies had spawned "dazzling results" during the past three centuries.[105]

It was true that the exterior of the pink-and-purple palace was a polyglot invention that issued forth from the Dutch colonial imagination. Yet, the brochure tried to accentuate that the inherent beauty and accomplishments of the different ethnic groups of the Indonesian archipelago should be allowed to speak for themselves: they should not be encased in flashy colonial packaging. Albeit unsuccessfully, it seemed as if the Dutch informational booklet also attempted to move beyond the "kidnapping language" of a Western scholarly idiom that appropriated native cultures in order to render them intelligible, habitable, and "natural."[106] At any rate, the Dutch delegation could make its mark by celebrating a colonial method that had yielded a superior appreciation of the customs and traditions of Indonesians, which implied an inviolable commitment — or a "metaphysical" obligation, as Edward Said might call it — to honor and preserve all ethnic cultures.[107] And the resplendence of these cultural and artistic practices would be communicated directly to the Western world, in an unmediated fashion, through the Dutch pavilion's exquisite exhibit of elegant ethnographic artifacts.

Herein resided a curious paradox of the Dutch colonial style as it was championed at the Exposition. While Indonesian peoples and cultures should be allowed to speak for themselves, Dutch archeologists had been the ones to identify, unearth, excavate, and describe a previously unmapped landscape dotted with long-forgotten Hindu and Budhist temples. Dutch philologists, too, were portrayed as dedicated scholars who had decoded and reproduced all sorts of ancient Javanese manuscripts. They had also treasured mysterious Balinese texts — inscribed on the fan-shaped leaves of a lontar palm (or palmyra palm, *borassus flabellifer*) — that would otherwise have descended into either physical disrepair or intellectual oblivion. An authoritative compendium published in 1935 in two hefty volumes on the cultures, political organization, and economic conditions of the Dutch East Indies repeated the exact same opinion. "Dutch historians have investigated the old history of Java. Western scholars have deciphered the inscriptions on the ruins of old Hindu monuments and solved the riddle of their origins and meaning, while only Dutch scholars have compiled all the dictionaries of indigenous languages."[108]

In addition, since 1918 or so, a few lonely ethnomusicologists had criss-crossed the enormous span of the archipelago with state-of-the-art recording equipment to preserve the distinctive musical traditions of a multitude of ethnic groups. Jaap Kunst's travels reached from the island of Nias off the northwestern coast of Sumatra to Sumba, Flores, and New Guinea in eastern Indonesia, while Johan Sebastiaan Brandts Buys focused his attention on regional folk-musical traditions in Java and Madura. Scholarly research on local music was still "a virgin scientific territory," because musicological scholarship almost everywhere in the world was steeped in a "latent Eurocentrism." This obsession with classical European music, the ethnomusicological pioneer

Jaap Kunst argued, prevented musicologists from exploring broad, comparative questions about the distinctive role of musical practices in the origins of different cultures.[109]

Kunst's urgent goal was to safeguard for further research the exotic sounds of music of as many different ethnic cultures as possible, as he wrote to Johan Huizinga, before they would "disappear as snow melts in the sun."[110] Following an active lobbying campaign, the Indies' *Volksraad* authorized Kunst in early 1930 to create a government-sponsored archive of phonographic recordings, photographs, and actual musical instruments.[111] This appointment would enable him to counter the "fatal work of the radio," which had a destructive effect on native musical practices that was far "greater than either a sledge hammer or a stick of dynamite."[112] But these sincere efforts to preserve the musical heritage of all sorts of ethnic groups throughout the archipelago for further research by Western ethnomusicologists underscored, again, the internal tensions in the Dutch representation of good colonial governance. It was a paradox that hinged on a genuine desire to enable Indonesians to convey their own refined sensibilities or musical sophistication directly to the Western world, even though the expression of their cultural achievements was always filtered through the scholarly looking glass of devoted European historians, linguists, or musicologists.

The patronizing judgments about the academic writings of Indonesian intellectuals, moreover, provided further testimony of these internal contradictions. So far, the *Encyclopaedie van Nederlandsch-Indië* announced unambiguously in 1918, the Dutch Javanologist Dr. Jan Laurens Andries Brandes "has written the most important work about Javanese literature," although it added, with a note of surprise, that Dr. Hoesein Djajadiningrat in his dissertation had "furnished some interesting addenda and even a few corrections!"[113] In the same year a much-maligned delegate to the congress on "Javanese Cultural Development" in Solo made the pronouncement that "Javanese culture was being destroyed by internal wars until God's hand placed Dutchmen in the Indies to rescue it!"[114] Albeit of a much higher intellectual caliber, the weighty two-volume compendium on *Neerlands-Indië* nonetheless reproduced the same pejorative tone in 1935: "while some natives may have defended a meritorious scholarly dissertation [at a Dutch university] their intellectual contributions have no significance, and as soon as their academic studies are behind them, they rarely engage in further research."[115]

The insightful Dutch archeologist, Willem Frederik Stutterheim, examined these problematic issues through a more populist prism. Preserving "the cultural trust" of a nation made little sense "if its own people cannot comprehend its spiritual worth and meaning." As long as the Javanese masses in the countryside viewed their island's artistic treasures as the tangible remnants of a historic "lineage of lofty, superior creatures" with whom they shared no common identity whatsoever, then cultural preservation merely indulged the intellectual fancy of Western scholars and a few Javanese aristocrats. As Stutterheim wrote in 1939, simple peasants saw pre-historic arrows and agricultural implements as "the Thunder God's teeth." They believed that the burial temples of Javanese rulers constituted "the houses and kitchens" of legendary, supernatural heroes, while the ancient sculptures within represented "the handicrafts of the Gods that had tumbled from the heavens." As long as Java's peasants toiling in the rice fields envisioned the pre-historic temple sites excavated from the soil by Western archeologists as "fossilized ancestors" who might unleash "magical dangers," then the efforts at protecting Java's cultural trust possessed only a dubious value, unless accompanied by popular education at the village level.[116]

Nevertheless, the official Netherlands' propaganda in Paris revealed an almost smug sense of vocation to honor and conserve the myriad native cultures of the Indonesian islands and to empower them to manifest their grace and sophistication directly to the public. It was true that in 1928 the acclaimed Dutch historian Johan Huizinga had remarked upon the irony — as well as the tragedy — of the Western world's tendency to become enraptured by and "receptive to the beauty of the East as soon as it had subjected and culturally assaulted it." But in colonial Indonesia, at least, Dutch scholars had fortunately engaged in "avid research" and had performed a rescue mission since the early twentieth century. Committed European researchers had nurtured a "respectful admiration" for the literature, architecture, textiles, music and theater, or the legal traditions of a wide diversity of Indonesian cultures.[117]

In the course of their scholarly investigations, they had supposedly managed to imbue native intellectuals with a new interest in their own historic civilizations. And eventually, through a trickle-down process, humble peasants in the countryside fields might learn to understand the true nature of their own cultural heritage, too. Even though it ranked as only the third largest colonial power in the world, the Dutch nation was first in its "imperialism-in-depth [rather] than in-breadth."[118] Hence, the deep knowledge of their colonial subjects proved "that Dutch imperialism differed in kind" and distinguished the Dutch East Indies representation at the Colonial Exposition from the gaudy depiction of primitive societies in the pavilions of other imperialist powers.[119] To most people familiar with the elegant dance forms of Java, "the African performers they saw at the Exposition produced shock rather than delight." The same Dutchman claimed that among the Exposition's diverse cultural demonstrations from Asia, he was convinced that visitors returned home with "the most vivid memories of the dignified Balinese dancers."[120]

Both Huizinga in 1928 and the Dutch brochure at the *Exposition coloniale* in 1931 singled out for praise the ardent research of the last two generations of dedicated European scholars. However, the intellectual engagement of the Dutch colonial community with Java went back much further, albeit mostly for instrumental purposes: as Cees van Dijk has recently stated, it was primarily motivated by commercial interests.[121] Since its early presence in Java in the early seventeenth century, the Dutch East India Company (*Vereenigde Oost-Indische Compagnie* or VOC) had negotiated trade agreements and formalized its contracts with the Mataram Kingdom in Javanese. For this purpose, the VOC employed a constantly changing assortment of interpreters and translators, most of whom were Eurasians.[122]

Besides, Governor-General Antonio van Diemen, who held office from 1635 to 1645, reputedly personified an exceptional European in seventeenth-century Asia, a kind of statesman unknown in the colonial territories of other European countries, because he "felt that in pursuing the interests of the VOC, it was wrong not to inquire into the concerns of Asian people and to consider the legitimacy (*rechtmatigheid*) of their claims."[123] The VOC also stipulated that the Javanese themselves could not be enslaved; but again, this regulation issued not from esteem for the Javanese but from a fear that too large a group of slaves with the same ethnicity might band together and pose a threat to the social order. As a result, the Dutch community in Batavia imported slaves from the Malabar coast of western India, the neighboring island of Bali, or from the southern part of the nearby island of Celebes (Sulawesi).[124]

During the early nineteenth century, when the VOC had died its natural death and Java had been transformed from a grasping trade *emporium* into a stately *imperium*, Governor-General Van den Capellen undertook some preliminary steps to train genuine Dutch "Java experts." Finally, in 1832, the first official, government-sponsored Institute for the Study of Javanese language and culture was founded in Solo; its existence was short-lived, however, since it was abolished again in 1843.[125] Hoping to make future colonial civil servants fluent speakers of both high and low Javanese (*krama* and *ngoko*), and to instruct them in Javanese customary law, jurisprudence, mythology, history, religion, and other cultural practices, the teaching success of the Institute was alleged to have been a dismal failure. A member of a committee of inquiry in 1838 reported that upon completion of the two-year curriculum, none of the students (*élèves*) could utter a complete sentence in Javanese. They also knew nothing about the Javanese past except a few trite tidbits about the history of the shadow puppet theater (*wayang*). But worst of all, the graduates were so completely ignorant about the *Cultuurstelsel* (Cultivation System) that they could not even answer the most "elementary questions about surface measurements"![126]

The founding of the Institute had coincided with the creation of the Cultivation System, which placed a premium on government officials who could converse in Javanese. Being able to "bargain and negotiate" in Javanese with village heads and district chiefs made it easier, of course, to impose land rents or to define cash-crop quotas for coffee, indigo, or sugar.[127] Communicating in the language of a Javanese village leader (*lurah*) rather than in Malay — which was, after all, a speech that did not belong to anyone but "floated" as a *lingua franca* in-between the multi-lingual daily life of Indonesians and the administrative realm of white-skinned foreigners — might also enhance the prestige of the colonial civil service.[128] Malay did not distinguish between high and low speech levels and did not enable speakers to register their differences in status through linguistic subtleties. Hence, learning to speak proficient Javanese would enable Dutch administrators to infuse all the native Javanese, even the most exalted aristocrat, with a perpetual awareness of their subordinate status.[129]

For the duration of the nineteenth century, the training of civil servants was geographically separated and institutionally divorced from serious research on Javanese language and history, because "coffee is more important than Kawi" (archaic Javanese), Johannes van den Bosch declared bluntly in the mid-1830s.[130] From then until the early twentieth century, the colorful "field workers and pioneers" of Dutch scholarship, who labored with all their linguistic might on a wide variety of dictionaries, grammars, or Bible translations into various indigenous languages, fell outside the orbit of official civil-service training.[131] To be sure, until its closure in 1900, the civil-service instruction program in Delft taught students during their three-year schedule of courses the "principles" of both Malay and Javanese, but it was an idiosyncratic crew of outsiders who conducted linguistic, philological, or historical research on the complexities of Javanese and other ethnic languages and cultures.[132]

All of this changed after the implementation of the Ethical Policy. Since the turn of the century, the Indies state embraced its role as a faithful sponsor of ethnographers, and information about local cultures improved in terms of quantity as well as quality.[133] Linguists, archeologists, legal scholars, and musicologists also produced more sophisticated insights, while eventually the Java Institute was revived once more in 1921. Their collective fund of scholarly "intelligence" was reconstructed from being the esoteric wisdom — or the whimsical hobby — of various intellectual oddballs into a tool that was essential to the pursuit of a truly "enlightened" colonial administration. Hence, the Dutch propaganda booklet at the Colonial Exposition in 1931 highlighted the prodigious research of the past two generations of Dutch investigators, thus exalting the Indies government's recognition of the crucial importance of precise "Oriental" knowledge as the handmaiden of power. The bulletin also magnified the sensitivities of the Dutch community at large to native traditions, as if each and every colonial resident of the Indies was an amateur scholar of local languages and cultural traditions in his or her own right.

In fact, the Dutch East Indies representation at the Colonial Exposition had sparked a curious controversy within the Dutch colonial community in Indonesia itself. An anonymous letter to the editor of the prominent, if conservative, Javanese newpaper *Het Soerabajasch Handelsblad* on March 28, 1931, for example, from someone who signed his or her missive with the sobriquet "Observer," registered a peculiar Dutch concern regarding the Indies participation in the Exposition. The initial plan to send aristocratic palace dancers from the Sultans' courts of either Yogyakarta or Solo to Paris prompted a series of delicate questions. "What should a sensitive and genteel Javanese nobleman feel when throngs of boisterous party-goers gawk at him?" Would such a finely tuned soul feel merely embarrassed or truly humiliated in front of an endless stream of "tourists, who saunter from one spectacle to the next, alternating the sounds of African drums with the sights of voluptuous belly dancers and self-lacerating fakirs?"[134] "Observer" feared that:

> One can only expect from the majority of this kind of raucous public that it will giggle and slap each other on the back with hilarity about all this funny commotion. The tittering crowds will return home with the idea that these highly cultured Dutch subjects from Java, whose level of civilization is in no way inferior to the average visitor to the Colonial Exposition, should be viewed in the same light as the primitive inhabitants of Senegambia or Somalia....[135]

In an earlier edition of the same daily newspaper, another Dutch colonial resident, who called himself "Mr. Dr. F. Valentijn" wrote on March 21, 1931, that he harbored disconcerting memories of the way in which European cities put colonized peoples from Africa or Asia on crude display. Anyone who dared to look inside an auditorium during the early morning before the first performance, he noted, "could catch a glimpse of a sad group of dark-skinned people, dressed in warm European clothes to ward off the bone-chilling climate, having just emerged from a cheap hotel in a city slum."[136] In his childhood, Mr. Dr. Valentijn continued, he had seen Ashantis, Abissynians, and Bedouins paraded in front of a ribald crowd of European citydwellers who ogled these unfamiliar people like animals in a zoo. During the performance of all the different ethnic peoples from either Africa or Asia, "each group's appearance and costumes were different and unique. But their demeanor, their dancing, and their manners evoked the exact same impression." Valentijn wrote that he could not help but remember such shameful sideshows when he read about "the plan to make refined, aristocratic dancers and musicians from Java perform at the Colonial Exhibition in Paris."[137]

In the eyes of the snickering journalists at *Timboel* in Solo, the committee of Dutchmen charged with organizing the Indies delegation had indulged in a series of "bizarre escapades and antics" (*capriolen*) in trying to draft *kraton* musicians and dancers from either Yogyakarta or Solo to represent the Indies in Paris. The official chairman was former Governor-General Dirk Fock but its pivotal presence was the committee's technical adviser to the construction of the Dutch pavilion, P.A.J. Moojen, whom *Timboel* described as "a mediocre (but harmless) painter and a questionable (but not so harmless) architect." According to *Timboel,* Moojen and his colleagues engaged in a "comedy of ineptitudes" by managing to snub and annoy the genteel retainers of the quasi-autonomous sultans' courts in central Java.[138] As a result, the ancient rulers of both Yogyakarta's and Solo's *kratons* equivocated in their permission to send renowned court artists to Paris.

Instead, Balinese musicians and a troupe of nubile *legong* dancers were dispatched to Paris. An Indies medical officer charged with evaluating the health of the delicate performers, however, had withheld approval for the little girls' departure because their physical condition predisposed them towards tuberculosis. But the young girls went anyway, first to be "dragged all over Holland and then to be put on display as a cabinet of curiosities in Paris."[139] And the Parisian public attended their performances in droves, enticed by newspaper articles that had reported that the smallest among the ravishing Balinese dancers "are five-years old, while the oldest dancers are only twelve."[140]

In the self-conscious language of the Exposition organizers, which tried to rise above the long-standing convention of salacious exhibitions of "exotic" people in the European metropole, these highly touted pre-pubescent girls from Bali would enter a decorous world. The Exposition was intended to be a "microcosm" that would summarize with grace as well as integrity the essence of human experiences from all over the world.[141] But the managers of the Exposition appeared conscious of the sleazy vo-

The very young Balinese dancers who enticed the Parisian public. Photo: Keystone (Coll. Moojen, KIT)

yeurism that had disfigured previous colonial exhibitions. Accordingly, the "Word of Welcome" in the Exposition's Official Guidebook placated spectators that they would not be exposed to a manipulation of the base instincts of a coarse public.[142] Instead of mounting all sorts of sordid vaudeville shows featuring undulating bellies or writhing bodies dripping in sweat, the Exposition would unveil a stylish panorama of the majesty of the colonial enterprise.[143]

However, in their counter-manifesto "Don't Visit the Colonial Exposition," the Paris Surrealists urged everyone to boycott this appalling circus, which would inundate viewers with nothing but "vulgar pleasures" (*réjouissances grossières*). In the name of Lenin, who was the first to recognize that "colonized people are the allies of the world's proletariat," Parisians should stay away from the Bois de Vincennes to register their opposition to the murderous exploitation and titillating portrayal of indigenous people.¹⁴⁴ A Counter-Expo carrying the grandiose title "The Truth about the Colonies" was expected to unmask the idea of the great French empire as an "intellectual swindle" (*concept escroquerie*).¹⁴⁵

L'Humanité, the official newspaper of the *Parti Communiste Français* (PCF or the French Communist Party), impressed upon the nation's working class and other party members on May 6, 1931, that the "apotheosis of colonialism in the Bois de Vincennes is the apotheosis of crime." It is "our duty to remind you of the historical truth," a front-page article in *L'Humanité* intoned, that the "transplantation of capitalist culture to the colonies means the despoliation of entire villages by fire as well as horrifying massacres, whether in Dahomey or Tonkin .. [hence] French workers should not be captivated by the more attractive aspects of the Festival in the Bois de Vincennes."¹⁴⁶

Of course *L'Humanité* elaborated on a venerable tradition of anti-colonialism on the part of certain segments of the French left, which since the turn of the century had maintained that the working class was never fooled by colonizers' "mirage of words or the seductions of humanitarian phraseology." Instead, committed socialists had always known that "colonization is based on violence, war, the sacking of towns, the sharing of loot, and slavery."¹⁴⁷ But despite *L'Humanité*'s warning not to be "lured" into visiting the fairgrounds, French workers could not resist the promise of tantalizing spectacles. While as many as six million French men and women gaped at the sights and sounds of the official festival, the counter-expo attracted no more than five thousand workers on day trips organized by labor syndicates. As Jacques Marseille has noted wistfully, the French proletariat was apparently more interested in exploring the exotic delights of Arabic *souks* or Balinese dancers in the Bois de Vincennes than in learning the sobering "Truth" about the colonies.¹⁴⁸

Nonetheless, Matu Mona maintained in his novel about "The Indonesian Scarlet Pimpernel" that "in general, working-class Parisians harbored an antipathy to the Colonial Exposition that was taking place [in 1931], because as members of the Socialist Party they strongly objected to downtrodden and enslaved people (*manoesia jang biadab dan ta' merdeka*) being displayed in such a way that observers, who claimed to be intelligent, were made to feel as if they were sightseeing in a museum."¹⁴⁹ One of the novel's protagonists, a fiery Indonesian political radical named Paul Mussotte — which was a thinly disguised and French-sounding reference to the Indonesian communist Musso — went even further in his attack. He made an ardent plea to his ideological comrades in Paris that the Exposition be disrupted through direct political action: "three bombs would be enough," he avowed, to close down this bourgeois spectacle once and for all (*tiga boeah bom sadja tjoekoep oentoek memoesnahkan tentoonstelling kaoem berdjoeis itoe*).¹⁵⁰

Mussotte intoned that the Exposition "should not stay open, because it insults the feelings of people from the East." In an explosive speech addressed to a gathering of working-class socialists in Paris, he challenged his audience with the provocative question whether "the mentality of the people here, my French comrades, has already emerged from the revolutionary era and become bourgeois again (*soedah mendjadi tabiat berdjoeis kembali*)."¹⁵¹ He declared:

I am one of those people from the East — one of those who is being exhibited as *un peuple Indonésien* ... My body and soul and the honor of my compatriots with colored skins have been trampled upon and ravaged (*indjak-indjak dan dinodai*): they have been stripped naked (*diterlandjangi*) before the eyes of civilized people with white skins. Comrades, if white-skinned people were to be put on display like this at an Exposition in the East, if you were told to undress or to cook a snake and be forced to eat food that smells rotten to you, wouldn't your soul be in pain as if you were deeply wounded (*tersajat*)? If this Exposition had taken place in the Orient it would surely have been reduced to ashes and smoke even before it opened, because we Eastern people don't wait long before we take action. Was it not François [a French Socialist fellow-traveler] himself who said: do what you have to do today, don't wait until tomorrow? Are you, comrades, using the name Socialist only as a mask, while your conduct is no different from that of the bourgeoisie?[152]

Matu Mona's literary license did not emerge in a vacuum; instead, his novel embellished a real historical event. On June 28, 1931, the florid pink-and-purple Dutch colonial palazzo in the Bois de Vincennes, with its fabulously valuable collection of textiles, jewelery, unique seventeenth-century maps, wooden carvings, and other ethnographic artifacts inside, was reduced to a pile of debris. A fire signal had sounded towards midnight on the previous day, calling out the Exposition's fire brigade, which arrived at the site within two minutes and investigated the alarm. The firefighters could not find anything suspicious and after an hour or so, they returned to their station. Early in the morning of June 28, however, a blazing fire engulfed the magical palace.[153]

In a flash the "imposing silhouette of Balinese turrets rising high above the exhibition terrain" had been transformed into a paltry heap of smoldering cinders. Only a week after the royal visit of Queen Wilhelmina and Princess Juliana to the Exposition, a burning inferno had caused a disaster of "national magnitude" because the gorgeous building personified "our glory in the noble competition of peoples (*edelen volkerenwedijver*) in the Bois de Vincennes," the *Nieuwe Rotterdamsche Courant* grieved on June 29.[154] It was a "catastrophe ... a national calamity," the *Algemeen Handelsblad* lamented in similar fashion, and we have to express "our sadness and sympathy on behalf of our entire country," if only because the financial damage due to the fire was estimated at at least one-and-a-half million guilders, representing the approximate cost of the pavilion's construction; newspapers in The Hague and Haarlem ranked the total financial loss as high as ten million guilders.[155] The *Algemeen Handelsblad*'s regular correspondent in Paris mourned that it was difficult to comprehend how "our proud pavilion, which was the most-admired building of the entire Exposition, could be cut down to such an inconceivably thin layer of ashes."[156]

Most Parisian newspapers, of course, reported on the fire too. *Le Figaro* used poetic language: "Horror! Despair! While everyone slept in the park of Vincennes, a shower of flames lit up the sky and embraced the birth of dawn, casting a scarlet glow upon all

Netherlands pavilion reduced to a pile of rubble. Photo: Chevojon frères (Coll. Moojen, KIT)

the surrounding trees and buildings, throwing the indigenous population into a panic and making the [animals] in the zoo yelp and howl .. And then, within a few moments, nothing remained of the magnificent Dutch East Indies palace, which was one of the most beautiful and interesting at the Exposition."[157] Other daily papers in Paris reprinted the lachrymose words of consolation transmitted in official telegrams to the government of the Netherlands by Prime Minister Paul Doumer and the French Minister of Colonial Affairs, Paul Reynaud. The Exposition's commissioner-general, Louis Lyautey, wired his condolences to Queen Wilhelmina who was on a holiday in the Vosges mountains of the department of Haut-Rhin at that time, indicating that "the destruction of the magnificent Netherlands pavilion, which comprised the greatest artistic achievement of our Exposition, and the loss of the invaluable treasures it contained have distressed us inconsolably."[158]

But the exaggerated French estimates of the financial losses due to the fire varied to a ludicrous degree. *L'Homme Libre* quoted the reasonable number of twenty-five million francs, while *Le Petit Journal* claimed it was sixty million francs; *L'Echo de Paris* weighed in with the highest sum in this guessing game, asserting that the destruction of the pavilion and its contents implied a financial damage of as much as eighty million francs.[159] The French government, meanwhile, generously granted its fellow colonizers from Holland a "handsome" sum of money to help defray the costs of rebuilding their pavilion, while Belgian authorities graciously offered to make a section of their Congo pavilion available, which would enable the Dutch to reconstitute an exhibit at the Exposition.[160]

By the next day, several French newpapers reported that according to the Parisian prefect of police the fire could not be attributed to arson or "malfeasance" (*malveillance*), and that an inquiry had established that sabotage was not a factor in the catastrophe. The police chief had concluded that the "makeshift character" of the Exposition buildings had rendered the Dutch pavilion, as was the case with all the other structures, extremely susceptible to fire.[161] But an electrical short-circuit as the cause of the fire was also ruled out. According to the chief engineer for the French company that supplied electricity to all the buildings in the Bois de Vincennes, the Dutch pavilion's electrical installation had been far superior to that of many other Exposition buildings. In fact, the Dutch electrical system was technically so sophisticated that during the early Spring "Parisian engineers had requested permission to show the Dutch wiring design to electricians who were working on other pavilions in order to teach them how they might construct the safest installation."[162]

Dismissing both sabotage and electrical failure as the catalyst of the fire produced a mysterious dilemma, but it seemed as if only *Le Figaro* openly addressed this quandary. Neither malfeasance nor a malfunctioning of the building's electrical system could be identified as the fire's triggering agent, "because the wires in the sub-station were entirely intact." If neither structural factors nor human agency had unleashed the fire, *Le Figaro* reflected sardonically, then any rational human being must continue to wonder how and why it had erupted?[163]

On June 30, however, *Le Figaro* changed its jocular tone and struck a more foreboding sound. The paper ran a front page article, posing the question whether the fire was accidental or the result of deliberate arson: "Accident or Assault?" (*Accident ou Attentat?*).[164] The *Algemeen Handelsblad* in Amsterdam also circled around this issue in a gingerly fashion. The four levers of the central fusebox had been lowered, meaning that the electricity had been entirely shut off before midnight on June 27th. A large ventilation grate in the building's entry hall, however, had connected the interior with the world outside. The paper noted judiciously that "it is possible that something was hurled inside the pavilion through this grate in order to set it on fire. Whether this actually occurred, however, no one can say with any certainty."[165] Without engaging in further analysis, the *Avondpost* in The Hague printed a rhetorical question on its front page: "Short-circuit or deliberate act?" The *Avondpost* intimated, too, that some witnesses claimed to have heard or seen several explosions, although the paper did not elaborate on the possibility that bombs or other explosive devices had actually been planted or thrown.[166]

Le Figaro's questioning of the incident was more emphatic. The paper pointed to a possible linkage with a previous blaze at the Exposition. A few weeks before the Dutch East Indies pavilion was diminished to a smoking mound of rubble, fire had erupted in the Madagascar palace. Fortunately, in the Malagasy case, the flames were quickly extinguished without leaving much visible damage. Such a recurrence within the space

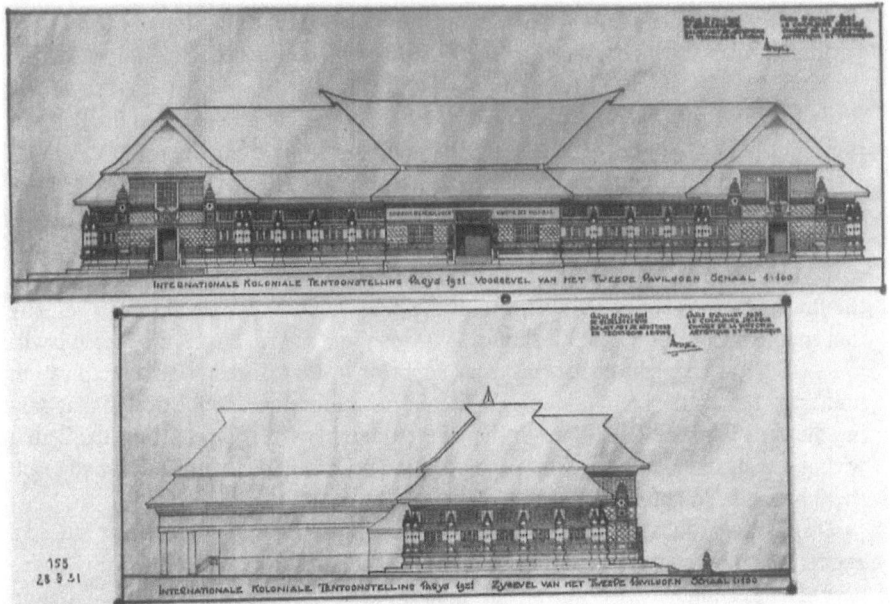

Architectural design for the second Netherlands pavilion. Photo: Chevojon frères (Coll. Moojen, KIT)

of a few weeks, however, "prevents us from relying too easily on destiny" and should make us think twice before we "simply resign ourselves to fate." After all, the fire in the Dutch palace had been ablaze for almost five hours long. But this did not make sense if we consider the provisional construction and the lightweight, inexpensive materials used in the Exposition's structures, the journalist for *Le Figaro* pondered. "Beneath an artistic mask, [the buildings] are nothing but skeletons stuffed with flimsy substances. One must wonder at once: why did fire burn for as long as four to five hours?"[167] Until the experts — the architects, electricians, and the specialists from the fire brigade — had reached a "spontaneous accord," *Le Figaro* urged everyone not to regard the anti-imperialist Communist agitation in the Far East as one of those "old-wives tales (*contes bleus*) we like to dismiss out of hand." While the Dutch are busily thinking about rebuilding the pavilion in due course, *Le Figaro* intoned, they must also respond, with a frank perspective and without despair, to the kinds of devastating blows meted out "in the cunning war of barbarism (*guerre sournoise de la barbarie*)."[168]

L'Humanité, for its part, chose not to address the issue of anti-imperialist "direct action" or the subversive anti-capitalist behavior of so-called barbarians. About a week later the daily Communist newspaper simply noted that the passage of time would show that colonial societies could never be "saved" from Communism. The methodical enslavement and subjection of entire races to European capitalism comprised the core of modern colonialism. *L'Humanité* prophesied that in due course mistreated native people would muster enough courage to act in their own self-interest and embrace

Indies Pavilion in Flames

Official inauguration of the second Netherlands pavilion in early August, 1931. Photo: Chevojon frères (Coll. Moojen, KIT)

the goals of Communism, but the French Communist Party's newspaper dodged the question of Communists' responsibility for the fire. *Timboel*, however, claimed that it was a well-known fact that "Bolsheviks in Berlin and Paris were mounting anti-imperialist campaigns," even if the writer for *Timboel* did not directly link Bolshevik activities to the Dutch pavilion's fire.[169]

Instead of heeding *Le Figaro*'s counsel and exploring whether Indonesian nationalists might have legitimate reasons to engage in inflammatory anti-imperialist "direct action," the two major Dutch newspapers, at least, dropped the topic of arson or sabotage. But they reported with glee on the frantic activities of the Exposition's executive committee in the Netherlands, which resolved on July 3 to construct a new set of buildings that could be "open to the public in early August."[170] The committee was inundated with an avalanche of offers from people and organizations in Holland and the Indies to make available a whole new set of artworks, ethnographic artifacts, and textiles for display in the newly constructed buildings.

At the time the fresh structures were inaugurated with great fanfare in August, less than seven weeks later, the incinerated flower-festooned palace had become little more than a nostalgic memory. Few Dutch people in Paris, the Dutch East Indies, or in the Netherlands iself still speculated whether anti-colonial fervor in Indonesia had spilled over into "direct action." In the public imagination, it seemed, the sudden transformation of the violet-and-maroon palace into a scorched stack of timber and dust could only be attributed to destiny or bad luck. What had happened on that ghastly early

The second Netherlands pavilion at the Colonial Exposition. Photo: Chevojon frères (Coll. Moojen, KIT)

morning of June 28, 1931, allowed little Holland to show the world its gritty, stubborn spirit: that a small nation could be great in overcoming adversity! In fact, the *Algemeen Handelsblad* trumpeted a quintessential badge of Dutchness in a headline two days after the fire : *Je Maintiendrai*.[171]

The next-to-last Governor General of the Dutch East Indies, Bonifacius Cornelis de Jonge, who was present at the official opening of the second Dutch pavilion in August, 1931, while on his way to the Indies to assume his exalted position of power, would later invoke this official credo with demagogic flair: "our country became great under the motto *Je Maintiendrai*." This dogma "flows in our blood" and constitutes a sacrosanct principle, he said in 1933, that no Dutch person "can betray" wherever he or she may be. While the *Algemeen Handelsblad* used the emblem *Je Maintiendrai* as the title for a story about a very specific event, De Jonge summoned this slogan as a lofty symbol for the long-standing and enduring colonial relationship between Holland and Indonesia: "What we have created in *Indië* during the past 300 years shall be maintained by all of us, regardless of our race or social status, not only in times of prosperity but, above all, in times of hardship."[172] *Je Maintiendrai* reverberated a bit like an incantatory refrain in both sophisticated and more simple-minded arguments designed to legitimate the perpetuation of Dutch colonial rule: "The Netherlands must 'maintain' its influence and power in the Indies, for the sake of the native population, for Holland's sake, and as our duty to the world."[173]

Echoing this archetypal Dutch injunction, former Governor-General Fock, in his role as chairman of the Dutch Exposition committee, published a self-righteous article on "The Task of Colonial Powers" in the twice-monthly bulletin issued by the press bureau of the International Colonial Exposition. Ironically, his hortatory discussion of Europeans' duty "to maintain themselves" in the face of colonized people's yearning for independence appeared at almost the exact same time as the fateful fire. His article emphasized the need for "solidarity" and the formulation of uniform policies among all the European colonizers towards nationalist movements and Communist upheaval. This celebration of the bonds of brotherhood between colonizing nations found further comfirmation in "the heavy-duty capitalist" (*zwaar-kapitalistisch*) orientation of an academic conference on colonial policy that coinciding with the Exposition and was organized by another colonial expert from Holland, Professor Dr. M.W.F. Treub.[174]

Many Dutch and French newpapers reprinted the most salient passages of Fock's article.[175] It was even reproduced in *La Tribune Indochinoise* on July 1, 1931, which reported with more than a hint of cynicism his emphasis on the fact that "even people of the Far East themselves recognize that it will be many years (*longues années*) before they are capable of exercising the right to independence."[176] In his commentary, Fock pontificated that:

> Actually granting independence to the people of the islands of the Dutch East Indies would unleash a veritable disaster. I am convinced the same holds true for the peoples of French Indo-China. For the sake of the native populations themselves, France and the Netherlands must contain their aspirations for independence. We have to oppose energetically the corrosive leadership of the Communists, who both promote and abuse the idea of independence in the hope of fostering a potential for revolution by fomenting of social disorder. Whatever it may cost, it is of existential importance that we liberate the native population from the deadly actions of Communism. But our principal duty resides no less in educating the [native] populations than it hinges on our respect for their arts and civilization. Contributing to the collaboration of the civilizations of the Orient and the Occident is a difficult but admirable task. In this sense the Exposition possesses a singular importance in revealing what different colonizing powers have accomplished in their colonial domains; it also allows us to envision the future fate of humanity by our perseverence in this task.[177]

The celebration of colonialism's *mission civilisatrice* at the Paris Exposition in 1931 was the "swan song," as Gwendolyn Wright has called it, of European imperialism in general.[178] The burning of the Dutch Exposition palace on June 28, 1931, symbolically portended a similar conflagration in the Dutch East Indies a mere fourteen years later. We could either summon Pramoedya Ananta Toer's trope for the Dutch colonial state as a "glass house" which was only glued together by police surveillance, or we could describe the labyrinthine Dutch East Indies governing system as a metaphorical fantasy palace, a castle in the air, or a house of cards. Regardless of the figures of speech we devise, however, the solidly constructed Dutch colonial mansion proved to be a rickety structure that collapsed in a sudden and traumatic fashion after World War II. Albeit unwittingly, the highly acclaimed Indies pavilion in the Bois de Vincennes in 1931 already emblematized the subcutaneous frailty of Dutch colonial constructions. Despite its careful design and architectural creativity, the palace turned out to be a contraption that was as flammable as a bamboo hut, because the glamorous building could be converted into a pitiful pile of rubble in a matter of hours.

Whether the fire was accidental or whether the pavilion burned down due to incendiary anti-imperialist action was not an issue Dutch politicians or journalists were willing to address, at least not in public. Nonetheless, the pavilion's sudden metamorphosis into a tiny mound of "ashes and smoke," as the imaginary Paul Mussotte called for in Matu Mona's novel *Spionnagedienst. Patjar Merah Indonesia*, yielded an apocalyptic vision. Although the Dutch colonial community was either incapable or reluctant to acknowledge it, the pavilion's allegorical heap of embers continued to smolder, only to reignite into a flaming, and ultimately victorious, assault on the meticulously crafted edifice of Dutch colonialism in Indonesia during the War of Independence between 1945 and 1949.

The fiery destruction of the Dutch pavilion in Paris in 1931 can be endowed with other prophetic features. We could see it as a symbolic preview of President Sukarno's rousing statement in a nationally broadcast radio address in December, 1962, for instance, when he said that unlike other nations which came to life in the gentle, silvery glow of a full moon, the Indonesian Republic was "born in fire!"[179] But the short-lived, if memorable, building at the Colonial Exposition in the Bois de Vincennes presaged something more tangible, too. In 1980, a phoenix-like reincarnation seemed to arise out of the ashes of the phantom palace of Dutch colonialism in Paris: the Suharto-sponsored "Indonesia Museum" in Jakarta's *Taman Mini* park.

The moving force behind the construction of *Taman Mini* and eventually, the "Indonesia Museum," was Mrs. Suharto. In the course of a visit to Disneyland in California in 1971, Mrs. Suharto had been struck, as if by a bolt of lightning, with an inspiration to create a park that could celebrate "Beautiful Indonesia" in miniature. Mrs. Suharto's "Disneyland dream" was converted into reality on International Women's Day in 1975, when, in the highly publicized company of Imelda Marcos of the Philippines, she inaugurated *Taman Mini* with great fanfare.[180] The "Indonesia Museum" was completed in 1980. The Museum's Balinese turrets or its stilted dioramas depicting the archipelago's ethnic traditions bear an uncanny likeness to the interior and exterior of the burned-down Dutch pavilion in the Bois de Vincennes in 1931.[181] *Plus ça change ...*

Epilogue

"Paradise Lost":

Nostalgia and the Re-Imagined Community of the Dutch East Indies

Once upon a time a paradise on earth existed for the Netherlands: it was located in southeast Asia and in daily discourse (*dagelijkse wandeling*) it was called "Our Indies." It was a paradise blessed with an abundance of crops and people who harvested them capably, deftly, and cheaply. In a subtle fashion and with a gentle hand the white civil servants governed the colony via indigenous rulers and retainers ...'Our Indies' was a model colony, polished more cleanly than the mother country itself.[1]

> Jan Bosdriesz and Gerard Soeteman,
> *Ons Indië voor de Indonesiërs*, 1985

"Our Indies," the model colony, supposedly gleaming more brightly than the mother country itself, was depicted, as late as 1985, as a *Paradise Lost* from which the Dutch were banished as John Milton's Adam and Eve, "Looking back, all th'eastern side beheld, of Paradise, so late their happy seat."[2] Even though "shame and regret" also saturate the remembrance of the colonial era, a deep-seated sense of yearning is the most prominent fixture in the hearts and minds of a large number of Dutch people.[3] While living productive and well-adjusted lives in the wet, frosty climate of the contemporary Netherlands, many Dutch folk still pine for the luxuriant colonial culture in Indonesia's tropical warmth that they were forced to leave behind. The fact that "Our Indies" now belong to the colonial other, to Indonesians, lingers on as a "collective trauma."[4]

Numerous former colonial residents remember the Dutch East Indies as an intimately familiar home in an arcadian world that was demolished by the inexorable decolonizing tide of history —or, in the eyes of some, by American diplomatic pressures after 1945, which prematurely imposed on the Dutch nation the reality of Indonesian independence. Nostalgia evokes the anguish of remembering, and scores of people continue to extol the Indies as Holland's Atlantis, a community and a past that can be recaptured only through the imagination.[5] As one former Dutch resident of the Indies put it: "Memory is the only paradise from which we can not be expelled."[6] The former Governor of Surakarta (Solo), the conservative M.B. van der Jagt, inadvertently provided more honest reasons for the nostalgia of Dutch people who cannot overcome their longing for the "Paradise Lost" in southeast Asia: "with the transfer of sovereignty to the Indonesian Republic, Holland was forced to abandon its valuable creation, which represented the work of three-and-a-half centuries — [it lost] its Indies *imperium*, its tropical treasure trove with unlimited economic possibilities, its historically secured rights and its voluntarily assumed duties!"[7]

Despite the official Dutch surrender of sovereignty almost a half-a-century ago, quite recently, during the national "Book Week" in 1992 — a well-entrenched annual ritual in celebration of authors, books, and the written word — the official theme was a melancholy commemoration of Dutch colonial literature. The windows of bookstores in every Dutch city displayed dozens of new or reissued novels, memoirs, and monographs about the history and colonial culture — *tempo doeloe*, the "good old days" — of the Dutch East Indies. Large stacks of southeast Asian travel guides and Indonesian cookbooks found their way into the showcases of bookstores, too. In fact, the special "Book Week" issue of the magazine *Nusantara* listed a mind-boggling total of more than 250 books on Indonesia currently in print in the Netherlands, thus feeding the Dutch intellectual appetite for fiction and scholarship about their erstwhile tropical domain. Such books seem to soothe what Johan Huizinga has called in a domestic Dutch context a *geestelijk heimwee*, which in this case entails a "spiritual homesickness" for the creature comforts and natural splendor of the bygone days of living in the Dutch East Indies.[8]

But a feeling of nostalgia for a colonial setting of the past can also function as a form of mystification, which converts former agents of colonial rule into guileless spectators by endowing the process of remembering former colonial societies with an elegiac aura. On occasion it seems as if nostalgia can exonerate European protagonists in the colonial drama *ex post facto*. Romanticized memories of the past can nurture the impression that earlier policies of racial mastery and economic inequality were inevitable, natural, or harmless: *zo was het nu eenmaal!* (that is simply the way it was!) Nostalgia frequently entails an actual "abdication of memory," Christopher Lash recently argued. By looking at the past through a hazy, soft-colored lens as an era that is irretrievably disconnected from contemporary moral or political judgments, nostalgia is linked to a "declining faith" in progress; it fosters a vision of history as a time of eternal "childlike innocence" or "charming simplicity," as if the past no longer holds a constitutive meaning for either the present or the future.[9]

"Imperialist nostalgia," whether the Dutch tendency to reminisce about the good old days of *tempo doeloe* or the "Raj Revival" in England, softens the historical reality of colonialism's injustice, if only because the persistence of poverty or the lack of political freedoms in contemporary Indonesia retroactively seems to vindicate colonial rule as necessary, as "decorous and orderly," or perhaps even as beneficial.[10] Hence, a historian who belabors the more egregious aspects of Dutch colonial practices in the past is sometimes accused of having written a "biased" or "subjective" historical narrative, implying that others who skate warily on the surface of some of the more problematic actions of our Dutch forebears in Indonesia are allegedly more "objective" in their description of colonial history.[11]

However, nostalgia also competes with bitter memories of racism, exploitation, suffering, and decolonization.[12] Similar allegations of ideological partisanship have been levelled in the other direction; charged with participating in a diabolic plot to bury the real historical "truth" about Dutch colonial society in the Indies, others within the historical profession are accused of residing in a scholarly "Sodom and Gomorrah" filled with hypocrisy and sophistry.[13] In their obstinate refusal to cast a blunt analytical glance at the more deplorable aspects of the Dutch colonial past, this antithetical cohort of prejudiced historians has presumably indulged in a similar kind of self-serving "subjectivity."

Hence, on the opposite end of the historiographical spectrum some scholars have maligned the Dutch colonial record in Indonesia by cloaking it in guilt and recrimination. According to a number of chroniclers, the three-hundred years of Dutch colonial rule in southeast Asia accomplished nothing even remotely positive. And worse yet, in the eyes of some among them the Dutch military troops during the police actions in 1947-48 engaged in excessive brutality, a painful accusation that has again come to the forefront of public attention in recent years. Obviously this purely negative description of the Dutch colonial project constitutes the flip side of dreamy nostalgia. In its categorical bleakness, this historiographical style obscures "genuine" understanding just as much as an overly sentimental portrayal shrouds "real" knowledge, too. On the whole these stridently conflicting opinions suggest that historians are caught in the rigid bipolarity of a moral universe that divides the past into two extremes of either black or white.

But would it not make more sense to acknowledge that all historical representations are inherently subjective ventures? Should not we try to expose the middle ground of collective memory, which can rise above and beyond a bifurcation of the world into either good or evil? As Eric Hobsbawm noted matter-of-factly, last year: "historians' business is to remember what others forget." But historians, he added, are invariably more than professional "remembrancers and compilers."[14] After all, a historian's creative act determines which memories should be rescued from oblivion by "selecting, pruning, editing, commenting ... and delivering judgments."[15] It also depends upon a historian's intellectual discretion to decide which memories are better left alone because it is preferable to let certain sleeping dogs rest in peace, at least for the time being. Historians, in other words, must always try to travel an intermediate passage in-between "the weight of memory and the terror of erasure."[16]

The historical record — as it lies buried in official archives, informal correspondence, honest or disingenuous memoirs, and in a panoply of good or mediocre novels — is unearthed by human beings who approach each pile of hand-written documents or printed pages with a highly personal imagination. Inevitably, they bring to bear a very private range of social and political sensibilities. Being a member of a particular national culture also delicately molds and shapes the "historian's business" of identifying scholarly questions, digging up sources and data, and interpreting the exposed information about a given social reality in the past. It was a serendipitous irony, in this context, that the Dutch Book Week's wistful tribute to colonial literature in 1992 more or less overlapped with the celebration of the "Festival of Indonesia" in the United States. Both events painted a picture of the exact same cultural universe of the Indonesian archipelago, but the resulting portraits revealed no likeness whatsoever.

During a year-long series of events in honor of Indonesian society mounted in a variety of major cities in the United States, the Suharto government, in its careful orchestration of modern Indonesia for the potential "tourist gaze" of the American public, had taxonomized its ethnically diverse cultures and cloaked them in a series of neat, stylized bundles — not unlike the portrayal of exotic peoples at the International Colonial Exposition in Paris in 1931. In addition, the "Festival of Indonesia" rank-ordered Indonesian ethnic identities according to a distinct hierarchy of cultural merit and refinement. As the political fulcrum of the nation, Java's position on top was unassailed. Bali, due to the lucrative flow of foreign currency its thriving tourist trade garners for the nation, was equally unchallenged in second place. Other burgeoning sites of foreign tourism — Toraja country in Central Sulawesi, for instance, or the Minangkabau region and the Toba Batak territory in Sumatra followed in close succession.[17] Inevitably the ethnic groups perceived to be the least sophisticated — or most "primitive" — occupied the lower rungs on the hierarchical ladder. This cunning, and officially sanctioned, process of classifying and staging Indonesian cultures for the imagination of the outside world, however, depicted all of them as pure and uncontaminated by three centuries of Dutch colonial practice.

The fortuitous juxtaposition of the Book Week in Holland and the Festival of Indonesia in the United States forces us to recognize that historical memories of an identical social world can be constructed in diametrically opposed ways. Even if each of these narratives about the former tropical gothic of the Dutch East Indies in its unique way tries to establish a certain "paradigmatic authority," both stories also betray a palpable tension between their depiction of the past and the "actual" historical record in its chaotic complexity.[18] In sum, the historical memory of Indonesians as well as Dutch people appears equally entangled in a spider's web of remembering and forgetting, as if imprisoned, in the words of Pierre Nora, in a "dialectic between *souvenir* and *amnésie.*"[19]

Such an interaction between remembrance and amnesia emerges from deliberate as well as unconscious motives, because omission is as vital to the social health of a community as is memory, and we must know "the right time to forget as well as the right time to remember."[20] In his classic definition of the "essence" of the nation, Ernest Renan also accentuated the necessity of all citizens to concur on the "range of things" they should collectively try to forget.[21] Any consensus regarding those aspects of the past that should be recalled, because they bolster a sense of collective identity or national integrity, implies, almost automatically, a similar unspoken agreement as to what should be overlooked. But this consensus is always fragile and transitory, because the process of remembering and forgetting is forever in flux. We might think of historical narratives as constituting a nation's official museum of memory, but one in which space is woefully limited. At particular moments in time, when a specific historical narrative has lost its luster or imaginative appeal, it must be removed from the "memory palace" in order to make room for a sparkling new story.[22]

Historical chronicles are crucial building blocks in the construction of national identity: they function as "meta narratives" that keep alive and consecrate the common genealogy of the nation, even if they embellish a miscellany of myths and half-truths in addition to "real" historical facts.[23] Hence, history as "fact" alternates with history as "fantasy" or "parable." Even the most diligent practitioners of the historian's craft, earnest in their efforts to seek "truth" and to represent the past in order to render it vibrant and intelligible, are mythmakers at the same time. Replicating the painstaking labors of archeologists, most historians, whether they do so deliberately or unconsciously, tend to excavate, dismantle, and refashion an endless array of tangible "structures of knowledge" about the past.[24] As a result, they are unwittingly engaged in "the invention of tradition" and participate in a scholarly ritual of "literary creation" or "textual construction."[25]

Indeed, if professional historians, despite their best intentions, compose or perpetuate certain interpretive fictions about the past, then it is hardly a surprise that most members of a national community also reimagine history by telling stories that celebrate positive characteristics or happy events, while glossing over others that are either ambiguous or painful. For instance, the appealing, almost hagiographical, portrait painted by the Polish poet Zbigniew Herbert of the "collective heroism" of the seventeenth-century Dutch bourgeoisie and its "healthy, concrete, down-to-earth attitudes," makes it easy to bury in the "graveyard of history" the Dutch East India Company's record of taking advantage of Indonesian people for the sake of financial profit.[26] Or, to invoke another obvious example, the heartfelt dedication of many Dutch civil servants to nurture and tutor their native pupils constitutes a "genuine historical image as it flares up" most brilliantly in the collective memory the nation, as Walter Benjamin expressed it.[27] This heart-warming record of empathetic devotion to the well-being of the Indonesian population on the part of large numbers of Dutch colonial administrators, in turn, may foster a tendency to skip over the heartless actions of just as many European planters on tobacco and rubber plantations on the east coast of Sumatra.

Thus, the stories Dutch people concoct about their contested history of colonial culture in the wondrous world of the Indonesian archipelago combine the "lore of faraway places ... with the lore of the past."[28] In the course of rehearsing, revising, and retelling these stories, their perennially changing plots help to negotiate and accommodate a shifting national identity. A litany of tales about the time-honored traditions of Dutch tolerance and the "ethical" governance of the Dutch East Indies molds historical memories and shapes Dutch visions of empire. And by resorting to "tricks of memory and by leaping over time," it becomes easy to believe in a Dutch cultural record in colonial Indonesia that was characterized primarily by wisdom, thoroughness, and respect for native customs and traditions.[29]

Dutch people's stories about their previous existence in colonial Indonesia thus employ a series of signs and symbols that reinforce a variety of convictions about the quintessential "Dutchness" of their past. This symbolic sense of what constitutes "Dutchness" fluctuates somewhat paradoxically between a characteristic tenacity in the face of adversity versus a Dutch propensity to embrace a cautious, calculated neutrality. It also hinges on a contradictory celebration of the typically Dutch habit of accommodation or judicious compromise, on the one hand, and a Dutch tendency to make moral decisions and unyielding commitments to ethical goals, on the other. In the European metropole, at least, these historical narratives reside in a bustling world that legitimates a pandemonium of co-equal voices and conflicting opinions. Hence, chronicles about the past in Holland itself are embedded in an intellectual climate that recognizes their emblematic character and subtly "corrects and purifies" the collective memory of the past.[30] As a result, the historical narratives about the tolerant "ecumenical culture" of the Dutch nation are subject to constant amendation, which exposes some of them as fairy tales.[31]

However, when the surrounding decor of such stories is located in the bounteous world of the former Dutch East Indies, they strike a more discordant note. They ring false because of a disjunction between their symbolic references to the tolerance and civic freedoms that presumably comprise the core of Dutch history in northern Europe and the stark realities of Dutch colonial society in Indonesia on the other side of the globe. "Dutchness" situated in Indonesia revealed its dark underbelly and spawned an inverted world. Being divorced from the daily habit of cultural contestation within the nation in the European metropole, "true" Dutch values were garbled in translation and acquired a different, and more problematic, moral resonance. After all, the halcyon days of Dutch East Indies culture in the past did not transpire in a democratic universe filled with co-equal, contentious voices that granted Indonesians the same right to speak as Dutch men and women. Indonesians' critiques of colonialism's inherent racism or economic inequalities were mostly silenced or ignored. Hence, in trying to recover the reality of Dutch East Indies society, historians must read in between the lines of every narrative and apply personal, moral judgments, even if the images they are impelled to construct reveal a murky mixture of black and white.

Most of the historical imaginings of "Our Indies," whether they are conjured up by elderly *adat* scholars, former government officials and private Indies residents, or even by an occasional modern-day historian, frequently boil down to a story grounded in a natural sense of superiority and a simple faith in the right to rule. Even if these narratives are modulated by a self-imposed ethical duty to "civilize" and "uplift," they nonetheless devise a tale that is a far cry from the renowned Dutch habit of compromise — of honestly negotiating over contested space or resolving moral ambiguities. Hence, attempting to recapture the ambience of an evaporated colonial culture is often more than an innocent, sentimental journey. This poetry of nostalgia tends to uphold, too, dearly beloved myths about ourselves that plague a candid reimagination of the colonial era.[32] At the same time, of course, the moralistic language of culpability and indictment hinders an honest assessment, too. Yet, in the many memoirs of ex-civil servants who represent their past labors on behalf of Indonesians as a kind of altruistic development work *avant la lettre*, Johan Huizinga's spiritual homesickness — or what Rudy Kousbroek has described as "the poisoned well of nostalgia" — can emerge as an obstacle to the honest reconstruction of the social world and political realities of the Dutch East Indies.[33]

NOTES

INTRODUCTION

1. *Interview Magazine*, May, 1989, p. 130.
2. Oliver A. Rink, *Holland on the Hudson. An Economic and Social History of Dutch New York* (Ithaca: Cornell University Press, 1986), p. 156, 18.
3. Henk van Nierop, "Gewone mensen in een ongewone eeuw," *NRC Handelsblad*, November 30, 1991.
4. Simon Schama, *The Embarrassment of Riches. An Interpretation of Dutch Culture in the Golden Age* (New York: Alfred A. Knopf, 1987), passim.
5. About the Dutch negotiation over contested space in either colonial North America or South Africa, see Carmel Shire, "Dutch-Indigenous Relations in New Netherland and The Cape in the 17th Century," and Paul Huey, "The Dutch at Ford Orange," in Lisa Falk, ed., *Historical Archaeology in Global Perspective* (Washington D.C.: Smithsonian Institution Press, 1991), pp. 11-69.
6. Donald Harman Akenson, *God's Peoples. Covenant and Land in South Africa, Israel and Ulster* (Ithaca: Cornell University Press, 1992). See especially the chapter on "The Afrikaners: A Culture in Exile, 1806-1948," pp. 45-96.
7. Anthony Trollope, *South Africa*, 2 vols. (London: Chapman and Hall, 1878), 2, p. 10.
8. Liah Greenfield, *Nationalism: Five Roads to Modernity* (Cambridge: Harvard University Press, 1992), p. 18.
9. Tom Nairn, *The Break-Up of Britain: Crisis and Neo-Nationalism* (London: New Left Books, 1987), passim.
10. Benedict Anderson, in *Imagined Communities. Reflections on the Origin and Spread of Nationalism* (London/New York: Verso, 1983), uses the word "conjuring" throughout the text, while "communities, fuzzy and enumerated," appears in Partha Chatterjee, *The Nation and its Fragments* (Princeton: Princeton University Press, 1993), pp. 223-24. Peter Carey, in "Myths, Heroes, and Wars," in Colin Wild and Peter Carey, eds., *Born in Fire. The Indonesian Struggle for Indepedence* (Athens: Ohio University Press/BBC Publications, 1986), writes that the existence of every nation results from a "creation of the imagination," p. 6.
11. Edward W. Said, *Culture and Imperialism* (New York: Alfred A. Knopf, 1993), p. 10.
12. Antoinette Burton, *Burdens of History. British Feminists, Indian Women, and Imperial Culture, 1865-1915* (Chapel Hill: University of North Carolina Press, 1994), p. 36.
13. Kwame Anthony Appiah, *In My Father's House. Africa in the Philosophy of Culture* (New York: Oxford University Press, 1992), p. 48.
14. See Timothy Brennan's discussion of "National Fictions, Fictional Nations," in *Salman Rushdie & the Third World* (New York: St Martin's Press, 1989), pp. 13, 16-31.
15. In this context it is interesting to note Simon Schama's observation in his recent *Landscape and Memory* (New York: Alfred A. Knopf, 1995), that the word landscape was imported into the English language in the late sixteenth century from the Dutch word *landschap*, which like its Germanic root *landschaft* came to signify "a unit of human occupation, indeed a jurisdiction," p. 10.
16. Richard Johnson, "Towards a Cultural Theory of the Nation: A British-Dutch Dialogue," in Annemieke Galema, Barabara Henkes, and Henk te Velde, eds., *Images of the Nation. Different Meanings of Dutchness, 1870-1940* (Amsterdam/Atlanta: Rodopi, 1993), Amsterdam Studies On Cultural Identity, 2, pp. 204-207.
17. Johnson, "Towards a Cultural Theory of the Nation," p. 170, fn. 22.
18. Charles Tilly, "A Bridge Halfway: Responding to Brubaker," *Contention. Debates in Society, Culture, and Science*, 4, No. 1 (Fall 1994), pp. 17-18, and Herman Lebovics, *True France. The Wars over Cultural Identity, 1900-1945* (Ithaca: Cornell University Press, 1992), passim.
19. Reprinted in the column "One hundred years ago," *The Spectator*, September 10, 1994.
20. See for example Stuart Hall, "Cultural Identity and Diaspora," in Jonathan Rutherford, ed., *Identity, Community, Culture, Difference* (London: Routledge, 1990), pp. 222-237.
21. Piet Korthuys, *In de ban van de tropen* (Wageningen: Zomer & Keuning, 1947), p. 9, and J.M. Coetzee, *White Writing. On the Culture of Letters in South Africa* (New Haven: Yale University Press, 1988), p. 49.
22. Leonard Blussé, "Retribution and Remorse: The Interaction between the Administration and the Protestant Mission in Early Colonial Formosa," in Gyan Prakash, ed., *After Colonialism. Imperial Histories and Postcolonial Displacements* (Princeton: Princeton University Press, 1995), p. 156.
23. C.R. Boxer, *The Dutch Seaborne Empire, 1600-1800*, quoted by Blussé in "Retribution and Remorse," p. 156.

22. Derek Walcott, *The Antilles: Fragments of Epic Memory. The Nobel Lecture* (New York: Farrar, Straus and Giroux, 1992), n.p.
23. Martin Green, *Dreams of Adventure and Deeds of Empire* (New York: Basic Books, 1979), passim.
24. Quoted by Cees Fasseur, *De Indologen. Ambtenaren voor de Oost, 1825-1950* (Amsterdam: Bert Bakker, 1992), p. 91. In a recent English translation of his book on the Cultivation System, *The Politics of Colonial Exploitation. Java, The Dutch, and the Cultivation System* (1975; repr. Ithaca: Cornell University Southeast Asia Publications, 1992), Fasseur invokes a comparable metaphor when he titles the third chapter, alluding to a phrase from John Sydenham Furnivall, "The Cork on which the Netherlands Floats," p. 56.
25. Burton, *Burdens of History*, p. 31. A thorough analysis of the ways in which colonial rule engaged in a constant reconfiguration of the norms and forms of female behavior can be found in KumKum Sangari and Sudesh Vaid, eds., *Recasting Women. Essays in Colonial History* (New Brunswick: Rutgers University Press, 1991).
26. Corinne A. Kratz, "We've Always Done It Like This ... Except for a Few Details": 'Tradition' and 'Innovation' in Okiek Ceremonies," *Comparative Studies in Society and History*, 35, No. 1 (January 1993), especially pp. 45-51.
27. Rudy Kousbroek, "De Mems in de koloniale samenleving," in *Deugd en ondeugd. Jaarboek voor vrouwengeschiedenis 13* (Amsterdam: Internationaal Instituut voor Sociale Geschiedenis, 1994), pp. 149-162. In *Het Oostindisch Kampsyndroom* (Amsterdam: Meulenhoff, 1992) he notes that "jaunty, conceited, merciless Indies *mems* [were] more colonial in their ideas than their menfolk: gossipy, provincial, and hypocritical," p. 191. In her thoughtful response, Mieke Aerts raises questions about Kousbroek's provocative statements that are similar to mine; see "Gemengde gevoelens bij gemengde berichten uit de Oost," in *Deugd en Ondeugd*, pp. 163-174.
28. Kousbroek, *Het Oostindisch kampsyndroom*, pp. 355-56; see also pp. 72, 191, 221, and 234, and his Introduction, "Cliché en Code," to C. Binnerts, *Alles in order, heren...! Een dagboek van het eiland Flores uit het jaar 1943* (1947; repr. Baarn: Hollandia, 1988), pp. 5-14.
29. Aerts, Gemengde gevoelens bij gemengde berichten," in *Deugd en ondeugd*, p. 164.
30. See, among others, Burton, *Burdens of History*; Laura E. Donaldson, *Decolonizing Feminisms. Race, Gender, and Empire Building* (Chapel Hill: University of North Carolina Press, 1992); Margaret Strobel, *European Women and the Second British Empire* (Bloomington: Indiana University Press, 1991); Nupur Chaudhuri and Margaret Strobel, eds., *Western Women and Imperialism. Complicity and Resistance* (Bloomington: Indiana University Press, 1992); Ann Laura Stoler, "Carnal Knowledge and Imperial Power. Gender, Race, and Morality in Colonial Asia," in Micaela di Leonardo, ed., *Gender at the Crossroads: Feminist Anthropology in the Post-Modern Era* (Berkeley: University of California Press, 1991), pp. 51-101; Elsbeth Locher-Scholten, "Orientalism and the Rhetoric of the Family: Javanese Servants in European Household Manuals and Children's Fiction," *Indonesia*, No. 58 (October 1994), pp. 19-40. I have tried to address some of these issues in Frances Gouda, "The Gendered Rhetoric of Colonialism and Anti-Colonialism in Twentieth-Century Indonesia," *Indonesia*, No. 55 (April 1993), pp. 1-22; Idem, "Das 'unterlegene' Geschlecht der 'überlegene' Rasse. Kolonialgeschichte und Geschlechterverhältnisse," in Hanna Schissler, ed., *Geschlechterverhältnisse im historischen Wandel* (Frankfurt/New York: Campus, 1993), pp. 185-203; Idem, "Nyonyas on the Colonial Divide: White Women in the Dutch East Indies, 1900-1942," *Gender and History*, 5, No. 3 (Autumn 1993), pp. 318-342, and Idem, "Teaching Indonesian Girls in Java and Bali, 1900-1942: Dutch progressives, the infatuation with 'Oriental' refinement, and 'Western' ideas about proper womanhood," *Women's History Review*, 4, No. 1 (1995), pp. 25-62.
31. Kousbroek, "De Mems in de koloniale samenleving," in *Deugd en ondeugd*, p. 149. A British feminist response to Kipling's poem "Female of the Species" was an alternative version, "The Mother of the Man," while Millicent Garrett Fawcett responded to his claim that women were deadlier than men with a defiant "That's me!" See Burton, *Burdens of History*, p. 15.
32. Loes Nobel, "Tirto" and "De uitnodiging," in *Gebroken rijst. Indische verhalen* (Baarn: Hollandia, 1978), pp. 13-17, 95-98.
33. J.A.A. van Doorn, *De laatste eeuw van Indië. Ontwikkeling en ondergang van een koloniaal project* (Amsterdam: Bert Bakker, 1994), passim.
34. Margaret Strobel uses this phrase in both *European Women and the Second British Empire* and *Western Women and Imperialism. Complicity and Resistance*.
35. For an examination of the role of the *njai*, see Nicole Lucas, "Trouwverbod, inlandse huishoudsters, en Europese vrouwen," pp. 78-97, and Tessel Pollmann, "Bruidstraantjes. De koloniale roman, de njai en de apartheid," pp. 98-125, in Jeske Reijs, et al, eds., *Vrouwen in de Nederlandse koloniën. Zevende jaarboek voor vrouwengeschiedenis* (Nijmegen: SUN Uitgeverij, 1986); see also Elsbeth Locher-Scholten, "The Nyai in Colonial Deli: A Case of Supposed Mediation," in Sita van Bemmelen, et al, eds., *Women and Mediation in Indonesia* (Leiden: KITLV Press, 1992), pp. 255-280.

36. M. Muchie, "II. Theories on Development — A synopsis," in M. Muchie, H.L. Wesseling, and O. Prakash, eds., *North-South Perspectives. Debates on Colonialism and North-South Relations* (Amsterdam: Royal Tropical Institute, 1989), pp. 40-43.
37. David Spurr, *The Rhetoric of Empire. Colonial Discourse in Journalism, Travel Writing, and Imperial Administration* (Durham: Duke University Press, 1993), p. 184.
38. Nicholas Thomas, *Colonialism's Culture. Anthropology, Travel and Government* (Princeton: Princeton University Press, 1994), p. 3.
39. Thomas, *Colonialism's Culture*, p. 3. For a discussion of the internal disagreements and conflicting visions within the Dutch colonial community, see P.J. Drooglever, "Koloniaal beleid en Indische samenleving tot 1942," in *Idem*, ed., *Indisch intermezzo. Geschiedenis van de Nederlanders in Indonesië* (Amsterdam: De Bataafsche Leeuw, 1991), pp. 19-32.

CHAPTER 1

1. Quoted by Taufik Abdullah, "Historical Reflections on Three Novels of Pre-War Indonesia," in *Idem*, ed., *Papers of the Fourth Indonesian-Dutch History Conference*, 2 vols. (Yogyakarta: Gadjah Mada University Press, 1986), 2, *Literature and History*, p. 230.
2. Hans Rijkx, We'll Meet Again (Don't Know Where, Don't Know When...) *Mijn leven als tabaksplanter en mijn belevenissen als krijgsgevangene van het keizerlijk Japans leger* (Santpoort: Hans Rijkx, 1990), pp. 88-89.
3. Piet Korthuys, *In de ban van de tropen* (Wageningen: Zomer & Keuning, 1947), pp. 13-14.
4. Siem Boom, "Thuis in de heimwee," *Pasarkrant. Uitgave van de stichting Tong Tong*, Summer Edition 1994, pp. 1, 7.
5. Meena Alexander, *Fault Lines. A Memoir* (New York: The Feminist Press, 1993), p. 11.
6. Doris Lessing, *Under My Skin. Volume One of My Autobiography to 1949* (New York: Harper Collins, 1994), p. 59.
7. Paula Gomes, *Sudah, laat maar* (Amsterdam: Querido, 1975), p. 18.
8. Rudy Kousbroek, "De Mems in de koloniale samenleving," in *Deugd en ondeugd. Jaarboek voor vrouwengeschiedenis 13* (Amsterdam: Internationaal Instituut voor Sociale Geschiedenis, 1994), p. 151.
9. Alexander, *Fault Lines. A Memoir*, p. 5.
10. For a lucid discussion, see Elsbeth Locher-Scholten, "Nederland leert niet van oorlogsmisdaden," *NRC Handelsblad*, May 20, 1994. The political scientist Arend Lijphart first used the terms "trauma" and "pathology" in *The Trauma of Decolonization: The Dutch and West New Guinea* (New Haven: Yale University Press, 1966). With psychoanalytic overtones, he called the Dutch attachments to its last colonial possession in southeast Asia "definitely pathological: it was a symptom of a serious and profound inferiority complex" and evidence of "the temporary insanity" of the Dutch nation, p. 288.
11. Sigmund Freud, *Civilization and its Discontents* (New York: W.W. Norton, 1961). Freud initially titled his essay "the unhappiness in culture" (*Das Unglück in der Kultur*) but later changed it to *Unbehagen*. See James Strachey's Editorial Introduction, p. 5.
12. Ian Buruma, *The Wages of Guilt. Memories of War in Germany and Japan* (New York: Farrar, Straus, Giroux, 1994), p. 5.
13. H.L. Zwitzer's review of Ad van Liempt, *Een mooi woord voor oorlog. Ruzie, roddel en achterdocht op weg naar de Indonesië-oorlog* (The Hague: SDU, 1994), in *NRC Handelsblad*, June 18, 1994.
14. Colin White and Laurie Boucke, *The UnDutchables. An Observation of the Netherlands: its Culture and Inhabitants* (Montrose, CA: White/Boucke Publishers, 1993), pp. ii, 92-93.
15. Quoted by Chris van Esterik, "Indië verloren, moralisme behouden," *NRC Handelsblad*, June 9, 1995.
16. On the strategic use of arbitrary, unpredictable power — or "terrorism" — in colonial societies, see Michael Taussig, *Shamanism, Colonialism, and the Wild Man. A Study in Terror and Healing* (Chicago: University of Chicago Press, 1987).
17. Anath Abeyesekere, *The Apotheosis of Captain Cook. European Mythmaking in the Pacific* (Princeton: Princeton University Press, 1992), pp. 14, 23. For a gentler reading of Captain Cook's behavior, see Peter H. Wood, "North America in the Age of Captain Cook: Three Glimpses of Indian-European Contact in the Age of the American Revolution," in Stuart B. Schwartz, ed., *Implicit Understandings. Observing, Reporting, and Reflecting on the Encounters Between Europeans and Other Peoples in the Early Modern Era* (New York: Cambridge University Press, 1994), pp. 484-501.
18. Theodore Friend employs this Hegelian dichotomy in "Lordship and Bondage: The Philippines, Indonesia, and Japanese Impact, 1942-1945," Occasional Paper No. 19, Asia Program, Woodrow Wilson International Center for Scholars, Washington DC. See also Gayatri Chakravorty Spivak, "Can the Subaltern Speak?," in

19 Cary Nelson and Lawrence Grossberg, eds., *Marxism and the Interpretation of Culture* (Urbana: University of Illinois Press, 1988), pp. 271-313, and Stephen J.Greenblatt, *Learning to Curse. Essays in Early Modern Culture* (New York: Routledge, 1990).
19 Jeffrey B. Kingston, "Manipulating Tradition: The State, Adat, Popular Protest, and Class Conflict in Colonial Lampung," *Indonesia*, No. 51 (April, 1991), pp. 21-46.
20 Rian van Kuppenveld, "Koelies? Het zijn beesten die wel wat op menschen gelijken," *Het Parool. Zaterdags Bijvoegsel*, March 24, 1987.
21 Sutan Sjahrir, *Indonesische overpeinzingen* (Amsterdam: De Bezige Bij, 1945), p. 85.
22 *The New Republic*, October 29, 1945.
23 E.J. Dommering, "De Nederlandse publieke discussie en de politionele acties in Indonesië," *Nederlands juristenblad*, No. 8, March 4, 1994, p. 277-290.
24 Nicolaas van Sas, "Varieties of Dutchness," in Annemarie Galema, Barbara Henkes & Henk te Velde, eds., *Images of the Nation. Different Meanings of Dutchness, 1870-1940* (Amsterdam/Atlanta: Rodopi, 1993), p. 15. In the Netherlands, a strong resistence against efforts to define "Dutchness" exists, too, because it conjures up antiquated, and perhaps politically harmful, "nationalistic" historiography. For an art historian's dismissal of efforts to identify "what makes Dutch art Dutch art," see E. de Jongh, "Real Dutch art and no-so-real Dutch art: some nationalistic views of seventeenth-century Netherlandish painting," *Simiolus. Netherlands Quarterly for the History of Art*, 20, Nos. 2/3 (1990-91), pp. 197-206.
25 See the contributions by Josien Blok, Marjan Schwegman, and Jan Bank to the section *polemiek* in *Deugd en ondeugd. Jaarboek voor Vrouwengeschiedenis 13*, pp. 123-36.
26 Gerard Mulder and Paul Koedijk, *H.M. van Randwijk. Een biografie* (Amsterdam: Raamgracht/Nijgh & Van Ditmar, 1988), p. 591. Whether intentionally or not, Van Randwijk's formulation echoed Soewardi Soerjaningrat's (Ki Hadjar Dewantoro) famous statement in *De Expres* in November, 1913: "if I were to be a Dutchman, I would be ashamed to celebrate the independence of my country in these colonized lands ..." See Benedict Anderson, *Imagined Communities. Reflections on the Origins and Spread of Nationalism* (London/New York: Verso, 1983), pp. 107-8.
27 Mulder and Koedijk, *H.M. van Randwijk. Een biografie*, pp. 591-95.
28 Quoted by Dommering, "De Nederlandse publieke discussie en de politionele acties," p. 281.
29 Graa Boomsma, *De laatste tyfoon* (Amsterdam: Prometheus, 1992), p. 55, and an interview published in *Nieuwsblad van het Noorden*, March 6, 1992.
30 Arjo Klamer uses the term "Citadel" in *Verzuilde dromen. 40 jaar SER* (Amsterdam: Contact, 1990), pp. 174-176.
31 Especially historians of British colonialism in India have focused their recent work on these issues. See, among others, Bernard S. Cohn, "Representing Authority in Victorian India," in Eric Hobsbawm and Terence Ranger, eds., *The Invention of Tradition* (Cambridge: Cambridge University Press, 1983); Nicholas B. Dirks, *The Hollow Crown. Ethnohistory of an Indian Kingdom* (Cambridge: Cambridge University Press, 1987); Ranajit Guha, "Dominance without Hegemony and its Historiography," in *Idem.*, ed., *Subaltern Studies*, VI (New Delhi: Oxford University Press, 1989); Lata Mani, "Cultural Theory, Colonial Texts: Reading Eyewitness Accounts of Widow Burning," in Lawrence Grossberg, et al, eds., *Cultural Studies: Now and in the Future* (New York: Routledge, 1992); Carol A. Breckenridge and Peter van der Veer, eds., *Orientalism and the Postcolonial Predicament* (Philadelphia: University of Pennsylvania Press, 1993), and Gyan Prakash, ed., *After Colonialism. Imperial Histories and Postcolonial Displacements* (Princeton: Princeton University Press, 1995).
32 For a discussion about Indonesia, see Robert van Niel, "Colonialism Revisited: Recent Historiography," *Journal of World History*, 1, No. 1 (1990), pp. 109-124, and Maarten Kuitenbrouwer, *The Netherlands and the Rise of Modern Imperialism. Colonies and Foreign Policy, 1870-1902*, (1989; repr. New York/Oxford: Berg Publishers, 1991).
33 Paul van 't Veer, *Vriend en vijand in de kolonie* (Amsterdam: De Arbeiderspers, 1956), pp. 14-15.
34 Ann Laura Stoler, "Rethinking Colonial Categories: European Communities and the Boundaries of Rule," *Comparative Studies in Society and History*, 31, No. 1 (1989), p. 135.
35 Lessing, *Under My Skin*, p. 202.
36 Salman Rushdie, *Imaginary Homelands. Essays and Criticism, 1981-1991* (London: Granta Books/Viking, 1991), p. 12.
37 Willem Walraven, *Brieven aan familie en vrienden, 1919-1941*, 2nd ed. (Amsterdam: G.A. van Oorschot, 1992), p. 379.
38 Gerard P.A. Termorshuizen, "The Novels of Maurits: A Portrait of a Society," in Abdullah, *Papers of the Fourth Indonesian-Dutch History Conference*, 2, pp. 185, 187.
39 Hannah Arendt, *Eichmann in Jerusalem. A Report on the Banality of Evil* (New York: Viking, 1964), p. 285.

40 Arendt, *Eichmann in Jerusalem*, p. 288. L. Noë, in "De nationale beweging," noted that this sense of racial superiority is especially "egregious if absorbed by people with little civilization themselves, who practice professions that place them in a caste which is not entitled to respect; the *inlander* most frequently encounters this kind of Dutchmen." in D.G. Stibbe, ed., *Neerlands Indië. Land en volk; geschiedenis en samenleving; bedrijf en bestuur*, 2 vols. (Amsterdam: Elsevier, 1935), 2, p. 242.

41 Ashis Nandy, *The Intimate Enemy. Loss and Recovery of Self under Colonialism* (Delhi: Oxford University Press, 1983), p. 72.

42 Thomas Karsten, "Rassenwaan en rassenbewustzijn," in *De Taak. Algemeen Indisch Weekblad*, 1, No. 18, December 1, 1917, pp. 205-206.

43 E. du Perron, in *De smalle mens II* (Amsterdam: G.A. van Oorschot, 1965), used the term hypocrisy, p. 238. Ian Buruma, in "Revenge in the Indies," *New York Review of Books*, August 9, 1994, employs the word bluff.

44 Taufik Abdullah, "The Making of a Schakel Society: The Minangkabau Region in the Late Nineteenth Century," in *Papers of the Dutch-Indonesian Historical Conference, Noordwijkerhout, 1976* (Leiden/Jakarta: Bureau of Indonesian Studies and Indonesian Steering Committee, 1978), pp. 143-153. Clifford Geertz has called this a "poetics of power, not a mechanics ... the Balinese state drew its force, which was real enough, from its imaginative energies, its semiotic capacity to make inequality enchant." In *Negara: The Theatre State in Nineteenth-Century Bali* (Princeton: Princeton University Press, 1980), pp. 124-25.

45 Amry Vandenbosch, *The Dutch East Indies. Its Government, Problems, and Politics* (Berkeley: University of California Press, 1941), p. 70.

46 "Kapers op de koloniale kust," in *Weerzien met Indië* (Zwolle: Waanders, 1994), No. 15, p. 347.

47 P.M.B. Blaas, "De prikkelbaarheid van een kleine natie met een groot verleden: Fruin's and Blok's nationale geschiedschrijving," *Theoretische Geschiedenis*, 9 (1982), pp. 271-304.

48 Concerns with revenue played their part, too. An expert on Dutch opium policies in the Indies, J.F. Scheltema, noted that "all good intentions and humanitarian impulses in the Indies succumb to pressure for profits," as examined by James R. Rush, *Opium to Java. Revenue Farming and Chinese Enterprise in Colonial Indonesia, 1860-1910* (Ithaca: Cornell University Press, 1990), pp. 237-38.

49 Cees Fasseur, "Nederland en Nederlands-Indië, 1795-1914," in *Algemene Geschiedenis der Nederlanden*, 15 vols. (Haarlem: Fibula van Dishoeck, 1983), 11, pp. 362-63.

50 Quoted by Cees Fasseur, "Vier eeuwen In(dones)ië," in *De weg naar het paradijs en andere Indische geschiedenissen* (Amsterdam: Bert Bakker, 1995), p. 9.

50 The missionary D.J. van der Linden wrote about the native "blood that is glued to the *batig slot*," quoted by Th. van den End, "Transformatie door informatie? De bijdrage van de Nederlandse zending aan de opinievorming over het koloniaal bestel," *Tijdschrift voor Geschiedenis*, 105, No. 3 (1992), p. 441. J.E. Stokvis, *Van wingewest naar zelfbestuur in Nederlandsch-Indië* (Amsterdam: Elsevier, 1922), p. 96; Coenraad Theodoor van Deventer in his "Eereschuld" article in *De Gids* (1899) estimated the Indies profits at the same number; N.P. van den Berg, in "Debet of credit?" (1885) came up with the higher amount of 844 million, whereas the Dutch Socialist F. Domela Nieuwenhuis mentioned in the Second Chamber of the Parliament in The Hague in 1888 that the figure was 850 million guilders.

52 See Cees Fasseur, ed., *Geld en geweten. Een bundel opstellen over anderhalve eeuw Nederlands bestuur in de Indonesische archipel*, 2 vols. (The Hague: Martinus Nijhoff Press,1980); Idem, *Kultuurstelsel en koloniale baten. De Nederlandse exploitatie van Java, 1840-1860* (Leiden: E.J. Brill, 1978), and Idem, "Nederland en Nederlands-Indië, 1795-1914," in *Algemene Geschiedenis der Nederlanden*, 11, pp. 349-372. See also Elsbeth Locher-Scholten, *Ethiek in Fragmenten. Vijf studien over koloniaal denken en doen van Nederlanders in de Indonesische Archipel, 1877-1942* (Utrecht: HES Publishers, 1981), and Hans van Miert, *Bevlogenheid en onvermogen. Mr. J.H. Abendanon en de ethische richting in het Nederlandse kolonialisme* (Leiden: KITLV Press, 1991); an analysis by a left-leaning participant can be found in D.M.C. Koch, *Batig slot. Figuren uit het oude Indië* (Amsterdam: De Brug/Djambatan, 1960), and *Verantwoording. Een halve eeuw in Indonesië* (The Hague/Bandung: Uitgeverij W. van Hoeve, 1956).

53 The colonial budget rose from 160 million guilders in 1901 to 300 million guilders in 1913. Allocations to the educational system for Indonesiers rose between 1901 and 1918 from 1.5 percent of overall government expenditures to 4.5 percent. The law on Decentralization of 1903 gave a minimal amount of independent authority to Indonesians, which would eventually be expanded, *de jure* but not *de facto*, with the establishment of the *Volksraad* (People's council) in 1918. See Elsbeth Locher-Scholten, "Een liberaal autocraat, goverrneur-generaal mr. J.P. graaf van Limburg Stirum," in *Ethiek in Fragmenten*, pp. 67-83.

54 Idenburg's report to the Queen, quoted by Elsbeth Locher-Scholten, "Dutch Expansion in the Indonesian Archipelago Around 1900 and the Imperialism Debate," *Journal of Southeast Asian Studies*, 25, No. 1 (March 1994), p. 106.

55 Quoted in W.H. van Helsdingen and H. Hoogenberk, eds., *Daar werd wat groots verricht...Nederlandsch-Indië in de XXste eeuw* (Amsterdam: Elsevier, 1941), pp. 425-33.

56 See, among others, Cees Fasseur, *De Indologen. Ambtenaren voor de Oost, 1825-1950* (Amsterdam: Bert Bakker, 1992), especially section IV on "Minerva en Insulinde," pp. 359-477; *Wij gedenken...Gedenkboek van de vereniging van ambtenaren bij het binnenlands bestuur in Nederlands-Indië* (Utrecht: N.V.A. Oosthoek, 1956); J.A. Jonkman, *Het oude Nederlands-Indië. Memoires* (Assen: van Gorcum, 1971); J.V. de Bruyn, *Het verdwenen volk* (Bussum: Holkema en Warendorff, 1978); J.J. van Velde, *Brieven uit Sumatra, 1928-1949* (Franeker: T. Wever, 1982); A. Visser, *Een merkwaardige loopbaan. Herinneringen van een bestuursambtenaar in Nederlands-Indië/Indonesië, 1932-1950* (Franeker: T. Wever, 1982); W.Ph. Coolhaas, *Controleur BB. Herinneringen van een jong bestuursambtenaar in Nederlands-Indië* (Utrecht: HES Uitgevers, 1985), and S.L. van der Wal. ed., *Besturen overzee. Herinneringen van oud-ambtenaren bij het binnenlands bestuur in Nederlandsch-Indië* (Franker: T. Wever, 1977). For a discussion about the memoirs of the last generation of Dutch administrators in Indonesia, see G.J. Schutte, "De ervaringen van de laatste generatie Indischgasten," *Tijdschrift voor Geschiedenis*, 97 (1984), pp. 216-224 and Leonard Blussé, "A View from the Veranda: the 'Colonial Situation' as mirrored in the fiction of Colonial Civil Servants," in *Journal of The Japan-Netherlands Institute*, 2 (1990), pp. 131-150.
57 Cornelis Bastiaan Nederburgh made these proposals in 1902; see H.W. van den Doel, *De stille macht. Het Europees binnenlands bestuur op Java en Madoera, 1808-1942* (Amsterdam: Bert Bakker, 1994), pp. 171-73 and the discussion in Fasseur, "Max Havelaar en de publieke zaak," in *De weg naar het paradijs*, pp. 25-26.
58 G.L. Gonggrijp, "Over fatsoenlijke huizen van ontucht en fatsoenlijke werving," 75th letter to Johan Fabricius, January 8, 1913, in *Brieven van opheffer*, 4th ed. (Maastricht: Leiter-Nypels, n.d.), p. 289.
59 Saul Friedländer, *When Memory Comes* (New York: Farrar, Straus, and Giroux, 1979), p. 5.
60 Audrey R. Kahin and George McT. Kahin, *Subversion as Foreign Policy. The Secret Eisenhower and Dulles Debacle in Indonesia* (New York: Free Press, 1995), p. 21.
61 Koch, *Verantwoording. Een halve eeuw in Indonesië*. Marcel Koch applied to De Jonge the polemic of the arch-conservative Indies journalist Carel Wijbrands: "Er maar een goed regeerstelsel: *ik* ben de baas, — dan zal ik jelui wel pap voeren," p. 182.
62 B.C. de Jonge to W. Roëll on July 2, 1933, in Appendix, "Brieven," in S.L. van der Wal, ed., *Herinneringen van Jh. Mr. B.C. de Jonge, met brieven uit zijn nalatenschap* (Groningen: Wolters Noordhoff, 1968), p. 423.
63 Emile Schwidder and Fritjof Tichelman, eds., *A. Baars en H. Sneevliet. Het proces Sneevliet 1917* (Leiden: KITLV Press, 1991), Reprint Series, No. III, pp. 238-39.
64 Elsbeth Locher-Scholten, "Kritiek en Opbouw (1938-1942). Een rode splinter," in *Ethiek in fragmenten*, p. 174.
65 Z. Stokvis, "Een handboek voor den koloniale leider," *De Socialistische Gids*, reprinted as "Het boek van De Kat Angelino," in *Timboel. Algemeen Periodiek voor Indonesië*, 5, No. 4, March, 1931, pp. 59-63.
66 Stokvis, "Het boek van De Kat Angelino," in *Timboel. Algemeen Periodiek voor Indonesië* (1931), pp. 59-63.
67 Dr. H. Kraemer, "Het boek van De Kat Angelino," reprinted from *Koloniale Studiën*, in *Timboel. Algemeen Periodiek voor Indonesië*, 5, No. 16, September, 1931, pp. 242-43.
68 Harry A. Poeze, ed., *Politiek-Politioneele Overzichten van Nederlands-Indië*, 3 vols. (The Hague: Martinus Nijhoff Press, 1982), 1, 1927-1928, passim.
69 In the course of the 1920s, Sarekat Islam became internally divided between the red *Sarekat Rakyat* and the anti-communist *Sarekat Hijau*. See Harry A. Poeze, *Politiek-Politioneele Overzichten*, 1, p. xxxvii. See also H.J.H. Alers, *Om een rode of groene Merdeka. Tien jaren binnenlandse politiek. Indonesië, 1943-1953* (Eindhoven: Vulkaan/de Pelgrim, 1956), passim, and Shiraishi, *An Age in Motion*, especially pp. 41-90.
70 Ahmat B. Adam, *The Vernacular Press and the Emergence of Modern Indonesian Consciousness, (1855-1913)* (Ithaca: Cornell University Southeast Asia Program, 1995), Studies on Southeast Asia, No. 17, p. 161. See also Kees van Dijk, "The threefold suppression of the Javanese: The fight against capitalism, the colonial state, and the traditional rulers," in Robert Cribb, ed., *The Late Colonial State in Indonesia. Political and Economic Foundations of the Netherlands Indies, 1880-1942* (Leiden: KITLV Press, 1994), Verhandelingen No. 163, pp. 261-78.
71 Adam, *The Vernacular Press and the Emergence of Modern Indonesian Consciousness*, pp. 161-73.
72 M.C. Ricklefs, *A History of Modern Indonesia* (Bloomington: Indiana University Press, 1981), pp. 156-166. See also Donald Hindley, *The Communist Party of Indonesia, 1951-1963* (Berkeley: University of California Press, 1964), pp. 18-26; Ruth T. McVey, *The Rise of Indonesian Communism* (Ithaca: Cornell University Press, 1965), passim, and Rudolf Mrázek, *Sjahrir. Politics and Exile in Indonesia* (Ithaca: Cornell University Studies on Southeast Asia, 1994), No. 14, pp. 75-81, 91-95.
73 Theodore Friend, *The Blue-Eyed Enemy. Japan against the West in Java and Luzon* (Princeton: Princeton University Press, 1987), p. 18.
74 Robert Cribb, "Introduction," in Cribb, *The Late Colonial State in Indonesia*, p. 7.
75 M.G. Hoogstraten, *Nederlanders in Nederlands-Indië. Een schets van de Nederlandse koloniale aanwezigheid in Zuidoost Azie tussen 1596 en 1950* (Zutphen: Thieme, 1986), p. 76. See also Susan Abeyasekere, "The

Soetardjo Petition," *Indonesia*, No. 15 (April 1973), pp. 81-107; for a more general exploration, see L. Turksma, *Nederlanders in Nederlands-Indië: Een sociologische interpretatie van een voltooid verleden tijd* (Amesfoort: Acco, 1987).

76 The Indonesian *Volksraad* member was Mulia, quoted by Bastiaan Jan Brouwer, *De houding van Idenburg en Colijn tegenover de Indonesische beweging* (Kampen: J.H. Kok, 1958), p. 173.
77 H. van den Brink, *Een eisch van recht* (Amsterdam: Kirchner, 1946), p. 57.
78 Noto Soeroto, "Aziatisch imperialisme," in *Wederopbouw. Maandschrift gewijd aan de jong-Javanen beweging en het Javaansch geestesleven*, 3, Nos 1-4, January, 1920, pp. 16-17. See also the arguments of E.D. van Walree in "Mededingend Japan," in *De economische eenheid van het land* (Haarlem: Tjeenk Willink, 1936), who used his forty-year experience in Japan — he had been appointed as the first official Dutch consul in Yokohama in 1896 — to analyze the alarming growth of the forces of militarism within Japanese society, pp. 26-38.
79 For a thorough analysis of this organization, see P.J. Drooglever, *De Vaderlandsche Club. Totoks en de Indische politiek* (Franeker: T. Wever, 1982), passim.
80 Theodore Friend estimates that the pre-war European population of Java was 300.000; See *The Blue-Eyed Enemy*, p. 71. A Japanese military administrator in Java during World War II, Myoshi Shunkichiro, guessed the European population of Java to be as high as 600,000 before the war; See Anthony Reid and Oki Akira, eds., *The Japanese Experience in Indonesia: Selected Memoirs of 1942-45* (Athens, Ohio: Ohio University Center for International Studies, 1986), southeast Asian Series, no. 72, pp. 113-125. The Dutch historian S.L. van der Wal, on the other hand, provided the lower estimate of 200,000 European citizens in the Indies, of which 50,000 had been born in the Netherlands and were *trekkers* (those who would return to the Netherlands) and the other 150,000 were *blijvers* (those who were born in the Indies and "stayed on"); See S.L. van der Wal, "Nederland en Nederlands-Indië, 1914-1942," in *Algemene Geschiedenis der Nederlanden* (1979), 14, p. 393.
81 See the essays in P.J. Drooglever, ed., *Indisch intermezzo: geschiedenis van de Nederlanders in Indonesië* (Amsterdam: De Bataafse Leeuw, 1991). Doris Lessing has described a similar process in southern Rhodesia in *Under My Skin*, p. 325.
82 C. van Heekeren, *Trekkers en blijvers. Kroniek van een Haags-Indische familie* (Franeker: T. Wever, 1980), passim. For an analysis of the historical origins of the mestizo culture in the Dutch East Indies until the late nineteenth century, see Jean Gelman Taylor, *The Social World of Batavia. European and Eurasian in Dutch Asia* (Madison: University of Wisconsin Press, 1983), passim.
83 Benedict Anderson, in *Imagined Communities*, has coined the phrase "Tropical Gothic" when he refers to European communities in a colonial setting, p. 137.
84 Dommering, "De Nederlandse publieke discussie en de politionele acties," p. 283.
85 Quoted by Ingrid Harms and Tessel Pollmann, "In Nederland door omstandigheden," *Bijvoegsel Vrij Nederland*, No. 19, May 15, 1982, p. 15.
86 The eyewitness was J.E. Hueting, who was interviewed on the VARA program "Achter het nieuws" (behind the news) on Dutch television.
87 Dommering, "De Nederlandse publieke discussie en de politionele acties," p. 283.
88 Lou de Jong, *Het koninkrijk der Nederlanden in de Tweede Wereldoorlog*, 12 vols. (Leiden: Martinus Nijhoff), Nederlands-Indië, 2 vols., 11a (1984) and 11b (1988).
89 Geert Mak, "Een debat tussen de wajangpoppen," *NRC Handelsblad*, January 17, 1995.
90 Jan Maarten Fielderdij Dop and Yvonne Simons, "De berechting van Indië deserteurs," *Bijvoegsel Vrij Nederland*, No. 49, December 10, 1983. The number of conscientious objectors and/or deserters comprised more than 6,000 men.
91 Hendrik Spiering, "Na tropisch surrealisme wachtte de schoenenbon," *NRC Handelsblad*, January 12, 1995, and Boomsma, *De laatste tyfoon*, p. 118.
92 The English translation of the first edition of 1987 was published by Oxford University Press in New Delhi in 1989, and KITLV Press in Leiden published a third Dutch edition in 1992.
93 Drooglever, in "Koloniaal beleid en Indische samenleving tot 1942," notes that "the position of the *koelies* was little better than slavery," in *Idem*, ed., *Indisch intermezzo*, p. 20.
94 Schwidder and Tichelman, *Het proces Sneevliet 1917*, p. 104.
95 Idenburg's letter to Kuyper on January 18, 1911, quoted by Brouwer, *De houding van Idenburg en Colijn*, pp. 30-31.
96 C.D. Lagerwerff, quoted by Van den End, "Transformatie door informatie?" in *Tijdschrift voor Geschiedenis* (1992), p. 436.
97 J. van de Brand, *De millioenen uit Deli* (Amsterdam/Pretoria: Hoveker & Wormser, 1903).
98 In 1913, however, Idenburg opposed the introduction of the penal sanction in Java, even though it was supported by planters and "sugar barons." In his considerations, he wrote to Abraham Kuyper that "the inter-

ests of the *inlanders* weigh more heavily," a choice that filled him with pride. In J. de Bruyn and G. Puchinger, eds., *Briefwisseling Kuyper-Idenburg* (Franeker: T. Wever, 1985), p. 345. Brouwer notes, however, that Idenburg rejected the penal sanction in Java for more mundane reasons, i.e. because labor shortages did not exist on densely populated Java, in *De houding van Idenburg en Colijn*, p. 31.

99 Anne Marie Christine Brunink-Darlang, *Het penitentiair stelsel van Nederlands-Indië, 1905-1940* (Alblasserdam: Kanters, 1986), p. 90.
100 Idenburg to Kuyper, March 6, 1912, and Kuyper to Idenburg, April 12, 1912, in De Bruyn and Puchinger, eds., *Briefwisseling Kuyper-Idenburg*, pp. 279, 286.
101 Constance van der Valk, "Zo waren onze manieren," *Algemeen Dagblad*, March 14, 1987.
102 Tessel Pollmann, "Het Comité Geschiedkundig Eerherstel Nederlandsch-Indië (60.000 aanhangers) begint een proces over het boek van dr. L. de Jong," *Vrij Nederland*, 46, July 20, 1985.
103 Sietse van der Hoek, "Niet alle kolonialen zijn rotschoften geweest," *De Volkskrant*, October 30, 1984; see also Jan Bank, "L.de Jong scheidt illusie en werkelijkheid in Indië," *De Volkskrant*, October 30, 1984; Ralph Boekholt, "Indisch X IJ Z," *Moesson*, November 15, 1984 and *Idem*, "Het Rhemrev-rapport en de rillingen van Nederland," *Moesson*, May 15, 1987; A.v.L., Review, Lou de Jong's 11a, *Moesson*, December 1, 1984, and February 1, 1985; n.a., "Omzien in anti-kolonialisme," *Indische Pensioenbond*, March, 1985, p. 43, and Frits Groeneveld, "Nederlands tijdperk in Indië door een antikoloniale bril beschouwd," *NRC Handelsblad*, October 30, 1984.
104 "Indië in de literatuur," in *Weerzien met Indië* (Zwolle: Waanders, 1994), No. 13, p. 315, and Karin de Mik, "Emoties lopen hoog op bij Fries schrijversproces," *NRC Handelsblad*, January 12, 1995.
105 as in Van Helsdingen and Hoogenberk, *Daar wordt wat groots verricht...Nederlandsch-Indië in de XXste eeuw*, passim.
106 Lessing, *Under My Skin*, p. 114.
107 Eric Hobsbawm, *The Age of Extremes. A History of the World, 1914-1991* (New York: Pantheon, 1994), pp. 217-18. Hobsbawm echoes the insights of D.A. Low, "Counterpart Experiences: India/Indonesia, 1920s-1950s," in *Idem*, ed., *Eclipse of Empire* (Cambridge: Cambridge University Press, 1992), pp. 120-47.
108 Hobsbawm, *The Age of Extremes*, pp. 217-18.
109 J.A.A. van Doorn, *De laatste eeuw Indië. Ontwikkeling en ondergang van een koloniaal project* (Amsterdam: Bert Bakker, 1994), p. 273.
110 M.B. van der Jagt, *Memoires van M.B. van der Jagt, oud-Gouverneur van Soerakarta* (The Hague: H.P. Leopold, 1955), p. 331.
111 *Elseviers Weekblad* in January, 1950, quoted by Hans Meijer, *Den Haag-Djakarta. De Nederlands-Indonesische betrekkingen, 1950-1962* (Utrecht: Het Spectrum, 1994), p. 177.
112 *Jakarta Post*, February 24, 1990.
113 See, for example, the elaborate, four-page advertising supplement in *The Washington Post*, "Indonesia: Unity in Diversity," September 14, 1990.
114 Lolke van der Heide, "In Indonesië is Nederland een afgesloten hoofdstuk," *NRC Handelsblad*, December 20, 1994.
115 Rudy Kousbroek, "Het Verloren Paradijs: gesloten wegens achterstallig onderhoud," *NRC Handelsblad*, December 9, 1994.
116 Nancy K. Florida, *Writing the Past, Inscribing the Future. History as Prophesy in Colonial Java* (Durham: Duke University Press, 1995), passim.
117 *Jakarta Post*, February 15, 1990.
118 Barry Wain, "Indonesia Squashes Its Gadflies," *Asian Wall Street Journal*, November 26, 1994.
119 See the description of these events in Goenawan Mohamad, *Buku Putih Tempo: Pembredelan Itu* (Jakarta: Alumni Majalah TEMPO, 1994).
120 "Indonesia's Phony Cleanup," Editorial, *New York Times*, November 4, 1994. See also a report issued by Amnesty International USA, *Indonesia, Operation Cleansing: Human Rights and APEC* (New York, 1994).
121 Quoted by Adam Schwarz, *A Nation in Waiting. Indonesia in the 1990s* (Boulder: Westview Press, 1994), p. 255-56.
122 Schwarz, *A Nation in Waiting*, p. 256. See also the general discussion in Michael R. Vatikiotis, *Indonesian Politics under Suharto: Development and Pressure for Change* (London: Routledge, 1993). On the ascendancy of Islamic influences in contemporary Indonesia, see Robert W. Hefner, "Islam, State, and Civil Society: ICMI and the Struggle for the Indonesian Middle Class," *Indonesia*, No. 56 (October 1993), pp. 1-36.
123 Rushdie, *Imaginary Homelands*, p. 3.
124 Quoted by Schwarz, *A Nation in Waiting. Indonesia*, p. 254.
125 Hamish McDonald describes the Suharto government as "The Feudal State" in *Suharto's Indonesia* (Sydney: Fontana/Collins, 1980), pp. 112-43. The activist was George Aditjondro, a leading Indonesian academic. He was released again after three days, but was interrogated in October, 1994, on charges of "insult-

ing a government body or authority." Aditjondro has indicated he wants to be tried because he would like to see "how the Suharto regime puts a joke on trial." Reported in an interview on the public radio station WAMU, October 29, 1994. See also an editorial in the *New York Times*, November 4, 1994.
126 Dirk Vlasblom, "De tyrannie der onzekerheid," *NRC Handelsblad*, July 8, 1994. See also another report issued by Amnesty International USA, *Indonesia: Power and Impunity — Human Rights under the New Order* (New York, 1994).
127 Guy Hunter, *South East Asia — Race, Culture, and Nation* (London: Oxford University Press, 1966), p. 29.
128 Ron Haleber, "Bij herdenkingen niet meten met twee maten," *NRC Handelsblad*, January 17, 1995.
129 "Het Indonesische beeld van Nederland," in *Weerzien met Indië* (Zwolle: Waanders, 1994), No. 20, p. 484. The phrase was coined by an Indonesian nationalist in a broadcast via Radio Bandung in 1945: "the voice of Holland is in our ears like the roaring of a toothless lion," quoted by Mrázek, *Sjahrir. Politics and Exile in Indonesia*, p. 299.
130 Yosef Hayim Yerushalmi, *Zakhor. Jewish History and Jewish Memory* (New York: Shocken Books, 1989), cites Deuteronomy, 8:11, 14, 19: "And if it shall come to pass if you indeed forget the Lord your God.... I bear witness against you this day that you shall utterly perish"; For any people or nation, he adds, there are certain fundamental elements of the past — historic or mythic, often a fusion of both — "that become Torah," pp. 108, 113.
131 Eugen Rosenstock-Huessy, *Out of Revolution. An Autobiography of Western Man* (Norwich, VT: Argo Books, 1969). p. 695.
132 Anil Ramdas, "Doorsnee," *NRC Handelsblad*, January 14, 1995.

CHAPTER 2

1 J.C. van Eerde, "Omgang met inlanders," in *Koloniale volkenkunde*, Mededeeling No. 1, Afdeeling Volkenkunde No. 1 (1914; repr. Amsterdam: J.H. de Bussy, 1928), p. 54. This book was translated into French, with a laudatory preface by Joseph Chailly [Bert], as *Ethnologie coloniale. L'Européen et l'indigène* (Paris: Editions du Monde Nouveau, 1927).
2 Van Eerde, "Omgang met inlanders," p. 156.
3 A.D.A. de Kat Angelino, *Colonial Policy*, 2 vols., trans. and abridged by G.J. Renier (1930; repr. Chicago: University of Chicago Press, 1931), 2, pp. 648-650. De Kat Angelino's authoritative book was described by Mohammad Ali, in Soedjatmoko et al, eds., *An Introduction to Indonesian Historiography* (Ithaca: Cornell University Press, 1965), as reeking of "dust and camphor, notwithstanding its positive qualities and the high level of learning to which it bears testimony," p. 351. See also A.P. Taselaar, "A.D.A. de Kat Angelino en de grondslagen van zijn koloniale theorie," *Bijdragen en Mededelingen betreffende de geschiedenis der Nederlanden*, 107, No. 2 (1992), pp. 264-284, and J.L. Heldring, "Ons Nederlands erfgoed," *NRC Handelsblad*, November 12, 1994.
4 Z. Stokvis, "Een handboek voor den koloniale leider," in *Socialistische Gids*, reprinted as "Het boek van De Kat Angelino," in *Timboel. Algemeen Periodiek voor Indonesië*, 5, No. 4 March 1, 1931, p. 60, and Cees Fasseur, "Rulers and Ruled: Some Remarks on Dutch Colonial Ideology," in *Journal of the Japan-Netherlands Institute*, 2, (1990), p. 20.
5 H.W. van den Doel, *De stille macht. Het Europees binnenlands bestuur op Java en Madoera, 1808-1942* (Amsterdam: Bert Bakker, 1994), passim. "Silent Force" is a variation on the theme of "Hidden Force," which is the title of Louis Couperus's remarkable novel published in 1900.
6 Stokvis, "Het boek van De Kat Angelino," in *Timboel* (1931), p. 60.
7 Cornelis van Vollenhoven, "De Roeping van Holland," *De Gids* (1910); see the discussion in Henk te Velde, *Gemeenschapszin en plichtsbesef. Liberalisme en nationalisme in Nederland, 1870-1918* (The Hague: SDU, 1992), pp. 231-235.
8 Te Velde, *Gemeenschapszin en plichtsbesef*, p. 231.
9 For a lucid discussion of adat among the Karo Batak in Sumatra and its changing meanings over time, see Mary Margaret Steedley, *Hanging Without a Rope. Narrative Experience in Colonial and Postcolonial Karoland* (Princeton: Princeton University Press, 1993), pp. 40-41.
10 Creusesol, *Oudgasten en Indischmannen*, quoted by D.J. van Doorninck, *Leven op Java. Critische opstellen* (Zwolle: J. Ploegsma, 1915), pp. 30-31.
11 J.A.A. van Doorn, *De laatste eeuw van Indië. Ontwikkeling en ondergang van een koloniaal project* (Amsterdam: Bert Bakker, 1994), p. 153.

12 He opened his study by asserting unequivocally that "no other tropical colony was more significant to the mother country than the Dutch East Indies," see G. Gonggrijp, *Sociaal economische betekenis van Nederlands-Indië voor Nederland* (1928; repr. Utrecht/Brussel: Het Spectrum, 1948), pp. 3, 48.
13 E.S. de Klerck, History of the Netherlands East Indies, 2 Vols (Rotterdam: W.L. & J. Brusse, 1938), 1, pp. 610-611.
14 The Netherlands Chamber of Commerce of New York, "Foreign Capital in the Dutch East Indies," October 20, 1924, New Series No. 21, in National Record Center, Suitland, Maryland, Record Group 165 (hereafter RG 165), Records of the War Department, "General and Special Staffs." Regional File, 1922-1944, Netherlands East Indies, Box No. 2632.
15 The Netherlands Chamber of Commerce of New York, "Foreign Capital in the Dutch East Indies," October 20, 1924, RG 165, Box No. 2632.
16 H.L. Wesseling, "Dutch Historiography on European Expansion since 1945," in H.L. Wesseling and P.C. Emmer, eds., *Reappraisals in Overseas History. Essays on Post-War Historiography about European Expansion* (Leiden, 1979), p. 138-139. However, Paul van 't Veer adds a sinister twist to the Dutch decision to surrender voluntarily its territorial holdings on the West coast of Africa in 1870. The Dutch settlements on the Gold Coast, he argues, had served as a "supply center" of African slaves transported by Dutch ships — a slave trade, he claims, that was monopolized by the Dutch — to furnish labor to the plantation economies of Suriname and other Caribbean colonies. By 1870 the Gold Coast had been rendered worthless, since slavery in Dutch colonies had finally been abolished in 1863, thirty years after the abolition of slavery in British colonies (1833). See *Vriend en vijand in de kolonie. Enkele variaties op het thema der menselijke verhoudingen onder koloniale omstandigheden* (Amsterdam: Arbeiderspers, 1956), p. 45.
17 See, among others, S.L. van der Wal, who used the word "abstention," in "De Nederlandse expansie in Indonesië in de tijd van het moderne imperialisme: de houding van de Nederlandse regering en de politieke partijen," *Bijdragen en Mededelingen betreffende de geschiedenis der Nederlanden*, 86 (1971), pp. 47-55, and B.W. Schaper, who employed the term "reluctant imperialism," in "Nieuwe opvattingen over het moderne imperialisme," Idem, pp. 4-21. See also Ivo Schöffer, "Dutch 'Expansion' and Indonesian Reactions: Some Dilemmas of Modern Colonial Rule (1900-1942)," in H.L. Wesseling, ed., *Expansion and Reaction. Essays on European Expansion and Reactions in Asia and Africa* (Leiden, 1978). For a recent historiographical discussion, see Elsbeth Locher-Scholten, "National Boundaries as Colonial Legacy: Ethical Imperialism in the Indonesian Archipelago around 1900," Occasional Paper No. 44, Asia Program, Woodrow Wilson International Center for Scholars (1992), and Maarten Kuitenbrouwer, *The Netherlands and the Rise of Modern Imperialism. Colonies and Foreign Policy, 1870-1902* (1989; repr. New York/Oxford: Berg Publishers, 1991), pp. 1-30.
18 Cees Fasseur, "De weg naar het paradijs," *Spiegel Historiael*, (December, 1987), criticized by Ewald Vanvugt in "Nog altijd oostindisch blind. Actuele koloniale geschiedschrijving,"in *Het dubbele gezicht van de koloniaal. Nederlands-Indië herontdekt* (Haarlem: In de Knipscheer, 1988), pp. 169-172. The British critic of colonialism, J.A. Hobson, also called the avowal of "moral imperialism" in Britain a contradiction in terms. "The claim of a 'trust' is nothing less than an impudent act of self-assertion," quoted in Philip Curtin, ed., *Imperialism* (New York: Walker, 1971), p. 331.
19 J. van Goor, who uses the term "rounding off," has shown that Dutch nationalist sentiments were tangled up with specific Dutch colonial confrontations, such as the struggle with a demonized enemy in Lombok, in "De Lombok expeditie en het Nederlandse nationalisme," *in Idem*, ed., *Imperialisme in de marge. De afronding van Nederlands-Indië* (Utrecht: HES, 1986), pp. 19-70. However, to the extent that Dutch nationalist sentiments were invested in the imperial enterprise, they tended to focus more on the embattled Boers in Transvaal rather than on southeast Asia. See Kuitenbrouwer, *The Netherlands and the Rise of Modern Imperialism*, p. 27. Albeit in a tongue-in-cheek fashion, H.L. Wesseling asked the rhetorical question whether Dutch Imperialism ever existed in "Bestond er een Nederlands imperialisme?" *Tijdschrift voor Geschiedenis*, 99 (1986), pp. 214-225.
20 David Kenneth Fieldhouse, *Economics and Empire, 1830-1914* (Ithaca: Cornell University Press, 1973), passim.
21 Sheldon Pollock, "Deep Orientalism? Notes on Sanskrit and Power Beyond the Raj," in Carol A. Breckenridge and Peter van der Veer, eds., *Orientalism and the Postcolonial Predicament* (Philadelphia: University of Pennsylvania Press, 1993), p. 77.
22 Henrika Kuklick has argued that "the history of colonial anthropology shows us little about the development of anthropology as a discipline," in *The Savage Within. The Social History of British Anthropology, 1885-1945* (New York: Cambridge University Press, 1991), p. 183, 240. For a critique, see George W. Stocking Jr., *Victorian Studies*, 36, No. 2 (Winter 1993), pp. 232-33, and Adam Kuper, "Boy's Own Cultures," *Times Literary Suppement*, June 26, 1992, p. 6.

23 Nancy L. Stepan, *The Idea of Race in Science: Great Britain, 1800-1960* (Hamden, CT: Archon Books, 1982), pp. xv-xvi.
24 Ethnology, in this context, refers to the general study of cultural differences in a general search for causes and effects. Hence, ethnology was essentially a theoretical or "interpretive" effort, while ethnography, in contrast, was the intensive investigation of a particular people in order to describe their vital social customs, cultural institutions, and religious concepts. See the discussion in James A. Boon, *Affinities and Extremes. Crisscrossing the Bittersweet Ethnology of East Indies History, Hindu-Balinese Culture, and Indo-European Allure* (Chicago: University of Chicago Press, 1990), passim, and Herman Lebovics, *True France. The Wars over Cultural Identity, 1900-1945* (Ithaca: Cornell University Press, 1992), especially pp. 28-32.
25 See Gwendolyn Wright, *The Politics of Design in French Colonial Urbanism* (Chicago: University of Chicago Press, 1991), p. 12, and passim, and a comparable analysis in Paul Rabinow, *French Modern. Norms and Forms of the Social Environment* (Cambridge: MIT Press, 1989).
26 The French term was *pépinière d'énergie*. See H.L. Wesseling, "Nederland als koloniaal model," in *Indië verloren, rampspoed geboren, en andere opstellen over de geschiedenis van de Europese expansie* (The Hague: Bert Bakker, 1988), p. 152.
27 Lebovics, *True France*, pp. 30-31.
28 Roy R. Ellen, "The Development of Anthropology and Colonial Policy in the Netherlands, 1800-1960," *Journal of the History of the Behavioral Sciences*, 12, No. 4 (October 1976), pp. 304-305.
29 P.E. Josselin de Jong, ed., *Unity in Diversity. Indonesia as a Field of Anthropological Study* (Dordrecht: Foris Publications, 1984), pp. 1-10.
30 Philip Quarles van Ufford, "Contradictions in the Study of Legitimate Authority in Indonesia," *KITLV Bijdragen*, 143, No. 1 (1987), pp. 143-144.
31 O.W. Wolters, *History, Culture and Religion in Southeast Asian Perspectives* (Singapore: Institute for Southeast Asian Studies, 1982), p. 63.
32 Edward Said, *Orientalism* (New York: Vintage Books, 1978), p. 72.
33 Talal Asad, "From the History of Colonial Anthropology to the Anthropology of Western Hegemony," in George W. Stocking Jr., ed., *Colonial Situations. Essays on the Contextualization of Ethnographic Knowledge, History of Anthropology*, vol. 7 (Madison: University of Wisconsin Press, 1991), p. 315.
34 Clifford Geertz, review of *Bali, Studies in Life, Thought, and Ritual. Selected Studies on Indonesia*, vol. 5 (The Hague/ Bandung: W. van Hoeve, 1960), in *KITLV Bijdragen*, 117, No. 4 (1961), p. 495.
35 W.F. Wertheim, "Counter-Insurgency Research at the Turn of the Century: Snouck Hurgronje and the Acheh War," *Sociologische Gids*, 19 (1972), pp. 320-328. For a strongly worded indictment of Snouck Hurgronje, see also Vanvugt, "Snouck Hurgronje —hooggeleerd spion, avonturier, en kamergeleerde," in *Het dubbele gezicht van de koloniaal*, pp. 54-64.
36 Said, *Orientalism*, p. 263.
37 J.C. van Eerde, "A Review of the Ethnological Investigations in the Dutch Indian Archipelago," Report of the International Circumpacific Investigation Commission of the Koninklijke Akademie van Wetenschappen on "The History and Present State of Scientific Research in the Dutch East Indies," (Amsterdam: J.H. de Bussy, 1927), p. 15.
38 Raymond Kennedy, *The Ageless Indies* (1942; repr. New York: Greenwood Publishers, 1968), p. 168, and Idem., "The Colonial Crisis and the Future," in Ralph Linton, ed., *The Science of Man in the World Crisis* (1945; repr. New York: Octagon Books, 1980), pp. 307-347. For Bali, see Miguel Covarrubias, *Island of Bali* (1937; repr. Singapore: Oxford University Press, 1972), who argued that "the Dutch have been called the best colonizers in the world .... it is lucky for Bali that of the imperialists, it is Holland that rules there," p. 403, and Vicki Baum, *A Tale from Bali. The Powerful Account of a Holocaust in Paradise* (1937; repr. Singapore: Oxford University Press, 1973), who asserted that ".... the Dutch have carried out an achievement in colonization that reflects the highest credit on them," p. x.
39 Sumner Welles made the statement, quoted by Wiliam Roger Louis, *Imperialism at Bay. The United States and the Decolonization of the British Empire, 1941-1945* (New York: Oxford University Press, 1978), p. 237.
40 P. Leroy-Beaulieu, *De la colonisation chez les peuples modèrnes* (Paris: n.p., 1872), p. 293.
41 See H.L. Wesseling, "Nederland als koloniaal model," in *Indië verloren, rampspoed geboren*, for a detailed list of the names of the participants in, and the specific assignments of, the study missions as well as a discussion of the sixteen different French journals and magazines focusing on colonial affairs founded in the period 1891-1904, pp. 156-158.
42 Wesseling, "Nederland als koloniaal model," pp. 157-58.
43 G. Angoulvant, *Les Indes Néerlandaises. Leur role dans l'économie internationale*, 2 vols. (Paris: Editions du Monde Nouveau, 1926), 1, pp. xvi-xvii.
44 Joseph Chailly [Bert], "Preface," to J.C. van Eerde, *Ethnologie Coloniale. L'Européen et l'Indigène*, p. vii. Georges Henri Bousquet, although quite critical of Dutch colonial governance, nonetheless made the same

argument: "I cannot too strongly advise French colonials to go and study [Dutch] material accomplishments [in Indonesia] on the spot .... such investigation could only benefit the French empire," *A French View of the Netherlands Indies*, tr. Philip E. Lilienthal (1938; repr. London/New York: Oxford University Press, 1940), p. 119.

45   See J.W.B. Money, *Java, or How to Manage a Colony* (London: Hurst & Blackett, 1861). See also Amry Vandenbosch, *The Dutch East Indies; Its Government, Problems, Politics* (1938; repr. Berkeley: University of California Press, 1944); H.L. Wesseling, "The Impact of Dutch Colonialism on European Imperialism," in *Papers of the Dutch-Indonesian Historical Conference, Noordwijkerhout*, May 1976 (Leiden/Jakarta: Bureau of Indonesian Studies, 1978), pp. 19-22, and Jean Stengers, "Léopold II et le modèle coloniale Hollandais," *Tijdschift voor Geschiedenis*, 90 (1977), pp. 51-84.

46   Clive Day, *The Policy and Administration of the Dutch in Java* (New York: Macmillan, 1904), and John S. Furnivall, *Studies in the Social and Economic Development of the Netherlands East Indies* (Rangoon: University of Rangoon/Burma Book Club, 1933), or *Idem, Netherlands India: A Study of Plural Economy* (Cambridge: Cambridge University Press, 1944).

47   Eliza R. Scidmore, *Java. The Garden of the East* (1899; repr. Singapore: Oxford University Press, 1984), p. 71.

48   André Roosevelt argued that "the Dutch do not move quickly, but they are extraordinarily steady." See his Introduction to Hickman Powell, *The Last Paradise. An American's "Discovery" of Bali in the 1920s* (1930; repr. Singapore: Oxford University Press, 1982), p. xvii. Nicholas Roosevelt, in *The Philippines. A Treasure and A Problem* (New York: J.H. Sears, 1926), refers to "that thoroughness which is so characteristic of Dutch colonial enterprise," p. 135. John Sydenham Furnivall, in *Progress and Welfare in Southeast Asia. A Comparison of Colonial Policy and Practice* (New York: Institute of Pacific Relations, 1941) wrote similarly that "thorough has always been the motto of the Dutch," p. 32. Covarrubias, in *Island of Bali*, further noted that "the Dutch have shown a more humanitarian treatment of the people than most imperialistic colonizers," p. 404.

49   M.G. van Hoogstraten, *Nederlanders in Nederlands-Indië. Een schets van de Nederlandse koloniale aanwezigheid in Z-O Azië tussen 1596 en 1950* (Zutphen: Thieme, 1986), p. 55. H. van den Brink, in *Een eisch van recht* (Amsterdam: Kirchner, 1946), mentioned that "during the period 1925-1936, on the average only 9 percent of the Dutch East Indies budget was allocated to education; the comparable proportion in the Philippines was 23 percent, and in Siam (Thailand) 17 percent," p. 33.

50   B.R. Mitchell, *European Historical Statistics, 1750-1970* (New York: Columbia University Press, 1978), p. 6.

51   M.C. Ricklefs estimates the indigenous population at 37 million in 1905. See *A History of Modern Indonesia* (Bloomington: Indiana University Press, 1981), pp. 138, 146-147: John Smail argues it was higher, i.e. 40 million; see *In Search of Southeast Asia. A Modern History* (Honolulu: University of Hawaii Press, 1985), p. 298; for Dutch population figures, see Mitchell, *European Historical Statistics*, p. 6.

52   H.L. Wesseling, "The giant that was a dwarf, or the strange history of Dutch imperialism," in A. Porter and R. Holland, eds., *Theory and Practice in the History of European Expansion Overseas: Essays in Honour of Ronald Robinson* (London: Frank Cass, 1989), pp. 58-71.

53   Cees Fasseur, *The Politics of Colonial Exploitation. Java, the Dutch, and the Cultivation System*, trans. R.E. Elson and Ary Kraal (Ithaca: Cornell University Studies on Southeast Asia, 1992), pp. 56-63, and John Sydenham Furnivall, *Progress and Welfare in Southeast Asia. A Comparison of Colonial Policy and Practice*, p. 38.

54   Cees Fasseur, "Nederland en Nederlands-Indië, 1795-1914," in *Algemene Geschiedenis der Nederlanden*, 15 vols. (Haarlem: Fibula van Dishoeck, 1983), 11, pp. 362-63.

55   G.H. van Soest, *Geschiedenis van het kultuurstelsel*, 3. vols (Rotterdam: Nijgh, 1869-1871), 3, p. 223, quoted by R.E. Elson, "Peasant Poverty and Prosperity Under the Cultivation System in Java," in Anne Booth, W.J. O'Malley, and Anna Weidemann, eds., *Indonesian Economic History in the Dutch Colonial Era* (New Haven: Yale University Southeast Asian Studies, Monograph Series 35, 1990), p. 25. Elson adds, however, that the 1840s was a decade of widespread experimentation with various kinds of crops and soil types. The harvest failures occurred when sugar cane was planted in too mountainous a region so the crop could not be properly irrigated (Cirebon) or indigo was cultivated in inappropriate soil (Banten). Other disastrous results ensued when the cultivation system tried to introduce exotic new crops such as silkworms and cochineal, p. 30.

56   Elson, "Peasant Poverty and Prosperity," in Booth et al, *Indonesian Economic History in the Dutch Colonial Era*, pp. 33-35.

57   Thomas Karsten, "Vreemd en eigen," *Djawa. Driemaandelijks Tijdschrift uitgegeven door het Java-Instituut*, 3, No. 2, (June 1923), p. 73. Karsten, though, attributed the economic development and "national awakening" of the Netherlands in the late nineteenth century to the "genuine stimulus" provided by the revived memories of both the energy and creativity of the Golden Age of the Dutch Republic.

58 Cees Fasseur, "Vier eeuwen In(dones)ië," in *De weg naar het paradijs en andere Indische geschiedenissen* (Amsterdam: Bert Bakker, 1995), p. 9.
59 Theodore Friend, *The Blue-Eyed Enemy. Japan against the West in Java and Luzon* (Princeton: Princeton University Press, 1988), pp. 17-20, and Audrey and George McT. Kahin, *Subversion as Foreign Policy. The Secret Eisenhower and Dulles Debacle in Indonesia* (New York: Free Press, 1995), p. 29.
60 W.H. van Helsdingen quoted in the *Nieuwe Haagsche Courant*, November 19, 1945.
61 See L.E. Davis and R.A. Huttenback, *Mammon and the Pursuit of Empire* (Cambridge: Cambridge University Press, 1988), who argue that with the exception of India, the financial rewards of British imperialism were limited, passim. For France, see Kennedy, "Colonial Crisis," in *The Science of Man*. Kennedy underscores the official tendency to encourage independent native production for the international market, which may have represented a conscious imitation of the pattern of small peasant or artisanal proprietorship in France. This economic policy made the French colonies "less prosperous in terms of profit and revenue" than either the Dutch East Indies or British India, pp. 329-330.
62 Theodore Friend, *The Blue-Eyed Enemy. Japan against the West*, pp. 17-20.
63 A.R. Zimmerman in *De Telegraaf*, March 25, 1928. An English translation of his article, "The construction of the Kingdom," was dispatched to the U.S. State Department by Richard M. Tobin. who was a political officer in the American Legation in The Hague. National Archives, Washington D.C., Records of the State Department, 1910-1929, M-682, Roll 30, 856D.01-.049.
64 See Wesseling, "Indië verloren, rampspoed geboren," in *Indië verloren*, pp. 285-308, and P.F. Maas, *Indië verloren. Rampspoed geboren* (Amsterdam: De Bataafsche Leeuw, 1983), passim.
65 P.E.B. de Josselin de Jong, ed., *Unity in Diversity. Indonesia as a field of anthropological study* (Dordrecht: Foris Publications, 1984), pp. 2-3.
66 Bernard ter Haar, "Een keerpunt in de Adatrecht-politiek," *Koloniale Studiën*, 12 (June 1928), p. 260, quoted by De Kat Angelino, *Colonial Policy*, 1, "General Principles," p. 461.
67 Clifford Geertz, "'Popular Art' and the Javanese Tradition," *Indonesia*, No. 50 (October 1990), p. 79.
68 John Pemberton, *On de Subject of "Java"* (Ithaca: Cornell University Press, 1994), p. 12.
69 Anna Lowenhaupt Tsing, *In the Realm of the Diamond Queen. Marginality in an Out-of-the-Way Place* (Princeton: Princeton University Press, 1993), p. 24; see also the analysis in Steedley, *Hanging Without a Rope*, pp. 74-76.
70 De Kat Angelino, *Colonial Policy*, 1, pp. 459-460.
71 See the discussion in Van den Brink, *Een eisch van recht*, p. 72.
72 J.A. Jonkman, *Het oude Nederlands-Indië. Memoires van Mr. J.A. Jonkman* (Assen: van Gorcum, 1971), p.22. Jonkman referred to a lecture, given by Cornelis van Vollenhoven, to the Utrecht Studenten Corps in 1916.
73 De Kat Angelino, *Colonial Policy*, 1, pp. 186-187.
74 J.H.A. Logemann, *Over enkele vraagstukken eener Indische staatsrechtbeoefening* (Leiden: E.J. Brill, 1927), p. 20.
75 De Kat Angelino, *Colonial Policy*, 1, p. 464.
76 Ido de Haan, *Zelfbestuur en staatsbeheer. Het politieke debat over burgerschap en rechtsstaat in de twintigste eeuw* (Amsterdam: Amsterdam University Press, 1993), p. 87, and Chapter III in general.
77 Ph.A. Kohnstamm, in "politieke moraliteit," (1924), quoted by Te Velde, *Gemeenschapszin en plichtsbesef*, pp. 200-202.
78 De Haan, *Zelfbestuur en staatsbeheer*, p. 78.
79 Charles Hirschman, "The Meaning and Measurement of Ethnicity in Malaysia: An Analysis of Census Classifications," *Journal of Asian Studies*, 46, No. 3 (August 1987), pp. 552-82, and the discussion of Benedict Anderson, "Census, Map, Museum," in *Imagined Communities. Reflections on the Origin and Spread of Nationalism*, 2nd ed. (1983; repr. New York: Verso, 1990), p. 164.
80 Van Doorn, *De laatste eeuw van Indië*, p. 158.
81 Oswald Spengler, *The Decline of the West. Form and Actuality*, trans. Charles Francis Atkinson, 2. vols (New York: Alfred A. Knopf, 1926), 1, pp. 106-107.
82 Cornelis van Vollenhoven, in *Het Adatrecht van Nederlandsch-Indië* (Leiden: E.J. Brill, 1918-1933) asserted there were 19 different adat law circles; see Koentjaraningrat, *Anthropology in Indonesia, A Bibliographical Review* (The Hague: Martinus Nijhoff, 1975), pp. 89-92. In *Een adatwetboekje voor heel Indië* (1910; repr. Leiden: E.J. Brill, 1925), Van Vollenhoven noted the existence of twenty different adat law circles and mentioned that other scholars have argued in favor of at least a hundred, p. 5.
83 T.J. Bezemer, "Volken en volksinstellingen," in D.G. Stibbe, ed., *Neerlands Indië. Land en volk; geschiedenis en bestuur; bedrijf en samenleving* 2 vols. (Amsterdam: Elsevier, 1935), 1, p. 61.
84 Van Eerde, *Koloniale volkenkunde*, p. 125.
85 Pemberton, *On de Subject of "Java"*, pp. 79, 84.
86 Pemberton, *On the Subject of "Java"*, p. 79.

87 See, for example, Tine G. Ruiter's description of a series of Dutch colonial adat "inventions" among the Karo Bataks in "Dutch and Indigenous Images in Colonial North Sumatra," paper presented at the annual meeting of the Asian Studies Association, April 1995. On Tanimbar, the civil authorities were responsible for abolishing the tradition of men's inventive and flamboyant headdresses, in collusion with Catholic missionaries; see Ewald Vanvugt, *Een propagandist van het zuiverste water. H.F. Tillema (1870-1952) en de fotografie van tempo doeloe* (Amsterdam: Jan Mets, 1993), p. 157. See also a comparable discussion in Oscar Salemink, "Mois and Maquis: The Invention and Appropriation of Vietnam's Montagnards from Sabatier to the CIA," in Stocking Jr., *Colonial Situations*, especially pp. 248-55.

88 See, for example, the recent analyses of the influence of Dutch colonial "conjuring" on the meaning of Minangkabau culture in Joel S. Kahn, *Constituting the Minangkabau: Peasants, Culture, and Modernity in Colonial Indonesia* (Providence/Oxford: Berg Publishers, 1993), and Freek Colombijn, *Patches of Padang: The History of an Indonesian Town in the Twentieth Century and the Use of Urban Space* (Leiden: Research School CNWS, 1994).

89 Mr. Dr. J. Paulus, ed., *Encyclopaedie van Nederlandsch-Indië*, 2nd edition (The Hague/Leiden: Martinus Nijhoff/E.J. Brill, 1917), pp. 543-552. The 1927 Supplement, vol. V, was edited by D.G. Stibbe and C. Spat; the 1932 Supplement, vol. VI, by D.G. Stibbe and J. Stroomberg, and the 1935 Supplement, vol. VII, by D.G. Stibbe and F.J.W.H. Sandbergen.

90 ARA, The Hague, 2nd Division, Losse aanwinsten van Indische bestuursambtenaren, No. 5, J.J. Wesseling, periode 1936-1950, "Wat deden wij Nederlanders in Indonesië?"

91 *Encyclopaedie van Nederlandsch-Indië*, vol. I, 1917, p. 6.

92 *Encyclopaedie van Nederlandsch-Indië*, vol. I, 1917, pp. 6-7.

93 Roy F. Ellen noted "the fragmentation of the human sciences of the colonies," in "The Development of Anthropology and Colonial Policy," in *Journal of the History of the Behavioral Sciences* (1976), p. 316.

94 Encyclopaedie van Nederlandsch-Indië, vol. IV (1921), pp. 538-39, and *Encyclopaedie van Nederlandsch-Indië*, Supplement, vol. V (1927), p. 246.

95 *Encyclopaedie van Nederlandsch-Indië*, vol. I (1917), p. 53, and *Encyclopaedie van Nederlandsch-Indië*, vol. II (1918), pp. 82-89.

96 Cornelis van Vollenhoven, *De ontdekking van het adatrecht* (1908; repr. Leiden: E.J. Brill, 1928).

97 Van Vollenhoven, *De ontdekking van het adatrecht*, pp. 1-3. For biographical information, see F.D.E. van Ossenbruggen, "Prof. Mr. Cornelis van Vollenhoven," in *Honderd jaar studie van Indonesië. Levensbeschrijvingen van twaalf Nederlandse onderzoekers* (The Hague: Smits, 1976), pp. 59-100.

98 Cornelis van Vollenhoven, *Miskenning van het Adatrecht. Vier voordrachten aan het Nederlandsch-Indisch bestuursacademie* (1909; repr. Leiden: E.J. Brill, 1926), pp. 20, 42-43.

99 Van Vollenhoven, *Miskenning van het Adatrecht*, p. 60.

100 Cees Fasseur, "Colonial Dilemma: Van Vollenhoven and the Struggle between Adat Law and Western Law in Indonesia," in W.J. Mommsen and J.A. de Moor, eds., *European Expansion and the Law* (Oxford/New York: Berg, 1990), p. 248.

101 Van Vollenhoven, *Miskenning van het Adatrecht*, pp. 16, 40. The Dutch phrases are *geen heilig huisje* and *oordeelkundig onderzoek*.

102 Van Vollenhoven, *Miskenning van het Adatrecht*, p. 84.

103 Benedict Anderson, "Census, Map, Museum," in *Imagined Communities*, pp. 163-186.

104 Van Vollenhoven, "Exacte Rechtswetenschap," quoted in Dutch by Koentjaraningrat, *Anthropology in Indonesia*, pp. 92-93. The translation is mine.

105 Van Vollenhoven, *De ontdekking van het adatrecht*, pp. 127-128. He praised the work of F.D.E. van Ossenbruggen for placing his studies of adat law in this rich cultural context.

106 Van Vollenhoven, Miskenning van het adatrecht, p. 90.

107 For a recent, general discussion of the complicated system of jurisprudence in the Indies, see Albert Dekker and Hanneke van Katwijk, *Recht en Rechtspraak in Nederlands-Indië* (Leiden: KITLV Press, 1993). See also Arjun Appadurai's essay, "Number in the Colonial Imagination," in Breckenridge and Van der Veer, *Orientalism and the Postcolonial Predicament*, for a lucid discussion of empirical statistics as a tool of translation — or a "meta-language" — that connected the European metropole to the colonies, pp. 314-340.

108 Fasseur, "Colonial Dilemma: Van Vollenhoven and the Struggle between Adat Law and Western Law in Indonesia," in Mommsen and De Moor, eds., *European Expansion and the Law*, p. 254.

109 Van Vollenhoven, *Een adatwetboekje voor heel Indië*, pp. 4-7.

110 Alan Howard, "History in Polynesia: Changing Perspectives and Current Issues," *KITLV Bijdragen*, 149, No. 4 (1993), p. 648.

111 Van Vollenhoven, Adatrecht II, p. 879, quoted by Rn. Mr. Soepomo, "De sociaal-culturele taak der Indonesische intellectuelen," in *Triwindoe-Gedenkboek Mangkoe Nagoro VII* (Soerakarta: Comité Triwindoe-Gedenkboek, 1939), p. 61.

112 "Cornelis van Vollenhoven," in *Encyclopaedie van Nederlandsch-Indië*, Supplement VII (1935), p. 450.
113 "Cornelis van Vollenhoven," *Encyclopaedie van Nederlandsch-Indië*, Supplement VII (1935), p. 441.
114 David Ludden, "Oriental Empiricism: Transformations of Colonial Knowledge," in Breckenridge and Van der Veer, *Orientalism and the Postcolonial Predicament*, pp. 250-278.
115 Christiaan Snouck Hurgronje, "Opleiding en positie bestuur," IV-3, advice addressed to the Governor General, July 5, 1904, in E. Gobée and C. Adriaanse, eds., *Ambtelijke adviezen van C. Snouck Hurgronje* (The Hague: Martinus Nijhoff, 1957), vol. 1, pp. 496-97.
116 Snouck Hurgronje, "Opleiding en positie bestuur," p. 498.
117 J.V. de Bruyn, *Het verdwenen volk* (Bussum: van Holkema & Scheltema, 1978), p. 42.
118 In *De Gids* he wrote in 1923 that "the time was ripe to reform the governance of the Netherlands Indies forcefully in order to give the native population the largest measure of autonomy in the shortest possible time." Quoted by Ewald Vanvugt, "Multatuli, Poncke en de anderen," *Vrij Nederland*, 56, No. 5, January 4, 1995, p. 41.
119 Quoted by Rudolf Mrázek, *Sjahrir. Politics and Exile in Indonesia* (Ithaca: Cornell University Studies on southeast Asia, 1994), No. 14, p. 18.
120 Snouck Hurgronje, "Zelfstandigheid inlands bestuur," IV-12, September 8, 1904, in Gobée and Adriaanse, *Ambtelijke adviezen*, p. 550. See also Cees Fasseur, *De Indologen. Ambtenaren voor de Oost, 1825-1950* (The Hague: Bert Bakker, 1993), pp. 378-384.
121 Quoted by Rabinow, *French Modern*, pp. 165-166.
122 Fasseur, *De Indologen*, p. 277-278. He also notes that the Ecole Coloniale emerged from the Ecole Cambodgiènne, founded in 1866, to familiarize Indo-Chinese young men with French civilization and language. In Great Britain, too, the training of Indian Civil servants emphasized the Western tradition and knowledge of Latin and Greek, English history, and the natural sciences, p. 285.
123 Emile Boutmy, *Le recrutement des administrateurs coloniaux* (Paris: Armand Colin, 1895), pp. 11, 37, 40, 46.
124 Salemink, "Mois and Maquis," in Stocking Jr., *Colonial Situations*, pp. 243-64.
125 Van 't Veer, *Vriend en vijand*, p. 11. See also Kennedy, "Colonial Crisis," in Ralph Linton, *Science of Man*, p. 330.
126 Quoted by Raul Girardet, *L'Idée coloniale en France de 1871 à 1962* (Paris: La Table Ronde, 1972), p. 158.
127 Quoted by Rabinow, *French Modern*, p. 163.
128 Bousquet, *A French View*, pp. 112-119.
129 Quoted by Kees Groeneboer, *Weg tot het Westen. Het Nederlands voor Indië, 1600-1650* (Leiden: KITLV Press, 1993), Verhandelingen 158, pp. 423-24.
130 Bousquet, *A French View*, p. 129, and Groeneboer, *Weg tot het Westen*, p. 423.
131 C. van Heekeren, *Trekkers en blijvers. Kroniek van een Haags-Indische familie* (Franeker: T. Wever, 1980), p. 80.
132 I.A. Nederburgh used this term in his inaugural lecture to the Indology Faculty in Utrecht; see Fasseur, *De Indologen*, p. 420, and also pp. 412-414; see also Jonkman, *Het oude Nederlands-Indië*, p. 29, and Wesseling, *Indië Geboren*, p. 42.
133 Rudy Kousbroek, in *Het Oostindisch kampsyndroom* (Amsterdam: Meulenhoff, 1992), also calls Colijn a "cheesehead (kaaskop) Khomeiny," p. 24.
134 The quote from the proceedings of the Second Chamber of the Estates General is reproduced by Susan Abeyasekere in "The Soetardjo Petition," *Indonesia*, No. 15 (April 1973), p. 102, and also by Bastiaan Jan Brouwer, *De houding van Idenburg en Colijn tegenover de Indonesische beweging* (Kampen: J.H. Kok, 1958), p. 184.
135 Brouwer, *De houding van Idenburg en Colijn*, pp. 179-80. This formulation echoed the language of the original Anti-Revolutionary Party Program, *Ons Program*, which Abraham Kuyper had drafted in 1879.
136 H. van den Brink used this phrase in response to a telegram which textile manufacturers sent to the Queen urging her to maintain Dutch authority in the Indies "for the sake of the native population," in *Een eisch van recht*, p. 73.
137 Brouwer, *De houding van Idenburg en Colijn*, pp. 185-86.
138 "Het rijk van Gadjah Mada," *Wederopbouw. Maandschrift gewijd aan de jong-Javanen-beweging en het Javaansch geestesleven*, 3, Nos. 1-4 (January 1920), p. 6. Bernard Dahm used the word "conceit" in *Sukarno and the Struggle for Indonesian Independence* (Ithaca: Cornell University Press, 1969), p. 348.
139 Mrázek, *Sjahrir. Politics and Exile in Indonesia*, p. 53.
140 Elizabeth E. Graves, *The Minangkabau Response to Dutch Colonial Rule in the Nineteenth Century* (Ithaca: Cornell University Southeast Asia Program Monograph Series, 1981), No. 60, p. 144.
141 Dahm, *Sukarno*, p. 194.
142 Emile Schwidder and Fritjof Tichelman, eds., *A. Baars en H. Sneevliet: Het proces Sneevliet 1917* (1918; repr. Leiden: KITLV Press, 1991), p. 316. See also Liesbeth Dolk, *Twee zielen, twee gedachten. Tijdschriften en intel-

lectuelen op Java (1900-1975) (Leiden: KITLV Press, 1992), Verhandelingen 159, p. 45. Although Darna Koesoema was an editor of the Sundanese nationalist journal *Padjadjaran*, he subscribed to a more broad-based, "Insulinde-type" nationalism. He published his translation and commentary in *Pertimbangan* on March 22, 1917 in which he emphasized, however, that the differences between the Russian and Javanese situations outweighed the similarities.

143 Henk Sneevliet, "Zegepraal," in *De Indiër*, March 19, 1917, reproduced in Schwidder and Tichelman, *A. Baars en H. Sneevliet: Het proces Sneevliet 1917*, pp. 5-9.

144 Takashi Shiraishi, *An Age in Motion. Popular Radicalism in Java, 1912-1926* (Ithaca: Cornell University Press, 1990), p. 85.

145 Schwidder and Tichelman, "II. Vervolging en proces," Introduction to *Het proces Sneevliet 1917*, pp. xxix-xxxi.

146 Dr. Radjiman to the annual meeting of Boedi Oetomo in Yokyakarta in 1914, as discussed by Darna Koesoema in *Pertimbangan*, March 22, 1917, quoted in *Het proces Sneevliet* 1917, p. 317.

147 For an elaboration of American diplomats' critiques, see Frances Gouda, "Visions of empire. Changing American Perspectives on Dutch Colonial Rule in Indonesia between 1920 and 1942," *Bijdragen en mededelingen betreffende de geschiedenis der Nederlanden*, 109, No. 2 (1994), pp. 237-258.

148 National Archives in Washington D.C., Records of the Department of State, Memorandum in response to a strictly confidential dispatch from Walter A. Foote on "The Possible Reorganization of the Government of Netherland India," of May 21, 1935. Division of Western European Affairs, Department of State, June 20, 1935. Record Group 59, Incoming Correspondence, 1930-1939, 856D.00/67.

149 Roger K. Paget, ed., *Indonesia Accuses! Soekarno's Defense Oration in the Political Trial of 1930* (Kuala Lumpur: Oxford University Press, 1975), p. 88.

150 G.L. Tichelman and H. van Meurs, eds., *Indië roept* (Amsterdam: Van Holkema & Warendorf, 1947), pp. 4-5. See also the introduction to an ethnographic overview of Indonesia, written by H.Th. Fischer and published in 1948, which was also still titled *Inleiding tot de volkenkunde van Nederlands-Indië* (Utrecht: De Erven F. Bohn, 1848). Without registering any anxiety about the continuation of the Indies as a Dutch political entity, Fischer counseled that "the many people who will be employed in Nederlands-Indië should receive a thorough ethnographic preparation," p. 60.

151 The author was J.J. van Loghem, quoted by A. de Knecht-van Eekelen, "Tropische geneeskunde in Nederland en koloniale geneeskunde in Nederlands-Indië," *Tijdschrift voor Geschiedenis*, 105, No. 3 (1992), p. 427.

152 Rita Smith Kipp, *The Early Years of a Dutch Colonial Mission. The Karo Field* (Ann Arbor: University of Michigan Press, 1990), p. 25. See also Jan Willem Gunning J.H.zn E.I., *Hedendaagsche zending in onze oost*, 2nd edition (The Hague: Den Zendingsraad, 1914), who maintained that the H.H. XVII — i.e. the governing council of the East India Company — "considered the Indies Church as its patrimony, which not infrequently degenerated into arbitrary treatment," p. 19.

153 Sartono Kartodirdjo, *Pengantar Sejarah Indonesia Baru: 1500-1900. Dari Emporium Sampai Imperium* (Jakarta: Gramedia, 1992); Gunning, *Hedendaagsche zending*, p. 79.

154 "La mission Protestante," in the official Dutch brochure for the *Exposition coloniale internationale à Paris. Les Indes Néerlandaises* (Amsterdam: J.H. de Bussy, 1931), p. 78. Gunning, in *Hedendaagsche zending*, called it "the totally neglected Indies Church," p. 84.

155 Jane Levy Reed, ed., *Towards Independence. A Century of Indonesia Photographed* (Seattle: University of Washington Press, 1991), p. 79.

156 Gunning, in *Hedendaagsche zending*, noted that "the policy of religious neutrality, embraced by the state, actually privileged Islam," p. 86.

157 *Exposition coloniale internationale à Paris. Les Indes Néerlandaises*, p. 78.

158 J.W. Gunning and D. Crommelin, "Eeredienst en zending. De Protestantsche Kerk — Protestantsche zendingscorporaties, haar arbeidsvelden en resultaten," in D.G. Stibbe, ed., *Neerlands-Indië. Land en volk; geschiedenis en bestuur; bedrijf en samenleving*, 2 vols. (Amsterdam: Elsevier, 1935), 2, p. 321.

159 Gunning, *Hedendaagsche zending*, pp. 397-400. The first appointee to the Zendings-Consulaat was Dr. C.W.Th. Baron van Boetzelaer van Dubbeldam. One of his successors was Dr. Slootemaker de Bruine, who heard a complaint from Jaap Kunst about the Rheinische Missiongesellschaft's destruction of native musical traditions on Nias in the late 1920s. Because the German Lutheran missionary organization was not affiliated with the Missionary Consulate, however, the Consul had no authority over the German mission's harmful activities in Nias. See Jaap Kunst, *De inheemsche muziek en de zending* (Amsterdam: H.L. Paris, 1947), p. 12.

160 Anderson, "Census, Map, Museum," in *Imagined Communities* (1990), p. 170. About the Pietists, see Jon Miller, "Piety and Patriarchy: Gender Relations in a Nineteenth-Century Evangelical Mission," paper presented at the annual meeting of the American Anthropological Association, Washington D.C., November,

1993. The Pietist Evangelical Mission Society, based in Basel, Switzerland, took over the southeastern Borneo "field" from the Reinische Missionsgesellschaft on January 1, 1923, because they were searching for a new "field" when it became clear that the Swiss missionaries could not reestablish their foothold in Gold Coast, Africa, from which they were evicted during the World War I. See *Encyclopaedie van Nederlandsch-Indië*, Supplement VII (1935), pp. 474-475.

161 Th. van den End, "Transformatie door informatie? De bijdrage van de Nederlandse zending aan de opinievorming over het koloniaal bestel," *Tijdschrift voor Geschiedenis*, 105, No. 3 (1992), p. 430, and pp. 429-45 in general.

162 "La mission Protestante," *Exposition coloniale internationale. Les Indes Néerlandaises*, p. 78-79. The entry for "Protestant Mission" in the *Enclyclopaedie van Nederlandsch-Indië*, Supplement VII, (1935), provided an exhaustive survey of the different missionary societies that were active in each and every region of the archipelago, pp. 468-491.

163 Gunning and Crommelin, "Statistiek der Protestantsche Zending in Nederlandsch-Indië, 1928," appended to the chapter "Eeredienst en zending. De Protestantsche Kerk," in Stibbe, *Neerlands-Indië. Land en volk; geschiedenis en bestuur; bedrijf en samenleving*, 2, p. 329, and P.J. van Santen en Jos. van de Kolk, "De Rooms-Katholieke kerk en hare missie onder de inlanders," in *Idem*, 2, p. 338.

164 Van den End, in "Transformatie door informatie" notes that before 1942, missionaries mostly ignored and hardly ever mentioned the nationalist movement, in *Tijdschrift voor Geschiedenis* (1992), p. 442.

165 Willem Walraven, *Brieven aan familie en vrienden, 1919-1941*, 2nd ed. (Amsterdam: G.A. van Oorschot, 1992), pp. 379-80.

166 See the discussion in J.A. Verdoorn, *De zending en het Indonesisch nationalisme* (Amsterdam: Vrij Nederland, 1945), pp. 1, 24, 51-54, 83. The orthodox Calvinist missionary in Makassar, H. van den Brink, in *Een eisch van recht*, agreed wholeheartedly with Verdoorn's assessment. He mentioned that the Synod of the Dutch-Reformed Church in the Spring of 1946 had called for the independence of Indonesia because "the time has come in which following God's will on earth means the suspension of Dutch authority in the Indies." With regret he noted that Synod of the Gereformeerde Kerk had not yet issued a similar pastoral missive, p. 59, fn. 1.

167 See the discussion in Lewis Pyenson, *Empire of Reason. Exact Sciences in Indonesia, 1840-1940* (Leiden/New York: E.J. Brill, 1989), p. 185.

168 J.S. Furnivall, *The Fashioning of Leviathan* (Rangoon: Zabu Meitswe Pitaka Press, 1939). I am indebted to Danilyn Fox Rutherford for alerting me to this source.

169 Michel Foucault, *Discipline and Punish. The Birth of the Prison* (1975; repr. New York: Vintage Books, 1979). See also the dissertation of Peter Zinoman, which analyzes the ideological mobilization and the formation of nationalist politicians in the French prison system of colonial Vietnam, Department of History, Cornell University, 1994.

170 Mrázek, *Sjahrir. Politics and Exile in Indonesia*, pp. 143, 147, 153.

171 Maurits Wagenvoort, *Nederlandsch-Indische mensen en dingen*, quoted by D. J. van Doorninck, *Hollanders op Java en in Holland* (Haarlem: H.D. Tjeenk Willink, 1912), p. 43.

172 Mr. R.A.A. Fruin, in *Handelingen van de Volksraad*, 1931-32, p. 759, quoted by Danilyn Fox Rutherford, "Racial Identity, Colonization, and New Guinea as Empty Space," dissertation-in-progress, Department of Anthropology, Cornell University, p. 28.

173 C.K. Elout, *De groote oost* (The Hague: W.P. van Stockum, 1930), p. 242. Accusing De Graeff of "dissociative tendencies" resembled the ascription of "mental illness," as Michel Foucault has suggested, to those who did not conform; it illuminated the ways in which "barriers [were] erected and all rituals of exclusion [were] organized." See *Mental Illness and Psychology* (1954; repr. New York: Harper & Row, 1976), p. 78.

174 Quoted by Antoinette Burton, *Burdens of History. British Feminists, Indian Women, and Imperial Culture, 1985-1915* (Chapel Hill: University of North Carolina Press, 1994), p. 38.

175 H.M.J. Maier, "From Heteroglossia to Polyglossia: The Creation of Malay and Dutch in the Indies," *Indonesia*, No. 56, (October 1993), p. 38. Theodore Friend notes about the same volume that it collects "informed analysis and nostalgic justification," in *The Blue-Eyed Enemy. Japan Against the West*, p. 298.

176 A.D.A. de Kat Angelino, "De ontwikkelingsgedachte in het Nederlands overzees bestuur," in H. Baudet and I.J. Brugmans, eds., *Balans van beleid. Terugblik op de laatste halve eeuw van Nederlands-Indië* (1961; repr. Assen: Van Gorcum, 1984), p. 49.

177 Catherine Bodard Silver, *Frédéric Le Play: On Family, Work, and Social Change* (Chicago: University of Chicago Press, 1982), and Walter L. Goldfrank, "Reappraising Le Play," in Anthony Oberschall, ed., *The Establishment of Empirical Sociology* (Chicago: University of Chicago Press, 1972). See also Lebovics, *True France*, Chapter 1 and Girardet, *L'Idée coloniale en France*, pp. 157-58.

178 G.J. Held, "Applied Anthropology in Government: the Netherlands," in A.L. Kroeber, ed., *Anthropology Today: An Encyclopedic Inventory* (Chicago: University of Chicago Press, 1953), p. 868; See also Koentjaraningrat, *Anthropology in Indonesia*, pp. 114-133.
179 Clifford Geertz, "Local Knowledge: Fact and Law in Comparative Perspective," in *Local Knowledge. Further Essays in Interpretive Anthropology* (New York: Basic Books, 1983), p. 185.
180 For a detailed analysis of the British reconfiguration of adat in negeri sembilan in Malaysia, see Michael G. Peletz, "Sacred Texts and Dangerous Words: The Politics of Law and Cultural Rationalization in Malaysia," *Comparative Studies in Society and History*, 35, No. 1 (January 1993), pp. 66-109.
181 Fasseur, "Colonial Dilemma: Van Vollenhoven and the Struggle between Adat Law and Western Law in Indonesia," in Mommsen and De Moor, eds., *European Expansion and the Law*, p. 248.
182 Geertz, Review of *Bali, Studies in Life*, in *KITLV Bijdragen* (1961), p. 496.
183 W.H. Rassers, "On the Meaning of Javanese Drama," pp. 1-61, and "On the Origins of the Javanese Theatre," pp. 93-215, in idem., *Panji the Culture Hero: A Structural Study of Religion in Java* (1925; repr. The Hague: Martinus Nijhoff/KITLV Translation Series, 1959), pp. 1-61. See also the discussion in H. Kraemer, "De Wajang als uiting van Javaanse cultuur," in *Referaten, Indische dag gehouden op initiatief van het studentencorps aan de Vrije Universiteit* (Heemstede: Kramer, 1941), pp. 37-39.
184 Fischer, *Inleiding tot de Volkenkunde van Nederlands-Indië*, p. 57.
185 On Von Hornbostel's ancient Chinese wind-quintet theory, see especially the letters of November 22, 1923, and February 25, 1926 from Kunst to Von Hornbostel; Archives of Jaap Kunst, Dossier n.n., Ethnomusicologisch Instituut "Jaap Kunst," University of Amsterdam.
186 Regarding the etymology of slendro, see letter from F.D.K. Bosch to Kunst on March 9, 1922 and a later, undated letter from Kunst to Bosch, in which he writes "if salendro=Cailendra, it would immediately explain why slendro seems to emerge in Central Java, where it maintains a hegemony in certain residencies (Banjoemas, Rembang, and to a lesser degree in Djokja and Solo). In East Java slendro and pelog are more or less equally popular, as far as Madioen, Kediri and Soerabaja are concerned; farther to the east, pelog predominates, and the Balinese use pelog almost exclusively." In archives of Jaap Kunst, dossier n.n.
187 Willem Frederik Stutterheim to Jaap Kunst, July 13, 1925, Archives of Jaap Kunst, Dossier 895.
188 See, for instance, "Music and Dance on the Kai Islands," in *Jaap Kunst. Traditional Music and its Interaction with the West* (Amsterdam: Royal Tropical Institute and University of Amsterdam/ Ethnomusicology Centre 'Jaap Kunst,' 1994), pp. 206-209. See also the discussions by Elisabeth den Otter in the same volume, "Music in the Tropenmuseum: from Jaap Kunst to the Present," pp. 25-35, and Maya Frijn, "Introduction to Part II. From Endangerment to Preservation: Western Interest in Traditional Culture," pp. 51-55. Stanley Tambiah, in *Culture, Thought, and Social Action* (Cambridge: Harvard University Press, 1985), has raised questions that are similar to Kunst's, pp. 123-24.
189 Jaap Kunst in *De inheemsche muziek en de zending* (Amsterdam: H.J. Paris, 1947), p. 6. This article was recently translated as "Indigenous Music and the Christian mission," in *Jaap Kunst. Traditional Music and its Interaction with the West*, pp. 57-87. See also Maya Frijn, "Introduction to Part II," in Jaap Kunst, p. 53.
190 Jaap Kunst, "Proeve van een autobiografie. Voor Katy, Sjuwke, Jaap en Egbert," typescript, n.d. in archives of Jaap Kunst, n.n.
191 Curt Sachs, *The Rise of Music in the Ancient World in East and West* (1943), p. 11, quoted by Kunst in *De inheemsche muziek en de zending*, p. 6 or "Indigenous Music and the Christian mission," in *Jaap Kunst. Traditional Music and its Interaction with the West*, pp. 59, 61.
192 Ellen, "The Development of Anthropology," in *The History of the Behavioral Sciences* (1976), p. 619, and Geertz, *Bali, Studies in Life*, in *KITLV Bijdragen* (1961), pp. 469-470. On the idea of "cultural wrapping," see Fredric Jameson, *Politics of Post-Modernity, or the Cultural Logic of Late Capitalism* (Durham: Duke University Press, 1991), pp. 101-129.
193 Piet Korthuys, *In de ban van de tropen* (Wageningen: Zomer & Keuning, 1947), p. 204.
194 The phrase *rumah kaca* is associated with Pramoedya Ananta Toer. See *House of Glass*, tr. Max Lane (Sydney: Penguin Books Australia, 1992), and Tsuchiya Kenji, "The Colonial State as a 'Glass House:' Some Observations on Confidential Documents Concerning Japanese Activities in the Dutch East Indies, 1900-1942," *Journal of the Japan-Netherlands Institute*, 2 (Tokyo, 1990), pp. 67-76. However, J.C. Baud, the Dutch Minister of Colonies between 1840 and 1848, used the phrase as early as 1847 when he noted that "colonial administration was ... in a glass house, visible on all sides." See Fasseur, *The Politics of Colonial Exploitation*, p. 15.

CHAPTER 3

1. G.L. "Het Javaanse meisje," in *De Taak. Algemeen Indisch Weekblad*, 1, No. 49, July 6, 1918, pp. 588-89.
2. *Priyayi* in the twentieth century also referred to the class of native officials incorporated into the colonial bureaucracy, as if a *noblesse d'épée* was expanded with a *noblesse de robe*.
3. Christopher Lash, *The True and Only Heaven. Progress and Its Critics* (New York: Norton, 1992); See the chapter on nostalgia, pp. 82-119.
4. Thomas Haskell, "Capitalism and the Origins of the Humanitarian Sensibility," Part 1, *The American Historical Review*, 90. No. 2 (April 1985), pp. 339-361, and Part 2, *Idem*, 90, No. 3 (June 1985), pp. 547-566.
5. Clifford Geertz, *The Religion of Java* (Chicago: University of Chicago Press, 1960), pp. 231-32, and *Idem, Islam Observed. Religious Development in Morocco and Indonesia* (Chicago: University of Chicago Press, 1968), pp. 11, 38.
6. J.A. Groot-Enzerink, "Aanraking tusschen de onderwijzeressen en de families der leerlingen van de dagschool," April, 1913, ARA, 2nd Division, Collection 424, Archives of Coenraad Theodoor van Deventer and Elisabeth M. L. van Deventer-Maas for the years 1857-1942, No. 2.
7. C.J.A. Lichtenbelt, "Het gewijzigde Hindoe-Bali schoolplan," n.d. (approximately 1938). ARA, Collection 416, Archives of C.J.A. Lichtenbelt for the years 1927-1939, No. 6.
8. "Primary instruction takes place in approximately 30 different types of schools — a primary classification in this chaos is the distinction between schools which instruct in native languages and those employing the Dutch language"; in *Exposition coloniale internationale à Paris. Les Indes Néerlandaises* (Amsterdam: J.H. de Bussy, 1931) The booklet proudly announced, too, that the state subsidized all the myriad public and private schools in the Indies on a co-equal basis, p. 64.
9. In May, 1912, only 360 girls attended grades 1 through 7 of the Dutch native schools in Java and Madura. See Letter from G.A.J. Hazeu to C.T. van Deventer, June 5, 1912, ARA, Collection 424, Van Deventer and Van Deventer-Maas, No. 2.
10. Kees Groeneboer, *Weg tot het Westen. Het Nederlands voor Indië, 1600-1950* (Leiden: KITLV Press, 1993), Verhandelingen 158, Appendix XVIII, p. 498. Groeneboer also reports the number of European students registered in the public and private *Hollands-Indische Scholen* (HIS), which revealed an almost fifty-fifty division between boys and girls. Most of these European students were probably Indo-Europeans, since few, if any, Dutch-born European children would have attended the Dutch native schools.
11. Groeneboer, *Weg tot het Westen*, Appendix XVIII, p. 498. The differential between male and female students in private Dutch native schools was smaller than in public ones, owing to the fact that some private *Hollands-Indische Scholen* were not co-educational and thus more acceptable to girls' parents.
12. G.L. Gonggrijp sr., "Volksonderwijs in Ned-Indië," in *Prae-adviezen van het koloniaal onderwijs congres*, October 22-24, 1919, in D. Wouters and J. van Hulzen, eds., *Insulinde. Schetsen van land en volk van Nederlands-Indië* (Groningen: P. Noordhoff, 1924), p. 288. The husband of Kartini's sister, Achmad Sosrohadikoesoemo, in "Het nijpend gebrek aan inlandsche vrouwelijke leerkrachten," in *De Taak. Algemeen Indisch Weekblad*, 1, No. 4, August 25, 1917, also quoted numbers for government schools. Between 1908 and 1914, the number of girls attending school had risen from 2,943 to 11,748, which implied an increase of 300 percent, p. 31.
13. Groeneboer, *Weg tot het Westen*, Appendix XVII, p. 497. The increase in the number of female students between 1915 and 1920 might be linked to the dissemination of Kartini's ideas and the impetus generated by the Kartini and Van Deventer Foundations. See also the discussion in Rudolf Mrázek, *Sjahrir. Politics and Exile in Indonesia* (Ithaca: Cornell Studies on Southeast Asia, 1994, No. 14), p. 23, who cites slightly different numbers for 1915.
14. Groeneboer, *Weg tot het Westen*, Appendix XVII, p. 497. Private European schools also revealed a greater gender equity among their student populations.
15. Takashi Shiraishi, *An Age in Motion. Popular Radicalism in Java, 1912-1926* (Ithaca: Cornell University Press, 1990), p. 28-31.
16. The young Sumatran Amir also used the term *kaoem sana* in "Multatuli (1820-1887)," in *Jong Sumatra*, 3, No. 2-3 (February-March 1920), pp. 35-37, quoted at length by Liesbeth Dolk, *Twee zielen, twee gedachten. Tijdschriften en intellectuelen op Java (1900-1957)* (Leiden: KITLV Press, 1993), Verhandelingen 159, p. 49.
17. In "Notosoeroto-Frans ... What Next?" the editors of *Timboel. Algemene Periodiek voor Indonesië*, 4, Nos 11-12, (June 1930), wrote about two Westernized Indonesians, one a central-Javanese poet and the other "an Indonesian with a Dutch name": "*Sana* has the right to say whatever it wants to, while *sini* has just as much right to proclaim as its opinion the exact opposite," p. 136.
18. Quoted by Mrázek, *Sjahrir. Politics and Exile in Indonesia*, pp. 68-69; see also pp. 45-48.

19 W. Schmidt, "Het meisjesonderwijs in Ned.-Indië," *De Opbouw*, April 1940 (Assen: van Gorcum, 1940), p. 14, in KITLV, Leiden, personal archives of Mrs. M.J.Th. Lievegoed-van Buren Schele, (H 974\8).
20 Quoted by Joost Coté, "Writing between the Lines: R.A. Kartini and Indonesian Nationalism in Two Decades of Correspondence, 1904-1924," paper presented to the Study Group on the History of the Education, Monash University, 1994, p. 21.
21 Sara Suleri, *The Rhetoric of English India* (Chicago: University of Chicago Press, 1992), p. 13.
22 Document 97, Letter from Kartini to Rosa Manuela Abendanon-Mandri, September 3, 1903, in F.G.P. Jaquet, ed., *Kartini. Brieven aan mevrouw Abendanon-Mandri en haar echtgenoot met andere documenten* (Dordrecht: Foris Publications, 1987), p. 280. Joost Coté has recently produced a new English translation of the Jaquet edition. See *Letters from Kartini. An Indonesian Feminist, 1900-1904* (Melbourne: Hyland House, 1992, in association with Monash Asia Institute, Monash University). The translations of Kartini's letters in this chapter, however, are mine.
23 Fredric Jameson, *The Politics of Post-Modernity, or the Cultural Logic of Late Capitalism* (Durham: Duke University Press, 1991), pp. 101-129, and James Clifford, "On Collecting Art and Culture" in *The Predicament of Culture. Twentieth-Century Ethnography, Literature, and Art* (Cambridge: Harvard University Press, 1988), pp. 215-251.
24 W.F. Wertheim cited the last four lines of Bertold Brecht's *Three Penny Opera* to describe the attitudes of the Dutch elite towards the silent masses of Java: "Denn die Einen sind im Dunkeln, und die Andern sind im Licht, und man siehet die im Lichte, Die im Dunkeln sieht man nicht," in *Elite en massa. Een bijdrage tot de ontmaskering van de elitewaan* (Amsterdam: Van Gennep, 1975), pp. 126, 177.
25 See the discussion in Frans Hüsken, "Declining welfare in Java. Government and private inquiries," in Robert Cribb, ed., *The Late Colonial State in Indonesia. Political and economic foundations of the Netherlands Indies, 1880-1942* (Leiden: KITLV Press, 1994), Verhandelingen No. 163, pp. 213-27.
26 Document 81, Letter from Kartini to R.M. Abendanon-Mandri, December 12, 1902, in Jaquet, *Brieven*, p. 241.
27 Document 81, Letter from Kartini to R.M. Abendanon-Mandri, December 12, 1902, in Jaquet, *Brieven*, p. 241.
28 Louis Couperus, *The Hidden Force* (1900; repr. Amherst: University of Massachusetts Press, 1985), p. 124.
29 Benedict R. O'G. Anderson, "The Languages of Indonesian Politics," in *Language and Power. Exploring Political Cultures in Indonesia* (Ithaca: Cornell University Press, 1990), p. 145.
30 Joost Coté notes in his Introduction to *Letters from Kartini* that the education of the "new woman, like the real Javanese, was to be a reconstituted subject of the colonial order," p. xii.
31 Kartini's letter was addressed to Stella Zeehandelaar, an early twentieth-century Dutch suffragist. The Japanese translation of "modern girl" is "a girl of a new age." See Kenji Tsuchiya, "Javanology and the Age of Ranggawarsita: An Introduction to Nineteenth-Century Javanese Culture," in *Reading Southeast Asia* (Ithaca: Cornell University Southeast Asia Publications, 1990), Translation Series, 1, p. 74.
32 ARA, Collection 424, Van Deventer and Van Deventer-Maas, No. 25. Letter from Kartini to Ms. Mien Bosch, July 5, 1903. This letter is not reproduced in either Jaquet's or Coté's recent editions of Kartini's Letters. In a letter to Rosa Abendanon-Mandri, Kartini described Ms. Bosch as a bright teacher with a degree in French language and literature who was also known as a writer of book and/or theater reviews (*recenseuse*). See Document 105, letter of June 15, 1903, Jaquet, *Brieven*, p. 299. Coté, however, translates this passage as Ms. Bosch being a "good storyteller" (i.e. *raconteuse*), *Letters from Kartini*, p. 417.
33 Letter from Kartini to Mien Bosch, July 5, 1903, ARA, Collection 424, Van Deventer and Van Deventer-Maas, No. 25.
34 Sitisumandari Suroto, who articulates the New Order interpretation of Kartini's legacy, in *Kartini. Pionierster van de Indonesische onafhankelijkheid en vrouwenemancipatie* (1977; repr. Franeker: T. Wever, 1984).
35 ARA, Collection 401, Archives of Johan David Leo Le Febvre, No. 6. Lecture delivered by Mrs. P.C. Le Febvre-Pleyte, "Verhandeling over de positie van de Indonesische vrouw," n.d. (approximately 1950). Johan David Leo Le Febvre had been a labor inspector and administrator in Sumatra; in both capacities he had criticized the capitalist practices and colonial policies of the Dutch in Indonesia. Eventually he was forced to resign from the colonial civil service; he returned to Europe, settled in Hamburg, Germany, and devoted the rest of his life to journalism and his struggle against fascism and colonial exploitation. The Indonesian nationalist politician Sutan Sjahrir referred to Le Febvre in his memoirs as "The Father of Indonesians."
36 Toeti Herati Noerhadi, "Women's Selfconcept: facts and fears in transition from Kartini's letters to contemporary popular novels written by women," in Taufik Abdullah, ed., *Papers of the Fourth Indonesian-Dutch History Conference*, 2. vols. (Yogyakarta: Gadjah Mada University Press, 1986), 2, *Literature and History*, p. 240.

37 Danilyn Rutherford, "Unpacking a National Heroine: Two Kartinis and Their People," *Indonesia*, No. 55 (April 1993), pp. 23-40.
38 Rudy Kousbroek, *Het Oostindisch kampsyndroom* (Amsterdam: Meulenhoff, 1992), p. 209. He adds that Pramoedya apparently emphasized the "proletarian" shape of Kartini's nose, which was not straight and narrow like the aquiline noses of her Hindu-Javanese paternal forebears. Instead, her nose was squat and flat, supposedly reflecting her mother's common ancestry, p. 210.
39 Rutherford, "Unpacking a National Heroine," in *Indonesia* (1993), p. 27. See also, among others, Jean Taylor, "Raden Adjeng Kartini," *Signs: Journal of Women in Culture and Society*, 1, No. 3 (Spring 1976), and Idem, "Education, colonialism and feminism: An Indonesian case study," in R.G. Altbach and Gail P. Kelly, eds., *Education and the Colonial Experience* (New Brunswick: Transaction Press, 1984); Cora Vreede-de Stuers, "Kartini, petit 'cheval sauvage' devenu héroine de l'indépendence Indonésienne," *Archipel*, 13 (1977); A.G.T. Zainu'ddin, "Education for girls in the Netherlands Dutch East Indies: A mighty factor in the upbringing of the people," *Canadian History of Education Association/ACHE Bulletin*, No. 2 (1988), and Idem, "What should a girl become? Further reflections on the letters of R.A. Kartini," in David F. Chandler and Merle C. Ricklefs, eds., *Nineteenth and Twentieth Century Indonesia: Essays in Honour of J.D. Legge* (Monash University, 1988).
40 Letter from J.H. Abendanon to R.M. Abendanon-Mandri, 1880, quoted by Rob Nieuwenhuys, "Kartini, legende en werkelijkheid," in *Tussen twee vaderlanden* (1959; repr. Amsterdam: Van Oorschot, 1988), p. 203.
41 C.Th. van Deventer, "Onder de hoede van Kartini's naam," lecture delivered at the creation of the Kartini Foundation on June 27, 1913. ARA, Collection 424, Van Deventer and Van Deventer-Maas, No. 1.
42 *Jubileum-verslag uitgegeven ter gelegenheid van het 25-jarig bestaan der vereeniging Kartinifonds te 's Gravenhage, 1913-27 juni-1938* (The Hague, Raad van Beheer, 1938), pp. 17-18; see also Van Miert, *Bevlogenheid en onvermogen*, pp. 89-95.
43 ARA, Introduction to Collection 424, Van Deventer and Van Deventer-Maas; see also W.A. van Goudoever, *Onder de hoede van een naam. Leven en werken van Elisabeth M.L. van Deventer-Maas, 1857-1942* (Amsterdam: P.N. van Kampen, 1958), passim.
44 *Jubileum-verslag .... der vereeniging Kartinifonds*, p. 22.
45 *Jubileum-verslag .... der vereeniging Kartinifonds*, Bijlagen I-XI, pp. 106-115. The Dutch socialist Henk Sneevliet concluded in 1917 that only 0.7 percent of the total male or female native population received some form of schooling. See Emile Schwidder and Fritjof Tichelman, eds., *A. Baars en H. Sneevliet. Het Proces Sneevliet 1917* (1918; repr. Leiden: KITLV Press, 1991), p. 187.
46 J.A. Joekes, eulogy at the cremation of Elisabeth van Deventer-Maas in Driehuis Westerveld, March 30, 1942, ARA, Collection 424, Van Deventer and Van Deventer-Maas, No. 24.
47 Eduard du Perron described Kartini's language as "loathsome with all the dreadful qualities of a certain kind of woman who writes in the throbbing, heartfelt tone (*hijgende-harttoon*) of *De Hollandsche Lelie*, a magazine worshipped by [Kartini] in a touching and ridiculous fashion: a provincial, heavy-handed writing style that pined for the 'Higher Life' (*Hoger-Leven-smachtstijl*) of which only Holland possesses the secret," quoted by Kousbroek, *Het Oostindisch kampsyndroom*, p. 211.
48 It is interesting to note that the entry for "indigenous women's movement" in the *Encyclopaedie van Nederlandsch-Indië* Supplement VII (1935), stated that the "fragility of the bonds between spouses constituted a social hindrance that should be regarded as more serious than the practice of polygamy in the Islamic world," p. 451. With regard to child marriages that did not postpone a husband's sexual access to a young girl until she was older — as in *kawin gantoeng* — the Indies government decided in December, 1925, not to restrict such marriage arrangements through government interference. Instead, "improvement should grow out of the evolution of ideas within indigenous society." With "tact and circumspection" Dutch civil servants ought to prompt native *regenten* to discourage the practice of child marriage as much as possible. See the discussion in Egbert Adriaan Boerenbeker, *De vrouw in het Indonesische adatrecht* (The Hague: J.C. van Langen, 1931), p. 59.
49 Document 28, Letter and story from Kartini to R.M. Abendanon-Mandri, August 8/9, 1901, in Jaquet, *Brieven*, p. 69.
50 Th.J.A. Hilgers and C. Lekkerkerker, "De positie der vrouw," in *Populaire schetsen over land en volk in Indië (een boekje voor allen die naar Indië vertrekken)* (Amsterdam: J.H. de Bussy, 1920), pp. 87-88.
51 John Pemberton, *On the Subject of "Java"* (Ithaca: Cornell University Press, 1994), p. 212-13.
52 Her husband-to-be was Djojoadiningrat (or DjoijoAdhiningrat), the Regent of Rembang. Jaquet, *Brieven*, Document 124, Letter to R.M. Abendanon-Mandri, November 3, 1903.
53 Kartini, *Give The Javanese Education!*, a memorandum written in response to a request from Mr. J. Kringenberg, an official in the Dutch Ministry of Justice, January 29, 1903; in Coté, *Letters from Kartini*, Appendix One, p. 540. Hildred Geertz, in her Introduction to *Letters of a Javanese Princess*, trans. Agnes L. Symmers (New York: Norton Library, 1964) elaborates upon Kartini's deepening involvement in Islam.

54 Kartini's letter to Stella Zeehandelaar, November 6, 1899, translated by E.M. Beekman, in "Kartini," *Fugitive Dreams. An Anthology of Dutch Colonial Literature* (Amherst: University of Massachusetts Press, 1988), p. 262.
55 Census of 1930. See the analysis in Elsbeth Locher-Scholten, "Orientalism and the Rhetoric of the Family: Javanese Servants in European Household Manuals and Children's Fiction," *Indonesia*, No. 58 (October 1994), pp. 19-40. However, Beekman argued in *Fugitive Dreams* that Kartini showed "real compassion for the plight of ordinary people," p. 236.
56 See, for instance, Document 81, Kartini's letter to R.M. Abendanon-Mandri, December 12, 1903, in Jaquet, *Brieven*, p. 241.
57 Document 28, August 8/9, 1901, "Eenige uurtjes uit een meisjesleven. Sentimenteele herinneringen eener oude vrijster," in Jaquet, *Brieven*, p. 63.
58 Van Miert, *Bevlogenheid en onvermogen*, p. 95. and Document 33, Letter from Kartini to R.M. Abendanon-Mandri, April 9, 1901, in Jaquet, *Brieven*, p. 79.
59 Letter from Kartini to Mien Bosch, July 5, 1903, ARA, Collection 424, Van Deventer and Van Deventer-Maas, No. 25.
60 Document 58, Letter from Kartini to R.M. Abendanon-Mandri, June 10, 1902, in Jaquet, *Brieven*, p. 170; For a somewhat different translation, see Joost Coté's *Letters from Kartini*, p. xviii. On Gregor Mendel's theory of mutation, see Peter J. Bowler, *Evolution. The History of an Idea* (1983; repr. Berkeley: University of California Press, 1989), p. 270-275 and below, Chapter Four.
61 Bernard S. Cohn, "Representing Authority in Victorian India," in Eric Hobsbawm and Terence Ranger, eds., *The Invention of Tradition* (Cambridge: Cambridge University Press, 1983), pp. 165-209. Cohn also notes, though, that the British were equally convinced that Indians' weakness and incompetence had made them unsuitable for self-rule and had caused the sub-continent to be subjugated by a sequence of foreign rulers, the last of which were the English.
62 Hamish McDonald, *Suharto's Indonesia* (Blackburn, Victoria: Fontana/Collins, 1980), p. 4.
63 Ian Buruma, "Revenge in the Indies," *New York Review of Books*, August 11, 1994.
64 Anderson, "Sembah-Sumpah: The Politics of Language and Javanese Culture," in *Language and Power*, pp. 204-207. See also Peter Carey and Vincent Houben, "Spirited Srikandhis and Sly Sumbadras: The Social, Political, and Economic Role of Women at the Central Javanese Courts in the 18th and early 19th Centuries," pp. 12-42, and Madelon Djajadiningrat-Nieuwenhuis, "Ibuism and Priyayization: Path to Power?", pp. 43-51, in Elsbeth Locher-Scholten and Anke Niehof, eds., *Indonesian Women in Focus. Past and Present Notions* (1987; repr. Leiden: KITLV Press, 1992).
65 Walter L. Williams, ed., *Javanese Lives. Women and Men in Modern Indonesian Society* (New Brunswick: Rutgers University Press, 1991), p. 208.
66 For a detailed exploration of the Balinization of Bali, see Tessel Pollmann, "Bali: Koloniaal cultuurreservaat in 'ons Indië,'" *De Gids*, 154, Nos. 5/6 (May-June 1991), pp. 386-417; for an English version of this essay, see *Indonesia*, No. 49 (April 1990), pp. 1-35.
67 See the fascinating if contentious discussions about this topic by Prof. P.G. Groenen, Dr. Victor Emanuel Korn, Dr. C. Lekkerkerker, Dr. C.W. Th. Boetzelaar van Dubbeldam, Dr. B.J. Haga, Mr. P. Bergmeijer, and Mr. K.J. Brouwer, in the minutes of a meeting of the *Indisch Genootschap* on December 16, 1932, chaired by Prof. Dr. J.H. Boeke. ARA, Collection 416, archives of Ms. C.J.A. Lichtenbelt, No. 16. In English, see Raymond Kennedy, "The Battle for the Souls of Bali," in *The Ageless Indies* (1942; repr. New York: Greenwood Press, 1968), pp. 145-148.
68 The Dutch colonial civil servant, Dr. V.E. Korn, angrily denounced the Dutch tendency to represent Bali as a "dream paradise" and criticized the construction of paved roads built by compulsory feudal labor services for the benefit of tourists. He cited the example of a poor peasant who pointed to a newly restored temple and said: "yes, the temple is beautiful but the stomach is empty." Cited by Pollmann, "Bali: koloniaal cultuurreservaat," in *De Gids*, p. 398.
69 For a general discussion about the anthropological infatuation with Bali, see James A. Boon, *The Anthropological Romance of Bali, 1597-1972: Dynamic Perspectives on Marriage and Caste, Politics and Religion* (New York: Cambridge University Press, 1977). For specific examples, see, among others, Jane Belo ed., *Traditional Balinese Culture* (New York: Columbia University Press, 1970); Colin McPhee, *A House in Bali* (1944; repr. New York: Oxford University Press, 1979); Margaret Mead, *Blackberry Winter. My Early Years* (New York: Washington Square Press, 1975), and Idem, *Letters from the Field, 1925-1975*, ed., Ruth Nanda Ashen (New York: Harper and Row, 1977). For self-indulgent and voyeuristic accounts of "natural" Bali, see Hickman Powell, *Bali, the Last Paradise* (1930; repr. New York: Oxford University Press, 1982), and K'Tut Tantri, *Revolt in Paradise. One Woman's Fight for Freedom in Indonesia* (1960; repr. New York: Clarkson N. Potter, 1989).

70 Dr. G. Krause, quoted in "Lichtpunten uit het verleden. In het heden voor de toekomst," *Wederopbouw. Maandschrift gewijd aan de jong-Javanen beweging en het Javaansch geestesleven,* 2, No. 2 (December 1919), pp. 203-205.
71 Kennedy, *The Ageless Indies,* p. 147.
72 *Encyclopaedie van Nederlands-Indië,* vol. 1 (1917), p. 116.
73 C.C. Berg, "Zorg voor de moedertaal," in *Triwindoe-Gedenkboek Mangkoe Nagoro VII* (Soerakarta: Comité Triwindoe-Gedenkboek, 1939), p. 218. See also Idem, "het Kramaiseringsverschijnsel," in *Inleiding tot de studie van het oud-Javaansch* (Soerakarta: De Bliksem, 1928), pp. 188-96.
74 Goenawan Mohamad, "*Pasemon.* On Allusion and Illusions," Acceptance speech delivered at the award ceremony of the 1992 Professor Teeuw Award, University of Leiden, May 25, 1992.
75 J.L.A. Brandes used these terms; see the discussions in Anderson, "*Sembah-Sumpah:* The Politics of Language and Javanese Culture," in *Language and Politics,* p. 206, and James T. Siegel, *Solo in the New Order. Language and Hierarchy in an Indonesian City* (Princeton: Princeton University Press, 1986), Introduction.
76 E.M. Uhlenbeck, *Studies in Javanese Morphology* (The Hague: Martinus Nijhoff, 1968), as discussed in Anderson, *Language and Power,* pp. 205-207. See also the descriptions in Heather Sutherland, *The Making of a Bureaucratic Elite. The Colonial Transformation of the Javanese Priyayi* (Singapore: Heinemann, 1977); and Robert van Niel, *The Emergence of The Modern Indonesian Elite* (The Hague: W. van Hoeve, 1970).
77 Pemberton, *On the Subject of "Java",* p. 94.
78 Document 81, Letter from Kartini to R.M. Abendanon-Mandri, December 14, 1902, in Jaquet, *Brieven,* p. 244.
79 Beekman, *Fugitive Dreams,* p. 238.
80 Quoted by Rob Nieuwenhuys, "Kartini," in Peter van Zonneveld, ed., *Oriëntatie. Literair-cultureel tijdschrift in Indonesië [1947-1953]* (repr. Schoorl: Conserve, 1988), p. 32.
81 In contrast, according to C.Th. van Deventer, *selir* wives in polygamous households among common people in the *desa* had a more co-equal status with primary wives; see the discussion in Boerenbeker, *De vrouw in het Indonesische adatrecht,* p. 82.
82 Pramoedya Ananta Toer, *Gadis Pantai* (Jakarta: Hasta Mitra, 1987), quoted by Tineke Hellwig, *In the Shadow of Change. Images of Women in Indonesian Literature* (Berkeley: Center for Southeast Asia Studies, Monograph No. 35, 1994), p. 85. While Hellwig translates *Gadis Pantai* as Beach Girl, Harry Aveling gives this novel the more appropriate English title of *The Girl from the Coast* (Singapore: Select Books, 1991).
83 Rutherford, "Unpacking a National Heroine," in *Indonesia* (1993), p. 39.
84 Excerpt from a lecture by Dr. A. M. Brouwer; in Wouters and Van Hulzen, *Insulinde,* p. 76.
85 Kartini's letter to Stella Zeehandelaar, January 12, 1900, in which she ridiculed Dutch plantation overseers and bridge engineers, "and perhaps tomorrow, station masters too," for insisting that their subordinates address them as *kandjeng,* a respectful form of address — your excellency — reserved for Javanese aristocratic rulers. She noted that she "used to think that only the stupid Javanese went in for this pomp and circumstance, but now I see that the civilized, enlightened Westerner.... is actually crazy about it." Quoted in Tsuchiya Kenji, "Kartini's Image of Java's Landscape," *East Asian Cultural Studies,* 25, No. 1-4 (March 1986), p. 78. See also Rob Nieuwenhuys, *Mirror of the Indies. A History of Dutch Colonial Literature* (1972; repr. Amherst: University of Massachusetts Press, 1982), pp. 158-162.
86 Letter from Kartini to E.C. Abendanon, November 21, 1902; quoted by Kenji, "Kartini's Image of Java's Landscape," pp. 77-78.
87 See Carey and Houben, "Spirited Srikandhis and Sly Sumbadras," and Djajadiningrat-Nieuwenhuis, "Ibuism and Priyayization," in Locher-Scholten and Niehof, eds., *Indonesian Women in Focus,* passim.
88 For a historical discussion of women's inheritance and property rights under Islamic law and the restrictions which different Muslim societies have imposed over time, see Leila Ahmed, *Women and Gender in Islam. Historical Roots of a Modern Debate* (New Haven: Yale University Press, 1992), pp. 110-113. See also Boerenbeker, *De vrouw in het Indonesische adatrecht,* pp. 142-47. Diane Lauren Wolf, in *Factory Daughters. Gender, Household Dynamics, and Rural Industrialization in Java* (Berkeley: University of California Press, 1992), elaborates on the situation in contemporary Java. Albeit in the different legal context of Palembang, a dissertation on *Adatdelichtenrecht in de rapat-marga-rechtspraak van Palembang* (Bandung: Nix, 1939) by Willem Frans Lublink-Weddik made the point that "a woman's accusation that her honor has been violated by a particular man is customarily accepted by the *adat* judge," p. 186. Similarly, Lublink-Weddik noted "that physically touching an unmarried woman (and widowed or divorced women) is a punishable act if the woman deems it an insult to her integrity," p. 197.
89 Elsbeth Locher-Scholten, "Female Labour in Twentieth-Century Java. European Notions—Indonesian Practice," in *Idem* and Niehof, eds., *Indonesian Women in Focus,* pp. 77-103, and Cora Vreede-de Stuers, "On the subject of the R.U.U.: The history of a set of matrimonial laws," in B.B. Hering ed., *Indonesian*

Women. Some Past and Current Perspectives (Brussels: Centre d'études du Sud-Est Asiatique et l'extrème Orient, 1976), pp. 80-150.

90 For an examination of women's role as mediators or "cultural brokers" throughout the archipelago, see Sita van Bemmelen, Madelon Djajadiningrat-Nieuwenhuis, Elsbeth Locher-Scholten, and Elly Touwen-Bouwsma, eds., *Women and Mediation in Indonesia* (Leiden: KITLV Press, 1992). A discussion of the differences in the status of Muslim women in Indonesia relative to the Middle East appears in Nikki R. Keddie, "The Past and Present of Women in the Muslim World," *Journal of World History*, 1, No. 1 (1990), pp. 105-108.

91 Locher-Scholten, "Female Labour in Twentieth-Century Java," in *Idem* and Niehof, *Indonesian Women in Focus*, pp. 77-79; For further details, see Chapter Five below.

92 Schmidt, "Het meisjesonderwijs," in *De Opbouw* (1940), pp. 14-15.

93 Confidential bulletin, "Denkbeeld tot oprichting eener Vereeniging Kartinifonds," February 26, 1913, ARA, Collection 424, Van Deventer and Van Deventer-Maas, No. 1.

94 Sosrohadikoesoemo, "Het nijpend gebrek," *De Taak*, August 25, 1917, pp. 31-33.

95 G.L. Geschiere, "De meningsvorming over het onderwijsprobleem in de Nederlands-Indische samenleving in de twintigste eeuw: de controverse 'westersch' of 'nationaal' onderwijs," *Bijdragen en Mededelingen omtrent de Geschiedenis der Nederlanden*, 22, No. 1 (1968), pp. 43-86.

96 Schmidt, "Het meisjesonderwijs," in *De Opbouw* (1940), pp. 9-11.

97 J.A.A. van Doorn mentions, for example, that Cornelis van Vollenhoven and Hendrik Colijn "found themselves in the same camp," in *De laatste eeuw van Indië. Ontwikkeling en ondergang van een koloniaal project* (Amsterdam: Bert Bakker, 1993), p. 71.

98 Gauri Viswanathan, *Masks of Conquest. Literary Study and British Rule in India* (New York: Columbia University Press, 1989) has argued that the "master narrative" of English history and literature was first implemented as an educational system in India; its purpose was to glorify Western culture and to entrench an awareness in Indians of their inherent, racial inferiority, passim. See also Edward Said, *Culture and Imperialism* (New York: Alfred A. Knopf, 1993), pp. 42, 109. It would be difficult to make a similar argument for the Dutch East Indies; see Cees Fasseur, *De Indologen. Ambtenaren voor de Oost, 1825-1950* (The Hague: Bert Bakker, 1993), pp. 285-291.

99 Quoted by Coté, "Writing between the Lines: R.A. Kartini and Indonesian Nationalism" (1995), pp. 20-21.

100 Letter of F.A. Volkers-Schippers, Director of the Van Deventer school in Semarang, to the Board of Directors of the Kartini Foundation in The Hague, June 1, 1924. ARA, Collection 424, Van Deventer and Van Deventer-Maas, No. 9.

101 Obituary of Mr. C.Th. van Deventer in *De Taak. Algemeen Indisch Weekblad*, 1, No. 1, August 4, 1917, pp. 2-3.

102 Mrs. C. Langelaan-Stoop in her eulogy at the cremation of Elisabeth van Deventer-Maas in Driehuis-Westerveld, March 30, 1942, ARA, Collection 424, Van Deventer and Van Deventer-Maas, No. 24. An obituary in *Het Vaderland*, on March 27, 1942, praised her as a woman "with a broadminded perspective and a serious interest in educational questions, who devoted all her attention to the Indonesian family, which could only be 'raised' (*opgevoed*) by preparing the native woman for her task as housewife and mother."

103 B. van den Sigtenhorst Meyer, "Sonate voor viool en piano opgedragen aan Z.H. Pangeran Adipati Ario Mangkoe Nagoro VII," *Triwindoe-Gedenkboek*, pp. 49-51.

104 E. van Deventer-Maas, untitled entry, in *Het Trinwindoe-Gedenkboek, p.* 113. See also the contribution by Ms. M. Jellema, the director of the Van Deventer school in Solo in 1939, "Z.H. Pang. Ad. Ar. Mangkoe Nagoro VII en de Solo'sche Van Deventer School," pp. 185-191.

105 Letter from Ms. H.A. Haighton to Mrs. Van Deventer-Maas, September 23, 1937. ARA, Collection 424, Van Deventer and Van Deventer-Maas, transcribed by Van Goudoever in No. 39.

106 Letter from Sri Wahijah to Mrs. Van Deventer-Maas, June 1, 1931, Ibid., No. 39.

107 Letter From Srijoewati to Mrs. Van Deventer-Maas, May 23, 1930. *Ibid.* No. 39. Letter from Sri Martini to Mrs. Van Deventer-Maas, June 20, 1935, *Ibid.*, No. 16.

108 Renato Rosaldo, "Imperialist Nostalgia," *Representations*, 26 (Spring 1989), pp. 107-108.

109 Anderson, *Language and Power*, p. 30. Rudolph Steiner, Maria Montessori, and the progressive Dutch educator Frans Lighthart were the European thinkers who influenced Ki Hadjar Dewantoro.

110 Groeneboer, *Weg tot het Westen*, p. 366. See also Kenji Tsuchiya, *Democracy and Leadership: The Rise of the Taman Siswa Movement in Indonesia* (Honolulu: University of Hawaii Press, 1987), Translation Series No. 18, passim.

111 Ricklefs, *A History of Modern Indonesia*, pp. 166, 180.

112 Groeneboer quoted these high numbers in *Weg tot het Westen*, p. 367.

113 The *ulama* were spiritually linked to an increasingly conservative *kaum tua* group (community of the "old"), which had evolved, ironically, from a secular anti-tax rebellion in 1908. See Ken Young, *Islamic Peasants and the State: The 1908 Anti-Tax Rebellion in West Sumatra* (New Haven: Yale University Southeast Studies Monograph, No. 40, 1994).
114 Taufik Abdullah, *Schools and Politics: The Kaum Muda Movement in West Sumatra (1927-1933)* (Ithaca: Cornell University Southeast Asia Program Monograph Series, 1971), pp. 59 and 216-25.
115 The Director of Education and Religion, K.F. Creutzberg during the early 1920s, quoted by Groeneboer in *Weg tot het Westen*, p. 365.
116 Taufik Abdullah, *Schools and Politics: The Kaum Muda Movement*, p. 221.
117 Abdurrachman Surjomihardjo, "Taman Siswa and the Wild Schools," in Colin Wild and Peter Carey, eds., *Born in Fire: The Indonesian Struggle for Independence. An Anthology* (London/ Athens: BBC Publications/Ohio University Press, 1986), p. 43.
118 Pemberton, *On the Subject of "Java"*, pp. 220-21.
119 Letter from Adi to Ms. Hoorn, February 20, 1932. ARA, Collection 424, Van Deventer and Van Deventer-Maas, No. 16.
120 *Ibid.*, No. 16.
121 Letter from Binti to Ms. Hoorn, March 26, 1932. *Ibid.*, No. 16. The emphasis is mine.
122 Letter from Soeparni to Ms. Hoorn, March 14, 1932. *Ibid.*, No. 16.
123 Letter from Sarlyne to Ms. Hoorn, March 14, 1932. *Ibid.*, No. 16.
124 Quoted by Sneevliet and Baars, *Het proces Sneevliet 1917*, p. 185.
125 M.A.M. Renes-Boldingh, *Adat* (Nijkerk: G.F. Callenbach, n.d., probably early 1930s), pp. 10, 20.
126 Michael Taussig, *Mimesis and Alterity. A Particular History of the Senses* (New York/London: Routledge, 1993), pp. 78-79, and Homi Bhabha, *The Location of Culture* (New York/London: Routledge, 1994), p. 26. See also *Idem*, "Of Mimicry and Man: the Ambivalence of Colonial Discourse," *October 28* (Spring 1984), pp. 125-33.
127 Rutherford, "Unpacking a National Heroine," in *Indonesia* (1993), p. 30.
128 Jaquet, Introduction to *Brieven*, p. x.
129 F.A. Volkers-Schippers, *Widoerileergang. Hoe men elementair naai-en huishoudonderricht kan geven aan de volksvrouw op Java* (Batavia: Volkslectuur, 1937), n.p. The first issue of *Widoeri* appeared on March 1, 1932. See ARA, Collection 424, Van Deventer and Van Deventer-Maas, No. 137.
130 Mrs. A.J. Resink-Wilkens, in *Widoeri*, August 1, 1935, repr. in *Widoerileergang*, p. 5.
131 *Widoerileergang*, pp. 5-7. These drawings were also published in A.J. Resink-Wilkens, "Huishoudonderwijs voor het desa meisje," in M.A.E. van Lith-van Schreven and J.H. Hooykaas-van Leeuwen Boomkamp eds., *Indisch vrouwenjaarboek 1936* (Jogjakarta: Kolff-Buning, 1936), pp. 61-67.
132 H.W. Ponder, *Javanese Panorama. More Impressions of the 1930s* (1942; repr. Singapore: Oxford University Press, 1990), p. 131.
133 *Widoerileergang*, pp. 7, 11.
134 Schmidt, "Het meisjesonderwijs," in *De Opbouw* (1940), p. 4.
135 Pemberton, *On the Subject of "Java"*, p. 220.
136 Mrs. Reitsma-Brutel de la Rivière, *Weekblad Indië*, November 5, 1920, in Hilgers, *Populaire schetsen*, p. 51.
137 Letter from Srijoewati to Mrs. Van Deventer-Maas, May 23, 1930, ARA, Collection 424, Van Deventer and Van Deventer-Maas, transcribed by Van Goudoever, No. 39.
138 Overzicht van het Hindoe-Bali plan in gewijzigde vorm, n.d. (probably 1938), ARA, Collection 416, Lichtenbelt, No. 8.
139 Letter from C.J.A. Lichtenbelt to the Director of Education and Religion of the Dutch East Indies, Pieter Johan Adriaan Idenburg, December 19, 1937. *Ibid.*, No. 3. In an earlier letter from Rudolf Bonnet to C.J.A. Lichtenbelt, January 6, 1936, *Ibid.*, No. 3., Bonnet had told her, however, that Spies was at that moment deeply involved in designing "a hotel in Balinese style for the KPM (the *Koninklijke Pakket Maatschappij*, the Dutch shipping company in the Indonesian archipelago) on Bratan lake and would not get around to the design for the Hindu-Bali school in the near future."
140 Rudolf Bonnet, "Aanmerkingen op het afwijzend oordeel [van een Europees hoofd eener H.I.S.] over de oprichting eener Bali-Hindoeschool," September, 1935, *Ibid.*, No. 10.
141 The Dutch civil servant and Bali expert, F.A. Liefrinck, made the statement "Geboren democraten and geboren kunstenaars" (born democrats and born artists). Quoted by Pollmann in "Bali: koloniaal cultuurreservaat," p. 390.
142 Bonnet, "Aanmerkingen," ARA, Collection 416, Lichtenbelt, No. 3. The emphasis is mine.
143 Letter from B. Schrieke to J.A. Joekes, March 8, 1939, *Ibid.*, No. 3.

144   Letter from W.F. Stutterheim to C.J.A. Lichtenbelt, June 1, 1936, in *Ibid.*, No. 3. Stutterheim also told her, in a postscript to this letter, that she should not call the school "Bali-Hindoe" school, which she had done until now, "because [Bali] has nothing to do with Hinduism."
145   Letter from C.J.A. Lichtenbelt to Rudolph Bonnet, January 21, 1938, *Ibid.*, No. 3.
146   Letter from C.J.A. Lichtenbelt to J.A. Joekes, March 28, 1939, *Ibid.*, No. 3.
147   Mrs. Van Loo-Rootlieb, "De taak der Europeesche vrouw en het vrouwelijk pauperkind in Indië," reported in *De Indische Verlofganger*, November 25, 1925. See also "De taak der Europeesche vrouw in Indië," *De Nieuwe Courant*, November 18, 1925.
148   Quoted by Th. Stevens, "Indo-Europeanen in Nederlands-Indië; sociale positie en welvaartsontwikkeling," in P.J. Drooglever, ed., *Indisch intermezzo. Geschiedenis van de Nederlanders in Indonesië* (Amsterdam: De Bataafse Leeuw, 1991), p. 39.
149   Van Loo-Rootlieb, "De taak der Europeesche vrouw en het vrouwelijk pauperkind in Indië." For an examination of prostitution, see Liesbeth Hesselink, "Prostitution: A Necessary Evil, Particularly in the Colonies. Views on Prostitution in the Netherlands Indies," in *Indonesian Women in Focus*, pp. 205-224.
150   Ch. Sj. Datoe Toemenggoeng, "Bestrijding van de vrouwenhandel," in Van Lidt-van Schreven, *Indisch vrouwenjaarboek 1936*, p. 55.
151   "Circulaire," in *Afdeeling Semarang en omstreken der Vereeniging tot oprichting van jonge vrouwenscholen in Ned-Indië. Verslag over de jaren 1918 en 1919* (Semarang: H.A. Benjamins, 1920), Appendix II, p. 5.
152   "Vereeniging tot oprichting van jonge vrouwenscholen in Ned-Indië," in *Encyclopaedie van Nederlandsch-Indië*, Supplement VII (1935), p. 438.
153   M. Misset-Stein, "De vrouw in het Pro Juventute-werk," in Van Lidt-van Schreven, *Indisch vrouwenjaarboek 1936*, pp. 27-28.
154   For an analysis of the rhetoric of pauperism in the European metropole in the nineteenth-century, see Frances Gouda, *Poverty and Political Culture: The Rhetoric of Social Welfare in the Netherlands and France, 1815-1854* (Lanham, MD/Amsterdam: Rowman & Littlefield/Amsterdam University Press, 1995), especially Chapter Two.
155   Paul van der Veur, *Introduction to a Socio-Political Study of the Eurasians of Indonesia* (Ithaca: Cornell University Ph.D. dissertation, 1955), pp. 24-25. L.J. Hissink-Snellebrand gave the lower number of 60,000 in 1911. See "Lezing gehouden op den 23en Februari 1991 te Amsterdam voor de Vereeniging "Oost en West," (Amsterdam: Meulenhoff, 1911), in KITLV, archives of the Secretariaat van de Koninklijke Vereeniging "Oost en West" (H 1077). However, Cees Fasseur, in "Hoeksteen en struikelblok. Rasonderscheid en overheidsbeleid in Nederlands-Indië," *Tijdschrift voor Geschiedenis*, 105 (1992), mentions that the last time the Dutch colonial state in Indonesia did an inventory of pure-blood and mixed-blood members of the European community was in 1855. Thus, it is difficult to determine the size of the Eurasian population between 1900 and 1942 with any precision, pp. 222-224.
156   Beate van Helsdingen-Schoevers, *De Europeesche vrouw in Indië*, in R.A. van Sandick ed., *Onze Koloniën* (Baarn: Hollandia Drukkerij, 1914), p. 14.
157   For a lucid exploration of the issue of milieu, see Ann Laura Stoler, "Carnal Knowledge and Imperial Power: Gender, Race, and Morality in Colonial Asia," in Micaela di Leonardo, ed., *Feminist Anthropology in the Post-Modern Era* (Berkeley: University of California Press, 1991), pp. 77-80.
158   Jean Gelman Taylor, *The Social World of Batavia. European and Eurasian in Dutch Asia* (Madison: University of Wisconsin Press, 1983), p. 14. and passim.
159   Elout wrote about Java in *De groote oost* that "in the olden days, the typical *Indischman* did not need to read much [about native culture] because he experienced it in his daily life thanks to the much maligned but equally misunderstood figure of the *njai*," pp. 237-38. About concubinage on the east coast of Sumatra, see the description in C.J. Dixon, *Een assistent in Deli* (Amsterdam: J.H. de Bussy, 1930).
160   Elsbeth Locher-Scholten, "The Nyai in Colonial Deli: A Case of Supposed Mediation," in Van Bemmelen, et al, eds., *Women and Mediation*, pp. 265-280.
161   Madelon Szekely-Lulofs touches upon this ambivalence in both *Coolie* (1932; repr. Singapore: Oxford University Press, 1987) and *De andere wereld* (Amsterdam: Elsevier, 1934). For an analysis see Lilly Clerkx, *Mensen in Deli. Een maatschappijbeeld uit de belletrie* (University of Amsterdam: Sociologisch-Historisch Seminarium voor Zuidoost Azië, 1961), publikatie No. 2, p. 100.
162   The former officer was S.E.W. Roorda van Eysinga, quoted in "Het Koninklijk Nederlands-Indisch Leger," in *Weerzien met Indië* (Zwolle: Waanders, 1994), No. 12, p. 289.
163   D.G. Stibbe, ed., *Encyclopaedie van Nederlandsch-Indië* (1919), vol. 3, pp. 514-515.
164   *Encyclopaedie van Nederlandsch-Indië*, vol. 3 (1919), pp. 514-515. Supplement VII (1935) of the *Encyclopaedie*, mentions in the entry for the "indigenous women's movement" (*inlandsche vrouwenbeweging*) that the Indies chapter of the Netherlands Women's League for the Improvement of Moral Consciousness inspired the creation of the women's organizations *Madjoe Kemoelian* in Bandoeng and *Hati Soetji* in Bata-

via, which were "dedicated to combat prostitution and the so-called trade in women and girls," p. 452. See also Liesbeth Hesselink, "Prostitution: a necessary evil, particularly in the colonies; Views on prostitution in the Netherlands Indies," in Locher-Scholten and Niehof, *Indonesian Women in Focus*, pp. 205-224.
165 Philippa Levine, "Venereal Disease, Prostitution, and the Politics of Empire: The Case of British India," *Journal of the History of Sexuality*, 4, No. 4 (1994), p. 602. See also Jacqui Alexander, "Redrafting Morality: The Postcolonial State and the Sexual Offences Bill of Trinidad and Tobago," in Chandra Talpade Mohanty, Ann Russo, and Lourdes Torres, eds., *Third World Women and the Politics of Feminism* (Bloomington: Indiana University Press, 1990), p. 133.
166 J.J. Einthoven, "Sexueele voorlichting voor het rijpere meisje," in Van Lith-van Schreven, *Indisch vrouwenjaarboek 1936*, p. 137.
167 Q., "Het concubinaat in de Indische kazerne," in *De Taak. Algemeen Indisch Weekblad*, 1, No. 48, June 29, 1918, pp. 577-78. See also Hanneke Ming, "Barracks Concubinage in the Indies," *Indonesia*, No. 35 (April 1983), pp. 65-94. Douglas Porch, in *The French Foreign Legion: A Complete History of the Legendary Fighting Force* (New York: Harper Collins, 1991), argues, however, that homosexuality was not at all prevalent in the Legion, p. 310.
168 Van Helsdingen-Schoevers, *De Europeesche vrouw in Indië*, p. 8.
169 See Elsbeth Locher-Scholten's "The *nyai* in Colonial Deli: A Case of Supposed Mediation," in Van Bemmelen, et al, eds., *Women and Mediation*, for a description of the institutionalization of concubinage among Europeans on the east coast of Sumatra, pp. 265-280.
170 On the agency of white women, see Tessell Pollmann, "Bruidstraantjes. De koloniale roman, de njai en de apartheid," in Jeske Reijs, et al. eds., *Vrouwen in de Nederlandse koloniën. Zevende jaarboek voor vrouwengeschiedenis* (Nijmergen: SUN, 1986), pp. 98-125.
171 Pamela Pattynama, "Oorden en woorden. Over rassenmenging, interetniciteit, en een Indisch meisje," *Tijdschrift voor vrouwenstudies*, 15, No. 1 (1994), p. 41. See also Ann Laura Stoler's analysis of the issue of *métissage* in "Sexual Affronts and Racial Frontiers: National Identity, 'Mixed Bloods' and the Cultural Genealogies of Europeans in Colonial Southeast Asia," *Comparative Studies in Society and History*, 34, No. 3 (July 1992), pp. 514-551.
172 Hissink-Snellebrand, "Lezing gehouden op den 23en Februari 1991 te Amsterdam," p. 8. See also Van Helsdingen-Schoevers, *De Europeesche vrouw*, passim.
173 In Pramoedya Ananta Toer's *This Earth of Mankind* (Bumi Manusia), the Javanese protagonist, Minke, at first echoed the moral prejudices and disdain toward the *njai* in the Indies around the year 1900, although he later changed his views. See *Awakenings* (1980; repr. Syndney: Penguin Books, 1991), pp. 15, 33. See also the discussion in Hellwig, *In the Shadow of Change*, pp. 69-95.
174 Hissink-Snellebrand, "Lezing gehouden op den 23en Februari 1991 te Amsterdam," p. 5.
175 ARA, Collection 198, archives of Johannes Hermanus Gunning (1859-1951), No. 42. Letter from C.H.C. Gunning to her father, J.H. Gunning, May 24, 1919.
176 On the "Gaze of Empire," see Ella Shohat, "Imaging Terra Incognita: The Disciplinary Gaze of Empire," *Public Culture*, 3, No. 2 (Spring 1991), pp. 62-68.
177 Pamela Pattynama, "Indo-European Hybridity and 'Modernity' in Dutch Colonial Culture: An Analysis of Louis Couperus' *The Hidden Force*," in Frances Gouda and Julia Clancy-Smith, eds., *Colonial Discourses and Gendered Rhetoric in the French and Dutch Empires* (Charlottesville: University Press of Virginia, forthcoming).
178 Quoted by Tineke Hellwig, *Adjustment and Discontent. Representations of Women in the Dutch East Indies* (Windsor, Ontario: Netherlandic Press, 1994), p. 33.
179 Annemarie Cottaar and Wim Willems, *Indische Nederlanders. Een onderzoek naar beeldvorming* (The Hague: Moesson, 1984), p. 100. Olof Nieuwenhoff, in *De Locomotief*, April 4, 1888, predicted that future historians would cite Maurits' (pseudonym for P.A. Daum) novel *Hoe hij Raad van Indië werd* "as one of the most important historical documents of our day." The dust jacket of J. Kleian, *Njai Mirdja* (Hoorn: De Steenuil, n.d.) advertises the book as "painting an exceptionally realistic portrait of the relationships between white and brown in the pre-war Indies." See also P.M.H. Groen, "Ten Thousand Things and A Jewelled Hair-Comb as Historical Sources: Fiction or Fact," pp. 87-123, and Sartono Kartodirdjo, "The Historical Novel *Pah Troeno*: A Mirror of Social Realities in the Colonial Past," in Abdullah, *Papers of the Fourth Indonesian-Dutch History Conference*, pp. 165-83.
180 Toni Morrison, *Playing in the Dark. Whiteness and the Literary Imagination* (Cambridge: Harvard University Press, 1992), p. 38.
181 The dismissal of the *njai* as a necessary evil appears in Annie Foore's short story "Geketend," in *Indische huwelijken* (Rotterdam: D. Bolle, 1895), p. 113. The term race melodrama is derived from Susan Gillman, "The Mulatto, Tragic or Triumphant? The Nineteenth-Century American Race Melodrama," in Shirley Samuels,

ed., *The Culture of Sentiment. Race, Gender, and Sentimentality in 19th Century America* (New York: Oxford University Press, 1992), p. 222.
182 Melantjong, *Njai Belanda* (1904; repr. Rotterdam: D. Bolle, 1927), p. 32.
183 Simon Franke, *Njai Sarina* (Amsterdam: Scheltens & Giltay, n.d.), p. 123.
184 Johan Fabricius, *Halfbloed* (The Hague: H.P. Leopold, 1946), p. 8.
185 Kleian, *Njai Mirdja*, p. 148. For a general exploration of these issues, see Lily Clerkx, *Mensen in Deli. Een maatschappijbeeld uit de belletrie*, pp. 87-101.
186 G.J. Resink, "Between the Myths: From Colonial to National Historiography," in *History between the Myths. Essays in Legal History and Historical Theory* (The Hague: W. van Hoeve, 1968), p. 37.

CHAPTER 4

1 P. Fournier, "De beteekenis van het overheerschingstijdperk," *Wederopbouw. Maandschrift gewijd aan de jong-Javanen beweging en het Javaansche geestesleven*, 3, No. 2 (February 1920), pp. 32-33.
2 *Djawa. Driemaandelijks Tijdschrift uitgegeven door het Java-Instituut*, 1, No. 1 (1921), Editorial statement of purpose, n.p. See also Linda Berman-Hall, Editorial Preface to Johan Sebastiaan Brandts Buys, *Music in Madura*, "Ethnomusicology in the Dutch East Indies during the Interbellum Period: The Life and Times of J.S. Brandts Buys, 1897-1939" (Ithaca: Cornell University Southeast Asia Publications, forthcoming), p. 18, and Kenji Tsuchiya, "Javanology and the Age of Ranggawarsita: An Introduction to Nineteenth-Century Javanese Culture," *Reading Southeast Asia* (Ithaca: Cornell University Southeast Asia Publications, 1990), Translation Series, 1, p. 91.
3 Dr. G.J. Nieuwenhuis, "Oosten en Westen," *Djawa*, 3, No. 1 (1923), p. 5. The first Dutch edition of Huizinga's *Herfsttij der Middeleeuwen* (The Waning of the Middle Ages) was published in 1919; the second edition in 1921. An English translation was published in 1924 in the United States. Douglas E. Haynes, in *Rhetoric and Ritual in Colonial India. The Shaping of a Public Culture in Surat City, 1852-1928* (Berkeley: University of California Press, 1991), argues, too, that British colonial rulers in India "located Indian society in a backward stage of historical evolution, awkwardly analogous to the time when English society had in theory been controlled by its aristocracy. It generally implied, however, that India was somehow permanently stuck in that stage," p. 104.
4 Nieuwenhuis, "Oosten en westen," *Djawa*, p. 5. The analogy between Huizinga's *Waning of the Middle Ages* and modern Javanese culture also resurfaced in A.D.A. de Kat Angelino, *Colonial Policy*, 2 vols. (The Hague: Martinus Nijhoff, 1931), 1, pp. 88-91. See also Berman-Hall, "Ethnomusicology in the Dutch East Indies," p. 22.
5 Tjipto addressed the Congress on "Javanese Cultural Development" in Solo in early July, 1918. His statement was reported in the minutes of the "Congres voor Javaansche Cultuur-Ontwikkeling" in Solo, 5-7 Juli, 1918, (reprinted from "De Locomotief"); *Djawa*, 1, No. 4 (December 1921), Bijlage a, p. 315.
6 Nancy Stepan, in *The Idea of Race in Science: Great Britain, 1800-1960* (Hamden, CT: Archon Books, 1982), uses the word naturalness to describe Europeans' deeply held convictions of the inequalities of the human races, p. xxi.
7 David Spurr, *The Rhetoric of Empire. Colonial Discourse in Journalism, Travel Writing and Imperial Administration* (Durham: Duke University Press, 1993), p. 136.
8 Although some people might insist on quotation marks around "primitive" to underscore the problematic nature of the word —or to emphasize that the label "primitive" is a cultural construction that often denotes the former subjects of colonial domination— doing so implies that we should also put "Western" in quotation marks. Not wanting to mar the text with an endless series of quotation marks, I will not place them around words such as primitive, backward, otherness, us, them, West, or East. For a detailed discussion of these issues, see Marianne Torgovnick, *Gone Primitive. Savage Intellectuals, Modern Lives* (Chicago: University of Chicago Press, 1990), pp. 12-20.
9 Torgovnick, *Gone Primitive*, pp. 8, 245-246, and Tzvetan Todorov, *On Human Diversity. Nationalism, Racism, and Exoticism in French Thought* (1989; repr. Cambridge: Harvard University Press, 1993), p. xi.
10 From Denis Diderot's eudaemonist utopian vision, "Orou and the Chaplain," in *Love in Tahiti*; see Frank E. Manuel and Fritzie P. Manuel, eds., *French Utopias. An Anthology of Ideal Societies* (New York: Schocken, 1971), p. 159.
11 Josien Blok, "D'où venons-nous? Que sommes-nous? Où allons-nous?" in *Deugd en ondeugd. Jaarboek voor Vrouwengeschiedenis 13* (Amsterdam: Internationaal Instituut voor Sociale Geschiedenis, 1994), p. 131.
12 Reprinted in Dennis Porter, *Haunted Journeys. Desire and Transgression in European Travel Writing* (Princeton: Princeton University Press, 1991), pp. 120-21.

13 Claude Lévi-Strauss, in *Tristes Tropiques* (New York: Atheneum, 1975), noted that anthropology as a scholarly excercise of Westerners "should be renamed entropology," because contact between the West and non-Western others imposes upon the latter a process of "entropy," which produces a higher degree of uniformity in human behavior; the bottom line, according to Lévi-Strauss, is that "all human creativity is essentially entropic," p. 385.
14 For the Dutch East Indies, see Roy F. Ellen, "The Development of Anthropology and Colonial Policy in the Netherlands: 1800-1960," *Journal of the History of the Behavioral Sciences*, 12, No. 4 (October, 1976), pp. 303-325. For a general discussion, see, among others, Talal Asad, ed., *Anthropology and the Colonial Encounter* (London: Verso, 1973); Johannes Fabian, *Time and the Other. How Anthropology Makes its Object* (New York: Columbia University Press, 1983); Edward Said, "Representing the Colonized. Anthropology's Interlocutors," *Critical Inquiry*, 15, No. 2 (Winter 1989), pp. 205-225, and George W. Stocking, Jr. ed., *Colonial Situations. Essays on the Contextualization of Ethnographic Knowledge* (Madison: University of Wisconsin Press, 1991), History of Anthropology, vol. 7.
15 Lewis Pyenson, *Empire of Reason. Exact Sciences in Indonesia, 1840-1940* (Leiden/New York: E.J. Brill, 1989), p. 182. The Dutch were pioneers in experiments in physical chemistry at a time when the field had barely received sanction as a discipline, p. 3.
16 Records of the Department of State, National Archives, Washington D.C., as discussed in Frances Gouda, "Visions of Empire: Changing American Perspectives on Dutch Colonial Rule between 1920 and 1942," *Bijdragen en Mededelingen betreffende de Geschiedenis der Nederlanden*, 109, No. 2 (1994), pp. 237-258.
17 Adam Messer, "Effects of the Indonesian National Revolution and the Transfer of Power on the Scientific Establishment," *Indonesia*, No. 58 (October 1994), p. 42.
18 A.M.C. Sengör, *Asian versus European Conceptions of Geology: Developments of Thoughts on the Structure and Tectonic Evolution of Asia* (New York: Cambridge University Press, 1995), p. 212.
19 Pyenson, *Empire of Reason*, pp. 177-80. See also Messer, "Effects of Transfer of Power on the Scientific Establishment," p. 43-44. The best survey of scientific research in the Dutch East Indies before World War II is P. Honig and F. Verdoorn, eds., *Science and Scientists in the Netherlands Indies* (New York: Board for the Netherlands Indies, Surinam, and Curaçao, 1945).
20 Paeleoanthropologists, today, are still engaged in an earnest search for "missing links." See the recent discussion about new findings in Ethiopia in "Out of Africa, A Missing Link," *Newsweek*, October 3, 1994, pp. 56-57, and "New Fossils Take Science Close to Dawn of Humans, *New York Times*, September 22, 1994.
21 Derek Walcott, *The Antilles: Fragments of Epic Memory. The Nobel Lecture* (New York: Farrar, Straus and Giroux, 1992), n.p. Paul Rabinow, in *French Modern. Norms and Forms of the Social Environment* (Cambridge: MIT Press, 1989) defines this Lamarckian vision of environment as one of "fundamental pathos: an active organism seeks endlessly to attach itself to its milieu, which is fundamentally indifferent to its survival," p. 129.
22 Stephen Jay Gould, "The Celestial Mechanic and the Early Naturalist," *Natural History*, 103, No. 11 (November 1994), p. 6.
23 Jan Pieterse Nederveen, *Wit over zwart. Beelden van Afrika en zwarten in de westerse populaire cultuur* (Amsterdam: KIT publications, 1989), p. 233.
24 Ph.H. Coolhaas, "Ontstaan en groei," in *Wij gedenken. Gedenkboek van de Vereniging van ambtenaren bij het Binnenlands Bestuur in Nederlands-Indië* (Utrecht: Oosthoek, 1956), pp. 62, 70-71. The Dutch words are *kinderlijk* and *kinderachtig*.
25 Hendrik Colijn made the actual statement; see the discussion in Bernard Dahm, *Soekarno en de strijd om Indonesië's onafhankelijkheid* (Meppel: Boom, 1964), p. 341.
26 Danilyn Rutherford uses this apt phrase in "European Identity, the Idea of Colonization, and New Guinea as Empty Space," unpublished dissertation chapter, Department of Anthropology, Cornell University, 1995.
27 Charles Darwin, *The Origins of the Species and the Descent of Man*, quoted by James A. Boon in *Other Tribes, Other Scribes. Symbolic Anthropology in the Comparative Study of Cultures, Histories, Religions, and Texts* (Cambridge: Cambridge University Press, 1982), p. 40.
28 Nora Barlow, ed., *The Autobiography of Charles Darwin, 1809-1882* (1876; New York, Norton, 1993), p. 80; see also Pat Shipman, *The Evolution of Racism. Human Differences and the Use and Abuse of Science* (New York: Simon & Schuster, 1994), p. 19.
29 ARA, 2nd Division, Collection 400, Archives of Louis Constant Westenenk, No. 55, "Over het orang pendek vraagstuk," (n.d., approximately 1930).
30 Peter J. Bowler, *Evolution. The History of an Idea* (Berkeley: University of California Press, 1989), pp. 91-92.
31 Arthur Lovejoy, *The Great Chain of Being* (Cambridge: Harvard University Press, 1936), passim.
32 "Heredity Can Be More Than Genes, a New Theory Proposes," *New York Times*, January 3, 1995.
33 Although in 1908 Herman Bernelot Moens, a young Dutch biologist in Maastricht who was interested in the question of human evolution and regression, proposed that a Negro be mated with a gorilla; he wrote a

pamphlet entitled *Recherches expérimentales sur l'origine de 'homme*, which the famous Ernst Haeckel greeted with enthusiasm. Quoted by Jan Breman, "Introduction," in *Idem*, ed., *Imperial Monkey Business. Racial Supremacy in Social Darwinist Theory and Colonial Practice* (Amsterdam: VU University Press, 1990), CASA Monographs 3, p. 2.

34   P.H.M. Travaglino, "Het karakter van den inlander," *Tijdschrift van de Politiek Economische Bond*, 1 (1920-21), pp. 342-43. See also *Idem*, "De psychose van den inlander in verband met zijn karakter," *Geneeskundig Tijdschrift voor Nederlandsch-Indië*, LX, No. 2 (Batavia: Javasche Boekhandel and Drukkerij, 1920), pp. 99-111.

35   See the discussion in Ashis Nandy, *The Intimate Enemy. Loss and Recovery of Self under Colonialism* (Delhi: Oxford University Press, 1983), p. 13, and Octave Mannoni, "Psychoanalysis and the Decolonization of Mankind," in J. Miller, ed., *Freud* (London: Weidenfeld & Nicholson, 1972), pp. 86-95.

36   Travaglino, "Het karakter van den inlander," in *Tijdschrift van de Politiek Economische Bond*, pp. 342-43.

37   Travaglino, "Het karakter van de inlander," p. 343, quoted and discussed in great detail in Paul van Schilfgaarde, "De psyche van de Javaan," *Djawa*, 5, No. 1 (1925), pp. 109-111.

38   Johan Huizinga, *The Waning of the Middle Ages* (New York: Anchor Books, 1954), pp. 200, 205, and Barbara Tuchman, *A Distant Mirror. The Calamitous 14th Century* (New York: Alfred A. Knopf, 1978).

39   Although a contemporary, A.B. Cohen Stuart, argued in 1918 in favor of a much more recent historical precedent: "Old Javanese culture, today, can more or less be compared with Christendom's adjustment to the modern values of Western Europe in the nineteenth century," in "Hedendaagsch Javaans geestesleven," *Koloniale Studiën*, 2, No. 2 (1918), p. 83.

40   Norman F. Cantor, *Inventing the Middle Ages. The Lives, Works, and Ideas of the Great Medievalists of the Twentieth Century* (New York: William Morrow, 1991), p. 186.

41   The reviewer J.A.N. Knutter, in "Nabloei," in *De Nieuwe Tijd* (1920), mentioned that the allusion to the inexorable ebb and flow of oceanic tides might indicate that Huizinga embraced a cyclical view of historical processes. This was not the case; in order to avoid further misunderstandings, Huizinga authorized the titles *The Waning of the Middle Ages* and *Le déclin du Moyen-Age* when his book was translated into English and French. See the discussion in Anton van der Lem, *Johan Huizinga. Leven en werk in beelden en documenten* (Amsterdam: Wereldbibliotheek, 1993), p. 139.

42   Cantor identifies this as a main argument in Huizinga's *The Waning of the Middle Ages*; See *Inventing the Middle Ages*, p. 397.

43   C.W. Vollgraff, in *Herdenking van Johan Huizinga* (Haarlem: Tjeenk Willink, 1945) uses this imagery to describe the decline of the Middle Ages, p. 24.

44   Van der Lem, *Johan Huizinga. Leven en werk in beelden en documenten*, p. 140; Van der Lem notes, too, that Huizinga was well-versed in the ethnographic literature on Indonesia. In fact, in the first edition of *Herfsttij*, he actually drew a series of deliberate analogies between medieval Europe and Javanese history, which were dropped from later editions, p. 142.

45   Theodoor Pigeaud called the literary flourishing in the *kratons* of Central Java in the second half of the eighteenth-century a "renaissance." But the sudden outburst of literary activity did not necessary issue from organic change or from "natural" internal forces; instead, the greater Dutch presence in Central Java reconfigured the internal rivalry between the various sultans' courts in Yogyakarta and Surakarta. Rather than struggle for political supremacy and strive for the subjugation of other courts, since the mid-eighteenth century each sultan's court aimed to achieve cultural primacy by trying to substantiate its claim to be the legitimate articulator of Javanese tradition. According to Kenji Tsuchiya, the sublimation of internecine military strife by converting it into a cultural competition was due to the Dutch ability to act as "arbitrators in civil strife." Perhaps this constituted an early precedent, too, for Dutch attempts to "culturalize" relations of power in the twentieth century as well as Suharto's contemporary efforts to "culturalize" internal Indonesian conflicts. See Tchuchiya, "Javanology and the Age of Ranggawarsita," in *Reading Southeast Asia*, 1, p. 93.

46   Resident Ch.Chr. Ouweling, *Memorie van Overgave*, May 19, 1930, quoted by P.M.H. Groen, "*Ten Thousand Things* and *The Jewelled Hair-Comb* as Historical Sources: Fiction or Fact?", in Taufik Abdullah, ed., *Papers of the Fourth Indonesian-Dutch History Conference*, 2 vols. (Yogyakarta: Gadjah Mada University Press, 1986), *Literature and History*, 2, p. 109.

47   P. Polman O.F.M., *Huizinga als kultuurhistoricus* (Haarlem: Tjeenk Willink, 1946), p. 9.

48   L.S.A.M. von Römer, "Cultuurstrijd," in *Wederopbouw. Maandschrift van de jong-Javanen beweging en het Javaansche geestesleven*, 2, No. 5 (1919), p. 84.

49   Von Römer asserted his pride in his mixed-blood status in his address to the congress on "Javanese Cultural Development" in Solo on July 6, 1918 (reprinted from "De Locomotief); See *Djawa*, 1, No. 4 (December 1921), Bijlage a, p. 318.

50   Von Römer, "Cultuurstrijd," in *Wederopbouw*, 2, No. 5 (1919), p. 84.

51 Fournier, "De beteekenis van het overheerschingstijdperk," *Wederopbouw*, 3, No. 2 (1920), pp. 32-33.
52 Von Römer, "Cultuurstrijd," in *Wederopbouw*, 2, No. 5 (1919), p. 84.
53 Soetan Sjahrir, *Indonesische overpijnzingen* (Amsterdam: De Bezige Bij, 1945), p. 63. See also the discussion of this particular passage in D. de Vries, *Culturele aspecten in de verhouding Nederland-Indonesië* (Amsterdam: Vrij Nederland, 1947), pp. 91-92.
54 Benedict R. O'G Anderson, "Introduction," *Language and Power. Exploring Political Cultures in Indonesia* (Ithaca: Cornell University Press, 1990), p. 7.
55 Cantor, *Inventing the Middle Ages*, p. 40.
56 See Johannes Fabian's chapter on "The Other and the Eye: Time and the Rhetoric of Vision," in *Time and the Other. How Anthropology makes its Object* (New York: Columbia University Press, 1893), pp. 135, 143.
57 Tessell Pollmann, Review of A.J. Bernet Kempers, *Monumental Bali: Introduction to Balinese Archeaology and Guide to the Monuments* (Singapore: Periplus, 1991), in *Indonesia*, No. 54 (October, 1992), p. 139.
58 Margaret Mead, "The Arts in Bali," in Jane Belo, ed., *Traditional Balinese Culture* (New York: Columbia University Press, 1970), pp. 331-33.
59 Quoted by Carol J. Oja, *Colin McPhee: Composer in Two Worlds* (Washington D.C.: Smithsonian Institution Press, 1990), p. 144.
60 For developments in nineteenth-century geology, see Mott T. Greene, *Geology in the Nineteenth Century. Changing Views of a Changing World* (Ithaca: Cornell University Press, 1982); for the biological sciences, see Peter J. Bowler, *Evolution. The History of an Idea*; Idem., *The Non-Darwinian Revolution. Reinterpreting a Historical Myth* (Baltimore: Johns Hopkins Press, 1988), and David Young, *The Discovery of Evolution* (New York: Cambridge University Press, 1993).
61 Bernard McGrane, *Beyond Anthropology. Society and the Other* (New York: Columbia University Press, 1989), p. 91. For a critique of McGrane's *Beyond Anthropology* as "unsatisfyingly crude," see Nicholas Thomas, *Colonialism's Culture. Anthropology, Travel and Government* (Princeton: Princeton University Press, 1994), pp. 67-68. Darwin borrowed the phrase "daughter of time" from Linneaus; see Jonathan Wiener, *The Beak of the Finch. A Story of Evolution in Our Time* (New York: Alfred A. Knopf, 1994), p. 25.
62 Quoted by Shipman, *The Evolution of Racism*, p. 92. See also Ernst Mayr, *One Long Argument. Charles Darwin and the Genesis of Modern Evolutionary Thought* (Cambridge: Harvard University Press, 1991), for a lengthy discussion of the work of August Weismann, who devoted his career to a refutation of the Lamarckian idea of the inheritance of acquired characteristics, pp. 112-124.
63 Bowler, *Evolution*, pp. 257-268, and George W. Stocking, Jr, "Lamarckianism in American Social Science," in *Race, Culture, and Evolution. Essays in the History of Anthropology* (1968; repr. Chicago: University of Chicago Press, 1982), pp. 234-269; for the Dutch context, see Piet de Rooy, "Bouleren met de evolutie. Over de samenhang tussen apen, negers en proletariaat," *De Gids*, 154, No. 5/6, (June 1991), special issue on "Colonialism, Racism, and Cultural Policy," pp. 351-352. See also his lucid essay in English, "Of Monkeys, Blacks, and Proles: Ernst Haeckel's Theory of Recapitulation," in Jan Breman, ed., *Imperial Monkey Business. Racial Supremacy in Social Darwinist Theory and Colonial Practice* (Amsterdam: VU University Press, 1990, CASA Monographs 3), pp. 7-34.
64 The question was posed by Edward Drinker Cope in *The Origins of the Fittest. Essays in Evolution* (1887; repr. New York: AMS Press, 1974).
65 Ernst Heackel, *The Wonders of Life* (New York: Harper, 1904), p. 390; quoted by Daniel Gasman, *The Scientific Origins of National Socialism: Social Darwinism in Ernst Haeckel and the German Monist League* (London: MacDonald, 1971), p. 86.
66 McGrane, *Beyond Anthropology*, pp. 91-94, and Bowler, *Evolution*, p. 257.
67 E.B. Tylor, *Anthropology, an Introduction to the Study of Man and Civilization* (1881; repr. New York: D. Appleton, 1913), p. 388. See also Brian V. Street, *The Savage in Literature. Representations of 'primitive' society in English Fiction, 1858-1920* (London/Boston: Routledge, Kegan, and Paul, 1975), who begins his discussion in the year Darwin's *Origin of Species* was published.
68 McGrane, *Beyond Anthropology*, p. 95. See also the discussion of Michael Adas in *Machines as the Measure of Man. Science, Technology, and Ideologies of Western Dominance* (Ithaca: Cornell University Press, 1990), pp. 164-65, or 308-311.
69 William Petty, *The Petty Papers* (1677), quoted by McGrane, *Beyond Anthropology*, p. 42. The gorilla, Petty contemplated, most resembles human beings in form; the parrot best imitates the human capacity for producing variable sounds, whereas the elephant most effectively replicates human memory and the ability to understand language, while the bee ranks highest in terms of spirituality and power.
70 Mott T. Greene, *Natural Knowledge in Preclassical Antiquity* (Baltimore: The Johns Hopkins University Press, 1992), pp. 6-7. See also Adam Kuper, *The Invention of Primitive Society* (London: Routledge, 1988), passim.
71 McGrane, *Beyond Anthropology*, p. 56.

72 F.D.E. van Ossenbruggen, "Het magisch denken van den inlander," George Nypels, ed., *De Indische Gids* (also the new series of *Tijdschrift voor Nederlandsch-Indië*), 48, No. I-VI (1926), pp. 290-99. Lecture delivered to students of the *Handelshoogeschool* in Rotterdam, December 1, 1925.
73 Van Ossenbruggen, "Het magisch denken van den inlander," *De Indische Gids*, 48, No. I-VI (1926), pp. 290-99.
74 "Preface" to the *Second Discourse*, p. 130, quoted by Todorov, *On Human Diversity*, p. 278.
75 Ronald L. Meek, *Social Science and the Ignoble Savage* (Cambridge: Cambridge University Press, 1976), p. 80.
76 Jean Jacques Rousseau, "Lettre à Beaumont," (1762), in *Oeuvres complètes* (Paris: Gallimard, 1959-1969), 4, p. 936, quoted by Todorov, *On Human Diversity*, p. 279-280.
77 Todorov, *On Human Diversity*, pp. 279-281. For a comparable reading, see Meek, *Social Science and the Ignoble Savage*, pp. 76-90.
78 J.C. van Eerde, *Koloniale Volkenkunde*, First Part, "Omgang met inlanders," Mededeeling No. 1, Afdeeling Volkenkunde, No. 1, Koninklijk Koloniaal Instituut (1914; repr. Amsterdam: De Bussy, 1928), p. 48.
79 G.L. Gonggrijp, *Brieven van opheffer aan de redactie van het Bataviaans Handelsblad*, 4th Edition (Maastricht: N.V. Leiter-Nypels, n.d.), p. 149; see also Rudy Kousbroek, *Het Oostindisch kampsyndroom* (Amsterdam: Meulenhoff, 1992), p. 137.
80 Gonggrijp, *Brieven van opheffer*, p. 137.
81 C.K. Elout, *De grote oost* (The Hague: W.P. van Stockum, 1930), p. 240.
82 C. van Heekeren, *Trekkers en blijvers. Kroniek van een Haags-Indische familie* (Franeker: T. Wever, 1980), p. 117.
83 Nora Barlow, ed., *Charles Darwin's Diary of the Voyage of the H.M.S. Beagle* (1934), quoted by Michael Taussig, *Mimesis and Alterity. A Particular History of the Senses* (New/London: Routledge, 1993), p. 81. See also the discussion of these notions in J.F.G. Brumund, *Het volksonderwijs onder de Javanen* (Batavia: Van Haren Noman & Kolff, 1857), and "Boeroe boedoer," *Tijdschrift Nederlandsch-Indië*, 2 (1858), pp. 279-280, quoted by J.H.F. Kohlbrugge, *Een en ander over de psychologie van den Javaan* (Leiden: E.J. Brill, 1907), a lecture delivered to the 17th general meeting of the Association for the promotion of research in physics in the Dutch colonies, May 14, 1907, p. 39.
84 Quoted by Cees Fasseur, *De Indologen. Ambtenaren voor de Oost, 1825-1950* (Amsterdam: Bert Bakker, 1992), p. 91.
85 Brumund, "Boeroe boedoer," *Tijdschrift Nederlandsch-Indië*, pp. 279-280. See also the discussion in Kees Groeneboer, *Weg tot het Westen. Het Nederlands voor Indië, 1600-1950* (Leiden: KITLV Press, 1993), Verhandelingen 158, pp. 172-73.
86 This phrase was coined by Anna Lowenhaupt Tsing, *In the Realm of the Diamond Queen. Marginality in an Out-of-the-Way Place* (Princeton: Princeton University Press, 1993).
87 C. Lekkerkerker, "Bali: Zending en Missie [Er is niets nieuws onder de zon]." Lecture delivered to the meeting of Indisch Genootschap, December 16, 1932. ARA, Collection 416, Archives of C.J.A. Lichtenbelt for the years 1927-1939, No. 16; also in *Koloniaal Tijdschrift*, 22, No. 1 (1932).
88 Tjipto Mangoenkoesoemo, "Eigen en vreemd regime," (Dr. Tjipto Mangoenkoesoemo's strijd voor Bali. Een gedocumenteerde rede), *De Beweging. Algemeen Politiek Weekblad*, 1, No. 30, July 26, 1919, p. 792.
89 Dr. H. Kraemer, "Repliek op 'Bali en de zending,'" *Djawa*, 13, No. 1 (1933), p. 43. An advocate of the entry of Christian missions in Bali, Kraemer nonetheless conceded this point.
90 Roelof Goris, "Bali's oude geschiedenis," *Timboel. Algemeen Periodiek voor Indonesië*, 1, No. 17 (September 1927), p. 270.
91 Dr. F.D.K. Bosch, "Bali en de zending," *Djawa*, 13, No. 1 (1933), pp. 3, 39.
92 "Tagore's bezoek. De wijsgeer over Bali: Rabindanath Tagore bespreekt de verhouding van Oost en West," in the section "review of the media" (*persoverzicht*) in *Timboel. Algemeen Periodiek voor Indonesië*, 1, No. 16 (September 1927), pp. 254-55. With regard to the grace and elegance of Javanese dance, Tagore apparently noted that "We wrote the *Mahabharata*, but the Javanese are the ones who know how to dance it!" Quoted by Dr. A. Baudisch, "Bekenntnis und Dank," in *Triwindoe-Gedenkboek Mangkoe Nagoro VII* (Soerakarta: Comité Triwindoe-Gedenkboek, 1939), p. 117.
93 Rudolf Bonnet to Jaap Kunst, April 23, 1933, No. 31, Archives of Jaap Kunst, Dossier 126, Ethnomusicologisch Instituut "Jaap Kunst," University of Amsterdam.
94 Bonnet to Kunst, April 23, 1933, Dossier 126, No. 31.
95 Hildred Geertz, "Balinese Imaginings. Paintings collected by anthropologists in the 1930s reveal the pervading anxieties of an Indonesian people," *Natural History*, 104, No. 2 (February 1995), p. 62.
96 Sujeta Neka, *The Development of Painting in Bali* (Ubud: Yayasan Dharma Seni Museum Neka, 1989), p. 24.
97 Geertz, "Balinese Imaginings," *Natural History*, p. 62.

98 Bonnet to Kunst, April 23, 1933, No. 31. Bonnet also told Kunst in a postscript, perhaps with a hint of envy, that Walter Spies "was accompanying rich Americans to Bangkok and Angkor Wat!"
99 Oswald Spengler, *The Decline of the West. Form and Actuality*, trans. Charles Francis Atkinson, 2 vols. (New York: Alfred A. Knopf, 1926).
100 De Kat Angelino, *Colonial Policy*, 1, p. 178.
101 Spengler, *The Decline of the West*, 1, pp. 106-107.
102 Greene, *Natural Knowledge in Pre-Classical Antiquity*, p. 22.
103 Jaap Kunst to Rudolf Bonnet, January 13, 1939, No. 49, Archives of Jaap Kunst, Dossier 126.
104 J.H. Boeke, "De Nederlandse bestuurspolitiek in Indonesië, gezien door de ogen van een Engelsman," in *Indonesië*, 1 (1947-48), quoted by J.A.A. van Doorn, *De laatste eeuw van Indië. Ontwikkeling en ondergang van een koloniaal project* (Amsterdam: Bert Bakker, 1994), p. 70. See also the discussion in Jacob van Gelderen, *Voorlezingen over de tropisch-koloniale staathuishoudkunde* (Haarlem: H.D. Tjeenk Willink, 1927), passim.
105 Van Gelderen, *Voorlezingen over tropisch-koloniale staathuishoudkunde*, pp. 17, 24.
106 Houbolt, "Oosten en westen," *Djawa*, 3, No. 2 (1923), p. 76.
107 Dr. F.D.K. Bosch, "Een ontoelaatbaar experiment," *Djawa*, 12. No. 4/5 (1932), p. 258; also published in *De Stuw*, 2, No. 17.
108 Ir. Thomas Karsten, "Vreemd en eigen," *Djawa*, 3, No. 2 (1923), p. 74.
109 ARA, Collection 416, Archives of C.J.A. Lichtenbelt, No. 16, Dr. V.E. Korn, "Christelijke Actie op Bali," lecture delivered to a meeting of the Indisch Genootschap, December 16, 1932.
110 *Ibid.*, Dr. B.J. Haga, Lecture to the Meeting of the Indisch Genootschap.
111 See the critical discussion in Th.J.A. Hilgers and C. Lekkerkerker, *Populaire schetsen over land en volk van Indië* (Amsterdam: J.H. de Bussy, 1920), p. 53.
112 Quoted by Gerard P.A. Termorshuizen, "The Novels of Maurits: A Portrait of a Society," in Abdullah, *Papers of the Fourth Indonesian-Dutch History Conference*, p. 201. The same reference to *Indië* as a "country of monkeys" is repeated in Piet Korthuys, *In de ban van de tropen* (Wageningen: Zomer & Keuning, 1947), who also refers to the Javanese as "cattle," pp. 29, 95.
113 Pramoedya Ananta Toer, *This Earth of Mankind* (*Bumi Manusia*), in *Awakenings* (1980; repr. Sydney: Penguin Books, 1991), pp. 21, 27.
114 Graham Saunders, "Early Travellers in Borneo," in Michael Hitchcock, Victor T. King, and Michael J.G. Parnwell, eds., *Tourism in South-East Asia* (London: Routledge, 1993), pp. 271-85.
115 Stephen Jay Gould, *The Flamingo's Smile. Reflections in Natural History* (New York: W.W. Norton, 1985), pp. 263-264.
116 Montesquieu, *The Persian Letters*, trans. George R. Healy, in The Library of the Liberal Arts (Indianapolis: Bobbs-Merrill, 1964), Letter XI, p. 23.
117 Montesquieu, *Persian Letters*, Letter XII, p. 25.
118 Article in *De Java Bode*, July 2, 1932, repr. in Wim Wertheim and Hetty Wertheim-Gijse Weenink, *Vier wendingen in ons bestaan. Indië verloren, Indonesië geboren* (Breda: De Geus, 1991), Appendix 2, p. 354.
119 ARA, Collection 400, Westenenk, No. 55, "Over het orang pendek vraagstuk," p. 2.
120 Stephen Jay Gould, in "So Near and Yet so Far," uses the same family metaphor: "honored ancestors or extinquished cousins?" in *New York Review of Books*, October 20, 1994.
121 *Soerabaiasch Handelsblad*, June 2, 1927, in ARA, Collection 400, Westenenk, No. 55, "Over het orang pendek vraagstuk," p. 23.
122 *Bataviaans Nieuwsblad*, September 5, 1929, in ARA, Collection 400, Westenenk, No. 55, "Over het orang pendek vraagstuk," pp. 23-25.
123 William Marsden, *The History of Sumatra*, 3rd edition (London: 1811), quoted by James A. Boon, *Affinities and Extremes. Crisscrossing the Bittersweet Ethnology of East Indies History, Hindu-Balinese Culture, and Indo-European Allure* (Chicago: University of Chicago Press, 1990), p. 32.
124 Wilhelm Volz, *Im Dämmer des Rimba. Sumatras Urwald und Urmensch* (Breslau: Ferdinand Hirt, 1921), pp. 59, 80, 89.
125 Léopold de Saussure, *Psychologie de la colonization française* (1899), quoted by Raul Girardet, *L'Idée coloniale en France de 1871 à 1962* (Paris: La Table Ronde, 1972), pp. 157-58, and James Hunt, "on the Negro's Place in Nature," (1863-64), quoted by Adas, *Machines as the Measure of Man*, p. 303.
126 Madelon Szekely-Lulofs, *Coolie*, trans. G.J. Renier and Irene Clephane (1932; repr. Singapore: Oxford University Press, 1982), pp. 187, 61, 9.
127 Szekely-Lulofs, *Coolie*, "A word to my British readers," pp. ix-x.
128 D.M. Roskies, "Imperial Perceptions: Examples of Colonial Fiction from the Netherlands East Indies," Occasional Paper No. 9, Centre for South-east Asian Studies, University of Kent (March 1988), p. 15.

129 Roskies, "Imperial Perceptions," p. 14, and Lili Clerkx, *Mensen in Deli. Een maatschappijbeeld uit de belletrie*, Publication No. 2, (University of Amsterdam: Sociologisch-Historisch Seminarium voor Zuidoost Azie, 1961), p. 45.
130 Elout, *De grote oost*, pp. 240-241.
131 J.Th. Blumberger, *De nationalistische beweging in Nederlandsch-Indië* (Haarlem: Tjeenk Willink, 1931), p. 235.
132 ARA, Collection 400, Westenenk, No. 55, "over het orang pendek vraagstuk," p. 26.
133 Letter from Eugène Dubois to L.C. Westenenk, July 1, 1928, ARA, Collection 400, Westenenk, No. 55.
134 Eugène Dubois, *Pithecantropus erectus. Eine Menschenaehnliche Uebergangsform aus Java* (Batavia: Landsdrukkerij, 1894). For a hagiographical portrait of Dubois, see Jan Feith, *Holland over zee* (Baarn: Hollandia Drukkerij, 1941), pp. 46-47. For more detailed studies of Eugène Dubois's role in evolutionary biology and the science of ecology, see Bert Theunissen, *Eugène Dubois and the ape-man from Java: the history of the first missing link and its discoverer* (Dordrecht/Boston: Kluwer, 1989), and Richard E. Leakey and L. Jan Slikkerveer, *Man-ape, ape-man. The quest for humans' place in nature and Dubois' missing link* (Leiden: Netherlands Foundation for Kenya Wildlife Service, 1993).
135 Quoted in "Wetenschappelijke exploraties," *Weerzien met Indië* (Zwolle: Waanders, 1994), No. 16, p. 379.
136 J.H.F. Kohlbrugge, *Die Morphologische Abstammung des Menschen. Kritische Studie über die neueren Hypothesen*, in Georg Buschan, ed., *Studien und Forschungen zur Menschen-und Volkerkunde* (Stuttgart: Verlag von Strecker & Schroder, 1908), p. 9.
137 Leakey and Slikkeveer, *Man-Ape, Ape-Man, The Quest for Human's Place in Nature*, p. 100-101.
138 W.T.A.H. Volz, "Uber das geologische Alter des Pithecantropus Erectus," *Globus*, XCII, No. 22 (1907), pp. 1-38. Carl C. Swisher's recent redating of Indonesian fossils to as much 1.8 million years old may prove Eugène Dubois correct after all. See "Asian Fossil Prompts New Ideas on Evolution," *New York Times*, February 24, 1994, and Stephen Jay Gould, "So Near and Yet So Far," *New York Review of Books*, October 20, 1994.
139 Theunissen, *Eugène Dubois and the Ape-Man from Java*, pp. 164-67.
140 For a popular discussion of these issues, see Maitland Armstrong Edey, *The Missing Link* (New York: Time-Life Books, 1972).
141 Bowler, *The Non-Darwinian Revolution*, p. 147.
142 Barlow, *the Autobiography of Charles Darwin*, p. 79.
143 Hermann Klaatsch, "Der gegenwartige Stand der Pithecantropusfrage," *Zoologische Zentralblad*, No. 6 (1899), p. 217.
144 Hermann Klaatsch, "Die fossilen Knochenreste des Menschen und ihre Bedeutung für das Abstammungsproblem," *Ergebnisse der Anatomie*, 9 (1899), p. 461; see also Idem., *The Evolution and Progress of Mankind* (London: T.F. Unwin, 1923).
145 Bowler, *Evolution*, pp. 232, 322.
146 Walter J. Garre, *The Missing Link: The Transition from Animal Instinct to the Human Mind. The Origin of the Human Mind* (New York: Philosophical Library, 1982), p. 35.
147 Mayr, *One Long Argument*, p. 8.
148 Thomas Henry Huxley, *Man's Place in Nature and Other Anthropological Essays* (1863; repr. New York: D. Appleton, 1900), p. 152-53.
149 Dubois' letter to W.H.F. Kohlbrugge, April 6, 1920, quoted by Theunissen, *Eugène Dubois and the Ape-Man from Java*, p. 169.
150 Kohlbrugge, *Die Morphologische Abstammung des Menschen*, pp. 86-87.
151 Barlow, *The Autobiography of Charles Darwin*, p. 131.
152 Gerard Baerends, Colin Beer and Aubrey Manning, eds., *Function and Evolution in Behavior. Essays in Honor of Professor Niko Tinbergen, F.R.S.* (Oxford: Clarendon Press, 1975), pp. 14-16. See also Niko Tinbergen, *The Study of Instinct* (1951; repr. Oxford: Clarendon Press, 1989), and Idem, *Social Behavior in Animals, with specific reference to vertebrates* (London: Chapman and Hall, 1990).
153 See, for instance, the recent book by Jeffrey Mousaieff Masson and Susan McCarthy, *When Elephants Weep. The Emotional Life of Animals* (New York: Delacorte Press, 1995), passim.
154 J.H.F. Kohlbrugge, "Die Gehirnfürchen der Javanen. Ein vergleichend-anatomische Studie," in *Verhandelingen van het Akademie van Wetenschappen, Afdeeling voor de Wis- en Natuurkunde* (Amsterdam: Johannes Muller, 1906), Tweede Sectie, 12, No. 4, p. 20, with 9 pull-out appendices containing diagrams of Javanese brains.
155 Franz Boas, *Kultur und Rasse* (Leipzig, 1914), rewritten as "The Problem of Race," in *Anthropology and Modern Life* (1928; repr. New York: Dover, 1986), p. 40.
156 Kohlbrugge cited as his source the work of E.P. and A.P. Penard, *De menschenetende aanbidders der zonneslag* (Paramaribo, 1907).

157 Meek, *Social Science and the Ignoble Savage*, p. 79, and Kohlbrugge, *Die Morphologische Abstammung des Menschen*, p. 86.
158 J.H.F. Kohlbrugge, *Blikken in het zieleleven van den Javaan en zijner overheerschers* (Leiden: E.J. Brill, 1907), and *Een en ander over de psychology van den Javaan*. See also Christiaan Snouck Hurgronje, "Blikken in het zieleleven van den Javaan?", *De Gids* (1908), 71, No. 3, pp. 423-447.
159 J.H.F. Kohlbrugge, "L'Anthropologie des Tenggerois. Indonésiens montagnards de Java," *L'Anthropologie*, 11 (1897), pp. 1-156. See also Idem., "De legende van Kyahi Koesoemo," *Tijdschrift voor Indische Taal,- Land,- en Volkenkunde uitgegeven door het Koninklijk Bataviaansch Genootschap van Kunsten en Wetenschappen*, 39 (1897), pp. 428-429.
160 J.H.F. Kohlbrugge, *Is grondvehuur aan suikerfabrieken een zegen of een vloek voor de Javaan?* (Haarlem: Tjeenk Willink, 1909).
161 J.H.F. Kohlbrugge, "Müskeln und periphere Nerven der Primaten mit besonderer Berücksichtigung ihrer Anomalien," in *Verhandelingen van het Akademie van Wetenschappen, Afdeeling voor de Wis- en Natuurkunde*, Tweede Sectie (Amsterdam: Johannes Muller, 1897), 5, No. 6, pp. 1-246; "Befrüchtung und Keimbildung bei der Fledermaus 'Nantharpya amplexicaudata'," *Verhandelingen van het Akademie van Westenschappen*, 17, No. 6, (1913), pp. 1-37. See also Marius Jacob Sirks, *Indisch natuuronderzoek; een beknopte geschiedenis van de beoefening der natuurwetenschappen in de Nederlandsche kolonien* (Amsterdam: Koloniaal Instituut, 1915).
162 J.H.F. Kohlbrugge, *Der Atavismus*. vol. 1, *Der Atavismus und die Deszendenzlehre*; vol. 2, *Der Atavismus und die Morphologie des Menschen* (Utrecht: Scrinerius, 1897).
163 *Koloniaal Weekblad* (Orgaan van de Vereeniging "Oost en West"), "Vragen van de dag," 11, No. 2 (January 12, 1911), p. 9. The question was "whether a blond European can adapt (*acclimatizeren*) to a tropical climate."
164 Ann Laura Stoler, "Sexual Affronts and Racial Frontiers: European Identities and the Cultural Politics of Exclusion in Colonial Southeast Asia," *Comparative Studies in Society and History*, 34, No. 3 (July 1992), p. 536.
165 Van Schilfgaarde, "Psyche van de Javaan," *Djawa*, 5, No. 1 (1925), p. 120.
166 Van Schilfgaarde, "Psyche van de Javaan," *Djawa*, 5, No. 1 (1925), pp. 121-122.
167 H.E.B. Schmalhausen, *Over Java en de Javanen* (Amsterdam: P.N. van Kampen, 1909), p. 57, and Kohlbrugge, *Blikken in het zieleleven van de Javaan*, p. 39-41.
168 J. de Jong, *Insulinde. Het geestesleven der volken van Indonesië* (Serie handleidingen voor de kennis van Indonesië) (Groningen/Batavia: J.B. Wolters, 1946), pp. 6-7.
169 Samuel van Valkenburg, *Elements of Political Geography* (New York: Prentice-Hall, 1939), p. 356, as discussed in Gerald Macdonald and John T. O'Hara, "Samuel van Valkenburg: Politics and Regional Geography," *Political Geography Quarterly*, 7, No. 3 (July 1988), p. 283-290.
170 The phrase was coined by J.B. Ruzius, *Heilig Indie*. Mr. D.J. van Doorninck, in *Hollanders op Java en in Holland* (Haarlem: Tjeenk Willink, 1912), offers a critical discussion of this notion, p. 29. See also Idem., *Leven op Java. Critische opstellen* (Zwolle: J. Ploegsma, 1915), pp. 8-9.
171 J.J.B. Ostmeier, "Een woord van protest en van opwekking," *Insulinde*, 1, 23 (December 1, 1910), p. 16.
172 Joseph Chailly-Bert, *Java et ses habitants* (Paris: Armand Colin, 1900), pp. 80-81.
173 Max Walther Koenicke, "Das Holländische Kolonialreich," in Dr. Karl F. Chudoba, eds., *Kriegsvortrage über 'Europa und die Kolonien'* (Bonn: Verlag Gebr. Scheur, 1943), p. 73. See also Irmgard Lober, *Das Niederländische Kolonialreich Weltgeschehen*, who argued that Holland, through its "energetic colonial policies has shown the world its legitimate right to possess overseas colonies," quoted in Feith, *Holland over zee*, p. 280.
174 Maurits Wagenvoort, *Nederlandsch-Indische mensen en dingen* (Amsterdam: J.H.de Bussy, 1903) p. 198.
175 Henri Borel, *Contra: een werkkring in Indie* (Baarn: Hollandia Drukkerij, 1913), p. 56, and the original unabridged edition of Bas Veth's *Het leven in Nederlandsch-Indië*, quoted by Van Doorninck, *Leven op Java*, p. 30.
176 W.F. Theunissen, "Onze psyche en hare wisselwerking met de omgeving," *Geneeskundig Tijdschrift voor Nederlandsch-Indië*, LXXI, No. 6 (Batavia/Weltevreden: G. Kolff, 1921), pp. 414-415. See also his "Psychopathische persoonlijkheden," *Geneeskundig Tijdschrift*, LVII, No. 2 (1917); Dr. F.H. van Loon, "Acute Verwardheids-toestanden in Nederlandsch-Indië," *Geneeskundig Tijdschrift*, LXII, No. 5 (1922), pp. 658-690, and H.L. Roelfsma, "Het zenuwlijden der blanken in de tropen," in *Geneeskundig Tijdschrift*, LXVII, No. 6 (1927), pp. 658-666.
177 Theunissen, "Onze psyche en hare wisselwerking met de omgeving," *Geneeskundig Tijdschrift*, (1921), p. 145.
178 Rob Nieuwenhuys, *Mirror of the Indies: A History of Dutch Colonial Literature* (1972; repr. Amherst: University of Massachusetts Press, 1982), pp. 136-37, and Hans Vervoort, "Kankeraars en vertellers. Bas Veth en P.A. Daum over Indië," *Vrij Nederland*, October 15, 1977.

179 Bas Veth, *Het leven in Nederlandsch-Indië* (1900; repr. and abridged, The Hague: Thomas & Eras, 1977), pp. 17, 111.
180 Veth, *Het leven in Nederlandsch-Indië*, p. 77.
181 Veth, *Het leven in Nederlandsch-Indië*, pp. 84, 92, 111-112.
182 Louis Couperus, *The Hidden Force* (1900; repr. Amherst: University of Massachusetts Press, 1985), p. 55; see also Pamela Pattynama's fascinating discussion in "Indo-European Hybridity and 'Modernity' in Dutch Colonial Culture: An Analysis of Louis Couperus' *The Hidden Force*," in Frances Gouda and Julia Clancy-Smith, eds., *Colonial Discourses and Gendered Rhetoric in the French and Dutch Empires* (Charlottesville: University Press of Virginia, forthcoming).
183 Augusta de Wit, *De godin die wacht* (1903; repr. Schoorl: Conserve, 1988), p. 83.
184 Veth, *Het leven in Nederlandsch Indië*, p. 68; D.C.M. Bauduin, *Het Indische leven* (The Hague: Leopold, 1927), p. 58, and C.H.W. van der Ven, "Zóó leven onze kinderen," in C.W. Wormser, ed., *Zóó leven wij in Indië* (Deventer: W. van Hoeve, 1945), pp. 172-73.
185 Karel Wybrands, "Karakter en onderwijs," in D. Wouters and J. van Hulzen, eds., *Insulinde. Schetsen van Land en Volk van Nederlandsch Oost-Indië* (Groningen: P. Noordhoff, 1924), p. 277.
186 Herman Salomonson, "De Europeesche samenleving," in D.G. Stibbe, ed., *Neerlands Indië. Land en volk; geschiedenis en bestuur; bedrijf en samenleving*, 2 vols. (Amsterdam: Elsevier, 1935), 2, p. 366.
187 Rabinow, in *French Modern* explores the French incorporation of neo-Lamarckian reasoning in French colonial policies in Indo-China; see especially Chapter III.
188 Jean Baptiste de Lamarck, *Zoological Philosophy: An Exposition with Regard to the Natural History of Animals*, trans. Hugh Elliot (1914; repr. New York: Hafner, 1963), pp. 11, 113.
189 Stephen Jay Gould, "Life's Little Joke," *Natural History*, 94 (October, 1988), pp. 16-23, and "A Short Way to Corn," in *The Flamingo's Smile*, pp. 371-373.
190 Kohlbrugge, *Die Morphologische Abstammung des Menschen*, p. 78.
191 Van Doorninck, *Hollanders op Java*, p. 43.
192 Adas, *Machines as the Measure of Man*, discusses Wallace's notions about the blending of species, pp. 307-311.
193 Daniel Trembly MacDougal, ed., Hugo de Vries, *Species and Varieties: Their Origin by Mutation* (Chicago: Open Court Pub. Co, 1904). De Vries's research was based on the evening primrose, *oenothera lamarckiana*, which turned out not be a parent form but hybrid itself.
194 Quoted by Wiener, *The Beak of the Finch*, p. 122.
195 See the lucid discussion in Piet de Rooy, "Of Monkeys, Blacks, and Proles: Ernst Haeckel's Theory of Recapitulation," in Breman, *Imperial Monkey Business*, pp. 22-23.
196 Bowler, *Evolution*, pp. 56, 276-77. The extraordinary research of the ornithologists Peter and Rosemary Grant on many generations of finches on Daphne Major in the Galapagos islands in the course of twenty-five years has confirmed this amended vision. Since a disastrous flood on the island in 1983, various strands of hybrid finches have reproduced much more successfully than purebred species; see Wiener, *The Beak of the Finch*, pp. 123-25.
197 L.J. Hissink-Snellebrand, Lezing gehouden op den 23en Februari, 1911 voor de Vereeniging 'Oost en West,' (Amsterdam: Meulenhoff, 1911) in KITLV, archives of the Koninklijke vereeniging "Oost en West," 1899-1971 (H 1077), pp. 15-16.
198 Kohlbrugge, *Blikken in het zieleleven van de Javaan*, p. 142.
199 *Koloniaal Weekblad*, "Vragen van de dag," 11, No. 2 (January 12, 1911), p. 9. See also the discussion about hybridity and miscegeneration in S.R. Steinmetz, J.A.J. Barge, A.L. Hagedoorn, and R. Steinmetz, *De rassen der mensheid. Wording, strijd, toekomst* (Amsterdam: Elsevier, 1938).
200 Chailly-Bert, *Java et ses habitants*, p. 87.
201 De Kat Angelino, *Colonial Policy*, 1, p. 190.
202 Kohlbrugge, in *Koloniaal Weekblad*, p. 10.
203 D.D. (E.F.E. Douwes Dekker), "Spreekt de waarheid en schiet goed," *De Indiër. Weekblad gewijd aan het geestelijk en maatschappelijk leven van Indië en Oost-Azië*, 1, No. 1 (October 23, 1913), pp. 6-8.
204 "Zelfvernietiging?" *Insulinde*, 1, No. 6 (March 16, 1910), pp.6-7; the emphasis on *produceren* is *Insulinde*'s. This editorial denounced an article, written by "Katjang Studiosus" in *Koloniaal Weekblad*, January 27, 1910, who had argued that "*Indos* should roll up their sleeves and try to disappear from this earth, because that would be the best solution for our descendants."
205 Korthuys, *In de ban van de tropen*, p. 73.
206 Dr. P.K. Kroest, "Raskruising op Java," *Geneeskundig Tijdschrift voor Nederlandsch-Indië*, LXX, No. 8 (1930), pp. 897-914.

Notes

207 Cees Fasseur, "Hoeksteen en struikelblok. Rasonderscheid en overheidsbeleid in Nederlands-Indië," *Tijdschrift voor Geschiedenis*, 105 (1992) p. 223. See a more detailed discussion of these issues in the next Chapter of this book.
208 Quoted by Mieke Bal, "'Door zuiverheid gedreven': het troebele water van *Het land van herkomst* van E. du Perron," in Ernst van Alphen en Maaike Meijer, eds., *De canon onder vuur. Nederlandse literatuur tegendraads gelezen* (Amsterdam: Van Gennep, 1991), p. 127.
209 Rutherford, in "European Identity, the Idea of Colonization, and New Guinea as Empty Space," p. 34.
210 Bauduin, *Het Indische leven*, p. 36.
211 Bauduin, *Het Indische leven*, p. 37.

CHAPTER 5

1   Robert Chauvelot, *Un roman d'amour à Java* (Paris: Eugène Fasquelle, 1919), pp. 117-18. This was not a dismissive attitude unique to Frenchmen. Justus van Maurik, in his *Indrukken van een totok. Indische typen en schetsen* (Amsterdam: Van Holkema & Warendorf, 1898), commented on "such well-built, large [Indies] women with their splendid opulent form," p. 139; Piet Korthuys in *In de ban van de tropen* (Wageningen: Zomer & Leuning, 1947), also refers to "heavy *Indo* ladies," and "European women with bulging fat deposits on their breasts and stomachs," p. 36.
2   Judith Belles-Knijnenburg, "Het vrouwelijke kantoorpersoneel van de Nederlands-Indische spoorwegmaatschappij, 1908-1925" (MA Thesis, department of social history, Erasmus University), quoted by Elsbeth Locher-Scholten, "Summer Dresses and Canned Food: European Women and Occidental Lifestyles in the Indies, 1900-1942," in Cees van Dijk and Henk Schulte Nordholt, eds., *Outward Appearances: Dressing the State* (forthcoming), p. 6.
3   C.H. Razoux Schultz-Metser, "De werkende vrouw," in C.W. Wormser, ed., *Zóó leven wij in Indië* (Deventer: W. van Hoeve, 1945), p. 48.
4   H. van der Spek-van Santen, "De alleenstaande vrouw in Indië," in M.A.E. van Lith-van Schreven and J.H. Hooykaas-van Leeuwen Boomkamp, eds., *Indisch vrouwenjaarboek 1936* (Jogjakarta: Kolff-Buning, 1936), p. 54.
5   1930 *Volkstelling* (Census), VI:96, 101, and VIII:122-125, quoted and analyzed by Locher-Scholten, "Summer Dresses and Canned Food: European Women and Occidental Lifestyles in the Indies, 1900-1942," p. 6.
6   Razoux Schultz-Metzer, "De werkende vrouw," in Wormser, *Zóó leven wij in Indië*, p. 47.
7   Although not referring specifically to Batavia, Simon van der Wal has called it "a small European world of employees in private entreprise (*particulieren*) and civil servants who displayed an oversensitivity to rank and status," in S.L. van der Wal, ed., *Besturen overzee. Herinneringen van oud-ambtenaren bij het binnenlands bestuur in Nederlandsch-Indië* Franeker: T. Wever, 1977), p. 9.
8   D.C.M. Bauduin, in *Het Indische leven* (The Hague: H.P. Leopold, 1927), mentions that "the anatagonisms and conflicts, the division into big and little clubs who don't greet each other but only slander each other already form on the mail boat to the Indies," p. 6.
9   Melantjong, *Njai Belanda* (1904; repr. Rotterdam: D. Bolle, 1927), p. 7.
10 Margaretha Ferguson, *Hollands-Indische Verhalen* (The Hague: Leopold, 1974), p. 126.
11 Melantjong, in *Njai Belanda*, described the romantic rivalries between women over eligible bachelors, passim; the phrase fighting each other like "polecats" appears in Michael Ondaatje's novel about his colonial ancestors in Ceylon, *Running in the Family* (New York: Vintage, 1982), p. 47.
12 C. van Heekeren, *Trekkers en blijvers. Kroniek van een Haags-Indische familie* (Franeker: T. Wever, 1980), p. 97.
13 Ms. Junius, upon her marriage, became known as Mrs. Ijzerman.
14 Annie Foore, *Bogoriana. Een roman uit Indië* (Haarlem: Tjeenk Willink, 1893), p. 10. For a personal account describing the dizzying cycle of teas, dinners, receptions, audiences, and other social rituals associated with the Governor General's residence, see Maria Schouten, ed., C.L.M. Bijl de Vroe, *Rondom de Buitenzorgse troon. Indisch dagboek* (Haarlem: Fibula van Dishoeck, 1980). Willem Walraven, in his *Brieven aan familie en vrienden, 1919-1941*, 2nd edition (Amsterdam: G.A. van Oorschot, 1992), ranted and railed against the petty status consciousness and sycophancy of the European community, passim.
15 Melis Stoke, *Wat men in Indië moet doen en laten* (The Hague: H.P. Leopold, 1939), p. 178.
16 "In the olden days," Bauduin wrote in *Het Indische leven* in 1927, "the Dutch housewife in the Indies wore the Indonesian sarong and kabaya in the morning, with bare legs; these exotic clothes were even part of the luggage (*uitrusting*) brought along from Holland ... but in these modern times, they have gone out of fashion" (p. 14).

17 Ivo Schöffer, "Dutch 'Expansion' and Indonesian Reactions," in Cees Fasseur, ed., *Geld en geweten. Een bundel opstellen over anderhalve eeuw Nederlands bestuur in de Indonesische archipel*, 2 vols. (The Hague: Martinus Nijhoff, 1980), 2, p. 12.
18 Karen Transberg Hansen, *Distant Companions. Servants and Employers in Zambia, 1900-1985* (Ithaca: Cornell University Press, 1989), p. 13 and the Introduction in general.
19 J. Kloppenburgh-Versteegh, *Het leven van de Europeesche vrouw in Indië* (Deventer: Dixon, 1913), p. 112, quoted by Elsbeth Locher-Scholten, "Orientalism and the Rhetoric of the Family: Javanese Servants in European Household Manuals and Children's Fiction," *Indonesia*, No. 58 (October 1994), p. 29.
20 Simon Franke, "Indonesisch personeel," in Wormser, *Zóó leven wij in Indië*, p. 250.
21 Ann Laura Stoler, "Making Empire Respectable: The Politics of Race and Sexual Morality in Twentieth-Century Colonial Cultures," in Jan Breman, ed., *Imperial Monkey Business. Racial Supremacy in Social Darwinist Theory and Colonial Practice* (Amsterdam: VU University Press, 1990), p. 64. See also the discussion in Locher-Scholten, "Orientalism and the Rhetoric of the Family," pp. 27-35.
22 M. Nittel-De Wolff van Westerrode, "Kijkjes in het leven van onze inlandsche bedienden," part VIII, in George Nypels, ed., *De Indische Gids* (also new series of *Tijdschrift voor Nederlandsch-Indië*), 48, Nos. I-VI (1926), p. 418.
23 Elsbeth Locher-Scholten, "Bruine handen. Kolonialisme in Indische meisjesboeken," *Lover. Literatuuroverzicht over feminisme, cultuur en wetenschap*, 21, No. 3 (September 1994), p. 58.
24 Chauvelot, *Roman d'amour à Java*, p. 171.
25 Melis Stoke wrote that Dutch men in the Indies embraced a "cult of hard work." He added, however, that "the columns of Dutch workers in the Indies resemble the armies of Napoleon: replacements (*remplacanten*) are easily found"; in *Wat men in Indië moet doen en laten*, p. 41. Charles Hampden-Turner coined the phrase "ambulatory cash registers" in *Maps of the Mind* (Cambridge: MIT Press, 1982), p. 31.
26 See Benedict Anderson's *Imagined Communities. Reflections on the Origin and Spread of Nationalism* (London/New York: Verso, 1983), on this score, pp. 137-139; see also Hortense Powdermaker, *Stranger and Friend. The Way of an Anthropologist* (New York: W.W. Norton, 1966), p. 274.
27 Madelon Szekely-Lulofs' novel *Rubber* (1931; repr. Singapore: Oxford University Press, 1987), heralded as "the 1930s novel which shocked European society," describes these tensions in lurid detail.
28 Marie van Zeggelen, *Indrukken van een zwervelinge. De Hollandse vrouw in Indië* (1910; repr. Schoorl: Conserve, 1989), p. 135.
29 For a discussion of the "incorporation" of wives into a masculine hierarchy, see the essays in Hillary Callan and Shirley Ardener, eds., *The Incorporated Wife* (London: Croom Helm, 1984).
30 Mary Poovey, *Uneven Developments. The Ideological Work of Gender in Mid-Victorian England* (Chicago: The University of Chicago Press, 1988), passim.
31 Walraven, *Brieven aan familie en vrienden*, p. 384.
32 Catherine Hall and Leonore Davidoff, in *Family Fortunes: Men and Women of the English Middle Class, 1780-1850* (Chicago: University of Chicago Press, 1987), elaborate on the fluidity, or the permeability, of the boundary between the private and the public, passim.
33 About the variations in policy in different colonial societies regarding the definition of citizenship for Eurasians, see Dr. S.R. Steinmetz, et al, *De rassen der mensheid. Wording, strijd, en toekomst* (Amsterdam: Elsevier, 1938), pp. 376-378.
34 Cees Fasseur, "Cornerstone and stumbling block: Racial classification and the late colonial state in Indonesia," in Robert Cribb, ed., *The Late Colonial State in Indonesia. Political and economic foundations of the Netherlands Indies, 1880-1942* (Leiden: KITLV Press, 1994), Verhandelingen No. 163, p. 37, and Anderson, *Imagined Communities*, p. 112.
35 See Ann Laura Stoler, "Rethinking Colonial Categories: European Communities and the Boundaries of Rule," *Comparative Studies in Society and History*, 31, No. 1 (1989), pp. 132-149 for a detailed discussion of this issue.
36 Van Maurik, *Indrukken van een totok. Indische typen en schetsen*, p. 11.
37 Toni Morrison, *Playing in the Dark. Whiteness and the Literary Imagination* (Cambridge: Harvard University Press, 1992), pp. 32-33.
38 Gail Ching-Liang Low, in "His Stories?: Narratives and Images of Imperialism," in Erica Carter, James Donald & Judith Squires, eds., *Space & Place. Theories of Identity and Location* (London: Lawrence & Wishart, 1993), approaches imperialism as "a culture of masculinity," p. 188.
39 Ladislao Szekely, *Tropic Fever. The Adventures of a Planter in Sumatra* (London: Hamish Hamilton, 1936), pp. 94, 85.
40 Quoted by Rudolf Mrázek, *Sjahrir. Politics and Exile in Indonesia* (Ithaca: Cornell Studies on Southeast Asia, No. 14, 1994), p. 28.

41 A novel focusing on the transformation of a vulnerable and socially ostracized working-class youth from Amsterdam into a white "*toewan*" in Deli is Madelon Szekely-Lulofs' *De andere wereld* (Amsterdam: Elsevier, 1934).
42 The phrase is discussed in Cees Fasseur, "De 'adeldom' van de huid. De rol van de Indische Nederlander in het Nederlands-Indisch bestuur," in Wim Willems, ed., *Sporen van een Indisch verleden, 1600-1942* (Leiden: University of Leiden's Centrum voor Onderzoek van Maatschappelijke tegenstellingen, 1992), No. 44, pp. 13-21.
43 This is the description on the cover of a novel by Willem Brandt (a pseudonym for Willem S.B. Klooster), *De aarde van Deli* (The Hague: W. van Hoeve, 1948). A distinct literary genre has glorified the strength and ingenuity of white planters in Deli, beginning with the intrepid Dutch pioneers Jacobus Nienhuys and P.W. Janssen in the second half of the nineteenth century.
44 C.K. Elout, *De groote oost* (The Hague: W.P. van Stockum, 1930), p. 8-10.
45 H.L. Burghardt-de Boer, *Als een dauwdrop is het leven. Een autbiografie* (Franeker: T. Wever, 1983), p. 90. However, as the daughter of the owner of the renowned Hotel de Boer in Medan, her recollections of Deli's culture are more subtle than this particular passage might suggest. See also Rudy Kousbroek's critique of Willem Brandt's *De aarde van Deli* and the genre of Deli novels in general in *Het Oostindische kampsyndroom* (Amsterdam: Meulenhoff, 1992), pp. 153-167.
46 The British Colonial Secretary, Lord Crewe, issued a confidential "Concubinage Circular" in 1909 stating that such practices would jeopardize the authority of colonial administrators and should be censured. See Helen Callaway, *Gender, Culture, and Empire. European Women in Colonial Nigeria* (Urbana: University of Illinois Press, 1987), p. 48, and Ronald Hyam, *Empire and Sexuality. The British Experience* (Manchester: Manchester University Press, 1991), passim; see also Ian Buruma, "Revenge in the Indies," *New York Review of Books*, August 11, 1994.
47 *Encyclopaedie van Nederlandsch-Indië*, vol. 3, (1919), p. 515.
48 Rob Nieuwenhuys, quoted by H.G. Surie, "Epilogue," to Victor Ido, *De Paupers* (1912; repr. The Hague: Thomas & Eras, 1978), n.p.
49 Cees Fasseur, "Hoeksteen en struikelblok. Rasonderscheid en overheidsbeleid in Nederlands-Indië," *Tijdschrift voor Geschiedenis*, 105 (1992) p. 223.
50 Quoted by Ingrid Harms and Tessel Pollmann, "In Nederland door omstandigheden," *Bijvoegsel Vrij Nederland*, No. 17, May 15, 1982, p. 11.
51 Raymond Kennedy, *The Ageless Indies* (1942; repr. New York: Greenwood Press, 1968), p. 161.
52 H.W. Ponder, *Javanese Panorama. More Impressions of the 1930s* (1942; repr. Singapore: Oxford University Press, 1990), p. 153.
53 Michael Taussig, *Mimesis and Alterity. A Particular History of the Senses* (New York/London: Routledge, 1993), p. 81.
54 Zareer Masani, *Indian Tales from the Raj* (Berkeley: University of California Press, 1987), pp. 155, 4.
55 Ponder, *Javanese Panorama*, p. 152.
56 Herman Salomonson, "De Europeesche samenleving," in D.G. Stibbe, ed., *Neerlands-Indië. Land en volk; geschiedenis en bestuur; bedrijf en samenleving*, 2 vols. (Amsterdam: Elsevier, 1935), 2, pp. 361-62.
57 Augusta de Wit, *De godin die wacht* (1903; repr. Schoorl: Conserve, 1988), p. 83.
58 Sutan Sjahrir, *Indonesische overpeinzingen* (Amsterdam: De Bezige Bij, 1945), pp. 144-147.
59 Mrázek, *Sjahrir. Politics and Exile in Indonesia*, p. 38.
60 Korthuys, *In de ban van de tropen*, pp. 102, 208, and Henk Smit, *Van katjong tot rijksambtenaar. Uit het leven van een (ver)indisch(t)e jongen* (The Hague: Moesson, 1982), p. 49.
61 National Archives, Washington D.C., Coert du Bois, U.S. Consul General in Batavia, to the Secretary of State in Washington D.C., Voluntary Report III, "The Problem of the Half Caste," October 9, 1928, pp. 1-2. M-682, Records of the Department of State Relating to the Internal Affairs of the Netherlands, 1910-1929, Roll 33, 856D.00-.40.
62 Van Maurik, *Indrukken van een totok. Indische typen en schetsen*, p. 140, and Ponder, *Javanese Panorama*, p. 154.
63 Elvire Spier, *De maan op het water* (Cadier en Keer: Uitgeverij 60+, 1993), p. 35.
64 Taylor, in *The Social World of Batavia*, describes the wealth and pivotal economic position of mixed-blood women in the Dutch East Indies, more or less until the late nineteenth century, passim.
65 L.W.C. van den Berg's preliminary advice offered to the Congress in 1887, quoted by W.F Wertheim, "Leven als vogelvrij-verklaarden," in Peter Boomgaard, Harry A. Poeze, and Gerard Termorshuizen, eds., *Aangeraakt door Insulinde* (Leiden: KITLV Press, 1992), pp. 131-32.
66 Wertheim, "Leven als vogelvrijverklaarden," in Boomgaard, et al, *Aangeraakt door Insulinde*, p. 132, and Albert Dekker and Hanneke van Katwijk, *Recht en rechtspraak in Nederlands-Indië* (Leiden: KITLV Press, 1993), p. 16.

67 Ann Laura Stoler, "Sexual Affronts and Racial Frontiers: European Identities and the Cultural Politics of Exclusion in Colonial Southeast Asia," *Comparative Studies in Society and History*, 34, No. 3 (July 1992), p. 544.
68 R.D. Kollewijn, "Huwelijk en onderhorigheid," *Triwindoe-Gedenkboek Mangkoe Nagoro VII* (Soerakarta: Comité Triwindoe-Gedenkboek, 1939), p. 87.
69 Mrinalini Sinha, "Chathams, Pitts, and Gladstones in Petticoats. The Politics of Gender and Race in the Ilbert Bill Controversy, 1883-1884," in Nupur Chaudhuri and Margaret Strobel, eds., *Western Women and Imperialism. Complicity and Resistance* (Bloomington: Indiana University Press, 1992), pp. 98-118.
70 Wertheim, "Leven als vogelvrij-verklaarden," in Boomgaard, et al, *Aangeraakt door Insulinde*, pp. 131-32.
71 Amirah Inglis, in *The White Woman's Protection Ordinance: The White Women's Protection Ordinance in Papua New Guinea* (London: Sussex University Press, 1975), discusses in great detail Australian efforts to shelter white women from the sexual danger embodied in indigenous men, by assuming that any interracial pairing between Australian women and Papuan men was inevitably a male violation of white women's virtue, passim. R.A.J. van Lier, in *Frontier Society. A Social Analysis of the History of Surinam* (The Hague: Martinus Nijhoff, 1971), reports that as early as 1711 Governor Jan de Goyer of Surinam stipulated in an edict "that a single white woman who had intercourse with a Negro was liable to flogging and expulsion, while a married woman would be branded as well." Indigenous men would receive the death penalty, pp. 76-77.
72 Anderson, *Language and Power*, p. 269, note 115. and Paul W. van der Veur, ed., *Towards a Glorious Indonesia. Reminiscences and Observations of Dr. Soetomo*, Monographs in International Studies, Southeast Asia Series, No. 81 (Ohio University: Center for International Studies, 1987), pp. 90-91, 98.
73 Mrázek, *Sjahrir: Politics and Exile in Indonesia*, pp. 111-112.
74 Mrázek, *Sjahrir: Politics and Exile in Indonesia*, pp. 111-112, and ARA, The Hague, 2nd Division, Algemene Secretarie en daarbij gedeponeerde archieven, 1942-1950, Nos. 4708 and 5505.
75 Sjahrir, *Indonesische overpeinzingen*, passim.
76 Walraven, *Brieven aan familie en vrienden*, p. 173. Pramoedya Ananta Toer, in *This Earth of Mankind* (*Bumi Manusia*) (1980; repr. Sydney: Penguin Books, 1991), created the brusque character of Robert Suurhof, among others, to register the pervasive ambivalence towards Indo-Europeans, from both a native and a Dutch perspective, passim.
77 However, as the *Encyclopaedie van Nederlandsch-Indië* (1919) mentioned, the concern with Indo-European paupers went back to the earliest years of Dutch settlement in the Indies. "Already in 1753, Governor General Mossel found it necessary to establish an orphanage in Chirebon, to prevent that the many poor bastards and orphans of European [men], who roamed around in the wild, would not degenerate and bastardize even further," vol. 3, p. 366.
78 Pauline D. Milone, review of Marguérite Schenkhuizen, *Memoirs of an Indo Woman: Twentieth-Century Life in the East Indies and Abroad* (Athens: Center for International Studies, Ohio University, 1993), in *Journal of Asian Studies*, 53, No. 3 (August 1994), p. 1021.
79 The statement was made by the Logemann Committee in 1927; quoted by Fasseur, "Cornerstone and stumbling block," in Cribb, ed., *The Late Colonial State in Indonesia*, p. 31.
80 De Hoog's speech in the *Volksraad*, in *Handelingen van de Volksraad, 1931-32*, pp. 809, 871, Quoted by Danilyn Rutherford, "Racial Identity, Colonization, and New Guinea as Empty Space," dissertation-in-progress, Department of Anthropology, Cornell University, 1994, p. 24.
81 *Handelingen van de Volksraad, 1931-32*, p. 809, quoted by Rutherford, "Racial Indentity, Colonization," p. 24-25. Thamrin was head of the *Orang Betawi* faction in the *Volksraad*.
82 *Handelingen van de Volksraad, 1935-36*, p. 182, quoted by Rutherford, "Racial Identity, Colonization," pp. 26-27.
83 *Encyclopaedie van Nederlandsch-Indië*, vol. 3 (1919), p. 367.
84 *Encyclopaedie van Nederlandsch-Indië*, vol. 3 (1919), p. 367.
85 Salomonson, in "Europeesche samenleving," in Stibbe, *Neerlands-Indië*, mentioned in 1935 that "year in, year out, the expansion of educational opportunities for the indigenous population releases more *inlandsche* manpower onto the intellectual labor market," p. 364.
86 Among employees in purely technical jobs, the proportion of Indonesians grew from 14 to 20 percent between 1928 and 1938. In administrative-technical positions the proportion increased from 22 to 42 percent, and among financial-technical personnel the share of native Indonesians relative to Indo-Europeans increased from 19 to 30 percent. See Th. Stevens, "Indo-Europeanen in Nederlands-Indië; sociale positie en welvaartsontwikkeling," in P.J. Drooglever, ed., *Indisch intermezzo. Geschiedenis van de Nederlanders in Indonesië* (Amsterdam: De Bataafse Leeuw, 1991), p. 42.
87 D.M.G. Koch, *Verantwoording. Een halve eeuw in Indonesië* (The Hague/Bandung: W. van Hoeve, 1956), p. 174. See also Stevens, "Indo-Europeaan in Nederlands-Indië, pp. 33-45.

88 E.M. Beekman uses the term "racially desultory" in his Introduction to Louis Couperus, *The Hidden Force* (1900; repr. Amherst: University of Massachusetts Press, 1985), p. 39.
89 Vincent Mahieu (pseudonym for J.J.Th. [Jan] Boon), "Het vriendje van de rups," in *Verzameld werk* (Amsterdam: Querido, 1992), p. 13.
90 Pamela Pattynama, "Over oorden en woorden. Rassenvermenging, interetniciteit, en een Indisch meisje," *Tijdschrift voor vrouwenstudies 57*, 15, No. 1 (1994), p. 37.
91 Elout, *De groote Oost*, p. 233.
92 This common ground, and others as well, confirmed the opinion of committed Dutch socialists earlier in the century, such as Asser Baars, that Indo-Europeanen "were doomed to move to the right." See Emile Schwidder and Fritjof Tichelman, "De ISDV," in Schwidder and Tichelman, eds., *Het proces Sneevliet 1917* (1918; reprint, Leiden: KITLV Press, 1991), p. lxvii.
93 P.J. Drooglever, *De Vaderlandsche Club, 1929-1942. Totoks en de Indische politiek* (Franeker: T. Wever, 1982), pp. 193-208. The phrase "Fata Morgana" was first used by Johan Winsemius in 1935.
94 "Ons Nieuw-Guinea lied," reproduced in "Geschiedenis van de Indo's tot 1942," *Weerzien met Indië* (Zwolle: Waanders, 1995), No. 26, p. 630.
95 Johan Winsemius, *Nieuw Guinee als kolonisatiegebied voor Indo-Europeanen en Europeanen* (Purmerend: J. Muusses, 1935), p. 335.
96 J.H. Schijfsma, "Kolonistenvrouw in Nieuw Guinea," in Van Lith-van Schreven, *Indisch vrouwenjaarboek 1936*, p. 73.
97 R. Herman Cohen, "Het blankenvraagstuk in Tropisch Queensland," *Mensch en Maatschappij*, May 1, 1931, quoted by P.E. Winkler in *Blank Nieuw-Guinea* (Utrecht: Nederlandsche Nationaal Socialistische Uitgeverij NENASU, n.d., probably 1934 or 1935), p. 7.
98 In *Onze Toekomst*, quoted by Winkler, *Blank Nieuw-Guinea*, p. 8.
99 Stoler, "Sexual Affronts and Racial Frontiers," in *Comparative Studies in History and Society* (1992), p. 548.
100 Dr. B. Vrijburg, one of the more enthusiastic advocates of the colonization of New Guinea by Dutch farmers imported straight from Holland — to substitute for the subsidized out-migration of Dutch dairy farmers to Normandy in France after World War I, designed to prevent a crisis of overproduction — owned a thriving dairy farm himself, south of Bandoeng, which he had called "de Friese Terp" (The Frisian Hillock); see Drooglever, *De Vaderlandsche Club*, p. 195.
101 *De Haagsche Post*, July 20, 1935, quoted by Schijfsma, "Kolonistenvrouw in Nieuw Guinea," in Van Lith-van Schreven, *Indisch vrouwenjaarboek*, p. 76.
102 Drooglever, *De Vaderlandsche Club*, pp. 195, 200.
103 Pattynama, in "Over woorden en oorden," in *Tijdschrift voor vrouwenstudies 57* (1994) presents the psychoanalytic insight that the *njai* may have represented, too, "the culturally absorbed sense of guilt and castration fears of European men," p. 36.
104 Ian Buruma," Revenge in the Indies," *New York Review of Books*, August 11, 1994.
105 Henk te Velde, *Gemeenschapszin en plichtsbesef. Liberalisme en Nationalisme in Nederland, 1870-1918* (The Hague: SDU, 1992), p. 157.
106 Quoted by Te Velde, *Gemeenschapszin en plichtsbesef*, p. 155; see pp. 153-161 for a lucid discussion of the manner in which the crowning of the eighteen-year old Queen Wilhelmina appealed to masculine sentiments of chivalry among her male subjects and produced a "romantic ecstasy." For a comparable discussion of the English novelist Haggard, see Ching-Liang-Low, "His Stories?: Narratives and Images of Imperialism," in Carter, Donald & Squires, *Space & Place*, pp. 187-219, who relies, in turn, on the psychoanalytic approach to German fascism of Klaus Theweleit, *Male Fantasies*, 2 vols (Oxford: Polity Press, 1989), passim.
107 Charles Boissevain, *Tropisch Nederland* (Haarlem: H.D. Tjeenk Willink, 1909), quoted by J. van Goor, "Indische reizen in de negentiende en twintigste eeuw. Van verkenning tot journalistiek toerisme," *Tijdschrift voor Geschiedenis*, 105, No. 3 (1992), pp. 457-58.
108 Joan Wallach Scott,in *Gender and the Politics of History*, New York: Columbia University Press, 1988), Doris Y. Kadish, in *Politicizing Gender. Narrative Strategies in the Aftermath of the French Revolution* (New Brunswick: Rutgers University Press, 1991), Lynn Hunt, in *The Family Romance of the French Revolution* (Berkeley: University of California Press, 1992), Helen Haste, in *The Sexual Metaphor. Men, Women, and The Thinking that Makes the Difference* (Cambridge: Harvard University Press, 1994), or Nancy Mairs, in *Voice Lessons. On Becoming a (Woman) Writer* (Boston: Beacon Press, 1994), albeit from different theoretical perspectives, have all argued convincingly that discursive symbols of femininity and masculinity embody and signify a variety of phenomena unrelated to sexual difference.
109 As Lynn Hunt has argued in *The Family Romance of the French Revolution*, family narratives and metaphors of motherhood and fatherhood are central to the constitution of "all forms of authority" and function as a primordial category for organizing "any kind of political experience," pp. 8, 196.

110 For an analysis of the role of the cantankerous Dutch *boers* in South Africa in the Dutch national imagination, see Te Velde, *Gemeenschapszin en plichtsbesef*, pp. 71-82.
111 Paul Scott, *The Day of the Scorpion*, book 2, *The Raj Quartet* (New York: Avon Books, 1979), pp. 403, 410, and Barbara N. Ramusack, "Cultural Missionaries, Maternal Imperialists, Feminist Allies. British Women Activists in India, 1865-1945," in Chaudhuri and Strobel, eds., *Western Women and Imperialism*, p. 133.
112 For a discussion of the use of pedagogical, heuristic, and constitutive metaphors, see Arjo Klamer, "Towards the native's point of view: the difficulty of changing the conversation," in Don Lavoie, ed., *Economics and Hermaneutics* (New York: Routledge, 1990), and Philip Mirowski, *More Heat than Light* (New York: Cambridge University Press, 1989).
113 Quoted by Cees Fasseur, *De Indologen. Ambtenaren voor de Oost, 1825-1950* (Amsterdam: Bert Bakker, 1992), p. 329.
114 M.B. van der Jagt, *Memoires van M.B. van der Jagt, Oud Gouverneur van Soerakarta* (The Hague: H.P. Leopold, 1955), p. 299.
115 *Provinciaal Blad van Midden Java*, Serie D, No. 5, December 30, 1939, p. 217. These metaphors have a long life. Not long before his death, W.F. Hermans recently characterized Holland as "a mother who lost her children and therefore takes care of every possible stepchild," in Remco Meijer, *Oostindisch doof. Het Nederlandse debat over de dekolonisatie van Indonesië* (Amsterdam: Bert Bakker, 1995), as quoted by Chris van Esterik, "Indië verloren, moralisme behouden," *NRC Handelsblad*, June 9, 1995.
116 Emily S. Rosenberg, "Gender," in "A Round Table: Explaining the History of American Foreign Relations," *Journal of American History*, 77, No. 1 (1990), p. 119. Callaway, in *Gender, Culture, and Empire. European Women in Colonial Nigeria*, discussed the reliance of the British colonial civil service on military organization and the ritual display of power and hierarchy. She argues, in fact, that the colonial arena was often represented as a space where heroic men of Protean strength and flawless judgment achieved their full masculine potential in a domain entirely inaccessible to women, passim.
117 H.J. Friedericy, *De eerste etappe*, in *H.J. Friedericy: Verzameld Werk* (Amsterdam: Querido, 1984), p. 328.
118 H.J. Friedericy, *De standen bij de Boegineezen en Makassarezen* (dissertation, University of Leiden, 1933).
119 *Handelingen van de Volksraad*, 1925, Eerste Gewone Zitting, Onderwerp 6, Stuk 3, Memorie van Toelichting, p. 7.
120 *Handelingen van de Volksraad*, 1925, p. 7.
121 H.E.B. Schmalhausen, *Over Java en de Javanen. Nagelaten geschriften* (Amsterdam: P.N. van Kampen, 1909), p. 49.
122 *Handelingen van de Volksraad*, 1925, p. 6. See also Elsbeth Locher-Scholten, "Female labour in twentieth-century Java: European notions — Indonesian practices," pp. 77-103, and Mies Grijns, "Tea-pickers in West Java as mothers and workers: Female work and women's jobs," pp. 104-119, in Elsbeth Locher-Scholten and Anke Niehof, eds., *Indonesian Women in Focus. Past and Present Notions* (1987; repr. Leiden: KITLV Press, 1992).
123 As the American Consul General in Batavia noted in 1925, "*adat* governs the natives almost exclusively in relations with each other and in practically all matters not regulated by Dutch codes. These laws of custom will probably continue to exist for generations to come and they are carefully respected by the Dutch." NA/State Dept, Consul-General Chas L. Hoover in Batavia to the Secretary of State in Washington D.C.,"The Government of Netherlands India and the Prospective Alterations in its Functions," April 1925, M-682, Roll 30, Political Affairs, 856D.00-.40.
124 Lata Mani, "Contentious Traditions: The Debate on Sati in Colonial India," in KumKum Sangari and Sudesh Vaid, eds., *Recasting Women. Essays on Colonial History* (New Brunswick: Rutgers University Press, 1990), pp. 90-91. For Indonesia, see several dissertations written at the University of Leiden, such as E.A. Boerenbeker, *De vrouw in het Indonesische adatrecht* (1931); S.R. Boomgaard, *De rechtstoestand van de getrouwde vrouw volgens het adatrecht van Nederlands Indië* (1926); L.B. van Straten, *De Indonesische bruidschat* (Leiden: n.p., 1927); see Sita van Bemmelen's critical analysis of a *adat* scholar's treatment of women's position in "Een adatrechtsstudie in historisch perspectief. J.C. Vergouwen over Toba-Batakse vrouwen," in Jeske Reijs, et al, eds., *Vrouwen in de Nederlandse kolonien. Zevende Jaarboek voor vrouwengeschiedenis* (Nijmegen: SUN Uitgeverij, 1987), pp. 52-77.
125 Joseph Chailly-Bert, *Java et ses habitants* (Paris: Armand Colin, 1900), p. 42.
126 Mr. S.L. Yap-Tan, in "De vrouw en het huwelijksrecht," in Van Lith-van Schreven, *Indisch vrouwenjaarboek 1936*, observed that the marriage law operating in the Dutch East Indies dated from 1838. He noted that "Dutch marriage law was dominated by the dogma of matrial power — the authority of the man over the person and property of his wife," p. 36.
127 Billie Melman, "Desexualizing the Orient: The Harem in English Travel Writing by Women, 1963-1914," *Mediterranean Historical Review*, 4, No. 2 (December, 1989), p. 327.

128 Memorie van Antwoord, November 10, 1925, *Handelingen van de Volksraad*, 1925, Tweede Gewone Zitting, Onderwerp 6, Stuk 1, afdeelingsverslag, pp. 1-3. For a white woman's curious response, see M. Nittel-De Wolff van Westerrode, "Doel en Streven van de vereeniging voor vrouwenkiesrecht," *Koloniale Studiën*, 1, extra politiek nummer (October, 1917), p. 119.
129 Jean-François Lyotard, "One of the Things at Stake in Women's Struggles," in Andre Benjamin, ed., *The Lyotard Reader* (Oxford: Basil Blackwell, 1989), p. 112.
130 John Strachey, *India* (London: Kegan, Paul, Trench, 1888), quoted by Lewis D. Wurgaft, *The Imperial Imagination. Magic and Myth in Kipling's India* (Middletown: Wesleyan University Press, 1983), p. 29. Couperus, in *The Hidden Force*, summoned all the tropes of the effeminate sexuality of native or mixed-blood men, p. 107 and passim.
131 Edward Said, *Orientalism* (New York: Vintage, 1979), p. 188.
132 Beekman, "Introduction," to Louis Couperus, *The Hidden Force*, p. 27.
133 Benedict Anderson, in "Professional Dreams: Reflections on Two Javanese Classics," in *Language and Power*, cites a plethora of Dutch sources from the turn of the century which registered Dutch observers' outrage with homosexual practices among the Dayaks, Buginese, Acehnese, or Balinese, pp. 277-78.
134 *Encyclopaedie van Nederlandsch-Indië*, vol. 3 (1919), p. 513. Pederasty, in this context, was a generic reference to sexual relations between men and did not necessarily imply a differential in age.
135 *Encyclopaedie van Nederlandsch-Indië*, vol. 1 (1917), p. 568. The entry for *priesters* (priests or shaman) related further that "the *bisoe* among the Boeginezen (Buginese) ... refrain from marriage and feign impotence. It is a normal practice for them to dress in female clothing and pretend to be women," in *Encyclopaedie van Nederlandsch-Indië*, vol. 3, (1917), p. 509.
136 See Ruth Nanda Anshen, ed., *Letters from the Field, 1925-1975*, World Perspectives, vol. 52 (New York: Harper and Row, 1977), p. 155. See also the discussion in Carol L. Oja, *Colin McPhee: Composer in Two Worlds* (Washington D.C.: Smithsonian Institution Press, 1990), pp. 143-47. Anderson notes, in "Professional Dreams" in *Language and Power*, however, that towards the end of the colonial era, discussions of homosexuality among indigenous men acquired a "calmer tone," p. 278. Hence, the sudden repression of European homosexuals may have served ulterior purposes.
137 Rudolf Bonnet to Jaap Kunst, March 1, 1939, No. 47, Archives of Jaap Kunst, Dossier 126. Etnomusicologisch Instituut "Jaap Kunst," University of Amsterdam.
138 Rudolf Bonnet to Jaap Kunst, March 1, 1939.
139 Quoted by Oja in *Colin McPhee*, p. 145.
140 Dr. Swart Abrahamsz in *De Javabode*, 1898; quoted by J.H.F. Kohlbrugge, *Blikken in het zieleleven van den Javaan en zijn overheerschers* (Leiden: E.J. Brill, 1907), pp. 19-20.
141 Beekman, "Introduction" to Couperus, *The Hidden Force*, p. 3.
142 Pans Schomper, *Indië vaarwel. De belofte van de eierboer*, as discussed in Lokien de Bie, "Indische herinneringen van Pans Schomper," *VPRP Gids*, December 17-23, 1994, p. 11.
143 Madelon Szekely-Lulofs, *Onze bedienden in Indië* (Deventer: W. van Hoeve, 1946), p. 80
144 Szekely-Lulofs, in *Onze bedienden in Indië*, p. 80, used the word "obscene,", whereas Rob Nieuwenhuis, in "Sinjo Robbie voor altijd," in Hans G. Visser, ed., *Indië in Holland. Schrijvers over hun rijk van Insulinde* (Amsterdam: de Bijenkorf, 1992), rhapsodized about the beguiling "erotic" qualities of Javanese life, pp. 10-12.
145 Mahieu (Boon), "Tjoek," in *Verzameld werk*, p. 157.
146 Szekely-Lulofs, *Onze bedienden in Indie*, p. 80. For thoughtful autobiographical memories about the *baboe*, see Eduard du Perron, *Country of Origin* (Amherst: University of Massachusetts Press, 1983) and Maria Dermout, *Nog pas gisteren*, in *Verzameld Werk* (1951; repr. Amsterdam: Querido, 1990).
147 Such as Annie Foore's short story "Willie's Mamma" in *Indische huwelijken* (Rotterdam: D. Bolle, 1895), pp. 39-103, and Marie van Zeggelen, *Koloniaaltje* (Amsterdam: Scheltema & Holkema, 1919).
148 See, among others, Annie Foore, "Geketend," in *Indische huwelijken*, and Carry van Bruggen, *Goenoeng-djatti* (1909; repr. Schoorl: Conserve, 1990), or Johan Fabricius, "Het duistere bloed," in *Achter de Molukken* (The Hague: W.P. Leopold, 1979). For further analysis, see Tessel Pollmann, "Bruidstraantjes. De koloniale roman, de njai en de apartheid," in Reijs et al., *Vrouwen in de Nederlandse kolonien*, pp. 98-125.
149 Adinda, *Vrouwen lief en leed in de tropen* (1892; repr. Schoorl: Conserve, 1989).
150 As in one of Thérèse Hoven's other novels, *Een bruidskrans en een doornenkroon* (The Hague, 1895).
151 Adinda, *Vrouwen lief en leed onder de tropen*, passim.
152 Margaretha Ferguson, in *Hollands-Indische verhalen*, argues that Dutch children already learned about "bossing around" their *baboe* while sailing through the Suez Canal to southeast Asia, p. 11.
153 Rudyard Kipling, *Something of Myself*, quoted by Wurgaft, *The Imperial Imagination*, p. 108.
154 Bauduin, *Het Indische leven*, p. 58.

155 On the "black peril" in the British empire, see Emily Bradley, *Dearest Priscilla: Letters to the Wife of a Colonial Civil Servant* (London: Max Parrish, 1950) and Joan Alexander, *Voices and Echoes. Tales from Colonial Women* (London: Quartet Books, 1983).
156 Benita Parry, *Delusions and Discoveries. Studies on India in the British Imagination* (London: Allen Lane, 1972), passim.
157 Korthuys, *In de ban van de tropen*, p. 46.
158 The proportion of women among emigrants to the Indies rose from 18.7 percent in 1905 to 40.6 percent in 1915, see Rob Nieuwenhuys, *Mirror of the Indies. A History of Dutch Colonial Literature* (1972; repr. Amherst: University of Massachusetts Press, 1982) p. 167. The British Women's Emigration Association, which incorporated several emigration societies in the 1880s and 1890s, encouraged the journey of English women to the colonies, see Strobel, *European Women*, pp. 25-27.
159 Pollmann used the controversial term *apartheid* in "Bruidstraantjes;" so did Beb Vuyk, *De eigen wereld en de andere* (Amsterdam: Querido, 1969), p. 16, Frans Schamhardt, "Introduction," in Walraven, *Brieven aan familie en vrienden*, p. 16, and Max Lane, "Introduction," in Pramoedya Ananta Toer, *Footsteps* (Sydney: Penguin Books, 1990), p. viii. See also Nicole Lucas, "Trouwverbod, inlandse huishoudsters en Europese vrouwen," in Reijs, *Vrouwen in de Nederlandse kolonien*, pp. 78-128, and Stoler, "Rethinking Colonial Categories" in *Comparative Studies in History and Society* (1987), pp. 146-149.
160 Charles H. Miller, *Khyber: British India's Northwest Frontier* (New York: MacMillan, 1977), p. 46.
161 Rudy Kousbroek, "De Mems in de koloniale samenleving," in *Deugd en ondeugd. Jaarboek voor vrouwengeschiedenis*, 13 (Amsterdam: Internationaal Instituut voor Sociale Geschiedenis, 1994), pp. 149-162. About Kousbroek's impact on shaping Dutch visions on the colonial past, see the response by Mieke Aerts, "Gemengde gevoelens bij gemengde berichten uit de Oost" in the same volume, p. 164.
162 Kousbroek, "De Mems in de koloniale samenleving," p. 161.
163 Powdermaker, *Stranger and Friend. The Way of an Anthropologist*, p. 103.
164 Burghardt-de Boer, *Als een dauwdrop het leven*, p. 91.
165 V.S. Pritchett, quoted in Michael Wood's preface to W. Somerset Maugham, *A Writer's Notebook* (New York: Arno Press, 1977), n.p.
166 National Archives, Washington D.C., Walter A. Foote, U.S. Consul in Medan, to Consul-General Coert du Bois in Batavia, July 16, 1929. His political report No. 6, entitled "Political Disturbances in North Sumatra" noted that "on July 6, 1929, Mrs. Landzaat-van Rijnberg, the wife of an assistant on the Parnobolon Estate of the Handelsvereniging "Amsterdam" was killed by a native coolie...His attempt to kill the little child [too] was frustrated by the *baboe* (the native nanny) who hid it in the servants' quarters," p. 2. Foote's report was forwarded to the State Department in Washington D.C. Records of the Department of State relating to the Internal Affairs of the Netherlands, 1910-1929, M-682, Roll 51, Sumatra, 856D.00-.40.
167 U.S. Consul Walter A. Foote to Consul-General Coert du Bois, July 16, 1929, political report No. 6, "Political Disturbances in North Sumatra."
168 U.S. Consul Walter A. Foote to Consul-General Coert du Bois, July 16, 1929, political report No. 6, "Political Disturbances in North Sumatra."
169 C.M. Bouwens-Hoek, "Setia sampai mati," archives of the "Indische Kulturele Kring," H 858, KITLV, Leiden.
170 C.J. Jongejans-van Ophuijsen, "De BB vrouw in de buiten-gewesten," in Van Lith-van Schreven, *Indisch Vrouwenjaarboek*, pp. 44-49, and Koch, *Verantwoording. Een halve eeuw in Indonesië*, p. 55.
171 See Van Zeggelen, *Indrukken van een zwervelinge*, for a moving description of Dutch women's nostalgia for the mother country and the ways in which three lonely women resolved the challenge of living in a small military outpost in Watansoppeng, high in the mountains of South Sulawesi in the early twentieth-century.
172 See Saszo Malko and Carolijn Visser, eds., *Herinneringen aan ons Indië* (Amsterdam: Sijthoff, 1988), p. 77. Examples of the autobiographical writing of Dutch women who thrived in remote locations, translated into English, are Beb Vuyk, *The Last House in the World*, and Maria Dermoût, *The Ten Thousand Things* (Amherst: University of Massachusetts Press, 1983).
173 See, among others, Friedericy, *De eerste etappe*, p. 385; P.A. Daum, *Hoe hij Raad van Indië werd* (1884; repr. The Hague: Thomas & Eras, 1978); Carry van Bruggen, *'N Badreisje in de tropen en andere verhalen* (1909; repr. Schoorl: Conserve, 1988); E.M. Beekman, in his Introduction to P.A. Daum's *Ups and Downs of Life in the Indies* (Amherst: University of Massachusetts Press, 1987), argues that the word *kranig* is derived from the Malay word *brani*, which could best be translated with bluster, swagger, or guts, or non-English words as bravado, bravura, or chutzpah, p. 26.
174 Virginia Woolf, *Three Guineas* (New York: Harcourt Brace, 1938), p. 167.
175 On women in a Dutch missionary society, see Rita Kipp Smith, *The Early Years of a Dutch Colonial Mission* (Ann Arbor: University of Michigan Press, 1990), p. 99, and "Why Can't a Woman be More Like a Man?

Bureaucratic Contradictions in the Dutch Missionary Society," paper presented at the meeting of the American Anthropological Society, November, 1993.
176 Antoinette Burton, "The White Woman's Burden. British Feminists and 'The Indian Woman," 1865-1915," in Chaudhuri and Strobel, *Western Women and Imperialism*, pp. 137-57.
177 Susan Pederson, "National Bodies, Unspeakable Acts: The Sexual Politics of Colonial Policy-Making," *Journal of Modern History*, 63, No. 4 (December 1991), pp. 647-80.
178 C.H. Razoux Schultz-Metzer, "I.E.V. Vrouwenorganisatie," p. 3, and T. Eckenhausen-Tetzner, "De huisvrouwenvereenigingen in Indië," pp. 5-9, in Van Lith-van Schreven, *Indisch vrouwenjaarboek 1936*.
179 Shirley Ardener, *Women and Space. Ground Rules and Social Maps* (London: Croom Helm, 1984), p. 14.
180 The term "spectacular" or "spectacularization" is derived from S. P. Mohanty, "Kipling's Children and the Colour Line," *Race & Class*, 31, No. 1 (1989), p. 37.
181 Stoler, in "Rethinking Colonial Categories,"in *Comparative Studies in History and Society* (1987) notes that policies prohibiting official, interracial *marriage* were late rather than early "inventions" in almost all colonial societies ranging from Mexico, Cuba, India, and Indonesia to the American South, p. 154.
182 What Carol Summers, in an African context, has called "Intimate Colonialism: The Imperial Production of Reproduction in Uganda, 1907-1925," *Signs*, 16, No. 4 (Summer 1991), pp. 787-807.
183 Alan Liu, "Local Transcendence: Cultural Criticism, Postmodernism, and the Romanticism of Detail," *Representations* 32 (Fall 1990), pp. 75-113.

CHAPTER 6

1 Erik Orsenna, *De koloniale tentoonstelling* (1988; repr. and trans. Tricht/Leuven: Goossens/ Kritak, 1989), p. 254. Orsenna's claim that thirty-four million people visited the Exposition is not pure fantasy. The Administrative Bureau of the Colonial Exposition reported that on September 30, 1931, 25,050,638 people had visited the Bois de Vincennes so far (Archives of P.A.J. Moojen, H 1169, No. 22, KITLV, Leiden). The final headcount of visitors at the closing of the fairgrounds on November 15, 1931, was a grand total of 33,489,000 people. See J.E. Findling and Kimberly D. Pelle, eds, *Historical Dictionary of World's Fairs and Expositions, 1851-1988* (New York, 1990). Six million of those tourists were French citizens; see Jacques Marseille, *L'Age d'or de la France coloniale* (Paris: Albin Michel, 1984), p. 135.
2 Prof. Mr. S.A. Oppenheim, "Wie Indië niet kent, kent Holland niet ...," *Nieuwe Rotterdamsche Courant*, morning edition A, January 2, 1927.
3 For a general discussion of the Chicago World Fair in 1933, see John E. Findling, *Chicago's Great World Fairs* (Manchester/New York: Manchester University Press/St. Martin's Press, 1994).
4 *L'Echo de Paris* predicted on April 7, 1931, that "this year's Spring will be a splendid one, although Spring is a bit like a woman's heart: one never knows what it has in store," p. 3. Until late June, however, the regular weather reports lamented the rain and cool temperatures, even if it did not stop people from visiting the Colonial Exposition.
5 O.G. Thoden van Velsen, "De koloniale tentoonstelling te Marseille," *Indië. Geillustreerd Weekblad voor Nederland en Koloniën*, 5, No. 6, May 10, 1922, p. 95.
6 "A l'Exposition Coloniale," *Le Petit Journal*, May 8, 1931.
7 From the regular correspondant in Paris, "In het Bosch van Vincennes — "Le Tour du Monde en un Jour," *Algemeen Handelsblad*, third evening edition, May 6, 1931.
8 Herman Lebovics, *True France. The Wars over Cultural Identity 1900-1940* (Ithaca: Cornell University Press, 1992), p. 74; see also Linda Nochlin, "The Imaginary Orient," in *The Politics of Vision: Essays on Nineteenth-Century Art and Society* (New York: 1989), pp. 33-59. It is interesting to note that the *Guide Officiel* of the 1922 *Exposition nationale coloniale* in Marseille was much less detailed about the historical circumstances under which Angkor Wat was built. Instead, the Official Guide of 1922 provided detailed information about French voyages of discovery in Indo-China, and the benefits the French administration had bestowed upon the region since then in the areas of education, physical health, missionary activity, agriculture, and economics. See *Guide Officiel*, 2nd ed. (Marseille: Samat/Imprimerie de la société du "Petit Marseillais," 1922), pp. 34-47.
9 For a vivid description of Angkor Wat's display of brute power, see David Chandler, "The Tragedy of Cambodian History Revisited," *SAIS Review* (Washington: Johns Hopkins University, 1995), in press.
10 Lebovics pointed out this analogy in *True France*, p. 59.
11 *L'Echo de Paris*, April 6, 1931, front page.
12 Lebovics, *True France*, p. 51.

13 Charles-Robert Ageron, "L'Exposition coloniale de 1931. Mythe républicain ou mythe impériale?", in Pierre Nora, ed., *Les lieux de mémoire*, 3 vols. (Paris: Gallimard, 1984), 1, *La République*, pp. 574-76.
14 Jacques Marseille, *L'Age d'or de la France coloniale*, p. 132.
15 "Nederlandsch paviljoen te Vincennes verbrand — Verbrande schatten en verloren arbeid," *Algemeen Handelsblad*, first evening edition, June 29, 1931.
16 Jakob Rosenberg, Seymour Slive, and E.H. ter Kuile, *Dutch Art and Architecture, 1600-1800* (London: Penguin, 1966), p. 73.
17 Catherine Hodeir and Michel Pierre, *1931: La mémoire du siècle. L'Exposition coloniale* (Paris: Editions Complexe, 1991), pp. 78-9.
18 Ageron, "L'Exposition coloniale de 1931. Mythe républicain ou mythe impériale?", in Nora, *Les lieux de mémoire*, 1, p. 576; F.W. Junghuhn, *De onuitputtelijke natuur* (Amsterdam: G.A. van Oorschot, 1966), p. 31.
19 Julia Clancy-Smith, *Rebel and Saint. Muslim Notables, Populist Protest, Colonial Encounters (Algeria and Tunisia, 1800-1904)* (Berkeley: University of California Press, 1994), p. 255.
20 Mounira Khemir, "Introduction," to *L'Orientalisme. L'Orient des photographes au XIXe siècle* (Paris: Centre nationale de la photographie/Institut du Monde Arabe, 1994), n.p. Although an editorial by Jerôme and Jean Tharaud, entitled "Exotisme," in *Le Figaro* on June 28, 1931, noted that "in Morocco we find again the forms of an ancient existence that is the foundation of our civilization, even if we have long since forgotten."
21 Mounira Khemir, "Introduction," to *L'Orientalisme*, n.p.
22 Naziha Hamouda, "Two Portraits of Auresian Women," in Elizabeth Edwards, ed., *Anthropology & Photography, 1860-1920* (New Haven: Yale University Press, 1992), p. 206.
23 Malek Alloula, *The Colonial Harem* (1981; repr. Minneapolis: University of Minnesota Press, 1986), No. 21, Theory and the History of Literature, p. 3.
24 Khemir, "Introduction," in *L'Orientalisme*, n.p.
25 Edward Said, *Culture and Imperialism* (New York: Alfred A. Knopf, 1993), "Introduction," p. xxi.
26 The official's name was Louis Massignon, who also served as one of Edward Said's prototypes of European Orientalist scholars in *Orientalism* (New York: Vintage, 1979). Quoted by Asaf Hussein, "The Ideology of Orientalism," in Asaf Hussein, Robert Olson, and Jamil Qureshi, eds., *Orientalism, Islam, and Islamicists* (Brattleboro, VT: Amana Books, 1984), p. 9. See also Muhammad Benaboud, "Orientalism and the Arab Elite," *Islamic Quarterly*, 26, No. 1 (1982), p. 7.
27 Marseille, *L'Age d'or de la France coloniale*, p. 87.
28 "En Indochine, les communistes provoquent de nouveaux troubles," *L'Echo de Paris*, April 21, 1931. See also the headlines in other daily newspapers in Paris such as *Le Petit Journal*, *Le Figaro*, and *L'Homme Libre*.
29 See Graeme Davison, "Exhibitions," in *Australian Cultural History* (Canberra: Australian Academy of the Humanities and the History of Ideas Unit, Australian National University), No. 2, 1982/83, p. 7, and Tony Bennett, "The Exhibitionary Complex," in Nicholas B. Dirks, Geoff Ely, and Sherry B. Ortner, eds., *Culture/Power/History. A Reader in Comtemporary Social Theory* (Princeton: Princeton University Press, 1994), p. 130.
30 Whitney Walton, *France at the Crystal Palace. Bourgeois Taste and Artisan Manufacture in the Nineteenth Century* (Berkeley: University of California Press, 1992), p. 221.
31 Quoted by Rosalind H. Williams, *Dream Worlds. Mass Consumption in Late Nineteenth-Century France* (Berkeley: University of California Press, 1982), pp. 63, 74. However, Eugen Weber, in *France. Fin de Siècle* (Cambridge: Harvard University Press, 1986), called the 1900 Exposition a "great success, despite disorder, congestion, and crowds," p. 124.
32 "On va voir à l'Exposition coloniale le premier 'Bibliobus,'" L'Echo de Paris, May 25, 1931.
33 Tzvetan Todorov, *On Human Diversity. Nationalism, Racism, and Exoticism in French Thought* (1989; repr. Cambridge: Harvard University Press, 1993), p. 265.
34 James Clifford, *The Predicament of Culture. Twentieth-Century Ethnography, Literature, and Art* (Cambridge: Harvard University Press, 1988), p. 13.
35 Catherine A. Lutz and Jane L. Collins, *Reading National Geographic* (Chicago: University of Chicago Press, 1993), p. 276.
36 Guy de Maupassant, "Marroca," in *The Collected Stories of Guy de Maupassant. 223 Classics by the Great French Master* (New York: Avenel Books, 1985), pp. 392-398.
37 Marseille reprinted the song's full text in *L'Age d'or de la France coloniale*, p. 15:
    Ne pleur'pas si je te quitte
    Petite Anna, petite Anna, p'tite Annamite,
    Tu ma donné ta jeunesse,
    Ton amour et tes caresses,

T'étais ma petit'bourgeoise,
Ma Tonkiki, ma Tonkiki, ma Tonkinoise.
Dans mon coeur j'garderai toujours
Le souv'nir de nos amours.

37 Marseille, *L'Age d'or de la France coloniale*, p. 129.
39 With regard to the opening of the Belgian pavilion on May 9, 1931, *L'Echo de Paris* struck a different tone: "Belgium, a nation that is a *parvenu* in the colonial enterprise, has nonetheless conquered and civilized a vast and rich empire"; see "Le pavillon de Belgique a été inauguré hier," May 10, 1931.
40 "Le magnifique effort hollandais à l'Exposition coloniale. Rivaux d'Angkor, les pavillons néerlandaises abriterons les richesses de l'Insulinde," *L'Echo de Paris*, April 11, 1931.
41 Ann Hale Mac Cormick, a foreign-affairs specialist and a member of the *New York Times*' editorial staff who served during World War II on the State Department's Advisory Committee on Post-War Foreign Policy, quoted by William Roger Louis, *Imperialism at Bay. The United States and the Decolonization of the British Empire, 1941-1945* (New York: Oxford University Press, 1978), pp. 159-60, 168.
42 Nam Dan - (L'Ami du Peuple Indochinois), "Conjectures," *La Tribune Indochinoise*, May 16, 1931.
43 Matu Mona, *Spionnagedienst (Patjar Merah Indonesia)* (Medan: Centrale Courant en Boekhandel, 1938).
44 Matu Mona, *Spionnagedienst*; regarding the Indonesian representation he wrote *Bangsa Indo-China mendapat perhatian besar... demikian djoega serimpi Bali dan Djawa*, p. 72. However, no Javanese *serimpi* dancers performed at the Exposition in Paris in 1931. Instead, Balinese *legong* dancers were dispatched to the Colonial Exposition.
45 Hodeir and Pierre, *1931: La mémoire du siècle*, pp. 68-9.
46 "Parijs," in *Timboel. Algemeen periodiek voor Indonesië*, 5, No. 10, June 10, 1931, p. 155. The word *timboel* means to rise to the surface, to emerge, to cause something to appear or to occur. In the very first issue of *Timboel*, 1, No. 1 (January 1927), the initial editors, R.T. Dr. Wediodiningrat and R.P. Mr. Singgih, inaugurated the magazine by emphasizing that "words are carriers of ideas, and we gave our magazine the name *timboel* so that our magazine will emerge as one of which people will say 'so in name, so in aim,'" a phrase they quoted in English rather than Dutch, p. 1.
47 George D. Larson, *Prelude to Revolution. Palaces and Politics in Surakarta, 1912-1942* (Dordrecht: Foris Publications, 1987), KITLV Verhandelingen No. 124, p. 138.
48 "Parijs," in *Timboel. Algemeen periodiek voor Indonesië*, 5, No. 10, June 10, 1931, p. 155.
49 Letter from Dr. L.J. van der Waals in The Hague to P.A.J. Moojen in Paris, December 30, 1932, in Archives of P.A.J. Moojen, H 1169, No. 22, KITLV, Leiden. The French expression is in the original.
50 "Le magnifique effort hollandais à l'Exposition coloniale," *L'Echo de Paris*, April 11, 1931.
51 "Les journalistes hollandais visitent le pavillon des Pays-Bas," under the headline "Le Ministre des colonies a inauguré hier la section métropolitaine de l'Exposition coloniale," *Le Petit Journal*, May 8, 1931. However, in an article on the fire of the Dutch pavilion on June 28, 1931, "La section néerlandaise est dévastée à l'aube par le feu," *Le Petit Journal* reported that the cost of construction had been twelve million francs.
52 *Le Petit Journal*, May 8, 1931.
53 "Les journalistes hollandais," *Le Petit Journal*, May 8, 1931.
54 "Parijs," *Timboel. Algemeen periodiek voor Indonesië*, 5, No. 10, June 10, 1931, p. 156.
55 "Le magnifique effort Hollandais," *L'Echo de Paris*, April 11, 1931.
56 "Vincennes en Nederland," *Nieuwe Rotterdamsche Courant*, evening edition D, May 8, 1931.
57 "Ned-Indië te Parijs — Decor en decorum," *Nieuwe Rotterdamsche Courant*, evening edition B, May 7, 1931.
58 John Pemberton, *On the Subject of "Java"* (Ithaca: Cornell University Press, 1994), p. 167.
59 Si Omong (a colonial wanderer), "De feeërieke rimboe te Vincennes. In het Nederlandsche paviljoen — een creatie!" *Algemeen Handelsblad*, second morning edition, May 9, 1931.
60 "Le magnifique effort Hollandais," *l'Echo de Paris*, April 11, 1931, p. 2.
61 "Parijs," *Timboel. Algemeen Periodiek voor Indonesië*, 5, No. 10, June 10, 1931, p. 156.
62 Thomas Karsten, "Van pendopo naar volksschouwburg," *Djawa. Driemaandelijksch Tijdschrift uitgegeven door het Java Instituut*, 1, No. 1 (January-April, 1921), p. 22. The writers of *Timboel* praised Karsten as a "talented, refined *eclecticus* who is full of attention and affection for the innovative forms of indigenous architectural beauty but who is too sensitive simply to paste them onto Western buildings." See "Een comedie van onbevoegdheden," *Timboel. Algemeen periodiek voor Indonesië*, 5, No. 7, April 16, 1931, p. 97.
63 Ir. H. Maclaine Pont, "Javaansche Architectuur," *Djawa*, 4, No. 2 (June 1924), p. 73.
64 "Parijs," *Timboel*, 5, No. 10, June 10, 1931, p. 156. The writer made a funny wordplay on the phrase "*épater le bourgeois.*"
65 Nicholas Thomas uses the term "promiscuity of objects" in *Entangled Objects. Exchange, Material Culture, and Colonialism in the Pacific* (Cambridge: Harvard University Press, 1991), p. 27-30.

66 Hodier and Pierre, 1931: *La mémoire du siècle*, p. 131, and "De brand te Parijs — de eerste uitgaven van de journalen onzer oudste zeereizen naar Indië, die mede verloren zijn gegaan," *Nieuwe Rotterdamsche Courant*, evening edition D, July 3, 1931.
67 "De brand van het Nederlandse paviljoen te Parijs," *Nieuwe Rotterdamsche Courant*, June 30, 1931.
68 Hodeir and Pierre, *1931: La mémoire du siècle*, pp. 65, 131.
69 Jacques Marseille, *Empire colonial et capitalisme français. Histoire d'une divorce* (Paris: Albin Michel, 1984), p. 55. Because the French economy was more self-sufficient in terms of agricultural supply and demand, and the French state had pursued protectionist policies in support of the domestic agricultural sector throughout the era of the Third Republic, the Great Depression's impact was slower in its negative effects on the French economy and perhaps less devastating than in other European countries or America.
70 Matu Mona, *Spionnagedienst*, p. 72.
71 The column of "Rondelet," *L'Echo de Paris*, May 23, 1931.
72 "L'Hôtellerie parisienne et l'Exposition coloniale," *Le Figaro*, May 7, 1931.
73 "Pour aller à l'Exposition coloniale," *L'Echo de Paris*, May 2, 1931; see also Hodeir and Pierre, *1931: La mémoire du siècle*, p. 13, and Lebovics, *True France*, p. 57.
74 Matu Mona, *Spionnagedienst*, p. 72.
75 "A L'Exposition coloniale," *L'Echo de Paris*, June 28, 1931.
76 Judith Williamson has noted that "by the 1880s, cameras were more mobile and could more easily enter the homespace," suggesting that by 1931, further facilitated by a reduction in the size of the average camera, they had become even more accessible to middle-class families. See "Family, Education, and Photography," in Dirks, Eley, and Ortner, *Culture/Power/History*, p. 238. For a description of simple Breton peasants' startled response to Parisians who "obsessively" walked around villages in Britanny trying to take pictures with their "Kodaks" in the mid-1930s, see Pierre Jakez-Hélias, *The Horse of Pride. Life in a Breton Village* (New Haven: Yale University Press, 1975), p. 314.
77 For a general discussion on the role of photography in the representation of colonial cultures, see Elizabeth Edwards' introductory essay on "Historical and Theoretical Perspectives" in Edwards, *Anthropology and Photography, 1860-1920*, p. 7, and pp. 1-17 in general.
78 Quoted by David Spurr, *The Rhetoric of Empire. Colonial Discourse in Journalism, Travel Writing, and Imperial Administration* (Durham: Duke University Press, 1993), p. 52.
79 Nicholas Thomas observes in *Entangled Objects* that "the artifacts of non-Western peoples were known over a long period as 'curiosities,'" p. 126. The word pastiche figures prominently in Fredric Jameson, "Postmodernism and Consumer Society," in Hal Foster, ed., *Postmodern Culture* (London/Sydney: Pluto Press, 1987), pp. 111-25. See also the discussion of Toby Alice Volkman, "Out of South Africa: *The Gods Must be Crazy*," in Larry Gross, John Stuart Katz, and Jay Ruby, eds., *Image Ethics. The Moral Rights of Subjects in Photographs, Film, and Television* (New York: Oxford University Press, 1988), p. 247.
80 Lutz and Collins, *Reading National Geographic*, p. 93.
81 Lebovics, *True France*, p. 57, and Raul Girardet, *L'Idée coloniale en France de 1871 à 1962* (Paris: La Table Ronde, 1972), pp. 121-22.
82 Marseille, *L'Age d'or de la France coloniale*, p. 129.
83 For a comparable observation regarding the London working class, see Brian Street, "British Popular Anthropology: Exhibiting and Photographing the Other," in Edwards, *Anthropology and Photography*, pp. 122-23.
84 Quoted by Hodeir and Pierre, *1931: La mémoire du siècle*, p. 13.
85 "Le discours de M. Jean de Castellane," in "Une grande journée nationale. Le Président de la République a inauguré hier l'Exposition coloniale de Vincennes," *L'Homme Libre*, May 7, 1931.
86 "Discours de M. de Castellane," under the headline "Le Président de la République a inauguré l'Exposition coloniale —Nortre avenir est outre-mer, déclare le maréchal Lyautey," *Le Figaro*, May 7, 1931.
87 Quoted by Hodeir and Pierre, *1931: La mémoire du siècle*, p. 26.
88 *Exposition coloniale internationale à Paris. Les Indes Néerlandaises* (Amsterdam: J.H. de Bussy, 1931), p. 61.
89 *Exposition coloniale internationale à Paris. Les Indes Néerlandaises*, pp. 76-77.
90 *Exposition coloniale internationale à Paris. Les Indes Néerlandaises*, pp. 76-77. C.J. Hasselman, in "Karakter van ons koloniaal beheer inzonderheid over Java sinds 1815. Verleden, heden, toekomst," in D.G. Stibbe, ed., *Neerlands Indië. Land en volk; geschiedenis en bestuur; bedrijf en samenleving*, 2 vols. (Amsterdam: Elsevier, 1935), 2, p. 42. reiterates the same theme: "It was the Dutch 'overlord' who had to disclose the Indies and present it to the rest of the world ... as well as to the Indonesians themselves," 2, p. 42. The ellipse is in the original.
91 "Universitaire studie als politiek probleem," *Nieuw Rotterdamsche Courant*, evening edition B, November 27, 1929.

92 In an editorial entitled "De litteraire faculteit," the editors attributed this statement to an earlier one made by Christiaan Snouck Hurgronje, *Timboel. Algemene periodiek voor Indonesië*, 4, No. 11-12 (November-December 1930), p. 151.
93 Kees Groeneboer, *Weg tot het Westen. Het Nederlands voor Indië, 1600-1950* (Leiden: KITLV Press, 1993), Verhandelingen No. 158, p. 425.
94 Groeneboer, *Weg tot het Westen*, pp. 415, 425.
95 Groeneboer, *Weg tot het Westen*, pp. 428-29, 433.
96 Quoted by Girardet, *L'Idée coloniale en France*, p. 128.
97 Although Paul Reynaud, by then a former Minister of Colonial Affairs in France, mentioned in a lecture on November 7, 1933, that the "moral crisis of people in Asia, in Indo-China even more than in the Dutch East Indies, is evident. Why have revolutionary movements achieved such a hold over Asian people? It is the fault of European administrators themselves. The West has imposed upon the East too much of its own culture and handed out too many diplomas ..." In "Rede van Mr. Paul Reynaud, oud Minister van Koloniën van Frankrijk," *Nieuwe Rotterdamsche Courant*, November 8, 1933.
98 Girardet, *L'Idée coloniale en France*, p. 157.
99 Quoted by Alice Conklin, *A Mission to Civilize: The Republican Idea of Empire in France and West Africa, 1895-1930*, dissertation, Department of History, Princeton University, 1989, pp. 333-334.
100 "A scrupulous respect for the manners, customs, and religion of the natives", as Gwendolyn Wright has argued in *The Politics in Design in French Colonial Urbanism* (Chicago: University of Chicago Press, 1991), implied the search for "a policy that would make European economic and political power work more effectively," p. 75.
101 Jean Bassac, "Le génie français et la colonization," *L'Homme Libre*, May 6, 1931.
102 The terms "wrapping" and "packaging" are derived from Fredric Jameson, *Politics of Post-Modernity, or The Cultural Logic of Late Capitalism* (Durham: Duke University Press, 1991), pp. 101-29, and Anthony Grafton (with April Shelford and Nancy Siraisi), *New Worlds, Ancient Texts. The Power of Tradition and the Shock of Discovery* (Cambridge: The Belknap Press of Harvard University Press, 1992), pp. 89, 254, and passim.
103 "De Parijshe (sic) tentoonstelling," *Timboel. Algemeen Periodiek voor Indonesië*, 1, No. 15 (August 1927), p. 234. This article focused on the Dutch East Indies entry to an international exhibition initially planned to take place in Paris in 1929.
104 "Deelneming van Nederlandsch-Indië, Suriname en Curaçao aan de koloniale tentoonstelling in Parijs — Rede van Minister Koningsberger," *Nieuwe Rotterdamsche Courant*, evening edition C, March 6, 1929.
105 *Nieuwe Rotterdamsche Courant*, evening edition C, March 6, 1929.
106 See Stephen Greenblatt, *Marvelous Possessions. The Wonder of the New World* (Chicago: University of Chicago Press, 1991), pp. 86-118.
107 Said, *Culture and Imperialism*, p. 10.
108 Hasselman, "Karakter van ons koloniaal beheer," in Stibbe, *Neerlands Indië*, 2, p. 42.
109 Ernst Heins, "Jaap Kunst and the Rise of Ethnomusicology," in *Jaap Kunst: Indonesian Music and Dance. Traditional Music and its Interaction with the West* (Amsterdam: Royal Tropical Institute/University of Amsterdam Ethnomusicology Centre 'Jaap Kunst,' 1994), pp. 14, 17.
110 Jaap Kunst to Johan Huizinga, March 3, 1929, in Archives of Jaap Kunst, Dossier 454, No. 40, Ethnomusicologisch Instituut "Jaap Kunst," University of Amsterdam.
111 Jaap Kunst wrote to Johan Huizinga on January 14, 1930, that his appointment as a musicological civil servant would commence officially on February 1, 1930; in Archives of Jaap Kunst, dossier 454, No. 50. Kunst's appointment was the culmination of a nasty competition with Johan Sebastiaan Brandts Buys. While Huizinga championed the appointment of Kunst, the Dutch composer Willem Pijper strongly advocated the choice of Brandts Buys. See his "Het onderzoek der Indonesische muziek," *De Muziek*, 2, No. 7 (July 1928), pp. 433-37.
112 Johan Huizinga, "De klank die wegsterft," *De Gids*, 91, No. 1 (January 1928), p. 118.
113 S. de Graaff en D.G. Stibbe, eds., *Encyclopaedie van Nederlandsch-Indië* (The Hague/Leiden: Martinus Nijhoff/E.J. Brill, 1918), vol. 2, p. 587. Ironically George Quinn does not mention Brandes at all in the historical section of *The Novel in Javanese* (Leiden: KITLV Press, 1992), Verhandelingen 148.
114 The speaker was Mr. Van Bergen; his statement was reported in the minutes of the "Congres voor Javaansche Cultuur-Ontwikkeling" te Solo, 5-7 Juli, 1918, (Uit "De Locomotief"), *Djawa*, 1, No. 4 (December 1921), Bijlage a, p. 320.
115 Hasselman, "Karakter van ons koloniaal beheer," in Stibbe, *Neerlands Indië*, 2, p. 42.
116 Dr. W.F. Stutterheim, "Zijne Hoogheid Mangkoe Nagoro en Java's oudheid," in *Triwindoe-Gedenkboek Mangkoe Nagoro VII* (Soerakarta: Comité Triwindoe-Gedenkboek, 1939), p. 36. He wrote this to praise the Sultan of the Mangkunegaran court for promoting popular education on the meaning of Java's cultural legacy.

117 Johan Huizinga, "De klank die wegsterft," *De Gids* (1928), p. 118. See also Renato Rosaldo, "Imperialist Nostalgia," *Representations*, 26 (Spring 1989), p. 109.
118 Elsbeth Locher-Scholten, "Dutch Expansion in the Indonesian Archipelago Around 1900 and the Imperialism Debate," *Journal of Southeast Asian Studies*, 25, No. 1 (March 1994), p. 110, who uses this phrase to highlight the imperial expansion of the Netherlands within, rather than beyond, the internationally recognized Dutch sphere of influence in southeast Asia around 1900.
119 Lewis Pyenson, *Empire of Reason. Exact Sciences in Indonesia, 1840-1940* (Leiden/New York: E.J. Brill, 1989), p. 184. Maarten Kuitenbrouwer, in *The Netherlands and the Rise of Modern Imperialism. Colonies and Foreign Policy, 1870-1902* (1989; repr. New York/Oxford: Berg Publishers, 1991), argues that in political terms, Dutch imperialism was no different from the expansionist actions of either Britain or France. However, he does not address the distinctive articulation of Dutch cultural policies.
120 J.W. Teillers, "Het tweede, tropische, tehuis," in *Triwindoe-Gedenkboek Mangkoe Nagoro VII*, p. 111.
121 C. van Dijk, "De VOC en de kennis van de taal- en volkenkunde van insulair Zuidoost-Azië," in J. Bethlehem and A.C. Meijer, eds., *VOC en cultuur: wetenschappelijke en culturele relaties tussen Europa en Azië ten tijde van de Verenigde Oostindische Compagnie* (Amsterdam: Schiphouwer & Brinkman, 1993), pp. 59-76.
122 E.J. Uhlenbeck, *A Critical Survey of Studies on the Languages of Java and Madura* (The Hague: Martinus Nijhoff, 1964), p. 43.
123 J.E. Heeres, "De Portugeezen in den archipel — de Oost-Indische Compagnie — Daendels — Raffles," in Stibbe, *Neerlands Indië*, 1, pp. 308-309. Even if he was more sensitive to native concerns, Van Diemen also "embodied both the great physical girth and well-balanced temperament of so many Dutch men of that era, whether they lived in the East, in the West, or at home: he proved to be a statesman, military commander, navy admiral, and merchant all in one," p. 308.
124 Groeneboer, *Weg tot het Westen*, pp. 45-46.
125 Kenji Tsuchiya, "Javanology and the Age of Ranggawarsita: An Introduction to the Nineteenth-Century Javanese Culture," in *Reading Southeast Asia* (Ithaca: Cornell University Southeast Asia Publications, 1990), Translation Series, 1, pp. 80-81. See also the discussion in Cees Fasseur, *De Indologen. Ambtenaren voor de Oost, 1825-1950* (Amsterdam: Bert Bakker, 1992), pp. 60-69.
126 Fasseur, *De Indologen*, p. 66.
127 Cees Fasseur, *The Politics of Colonial Exploitation. Java, The Dutch, and the Cultivation System* (1975; repr. Ithaca: Cornell University Southeast Asia Publications, 1992), p. 39.
128 I am indebted to Takashi Shiraishi for this formulation.
129 Fasseur, *De Indologen*, pp. 90-91. The Javanologist Taco Roorda made this argument in a fiery oration before King William II in 1841 on the occasion of the opening of the Royal Institute in Amsterdam.
130 Quoted by Fasseur, *De Indologen*, p. 84.
131 Rob Nieuwenhuys uses the term "pioneer" in his "Introduction" to Herman Neubronner van der Tuuk, *De pen in gal gedoopt. Brieven en documenten* (Amsterdam: G.A. van Oorschot, 1962), p. 7.
132 Fasseur, *De Indologen*, pp. 311, 339. The auxiliary languages — *bijtalen* — such as Sundanese, Balinese, Batak, Buginese, Madurese, and Makassarese had been abolished in 1897, p. 304.
133 H.Th. Fischer, *Inleiding tot de volkenkunde van Nederlands-Indië* (Utrecht: De Erven F. Bohn, 1948), p. 45.
134 "Observer," letter to the editor of *Het Soerabajasch Handelsblad*, March 28, 1931.
135 "Observer," in *Het Soerabajasch Handelsblad*, March 28, 1931. See also the discussion in "Een comedie van onbevoegdheden" in *Timboel. Algemeen periodiek voor Indonesië*, 5, No. 7, April 16, 1931, pp. 97-102.
136 Mr. Dr. F. Valentijn, letter to the editor of *Het Soerabajasch Handelsblad*, March 21, 1931.
137 Mr. Dr. F. Valentijn, *Soerabajasch Handelsblad*, March 28, 1931.
138 "Een comedie van onbevoegdheden," *Timboel. Algemeen periodiek voor Indonesië*, 5, No. 7, April 16, 1931, p. 98.
139 "Parijs," *Timboel. Algemeen Periodiek Voor Indonesië*, 5, No. 10, June 10, 1931, p. 156.
140 Hodeir and Pierre, *1931: La mémoire du siècle*, pp. 65-66. They describe the dancers, however, as hailing from the Javanese courts in central Java rather than Bali.
141 Said quoted this comment with regard to the International Exposition in Paris of 1867 in *Culture and Imperialism*, p. 119.
142 Quoted by Lebovics, *True France*, p. 52.
143 For the role of belly dancing at colonial exhibitions, see Leila Kinney and Zeynep Celik, "Ethnography and Exhibitionism at the *Expositions universelles*," *Assemblages*, 13 (December 1990), pp. 35-59.
144 Hodeir and Pierre, *1931: La mémoire du siècle*, pp. 112, 127.
145 Quoted by Lebovics, *True France*, p. 52, and Hodeir and Pierre, *1931: La mémoire du siècle*, p. 111.
146 Florimond Bonte, "L'Apotheose du crime — c'est aujourd'hui qu'elle ouvre 'leur' Exposition coloniale," *L'Humanité*, May 6, 1931.

147 Paul Louis, *Le Colonialisme* (1905), quoted by Patricia Leighten, "The White Peril and *L'Art nègre*: Picasso, Primitivism, and Anticolonialism," *Art Bulletin*, 72, No. 4 (December 1990), p. 619. Leighten emphasizes, though, that other prominent socialists such as Jean Jaures were more equivocal about the *mission civilisatrice* of colonialism, pp. 617-19.
148 Marseille, *L'Age d'or de la France coloniale*, p. 135.
149 Matu Mona, *Spionnagedienst*, pp. 73-74.
150 Matu Mona, *Spionnagedienst*, p. 76.
151 Matu Mona, *Spionnagedienst*, pp. 93, 77.
152 Matu Mona, *Spionnagedienst*, p. 77.
153 "De brand te Parijs — onderzoek naar de oorzaak," *Nieuwe Rotterdamsche Courant*, morning edition C, July 4, 1931.
154 "Het Nederlandsche paviljoen op de Internationale Koloniale tentoonstelling te Parijs afgebrand — Een nationaal verlies," *Nieuwe Rotterdamsche Courant*, evening edition D, June 29, 1931.
155 "De schade op 10 millioen gulden geschat," *De Avondpost*, June 29, 1931. "Het Nederlandsche Paviljoen op de Intern. Koloniale Tentoonstelling door brand vernield — Schade 10 millioen gulden," *Haarlemsche Courant*, June 29, 1931. It is difficult, of course, to gauge the actual financial damage caused by the fire. In the *Financieel verslag* (financial report), composed on behalf of the Dutch Exposition Committee on April 14, 1932, the treasurer listed that insurance companies paid out the sum of 459,152,88 guilders for the loss of the building, and the sum of 661,040,08 guilders for the destruction of the exhibition's contents. In Archives of P.A.J. Moojen, H 1169, No. 22, KITLV, Leiden. Since many of the objects on display were unique and irreplacable textiles, jewelery, or wooden artifacts, obviously their monetary value could only be estimated.
156 "Een onherstelbare ramp. Niets kon gered worden —vermoedelijke oorzaak kortsluiting. Schade tenminste 1 1/2 millioen," *Algemeen Handelsblad*, first evening edition, June 29, 1931.
157 "Le pavillon des Indes néerlandaises détruit par un incendie," *Le Figaro*, June 29, 1931. The dramatic ellipse was in the original article.
158 "L'Incendie du pavillon des Indes néerlandaises à l'Exposition coloniale," *L'Homme Libre*, June 29, 1931.
159 "L'Incendie," *L'Homme Libre*, June 29, 1931; "La section Néerlandaise est dévastée, à l'aube, par le feu — on parle de 60 millions de dégâts," *Le Petit Journal*, June 29, 1931, and "L'Incendie du pavillon hollandais — 80 millions de dégâts des richesses irremplaçables," *L'Echo de Paris*, June 29, 1931. *Le Figaro* did not venture a guess as to the financial impact of the disastrous fire.
160 "De brand in Parijs — la séance continue. De vlag in top. Bewijzen van instemming," *Nieuwe Rotterdamsche Courant*, evening edition D, July 3, 1931.
161 "Après l'incendie du pavillon de la Hollande," *L'Echo de Paris*, June 30, 1931, and "L'Enquête établit que la malveillance est étrangère au sinistre," *Le Petit Journal*, June 30, 1931.
162 The French engineer was P. Mallet, quoted by Prof. Ir. E.J.F. Thierens, President of the electrotechnics section of the Netherlands' Royal Institute of Engineers, "Rapport inzake de oorzaak van den brand in het eerste hoofdgebouw op de Internationale Koloniale Tentoonstelling in Parijs 1931," Delft, December 12, 1931, in Archives of P.A.J. Moojen, H 1169, No. 22, KITLV, Leiden.
163 "Le pavillon des Indes néerlandaises détruit par un incendie. Commes éclata l'incendie — les causes du sinistre," *Le Figaro*, June 29, 1931.
164 "L'Incendie du Palais de la Hollande: Accident ou Attentat?" *Le Figaro*, June 30, 1931.
165 "De brand in het Ned. paviljoen — bij de controle van de verdeelkast ... bleek dat de stroom inderdaad was uitgeschakeld," *Algemeen Handelsblad*, first evening edition, July 2, 1931.
166 "Hoe de brand ontdekt werd. Kortsluiting of moedwil? Explosies waargenomen," *De Avondpost*, June 29, 1931.
167 *Le Figaro*, June 30, 1931.
168 *Le Figaro*, June 30, 1931.
169 "Een nationaal schandaal," *Timboel, Algemene periodiek voor Indonesië*, 5, No. 12, August 8, 1931, p. 192.
170 "Een nieuw Nederlandsch paviljoen. Tot den bouw besloten —Begin Augustus de opening," *Algemeen Handelsblad*, first evening edition, July 4, 1931.
171 "Na de brand in Vincennes — 'Je Maintiendrai,'" *Algemeen Handelsblad*, first morning edition, June 30, 1931.
172 S.L. van der Wal, ed., *Herinneringen van jhr. mr. B.C. de Jonge met brieven uit zijn nalatenschap* (Groningen: Wolters Noordhoff, 1968), p. 164. De Jonge used these words in a spontaneous address to a crowd assembled in front of the Governor's palace in Batavia during the mutiny crisis on *De Zeven Provincien* in early 1933. The Dutch phrase was "*[onze] natie, welke groot geworden is onder de leuze: Ik zal handhaven*. According to the *Bataviaans Niewsblad* of February 8, 1933, never before in the history of Indonesia had "a representative of the Queen addressed the *burgerij* directly."

173 Dr. M.J.A. Steenhuis, "Netherlands' Rule in the Dutch East Indies," *Gazette de Hollande*, April 6, 1928; an English translation of this article was completed by the U.S. Embassy in The Hague and transmitted to the State Department in Washington D.C. by Richard M. Tobin on April 7, 1928. In National Archives, Washington D.C., Records of the Department of State, 1910-29, M-682, Roll 28, 856D.00-.40.
174 Treub was a former Dutch Minister of Finance and in 1931 the director of the *Ondernemersraad* (Council of Entrepeneurs). "Parijs," in *Timboel*, 5, No. 10, June 10, 1931, p. 155.
175 "Mr. D. Fock over de taak van koloniseerende mogendheden," *Nieuwe Rotterdamsche Courant*, evening edition D, July 3, 1931, and "Les devoirs des nations coloniales," *L'Echo de Paris*, June 30, 1931.
176 "Les devoirs des puissances coloniales," *La Tribune Indochinoise*, July 1, 1931.
177 "Les devoirs des puissances coloniales," *La Tribune Indochinoise*, July 1, 1931, and "Mr. D. Fock over de taak," *Nieuwe Rotterdamsche Courant*, July 3, 1931.
178 Wright, *The Politics of Design*, p. 305.
179 Peter Carey, "Introduction," to *Born in Fire. The Indonesian Struggle for Independence. An Anthology* (London/Athens: BBC Publications/Ohio University Press, 1986), p. xix.
180 As John Pemberton notes, Indonesian newspaper headlines announced on April 20, 1975, that Mrs. Suharto's "Dream Becomes Reality," *On the Subject of "Java"*, p. 153.
181 Pemberton, *On the Subject of "Java"*, pp. 152-53, 167.

Epilogue

1 Jan Bosdriesz and Gerard Soeteman, *Ons Indië voor de Indonesiërs. De oorlog, de chaos, de vrijheid, bewerkt naar een gelijknamige NOS documentaire door C. van Heekeren* (The Hague: Moesson, 1985), pp. 16, 18. The former Governor of Surakarta (Solo), M.B. van der Jagt, titled the Epilogue to his memoirs "Paradise Lost," see *Memoires van M.B. van der Jagt, oud-Gouverneur van Soerakarta* (The Hague: H.P. Leopold, 1955), pp. 329-35.
2 Merritt Y. Hughes, ed., John Milton, *Paradise Lost* (New York: The Odyssey Press, 1935), p. 411.
3 "Rudy Kousbroek over het Indië-Debat. Je kunt ook zondigen door iets na te laten," *Elsevier*, 51, No. 8, February 25, 1995, pp. 22-26.
4 Arendt Lijphardt, *The Trauma of Decolonization: The Dutch and West New Guinea* (New Haven: Yale University Press, 1966), passim.
Or as in the title of Margaretha Ferguson's book, *Nu wonen daar andere mensen* (The Hague: Leopold, 1974). Ferguson's title implies that citizens of the independent Republic of Indonesia are fundamentally different from their parents, who were *inlanders* in the colonial Dutch East Indies, although this is probably not the meaning Ferguson meant to convey.
5 E.M Beekman, in "Introduction," to A. Alberts, *The Islands* (Amherst: University of Massachusetts Press, 1983), p. 5.
6 C.M. Wijmans-Fetzer, H 851, Archives of the Indische Kulturele Kring, KITLV, Leiden.
7 Van der Jagt, *Memoires*, p. 330.
8 Johan Huizinga, "De betekenis van 1813 voor Nederland's geestelijke beschaving," in *De Nederlandse natie. Vijf opstellen door J. Huizinga* (Haarlem: Tjeenk Willink, 1960), p.108.
9 Christopher Lash, *The True and Only Heaven. Progress and Its Critics* (New York: W.W. Norton, 1992), pp. 82-119.
10 Renato Rosaldo, "Imperialist Nostalgia," *Representations*, 26 (Spring 1989), pp. 107-108, and Salman Rushdie, "The Raj Revival," *The Observer* (April 1, 1984), quoted by Nupur Chaudhuri and Margaret Strobel, eds., in "Introduction" to *Western Women and Imperialism. Complicity and Resistance* (Bloomington: Indiana University Press, 1992), p. 13.
11 See Jan Breman, "Voorwoord bij de derde druk," *Koelies, planters, en koloniale politiek. Het arbeidsregime op de grootlandbouwondernemingen aan Sumatra's oostkust in het begin van de twintigste eeuw*, 3rd ed. (Leiden: KITLV Press, 1992), and Vincent Houben, "'Colonial History' Revisited: A Response to Breman," *Itinerario*, 17, No. 1 (1993), pp. 93-97.
12 See the discussion in Elsbeth Locher-Scholten, "From Urn to Monument: Dutch Memories of the Second World War in the Pacific," paper presented to the Conference on *Memory and the Second World War in International Comparative Perspective*, Amsterdam, April 1995, pp. 13-14.
13 Cees Fasseur, "Koloniale mythen en hun makers," in *De weg naar het paradijs en andere Indische geschiedenissen* (Amsterdam: Bert Bakker, 1995), p. 269. See also the thoughtful discussion of these polarized views in Remco Meijer, *Oostindisch Doof. Het Nederlandse debat over de dekolonisatie van Indonesië* (Amsterdam: Bert Bakker, 1995).

Notes

14 Eric Hobsbawm, *The Age of Extremes. A History of the World, 1914-1991* (New York: Pantheon, 1994), p. 3. See also the more theoretical discussion in Richard Terdiman, "Deconstructing Memory: On Representing the Past and Theorizing Culture in France since the Revolution," *Diacritics* (Winter 1985), pp. 13-36.
15 Simon Schama, "Afterword," in *Dead Certainties. (Unwarranted Speculations)* (New York: Alfred A. Knopf, 1991), p. 322.
16 Meena Alexander, *Fault Lines. A Memoir* (New York: The Feminist Press, 1993), p. 42.
17 For a discussion about the repackaging and display of Toraja culture for "ethnic" tourism, see Toby Alice Volkman, "Visions and Revisions: Toraja Culture and the Tourist Gaze," *American Ethnologist*, 17, No. 1 (February 1990), pp. 91-110.
18 Steven Knapp, "Collective Memory and the Actual Past," *Representations* 26 (Spring 1989), pp. 123-149.
19 Saul Friedländer, "Some German Struggles with Memory," pp. 27-42 in Geoffrey H. Hartman, ed., *Bitburg in Moral and Political Perspective* (Bloomington: Indiana University Press, 1986), p. 27. and Pierre Nora, ed., *Les lieux de mémoire*, 4 vols. (Paris: Gallimard, 1984), 1, *La République*, "Introduction: "Entre mémoire et histoire: la problématique des lieux," p. xix.
20 Friedrich Wilhelm Nietzsche, "Vom Nutzen und Nachteil der Historie für das Leben," in *Werke in drei Banden*, quoted by Yosef Hayim Yerushalmi, *Zakhor. Jewish History & Jewish Memory* (New York: Shocken Books, 1989), p. 107.
21 Ernest Renan, "Qu'est-ce qu'une nation?", quoted by Benedict Anderson, *Imagined Communities. Reflections on the Origin and Spread of Nationalism* (London/New York: Verso, 1983), p. 15.
22 The term "memory palace" is derived from Jonathan Spense, *The Memory Palace of Matteo Ricci* (New Haven: Yale University Press, 1989).
23 Prasenjit Duara, "Rescuing History from the Nation-State," Occasional Paper No. 39, Asia Program, Woodrow Wilson International Center for Scholars, Washington D.C. (1990), p. 41.
24 The simile between the labors of archeologists and historians was articulated by Michel Foucault in "The Discourse on Language," in *The Archeology of Knowledge* (New York: Pantheon, 1972), and *The Order of Things: An Archeology of the Human Sciences* (New York: Random House, 1970), passim.
25 Eric Hobsbawm, "Inventing Traditions," in Eric Hobsbawm and Terence Ranger, eds., *The Invention of Tradition* (Cambridge: Cambridge University Press, 1983), p. 13. See also Paul A. Cohen, "The Contested Past: The Boxers as History and Myth," *Journal of Asian Studies*, 51, No. 1 (1992), p. 83. The term "textual construction" is derived from Bryan S.R. Green, *Knowing the Poor. A Case-Study in Textual Reality Construction* (London: Routledge, Kegan & Paul, 1977), especially the Introduction and Chapter I, pp. 1-55; Jack Goody coined the phrase "literary creation" in *The Domestication of the Savage Mind* (Cambridge: Cambridge University Press, 1977), p. 116.
26 Zbigniew Herbert, *Still Life with a Bridle. Essays and Apocryphas* (New York: The Ecco Press, 1991), p. 19, and Maurice Halbwachs, *La mémoire collective* (Paris: Presses universitaire de France, 1968), p. 38.
27 Walter Benjamin, "Theses on the Philosophy of History," in *Illuminations* (New York: Schocken Books, 1969), p. 256.
28 Benjamin, "The Storyteller. Reflections on the Works of Nikolai Leskov," in *Illuminations*, p. 85.
29 Luisa Passerini, *Fascism in Popular Memory: The Cultural Experience of the Turin Working Class* (New York: Cambridge University Press, 1988), pp. 67-68.
30 Eugen Rosenstock-Huessy, *Out of Revolution. Autobiography of Western Man* (Norwich, VT: Argo Books, 1969), p. 695.
31 See the general discussion in Ernst Zahn, *Regenten, rebellen, en reformatoren. Een visie op Nederland en de Nederlanders* (1984; repr. Amsterdam: Contact, 1989), passim.
32 Aram A. Yengoyan, "Of Islands and Legacies in Dutch Colonial Literature. A Review Article," *Comparative Studies in Society and History*, 27, No.3 (July, 1985), p. 480, and G.J. Schutte, "Koloniale geschiedschrijving," in W.W. Mijnhardt, ed., *Kantelend geschiedbeeld. Nederlandse historiografie sinds 1945* (Utrecht/Antwerp: Aula-Het Spectrum, 1983), p. 307.
33 Rudy Kousbroek, "De vergiftigde bron," in *Het Oostindisch kampsyndroom* (Amsterdam: Meulenhoff, 1992), pp. 185-88. About the contested story of the beneficial infrastructural effects of colonial administration in the twentieth century, see Jan Breman, "Civilisatie en Racisme," *De Gids*, 154, 5/6 (1991) p. 491, and J.Th.M Bank and P. Romijn, eds., *Reacties* (The Hague: SDU Uitgeverij, 1991), 14, part 2, pp. 761-814.

Index

Abdullah, Taufik 36
Abeyesekere, Anath 18
Abendanon, J.H. 84-85
Abendanon-Mandri, R.M. 84
Aboriginese (Australia) 129,151
Aceh 43,181
Adat (indigenous traditions) 18,24,40-41,43, 49-50,52-59,69-70, 73,75,78,81,87,94-96, 105,107,112,116,138,160,178-179,182- 183,192
Adat scholarship 41,43-44,53-59,70-71,73
Adinda (Therese Hoven) 183
Africa 2,4,6,42-43,60,67,200-205,212,214,216, 219,220
Agrarian Law (1870) 171
Alexander, Meena 16
Algemeen Handelsblad 211,212,229,231,234
Algeria 200-202
Ambarawa 111
Amboina 126
Amsterdam 30,218
Amuk (explosive, violent rage) 181,184
Anderson, Benedict 52,57,67,94
Angkor Wat, 196-198,206,210,211,217
Annam, 200,204,208
Animism 56
Anthropology 9,39,43-44,52,56-58,68,70,73, 112,120-123,127-130,146,171,207-209
Anti-Revolutionaire Partij 32
Apartheid 4,114,186
Appiah, Kwame Anthony 2
Aragon, Louis 213
Arendt, Hannah 22
Arjunawiwaha 63
Australia 14,20,74,173-174
Avondpost (The Hague) 231

Baars, A. 25-26,64
Babad (Javanese chronicle) 117
Baboe (nanny) 12-14,150,182-184
Bali 4-5,23,33,42-46,70,73,75-76,78,89,91-92, 96,108-110,115,127-128,133-137,155,209, 210,224,226
Banda 166,170

Bandung 103,121
Bangka 189
Bantam 132
Banyuwangi 132
Bataafse Petroleum Maatschappij (Royal Dutch Shell) 62
Batak 1,10,33,41,53-54,105,132,213
Batavia (Jakarta) 12,29,65-67,71,85-86,99,106, 108,112-113,134,158,160,219
Bateson, Gregory 91
Bauduin, D.C.M. 155
Bauhaus architecture 211
Beets, N. 30
Belo, Jane 91,182
Bemmelen, W. van 121
Benjamin, Walter 216,241
Berastagi 10,12
Bergson, Henri 175
Bersiap period 31,74
Bertsch, R.K.A. 176
Bhabha, Homi 105
Blackstone, William 58
Blijvers (permanent Indies residents) 28-29, 122,171
Boas, Franz 145-146
Boedi Kemuliaan hospital 108
Boedi Oetomo 26,65,108
Boeke, J.H. 131
Boers (South Africa) 1-2,42,175-176
Bois de Vincennes 5,194-237
Bois, Coert du 167,170,172
Boissevain, C. 175-176
Bon, Gustave le 69
Bonnet, R. 71,73-74,91,108-110,134,136, 181-182
Boomsma, G. 20,31,33
Borneo (Kalimantan) 56,67,138,139,189,210
Borobodur 63,126,211
Bosch, M. 82-83,88
Bosch, J. van den 24,224
Bosdriesz, J. 237
Bousquet, George Henri 61-62
Boven Digoel 19,170
Boxer, Charles 4

Brand, J. van den 31
Brandes, J.L.A. 222
Brandts Buys, J.S. 221
Breman, J. 31-32
Breton, Andre 213
Broca, Paul 152
Bruyn, J.V. de 59
Buginese 181
Buitenzorg (Bogor) 45,85-86,121,179n14
Burma 10
Burton, Richard Francis 179
Burton, Antoinette 2
Buruma, Ian 16,23,165

Calvinism 12,67
Cambodia 199,203
Cameroon 199
Carib people (Surinam) 146
Castellane, Jean de 217-218
Catholicism 1,66-67
Celebes (Sulawesi) 54,56,162,177,178,224
Ceram 59
Ceylon (Sri Lanka) 14,16
Chailly-Bert, Joseph 46,148,153,179
Chauvelot, Robert 157,158,160,161
China 4,7,18,20,24,29,31,45,60,71,113,153, 166,188,200,208,215
Christian Mission and missionaries 4, 21,24,31,66-67,71
Cirebon 47,210
Citizenship 17-18,20,23,29,56,62,163,169-171
Civilizing Mission (Mission civilisatrice) 21, 62,130-131,217,220,235
Clay, Jacob 121
Clifford, James 207,210
Cochin-China 203
Colijn, H. 62-63,97
Colonial rhetoric 4-6,9,14-15,22-26,28,39-42, 45-46,51-52,116,177-180,190-192,194- 195,240-241
Colonial Exposition (Paris) 5,194-237
Comité Geschiedkundig Eerherstel van Neder- lands-Indië 33
Communism 27,30,204,208,218,232-233,235
Communistische Partij Nederland 30
Concubinage (njai) 6-7,9,112-117,174-175, 183-84
Conquistadores 21

Cook, James 18-19
Coolies 8-9,18-19,31-32,112-113,141
Corporatist Regulation (sociale ordening) 52
Couperus, Louis 40,82,116,150,182
Covarrubias, Miguel 92
Crystal Palace Exhibition (London) 205-206
Cultural Symbiosis 34,51
Cultural Association 40,51,69,196
Cultural Difference (definitions of) 3-5,14-15, 22-26,29-50,95-98,130-134,160,161, 182-185,215-217,240-241
Cultural Assimilation 60,219-220
Cultural Synthesis 26,34,49-50
Cultuurstelsel (cultivation system) 24,47-48, 224
Curaçao 14,26,213

Darwin, Charles 57,121,122-123,128,138, 139,144,145,152
Daudet, Alphonse 67
Daum, P.J. (Maurits) 116
Day, Clive 38
Dayak 181-182
Delft 225
Deli (see also Sumatra) 8,19,31-32,36,112,114, 117,141,162,164,188,241
Demak 210
Democracy 17-18,100
Deventer, C.T. van 78-79,82-88,99,101
Deventer-Maas, E. van 78-79,82-85,87-88, 97-100,103,106,108
Diaspora 1-5,9,14
Diemen, A. van 223
Dieng plateau 196
Dijk, C. van 223
Dirks, Nicholas 21
Djawa (Journal of Java Institute) 118,119
Doorn, J.A.A. van 41,52,97n97
Doorninck, D.J. van 151
Doumer, Paul 230
Douwes Dekker, E.F.E. 153
Dubois, E. 142-145
Duchâteau, M. 170
Durkheim, Emile 60,61
Dutch Republic 1-2,23,40
Dutch East India Company (VOC) 4,66,112, 153,223-224

Index

L'Echo de Paris 197,215,230
Economic profitability (mise en valeur) 45-46,
　47,60-62,208,220
Education (schools) 22,26,33-34,46-47,59-60,
　63,66-67,75-76,78,80-85,87,96-98,100-
　102,104-105,107-108,110,112,134-136,
　150-151,218-219
Eerde, J.C. van 39-40,45-46,53,132
Egypt 83
Elout, C.K. 68,112,132
Eluard, Paul 213
Encyclopaedie van Nederlandsch-Indië 54-56,
　92,113,133,172,181
England 2,4,18,25,34,43,45-46,53,60,163,190,
　209,238
Enlightenment 78,96,130-132
Ethical Policy 23-26,28,50,69,87,97-99,225
Ethical Colonial residents 24-25,41,51-52,
　56-58,82-88,97-100,132,241,242
Evolutionary biology 5,43,120-138,147-148,
　155
Excessennota (memorandum on excessive
　violence) 30,238

Fabian, Johannes 127
Fasseur, C. 24,25,57,98,112
Ferguson, M. 159
Festival of Indonesia 35,239-240
Fieldhouse, David K. 43
Figaro, Le 215,229,230-232,233
Flores 221
Fock, D. 221,226,234
Foore, A. (F.J.J.A Junius) 159
Foucault, Michel 68,241n24
Fournier, F. 118,126
France 43,45-46,48,61,69,
Free Trade 42
Freedom of thought 1,2,17-18
Freud, Sigmund 16,124
Friedericy, J.H. 177-178
Friend, Theodore 27,48,50,69
Furnivall, John Sydenham 46,47,67

Gauguin, Paul 92,120
Gayo Highlands 140,173
Geertz, Clifford 44,49,70,73,78,87
Gendered Rhetoric 6-9,116,162-166,172,173-
　177,184,190-194

Geneeskundig Tijdschrift voor Nederlandsch-
　Indië 148
Gennep, Arnold van 56,60,81
Gerke, P.J. 104
Göbbels, Joseph 34
Gomes, P. 14,32
Gonggrijp, G.L. 25,132
Gonggrijp, G.F.E. 41
Goris, R. 133,181
Gould, Stephen Jay 123,139,151
Government monopolies 48,54
Graeff, A.C.D. de 68,188
Great Depression 12,16,28,104,114,170,213
Great Britain (see England)
Great Chain of Being 122,124,129-130,
　138-141
Greenfield, Liah 2
Groen, P.H.M. 17
Groningen 29
Gropius, Walter 211
Guadeloupe 60
Gunning, J.H. 66-67
Gunning, C. 115

Haar, B. ter 49,81,108
Haarlems Dagblad 229
Haatzaai artikelen (dissemination of hatred)
　65
Haeckel, Ernst 121,129,139,142,145
Haga, B.J. 91,137
Haggard, Henry Rider 175
Hatta, Mohammad 80
Healthcare 24-25
Heekeren, C. van 132-133,159
Helsdingen, W. H. van 48
Het Vrije Woord 65
Heterosexuality 6-7,180-181,184,190-192
Hinduism 110,133-137,218,221
Hissink-Snellebrand, L. J. 112,115,152
Historikerstreit 34
Hitchens, Christopher 1
Hitler, Adolf 17,19-20,33
Hobsbawm, Eric 34,239
L'Homme Libre 220,230
Homo sapiens 139-140,143,145,155
Homo troglodytes 139
Homosexuality 91-92,113,116,180-182,187
Hornbostel, Erich von 71

299

Huizinga, J. 118-119,125-126,136,222-223,238
Humanism 137,155
l'Humanité, 228,232-233
Human rights (in Indonesia) 36-37
Huxley, Thomas H. 144-145
Hybridity 29,114,116,152-154,162-163,165-174

Idenburg, A.W.F. 31-32
Idjitahad (individual rationality) 101
Ilbert Bill (India) 168
L'Illustration 215
Imperialism 2,9,14,21,24,137,98,185,223
India 4,21,28,34,81,88,89,98,112-113,118,129, 134,151,153,163,165,208
Indiër, De 65,153
Indische Partij (Indies Party) 27
Indo (Indo-Europeans) 60,82,112-117,126, 154,162-163,165-174
Indo-China 21,28,68,151,201,208,209
Indo-Europees Verbond (Indo-European League) 27,171
Insulinde 24,27,64,79,95,147-148,150,153-154
Inter-Governmental Group on Indonesia (IGGI) 35
Intermarriage (miscegenation) 150-154,162, 164-170,191-192
International Monetary Fund (IMF) 37
Islam 27,44-45,57,59,66,78,87,96,103-104, 127,133,145,146,179

Jagt, M. B. van der 34,237
Jahyavarman VII, King of Cambodia 197
Jambi 139
Japan 11-12,16,28,219
Java 4-7,12,18,22,24-28,32-33,35,54-57,75-76, 78-83,94-107,110-112,115,118-119,121, 124-127,132-133,137,140,142-143,145-148,151-154,160-166,221,240
Java Institute 118,224
Johnson, Richard 3
Jong, L. de 30-33
Jonge, B.C. de 25,111,134,234
Judaism 3-4,17
Juliana Foundation 111
Juliana, Princess of Orange Nassau 229

Kahin, George McT. 25,48
Kahin, Audrey W. 25,48
Kan, Wim 10
Kardinah (Kartini's sister) 80
Karsten, T. 22-23,212
Kartini, Raden Adjeng 76,79-88,94-99,103, 105-107,110
Kartini Foundation 84-86,97-99
Kartodikromo, Mas Marco 65
Kat Angelino, A.D.A. de 26,39-40,49,51,69,153
Kaum sana (colonial community, over there) 80
Kaum muda (community of the young) 80, 101-103
Kaum muda schools (West Sumatra) 101-102
Kaum sini (our community, here) 80
Kaum tua (community of the old) 102
Kaum ningrat (aristocratic community) 80
Kawi (archaic Javanese) 224
Kayam, Umar 35-36
Kemp, J.T. van der 66
Kennedy, Raymond 45,48,60,91-92,165
Kerinci 139,140
Kipling, Rudyard 7,184
Klungkung 134
Koch, D.M.G. 24-25,172
Koesoema, Darna 64-65
Kohlbrugge, J.H.F. 145-147,151,152-154,174
Kollewijn, R.D. 168
Korea 28
Korn, V.E. 91,137
Korthuys, P. 74
Kousbroek, R. 6,7,15,35,83n38,87n47,186,242
Kraemer, H. 133
Krama inggil (overly refined Javanese speech) 94
Krama (high Javanese speech) 94,224
Kraton (Sultan's courts in central Java) 53,209, 218,225-226
Kritiek en Opbouw 26,219
Kroest, P.K. 154
Kromo (Javanese peasants of humble descent) 25,63,78,82,
Krontjong music 11
Kudeta (1965) 35-36
Kunst, J.71-73,134,136,181,221-222
Kuyper, A. 31-32,63

Lamarck, Jean-Baptiste de 53,124,128-129, 138,139,151
Laos 203
Lash, Christopher 238
Lavisse, Ernest 219
Lebaran (end of Islamic fasting month) 103-104
Lebovics, Herman 43,69
Leiden 23-23,26-27,30-31,40,42,44,46,51-53, 56-57,59,61-62,64,67,69,79-81,86,89,94, 96,168
Leopold II, King of Belgium 46
Lessing, Doris 14,33
Lévy-Bruhl, Lucien 60
Liberalism 26
Lichtenbelt, C.J.A. 133-137
Liefhebbers (amateur scholars) 33,137,
Linnaeus 123,139,152
Liu, Alan 192
Locher-Scholten, E. 16,24,26,160
Lombok 43
Lombroso, Cesare 111
Loo-Rootlieb, Mrs. van 110-111
Lovejoy, Arthur 124
Louis XIV, King of France 197
Ludden, David 58
Lugard, Sir Frederick (Lord Lugard) 69
Lyotard, Jean-François 180
Lyautey, Louis-Hubert-Gonzalve 43,61,217
Lyell, Sir Charles 128,129

Maclaine Point, H. 212
Madagascar 43,60,196,200,231
Madura 118,183,221
Magelang 103
Magreb 201-203
Mahabharata 71,126-127,134
Maier, H. 69
Majapahit 133
Makassar 149
Malaka, Tan 164
Malang 12,67,85,111
Malay (see also Bahasa Indonesia) 1,33,59, 61,64,69,78,94,123,138,142-143,160, 224,225
Malaysia 52,70,165,213
Mangkoe Nagoro VII 94,99,102,135
Mangoenkoesoemo, Tjipto 119,133

Manouvrier, Leonce 143
Marcos, Imelda 236
Marin, Louis 69
Marsden, William 140
Marseille, Jacques 228
Marseille 196
Masani, Zareer 165
Mataram empire 223
Maupassant, Guy de 207
Max Havelaar Foundation 86
Maybury-Lewis, David 120
McPhee, Colin 91,128
Mead, Margaret 91,128,181
Mecca 68
Medan 12,13,31,105,160,162,170
Medici, Lorenzo de 127
Memsahib (British colonial matron in India) 7,163,179-180,184,186
Mendel, Johann Gregor 88,114,152
Merauke 68
Mestizo Culture (see hybridity)
Middle Ages 118-119,125-127,136,155
Milton, John 237
Minahassa 54,62,68
Minami 65
Minangkabau 23,53,62-63,83,101,240
Mise en valuer (see economic productivity)
Mission civilisatrice (see civilizing mission)
Mohamad, Gunawan 94
Moluccas 68,188
Mona, Matu 208,214,228-229
Money, J. W.B. 46
Montesquieu, Baron de 139
Moojen, P.A.J. 195,213,226
Morocco 199,201,203,207
Multatuli (E. Douwes Dekker) 24
Musso (alias Paul Mussotte) 228

Nationalism 1-3,13,19,24,26,42,52,64,68,120, 122,129,229-236
Nazi-Germany 19-20,128
Nederlands Zendings Genootschap (Netherlands Missionary Society) 66,67,190
Nederlandsch tijdschrift voor geneeskunde (Netherlands Journal of Medicine) 65
Negroes (Africa) 141
Netherlands Chamber of Commerce in New York 41-42

New Order Government 35-37,49,94
New Guinea 16,19,59,68,122,151,154,173-174, 188,221
New Republic, The (U.S.) 19
Ngaras (Javanese ceremonial gesture of respect) 103
Ngoko (low Javanese speech) 94,224
Nias 71,73,180,221
Nieuwe Rotterdamsche Courant 210,211,218, 222,229
Nieuwenjuis, G.J. 118,125-126,127
Njai (see concubinage)
Njonja (colonial matron in the Indies) 7-9,16, 88,159-163,183-190
Nobel, L. 8
Noblesse oblige 76,78,221
Noosten, H. 181
Nora, Pierre 240
Nostalgia 6,14,11.37,76,100,128,148,237-242
Notre Dame (Paris) 197
Nuremberg Trials 29

Oppenheim, A.S. 194
Orang Gugu (Gugu people) 123,140
Orang kecil (common folk; see also kromo) 53,78
Orang Kubu (Kubu people) 123,140
Orang letjo (midget man) 123,140
Orang pendek (short man) 123,139-140,142
Ordeningsgedachte (idea of social regulation) 50-52
Oriental knowledge 21,43,44,57-58,88,97,223, 224-226
Orsenna, Erik 194
Osborn, H.F. 123
Ossenbruggen, F.D.E van 130-131
Outer regions 42,44,47,66 114,158

Padang Highlands 176
Paganism (heidendom) 56
Palembang 96,139-140,
Pane, Armijn 10
Pangèstu (Javanese blessing) 103
Panji tales 63,126
Panza, Sancho 9
Papuans (New Guinea) 129,151,173-174
Paris 3,20,39,45-46,60-61,71,128,141-142, 148,159,194-237

Partai Komunis Indonesia (Indonesian Communist Party) 27
Partij van de Arbeid (Dutch Labor Party) 30
Paternalism 25
Pekalongan 86
Pembangunan (development) 49
Pemberton, John 53
Perron, E. du 154
Persdelicten (violations of press laws) 65
Petit Journal, Le 230
Petit Parisien, Le 216
Philippines 18,28,46,120-121,236
Philosophes (Enlightenment) 130-132
Piepers, M.C. 168
Pita Maha (Great Vitality) 135
Pithecanthropus erectus (Java Man) 142-143
Play, Frédéric le 69
Police Actions 17,30,33,38,65
Pollock, Sheldon 43
Polynesia 18-19
Ponder, Harriet W. 123
Powdermaker, Hortense 107,186
Pragmatism 18
Preanger (Priangan) 123,132
Primitive (definitions of) 5,82,108,119-121, 125,127,129-133,137,142,145,155,206, 216-217
Priyayi (Javanese aristocracy) 24,26-27,63,65, 76,78,87-89,94-98,100,104-108,115-117, 190,226
Pro Juventute 111
Puasa (Muslim fasting month) 103

Quinzaine Coloniale 45,61

Racial Consciousness 22-23,163-164,168-174
Radical Tories 25
Radjiman, Dr. 65
Ramayana 71,126
Ramdas, Anil 38
Randwijk, H. van 19-20
Rassers, W.H. 71
Rebutan (Javanese wedding ritual) 87
Rembrandt 48,199
Renaissance 126-127,129,137,155
Renan, Ernest 240
Rendra, W.S. 36
Renes-Boldingh, M. A.M. 105

Index

Resink, G.J. 117
Reynaud, Paul 230
Rhemrev, J.T.L. 31-32
Rink, Oliver 1
Rohe, Mies von der 211
Rokan Mountains 139,142
Romer, L.S.A. M. von 126-127
Roorda, T. 6,113,133
Roosenboom, J. 31
Rotterdam 33,48,116,131
Rousseau, Jean-Jacques 131-132,146
Royal Dutch East Indies Army (KNIL) 113,115
Russian Revolution 64-65
Rust en Orde (tranquility and order) 26,94
Rutherford, Danilyn 58n168,83,95,105,122, 154,171

Sabang 68
Sachs, Curt 71,73
Said, Edward 2,44,210
Saigon 60
Saint-Simonianism 52
Salatiga 67
Sarekat Islam (Islamic Union) 27
Schama, Simon 1-2
Schilfgaarde, P. van 125,147
Scidmore, Eliza 46
Security Council (United Nations) 20
Sejarah (historical chronicle) 117
Semarang 64-65,67,85,98,106,111,158,160
Sepoy Mutiny in India (1857) 88
Shiraishi, Takashi 27,64,80,224n128
Singkep 189
Singkies (newcomers, greenhorns) 33,165
Sjahrir, Sutan 19,27,37,59,63,68,79-80,83, 127,166,170
Sjahsam, Sutan 170
Sneevliet, H.J.F.M. 25-26,31,64-65,86,105
Snouck Hurgronje, C. 24,44,58-60,69,146,176
Social difference (definitions of) 5-8,158-159, 162-166,170-171,173-174,240-242
Social-Democracy (Socialism) 24,25,26,31
Soerabajasch Handelsblad 225
Soerioadikoesoemo 176
Soeriokoesoemo, Soetatmo 126
Soerjaningrat, Soewardi (Ki Hadjar Dewantoro) 19,100
Soeroto, Noto 28

Soetardjo petition 27-28,62-63
Soeteman, G. 237
Soetomo, Dr. 142,169-170
Solo (Surakarta) 53,71,84-85,99-100,119,126, 209,222,224-226,237
Sosrohadikoesoemo, Achmad 98
Spencer, Herbert 121,144
Spectator of London 3
Spengler, Oswald 52,136,141
Spier, E. 167
Spies, Walter 90,91,108,135-136
Stoke, M. (H. Salomonson) 159,166
Stokvis, Z. 24
Stokvis, E.J. 26,40,59
Stoler, Ann Laura 21,112,115
Stutterheim, W.F. 71,110,222-223
Suez Canal 49,149,206
Suharto 35-36,49-50
Suharto, Mrs. 236
Sukabumi 115
Sukarno 63,65
Suleri, Sara
Sumatra 7,41,43-44,53,56,68,138-142,164,188
Sumba 54,221
Sunkeman (Javanese gesture of obeisance) 103
Surabaya 12,67,158,160
Surinam 16,213
Suryavarman II, King of Cambodia 197
Sutrisno, Try 36
Swart Abrahamsz, Dr. 182
Szekely, L. 164
Szekely-Lulofs, M. 112,185

Taak, De 23,75-76,79,97,99,111,113,175
Tagore, Rabindranath 134,135
Tahiti 92,120
Taman siswa schools 101
Taman mini (Jakarta) 236
Tanguy, Yves 213
Taussig, Michael 105
Tegal 104
Tempo Doeloe (good old days) 11,53,238
Tengger 146
Thamrin, Muhammad H. 171
The Hague 16,24,26,28,34,85,87,94,98-99,110, 116-117,160
Theunissen, W. F. 149
Thomas, Nicholas 9

Timboel 26,134,209-210,212,218-222,225-226,233,235
Timor 59
Tinbergen, J. 50
Tinbergen, N. 145
Tjandi Foundation 86
Tjandi Mendut 211
Tjap Belanda (stamp of Dutchness) 51,111,218
Tjikini Hospital 12
Todorov, Tzvetan 120,207
Toer, Pramoedya Ananta 36,74,83,95,115,138,170,186,235
Toraja 33,240
Torgovnick, Marianne 120
Totok (European born) 65,112,157,160,164-165,167,170-172,174,187,189
Totokization (westernization) 160,165
Transvaal 2,42,176
Travaglino, P.H.M. 124-125,130
Trekker (temporary Indies resident) 28-29,122
Tretes 12
Treub, M.W.F. 235
Tribune Indochinoise 208,235
Triwindoe-Genkboek 99
Trollope, Anthony 2
Tunisia 201-203
Turgenev, Ivan 15
Tylor, Edward Burnett 56,121,129

U.S. Diplomats (in the Dutch East Indies) 65,120-121,167,170,172
Ubud 91,134,181
Union Coloniale Francaise 45
United Nations 20,36,37
United States of America 4,37,120,215
Utrecht 62

Vaderlandsche Club (Patriotic Club) 28,68,171-173
Valkenburg, S. van 148
Van Deventer Foundation 86
Veddahs (India) 129,151
Veer, P. van 't 21
Vening Meinesz, F. 121
Vereeniging Kolonisatie Nieuw Guinea (League for the Colonization of New Guinea) 173

Vermeer, Johannes 48
Veth, B. 149-151
Victoria, Queen of Great Britain 89
Vietnam 30,60,68,208
Volkers-Schippers, F.A. 98,107
Volksraad (Peoples Council) 24,27-28,48,68,158,171,178-180,222
Volksvrouwen (native women of humble descent) 78,81-82,87,94-95,106-107,112-115
Vollenhoven, J. van 220
Vollenhoven, C. van 24,40,51-52,56-58,60,69-70,97,126
Voogdijschap (guardianship) 24,108
Voûte, J. 121
Vries, Hugo de 152

Waals, L.J. van der 209
Walraven, W. 7,22,67,159,163,170,186
Washington D.C. 17,35,48,65,67,121,128,167,179,181,188,234,241
Wayang (shadow putter theater) 71,127,225
Wederopbouw 28,63,92,118,126-127
Wertheim, W. 81n24,165
Westenenk, L.C. 140-142
Widoeri Magazine 106-107
Wild School Ordinance 101-102
Wilhelmina, Queen of the Netherlands 24,51,173,188,208
Winsemius, J. 173
Wit, A. de 150
Wolters, Oliver 44
Wong cilik (see also orang kecil) 78
Woolf, Virginia 190
World Bank 37
World War II 10-11,14,16-17,19,27-28,48,59,121,208,235
Wright, Gwendolyn 235

Yerushalmi, Joseph 38
Yogyakarta 10,35,53,83,100-101,103,113,118,126,225-226

Zeggelen, M. van 162
Zweedijk, W.J.G. 211

Postscript to the New Edition Issued by Equinox Publishing in Jakarta

Since the original publication of this book in 1995, much has changed in writing the history of European imperialism in Latin-America, Asia or Africa. New approaches such as global, transnational and postcolonial history are now fashionable. In fact, during the past decade the meanings and implications of the interactive histories between the European metropole and its colonial possessions overseas have emerged as vibrant intellectual concerns, situating the migrations back and forth of people, commodities and ideas between West and East or North and South at the very center of historical analysis. As the editorial program of the newly established Journal of Global History stated in 2006: the journal will seek to transcend the dichotomy between "'the West and the rest' by straddling traditional regional boundaries."

These global processes of interaction, or the pushes and pulls between the political and cultural configurations of occidental and oriental landscapes, began in the early modern era of European colonial expansions into Latin America and Asia. During the nineteenth and twentieth centuries, the transnational travels of human beings and goods as well as socio-cultural practices and political ideas became both more intense and more complex. That Iberian, English, French, Dutch and other European imperialisms exerted a lasting impact on a wide range of Latin American, Asian and African societies is a well-established fact. The other side of the equation, however, is less transparent. As a result, during the past decade these new questions have become an urgent object of scrutiny for historians. For instance, one of the leading scholars of modern British history, Catherine Hall, provided throughout her recent *Civilising Subjects: Metropole and Colony in the English Imagination, 1830-1867* a thoughtful analysis of a simply formulated problem: "how did the empire make a difference at home?"

When I conducted the research for this book during the early 1990s, this kind of query was only rarely articulated in the historiographical literature. In retrospect, however, it was exactly this particular question that inspired me to write *Dutch Culture Overseas*. The possession of a lucrative colonial empire in Southeast Asia – and, to a lesser extent, in the Caribbean region – was a decisive factor in the political and economic history of the Netherlands, beginning with the "golden age" of the Dutch Republic in the seventeenth century and ending with the transfer of sovereignty to an independent Indonesian nation in 1949. As a small European democracy with a significant imperial presence in Asia, it is hard to deny that the modern political "identity" of the Netherlands was not moulded and shaped in large measure by its successful record of colonial mastery in the Dutch East Indies. Because of a slowly emerging postcolonial perspective among historians and political scientists who analyze, for instance, the influx and integration of immigrants in the contemporary Netherlands, the colonial past is increasingly defined as playing a constitutive role in the postcolonial present. Hence, I am grateful to Mark Hanusz at Equinox Publishing for his decision to give *Dutch Culture Overseas* a second lease on life in the hope that the book might add a useful historical dimension to current debates concerning continuity and change in Dutch society.

Amsterdam, May 2008

www.ingramcontent.com/pod-product-compliance
Lightning Source LLC
Chambersburg PA
CBHW020638230426
43665CB00008B/227